PHYSICAL MAP
OF THE ANCIENT WORLD

Scale of Miles
0   200   400

THE ANCIENT WORLD

THE ANCIENT

WORLD

Wallace Everett Caldwell

LATE OF THE UNIVERSITY OF NORTH CAROLINA

Mary Francis Gyles

BROOKLYN COLLEGE

Third Edition

HOLT, RINEHART AND WINSTON, INC.

New York · Chicago · San Francisco · Toronto · London

Binding: Panel from a fourth-century Christian
sarcophagus of marble. (The Metropolitan Museum
of Art, Rogers Fund, 1924)
Title page: Bronze ox, archaic Greek.

PREFACE TO THE THIRD EDITION

The aims of the late Professor Caldwell in writing this book have been kept firmly in mind during this revision. The third edition retains his plan of organization while incorporating recent evidence. Because of the great quantity of archaeological and other source material that has become available since the last edition was prepared, it has been necessary to rewrite the first third of the book extensively and to add two new chapters.

No one volume could deal exhaustively with the histories of ancient middle eastern, Greek, and Roman civilizations, so I have tried to select from the theories of specialists the interpretations that make possible a chronological account and a well-rounded history. My choices have been conservative, and I have tried by means of notes to indicate the most important areas where alternative explanations are offered by other scholars. I hope the notes will lead readers to explore the problems in greater depth and to make use of specialized publications, listed in the bibliography, which has been thoroughly revised for this edition.

Many individuals and institutions have helped make this book a reality. I am particularly indebted to the Caldwell family, to Professor William C. McDermott of the University of Pennsylvania for his useful criticisms on the previous edition, to Professor Samuel Noah Kramer of the University of Pennsylvania, to Professors John A. Wilson and Thorkild Jacobsen of The University of Chicago, and to Professor Sterling Dow of Harvard University for their generous answers to my questions and assistance with problems. Many other colleagues, at Brooklyn College and elsewhere, have helped me with encouragement and suggestions, and readers of various parts of the manuscript have given me valuable criticism. Libraries, museums, and embassies have all contributed to making my work possible. Finally, I owe a great debt to Mr. Dyno Lowenstein, cartographer, for the excellent maps, to my student assistants, Mr. Michael Berg and Mr. Lawrence Rosenberg, and to all my students for their interest, ideas, and encouragment. It is they who gave me the reason for undertaking the work.

Brooklyn, N.Y. M. F. G.
February 1966

PREFACE TO THE FIRST EDITION

In writing this book my aim has been to present the important facts and factors in the rise of western civilization during ancient times. I have endeavored to give as brief a statement of the political history as is consistent with sound scholarship for each of the major periods of antiquity. This has been followed with a survey of political, economic, and social institutions and activities and a description of religious life and of cultural achievements. Emphasis has been placed upon general tendencies and major developments with sufficient detail to illustrate and clarify them. Although I have followed the usual division into periods for purposes of analysis, the continuity of the whole story of human advance and the interaction of peoples upon each other have received proper consideration. Wherever titles or technical words or expressions have first been used, an explanation is given.

A book of this scope owes much to the researches and writings of the great scholars of the past and present. I wish to express particular indebtedness to the late Professor Breasted, and to Professors Olmstead, Woolley, Glotz, Tarn, Homo, Rostovtseff, Ferguson, and Westermann.

To my teachers, the late Professors H. A. Sill, G. W. Botsford, and J. H. Robinson, and to Professor Jean Capart of Brussels, and to the many colleagues and friends with whom I have discussed the problems of antiquity, I am deeply indebted. My thanks are also due to those of my students, particularly Messrs. Shaw, Grimes, Keeney, and Suskin, who assisted me in the laborious work of checking, to Dean C. H. Oldfather of the University of Nebraska who read the manuscript in the first draft and gave me the benefit of his knowledge and experience, and to Dr. Henry David and Mr. M. I. Finley, both of whom rendered valuable editorial assistance.

I hope that teachers and students will find the book useful as an approach to the great subject of human achievement in antiquity and that the general reader may discover herein facts and interpretations of the past which will add to his understanding of the present.

Chapel Hill, N.C.   W. E. C.
April 1937

CONTENTS

MAPS

INTRODUCTION

The word history, originally Greek and meaning inquiry, is used to designate both things that have happened in the past and the recorded memory of the past. In the first sense, history may be said to include everything that has ever happened. All things that have a past have a history. When applied to mankind, history consists of all those deeds and thoughts and beliefs that have contributed to the story of human achievement. As record, however, history consists only of those things that inquirers called historians have been able to ascertain and relate. The record is constantly growing as scholars find and examine new evidences of human activities which enable them to add to historical knowledge. The first task of the historian, therefore, is to gather together all the sources from which he may develop his story.

There are two main classes of sources: material remains and written records. Among material remains are such things as the skeletons and mummies of men themselves, buildings, walls, roads, and bridges; statues, reliefs, paintings, coins, and the many kinds of artifacts like clothing, jewelry, pottery, and tools. Material remains give definite information about the appearance and the dress of men in different lands and at different times and about their technical abilities and their artistic standards.

Written records include histories, poems, plays, novels, essays — all the literary forms that portray the life and thought of past epochs — as well as the existing great mass of documents, public and private. Treaties and diplomatic correspondence, constitutions, laws, and judicial decisions, the records of legislative bodies, decrees, and proclamations appear among public documents; letters, diaries, household accounts, estate records, and wills, among private documents. Public documents are of great value to the historian, as they furnish incontrovertible evidence of past events. Private papers give him an insight into the lives and thoughts of individuals. Literary records, while they provide pictures of the ideas and beliefs dominant in the many periods of the past, vary in their usefulness as historical sources according to the literary form and the reliability of the writer.

The types of sources which are available to historians vary with different periods. The only definite records of the earliest ages are the material remains of men, their artifacts, and their art. After the invention of writing there appeared lists of kings and magistrates, building and tombstone inscriptions, and finally records and literary works on stone, papyrus, clay tablets, and parchment. The enlargement of sources continues steadily, and for modern times the historian must use newspapers and magazines, pamphlets, and public archives.

The historian's task is by no means finished when, after a careful scientific study of the sources, he has arrived at a knowledge of individual occurrences. From the facts at his disposal he must make selections of those that seem important. Then he must arrange them in a time sequence, distinguish between the more and the less important, explain causal relationships, and make generalizations.

Selection depends upon the historian's theory of history. For many years history was considered primarily a record of political and military events. More recently, an interest in social and economic factors, in culture as expressed in literary works and in art, and in religion has broadened the scope of history to embrace these fields, which are all properly included in a history of civilization. History in action has been a continuous process. We are where we are today because we stand on the shoulders of those who in their turn stood on the shoulders of the men before them. The historian must concentrate on the facts that are in the main stream of this process or have a bearing on the public interest. The purely episodic or incidental, however interesting, must be passed by except as illustrative material.

Causal relationships are most difficult to ascertain. The life of man is an exceedingly complex thing; events are usually caused not by one but many influences, most of which go unrecorded. The historian cannot assign definite causes to historical happenings with final certainty; he can only describe the circumstances that led to or surrounded an event and express his judgment of the why and the wherefore. Needless to say, his explanations will be subjective, that is, they will depend upon his own attitude toward life, his philosophy of history, and his particular theory of causation.

Chronology, or time sequence, is the framework of history. Dates, if nothing else, serve as convenient pegs on which to hang facts which, when placed in their proper time relationships to other occurrences, provide an orderly sequence of events. Without dates the study of history would be well-nigh impossible. Yet, the problem of accurate dates in certain periods is frought with enormous difficulty. New dating methods, several of which are mentioned in Chapter 1, must eventually bring order out of the present chaos, but for the time being the results have sometimes increased the uncertainty of attempts at historical reconstruction. The early records help very little because ancient peoples, after the discovery of the year and the invention of the calendar, kept their records by the years of a king's reign or by means of the names of chief magistrates, such as the archons at Athens or the consuls at Rome. Some records are dated from extraordinary events of history or of nature, so astronomical events such as eclipses or the rising of stars serve modern scholars as a check in determining the actual dates of certain occurrences and frequently provide the only clue for arriving at a fixed chronology. Even with these checks there is much dispute among scholars about dates.

For the history of the ancient middle east especially, this dispute is significant. There are presently three major systems of chronology known respectively as high, low, and middle. I have chosen to use the middle chronology for this book in the full consciousness that time may prove one of the others more accurate. Considering the evidence so far available from the carbon-14 method, it is my opinion that either the middle or low chronology will prove the more acceptable.

After the historian has assembled his selected facts and arranged them in order, he divides them into periods. Since history is dynamic, constantly changing, such divisions are largely conventional. Certain generations seem to show distinctive characteristics in the geographical centers and in the motivating forces of their activities. Consequently they are set apart and designated ages, periods, epochs, or eras. Thus we have ancient, medieval, and modern history, and within these many subdivisions. There is much disagreement among historians however, as to where one period ends and another begins, so much do they overlap and pass from one to the other

The historian of civilization must further give the meaning of the much used words civilization and culture. A good definition of civilization emphasizes that it is an advanced state of social culture in which there is progress in the arts, science, and statecraft together with an improvement of material well-being. A culture, by contrast, need not be in an advanced state, and thus a distinction may be drawn between civilization and culture through the degree of control exhibited by different societies of men over their environment. But both civilization and culture are used interchangeably and with much broader meaning.

Anthropologists use "culture" to denote all the traits of a people—its practices, habits, tools, economic conditions, governmental organization, thoughts, and arts. We shall therefore use the word in this sense in dealing with the record of primitive men. When we reach the periods where civilization has attained the levels implied in the definition, we shall employ culture to denote religion, philosophy, and literary and artistic achievements.

The final question the writer and the student of history must answer is, Why should we study history? There are many reasons. The study of the past helps us to explain and understand the present. It gives us a sense of the historical process, of the continuity of the life of man, and it shows us our place in that process. It is travel in time instead of in space and it has travel's broadening effect in helping us to understand other people and to appreciate the great achievements of men. Finally, history is the laboratory of the social studies. There we can see in operation the forces that govern society; we can study past attempts at political, social, economic, or religious reform, and measure our own programs by the experience of men. We learn to approach our problems with the humility and open-mindedness that are essential to real intelligence.

1 · Preliterary History

HISTORY, AS IT IS USUALLY UNDERSTOOD, BEGINS
with the art of writing. The study of man's long sojourn on earth
before he learned to make written records is called prehistory
or, more accurately, preliterary history. The distinction in terminology is due not to a failure to recognize the significance and
grandeur of early human achievement but to the recognition that this
development can be treated only in outline. As Seton Lloyd put it, the
times to which archaeology alone bears witness are like a long, "voiceless prologue" to a play; the curtains are drawn, stage scenery is shifted,
and actors appear and disappear but with no word spoken. In the long
prehistoric prologue, discoveries and inventions were made, and great
deeds were wrought by men whose names are unknown to poet or historian. Preliterary history reveals no record of human thought or emotion, no insight into men's minds and hearts.

Sources   The fundamental sources for preliterary history are material objects such as tools, weapons, and pottery; the remains of dwellings, graves, and monuments; and the skeletons of men and animals,
whose time-resisting properties, or the chances of climate, have caused
to be preserved. Some additional information may be drawn from word-
of-mouth tradition later recorded, and from customs and institutions
that persisted into historic times. Finally, the studies made by anthropologists on living, primitive peoples may be used cautiously to throw
light on the culture and institutions of earlier peoples whose economies
were of a similar type. From these varied sources may be gathered, not
an account of what happened, but a series of general pictures of how
prehistoric men lived and toiled, along with some inferences about migration and the succession of cultures.

Chronology   The chronology of preliterary history is not absolute,
though new methods of dating permit more precision than the relative,
or comparative, systems that could be established by geology and archaeology. Through these sciences it was possible to distinguish the

1

succeeding strata of the earth's crust, or of a continuously inhabited
site, and to determine which levels were older or younger than others.
Human artifacts and skeletal remains found in geological deposits could
be arranged in sequence by the comparative age of the clay, gravel, or
sand in which they were found. Within a single geological period, the
archaeologist could establish a comparative chronology on the same
principle. For, when a succession of peoples lives in the same place for
a long period of time, there will be an accumulation of debris consisting
of ashes, bones, tools, pottery, and other remains. Obviously the materials used by the oldest inhabitants will be at the bottom, by more
recent ones above, and by the latest on top. Careful study of the layers,
or strata, furnishes relative dates for the cultures represented on the
site. Comparison with other sites to detect similarities helps to establish
relationships and often provides information on the spread of a culture
or the extent of a migration.

Since 1949, chemistry and physics have provided tests that make
the dating of the earth's age and the early life on it more precise. The
loss of radioactivity in various substances, such as uranium, potassium,
and strontium (a loss which can be detected and measured) furnishes
more accurate terminal dates for geological periods and gives some clue
to the total age of the earth, which is estimated to be at least four billion
years. But probably many millions of years passed before life appeared
on earth. Beginning in the seas, living creatures gradually crept over
the land. Plant life spread, then animals, and very late, in the Upper
Pliocene or Lower Pleistocene, man came.

Most significant for the dating of once living creatures, including
men, is the carbon-14 test. Carbon-14, a radioactive isotope of carbon,
is continually produced in the upper air through the action of cosmic
rays on nitrogen. Every living organism ingests it during life. Plants
absorb the equilibrium amount from atmospheric carbon dioxide, and
animals get their share from eating plants. But when the organism dies,
it ceases to take in carbon-14 and material begins to decay, emitting beta
particles in the process. The rate of decay is such that half the radioactivity is lost after about 5,800 years, and three-fourths after some 11,600
years.[1] Several instruments can measure the rate of decay, but allowance
for error must always be made because of the uncertainty of the value
of the half life, variations in methods used by different laboratories, the
statistical uncertainties, and the danger of contamination in the sample.
The possibility of error from all these sources increases with the age of
the sample so that accuracy is less the further back one goes, and the

[1] The half life of carbon-14 has been recalculated at 5730 ± 40 years (H. Godwin,
Nature 195, No. 4845, September 8, 1962, p. 984). At the time of writing (November 1965)
this recalculated half life has not officially replaced the "old" half life of 5568 ± 30 years,
but official replacement is likely in the near future.

carbon-14 test can seldom be used with any success on material older than 40,000 years.

Botanists also have made available some useful dating tools. The age of trees and the climatic changes they experienced during growth can be determined from the annual rings visible in the cross section of a tree trunk. Even more valuable for earlier periods are the pollen counts made on bores from swamps, peat bogs, and the like. The pollen studies reveal the flora existing at any given time and the climatic fluctuations of late-Pleistocene and post-Pleistocene times is largely deduced from changes shown by these data. Even the effects of human activity in clearing and planting can be seen in the pollen studies, and through them the world in which primitive man lived can be understood. At one time he hunted through semitropical foliage, later over grassy plains. Again he walked softly over fragrant pine needles, or in a different age looked up into the dim, mysterious green light of a tall beech forest. The type of game he hunted, the fruit he gathered, changed with the plants.

The Stone Age   Tools were the first traces of early men to be found and studied, and a relative historical framework was established on the basis of the shapes and techniques of workmanship which characterized them. Crude, chipped stones were labeled *paleoliths* (old stones); polished, specialized stone tools were called *neoliths* (new stones); and these terms were applied to the periods in which they were made. There remained a group of chipped stones, named *eoliths* (dawn stones), which were at first thought to be the simplest tools used or made by man. But subsequent studies show that the chipping is probably due to natural causes, so the term "eolith" is no longer generally used, nor is any age named "Eolithic." The Paleolithic and Neolithic periods of the Stone Age and their subdivisions were followed by the Copper, Bronze, and Iron ages, which succeeded one another as man gained mastery over metals. This simple classification, based on technology, does not in any way coincide with the geological epochs through which men are known to have lived. Nor is it reflective of human physical types or of economic organization. Yet it lingers on, in part because of habit, in part because no really adequate substitute has been devised. The Paleolithic Period has been divided into several stages, which were named after the places where specific tool types were first found. The Neolithic Period and the metal ages fall also into numerous subdivisions, named usually after types of pottery, of dwellings, or of tombs (see the chronological chart). Little consistency or order exists in the method of classification aside from the major divisions on the basis of tools. But tools, after all, represent only one of the techniques of living.

A more significant classification, proposed by V. Gordon Childe, is based on economy: (1) man, the food gatherer; (2) man, the food pro-

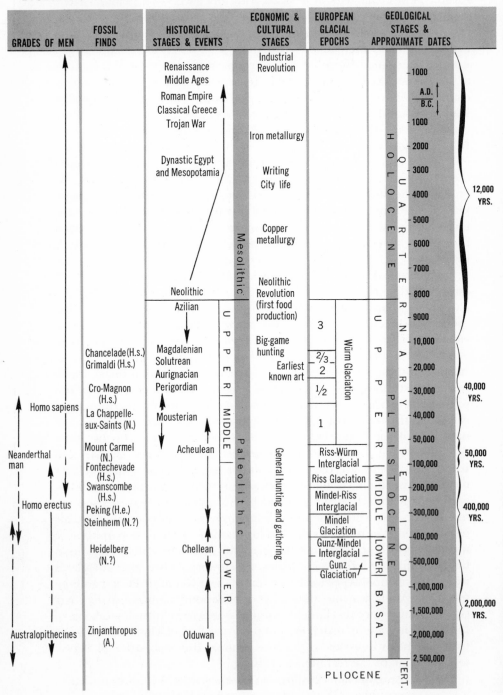

Chronological Chart. (Prepared by Bernard Wailes)

ducer; and (3) man, the city dweller. Roughly this classification can be correlated with the stone and metal ages. Man was a food gatherer throughout the Paleolithic Period. He became a food producer at the opening of the Neolithic Period and an urban dweller with the beginning of the metal ages. But both of these systems of classifications refer to stages in human development rather than to specific, datable periods of history. For example, the Neolithic (food-producing) stage began in Mesopotamia about 7000 B.C. but did not begin in the Mississippi Valley until another eight thousand years had passed.

MAN, THE FOOD GATHERER

For almost 98 per cent of man's existence on earth he was engaged in a precarious search for food. Plants and animals provided his nourishment, and he found his shelter in nature. He was forced to range afar in a hostile environment to satisfy his hunger. The most primitive of living men, the Australian aborigines—who gather grubworms to supplement their meager diet—are many times more secure than the earliest manlike creatures whose remains have been found.

Early Men Discoveries made in Africa since the 1920s have pushed back in time the limits of human prehistory and provided increased knowledge of the probable development of man. *Proconsul*, an ape which may have been ancestral to human stock, was found in Lower Miocene deposits in Kenya (about 14 million years old). More certainly human are the Australopithecines (Southern Apes), first found in southern Africa but since discovered in other parts of Africa as well. The Australopithecines were rather small by modern human standards, but their brains in proportion to their body size were somewhat larger than those of apes and they walked on two feet like later men. Two types of Australopithecines are recognized: *Australopithecus*, who may have lived on a diet which included meat; and *Paranthropus*, a somewhat more "primitive" form, whose diet was largely vegetarian. One of the most spectacular discoveries among the *Paranthropus* types was that of *Zinjanthropus*, whose bones were found by Dr. and Mrs. Leakey in the Olduvai Gorge (Bed I) in Tanganyika. This find was doubly important, since the bones of *Zinjanthropus* lay close to tools—suggesting that this manlike creature had made and used the tools. Previously, though "chopper" tools had been found in approximately contemporary deposits, none had been closely associated with the Australopithecines.

However, the connection between the Australopithecines and the use of tools is still uncertain, for the Leakeys later discovered the fragmentary remains of another type of man in the same bed. He must have coexisted with *Zinjanthropus*, but while some specialists call him an *Australopithecus*, others consider him to be an early form of *Homo erectus*, a

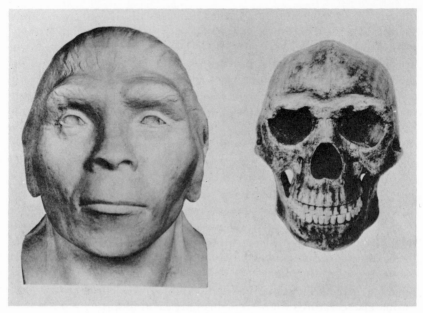

Reconstruction of Head of a *Sinanthropus* Woman Together with Skull. (American Museum of Natural History)

more advanced form of man. If the latter classification proves correct, *Homo erectus* may have made and used the tools rather than *Zinjanthropus* or any other Australopithecine.

The men from the Olduvai Gorge lived about one and three-quarter million years ago, according to the potassium-argon dating method.[2] This is perhaps a million years earlier than any evidence of bones or tools from Asia, for the first traces of *Homo erectus* to be found in eastern and southeastern Asia date to the Lower and Middle Pleistocene. At that time, *Homo erectus* may also have lived in Europe and Africa, but the evidence is slight and inconclusive.

Homo erectus was appreciably larger than any one of the Australopithecines, and had a larger brain—not very much smaller than the brain of modern man. Two slightly different types of *Homo erectus* are known: the Java man (*Pithecanthropus*), whose remains were found on that island, and the Peking man (*Sinanthropus*), whose bones were found near Peking in China. Peking man is the earliest man known to have controlled fire. Another manlike creature of unusual size also reported from China has been named *Gigantopithecus* (Giant Ape). It is known

[2] Corroborated by another dating method, recently developed, known as fission-track dating.

only from its enormous teeth, which suggests it to have been about thirteen feet tall. However, most anatomists are now agreed that this creature was not a man or manlike form but definitely an ape.

Tools Three essential features characteristic of the early types of men are found in all human beings. Their brains were large in proportion to their total size, they walked upright, and they possessed hands made amazingly useful by thumbs, which could be opposed to the other fingers to enable them to grasp and manipulate all sorts of objects. The unique hand, freed for use by the upright posture and guided by the remarkable brain, made tool users of men from the beginning. By means of tools they overcame their comparatively weak and defenseless physical condition and obtained the food necessary to their existence. These early men must have made tools of wood and other perishable materials, but the only tools that survive (with one or two exceptions) are those manufactured from stone, bone, ivory, and antler. The earliest known tools are from Africa south of the Sahara, where they are contemporary with the Australopithecines, though it is uncertain who made or used them.

These early tools are known as *choppers*, or *chopping tools*, and are collectively known as the Olduwan industry after the Olduvai sites where they were first recognized. They are simply suitable pieces of stone with a few flakes removed from one end so that a sharp cutting or chopping edge was obtained. The resultant flakes were also used as tools. This chopper-tool tradition eventually spread into Asia, where it formed the basis for the stone-tool tradition (often clumsily known as the "chopper/chopping-tool tradition"), which persisted in east and southeast Asia, with gradual modification, for most of the Paleolithic Period. In Africa the Olduwan industry slowly developed into the "hand-ax tradition," alternatively known as the Chelles-Acheul tradition after the two sites (Chelles-sur-Marne and Saint-Acheul) in northern France where it was first recognized. The *hand axes* are really just more elaborately made Olduwan choppers, with more flakes removed; they generally are flaked all over to produce an implement that is roughly pear-shaped in outline, with a cutting edge running all around. The Chellean industry is somewhat cruder than the later Acheulean, by which time the flaking technique was much more expert. The Chellean industry is the earliest to be recognized in Europe, and must have spread there from Africa.

The hand axes are known as core tools, as they were made by removing flakes from a piece of stone or flint until the "core" was the desired size and shape. This meant, of course, that many flakes were produced too, as with the Olduwan industry, and these flakes were frequently used as tools themselves. In northern France and southern England there are a few sites, contemporary with Chellean and the later Acheulean, which have flake tools only, and no hand axes. This lack of

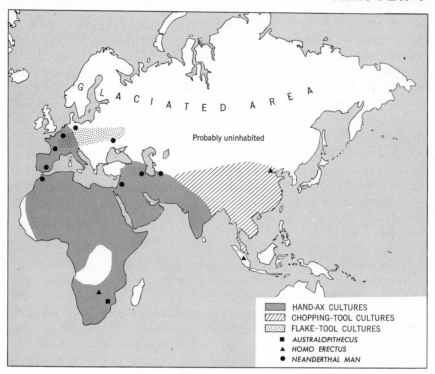

G LACIATED AREA

Probably uninhabited

	HAND-AX CULTURES
	CHOPPING-TOOL CULTURES
	FLAKE-TOOL CULTURES
■	*AUSTRALOPITHECUS*
▲	*HOMO ERECTUS*
●	*NEANDERTHAL MAN*

Principal Cultures and Early Men, Early Paleolithic Period, ca. 1,000,000–100,000 B.C.

hand axes suggested the possibility of a different industry, for which the name "Clactonian" is used (after Clacton-on-Sea, the English type site). But since Clactonian flakes are really indistinguishable from Chellean-Acheulean flakes and since none of the few Clactonian sites have produced very many tools, it does not seem justifiable to talk about a separate and distinct Clactonian flake tradition. Perhaps the Clactonian sites are Chelles-Acheul sites on which no hand axes were found. Even if hand axes really were not made, the similarity of Clactonian and Chelles-Acheul flakes indicate that the Clactonian is probably no more than a local variant of the Chelles-Acheul tradition.

The Chellean industry first appeared in Europe during the Gunz-Mindel Interglacial Period. The more developed Acheulean appeared during the Mindel-Riss Interglacial and continued into the Riss-Würm Interglacial. There is little evidence of man in Europe during the intervening glacial periods; apparently he retreated to warmer areas as the glaciers advanced and returned as the climate became warmer again. It is difficult to correlate events in Africa to those in Europe with any precision, but the appearance of the Chellean in Europe is roughly contemporary with its development in Africa, according to the few potassium-argon dates available. The Chelles-Acheul tradition thus appears to have developed simultaneously in Europe and Africa, from a basis of the earlier Olduwan chopper tradition of Africa.

The Pleistocene Environment The Pleistocene was an epoch of climatic disturbances. Four long ice ages, each with minor oscillations, spread over the northern continents, but long periods of warmth intervened between them. In Africa and the Mediterranean basin, periods of heavy rainfall (pluvials) coincided with the ice ages. Both have left their earthly marks in the moraines, or beds of gravel, deposited by the glaciers; in the formation of terraces on hillsides made by flooding and swollen rivers; and in great beds of windblown soil called *loess* by geologists. Plant and animal life varied with the climatic changes. In the warm interglacials hippopotamuses and tigers lived in Portugal, France, and southern England. In the periods of cold, woolly mammoths, woolly rhinoceroses, and other hairy beasts took their place. Great changes affected the animal life through the whole, vast age. Saber-toothed tigers, mastodons, and cave bears gave way near its end to the tigers, elephants, and bears of the present. A host of other creatures underwent gradual change, some by decreasing in size, but others grew larger, as did the horse. Men changed also. *Homo erectus* disappeared, to be succeeded by men with larger brains, the Neanderthal men. Before the end of the Pleistocene, during the last ice age, they in turn disappeared and were replaced by human types similar to modern men.

Neanderthal Man During the last interglacial, a sturdy race of men spread over Europe, Asia, and Africa. Named after the location in which the first specimen was found, the Neander River valley in Germany, the Neanderthals represented a considerable advance over their predecessors. Their brains were even more capacious than those of men today, but they looked slightly different. The skull was imperfectly centered on the spine and hung forward. Also, though the skull was higher and more domed than that of *Homo erectus* and the muzzle had receded, a bony ridge remained over the eyes and the chin was undeveloped. Yet Neanderthal men showed themselves to be proficient in technology and quite advanced socially. Indeed, they made positive contributions to human progress.

Neanderthals made their homes in caves wherever possible, even occasionally dispossessing the cave bear to do so. A well-defined hearth marked their habitation. Groups, whether in individual families or larger, lived and worked together, and several generations sometimes inhabited the same cave. For the first time, there was deliberate burial of the dead. When a member of the group died, he was buried in a carefully excavated grave near the fireplace. Stones were often placed protectively against the weight of the covering earth. The body was doubled

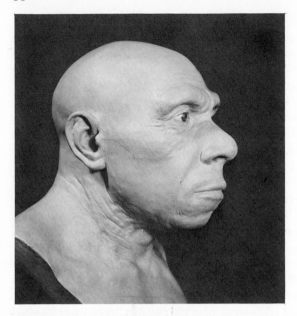

Reconstruction of Head of a Neanderthal Man. (American Museum of Natural History)

up, and tools and joints of meat were placed beside it for use in the next world. Other signs of a definite system of beliefs are the ritually arranged heaps of animal bones found in certain Alpine caves, the remains of a purposeful ceremony.

The technical achievement of the Neanderthals was important. Their tools were quite specialized, and the spear point was almost certainly

Paleolithic Tools (opposite page, approximately one-third natural size). (*Above*) Typical Acheulian core implements: (1) Coup-de-poing or cleaver, oval outline, flaked on both faces all around, edge moderately thin and straight (France). (2) Coup-de-poing of subtriangular outline — possibly a weapon (France). (*Center*) Typical Levalloisian implements: (1) Scraper of flake derived from prepared coup-de-poing or turtleback core with convex face, striking platform visible at bottom; cross section above (France and Egypt). (2) Knife of flake derived from prepared coup-de-poing core, concave or bulbar face with part of striking platform (France and Egypt). (3) Scraper or core of discoidal outline, showing large flake-beds and subsequent marginal chipping (France and Egypt). (*Below*) Typical Mousterian implements: (1) Coup-de-poing or small pointed core implement (France). (2) Pointed flake with marginal pressure retouch on convex face (France). (3) Pointed flake with chipped stem for hafting to spear (?) (North Africa). (4) Sidescraper of thick spall, crescentic edge, chipped on convex face only (France). (5) Sidescraper or slingstone (?), small, discoidal (France, Egypt, etc.). (6) Notched sidescraper with marginal chipping — rare (France); after G. and A. de Mortillet. (7) Bone implement (?) with blunt spatulate point (Switzerland); after O. Menghin. (8) Anvil or rest of bone fragment showing tool marks. France. (American Museum of Natural History)

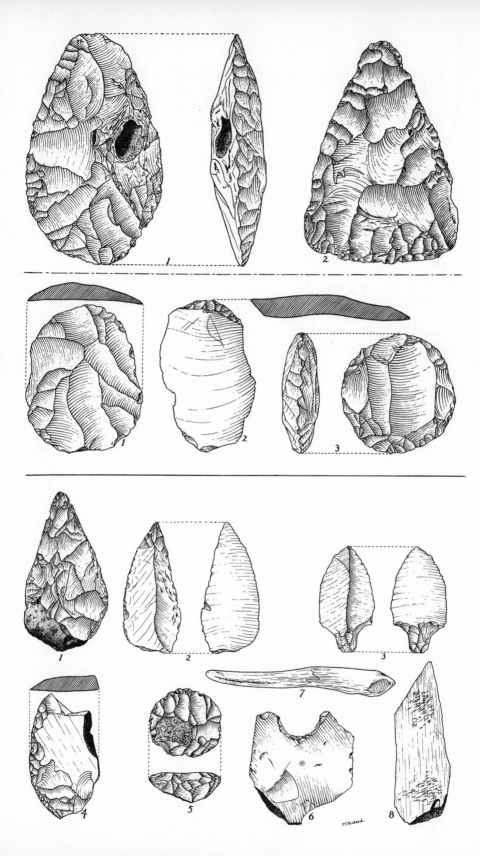

their invention. Points were made of stone and wood. Proof for the use of the wooden spear comes from a site in Palestine: "One of the skeletons . . . had a clean-cut hole passing through the head of the femur into the pelvis, and from this was obtained a plaster cast, reproducing the tip of a wooden spear which had been thrust into his vitals, and of which no other trace remained."[3] Other specialized tools included choppers and scrapers; the latter were probably used in the preparation of animal skins for clothing and cover. This specialized tool industry developed by the Neanderthal men was called Mousterian.

Everything indicates that Neanderthal men lived better and more comfortably than their predecessors. Successful hunters, they brought down very large game and were the first men to inhabit the frost zones. The mammoth and woolly rhinoceros fell victim to them, as did the cave bear. Ingenuity and social cooperation were necessary to hunt, kill, and butcher such large animals. Specialized tools alone were not sufficient. The relative frequency with which Neanderthal bones and tools are found over a three-continent range is witness to their achievement. Interesting discoveries at Krapina in Croatia and on Mount Carmel in Palestine seem to prove the membership of the Neanderthaloids in the recent human species. At both of these widely separated spots a series of skeletal remains has been found that may belong to families of crossbreeds between Neanderthal men and *Homo sapiens.*

Homo Sapiens   At the beginning of the last ice age in Europe, *Homo sapiens* (Wise Man) began to encroach upon the Neanderthaloids, and before the end of it he had displaced them entirely. The reason is not clear, because the techniques and tools of *Homo sapiens* were not at first superior and, indeed, were based on the Mousterian industries, and there was some interbreeding. Yet when the ice receded, no trace remained of Neanderthal men or of their industrial tradition. In their place, ranging over Europe, Africa, and Asia, lived *Homo sapiens.* Modern races were already differentiated into Negroid, Mongoloid, and Caucasoid types, and some anthropologists distinguish subraces, seeing in one skull type the ancestor of the Eskimo. Most famous of the early subraces were the Cro-Magnon people, who were rather tall with dolichocephalic skulls (long heads). But tall or short, all these men were members of the modern living species; all were *Homo sapiens.*

During the Upper Pleistocene, when *Homo sapiens* made his first appearance, the last ice age brought about an unusually wealthy environment for hunters in certain parts of Europe, Africa, and Asia. Open grassy plains supported vast herds of reindeer, bison, wild horses, mammoths, rhinoceros, and other grazing animals. Men followed on the

---

[3] Dorothea Garrod, *Environment, Tools and Man.* Cambridge, England: Cambridge University Press, 1946, p. 18.

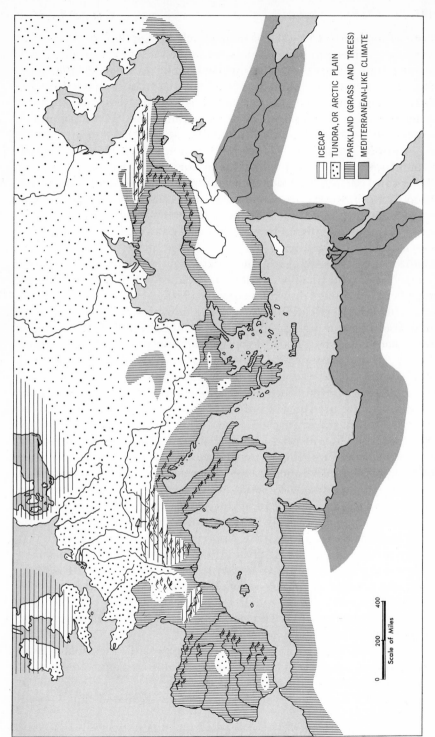

ICECAP

TUNDRA, OR ARCTIC PLAIN

PARKLAND (GRASS AND TREES)

MEDITERRANEAN-LIKE CLIMATE

Scale of Miles

0   200   400

The Last Ice Age, ca. 25,000 B.C., on a Map of Modern Europe and the Middle East

heels of the herds, and some of them traveled far, spilling over from the Eurasiatic plains into the Americas.[4] Also men went to Australia. It was at some time during the last ice age, marked by its late Paleolithic hunting cultures and the abundance of game, that man completed his encirclement of the globe and reached all continental land areas. In the older inhabited regions men were more numerous on the plains and in the river valleys, where they hunted together in large groups.

In open country the people lived in houses with floors dug below ground level and roofed with skins or turf supported on posts as in American Indian huts. Floor plans and post holes of such houses have been found in Russia. In mountainous areas the hunters lived in caves or rock shelters, as did their Neanderthal predecessors. In houses or in caves they warmed themselves by, and cooked over, fires in which they burned animal bones, since wood was scarce on the grasslands. They clothed themselves with garments of skin from which the flesh had been scraped, and which had been cut into shape with stone knives and sewn together with thongs drawn by bone needles.

The dead were carefully buried on their sides in doubled-up position, and red ocher was sprinkled on the body. Food offerings and tools were placed close by. A favorite burial place was near the hearth, just as it was for the Neanderthals. Perhaps it was believed that the dead needed warmth. The food offerings and tools indicate a hope of future existence, but the red ocher (which is believed to represent blood) and closeness to the fire show a confused notion that the afterlife might be confined to the grave.

Evidence abounds that within each hunting culture a well-defined system of beliefs, or religion, was developed. "Venus" figurines, ritual offerings, and cave paintings played a part, all of which could be signs of both worship and magic. Some anthropologists maintain that men painted bison, reindeer, and other animals because they wanted to insure a supply of them to be killed. Another possibility is that, like some living men of Paleolithic culture, they wished to assuage the *totem*, or great animal spirit, before killing. Whatever the explanation, magic was mixed with worship, an assumption proved by the location of the cave paintings, which are hidden away in the recesses of deep caverns where they could not possibly have been frequently seen or enjoyed. The inaccessibility of the paintings indicates that the act of creation was more important than the object produced.

The tools of the earliest modern men are indistinguishable from those of their Neanderthal neighbors, but improvements came swiftly, and by the middle of the last ice age specialized *blade tools* developed as the principal stone tool type. From carefully prepared flint nodules

[4] Human occupation in the Americas began more than thirty thousand years ago.

Rock Painting of Woolly Rhinoceros from the Cave of Font de Gaume, France. (American Museum of Natural History)

blades were struck off to form long, parallel-sided flakes. The blades were then worked into tools by pressure flaking, which produced fine edges and sharp points. Knives, chisels, scrapers, gravers, awls and stone points were made by this method. Other tools—harpoons, fishhooks, needles, and spear-throwers—were made of bone, horn, and ivory. With time, the technology became varied and rich, and two major traditions, the Perigordian and Aurignacian, together with several localized cultures, can be distinguished in Eurasia. But the technological distinctions cannot be attached to any race or subrace. At the caves of Grimaldi, Italy, Gravettian (one of the specialized blade industries first identified in France) techniques were used by both Grimaldians (possibly Negroids) and Cro-Magnons (Caucasoids), and the same Gravettian tradition was used in south Russia and central Europe by still other peoples.

Meat served as the principal food. Few indications exist for the use of wild grains, vegetables, or fruits, though an occasional cherry stone has been found. Rather, vast heaps of animal bones—mammoth,[5] bison, reindeer, fox, rhinoceros, horse, and fish—attest to men's success as hunters. They knew how to corral or trap the largest animals. In south Russia and central Europe they camped in the river valleys at spots along the game routes between summer and winter pastures. Lateral

[5] There is evidence of the hunting of mastodons in North America.

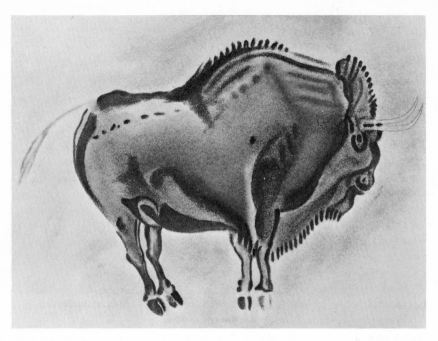

Rock Painting of Bison from Altamira, Spain. (American Museum of Natural History)

canyons were made to serve as natural corrals into which the animals were driven and killed. In Moravia, huge stones sharpened to a point have been found. On the average they weigh about fifteen pounds, but one stone shaped like a pear, or bomb, weighs more than a hundred and twenty pounds. Obviously these *gigantoliths* were suspended in a dead-fall to crush the skull of the unwary mammoth that wandered into the trap. Spears and javelins propelled by spear throwers increased the effectiveness of man's power and reach, and lessened his danger in hunting big game.

The variety of tools and the excellence of their forms, together with the multiplicity of materials from which they were made, hint that specialization in the crafts may have developed near the end of the ice age, though if comparison is made with the successful hunting cultures of the northwestern United States (which they much resemble) no certainty can be arrived at on this point. Among the Indian hunters of the American Northwest every man was an artist at tool-making. But though industry may have remained unspecialized, the existence of trade in raw materials is certain. Shells and the bones of sea fish are found far inland, and flint was carried long distances from the sources of supply. The river valleys provided highways even then, and there is good reason to suppose that men used rafts or some kind of primitive boat—just as the American Indian used canoes.

Late Paleolithic Art Beauty was sought by these early men and achieved in several ways. Utilitarian tools of bone, ivory, and horn were decorated with delicate carvings of animals, fish, and birds. Pure ornament of geometric or linear form was also used, and special efforts were lavished on the decoration of certain implements, which appear to be spear throwers. But the most striking manifestation of men's desire for beauty, and their skill in attaining it, is found in their painting.

The magnificent cave paintings in Spain and southern France, executed between 20,000 and 10,000 years ago, were first revealed by chance, and accident has continued to play a role in locating others. Men, chasing stray animals, have been led into the depths of the caves and startled to discover the decorated walls. Boys following a dog found stunning paintings in a previously undiscovered cave at Lascaux. A riotous series of pictures of animals cover its walls and ceiling. A herd of horses is shown, reindeer are swimming in a stream, a rhinoceros is grazing, and a man with a birdlike head is being thrown by a wounded bison.

Equally handsome are the paintings in the caves of Altamira in Spain and of Font-de-Gaume in France. Both were decorated by people of so-called Magdalenian culture (the last and most highly developed Paleolithic culture), which was localized to Spain and southern France. Engraving was combined with painting to achieve the desired effect, and ceilings, walls, narrow corridors, and almost inaccessible corners were covered. By taking advantage of freak shapes on the limestone-crystal walls and by the use of color, the artists produced realistic likenesses of animals. They chiseled outlines with a sharp tool, or sketched them with carbon, manganese, and red or yellow ocher. The outlined bodies were

Rock Painting of Mammoths and Reindeer from the Cave of Font de Gaume, France. (American Museum of Natural History)

then filled in with appropriate colors made from the same minerals. Bison were favored at Altamira but the artists at Font-de-Gaume preferred mammoths, rhinoceros, and reindeer. Their accuracy in drawing mammoths was questioned until one of these extinct beasts, frozen in the tundras of Siberia, proved the artists right and their modern critics wrong. Strange designs that look like tents or huts are sometimes pictured also, and occasionally there is the outline of a human hand.

In caves of southern Spain a different tradition of painting is found. The animals are not so realistically and colorfully rendered, but men are more frequently shown and an attempt is made to catch action. The total impression is one of a lively scene of "stick figures" in motion.

Among the peoples of late Aurignacian and Upper Perigordian culture, sculpture took the place of painting to some extent. Followers of a fertility cult, they carved figurines of women from stone or ivory, or modeled them from clay and ash. The figures are crude and misshapen, often without faces, and designed to emphasize female sex characteristics—a fact that has earned them the nickname "Venuses." They are grotesque and exaggerated, but purposeful statements of woman's regenerative qualities, not images of normal women. Peoples of other cultures modeled animal figures of clay and baked them. Most of these come from Moravia and usually represent bears and lions. In an inner room of a cave used by Magdalenians a pair of bison of considerable size were sculptured in unbaked clay. Reliefs of horses and bears have been found in central Europe, evidently made by the people of localized culture called Solutrean, who were justly famous too for the beauty of the stone points they manufactured.

Whether these men painted and carved for religious or magical purposes, or for their own pleasure, or to illustrate a myth (as did the Indians of the Pacific Northwest in making totem poles), they achieved great beauty. The richness of their art is a measure of their wealth and their success in exploiting their environment. The abundance of game increased the human population and at the same time encouraged greater social cooperation and provided leisure time, which could be devoted to art. Seldom since then have hunting cultures, or food gatherers, lived as well (the Indians of the Pacific Northwest are notable among those who did). Few have been able to create, or to afford, so much beauty even in their mundane tools.

The End of the Pleistocene   But rich as was his culture, man was still a food gatherer and at the mercy of his environment. Changes in this environment brought about changes in his life. About ten thousand years ago the ice age came to an end and the open country retreated northward before an advancing forest cover. Some large grazing animals, mostly reindeer, moved north also, and some men followed them. Other men, however, stayed to face the new forest conditions. The

Painting of a Reindeer Hunt from the Cueva de los Caballos, Albocacer, Spain. (American Museum of Natural History)

change came rapidly in terms of geological time, for the recession of the ice occurred about ten thousand years ago and within two thousand years the climate of Europe, the Mediterranean basin, north Africa, and the middle east was approaching that of the present.

The Mesolithic Period   Sir John Marshall, contemplating the rapid changes through which man passed after the end of the ice ages, suggested a theory of *challenge* and *response* to account for the transitions. By this theory man was forced to adapt to a new environment in order to survive (the challenge), and he did so successfully and quickly by changing his habits and customs (the response). It is stimulating to consider the idea in the light of the development which follows, though it must be cautiously noted that not all the puzzles of preliterary history can be solved by it. Certain groups of men seemed ready to adapt to change. Others refused and continued to survive into modern times following Paleolithic customs and living in precarious poverty.

In the brief span called the *Mesolithic* (middle stone) phase, which lasted only two or three thousand years in the middle east and not much longer in Europe, man's basic problem, as always, was food supply. The eventual solution to the problem posed by the changed climate made him a food producer rather than a food gatherer, but meanwhile, during the Mesolithic Period, he lived insecurely. His environment differed, for in Europe great forests rose and spread, while in North Africa many areas were drying out, and the big game animals were disappearing from both sections. Those remaining were not only smaller (therefore wanted in greater numbers) but also, being fleet, much harder to catch. It was in this time of need that the dog came to live with man and became his partner in hunting. Probably wild dogs had hung about the hunters for a long time, scavenging in their wake and thus partly domesticating themselves, but not until the Mesolithic Period did man welcome the dog's company. Sometimes the dog paid for his welcome by becoming a meal, and his presence may well have provided a pattern for the later domestication of more desirable food animals. In the primitive village cultures of the middle east the bones of the dog are found, and in the impoverished camps in the European forests the dog's bones lie beside man's.

Other changes came too. In the woodlands a whole array of new tools appeared for use in woodworking: axes, adzes, and gouges. Carpentry was developed to a high peak, and new inventions were made in wood. Runners for sleighs have been found in Mesolithic peat, the first known vehicle to be used for land transportation. Stone tools changed in shape and size. The first arrow points were found in Spain and are from the late Paleolithic, when the forest first began to spread, but they became common over all of forested Europe during the Mesolithic.

Many arrow points were small in size (*microliths*) and of very fine work-manship. Obviously both man and dog could use help in hunting the fleet red deer and the bird on the wing. The bow and arrow provided this help.

The tool tradition of North Africa and the middle east is also microlithic during this period. V. Gordon Childe's suggestion that the domestication of animals took place in the middle east earlier than else-where because men could chase them into the oases and river valleys and round them up with ease seems no longer acceptable in the light of more recent evidence. It is not now believed that desert conditions pre-vailed in North Africa and the middle east until historic man helped bring them about by deforestation and overgrazing. But by some means, pigs, sheep, goats, and cattle came to live with the dog and his master at the end of the Mesolithic Period in Egypt and Mesopotamia, and men's movements fell into a pattern made necessary by care of the grazing herds. Rapidly, not slowly as in past ages, men began to master the environment. But in the adjustment they profited from the knowledge of nature so painfully acquired through the long past.

Transition to Settled Life Anthropologists speculate that as the hunters turned from food gathering to food producing they carried their patterns of social, political, and religious life over into the new economy. Details of such change have been studied in many living socie-ties which have reached this stage, and the information, combined with evidence surviving in the myths, annals, and tales recorded by the earliest civilizations, makes possible a general reconstruction of human life during the transition.

Men lived in tribal groups or in smaller clans. Clansmen believed themselves to be related by blood kinship, though the fact of kinship must be doubted because adoptions were frequent. Membership in the clan was gained through a ceremony, and roughly the same rites were used to admit youths at puberty and adults who were newcomers from outside. Once an individual was a member of the clan (which was fol-lowed by automatic membership in the larger tribe), he was entitled to use the common property of the group, originally hunting and fishing grounds but later grazing and arable lands. Personal property existed, in tools, weapons, clothing, ornaments, and the right to certain lands. Inheritance descended in some tribes and clans through the mother, in others through the father, and near relationships were determined accordingly. In the matrilineal clan the young man considered the mother's relatives closer than the father's. The opposite was true in the patrilineal clan.

The clans were led by one or more "elders" or "chiefs," who were regarded with considerable esteem and rewarded with a larger share of "wealth" than an ordinary member possessed. Wars were fought between tribes — sometimes even between clans — over territorial rights and other causes of disagreement.

Members of each clan conceived of themselves as the related descendants of a common ancestor or *totem*, often the spirit of a plant or animal important to the group economy or significant in some other way to its well-being. The clan honored the totem at various ceremonies and rites, and sometimes abstained from eating the totem animal or plant at any other time, when it was *taboo* to do so. Other group activities of a religious nature were carried out, and myths were told of divine beings. Sympathetic magic was also universally practiced. When rain was wanted, a dance might be performed in which the pouring out of water occurred, as if men wished to show the responsible spirit what to do and how to do it. Before going to war, a ritual accompanied by prayer imitated the victorious return. All these customs, practiced by Paleolithic societies, were carried over into the food-producing economy, or Neolithic Period.

MAN, THE FOOD PRODUCER

The Neolithic Period, or food-producing stage, was characterized everywhere by the domestication of food animals and, more important, by the discovery of farming. Early investigators recognized the change visible in the stone tools, which they called *neoliths*, but they did not fully understand its significance, and the term has been abandoned. It was of no particular significance that the tools were polished. What was important was the increasing number of types and the specialization of implements needed for agriculture. Food production was taking the place of food gathering. Childe has pointed out that no other development made so vast a difference in human existence except possibly the modern industrial revolution. He guessed that women may have discovered farming, finding that seeds scattered around their dwellings would grow and thus provide a safe and easy supply of food. This is quite likely, since in living tribes at this stage the men often hunt, care for the animals, and make tools while the women tend the garden patches. The earliest farmers were not always stationary, but seminomads, who learned to put seeds in the ground while in summer pastures, to supply the growing plants with water, and to harvest the crop before they moved on in search of fresh grass or milder weather for their herds.

Early Village Economies   By 7000 B.C. in Mesopotamia, men lived along the northern hilly rim of the broad, double valley of the Tigris and Euphrates rivers. In the dry season they migrated into the valley with their herds, returning to higher ground in the flood season. A little later, the same thing happened along the Nile in Egypt, and then along the Indus in Pakistan. Gradually, as the river valleys became drier, or as men learned of their advantages, they moved down permanently to settle on the fertile bottom land, where they were rewarded with rich grain crops and lush pasturage. Apparently this took place about 5000 B.C. in Mesopotamia and perhaps a little later in Egypt.

In the intervening two thousand years, inventions had been made at an amazing pace. The necessity for year-round shelter caused men to build permanent houses, and they made use of the materials at hand. In Mesopotamia and Egypt mud was most plentiful, so buildings were made of packed earth, adobe, or crude mud brick. In some other areas stone and wood were used for construction. The necessity for storage and transport led to the development of basketry, and the necessity for cooking vegetable foods to the invention of pottery. Much of the early pottery has a "basket-weave" pattern on the exterior surface, indicating that baskets lined with clay served as the first cooking vessels and led naturally to the discovery of the advantages of baked clay. The weaving of flax, wool, and other fibers to make clothes and coverlets may also have stemmed from the knowledge gained in the weaving of baskets.

As each of these arts appeared, man soon showed himself dissatisfied with a severely utilitarian appearance. Within each cultural group specific decorative patterns were developed. The designs, ornaments, and techniques of pottery making have come to have peculiar importance for the archaeologist and historian because baked clay is

Predynastic (Late Neolithic) Pottery Jar from Egypt, Painted with Gazelles and Ostriches. (The Metropolitan Museum of Art, Rogers Fund, 1920)

well-nigh indestructible, and great quantities of it are available for study. Clans making distinctive wares can be located, their migrations traced, and the succession of peoples on a single site observed, often in some detail, through the stratification of the potsherds in the village mounds. Otherwise unrecorded groups are frequently named after their pottery, as are the Bell Beaker folk, the Red Ware folk, and the Painted Pottery folk. Improvements were made within the pottery tradition, and some clans learned to make slip wares, polished wares, or beautifully burnished wares. The better surfaces obtained made the pottery watertight, and thus more useful as well as more beautiful.

Wild wheat, spelt, and barley grew in the middle east. The peach, fig, date, and other fruits were also native to the region. Oxen, sheep, goats, swine, and asses made up the animal population, along with the lion and other wild creatures. Men of Mesopotamia were fortunate to have so varied a supply of plant and animal life on which to base their agricultural economy. Egypt's resources were equally good, though barley played a greater role than wheat in the early period. Much the same animal life as that of Mesopotamia was found also in Egypt, though ducks and geese were domesticated there, and the domestic cat was trained to assist in hunting wild birds in the marshes. Flax and papyrus reeds were native to the Nile Valley, and were used to weave clothes, baskets, and mats.

Stone tools took on a host of new shapes and forms. The hunting points were made in less quantity, while hoes, sickles, grinding stones, and other devices useful to agriculture increased. Care was lavished on a tool that a man expected to use over a long period, such as a good knife, ax, or sickle. It was smoothly polished with a finely ground edge, and perhaps grooved for hafting. Arrow and spear points were unpolished because they were often lost, but even these were improved, being flanged, prepared for shafting, and the like. Flint was in great demand for the manufacture of such tools and it was mined in many regions. Grim evidence of mining exists in the skeleton of a miner who was killed by the collapse of a shaft, his deerhorn pick in hand. Pits were sunk into the ground and shafts dug from them into the flint-bearing chalk. When near the close of the Neolithic Period men began to make copper tools, they had already acquired a considerable experience in the techniques of mining.

Religion   The changing needs brought about by settled life resulted in a changed relationship with the supernatural powers in which man had long believed. The spirit that had once controlled wild game and that man had solicited for success in hunting was now needed to protect domestic cattle and insure the fertility of the herds. Gods of vegetation and plants had to be cajoled or appeased. Flood or drought were matters of universal concern to the farmer, and the spirits of air

Neolithic Flint Knives
from Egypt. (The Metro-
politan Museum of Art,
Rogers Fund, 1907,
1910)

and water, which controlled these matters, needed to be made friendly. Man's relationship to supernatural powers beyond his control and understanding constituted the source of religious thought and experience. To secure the aid or avert the anger of these dimly understood forces, man practiced rituals of prayer, sacrifice, dance and feast, injunction and taboo; and the paraphernalia of sympathetic magic was exerted now toward agricultural ends. Sexual symbolism played an increasing role as man sought to increase, ensure, or renew the generative powers of nature. The winter season and the long wait between seedtime and harvest were particularly anxious intervals, so feasts of joy came to be celebrated in the spring and feasts of thanksgiving when the harvest had been safely gathered in.

Neolithic Progress Men of the Neolithic Period, after becoming successful farmers who could produce a surplus of food, tended rapidly to develop specialization in trade and industry. The potter concentrated on making pots, and exchanged his wares for grain and meat. Merchants began to travel afar and to ship goods in bulk. These developments were accelerated and helped by several inventions of the most far-reaching significance. Among them were the canal, the sail-boat, metal-working, and writing. They were made as men adapted themselves to life in the great river valleys of Mesopotamia and Egypt.

The Canal It is possible that neither the Tigris-Euphrates delta nor the Nile delta was built up in the fifth millennium B.C. to its present extent.[6] The rivers entered the sea some distance inland from their present mouths, and the marshes presently characteristic of the deltas extended farther up the river valleys. Canals made it possible to utilize the fertile but swampy land. Channels and ditches drew off the surplus water of flood seasons and drained the swamps, and provided water for irrigation in dry weather. Networks of canals of varying sizes were built in the valleys of the Tigris-Euphrates, the Nile, and the Indus during the late Neolithic Period.

The Wheel   The invention of the wheel revolutionized the transport of men and goods by land. Sleds continued to be used into the historical period in both Mesopotamia and Egypt, but wheeled carts were more commonly used in Mesopotamia. The discovery of the principle of the axle produced the free-turning wheel without which modern civilization could hardly exist. The earliest carts had both axle and wheel made of wood but no means of lubrication. Noise, shrieking noise, undoubtedly marked their progress from field to village in early Mesopotamia. Nor did they race across the land. The draft animals were oxen or asses, neither of which are known for their speed. But hitched to the cart, the slow ox or donkey could draw a heavy burden and cover a long distance at its own pace. The principle of the free-turning wheel applied to the pottery industry transformed that ancient craft as well, giving its products not only greater uniformity in shape but making possible a more rapid production of vessels.

Sailboats   Rafts and boats of some kind or other were already known before this time but they were not constructed to carry large cargoes. For example, the earliest boats on the Euphrates were made of hides and were small and frail. Sea-going boats and cargo ships together with the sail to propel them, were invented in the late Neolithic. By the time written records become available, ships were sailing down the Euphrates, the Nile, and the Indus, and sea trade had developed in the Persian Gulf and Indian Ocean, and around the coasts of the Mediterranean Sea and across it to the island of Crete.

Metal-working   Many scholars believe that the first metal to be worked was gold, and some evidence and considerable logic support the idea. Men searching for flint may have come across gold-bearing ores and picked up lumps of it because of its beauty. Gold is easily worked, being very malleable and soft as metals go, so it is easily shaped for ornament. Silver likewise lends itself to the experiments of inexperienced workmen. The third most malleable metal is copper, and it occurred frequently and in considerable quantity in the highlands of the middle east. Copper, like the rarer metals mentioned, is found in a pure state in nature, and it was soon discovered that it could be hammered into shape cold. Accident or experiment led to the further dis-

[6]Some studies suggest that the Tigris-Euphrates delta has not changed as much as was formerly believed.

covery that it could be molded more readily when heated. Later, in the attempt to make it harder, artisans were to add other metals, notably tin, and to invent bronze. The manufacture of iron came much later. It is a far more difficult medium to master, so it was not until the second millennium B.C., after a very long experience in the manufacture of copper and bronze, that men were able to deal with iron effectively. An occasional object made from meteoric iron is found from an earlier time, but its owner probably regarded it as a curiosity or magical charm.

The use of metal tools and weapons made all tasks easier and their accomplishment more efficient. The clans that possessed metal weapons had an advantage in warfare, and as the knowledge of metal-working and of agriculture spread westward into Europe the advantage was felt. The early metal age in Europe led to migrations, wars, and the stirring deeds of heroes; it was an epic age sung by the bards and poets.

Writing Indian tribesmen of North America who had reached a late Neolithic stage were leaving each other messages in picture writing. Two man figures walking and followed by two pictures of the sun indicated that two men had set out on a journey of two-days duration. Early writing in the middle east and Egypt developed in the same fashion. At first, each picture represented an object. Next, variations were used to express not an object but a sound, or group of sounds. In some systems of writing, notably Sumerian and Chinese, the pictures came to stand for syllables, or morphemes, and the signs came to be formalized and lost all pictorial qualities. The scribes were taught to recognize the sounds for which they stood. The Egyptian script developed toward an alphabet but never quite reached it. Several pictures originally stood for monosyllabic words consisting of a consonant and vowel ($\bigcirc$ *te*, $\Leftrightarrow$ *re*, $\square$ *pe*), in which the vowel was very weak. Dropping the vowel, these pictures came to represent the single consonants (*t, r, p*). The entire Egyptian language could have been written in an alphabet of consonantal signs numbering twenty-four, but it never became that simple, as biliteral and triliteral signs were retained, as well as a group of determinatives which remained true pictures of objects and were used at the end of a word to make doubly clear its meaning. Egyptian did however develop a separate set of symbols for numerical notation, which was a great advantage in mathematical calculations. The Egyptian system probably underlies the present alphabetic script. It spread into Sinai and then Syria, and the Phoenicians of the first millennium B.C. developed a true alphabetic system through their simplification of the Syrian version. From them it passed to the Greeks, Etruscans, and Romans—from whom western Europeans inherited it.

The Spread of Farming to Europe The agricultural economy spread slowly from Mesopotamia and Egypt by way of the river valleys. From Mesopotamia it moved up the Danube into the Alps, followed the river valleys into Germany, and spread into France and England. From

Egypt, the agricultural pattern crossed North Africa into Spain and traveled on into France, where it met and mingled with the alternate pattern advancing in the north. The method of transmission was simple. Groups, or clans, which practiced farming would move to a likely spot, settle down, and clear fields by chopping and burning. For a few years they planted crops, but after the initial fertility of the soil was reduced and the forest cover began to reseed itself, the group would abandon the site and move on and repeat the process. Several farming cultures fol-

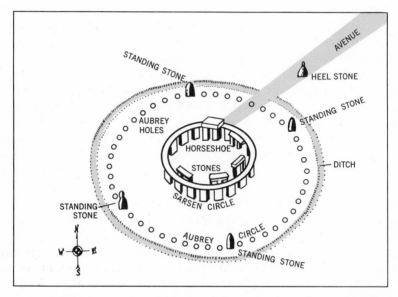

Plan of Stonehenge. The oldest features are believed to be the bank, ditch, Aubrey holes, and Heelstone (Sunstone). The purpose of the holes is unknown but cremated human remains, wood ash, and flints were found in them. From the center of Stonehenge, the sun is seen to rise near the tip of the Heelstone on the longest day of the year. The later Standing stones may mark off the year into four seasons through the appearance on certain dates of sunset over their tips. The last building period saw the erection of the bluestone horseshoe, with stones brought from quarries two hundred miles distant, and the Sarsen circle. These huge stones, which are capped with lintels of equally large size, have figures of stone axes of Aegean style incised upon them in shallow relief. Other features (not shown) include the Altar stone within the inner horseshoe, the "Slaughter" stone (whose purpose is unknown) at the head of the causeway, and a series of empty holes within the space between the Aubrey holes and the Sarsen circle which are called X, Y, and Z holes. Some of these features may represent changes of plan resulting from the various periods of building.

lowed one another across Europe, among them the Bell Beaker folk, the Danubians, the Swiss lake dwellers and the Indo-Europeans.

Trade with the more advanced and civilized east was maintained and grew apace. Enterprising easterners came to the river mouths to exchange their manufactured goods for the raw materials of the west, and well-established trade routes developed along the Dnieper, Danube, Rhone, and other navigable rivers. Amber, fine flint, raw metals, furs, and many other products reached the Mediterranean merchants, while bronze wares, wine, dyed textiles, and other specialties penetrated into Europe.

Change ordinarily came last to Scandinavia and the British Isles, but even they were not exempt from the currents radiating from the south and east. Beads made in the Aegean area came to Britain in the second millennium B.C., and ideas came along with such objects. Beginning in the third millennium B.C. and continuing into the second, monuments and tombs characterized by the use of huge stones (megaliths) follow a broad path from Malta, Sicily, and Sardinia into Spain and France and then to Britain. Stone circles exist in Brittany, England, Ireland, Scotland, and even Denmark. The most famous of these is Stonehenge near Salisbury, England. Its earliest building period dates from about 1900 B.C., though additions were made until about 1600 B.C. Stonehenge is tremendously impressive. It can be seen for miles over Salisbury Plain, crowning a hill free from all forest and magnificently open to the sky. Leading up to it is an embanked earthen avenue, which is easily traceable from the air. An outer bank and ditch bound a broad, grassy circle lying outside the inner horseshoe of standing stones. Imagination peoples it with rings of dancing sunworshipers.[7]

MAN, THE CITY DWELLER

While Europeans gradually learned to farm, the settled villagers in Mesopotamia and Egypt expanded and developed their economy, social institutions, and political organization and the physical size of their communities. The arts and crafts which grew up through the Neolithic Period required that men divide their labors, specialize, and depend more closely on one another to supply goods and services which not every man could provide for himself. Successful agriculture could supply a large population, and villages in fertile areas rapidly grew into towns and then into small cities. Political organization changed and developed as men sought protection, order, and advantage in trade.

---

[7] Gerald S. Hawkins, *Stonehenge Decoded.* Garden City, N. Y.: Doubleday & Co., 1965, pp. 98–118 and passim.

With this era of specialization, marked as it was by the systematic use of writing, true history may be said to begin. Man was less a victim of his environment, and took more successful steps to manipulate and control it.

Conclusion Through long centuries man slowly advanced his control over his environment. As a food gatherer he learned to make tools, to use fire, and to sustain himself and his family in a hostile environment through social cooperation. He made slow but continuous progress toward a more stable economy. Then, achieving the domestication of animals and the mastery of agriculture, he became a food producer, and the pace of his advance quickened. Invention followed invention to give him greater comfort and security. He learned to control his environment by digging canals, by inventing wheeled vehicles, by inventing the sailboat, and by manipulating metals into new forms. Finally, by the invention of writing he brought himself to a level of accomplishment undreamed of by his forebears. A sure means of communication over both distance and time was made available, and the danger of the loss of accumulated skills was ended. Literature and recorded history began, and it is to the earliest of the true civilizations, with its written records, that attention must now be given.

2 · Mesopotamia: The Land
of the Two Rivers

THE FOUNDATIONS OF WESTERN CIVILIZATION WERE laid in the middle east almost ten thousand years ago. While still relying primarily on hunting for a livelihood, men settled in villages along the rim of the Tigris-Euphrates Valley and on the terraces of the Nile canyon before or soon after 7000 B.C. Later, villages edged the flood plain of the Indus River in Pakistan. The settlers turned, in the course of time, to herding, and occupied their villages for only part of the year because of the necessity to seek ample pasturage for their flocks and herds. By the beginning of the fifth millenium, men were moving into the rich flood plains, with their lush foliage crops, and were turning to farming in the fullest sense.

The earliest settlements and the clearest uninterrupted record of village growth, from primitive camps to cities, are found in Mesopotamia. Every stage of Neolithic development — the domestication of animals, the change to farming, the use of canals, the invention of the sailboat and early use of the wheel, the discovery of metal-working and the development of the art of writing — is clearly shown. By contrast, the records from Egypt and Pakistan are incomplete and offer uncertainties in the attempt to reconstruct the course of events. Moreover, new dating methods indicate that men's progress toward an urban life occurred a little earlier in Mesopotamia than in Egypt or Pakistan. For these reasons, a study of early Mesopotamian history is undertaken first.

The Land of the Two Rivers The land known presently as Iraq was called *Mesopotamia* by the Greeks, a name that meant "between the rivers" and designated the entire broad, fertile plain watered by the Tigris and the Euphrates. Within the considerable area of Mesopotamia local names are given to particular sections. The people who are now called Sumerians called their land Kengir, though modern writers designate it Sumer; Akkadian territory is called Akkad and, much later, when Babylon became the leading city of the region, the area is known as

31

Babylonia. The general term that includes the entire area is
Mesopotamia.

Sources   The sources of information for the earliest periods in
Mesopotamia are entirely archaeological. They are supplemented in
time by epigraphic (inscriptions on clay, stone, or metal) and literary
texts, but until the beginning of the third millenium B.C., archaeology
alone is responsible for tracing the village settlements in the northern
hill country and the gradual occupation of the flood plain. Houses and
walls were made of sun-dried clay and brick, in the hills and on the plain.
When buildings fell down or were melted down by rains, new structures
were built on the debris, to collapse in their turn and be succeeded by
others. Mounds grew, in the course of the generations, on the accumulation of collapsed houses. Over a long period of time, and following
successive building and rebuilding in sun-dried brick, the mounds grew
to tower above the plain. When they are opened, the layout of the successive cities and the plans of the houses are revealed, and in the ruins
are found the implements and the writings of the inhabitants.

Writing began in Mesopotamia by about 3000 B.C. but the number
and nature of the documents make them most valuable after 2700.
Occasional inscriptions on stone are found, but most of the texts are
written on clay tablets that were dried in the sun or baked in kilns.
Many hundreds of thousands of such clay tablets have been found.
They consist of public and private records of all sorts: legal-economic
texts, omen texts, annals, poems, tales, religious documents, myths,
proverbs, wills, deeds, bills of sale, contracts, law codes, and scholarly
literature, including works on astronomy, mathematics, chemistry,
medicine, and pharmacology. They provide a wealth of material on
the history and literature of the Mesopotamian peoples in all major
periods. Decipherment has proceeded apace, so that the scholar is no
longer dependent on the scraps of information that can be gleaned from
later literature such as the Bible, the works of the Greek historian
Herodotus, or the late Babylonian chronicler Berossus, whose work
survives chiefly through quotation by Josephus in the Roman period.

The recovery and decipherment of contemporary texts has revealed in detail the history of Sumer, the earliest civilization of Mesopotamia—a civilization completely unknown to the Biblical writers or to the
Greeks. The archaeologist has supplemented the facts described by
the Sumerian documents to give a full picture of the material culture.
But archaeology alone could never have named the Sumerians, or described their political, social, and religious institutions or the wealth and
force of their thoughts and aspirations.

Geography   Mesopotamia is a land richly endowed for the development of civilization. Two very large rivers pour across an extensive
plain, whose fertility is renewed by the silt deposited annually during

the floods. The longer of the rivers, the Euphrates, rises in the mountains of Armenia, flows west for a distance, and then turns southeast onto the flood plain, across which it makes its leisurely way in bends and loops. The Tigris rises at no great distance from the upper Euphrates but rushes swiftly through the Assyrian hills and over the plain to the Persian Gulf, staying to the north or east of the longer river. It is deeper, swifter and more dangerous in flood than the Euphrates. In the fourth and third milleniums B.C. the two rivers entered the Persian Gulf separately, rather than together as they do now.

Both rivers served as highways for travel and as avenues for trade. By the third millenium they formed an important link in the international trade route extending from the Indus River to the Mediterranean and the Nile. It is unlikely that any one merchant made the entire journey, but goods of a luxury type, such as jade, sometimes did. From the Indus, ships crossed the Indian Ocean and sailed through the Persian Gulf to the river ports. Inland from a point roughly north of Damascus, the route led overland across the grassy highland that forms a part of the Fertile Crescent (grasslands extending through Syria), and then down the valleys to the coastal plain of Syria and thence to the shores of the Mediterranean. From there the routes branched to the north and south, by land and by sea.

The fertile plain offered every incentive to the farmer, once he had learned to drain it, adapt to it, and combat its dangers. During the Pluvial period coinciding with the last ice age, much of Mesopotamia was extensively covered with bogs and swamps. But by about 5000 B.C. it was dry enough to permit permanent settlement, though areas of swamp remained and were drained through canals by the early settlers. The plain was rich in plant and animal life useful to men. Wild grains, including two or three varieties of wheat and barley; wild fruits, the peach, fig, and date; nuts, such as the Persian walnut; and various edible vegetables grew luxuriantly. Reeds for baskets and mats were plentiful. Goats, oxen, and sheep profited from the excellent pasturage, and the omnivorous pig found plenty to sustain him. Lacking were stone, timber, and vegetable fibers suitable for textiles. Mud had to be used for building; sheepskin and wool for clothing and covering. Nevertheless it was a wealthy environment which offered not only the essentials for nourishment but the possibility of a surplus that could be used for trade.

Mesopotamia was marked by no geographical frontiers that could be easily defended, so invasions and immigrations were frequent. The first settlers were hill people from the north and east, and they were followed by other vigorous hill folk who unexpectedly and swiftly moved down the valleys into the plain. To the west and south were the grasslands of northern Arabia, where the rains were sufficient to provide fodder for the herds of sheep and cattle which groups of hardy Semitic peoples (p. 46) have tended since Neolithic times. The increase of population or a sequence of bad seasons drove them either into the hill country of Syria in the west or into Mesopotamia to the east. The history of Mesopotamia is marked by succeeding waves of peoples who swept into and settled on the plain.

Early Settlements on the Hills   Agriculture and village life did not begin in the river valley but on the hills above it. A growing number of the earliest village sites have been located and excavated, and the pattern of development is fairly clear. The first inhabitants built small mud-brick houses with regular rooms. They used microliths and polished stone tools, and invented sickles for reaping and grinding stones for milling their grain. They practiced a primitive agriculture and kept herds of sheep, beef and dairy cattle, and pigs. No pottery is to be found in the earliest sites, indicating a diet based on meat and grain, with little use of other plant foods. But as time passed and the villages underwent several periods of rebuilding, the houses increased in size and complexity, pottery appeared, and clay ovens were constructed for baking bread. Storage facilities for grain, consisting of bins sunk into the floor, were devised and expanded. The diet became more diverse and the livelihood secure. Mats and baskets were woven of reeds, cloth of wool. More and more of the stone tools were polished, and they changed slowly but consistently in shape and purpose. Hunting points decreased, though arrowheads and maces were still made and slings were used to fire clay pellets. Agricultural tools and household implements including hoes, sickles, knives, awls, grinding stones, mortars, and pestles took their place.

Similar villages growing in much the same way, though later in time, came to dot the Fertile Crescent all the way to the Mediterranean coast, and eastward into Elam and Iran. An active trade, which carried shells from the Persian Gulf far inland, developed between these villages, and finely made and decorated pottery was exchanged over wide areas. The donkey served as the chief beast of burden, and was used for the transport of farm products and trade goods.

The First Villages on the Plain   The first men to settle in the flood plain of the Tigris and Euphrates rivers had considerable experience in successful farming and village life behind them. Used to social cooperation and knowing the value of good land, they were attracted to the valley because of its fertility. Several waves of immigrants, whose relative state of sophistication is proved by the painted pottery they made, entered on one another's heels. Since these people can be identified only by their pottery and tools, they are named after the modern villages near which they are known to have settled; they cannot be identified as to race or language. Late in the fifth millenium, or early in the fourth, came the Ubaid culture, the Uruk (or Warka) culture, and others. The Ubaid people settled in a number of small villages up and down the banks of the two rivers, building houses of matting plastered over with mud and covered with flat or barrel roofs. They brought with them their herds of cattle, sheep, goats, and pigs, as well as their tools of flint and obsidian. Stone for new tools had to be obtained from the north. But the tools were the familiar ones of the types long used in the hill villages: hoes, sickles, grinding stones, slings, arrows, and maces. Their pottery was coarse and was decorated with geometric designs.

The Uruk culture included the making of fine pottery but, more important, the people made noteworthy advances in digging an extensive network of canals for drainage and irrigation. So successful were they in social cooperation to increase crop yields that the population grew enormously. Villages gave way to walled cities and towns in which temples were built, as well as private houses. Metal was cast in molds. In and along with the Uruk culture existed a more sophisticated pattern known as the Jamdat Nasr phase. It is likely that it evolved from the Uruk, but whether slowly or swiftly and whether as a result of new peoples coming among the older inhabitants, is uncertain. In the Jamdat Nasr phase, toward the middle of the fourth millenium, metallurgy made decisive advances. Tools and ornaments of gold and copper appeared. Soon after, before the end of the Jamdat Nasr phase, writing began.

THE SUMERIANS

Among the hill peoples who settled in Mesopotamia are the Sumerians. Their earliest settlements cannot be identified in the absence of written clues, but taking into account the archaeological evidence combined with their own historical tradition, it is probable that the Sumerians were not the dominant cultural group of the Jamdat Nasr period or even responsible for the development of writing, but that they inherited these civilized advances when they came into control of the towns of the lower valley toward the end of the fourth millenium or shortly thereafter.

Before the end of the third millenium the cities were large, prosperous, and thriving. Among them were Ur, Erech, Eridu, Nippur, Kish, Larsa, Lagash, and Umma. Occasional floods caused damage, and early excavations seemed to show that Ur was almost destroyed by an especially severe inundation sometime prior to 3000, but more extensive investigation proved that only one section of the city was badly damaged. No evidence of one great, disastrous flood has come to light, though Sumerian and later literary tradition persists in recounting the story of a flood that "destroyed the world and most of mankind." The later tales may have been based on the Sumerian version, which was in

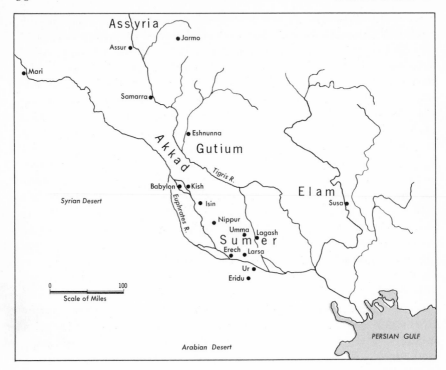

Ancient Sumer and Akkad, ca. 2500 B.C.

the form of an epic and told how Ziusudra built a giant boat to save himself and his family. The text (from Nippur) reads in part:

> All the windstorms, exceedingly powerful, attacked as one,
> At the same time, the flood swept over the cult centers.
>
> After, for seven days and seven nights,
> The flood had swept over the land,
> And the huge boat had been tossed about by the windstorms on
>   the great waters.
> Utu came forth, who sheds light on heaven and earth,
> Ziusudra opened a window on the huge boat,
> The hero Utu brought his rays into the giant boat.[1]

This poem, like other Sumerian documents, was written in cuneiform script on clay tablets.

Cuneiform Writing   During the Jamdat Nasr period, a system of writing was invented which is known as cuneiform, so named from the Latin word *cuneus*, meaning wedge, because of the wedge-shaped marks

---

[1] Trans. by Samuel Noah Kramer, *History Begins at Sumer*. Garden City, N.Y.: Doubleday & Company (Anchor Books), 1959, p. 153.

made by a blunt reed stylus on wet clay. The Sumerians adopted, and undoubtedly perfected, the system. Early cuneiform script contained pictures representing objects and ideas, but the pictures gave way to stylized symbols representing syllables. The Sumerian language was agglutinative, that is, it was made up of syllables, or rather morphemes, joined together to form phrases and sentences—as in the languages of the American Indians and in modern Turkish. Since letters were not a part of the original language, cuneiform did not develop toward an alphabetic system. Hundreds of signs were used, of which about two hundred were common. Cuneiform was difficult to learn but flexible enough to be adapted to other languages. Various Semites and Indo-European Hittites and Persians were able to use it, and even Egyptian scribes learned to write cuneiform for use in diplomatic correspondence. It continued to be used in Mesopotamia until the first century A.D., when it was finally superseded by the alphabet.

The Calendar The lunar calendar used by the Sumerians, based on the recurrent phases of the moon, was awkward, as it rapidly got out of harmony with the rotation of the crop seasons and had to be adjusted to them again. Still, it provided a system of chronology useful in keeping records. The year was divided into two seasons, summer and winter. There were twelve months with twenty-nine or thirty days, and an intercalary month was added when necessary to adjust the calendar to the crop seasons. For many centuries each city had its own names for the months and its own system of inserting extra months, but eventually the calendar of the city of Nippur was generally adopted and became official. In public records, years were recorded by means of some noteworthy event rather than by a system of formal numbering.

Government While the Sumerians shared a common language and culture, each of their cities constituted an independent, normally self-governing city-state. An insecure political union was occasionally attained when one city succeeded in conquering others and imposing its overlordship on them. Such unions were of short duration, and even when effected no real centralization of government was achieved. A conquered city continued to be ruled by local officials, who were looked upon as "vassals" of the ruler of the conquering city.

After 2700 B.C., the normal government was monarchial. The governments prior to that time, it is widely believed, could be called "primitive democracies."[2] Kingship probably grew out of the need for

[2] The term "primitive democracy" was first advanced by Thorkild Jacobsen in a paper and later amplified by him in "Mesopotamia" in *The Intellectual Adventure of Ancient Man* by Henri Frankfort *et al.* Chicago: The University of Chicago Press, 1946. In my view it is an unfortunate term to place before the beginning student since the Sumerian system resembled neither the classical democracy of the Greeks, nor the neoclassical concept of democracy discussed by seventeenth- and eighteenth-century philosophers, nor modern Western democratic governments.

The Ram in the Thicket
from the Royal Tombs
at Ur, Gold and Lapis
Lazuli. (The University
Museum, Philadelphia)

military leadership, and at first the king may have been chosen by the
assembly of citizens. In the course of time, the office of king became
hereditary and individual rulers sometimes claimed divine ancestry—
Gilgamesh of Erech, according to an early text, was two-fifths a god.
The monarch was advised by the Council of Elders, and he could call
together the Assembly, which was made up of all free men in the
city-state. A text from Erech indicates that the king and Assembly
could, if they wished, override the advice of the Council.

The principal source of information on the royal families between
about 2700 and 1750 B.C., though it is often confusing, is the Sumerian
king list. It says the kingship originally "descended from heaven,"
and thereafter it records the "carrying off" of the kingship from one
city to another. Typical is the statement: "Kish was defeated and its
kingship was carried off to Eanna." It is known, however, that some of
the dynasties listed consecutively in the king list were actually contemporary and parallel. For example, it is now known that Gilgamesh of
Erech was a younger contemporary of Mesannepadda of Ur. Both
kings probably reigned about 2600 B.C.

Political History   The best that can be done presently in reconstructing the political history of Sumer is to give a rather bare outline.
Between 2700 and about 2500 B.C., there were parallel dynasties of
kings at Kish, Erech, and Ur. Each controlled other city-states but none

Gold Vessels from the Royal Tombs at Ur. (The University Museum, Philadelphia)

dominated all of Sumer. A little before 2500, a king from Adab called Lugalannemundu conquered most, if not all, of the Sumerian states. He called himself King of the Four Quarters and the king list assigns him a remarkable reign of ninety years. After his death, division once more beset Sumer, and the king list records "the carrying off of the kingship" successively to Mari, Kish, and Akshak, back to Kish, and then to Erech.

The king of Erech was then defeated by Sargon of Akkad, possibly a little before 2300 B.C., and Sargon went on to conquer all of Sumer and extensive territories to the north, northeast, and northwest. The bounds of his empire are uncertain, though later tradition gives him everything from Egypt to India. Sargon's sons had to deal with revolts and rebellions, which they successfully overcame, and his grandson, Naram-Sin, claimed to have extended the vast empire into north Syria and Armenia.

A tragic end befell Naram-Sin's empire. A people called Guti, coming from the mountains of the east, took Akkad and nearly engulfed Sumer. The Akkadian domination was ended, though Akkad itself survived into the first millenium.

How long the Guti ruled Sumer is a matter of dispute, but for some time they were able to appoint and remove local governors and collect tribute. Yet there was an increasing independence perceptible in Lagash and perhaps other cities. Gudea, the most reknowned *ensi* ("governor") of Lagash, seems to have been quite free from any interference by them (see p. 47). But traditionally it was Utukhegal, the hero-king of Erech, who drove the Guti from Sumer. His victory gained him only a short period of dominance, for after seven years (by the king list) "Erech was smitten with weapons [and] its kingship carried off to Ur."

Ur-Nammu, founder of the Third Dynasty of Ur a little before 2100 B.C., extended his sway over most of Sumer, though he and his successors had to continue a defensive war against the Guti. Shulgi, son of Ur-Nammu, took the title King of Four Quarters (the title seems to have come to mean overlord, or perhaps emperor) and claimed to have conquered territory beyond the borders of Sumer. The next three kings of Ur were threatened by Amorites and, more seriously, by Elamites, whose incursions weakened and finally ended Ur's "empire" shortly before 2000 B.C.

In the aftermath of Ur's fall, rival dynasties at Isin and Larsa strove to control Sumer. Early in the eighteenth century B.C., Rim-Sin of Larsa defeated his rival at Isin and gained undisputed leadership, which lasted about thirty years. He was overthrown by Hammurabi, who went on to conquer all of Sumer. Independent Sumerian history ends forever with this conquest in about 1750 B.C.

Society The law codes of Sumer recognize only two classes: free men and slaves, but among the free men there were a number of subclasses, or occupational groups. The priests, princes, and soldiers constituted an upper class, even if this was not recognized by law. Below them were the majority of free citizens, who made their living by farming, cattle breeding, fishing, trading, and manufacturing goods for home use and for sale abroad. Others were merchants, scribes, doctors, carpenters, masons, smiths, and jewelers. There is some evidence to indicate that merchants and scribes ranked higher socially than men working in the crafts or in agriculture, as education was necessary for these professions and was highly valued. The Russian scholar N. M. Diakanoff classifies Sumerian society in four groups: nobles, commoners, clients, and slaves. In his view, the nobles held large landed estates, worked by clients, and they made up the Council of Elders in the city-state. The commoners filled the occupations noted above and constituted the Assembly. The clients worked for the temple or for the nobles and owned no land in their own right, though they may have received temporary assignments of plots as well as rations of food and wool.

Slavery, while apparently not on a large scale, was normal in Sumerian society. Some slaves were war captives, others were purchased abroad, and still others were natives who had sold their families or themselves into temporary bondage for three years. A man might also be enslaved as a punishment for crime. The slave could be beaten by his master but not killed, and Sumerian law gave slaves important legal rights. They could go into business, borrow money, and, if they could manage it, buy their freedom. The children of a free person (male or female) who had married a slave were free.

Women in Sumer could hold property, engage in business, and serve as witnesses. However, marriages were arranged by parents or guardians, and if there were no children of a marriage, the husband could take a second wife. Divorce was easy for men and extremely difficult for women. Wives probably had dower rights in joint property, but the true heirs were the children.

Children, natural-born or adopted, were the property of their father, who could sell them into slavery or even disinherit them. There is no reason to believe, however, that fathers frequently did either. On the contrary, texts showing the value placed upon the education and training of children make very real the affection and good wishes felt by normal parents in any age and the desire to have the children properly prepared for success in later life.

The Sumerian city-states of the late third and early second millen-iums attained considerable size. The populations, which have been estimated from the physical extent of the mounds and from written records, vary from 12,000 or 19,000 to 250,000 or more. The citizens lived in comfortable houses built of mud-brick and of a size commen-surate with their incomes. Homes of well-to-do owners were usually built around a paved courtyard, which served as a pleasant lounging area, and were two stories in height. The over-all appearance of the cities was impressive. A map of Nippur, drawn on a clay tablet and dat-ing from the beginning of the second millenium, indicates the princi-pal features of a town. The mound towered from sixty to a hundred feet over the plain, and was defended by a moat and a heavy brick wall pierced by seven gates; the city was bisected by a great canal eighty feet wide, and contained a park, the temple precinct of Enlil (its tutelary deity), and other temple areas.

Economic Life The economic life of Sumer was based on agricul-ture, though industry and trade were not without significance. The land sometimes yielded, according to Sumerian records, eighty-six times the sowing of a field of barley, and yields of a hundredfold or more may occasionally have been obtained on wheat. However, the aver-age yields of these grains must have been considerably less. Texts speak often of milk, cream, sheepfolds, groves (of fruit trees), and grain. Cheese and butter were made from the milk and cream, which was also consumed fresh, and wine was made from palms and dates. The grain furnished bread and beer. Sheep provided meat and wool; goats and dairy cattle produced milk, meat, and hides. Vegetables, including herbs, salad greens, beans, peas, lentils, and onions were marketed locally. The land was so fertile and rich that surpluses were easily and normally produced, though not all farm produce could be shipped. Grain, date and palm wine, beer, wool, hides, cheese, dried fish, and dried fruits could be exported. Beer was the most popular beverage. The date palm furnished fruit, wine, and an extract called *lal* ("honey"), which served as a sweet.

Land tenure varied from city to city, but some cities were subject to a kind of "divine ownership" by the tutelary god. Such cities, but not others, were under direct or indirect temple administration. There were many variations, but at Nippur, for example, land was held in freehold (subject to taxes in the name of the tutelary deity), rented for short periods, or leased for long terms. Theoretically, all the property of the city-state was owned by the patron god but in practice it was treated as private property. Still, the god's nominal ownership gave a legal basis for taxation, which was termed "rent," for the use of his land. A clear distinction was made between the land held directly in a god's name and managed by his priests, and that held permanently by families and individuals. The latter, while termed "tenants" of the god, could dispose of their holdings freely by sale or lease and, after payment of taxes, make any use they desired of the produce. On land forming a part of the god's demesne, or personal estate, all produce came into his storehouses and the workers were paid wages in barley and other foodstuffs.

Industry was diverse, and conducted by private individuals or in shops belonging to the estates of the gods. Long before 3000 B.C. stone tools had been displaced by implements made of copper, and by 3000 bronze was coming into common use. It was easier and cheaper to import metals than stone. Metalsmiths were kept busy making hoes, plows, knives, axes, sickles, razors, and a multiplicity of other wares. Weapons, armor, ornaments, and jewelry were also in demand, and the smiths were able to make all manner of cunningly wrought articles. The royal tombs of Ur, dating soon after 2700 B.C., provide many samples of their art. Furniture inlaid with gold, silver, and semiprecious stones; harps, silver harnesses for donkeys, bowls, helmets, swords, daggers, jewelry, and game boards are among the products represented.

But many other industries besides metal-working were profitable. Brickmakers and construction crews were kept busy building dwellings, shops, and public buildings. Since sun-dried brick was used for most building purposes, repairs were often needed and rebuilding occurred at frequent intervals. Brewers of beer and wine found sales through small shops and taverns, as well as through the merchants interested in export. Canal diggers were almost constantly at work. The tremendous volume of silt brought down by the Tigris and Euphrates rivers spread annually over the land and clogged the drainage and irrigation ditches.

Bull's Head of Gold and Lapis Lazuli Ornamenting a Harp Found in the Royal Tombs at Ur. (The University Museum, Philadelphia)

These had to be cleared, or bogs and marshes would form, the crops would rot in the fields, and the lower parts of the cities would be flooded. Drainage was of vital importance for the life and health of the city-state. The canals were equally important to the economy because of their function in irrigation. During the dry season water was brought through them from the rivers to the thirsty fields and garden plots. Constant, unending labor was necessary to maintain this complicated system, and while individual farmers were themselves responsible for small channels leading to their fields, the huge canals (such as the eighty-foot-wide ditch bisecting Nippur) required gangs of workmen to maintain them. There were many household industries, but pottery making was probably the most important. Since pottery vessels and baskets were the principal containers for goods to be exported, a surplus must necessarily have been produced. Weaving was also important, and included making baskets and matting as well as weaving textiles for rugs, covers, and clothing. Some of these goods too were exported.

If there were retail shops for local trade, they were undoubtedly connected with or part of private homes and tended to be small and designed to serve as outlets for the products made on the premises. Leatherworkers, perfumers, goldsmiths, silversmiths, and seal makers generally made and sold their goods in the same store, but could produce surpluses for export nonetheless.

Trade was active inside each city, between Sumerian cities, and with far countries such as Elam, Assyria, the Anatolian highlands, Syria, Egypt, Iran, the shorelands of the Persian Gulf, and the Indus Valley. Transport was by water wherever possible, at least for bulk cargoes, but an early text from Erech records the shipment of grain to a mountain city on the backs of donkeys, in exchange for building stone and stones for ornament. Sumerians had to import all stone as none was available in the valley. All metal, too, had to be imported. Copper and tin came from the hills along the Persian Gulf and from Anatolia (Asia Minor). Silver and lead came from the Taurus Mountains and gold from Anatolia or Egypt. Shell and mother-of-pearl were obtained from the Persian Gulf and the Indian Ocean. Wood was another material strongly desired and ardently sought by Sumerians. No trees suitable for building were native to Mesopotamia, and the merchants were forced to range far to obtain cedar and hardwoods. Most timber came from the mountains of the northeast, but some may have been brought from Lebanon and Syria.

To pay for the raw metals, stone, lumber, and other materials they imported, the Sumerians exported agricultural surpluses and manufactured products. Grain, according to the sources, was most welcome to the hill peoples, though other foods that could be preserved were also shipped. Fine pottery, metal vessels and tools, inlaid furniture, and other articles traveled farther. Items of Sumerian origin have been found in Syria and Egypt, and products probably Egyptian in Sumeria. Merchants, shipowners, boatmen, stevedores, and donkey drivers all played a role in this trade.

Religion The Sumerians explained the observable facts of nature and their own habits, customs, and institutions in relation to it in mythopoeic terms. The cosmos was to them an animate, living thing whose powers and forces were personified as spirits, or gods. The Sumerian creation myths embody and express this belief in an animate cosmos. "In the beginning" heaven and earth were united in the primeval waters, which gave birth to the "Mountain of Heaven" (An) and the earth (Ki). An (male) and Ki (female) united to bring forth a host of divinities called the Anunnaki, each of whom controlled some nat-

ural power. The most important of these was Enlil (air), who separated
An and Ki by force, carried off his mother, and by her begot other
important divinities. These various deities (forces) formed unions to
produce thousands of lesser gods and goddesses, each of whom personified an object (reed, brick, salt) or a specific power (love, hate, greed).
Each myth of divine marriage sought to explain some relationship
between natural phenomena. The entire spirit host was organized and
run as a state, ruled and guided by the major forces, who were: An, Ki
(also called Ninhursag), Enlil, Nanna (moon), Utu (sun), Enki (fresh
water and wisdom), and Inanna (love and "Queen of Heaven").

While each of the great forces might act independently within their
own realms, major decisions concerning the universe were debated and
decided by the Anunnaki meeting in an assembly over which An presided. When a decision was made, the appropriate god was delegated
to carry it out. Enlil, who because of the power of wind, storm, flood,
and rain, which he controlled, had also become god of war, was often the
executor of the decrees. He was loved, courted, and feared beyond any
other god, because rain and flood were benevolent to Sumer and
necessary to the land's well-being, yet dangerous, destructive, and un-
predictable in their unleashed force. The Sumerian attitude toward
Enlil is movingly stated in this short hymn:

> What has he planned . . . ?
> What is in my father's heart?
> What is in Enlil's holy mind?
> What has he planned against me in his holy mind?
> A net he spread: that is the net of an enemy.
> A snare he set: that is the snare of an enemy.
> He has stirred up the waters, and will catch the fishes.
> He cast his net and will bring down the birds.[3]

Such a view of the cosmos made the Sumerians feel humble. They
could feel no confidence in their ability to determine their own fate on
either an individual or community level. Rather, they believed that they,
the "black-headed people," had been created from clay to be the servants of the gods. Nor did they expect a better fate after death. The
nether world was a grim place under the earth, devoid of light and air,
where the dead existed as pale shades. It was ruled by a pitiless goddess
called Ereshkigal. Life, to the Sumerians, was infinitely better, or at least
more interesting, than death.

The only time Sumerians voluntarily, apparently, chose death was
at Ur, where mass graves have been found. Between fifty and seventy-
five people — servants, guards, and entertainers — joined important

---

[3]Trans. by Thorkild Jacobsen and reprinted from *The Intellectual Adventure of Ancient
Man* by Henri Frankfort *et al.* by permission of The University of Chicago Press, copyright 1946 by The University of Chicago, p. 144.

persons (male or female)[4] in huge death pits. The evidence indicates that the servants filed in wearing their finest clothes and jewels, drank a death potion (perhaps laudanum) and then disposed themselves peacefully to sleep and to die. They must surely have expected a better afterlife in the service of a divine master or mistress than was the lot of the ordinary mortal.

Religious beliefs also explained and guided political, social, and economic life in Sumeria. Some cities were "owned" by gods: Erech by Inanna, Ur by Nanna, and Nippur by Enlil. The tutelary deity in such a city was housed in a temple built on a "mountain," which was originally a raised platform but grew into a multistaged structure called a ziggurat. Built solidly of sun-dried brick, the ziggurat was decorated with baked brick or colored tile, and its terraces were planted with shrubs and flowers. The small temple on top contained an altar and couch, and was reached by an ornamental stairway. Near the base of the ziggurat were other buildings: temples to other gods, living quarters for the priests, storehouses, and the city archives. There was also a large open space in which the citizens could gather for meetings of the Assembly or for religious festivals. The whole great temple area, which was bounded by a wall, was called the *ekur*, and it, together with the palace and grounds that adjoined it, was the administrative heart of the city. The king or governor could enter the *ekur* by a private gate to sleep in the temple and receive the god's orders through dreams. The taxes, or "rents," of the god, which were paid in produce, were received into the storehouses along with the income from the god's personal estate. Official records, annals, and private business and property records were deposited in the archives. Individual citizens came to the *ekur* to ask the priests to interpret omens, to make sacrifices to the gods, to pay taxes and fees, and to enlist the services of a scribe. In the course of time the priestly caste which administered the area and assisted the ruler became more and more powerful politically and more and more important socially.

THE SEMITES

The term "Semite" has been applied to widely scattered groups of peoples who in historic times were found in Mesopotamia and on the grasslands west of the Euphrates in Syria and Arabia. Widely diverse in physical characteristics, they possessed a complex of language, ideas, customs, and institutions. The original Semites were

[4]Sir Leonard Woolley, *Excavations at Ur; A Record of Twelve Years' Work*, London: Ernest Benn, Ltd. 1954, *passim*; and more recently in Jacquetta Hawkes and Sir Leonard Woolley. *The History of Mankind*, vol. 1, *Prehistory and the Beginnings of Civilization*. New York: Harper and Row Publishers, 1963, p. 712.

a nomadic folk wandering in the grasslands with their herds. Their social organization was patriarchal. Their material culture was low, and their religion consisted in a belief in spirits, formless powers arbitrarily controlling the lives of men. Their language was capable of epigrammatic terseness and of word pictures glowing with imagery. The Semites showed marvelous adaptability and facility in learning. When overpopulation, bad seasons, or restlessness drove tribes into settled communities, they speedily blended with the older inhabitants and adopted their ways of living. In agricultural regions they became skillful farmers; in commercial centers many of them gained success as merchants. In western Arabia, in Syria, and in Mesopotamia they built powerful cities, conquered and organized great empires. They have contributed to the world some of its greatest religious leaders.

Akkad   At a very early time groups of Semites moved down the Euphrates from its middle stretches into the richer lands of the south. They may even have preceded the Sumerians along the gulf coast. There was always a strong Semitic element in the Sumerian cities, derived either from the north or from the grasslands of the west. The Semites were dominant in Akkad, a city-state in the region north of Sumer. The Akkadians adopted Sumerian practices in business and in agriculture, used Sumerian law and customs, and fitted the cuneiform script to their own language. When Sargon of Akkad defeated Lugalzaggesi of Umma and took all Sumer, he boasted of building roads to bind the empire together. He and his successors assigned Akkadian governors to oversee the rulers in each district, and Akkadians were permitted to reside freely in Sumerian cities. Their descendants remained there even after Akkadian control was ended by the Guti.

LAGASH

Lagash, one of the cities never mentioned in the Sumerian king list, has furnished one of the largest and most detailed collections of Sumerian records—especially after about 2500 B.C. They provide a clear picture of boundary disputes with neighboring Umma, military actions, methods of arbitration, the part played by oracles in the interior affairs of the city and in its relationships with other states, and the kind of treaties made between states. These texts also recount the abuse and corruption that grew to riddle the government of the *ensis*, and they tell of the social and ethical reforms of Urukagina, who tried to correct the evil conditions. His good work came to an end (though Urukagina himself may have survived) with the invasion of Lagash by Lugalzaggesi.

After the Guti ended Naram-Sin's control over Sumer, Lagash again became important. A new and strong dynasty of *ensis* ruled the city and came to be influential also in the affairs of Ur. The fourth of this line was Gudea (*ca.* 2100 B.C. or a little later). It is not certain whether

Seated Statue of Gudea, Diorite. (The Metropolitan Museum of Art, Dick Fund, 1959)

he paid tribute to the Guti, for his texts do not mention them. If so, he was permitted freedom in military and local affairs. The most interesting texts from the period of his governorship give an exciting insight into the wealth and resources of his state. The records describe how Gudea discovered the anger of Ningirsu (tutelary deity of Lagash) because his temple had fallen into disrepair and the attempts he made to be certain of the god's wishes and orders for its rebuilding. He slept many nights in temples until message-dreams had made the divine plan clear. Then he organized the citizens to carry it out. Architects drew up a "blueprint" of the temple, which is shown on the lap of one of the seated statues of Gudea. Stone was imported in some quantity for use in key parts of the building and to make a number of life-sized statues of Gudea. They are among the finest examples of Sumerian sculpture.

THE SUMERIAN REVIVAL, *ca.* 2150–2050 B.C.

Not long after Gudea's death, the ruler of Erech led a successful revolt against the Guti, but dominance over Sumer was soon wrested from him by Ur-Nammu, king of Ur, who founded the third dynasty of that city. Ur-Nammu, Shulgi, and their descendants led the most brilliant period in Sumerian history. A huge three-stage ziggurat was built in Ur, along with walls, temples, and palaces. After securing the defenses of Ur, Ur-Nammu turned to the internal problems of the state. He codified the laws and boasted that "the orphan did not fall prey to the wealthy" or "the widow to the powerful." His code exists only in fragments, but enough remains to show that the principle of an "eye for an eye, a tooth for a tooth" had given way to the less severe penalty of a money fine for the punishment of an injury.

Literature The period of the Sumerian revival might be called the golden age of Sumerian literature. S. N. Kramer dates the composition of the majority of Sumerian literary tablets to the period of the Third Dynasty of Ur, though by no means all of them were written in

Restoration of the Ziggurat of Ur-Nammu, Third Dynasty of Ur. (The University Museum, Philadelphia)

A Map of Ancient Nippur Drawn on a Clay Tablet ca. 2000 B.C. The walls
and principal drainage canal, along with the oblongs of various public
buildings, can easily be distinguished. City gates are labeled in cuneiform,
as are the other features. (The University Museum, Philadelphia)

Ur itself. The range of these documents is diverse, their contents rich.
Epics, tales, love poems, annals, medical prescriptions, mathematical
texts, laws and trial records, fables, and proverbs display the variety of
Sumerian interests, beliefs, and knowledge. This literature of the
"black-headed people" was to deliver an intense impact on all succeeding
peoples in Mesopotamia, even after Sumerian political hegemony was
ended and the very language was dead. Babylonians, Assyrians, and
Hittites copied and preserved these writings, constructing "dictionaries"
and "syllabaries" for themselves in order to gain access to it.

Causes of the Fall of Sumer   Technically, the conquest of Sumer
by the Amorite king Hammurabi about 1750 B.C. put an end to Sumerian independence, but it does not explain why the people and their

language ceased to exist (or why they ceased to maintain a separate identity). In all likelihood the reason for the absorption of the Sumerians into an Amorite-Akkadian population is exceedingly complex, but some probable reasons can be pointed out. From the time of the Akkadian conquest, the proportion of Semites to Sumerians was greatly increased, and the influx of Akkadian-speaking Amorites would have increased the proportion even more. Also contributing to the disappearance of the Sumerians, politically and linguistically, was the economic decline of most of their city-states. Many of them lost their harbors through the vagaries of the rivers or the extension of the coastline. For example, Ur and Eridu were both left high and dry by the shifting bed of the Euphrates and were abandoned by their citizens. Added to this misfortune was the decline of trade with the Indus Valley civilization in Pakistan. That culture was totally destroyed sometime between 1750 and 1500 B.C. The economic and political leadership of the lower valley of the Tigris-Euphrates rivers passed to Babylon.

THE INDUS VALLEY CULTURES

The history of the peoples of the Indus Valley parallels that of the Sumerians, though their development came a little later in time. Neolithic villages grew up along the northern line of hills in eastern Persia and Baluchistan above the flood plain of the Indus. Explorations have revealed some six or more farming cultures (named for modern mounds or from distinctive pottery), including the Amri, Kulli, and Shahi Tump peoples. By the opening of the third millennium, some of these villagers had descended into the plain to take up permanent residence, and their pottery underlies (Amri) or mingles with (Kulli) that of the Harappa people who conquered the valley and created its first civilization.

The origin of the Harappans is unknown, though from the evidence of the cemeteries they were made up chiefly of Caucasians with a sprinkling of Mongolians. About 2300 B.C. they conquered and lived with a Dravidian (proto-Australoid) people, and were always buried in separate cemeteries. The relative poverty of the Dravidian graves indicates that the Dravidians were in servitude to the Harappans. Perhaps they were "untouchables" even then, as they have been for so many centuries since.

The Harappan civilization is named for a village on the Ravi River, a tributary of the Upper Indus, near which the first of the cities was discovered in 1856. Builders of a railway were pleased to find the tremendous mound of baked brick and robbed it freely for use on the railway bed. Serious archaeological exploration did not take place until the 1920s, when an even larger city called Mohenjo-Daro was

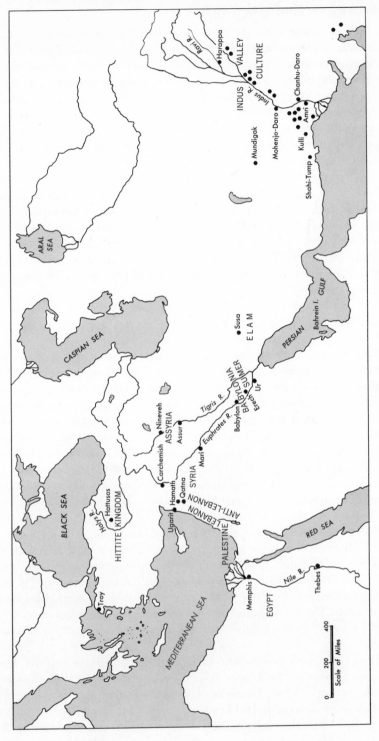

The Middle East and Indus Valley, ca. 1800 B.C.

found on the Indus River itself about 150 miles from its mouth. Medium-sized cities (Chanhu-Daro) and smaller towns of the same distinctive culture have been located up and down the river and even outside the watershed of the valley on the north, and well down to the south on the coastal plain. They all share a common cultural pattern but it is impossible to know whether they were under a common government.

The towns give an impression of formal planning, for they were laid out in a grid pattern with the principal streets running east and west, north and south. Houses and shops built of baked brick filled the blocks between them. Homes of the well-to-do were built around paved courtyards, often had two stories, and possessed bathrooms whose drains connected with brick sewers laid through the streets. The poor lived in "row-dwellings" which were connected with workshops.

On the western edge of the city stood a citadel, heavily walled with baked brick. On the enclosed platform, standing high above the town and surrounding plain, was a pool surrounded by structures resembling bathhouses. Since no identifiable temples have been found, it is believed that this curious "citadel" may have served the double purpose of a fort and a religious center.

Writing and Art   Stamp seals bearing short inscriptions in a pictographic script attest to the development of writing and indicate the availability of a system for keeping records, but no documents have been discovered. The seal inscriptions are too brief to allow much hope of deciphering the script, but the symbols are interesting and beautifully

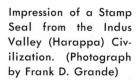

Impression of a Stamp Seal from the Indus Valley (Harappa) Civilization. (Photograph by Frank D. Grande)

drawn, and make use of animals native to the area. Tigers, elephants, and water buffalo figure in the writing and are also used as pure decoration. Handsome, naturalistic bronze sculpture was the greatest achievement of the Harappan artists, but a variety of articles were made in stone, metal, and clay. The beads were particularly fine. Children's toys made of clay have been found, including a monkey on a string. Clay whistles shaped like birds gave out bird calls when blown.

Economy Students of the Harappan culture, pointing to its uniformity and stagnation over the course of centuries (*ca.* 2300– *ca.* 1500 B.C.)[5] and to the evidence of two types of houses and two sets of cemeteries, believe that the economy was built on slave labor. Stuart Piggott points out that no change in metal tools and weapons (which though fairly advanced were poorly designed in comparison with Sumerian implements) took place in the course of almost a thousand years, and he assumes that neither master nor slave had any interest in their improvement. But there are many puzzles involved in an attempt to explain Harappan economy, society, and government. The lack of written sources is serious but certain texts from Ur, published by Kramer, give clues to the extent of their trade.

From the art, architecture, and rich material remains it must be assumed that the Indus Valley climate was more favorable in early times than it is now. Many animals whose bones have been found and which are pictured in the script (the tiger, rhinoceros, water buffalo, and elephant) are no longer native to the region. To bake sufficient brick for the construction of the cities required a supply of wood which does not now exist. It is therefore necessary to assume a wetter climate in the Harappan period, and one now characteristic of the regions of India dominated by the monsoon pattern. If this reconstruction is correct, the farmers of the Indus plain grew wheat, barley, cotton, field peas, and several fruits. From the surviving art it is certain that they kept domestic fowl, the Indian buffalo, oxen, goats, sheep, and pigs for meat. Transportation was provided by donkeys, oxen, elephants, and (probably) camels. Other domestic animals included the dog and cat.

There is ample evidence that the Indus Valley peoples traded with the Mesopotamians during the third millennium. Kramer theorizes that they may also have traded with Egypt, but so far there is no concrete evidence for such an assumption. Cylinder seals,[6] however, character-

[5] Sir Leonard Woolley, in Hawkes and Woolley, *The History of Mankind*, vol. 1, *Prehistory and the Beginnings of Civilization*, p. 389, gives the terminal date of 1500 B.C.

[6] A cylinder seal was, as its name suggests, a small cylindrical object made of baked clay or ornamental stone on which delicate scenes were carved in relief. When the seal was rolled over wet clay, the scene was clearly reproduced. Since the impression was designed to serve as an individual's signature, every effort was made to have each seal different and as unique as possible. The little cylinders, measuring in length about an inch or a little more, were perforated from end to end and were probably worn on a thread tied around the wrist or neck.

istic of Akkad and Sumer have been found in Mohenjo-Daro, and Indian stamp seals have been found in Mesopotamia. Texts from Ur speak of trade between that city and "Dilmun," and possibly also of trade between Dilmun and Egypt and Ethiopia. Excavations on the island of Bahrein in the Persian Gulf indicate that it was a way station on the long sea route, and French archaeologists have unearthed the ruins of a town called Mundigak in Afghanistan which probably served the same purpose on the overland route. Both sites show strong Mesopotamian influences in their architecture, but Mundigak also had granaries reminiscent of those at Harappa. Either might have been Dilmun, or perhaps Kramer is correct in speculating that Dilmun was the Indus civilization itself. The products traded (according to the Mesopotamian texts) were wood, various stones, and metals. Grain and textiles may also have played a part, along with spices and other luxury items.

The Fall of the Indus Civilization The end of the Indus cities was violent. Skeletons, bearing marks of sudden death, were found in rooms and corridors and along the streets. Possessions lay scattered about. The conquerors (perhaps the Aryans) destroyed, looted, and then moved on, leaving the cities ruined and deserted. A few former inhabitants struggled briefly to rebuild on the ruins, then gave up and left, and the mounds lay desolate and forgotten. By 1500 B.C., the Harappan language, writings, art, and techniques were lost. The Indus peoples were not so fortunate as the Sumerians, who in their slow decline mingled their blood with their Semitic successors and handed over to them a vast store of accumulated knowledge.

BABYLONIA

About 1984 B.C., the Semitic Amorites pushed into the Euphrates Valley and settled in Babylon, a rather unimportant town until then. Toward the end of the nineteenth century the Amorites began a struggle with Isin and Larsa for the control of Sumer, but it was not until about 1750 that their king Hammurabi succeeded in gaining control of the lower valley. Though the Amorites themselves did not speak of "Babylonia," it is customary for modern scholars to call the lower and central Tigris-Euphrates Valley region Babylonia from his time onward.

In addition to Sumer, Hammurabi conquered the Assyrians of the upper Tigris Valley and marched west into Syria to conquer the strong state of Mari. Directed by his letters, which may still be read, the king's agents built temples, repaired canals, kept order, and controlled local affairs throughout the empire. To reform injustices, Hammurabi compiled a code of laws based on Sumerian precedents and Semitic customs and traditions. A complete text of the code, inscribed in stone, was found in 1901 and stands now in the Louvre. It affords a good picture of life in Babylonia, though since it was a reform code not every phase of existence is covered. It is not likely that it had much effect on the practices in the individual states of the empire, nor did it set a precedent for later codes. It was probably designed to guide the "judges of Babylon" in cases of appeal, or for some similar purpose. Still, it remains a valuable historical source for a period of Babylonian history about which there is little other information.

Government Hammurabi was assisted by many subordinate officials, among whom were army officers, ambassadors, and governors of individual cities. Under the direction of the city governors (called *shapirum*) were local officials and panels of judges. The Babylonian army was made up of professional soldiers, who were supported by farmlands assigned to them. The king served not only as the executive officer of the state, controlling the civil administration, but also as commander in chief of the armies and as the final court of appeal in the judicial system.

"Elders" of the upper class (*amelu*) served as judges under the jurisdiction of the local governors in the respective city-states. The task was probably considered an honor. Certainly it was taken seriously, for the code made provisions for the disbarment of venal judges and for the recording of all decisions. Through the judicial interpretations deposited in the public archives, precedents were established, and decisions became easier with each succeeding case.

Society A wide variety of laws dealing with family life, property, contracts, and civil and criminal procedure is contained in the code of Hammurabi. Distinctions were made on the basis of a recognized class system consisting of "gentlemen," freemen, and slaves. A woman could become a priestess or a wine seller and manage her own affairs, but she had legal responsibilities to live up to in the practice of her profession. Every woman was entitled to a dowry from her father, to her husband's support while he lived, and to dower rights in his estate after his death. A man could have more than one wife, and concubinage was permitted, even encouraged, in default of heirs by the wife. Children were greatly valued, but were considered the exclusive property of the father. Children by a slave woman, if acknowledged by the father, could inherit part of his property. Adultery was severely punished, and divorce was easier for men than for women. Family law in general shows clearly its origins in the strong patriarchal customs of the Semites.

Slaves were protected by the code, but in much the same way as other valuable property. Injury to slaves entailed compensation for the owner. Still, slaves could be freed with ease, especially women who had borne children to their master, and their only distinguishing mark was a particular hair style.

Criminal law provided severe punishments based on the retributive principle of "an eye for an eye and a tooth for a tooth" (*lex talionis*) within—but not between—each class. Quite literally, the law states that

The Stele on which Hammurabi's Law Code Is Inscribed. Musée du Louvre. (Service de Documentation Photographique, Réunion des Musées Nationaux.)

if "a gentleman knocks out the tooth of another gentleman, his tooth shall be knocked out." But, if a gentleman knocked out the tooth of a free man (commoner), he was subjected only to a money fine. Malpractice of any sort in medicine, veterinary surgery, and the building trades was ruthlessly punished. Laws regarding theft reflected a strong sense of community responsibility for the protection of property.

Economy Agriculture was the chief basis of economic life, and this fact is reflected in Hammurabi's code and in the numerous records dealing with the disposition of lands and crops. Land was owned by the king, royal officials and soldiers, the temples, and small freeholders. It could be rented on shares or for a fixed rent, which could be canceled in case of flood or drought. Taxes were paid on the land, and landholders were subject to a *corvée* for the maintenance of canals and roads. No new crops had been added to those produced by the Sumerians, but the land retained its marvelous fertility.

The law regulated apprenticeships, fixed wages for workmen, and assigned liabilities for bad workmanship. Physicians were treated as craftsmen and assigned fees according to the type of case treated and the class of the patient. The fees of a veterinarian were similarly regulated. Both were penalized if their treatment failed to cure. Metallurgy, leather-working, pottery making, brickmaking, jewelry making, baking, and brewing were the major industries.

Trade was active between cities and along the trade routes to the east and to the Mediterranean. Partnerships, associations, and agencies for carrying on trade were common. Exports and imports remained the same as in Sumerian times except that more luxury articles were exchanged, and the means and methods of commerce had improved. Fixed weights of silver—the talent, mina, and shekel—facilitated the exchange of goods. Loans were available in grain or in silver, and rates of interest were legally fixed at one-third of the principal for grain and at one-fifth for silver. Maximum prices were set on many products, and the price of a drink at the wine seller's shop could be paid in a stated amount of grain or silver.

Babylonia After Hammurabi   Though Hammurabi's empire did not long survive him and Babylon itself suffered disastrous raids by Hittites, Assyrians, and Elamites during the course of the next few centuries, the culture of the city and of the region continued slowly to evolve. Perhaps the peak was reached, in a cultural sense, during the twelfth and eleventh centuries B.C., which saw the composition of the two great epics, *The Epic of Creation (Enuma Elish)* and *The Epic of Gilgamesh*. Both rank with the best in world literature.

The Epic of Creation explains how Marduk, Babylon's tutelary deity, shared in the creation of the universe and became the supreme god of Babylonia. The assembly of the gods, the Anunnaki, voted him the kingship and supreme command of their forces in the pending struggle against chaos (Tiamat). Marduk was the victor in the cosmic war and saved the older gods from destruction. When the struggle was over, he gave them all a great banquet in his newly built shrine, seeing to it that all were provided with the best food and an ample supply of good wine.

The Epic of Gilgamesh is more profound, posing two universal questions of the deepest human import: Why must a good man suffer and die? Can men ever attain immortality? Gilgamesh was a historical ruler of Erech in the early Sumerian period (see p. 38), and his adventures are described in a number of Sumerian poems. The Babylonian poet drew these together and connected them through statement of the major, tragic theme posed by the questions. Enkidu, friend and companion of Gilgamesh, is killed. Gilgamesh is filled with grief and rebellion, and sets out to discover how immortality may be achieved. Everyone tries to dissuade him from his quest, saying:

> Gilgamesh, whither are you wandering?
> Life, which you look for, you will never find.
> For when the gods created man, they let
> Death be his share, and life
> Withheld in their own hands.
> Gilgamesh, fill your belly —
> Day and night make merry,
> Let days be full of joy,
> Dance and make music day and night.
> And wear fresh clothes,
> And wash your head and bathe.
> Look at the child who is holding your hand,
> And let your wife delight in your embrace.
> These things alone are the concern of men.[7]

But Gilgamesh will not stop. He goes from adventure to adventure, finally reaching the only man to become immortal, Utnapishtim, who survived the great flood. Utnapishtim tells Gilgamesh his story but can offer no help save some information about a plant of eternal youth growing on the sea bottom. Gilgamesh obtains the plant, but a snake steals it away. Gilgamesh, tired, defeated, and without hope, returns to Erech knowing that man is mortal and that only the work of his hands may survive.

Art and Architecture   The art and architecture of Hammurabi's Babylon were not superior to that of Sumer, and were chiefly borrowed from it. Gods continued to be housed in temples of sun-dried brick faced with baked brick, but there is no evidence from this excavation level of Babylon itself, since the part of the city with the temples is under water. In other towns, the marks of Hammurabi's agents in repairing old temples and building new ones are frequent. In later periods, Babylon grew steadily, in spite of the destructive raids mentioned, and continued the earlier architectural tradition of building with sun-dried brick. Beautiful cylinder seals, many of which were works of art in miniature, were made by the thousands, and engraved vases, carved gem stones, and metal objects of great beauty, which were molded, cast solid or hollow cast, and decorated with engravings or

---

[7]Trans. by Thorkild Jacobsen and reprinted from *The Intellectual Adventure of Ancient Man* by Henri Frankfort *et al.* by permission of The University of Chicago Press, copyright 1946 by The University of Chicago, pp. 210–211.

Impressions Made by Cylinder Seals from Babylonia and Neighboring Areas. (The Metropolitan Museum of Art, the Cesnola Collection; purchased by subscription, 1874–1876)

repoussé (hammered) ornament, continued to witness to the quality of Babylonian craftsmanship over the generations.

Religion The traditional view of Babylonian religion has been that it was gloomy, fatalistic, and produced a feeling of helplessness in the believer, and it is true that certain texts point to such an interpretation. However, the existence of others lead to a happier view. The Babylonians of Hammurabi's time and afterward believed in the familiar Sumerian gods and practiced rites similar to those long used in the valley of the two rivers. Marduk was not accorded supremacy in the pantheon before the twelfth century, and he seems then to have been assigned by his worshipers many of the powers formerly ascribed to Enlil. As has been noted, this god, while greatly feared, was greatly respected and also loved.

The Kassites in Babylon The first half of the second millenium was marked by great movements of barbaric and semibarbaric tribes. It has been the traditional view to ascribe the original impetus behind these vast migrations to a movement of the so-called Indo-Europeans.[8] Whether or not their pressures began the movements, they, and many other peoples, poured into the middle east and into the Mediterranean basin. The Indus Valley civilization was probably destroyed by one of the Indo-European groups called Aryans, and some Indo-Europeans were among the general mixture of tribes that were to become the historic Hittites.

The Kassites,[9] another tribe of mixed origin, began infiltrating the upper part of Hammurabi's former empire from the time of Hammurabi's son onward, and they secured a firm footing there before 1600 B.C. In that year, Hittite raiders succeeded in storming and sacking Babylon. The weakened and half ruined city came under control of the Kassites. Their kings boasted of making horses "as common as straw" in Babylonia, and iron was introduced during their period. Otherwise they made few lasting changes in the lives of the valley peoples.

A long period of somnolence, broken occasionally by an Assyrian or Elamite raid, descended on Babylon, but its culture continued to develop. Gradually, techniques in the crafts were perfected, astronomical and mathematical knowledge was accumulated, and the slow evolution of civilized arts continued. Moreover, these arts and institutions passed steadily through trade to the Assyrians, Hurrians, Hittites, and Syrians. Later, under the ambitious rulers, Nabopolassar and Nebuchadrezzar, of the Neo-Babylonian (Chaldean) period, Babylonia was to compete with Egypt for control over much of the middle east. It is time therefore to explore the history of the civilization developed in the Nile Valley, a civilization which rivaled that of Mesopotamia in its early beginnings, in its power and attainment, and in its influence on later peoples.

---

[8]Technically the term refers only to peoples speaking closely related languages such as Greek, Latin, Celtic, German, and the like, but historically these peoples may also have shared certain social and political institutions and had similar religious beliefs and customs.

[9]It was formerly believed that their chiefs were Indo-European, but it is now doubtful that there were any Indo-Europeans among the Kassites.

3 · Egypt: The Two Lands

A THOUSAND MILES WEST OF SUMER IN THE VALLEY of the Nile, a second brilliant civilization grew and flourished. During the same span of time that saw Sumerians and Semites settle in the Tigris-Euphrates Valley, the Egyptians took their herds into the rich bottom land of the Nile valley and into its delta. There, like the Mesopotamians, they planted and harvested crops, made pottery, dug canals, built sailing ships, worked metals, and invented a system of writing. Yet despite these basic similarities, the civilization of Egypt was strikingly different from that of Mesopotamia. The Egyptians were relatively secure in their river valley, protected by desert and sea. They were seldom the prey of invaders or victims of the vagaries of nature. Consequently, the Egyptians' outlook, beliefs, customs, and institutions reflected the security, serenity, and contentment of their environment.

Sources The sources for the earliest periods of Egyptian history, like the sources for early Mesopotamian history, are wholly archaeological and vary considerably in quantity and value. The dry climate of Egypt has preserved organic and material remains in abundance, but there are gaps in the record of settlement in and along the Nile. No full and clear record of the transition between the Mesolithic and Neolithic stages is available, nor is the early Neolithic Period represented. A few artifacts of Paleolithic type attest to human occupation of the canyon rim and terraces, but the first village sites to be discovered are late Neolithic, dated to the fifth and fourth millenniums, and are found in the river valley or the Fayum oasis.

Egyptian building habits during early historical periods contributed to the extraordinary fullness of the archaeological record. Brick and clay were used for houses and temples, and graves were dug in the desert surface. Later, stone became the prime building material for temples, tombs, and all public monuments, though royal palaces and private dwellings continued to be built of brick or adobe. Egyptian religious belief required that all sorts of objects needed in life accompany the dead for use after death, and religious texts and magic pictures were painted and carved on tomb walls. In addition, kings recorded their achievements in pictures and inscriptions in the temples, and both they and the officials boasted of their deeds in their tombs.

Written sources become available about 3000 B.C. and multiply in quantity and usefulness thenceforward. Many of them are on stone, but religious and historical texts, literary and mathematical treatises, scientific works (in medicine, especially), letters, accounts, and many other kinds of public and private papers have been found on papyri (Egyptian "paper" made from strips of papyrus reed), which the dry climate has preserved. While these records on stone and papyrus are outnumbered by the clay tablets of Mesopotamia, the Egyptian documents provide more historical detail and a clearer picture of everyday life. Indeed, Egyptian history is so much better known than that of other ancient middle eastern countries (save for a few periods) that it serves as the base, or key, around which the rest of ancient Near Eastern history is built.

Written sources outside Egypt become valuable late in the second millennium and thereafter. Correspondence between Egypt and the Hittite, Assyrian, Babylonian, Syrian, and Palestinian princes, as well as Hittite and Assyrian documents, supplement the Egyptian records of the Empire and post-Empire periods. The Old Testament throws light on Egyptian relations with the Hebrew states and their Syrian neighbors in the first millennium. Finally, beginning in the fifth century B.C., Greeks became interested in Egypt and wrote of its history. The most notable of these writers were Herodotus and the later Diodorus. In the Ptolemaic period, an Egyptian priest called Manetho (*ca.* 290 B.C.) wrote a history of Egypt in Greek, making use of Egyptian records for his work. The body of his book is now lost, but an outline survives in the works of chroniclers of the Roman period. Manetho's list of thirty royal dynasties, or families, still provides the outline for writing Egyptian history. Despite numerous corruptions, Manetho's general accuracy has been largely corroborated by independent Egyptian records.

Geography Herodotus understood that "Egypt is the gift of the Nile," and obviously no large population could have inhabited the area without the river, for it would have been dry desert. The arable land of Egypt consists of ribbons of watered land on either bank of the Nile (which runs in a deep, winding valley) and the fan-shaped delta built up on the Mediterranean coast. The only other area that can be farmed is the Fayum, an oasis created by a secondary channel of the river branching to the west and paralleling the main stream for a short distance midway in Egypt. The fertility of this limited area was, and is, maintained solely by the river which has flooded annually from June

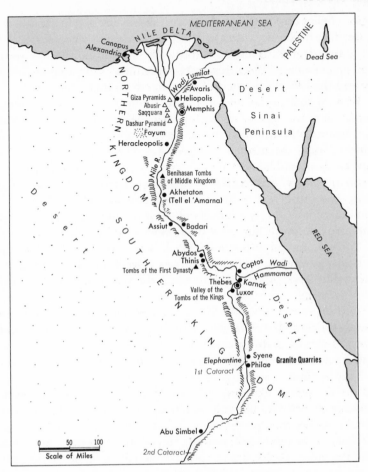

Ancient Egypt, ca. 2500–1400 B.C.

to December throughout the historical period. Almost no rain falls in the valley, though the delta receives light rains during part of the year.

Ancient Egypt consisted of the lower valley of the Nile from the first cataract (at Aswan) to the Mediterranean Sea. No tributaries entered the river throughout this long, lower course, but in the pluvial ages the Nile had formed outlets to the Red Sea. One of these, the Wadi Hammamat, was dry by the Neolithic Period, but its bed, leading from a point near Coptos to the Red Sea coast, served as an overland highway, and its walls provided a useful quarry. The second outlet branched off in the north, near the head of the delta. Now dry, it is called the Wadi Tumilat. It may have carried shipping from Egypt to the Red Sea during the period of the Old Kingdom, but it had to be opened by dredging in the Persian and Roman periods. The latest dredging operations recorded were those carried out by the Roman emperor Hadrian, early in the second century A.D., after which it silted up forever. This Red Sea mouth of the Nile, when open, provided a water passage from the Mediterranean to the east. Ships could enter either of the five main Mediterranean branches, sail upstream to the head of the delta, then turn down the easternmost branch and continue into the Red Sea.

No inhabited spot in Egypt was far from the Nile and its life-giving waters, and the river was so perfect a highway that the Egyptians seldom bothered to use wheeled vehicles. Even the prevailing winds were kind, blowing always upstream. The boatman never had to row except when crossing the river; he floated down and sailed up. In Egyptian hieroglyphics, the picture of a ship with sails raised is the verb "to sail upstream"; a ship with sails furled means "to sail downstream." This remarkable river cooperated in other ways with the men on its banks. Running as it did through a deep valley from twelve to thirty miles wide, it could not and did not make great changes in its bed. Compared to the Tigris or Euphrates, the Nile was unusually safe and dependable. The worst men had to fear was an excessive or inadequate flood or the crocodiles and hippopotamuses that inhabited its waters.

The dependability of the river was almost matched by the security given by the surrounding desert. There were few paths into Egypt that could be taken by invaders, and there were not many nearby peoples to be tempted into the valley. Small straggling bands of nomads could be and were absorbed, but in more than two thousand years Egypt suffered only one large-scale invasion. Its inhabitants were not plagued by wave on wave of hill peoples such as descended upon Mesopotamia.

Security and serenity marked also the landscape and climate. Egypt was warm and balmy, without violent extremes of temperature. Dry, pure air, and pleasant breezes mitigated the heat of summer. The valley walls, sometimes sheer cliffs, sparkled and glowed with varying colors in the brilliant sun, and the luxuriant plant life of the valley was a soft gray-green from the dust never washed away by rains. The sun seemed to fill the daytime sky, and it rose and set in splendor over the cliffs. At night the moon and stars seemed very close through the clear air. Egypt was beautiful, serene, never-changing, and hospitable to its people.

Plant life and other resources were abundant in the Nile Valley. Crops of barley, wheat, herbs, vegetables, fruits, flax, cane, and papyrus reeds grew abundantly to provide food, beer, and clothing, housing, and writing material. Long-horned oxen, goats, sheep, pigs, fish, ducks, geese, and several kinds of wild fowl furnished meat for the table. Oxen and donkeys were used to draw sleds or, rarely, wheeled carts, and the domestic cat was trained to help in hunting wild birds. The desert was the source of many sorts of building stones and semiprecious stones used for ornamental purposes. In the eastern desert and in Nubia were deposits of copper and gold, and natural salt deposits were available. Egypt lacked only the timber, tin, and iron considered desirable or necessary by ancient peoples.

Early Settlement   Evidence for settlement along the valley's rim and terraces, or along the edges of the Nile delta, is very scanty. But despite the lack of evidence, it must logically be supposed that men built their earliest villages safely above the marshy valley, just as they did in Mesopotamia and northern India. The earliest Neolithic settlements to be excavated were in the Fayum and at Badari on the edge of the valley. The peoples of these villages were already highly skilled and advanced in the Neolithic arts.

Physically, most of the early inhabitants of Egypt were short and slender, and had dark hair, often curly. The men wore short pointed beards and both sexes wore clothing of linen supplemented by animal skins. Settlers in one group, who may have entered Egypt from the Red Sea coast through the Wadi Hammamat, were somewhat larger in build, and their cultural patterns had curious and striking resemblances to the early Sumerians. The similarities appeared in art styles and building techniques of the latest Predynastic Period, but there is no sign of Sumerian or other Mesopotamian influence in language, script, or religion.

Both Hamitic and Semitic[1] peoples participated in the settlement of Egypt, and the Egyptian tongue came to embody elements from both language families. The broad connecting highway of the Nile contributed to the gradual intermingling of custom and language, and the conflicts and ambitions of the clans and their chiefs led step by step toward political union. Much of this progress can be traced in the late Neolithic Period, which in Egypt is called the *Predynastic Period.*

THE PREDYNASTIC PERIOD

In the Predynastic Period, during the fourth millennium, clans, each with chiefs and special totems, had long been settled up and down the fertile valley and across the delta. Clan members claimed communal lands for farming and grazing, and built villages where all could dwell in greater security. The valley settlements were ordinarily on the plain and because of the floods only those on the valley margins have been preserved.

The cultural pattern of the late Neolithic Period differed in Lower (northern) and Upper (southern) Egypt, but basic resources were the

[1] The terms "Hamitic" and "Semitic" like the term "Indo-European" properly designate language groups. The Hamitic group is presently represented by the language of the north African Berbers. The Semitic group includes Arabic and Hebrew. As with the Indo-Europeans, peoples originally speaking a language within one of these two may have shared other cultural and social institutions.

Ceremonial Maceheads from Predynastic Egypt, Alabaster and Red Stone. (The Metropolitan Museum of Art, Rogers Fund, 1910)

same for both areas. Flax provided clothing, oil, cord, rope, mats, covers, and the like. Flint and other stones were beautifully worked into all manner of tools. Knives had such finetoothed edges that the indentations were nearly invisible, and sickles were equally well done. Stones were shaped and polished to make maces, spearheads, and axes. Arrow points were delicately flaked, and throw sticks (shaped like boomerangs) were common. Pottery was well made and decorated with pictures of boats, men, animals, birds, and fish. Toward the end of the Predynastic Period quantities of fine stoneware were made: plates, bowls, jars, and vessels of many shapes and sizes. A variety of beautiful stones—rose granite, green diorite, porphyry, and others—were used to make these wares. Perhaps the loveliest of all were made of alabaster, so finely worked that it became translucent. From green slate were made palettes, often shaped like animals and sometimes engraved with pictures, on which the Egyptians mixed green paint for their eyelids. Houses were built of wattle or sun-dried brick or shaped of wet clay (adobe) and roofed with branches and reeds. Woven mats hung over the open doors and served as rugs on the dirt floors. The dead were buried in the desert doubled up in pit graves, which were sometimes lined with brick or wood. Occasionally the body was placed in a coffin of clay or in a huge clay jar. Tools, weapons, ornaments, and jars of food were placed in the grave for use in the next world.

Toward the end of the Predynastic Period, copper tools and gold ornaments became increasingly common, and suddenly writing appeared, already highly developed. The hieroglyphic script plainly betrays its ideographic origin, but examples of its formative stages are missing. They may be hidden under the delta mud or the desert sands, but there is no question that hieroglyphics were developed in Egypt itself. Every character is drawn from the life of the Nile Valley, and from its animal, bird, plant, fish, and human inhabitants.

The Two Lands Progress toward political unity characterized the end of the Predynastic Period. In the process of clan and tribal struggles, two distinct kingdoms emerged: the Southern Kingdom comprised the long narrow valley in the south and was ruled over by the "sons of Horus," whose totem was the hawk; the Northern Kingdom, the northern, delta region.[2] The two kingdoms existed long enough to set a pattern for much of Egypt's history, and though a conquest of the north by the south united Egypt into one kingdom and ended the Predynastic Period, the country was always called the Two Lands. Throughout later centuries, in times of weakness or trouble it tended to break along the original lines into delta (Lower Egypt) and valley (Upper Egypt) kingdoms. Only the power and administration of strong pharaohs (kings)[3] kept the country united and strong.

THE UNION OF EGYPT

Manetho wrote that "Menes united Egypt," but excavations of the tombs of the pharaohs of the first two dynasties have not made clear Menes' identity. According to W. B. Emery, the choice lies between Narmer, Hor-aha, and the ruler called The Scorpion, but the problem may never be resolved because of the Egyptian royal practice of using three "great names" (later five) by any one of which a pharaoh might be listed. It is enough to say that the union of Egypt was achieved and secured through the efforts and leadership of these three pharaohs of Upper Egypt, partly by conquest and partly by intermarriage with the royal family of Lower Egypt to give them a hereditary claim to both kingdoms.

From the time of the union, the ruler built two tombs for himself, one in Upper and one in Lower Egypt. The tombs have all been robbed, so it is impossible to say in which the royal personage was actually buried. Southern and northern tombs were equally handsome, and the bodies of servants were buried around both. Each was furnished with every object that might conceivably be wanted by any of the dead. The burials are

[2] Recently doubts have been expressed about the reality of this division, but the traditional view given here is still widely accepted.
[3] The title Pharaoh is the Hebrew form of the Egyptian *pr 3 ᶜ*, which meant "great house" (royal palace). It did not come into common usage before the Empire Period but for the sake of consistency it will be used throughout this discussion to designate the ruler of Egypt.

vaguely reminiscent of the practices at Ur, but the tomb complexes in Egypt are more elaborate. A great brick superstructure, whose walls featured ornamental, recessed paneling, was raised over a pit in which the royal personage was laid with rich furnishings and equipment. Outside and around the royal tomb clustered the individual brick tombs of the servants, guards, and entertainers. The practice of killing and burying servants to accompany the pharaoh or queen ceased during the second dynasty. Small tombs continued afterward to cluster about royal graves, but evidence indicates that the occupants died natural deaths and were buried at diverse times.

Every sign, from the evidence of the tombs to the artifacts, art, and the brief inscriptions available, shows that Egypt prospered and progressed under the union. The pharaoh, wearing the white crown of Upper Egypt in combination with the red crown of Lower Egypt, established a dual administration with his capital probably at Memphis. The administrative offices of southern Egypt occupied the *white house*, while those of northern Egypt were housed in the *red house*, though much of the separation may in fact have been fictional. Each kingdom was divided into administrative districts, customarily called by the Greek name *nomes*, which were established on the basis of old clan divisions and communal land claims. The clan chieftains formed a hereditary nobility under the pharaohs, and administrative officers were chosen from their ranks. Inheritance in Egypt, even for the royal family, was matrilineal, and though the pharaoh might have a harem if he chose, only a son of the queen had an undisputed right to inherit the throne.

A strong fortification called *Memphis* was built at the head of the delta, and a kind of capital grew up around it. Memphis was ideally located for trade and for communication with the rest of Egypt, the river bringing to it products for transshipment. Downstream from Africa came ivory, ebony, gold, ostrich plumes, and other luxuries; upstream from the Mediterranean, cedar of Lebanon and oil from Syria. Egypt in return shipped stoneware, metalware, leathergoods, linen, and jewelry.

The fine arts kept pace with trade and industry. Brick architecture was beautifully developed in the tombs of First Dynasty pharaohs, but stone came increasingly into use during the Second Dynasty. Sculpture in relief and, more rarely, in the round was executed, and techniques were improved and perfected. Bone, wood, ivory, and stone were carved or painted, and handsome furniture was inlaid with these materials. Game sets of great beauty were inlaid, and dice sticks of ivory determined the moves of the pawns over the squares on the boards. Gold jewelry of exquisite workmanship was set with turquoise, lapis lazuli, amethyst, garnet, and other semiprecious stones.

Religious beliefs, derived in part from the totems of predynastic times, underwent change. The hawk (Horus), bull (Apis), cow (Hathor), sun (Re), ibis (Thoth), and other totemic devices were anthropomor-

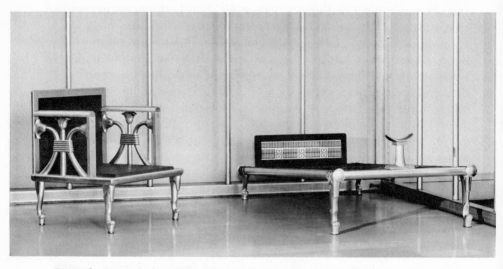

Reproduction of the Gold Furniture from the Tomb of Queen Hetepheres, Fourth Dynasty. (Museum of Fine Arts, Boston)

phized and shown partly or wholly in human form. Myths were elaborated and relationships established between various gods. Horus became the son of Re. Osiris, always mortal in form, is believed to have originated in a myth about one of the early kings who battled to unify Egypt, and Osiris' epic encounters with Set immortalized the varying fortunes in that long struggle. Before the end of the Second Dynasty the pharaoh was already a god, divine protector of Egypt's union both in life and in death. Formalized rituals in honor of the gods and of the divine pharaohs were well established, and records of their country-wide performance are extant from this archaic age. The stage was set for the full flowering of Egyptian culture, which took place between the Third and Fifth dynasties, a period sometimes called the Pyramid Age but more usually the Old Kingdom.

THE OLD KINGDOM

The unification of Egypt was achieved between 3400 and 3200 B.C. According to Manetho the first two dynasties lasted 550 years.[4] The Third Dynasty ushered in a period of prosperity, strength, and glory,

---

[4] Many scholars think this time too long, but W. B. Emery, who has excavated many of the royal tombs of the First and Second dynasties, is inclined to accept it. (See W. B. Emery, *Archaic Egypt.* Baltimore: Penguin Books, Inc., 1961, p. 29.) At best all Egyptian dates before 2000 B.C. are only close approximations. Not even carbon-14 tests have produced an accurate chronology.

whose material signs culminated in the building of towering pyramids to serve as royal tombs. The best-known rulers of the Old Kingdom were the Third Dynasty pharaoh Zoser (Tosorthros) and the Fourth Dynasty pharaohs Senefru, Khufu (Cheops), Khafre (Chephren), and Menkaure (Mycerinus). They perfected Egypt's administration, enlarged its trade, and created extensive trading contacts which stretched up the Nile to the second cataract in the south and reached to Sinai in the east and to Byblos on the Syrian coast. Egypt had unhindered access to the lumber and metals she coveted in these areas. Fifth Dynasty pharaohs developed religious, political, and legal institutions and traded far down the Red Sea coast with the land of Punt—believed to be Somaliland. The extension of power and increase of prosperity redounded to the royal credit and increased the royal authority. The pharaoh became a major god, and the Two Lands labored in his service.

Hieroglyphic and Hieratic Scripts Over the centuries the Egyptian language, which was partly Hamitic and partly Semitic in origin, was written in several different scripts. Hieroglyphics, whose invention and characteristics have been described (pp. 27, 67), always remained in use for formal inscriptions on stone. But the Egyptians invented simplified systems for business records; the most notable was hieratic writing, which was customarily executed with pen and ink on papyrus. In hieratic writing the animals, men, and other creatures of normal hieroglyphics were reduced to brief strokes and hooks that could be written as rapidly as any modern cursive script. The semialphabetic nature of Egyptian scripts made them less difficult to learn than cuneiform, for though the total number of signs ran into the hundreds, not all were in common use and some were merely determinatives having ideographic value.

The Calendar From the early Old Kingdom (*ca.* 2500 B.C.) onward, the Egyptians used three coexisting calendrical systems: a lunar calendar, which was the earliest devised; a civil calendar, probably first used about 2500 B.C., which was a schematization of the lunar calendar providing greater precision in recording dates; and the basic seasonal year, which regulated the agricultural life of Egypt. In the lunar calendar, a thirteenth intercalary month was inserted every three years so that the lunar calendar, seasonal year, and solar year of 365¼ days were kept in harmony. The civil calendar consisted of a year of exactly 365 days (twelve months of thirty days each with five added "festival" days), but since it did not take into account the ¼ day, the civil calendar diverged gradually from the seasonal year and only returned to harmony with it after a cycle of 1,460 years.

Government The pharaoh of united Egypt had always been considered a god, but Egypt's expansion in power and prosperity during the Old Kingdom lent him even greater authority and presence. The power of the royal army and the successful organization of the Egyptian labor force by the ruler decreased the influence and significance of the hereditary nobility. The pharaoh was free to choose his officials where he liked, without regard for inherited rights. Competent, educated men were sometimes promoted over the heads of aristocrats, and the most potentially rewarding occupation became that of the trained scribe.

The administration was highly centralized but varied to some degree with the ruler. A pharaoh was usually assisted by one or two viziers. The duality of administration was maintained for appearance, but the functions of officials overlapped considerably, and the pharaohs were strong enough to dispense with the political fiction of the Two Lands whenever they wished. No man and no god challenged the royal power.

Ceremoniously, the pharaoh came to be addressed by five names and titles. In the first two dynasties the pharaohs had three "great names": the *Horus* name, the *nebty* name (the two goddesses symbolizing Upper and Lower Egypt), and the *nesu-bit* name ("He of the sedge and the bee"). To these were added in the Old Kingdom the *Golden Horus* name and the *Son of Re* name, which was the personal name given at birth. In the Fifth Dynasty the pharaoh came to be formally recognized as "son of Re" and with this recognition was developed a useful legal fiction which justified the pharaoh's rights and power and even explained dynastic changes.

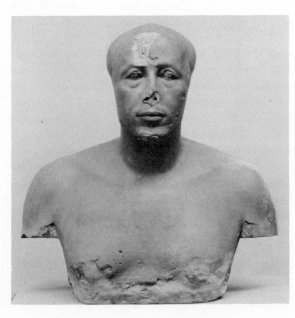

Portrait Bust of Prince Ankh Haef. Painted limestone from Giza. (Museum of Fine Arts, Boston)

Reproduction of the Pyramid-Temple Complex of King Sahure at Abusir, Fifth Dynasty. (The Metropolitan Museum of Art, Dodge Fund, 1911)

According to the myth *Re*, the sun god, had owned and ruled all Egypt, but in the course of time had decided to retire to the heavens and leave his son Horus (the hawk) to rule over the Two Lands. The living pharaoh was officially Horus (dead, he became Re), and each pharaoh was conceived by Re, who visited the queen in the form of the reigning pharaoh and begot his heir. Thus was royal inheritance through the queen justified and, with equal ease, infrequent dynastic changes were explained. The usurper had only to convince the Egyptians that Re had visited his own mother instead of the queen. Another legal fiction in the form of a myth was developed to aid this interpretation. The Egyptians conceived of a stable universal order, or "rightness of things," in which they came firmly to believe. This order was personified by the goddess Ma'at, who wore on her head the "feather of truth," and it involved notions of cosmic regularity, the political hierarchy, proper dealings with one's fellow men, ideal truth, and ideal justice. No one word can translate it. The pharaoh had his proper place in *Ma'at* as the "good god," ruler and protector of Egypt, and a usual boast of Old Kingdom pharaohs was that they had "upheld *Ma'at*" by fulfilling their duties to gods and men. If the pharaoh failed to uphold *Ma'at* or a usurper could convince the Egyptians that his predecessor had failed, Re's introduction of a new dynasty was thereby explained and justified. Both of these myths were useful from time to time throughout Egyptian history, and appear as strongly during late dynasties as they do during the fifth.

The pharaoh as Horus, son of Re, had great power, many preroga- tives and privileges, and heavy responsibilities. In his hands rested every final decision in administrative, executive, military, and judicial affairs. In addition, he was the living god and chief priest of all Egypt, representing the people before the great gods of heaven. Every ceremony and every sacrifice was offered in the pharaoh's name. The prosperity of the Two Lands was believed to depend on him, and he was thought to call forth the waters of the Nile. The pharaoh owned the Two Lands and had the power to regulate their every activity: he or- dained the season of planting, regulated the water supply, controlled quarries, mines, and workshops, and built all public buildings. The people came at his call to build his pyramid, to construct temples, or to fight in his army.

At times he was assisted by two viziers, who in the Fourth Dynasty were drawn from his sons but in later times from the nobility. Other officials were charged with carrying out the pharaoh's orders in what- ever sphere was assigned to them. Royal officers were chosen from a large group of princes, hereditary nobles, and educated scribes, and might be transferred at the pharaoh's will from one activity to another. The career of the Sixth Dynasty official Uni was typical. He boasted:

> When I was master of the footstool of the palace and sandal-bearer, the king of Upper and Lower Egypt, Mernere, my lord, who lives forever, made me count and governor of the south, southward to Elephantine, and northward to Aphroditopolis; for I was excellent to the heart of his majesty . . . .
>
> Never before was this office conferred upon any servant. I acted as governor of the south to his satisfaction . . . I accomplished all tasks; I numbered everything that is counted to the credit of the court in this south twice . . . .
>
> His majesty sent me to Ibhet to bring the sarcophagus named: "Chest-of- the-Living," together with its lid and the costly pyramidion for the pyramid called: "Mernere-Shines-and-is-Beautiful," of the queen.
>
> His majesty sent me to Hatnub to bring a huge offering table of hard stone of Hatnub. I brought down the offering table for him in only 17 days, it having been quarried in Hatnub . . . I hewed for him a cargo-boat of acacia wood of 60 cubits in its length and 30 cubits in its breadth . . . .
>
> I was one beloved of his father and praised of his mother; firstborn — pleasant to his brothers, the count, the real governor of the south, revered by Osiris, Uni.[5]

[5] Translated by James Henry Breasted in William C. McDermott and Wallace E. Caldwell, *Readings in the History of the Ancient World.* New York: Holt, Rinehart and Winston, Inc., 1951, p. 80. See also: Breasted, *Ancient Records of Egypt* 1. Chicago: Uni- versity Press, 1906, section 320, p. 147.

The diversity of duties to which officials could be assigned is well illustrated by Uni's experience. He had served as a nomarch, as judge, and as leader of a military expedition before receiving the important appointment as governor of the south.

Roughly, the royal hierarchy can be outlined as follows, though it must always be remembered that the pharaoh could make changes as he pleased. Under the pharaoh were the two viziers. If no viziers were appointed, governors of the north and south ranked as the principal royal officials of the two kingdoms. Under their supervision were the *nomarchs*, or *counts*, who were in charge of each nome. It was the nomarch's duty to collect taxes, raise the local levies and labor battalions, keep order, and superintend irrigation. Also serving under the governors were judges, who cooperated with the nomarch in each district, and the necessary military and naval officers to guard the country and maintain peace. A host of scribes assisted the officials, for every action and transaction had to be recorded.

Society The pharaoh and queen ranked as divine beings above mankind, before whom courtiers and officials must prostrate themselves. The pharaoh's godhead limited his choice of a queen to someone in his own family, sometimes a sister, and she was treated with a respect almost equal to that accorded to the pharaoh.

The pharaoh and queen lived in a royal palace not too far from the site of his pyramid, the construction of which began with his reign. Pleasure gardens, in which pools and lakes provided coolness and sport, surrounded the palace. A delightful tale about King Khufu and his magician Djedi gives a glimpse of the pharaoh's private life: Khufu fell into a state of great boredom one day. The courtiers, attendants, and officials strained to amuse or interest him but with no success. At last Khufu was attracted by the proposal to man two boats with beauties from the harem and set them to race across a lake. He watched the preparations with anticipatory pleasure, but just as the race began in earnest, the "coxswain" in one boat stopped and began to weep. She had dropped her "fish ornament" overboard and would not be consoled for its loss. Khufu promised her a new one, but it would not do; she wanted only the old. In this state of emergency the great magician Djedi was called. He "said his magic" and folded one-half of the lake over the other half, laying bare the bottom, from which the ornament was recovered. When it was restored to the happy girl, Djedi once more "said his magic," unfolded the lake, and laid it back in place so that the race could go on. Khufu was amused and pleased, and his courtiers were relieved.

The nobles who surrounded the pharaoh, and from whom he chose his officials, were less restricted than the royal family by formality and ceremonious custom, but their lives were modeled on the royal pattern. Like the pharaoh, a noble had only one wife. She was treated with the utmost honor and respect, and her children alone were heirs to the family property. This property included a pleasant home of brick, whose lounges and porticoes were colonnaded and opened into gardens planted with trees, shrubs, and flowers. Ornamental pools were filled with fish and adorned with water lilies (the lotus). The house was made beautiful by columns carved and painted to resemble palms, bundles of papyrus blossoms or lotus stems and flowers, and walls painted with outdoor scenes or hung with woven mats. The furniture, elegant and comfortable, was made of wood inlaid with ivory or colored stones.

Aside from a home built near the royal palace, the noble owned country estates, which he visited and inspected regularly, accompanied by scribes who kept his records. His life was no idle one, for he might be sent at a moment's notice on the pharaoh's business or be forced to move his residence to the district he was assigned to govern. Still he found time for relaxation and pleasure. A favorite sport was the hunting of wild birds in the marshes with the throw stick. Trained cats retrieved the dead or disabled fowl. Or the noble might take his family spear fishing, or boating on the river or the "lily lake." On a quiet evening at home, his wife joined him for a game much like chess. Dinner parties were frequent, and the guests were entertained by dancers, tumblers, musicians, storytellers, magicians, or wrestlers.

At the bottom of the official scale were the scribes, many of whom rose to the ranks of the nobility. The need for educated men was so great that few restrictions were placed on admission to the temple schools, and as a result the class system of Old Kingdom Egypt was not as rigid as that of Mesopotamia. If a man of humble origin succeeded in learning to read and write, then proved himself able in the service of pharaoh, noble, or temple, promotion could be rapid. Pharaohs rewarded faithful service lavishly — with lands, gold, and a fine tomb near the pharaoh's own pyramid.

Military competence could also bring forward a man of lower-class origin, and the expansion of Egypt outside its borders provided opportunities for advance by this path. Intermarriage with, or adoption by, a woman of rank also advanced a man to a higher class. Women of high rank had great freedom of action and control over property in Egypt.

Most of Egypt's population was legally free, for there were few slaves, and these were foreigners captured in war. However, many peasants were in a state of half-serfdom, sharecropping the lands of pharaoh, temples, or nobles, and subject to the royal levies for the army and corvées for pyramid building and for quarrying and mining operations in the desert. Their mobility was limited by economic circumstances and royal need. Some small farmers "owned" (subject to the pharaoh's will) their own land. Ranking below the farmers were the herdsmen of sheep, goats, or swine, and below them the boatmen and common sailors.

Merchants and shipowners formed no distinct class. Many of them were royal agents (scribes), for the pharaoh was ever the chief merchant of Egypt. Trade and industry resting in private hands were usually small-scale, or if large were backed by the wealth of the nobility and the temples. Merchants and shippers acted more often as commissioned agents than in a private capacity. The reason becomes clear from an examination of the Old Kingdom economy.

Economy   Theoretically, the pharaoh as the "good god" owned all of Egypt, and in fact he directly controlled much of it. The royal estates were immense, and the land granted to nobles, officials, temples, and private individuals was subject not only to royal taxation but also to repossession (the royal right of "eminent domain") at the pharaoh's will. This right was rarely exercised, and the owners of property treated land as freehold, buying it, selling it, renting it, willing it intact or divided to their heirs. But from all of it produce poured into the pharaoh's storehouses, to be used by him as needed. From his vast stores the armies were fed and the corvées of workmen in quarries and on the pyramids drew their daily rations of bread, beer, vegetables, and meat. Any surplus remaining in the royal warehouses could be sold at home or abroad.

The quarries and mines were located in the desert, and planned expeditions of a semimilitary type were necessary to exploit them. The pharaoh owned these natural resources and only he could provide labor to work them. Every one in Egypt, whether noble, priest, or free craftsman, was dependent on the pharaoh for stone and metal. The manufacturer of copper tools or of gold jewelry bought his supply of metal from the pharaoh's agents. Many craftsmen worked directly for the pharaoh in "factories" under official direction. The temples of the gods were built through royal bounty, and the tombs of nobles through the pharaoh's generosity or will. It is little wonder that the offering formula for sacrifices, no matter who made them, read: "An offering which the king gives," and it is no wonder that private trade and industry existed only on a small scale. No merchant or craftsman was in any way forbidden to ply his trade, nor were any legal hindrances placed in his way, but always the private citizen competed with, or was dependent on, the vast resources of the pharaoh.

Yet the royal domination of industry and trade brought a goodly measure of prosperity and well-being to the Egyptians. The great corvées for quarrying and building occupied the laborers during the flood season when all farming was suspended, and each man drew his "pay" in rations from pharaoh's stores. Craftsmen and artists labored constantly to supply the most beautiful objects for the household of the living pharaoh and to prepare the magnificent furnishings for his "house of eternity," the pyramid. The horde of royal officials bought freely also of beautiful wares to use in this life and the next. Pharaoh's agents sold Egypt's products abroad and shipped timber and metals home from Lebanon, Syria, and Nubia. Merchants from Syria traded in Egypt, and Egyptian goods were exported north and east. Payment was made by exchanging wares for other wares, on the basis of a well-known system of relative values (so many measures of wheat were equal to one goat), or through the use of established weights of copper or gold made up into rings. Egyptian mathematics and Egyptian weights and measures were based on a decimal system.

The bulk of the Egyptian population worked on the land, turning the ground with crude plows, breaking clods with hoes, and using goats or oxen to tread in the seed. After planting, the important task was to provide the growing crops with water, which was taken by canals and ditches to the fields or carried to higher levels in jars. At the harvest men reaped the grain while the women and children gleaned. After the grain was threshed on the threshing floor, it was stored in bins in the granaries, scribes keeping accurate account of every measure poured into the bins. The same careful account was kept of the flocks and herds and all other products of the land, principally for purposes of taxation. A tax was due to pharoah on all.

Religion   Every aspect of Egyptian life was permeated and guided by religion. For the average man the local deities, derived from the old clan totems, remained the center of religious belief and ritual, but through the activities of priests and pharaohs certain "great gods" came to be honored over all of Egypt. In the Fifth Dynasty the Re cult, fostered and promulgated by the identification of the pharaoh as Horus, son of Re, assumed such significance that many local gods were later identified with Re. Thus Amon, the ram-headed god of Thebes, came to wear the sun disk between his horns, and Sebek, the crocodile god, wore it on his head. Priesthoods in the service of certain gods sought to clarify the divine functions or to relate their god to other gods whose powers overlapped or were similar. One of the most ambitious of these "theologies" was the Memphite, which described Ptah (god of artisans) as the creator of the gods and the universe: "He existed from the beginning with all things in his thought." Ptah empowered Atum to carry out further creation, which Atum did through his "word." Also associated with Ptah in this "theology" were seven other divinities who formed with him and Atum an *ennead* (group of nine) — which was three groups of *triads* (three gods arranged in a family group of father, mother, and son). The ennead arrangement was adopted for other Egyptian gods also.

In popular thought Osiris, early hero-king, came quietly to dominate. He represented the fertility of Egypt itself — its fruitful black soil ever renewed by the Nile. Through Osiris came the hope of immortality for the ordinary man, an immortality to be spent in Osiris' blessed kingdom inhabited by the good and the just. According to the myth, Osiris was killed by his brother Set, his body dismembered and its parts scattered over the land. His sister-wife Isis and his son Horus mourned him and sought his remains. When all were found, Horus restored his father to life eternal, and Osiris became king of the dead. Horus overcame the evil Set and ruled over Egypt in Osiris' place.

Belief in an eternal life dominated Egyptian thought and guided the individual's activity. Kings and nobles alike were constantly preoccupied with the preparation and furnishing of their tombs, and even ordinary folk wanted their possessions with them in the grave.

The ideas held about life after death varied, but gradually it was assumed that three principles had eternal existence. The first principle was the *ba*. Originally the power that was possessed by a god and permitted him to assume any form, it became by the time of the Empire, or New Kingdom, a "soul" that animated the body of a dead man and enabled him to move freely in the afterlife. It was therefore important to preserve the body. The second principle was the *ka*, a spiritual element present in man during life and after death. John A. Wilson translates it as "vital force," whereas others think of it as "personality" or as a "double." After death it was closely connected with a statue (body substitute) of the deceased which was enclosed in the tomb. The third principle, which is not so clearly defined, was the *akh*, or "spiritual state," into which an individual entered after death.

Architecture and Art   The most significant developments in Old Kingdom architecture took place in connection with the royal tombs and their surrounding buildings. The tombs of First Dynasty pharaohs were mastabas, imposing brick structures with paneled faces built over pits. In the Second Dynasty rock-cut chambers came to be used in place of pits, but the tombs remained one-storied mastabas.

Under the Third Dynasty Zoser, a minister named Imhotep, renowned as a physician and worshiped by later generations as a god, designed the first pyramid for his royal master. Succeeding rulers of the Old Kingdom continued the pattern, seeking to erect ever larger and more imposing pyramids. The peak was reached in the Fourth Dynasty by Khufu, whose vast tomb at Giza provides one of Egypt's major tourist attractions. Khufu's pyramid was originally 755 feet square at the base and stood 481 feet high, covering some 13 acres of ground. Later tradition, reflected by Herodotus, said that it took 100,000 men twenty years to build. The huge stones of this and other pyramids were cut and fitted with marvelous precision, and were set in place at ever higher levels by dragging them up ramps and sliding them into position over a thin layer of wet mortar. Local stone was used for the core but fine white, imported limestone faced the pyramid. When the top was

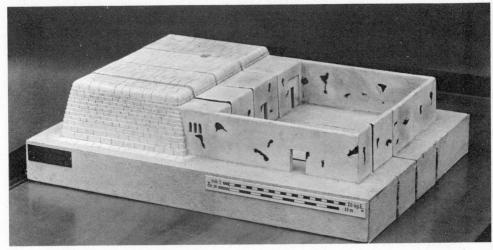

Model of a Mastaba Tomb of the Fifth Dynasty. (The Metropolitan Museum of Art, Dodge Fund, 1913)

reached, the ramps were cleared away and the pyramid stood unobstructed, smooth and gleaming in the sun, with its cap of gold.[6] Occasionally, more than one color of stone was used. The pyramid of Menkaure was finished partly in Mokattam limestone and partly in rose granite brought from the quarries near Aswan.

A pyramid was very nearly solid, being penetrated by only a few narrow passages and small chambers. A large room was ordinarily excavated in the rock beneath the structure, and it was reached by a passage running through and under the pyramid. This passage and all others were blocked with great stones after a burial, and the surface of the pyramid was finished to cover all trace of the entrances. Still, all pyramids were robbed, most of them in antiquity.

Imposing as it was, the pyramid was only the central structure in a complex of buildings. Temples stood at its feet, and the tombs of nobles, of lesser members of the royal family, and of officials spread around it in an ordered "city of the dead." Servants were no longer killed to accompany the dead pharaoh or queen, but courtiers wished to attend the pharaoh in death as in life. Then too they were dependent on him for the material to construct their mastabas. The tombs of the nobles were built at the same time that the stone was quarried for the pyramid and the workmen were at hand.

[6] Medieval Arab rulers used the pyramids as quarries and took the fine facing stones to build a handsome mosque in Cairo. Only the core of local stone remains in the pyramids at Giza, so their present appearance is stepped rather than smooth.

Statuette of Pepi I in Alabaster. Horus, the hawk god and son of Re, stands behind his shoulder. (The Brooklyn Museum)

The pyramid temples are unusual structures but have elements in common with those constructed for the gods. Either temple had an open forecourt, surrounded by a colonnade and a wall, which led to one or two pillared basilicas (halls) lighted by clerestories (windows built between two roof levels).[7] The central part of each hall was high, and it was flanked by two aisles with lower ceilings. Behind the halls lay a series of small sanctuaries. The pyramid temple sanctuaries contained ka statues of the dead pharaoh before which offerings were laid, and those of normal temples statues of gods.

Statues of men were made only for the use of the ka, and were shut away in the tomb, though those of pharaohs were exposed to view in ka temples. Since the purpose of sculpture was religious, realism was

[7] In most early temples there were no true clerestories but simple slits to admit light.

sought, and particular attention was given to the face. Bodies (which were not thought to express much individuality) were customarily standardized unless some peculiarity had to be shown. A very fat man was pictured in all his obesity and the deformity of a dwarf was meticulously rendered, but otherwise the artist concentrated his effort on making an accurate facial portrait and placed it on a conventional male or female body. Stiff poses, seated or standing, were originally arrived at through the need to balance evenly the weight of the heavy stone, but they became hallowed through usage and religious custom. The sculptors made no further experiments or advances. Their work was done for the dead or for the gods, not for the delight of living men. So standardized were the poses that Egyptian sculpture is said to obey a "law of frontality." Yet the sculptors' achievements were great, and certain Old Kingdom statues such as the Sheikh el-Beled, the Seated Scribe, the magnificent diorite ka statue of Khafre, and many others justly rank with the greatest in the history of art. The famous sphinx of Khafre, carved from a hillock in his pyramid quarry, is not so much a work of art as a marvel for its bulk.

The fate of painting was somewhat different from that of sculpture, for while the painter executed works in the tombs and temples, he also decorated the houses of the living. As a result, though much of the painting was stylized—especially that of a funereal or religious nature— there was more naturalism and freedom in it than in sculpture. Scenes from the farm or marsh were handled feelingly and with great skill, and animals and birds were portrayed lovingly. Men were curiously shown with face in profile, though the eyes were full-face; shoulders were to the front, but hips and legs were in profile. It was an impossible position for even the trained contortionist, but the Egyptian painter made it look pleasing and natural. The paintings were two dimensional, with neither depth nor perspective, and people of higher rank or importance were always shown larger than lesser folk. A pharaoh towered above all other creatures, even above buildings. Palaces and gardens were laid out flat, somewhat like an architect's plan, though living creatures in the scene were done in profile. In spite of all these conventions, Egyptian paintings bear an air of reality, a freshness, verve, and vitality that is ever attractive. They seldom fail to please and instruct the viewer.

The End of the Old Kingdom   No sudden disaster put an end to the period of strength and glory known as the Old Kingdom; rather, a slow breakdown in the centralized authority brought weakness and change. Weak pharaohs of the Sixth Dynasty, among them Pepi II, whose incredible reign lasted more than ninety years, progressively lost control over the royal officials. The nomarchs claimed hereditary rights and acted like petty kings in their own districts. Gradually each

Wooden Statue of an Egyptian Nobleman and Official of the Sixth Dynasty. (The Metropolitan Museum of Art, gift of Edward S. Harkness, 1926)

noble tried to turn himself into a pharaoh, and the Feudal Age resulted. The Seventh through the Tenth dynasties held only the most shadowy authority, and some of them were contemporary houses struggling with each other for power. The Two Lands were divided once more.

There were rebellions and disorders, and strife between the nobles; and there were inroads by Nubians into the south and desert folk from Libya and Asia into the delta. The economy of Egypt suffered and her foreign trade disappeared as her political weakness grew. Men looked back to the Old Kingdom and exalted the pharaohs in tales and legends, or composed poems and dialogues to express their own trouble, uncertainty, and misery. These tales, poems, and dialogues were written down, copied, and widely circulated during the Middle Kingdom.

THE FEUDAL AGE

The period of weakness and disunion brought cultural evolution. Legal and social justice became of deep interest to Egyptians of all classes, and the need to live by *Ma'at* to achieve this justice was strongly felt at all levels. Many of the writings of the period express this concern: the sage Ipuwer paints the terrible conditions of his time but prophesies that the future will bring better days under just pharaohs; "The Eloquent Peasant," victimized by an official, pleads before pharaoh and receives justice; "The Dialogue of a Misanthrope with his Soul" records a conversation between a pious man, tired of the evils of life and ready to commit suicide so that he may go to a better world, and his soul, which urges him to stay alive. A contrasting, hedonistic view is expressed in "The Song of the Harper," who sings that none return from the dead and it is best to enjoy life on earth to the full. But with most men piety prevailed and the *Coffin Texts* and *Pyramid Texts*, designed to direct the soul safely to heaven, were redacted and copied in great numbers. Most Egyptians agreed with Merikere, who wrote in his "Instructions": "Good conduct of the righteous is more acceptable to god than the ox of the evildoer."

THE MIDDLE KINGDOM

About 2000 B.C. the central authority was restored by hereditary princes of Thebes, who established the Eleventh Dynasty. When their line failed, another Theban family of nobles, listed as the twelfth dynasty, took up and completed the work of unification and centralization. Once again, rulers of the south had stepped forward to unite the Two Lands.

Under the Eleventh Dynasty rulers the powerful feudal nobility continued to act as a brake on the pharaoh's power. Compromises had to be

Wooden Funerary Model of Boat with Rowers, Eleventh Dynasty from Thebes. (The Metropolitan Museum of Art, Museum Excavations, 1919–1920; Rogers Fund supplemented by contribution of Edward S. Harkness)

made continually, but the increase of royal authority can be measured to some degree by the pharaoh's control over materials and labor. By the reign of Mentuhotep II, this control was sufficient to allow him to build the largest building since Old Kingdom times, a stone pyramid-temple. The pyramid was small, but the temple was large and handsome.

The Twelfth Dynasty rulers, the most famous of whom were the founder Amenemhat I and his descendants Sesostris III and Amenemhat III, gained such effective control that they were able not only to build tombs and temples but also to extend Egypt's power into Syria in the northeast and into Nubia in the south. They dug a canal around the first cataract so that shipping could sail upstream unhindered, built great fortresses up to the second cataract, and fortified the Sinai frontier. Trade with Syria, Crete, and the land of Punt was actively resumed by sea.

A large tract of wonderfully fertile land was opened to Egyptian farmers by these pharaohs when they built a great earthen embankment and a series of irrigation ditches which successfully controlled the flow of water into the Fayum. The area thus reclaimed was held as crown

Reproduction of Wall Painting Showing a Nobleman Netting Birds, Twelfth Dynasty from Beni Hasan. (The Metropolitan Museum of Art)

property and became a favorite residence of Twelfth Dynasty pharaohs. Amenemhat III built a great funerary temple there, which Greek tourists were later to call a labyrinth because of its size and complexity of plan.

Government The Theban rulers of the Middle Kingdom made the same claims to divinity, power, and authority as their Old Kingdom precursors had asserted so effectively. Amon was identified with Re, and the pharaoh called himself "son of Amon-Re." He used the same titulary of five "great names." But in fact and in practice, the Middle Kingdom pharaoh was not so powerful as the Third, Fourth, or Fifth Dynasty rulers. He was never freed from the need to rely on the hereditary nobles. They retained the right to govern the nomes, collect the taxes—of which they retained a portion—and control local labor, and they built handsome rock-cut tombs for themselves in their own districts, in which they boasted of their justice, mercy, and philanthropy.

Society When the Middle Kingdom pharaohs sought to climb to the uncontested position of past rulers, they found it difficult to overcome the known facts of their origin from the ranks of the feudal nobility. It was only toward the end of the Twelfth Dynasty, after a series of military victories against Egypt's enemies had increased the royal power, that their efforts were crowned with a measure of success. Middle Kingdom nobles did not think it worthwhile to remain in close attendance on the pharaoh—in life or in death—and only the necessary officials, servants, and retainers resided continually at court.

The population of Egypt may have dwindled during the period of weakness, for apparently more land was held by free farmers at this time than had been the case late in the Old Kingdom. The paucity of records from the Feudal and Middle Kingdom periods makes it impossible to see the facts clearly or to determine probable causes. The labor force of the Middle Kingdom also seemed unequal to that available in the Old Kingdom, though here the divided control exerted by nobles and pharaohs obscures the real situation.

Architecture and Art   Aside from the pyramid-temple of Mentuhotep, the Twelfth Dynasty funerary temple in the Fayum, and some temples to the gods in Thebes and elsewhere, the architectural achievements of the Middle Kingdom were not impressive. The greatest change lay in the gradual decline in building pyramids, most of which were brick, and the increasing construction of rock-cut chamber tombs. Monumental sculpture decreased in quantity, though excellent portrait and sphinx statues were made of Middle Kingdom pharaohs.

The most beautiful work was done in relief sculpture, painting, and the lesser arts. All show great taste and delicacy of execution. Hieroglyphs were exquisitely detailed and colored; and small objects, little wooden figures of men, boats, animals, and buildings—made to scale in sets and carved and colored with exacting realism—were created in large numbers to be placed in tombs. Carved ivory, stoneware, and lovely jewelry all show the same good taste, and workmanship and close attention to detail.

A major invention of the period was glassmaking, though the industry only became important later, in the period of the Empire. The discovery of the process may have come about accidentally from the overfiring of faïence ware (an industry begun in predynastic times). This ware is made of frit with a silicon glaze colored with other minerals. Blue hippopotamuses and other enchanting statuettes were made of faïence, as were cosmetic sets and jewelry. A few thick glass vessels date from the Middle Kingdom but glassware in quantity came later.

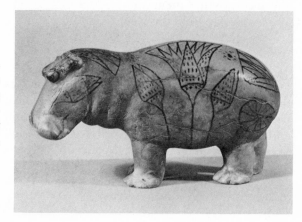

Statuette of a Hippopotamus Made in the Twelfth Dynasty, Blue Faïence. (The Metropolitan Museum of Art, gift of Edward S. Harkness, 1917)

Literature The Middle Kingdom is considered the golden or classical age of Egyptian literature. Letters, hymns to the gods, maxims, and "wisdom literature" are found on papyrus. Notable among the latter are the "Instructions" ascribed to Ptahhotep, an Old Kingdom vizier, whose work was popular in the Middle Kingdom. He wrote:

> Let not thy heart be puffed-up because of thy knowledge; be not confi-
> dent because thou art a wise man. Take counsel with the ignorant as well as
> the wise. The full limits of skill can not be attained, and there is no man
> equipped to his full advantage. Good speech is more hidden than the
> emerald, but it may be found with maidservants at the grindstones . . . .
> If thou art a leader commanding the affairs of the multitude, seek out
> for thyself every beneficial deed, until it may be that thy own affairs are
> without wrong. Justice (Ma'at) is great and its appropriateness is lasting;
> it has not been disturbed since the time of him who made it, whereas there
> is punishment for him who passes over its laws. It is the right path before
> him who knows nothing. Wrong-doing has never brought its undertaking
> into port.[8]

The most popular works of literature, however, were the tales of adventure and magic, like the stories of Djedi and King Khufu, the adventures of Sinuhe, and the fable of the Two Brothers. Though many of these works were composed earlier, Middle Kingdom scribes edited and transcribed the texts that contained reflections on social justice, comment on the foibles and tragedies of life, or tales of marvelous adventure for entertainment. None deals with the same epic, tragic themes found in the Babylonian poem of Gilgamesh, for the Egyptians seldom felt insecurity before their gods. Their troubles and complaints were earthly and arose from dealings among men. Egyptians believed a happy eternal life could be secured if man followed the proper directions. To achieve this end, Middle Kingdom scribes labored to compile all the known charms, directions, and instructions for reaching eternity, and incorporated them into a series of texts known as the *Coffin Texts*. These developed in the New Kingdom into the *Book of the Dead*.

THE HYKSOS CONQUEST

The end of the Twelfth Dynasty (about 1788 B.C.) was followed by turmoil and confusion. Pharaohs of the Thirteenth and Fourteenth dynasties alternately recovered and lost ground before their enemies and the hereditary nobles. Egypt, weakened, fell prey to invaders from Syria, a conglomerate horde made up largely of Semites. Soon after

---

[8]Translated by John A. Wilson in William C. McDermott and Wallace E. Caldwell, *Readings in the History of the Ancient World*. New York, Holt, Rinehart and Winston, Inc., 1951, pp. 82–83.

1750 B.C. the Hyksos (the Egyptian word meant Asiatics, though, according to Josephus, Manetho called them "Shepherd-kings")[9] descended on the delta and with their superior military techniques, possibly including horse-drawn chariots, overcame the Egyptians. Their king established the Fifteenth Dynasty, which with the contemporary Sixteenth vassal dynasty lasted just over a hundred years. Many scholars believe that the Hebrews entered Egypt with the Hyksos and that Joseph served under one of their last kings.

The Hyksos established their capital at Avaris in the eastern delta from which they ruled Egypt and southern Palestine through vassal princes in the different areas. Rude conquerors as they seemed to the Egyptians, who hated them cordially, the Hyksos brought new ideas and knowledge and gave the Egyptians and Syrians new tools, weapons, and engines of war. The empire itself was a source of considerable prosperity to its peoples. A well-traveled desert road connected Avaris with the Asiatic regions, and it and other routes were protected by fortifications and strong garrisons. The Hyksos kings gradually assumed Egyptian ways and customs, and claimed the full titles and powers of a pharaoh. But they delighted to honor the god Set, who was identified with a divinity of their own. After the expulsion of the Hyksos, Set was more firmly identified than ever in the Egyptian mind with evil—the opponent and enemy of the good Osiris and his son Horus.

Once again Egypt's salvation and unity came from the south. The Hyksos conquerors had permitted native princes to rule in Thebes as their vassals. Theban governors were responsible for the maintenance of order and were obliged to collect tribute and send it to Avaris. Rebellion began, according to an Egyptian text, after the Hyksos king ordered the Theban prince to "silence the bellowing of the hippopotamuses who were disturbing his sleep." One of the Egyptian rulers was obviously killed in the ensuing struggle—his mummy shows grievous head wounds—but step by step the Theban princes drove back the Hyksos and pushed them out of Egypt. Soon after 1575 B.C. a prince of Thebes called Amosis was in control of all Egypt. He was the founder of Manetho's Eighteenth Dynasty, and his successors, Amenhotep I and Thutmose I, were to establish their control firmly and go on to build an empire.

[9] Flavius Josephus. *Against Apion*, 1. 14.

4 · The Fertile Crescent and the Peoples of the Sea

URING THE THIRD MILLENNIUM B.C. THE PATTERN of urban civilization, hitherto centered in the great river valleys, reached out along the trade routes to change the lives of farming peoples in the Fertile Crescent of Syria-Palestine, in the uplands and along the coastal plain of Anatolia, and on the islands and European coasts of the Aegean Sea. In Syria groups of Semites built prosperous city-states; in Anatolia centers like Troy and other trading depots grew; and in the Aegean a brilliant culture arose on the island of Crete.

In the second millennium many of the lessons of civilization had to be taught anew to incoming tribes of Armenoids, Hurrians, various Indo-Europeans, and mixed tribes of Kassites, Hittites, Greeks, and Iranians. The newcomers proved apt pupils who established themselves among the older inhabitants and were assimilated or, in the case of the Hittites and Achaean Greeks, built civilized states of their own into which they absorbed older cultures. The invaders brought new blood, new languages, and new ideas, and enriched the life of the east with gifts of tools and techniques. Some of them were tamers of horses and workers in iron, and all were brave warriors.

Sources Archaeology provides the bulk of the evidence for the development of these regions during the third millennium. The climate and available resources made stone and timber the principal building materials, so towns and cities have survived, although in ruins. Not many organic remains have been preserved because of the rains and snows, but tools, pottery, weapons, and artifacts provide much information.

By the beginning of the second millennium, written sources become available from cities and states in Hittite Anatolia and Syria. The documents, in many tongues, though usually written in cuneiform on clay tablets, include city archives, treaties, diplomatic correspondence, law codes, business records, tales, and poems. The archives and corre-

90

spondence from Mari are among the earliest and most valuable for synchronizing the dates and events in Mesopotamia, Assyria, and Syria, but they are followed in time by many other records. The frequent discovery of datable Egyptian inscriptions and objects in Syrian cities has been helpful in correlating their histories with the Egyptian. Through fitting together in a vast jig-saw puzzle bits and pieces from all directions, the chronology and course of events in the entire middle east has been tentatively established.

Writing was also used on the island of Crete, but the scripts, Cretan hieroglyphics and the Linear A,[1] cannot be read with certainty. The only contemporary documents available for the Aegean world are the Greek texts in Linear B, found both at Knossos and on the Greek mainland and written between 1600 and 1200. There is an occasional reference by Egyptians and Syrians to the Aegean "peoples of the sea," and a few clues, some of them quite puzzling, in Greek myths, place names, and literature, but early Aegean history chiefly depends on the voiceless record of archaeology.

SYRIA AND PALESTINE

Syria and Palestine lay like a bridge between the great states of Mesopotamia and Egypt, and their combined land area provided passage for travelers from the south and east to Anatolia in the north. But the region was more than a highway. It had wealth and natural resources of its own, which made possible a rich life for its inhabitants.

Geography In Syria the terrain was diversified. From the upper reaches of the Euphrates, broad grasslands swept westward to the sea, to be interrupted by chains of hills before reaching it. The hills rose higher to the south to form Lebanon and Anti-Lebanon, parallel ranges of mountains. The two massifs and their dividing valley continued for some two hundred miles or more with few breaks; close to the seacoast in the north, they receded inland in the south. Much of the annual rainfall that was carried eastward from the Mediterranean was caught by these mountain chains, particularly by the seaward range of Lebanon, and their slopes were clothed with forests. The cedars of Lebanon were especially prized by all middle eastern peoples, but many other hardwoods growing on the mountains were also valuable.

---

[1] Linear A was a script developed and used in Crete in addition to a hieroglyphic writing. Presumably it embodies the Cretan language, but scholars in general do not accept any of the attempts so far made to decipher it. Linear B is a script that resembles Linear A and may have been derived from it. The language of the Linear B texts (they are on unbaked clay tablets) which have been found in Crete and Greece is archaic Greek. The key to the decipherment of the Linear B texts was discovered by Michael Ventris (see p. 112).

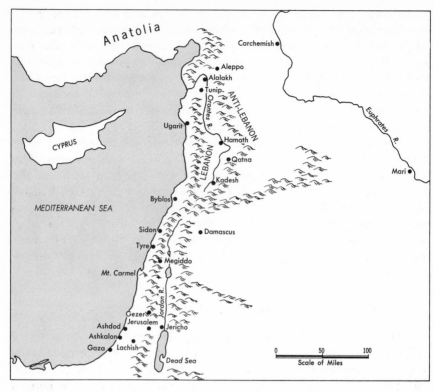

Ancient Syria, Second Millennium B.C.

In north Syria rose several cities. Ugarit (Ras Shamra) was a prosperous port on the coast, and Aleppo, on the plain to the northeast, straddled the direct route from Ugarit to the Euphrates. Northward, on the Euphrates itself, stood Carchemish, and downstream toward Babylon rose the state of Mari. On the Tigris lay hilly Assyria with its towns of Assur and Nineveh.

South of Ugarit on the coast, where the mountains of Lebanon neared the sea, was a narrow, fertile strip occupied by the Phoenicians. Their most famous cities were Byblos, Sidon, and Tyre. Inland, across Lebanon in the valley, ran the north-flowing Orontes River, along whose banks and tributaries were many cities: Alalakh, Qatna, Kadesh, and Hamath. East of these, across Anti-Lebanon, lay the grasslands over which nomads wandered. Near the end of the second millennium, the city of Damascus rose in an oasis on the edge of this plain and prospered greatly from its position at the head of a new caravan route to Mesopotamia.[2]

---

[2] This route did not become important until the camel was domesticated in the middle east at the end of the second millennium.

Below Tyre, Lebanon was broken by the valley of Esdraelon, a favorite battlefield throughout history, beyond which rose the peak of Mount Carmel. The mountains then bore east, leaving a widening plain and a piedmont of low hills covered with fertile soil. Mountain streams and winter rains watered the area sufficiently to support a cluster of towns, of which the fortified city of Megiddo was the most important. To the east the hills climbed again to the continuation of the Lebanon chain. Jerusalem was built in these highlands and became important in the first millennium. The mountains descended sharply to the trough where the Jordan River flowed. Rising in the Anti-Lebanon mountains, the Jordan passed through the little Sea of Galilee and then sank far below sea level and became lost in the Dead Sea. Just north of the Dead Sea, on the banks of the Jordan, stood the most ancient of Palestinian cities, Jericho. Jericho and the valley were guarded on the east by Anti-Lebanon. Beyond the mountains lay meager grasslands, which faded gradually into the dry sand and stone of the Arabian desert.

Between Megiddo and the borders of Egypt, the narrow, fertile coast land saw the rise of several strong fortified cities. The best known of these was Gaza. Late in the second millennium the Philistines conquered and settled the region, and for centuries it was called Philistia after them.

Early Settlement In the seventh millennium early Neolithic settlements rose all along the hill country from northern Mesopotamia to southern Anatolia and south to Palestine. One of the clearest archaeological records was found at Jericho, where the people progressed from a prepottery stage to civilization over the course of five thousand years. Many of the upland villages used elaborately painted pottery of excellent manufacture. One of the earliest and most beautiful of these wares, called Halaf, had a wide range over northern Mesopotamia and Syria. It coexisted in the same territory with Samarra, an earlier painted ware, and both preceded in date the Ubaid ware in Sumer. The villages in which these wares were made were solidly built, with clay, stone, and timber construction. They contained temples in which were found figurines, in the towns some small copper beads were found, though rarely. Tools and possessions were similar to the late Neolithic artifacts of Mesopotamia.

Mari The first strong civilized state to arise in Syria was Mari. It was founded on the bank of the middle Euphrates and grew to considerable size and importance by 2500 B.C. Its kings and people were Semitic, closely akin to the Akkadians, but they hired an army of Amorite "mercenaries." Mari profited from Elam's destruction of the Third Dynasty of Ur and for a time ruled several former Sumerian territories. But the Amorite mercenaries turned on their masters and took these lands one by one. Mari itself was forced to bow to an

Amorite king in the twentieth century, but the state remained powerful and independent and rivaled Babylon for two hundred years. The Amorite rulers, however, had to accept incoming Hurrian tribes (pp. 98 and 102) into the citizen body and to use Hurrians as hired soldiers.

During these two centuries, before its defeat by Hammurabi, Mari controlled a three-hundred-mile strip from the borders of Babylon to Carchemish. The capital city was large and the palace of the king became one of the show places of the world. Extensive archives were kept, including annals, business records, letters between officials within the country, and diplomatic correspondence between the rulers of Mari and the kings of other states. Most of the records are in Akkadian and written in cuneiform, though an occasional document in Hurrian has been found.

The state was organized like that of Babylon, at first with a strong military system. Noteworthy were the fortifications for defense and a system of fire signals which could flash a message across the country in a matter of hours. Despite these preparations, the Assyrians took Mari and ruled it for a generation, and Hammurabi later reduced its territories to a province of his empire. Mari was destroyed by raiders from Anatolia between 1600 and 1550, and the Hurrian state of Mitanni arose in the same general area.

Canaan   The Mari correspondence mentions several Syrian states, among them Byblos, Apum, and Hazor, and from other sources it is clear that a number of contemporary cities inhabited by Semites flourished in the plains and valleys of Syria and Palestine (called Canaan). The coastal towns and the cities of the south (Megiddo, Ai, and Beth-Shan) were strongly influenced by Egypt, with which contacts were close and direct. In the twenty-third and twenty-second centuries many Canaanite towns were destroyed, and those remaining decreased in population because of nomadic movements sending Amorites into Mesopotamia. The process was reversed about 2000 B.C., when town life began to flourish anew, though the Hyksos conquest temporarily shattered the peace in 1750. The Hyksos invaders included Hurrians, Iranian (perhaps Indo-European) charioteers, and a third people speaking an unidentified tongue. They settled among the Semites in the towns of southern Palestine and built forts and castles. The wealth of Canaan increased considerably because of its flourishing trade with the Hyksos—of whose "empire" Egypt was so unwilling a member (p. 89).

Immediately after the expulsion of the Hyksos from Egypt in *ca.* 1575 B.C. the pharaohs of the Eighteenth Dynasty began a steady advance into Syria. By the end of the reign of Thutmose III (*ca.* 1468–1437) Egypt controlled the entire area, even penetrating the upper Euphrates valley. North Syria fell away from Egypt to the Hittites before 1370, but the coastal cities and southern Canaan remained for another century in Egyptian hands. Some of the towns were gar-risoned by Egyptian troops; others were ruled by native princes who proved themselves loyal to the pharaoh.

Amorites and Hebrews   Side by side with the Semitic city dwellers of Canaan and north Syria dwelled a nomadic people who shared their ethnic origin and language. These wanderers were called Amorites, or "Westerners," by the Sumerians and Akkadians. Though the Amorites depended for their livelihood on herding and had at first no fixed abode, they did not resemble the nomadic peoples of more recent times. They did not have swift horses or camels, and depended on the ox and donkey to move them from place to place. Consequently, they could not easily cross desert areas to travel from one oasis to another, but were confined to the grassy plains of the Fertile Crescent itself, and moved slowly and spasmodically along the borders of the farming regions. Their men were available to serve as mercenaries for the city-states. The Amorites could easily exchange their pastoral life for a settled existence in the arable lands.

By 2000 B.C. they had done so, and were absorbed into the states of Mesopotamia and Syria. Other slow wanderers of varied ethnic origin replaced them on the grasslands. Among these were the tribes called Khabiru ("bandits") by the city dwellers, and it is from among them that the later Israelites may have come.[3]

Phoenicia   Some of the earliest Semitic cities of Syria arose on the narrow coastal plain of Lebanon, but unlike Mari they were not always independent. Byblos, the oldest port, may even have been an Egyptian colony. Certainly it and other cities of the area were strongly influ-enced by Egypt from its first dynasties onward, and only during periods of Egyptian weakness did Byblos, Sidon, and Ugarit achieve full in-dependence. Nevertheless, though Egyptian control may sometimes have proved irksome, the Phoenician cities prospered because of their command of an assured market for timber and textiles, and they became marts where Egyptian and Mesopotamian products, as well as the goods of every other region, were mingled and exchanged.

Cedar and hardwoods from the mountains and wool from the interior were the regional sources of wealth, and the Phoenicians exploited them profitably. Logs felled on the mountains came down chutes to the coast, where they were floated in rafts to the harbors. Here they were dressed into lumber or taken in tow for shipment to Egypt. Wool was woven into handsome textiles and dyed a rich crimson,

---

[3]A number of scholars have worked on this problem and the view stated here is widely accepted. However, alternative theories of the identity of the Khabiru have been offered. It should be noted that the early Israelites did not identify themselves as Khabiru. The name Hebrew became attached to the Israelites at a much later date.

Snake Goddess from Northern Syria, ca. 1200 B.C. (The Brooklyn Museum)

later called "Tyrian purple," with the color obtained from small mollusks, caught and dried on the seashore.

After the fall of the Egyptian empire Tyre, the newest Phoenician city—founded by villagers moving from the coast to an island that offered them safety and a good harbor—became the leading Phoenician state. The Tyrians continued to export timber and dyed textiles, but in addition established a famous glass industry. Glass was molded in the Egyptian fashion, and Tyre became famous for its fragile, lovely wares. The Phoenicians, led by the kings of Tyre, became the greatest traders of the Mediterranean world after the fall of Mycenae. They were cordially hated by later Greek rivals, who nevertheless learned the alphabet and the art of celestial navigation from them.

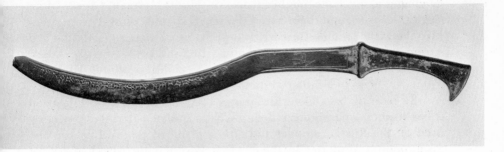

Assyrian Sword of Bronze Made for Adad-Nirari, King of Assyria ca. 1310–1280 B.C. (The Metropolitan Museum of Art, gift of J. Pierpont Morgan, 1911)

ASSYRIA

Semites of Akkadian stock lived along the upper Tigris throughout the third millennium. They called their land Assyria after its capital, Assur (or after their chief god, also called Assur). The Assyrians were sturdy farmers, but Assyria was too poor and isolated to achieve early significance. It was not until 2000 B.C., when the Amorites cut the normal trade routes from Mesopotamia up the Euphrates that Assyria gained prosperity and prominence. Its citizens, aided by their Akkadian rulers, succeeded in developing a new route up the Tigris, and Assyrian merchants set out to form commercial colonies in foreign lands. The best documented of these mercantile colonies was a settlement at Kültepe in southeastern Anatolia, which lasted for nearly a century (*ca.* 1875–*ca.* 1800 B.C.). Its records and letters give detailed information on trade routes, mercantile organization, agents, means of transport, messenger systems, wages and prices, and the values of goods relative to metals. The merchants' comments on political conditions in Assyria and in the Anatolian area where they lived are also revealing.

Assyria's brief period of international importance was ended by Hammurabi's conquest. Later, after the fall of the Amorite dynasty of Babylon, its way was blocked by the strong Iranian-Hurrian state of Mitanni on the west and by Hittites and Hurrians on other frontiers. A period of successful wars against Mitanni, under the Assyrian king Assur-uballit I, marked the beginning of its rise to power, and in the first millennium B.C. Assyria became the leading world power.

THE INDO-EUROPEANS

The various tribes and clans called collectively "Indo-European" which migrated into the east, middle east, Mediterranean, and west European areas during the second and first millenniums B.C. spoke languages akin to one another (Sanskrit, Hittite, Iranian, Greek, Latin, Celtic, German), and they shared similar social and cultural institutions. Like the early Semites, the early Indo-Europeans were nomads and had strong patrilineal tribal organizations. But unlike the Semites, their families were monogamous and only the children of the wife were ordinarily heirs to a father's estate.

By plotting back along the routes followed by the Indo-European tribes in their migrations, scholars have postulated that they formerly lived on the Russian steppes and on the plains of central Europe. The assumption is supported by the fact that most of these tribes had domesticated the horse, a native of the plains, and that their languages contained words for plants found in those lands, but there remains great uncertainty about their origins.

Certain customs and talents mark Indo-European tribes known most clearly to history (Greeks, Celts, Aryans, Germans, and the like). Their chiefs were primarily military leaders, and the clansmen gloried in battle, drinking, and song. Clans and tribes formed and reformed to follow the mightiest war chiefs. Even gods and goddesses were jealous and warlike, though they represented natural forces. Heading the Indo-European pantheons was the god of war and of the sky, who controlled storm and lightning. It became fashionable among some Indo-Europeans to cremate their dead and carefully bury the bones and ashes. They held their garments together with brooches (safety pins or fibulae), and were skillful and talented workers in metals, whether gold, copper, bronze, or, later, iron.

HURRIANS AND HITTITES

Peoples of many ethnic origins participated in the migrations pouring into the middle east just before and after 2000 B.C. The ultimate cause probably was the movement of the Indo-Europeans, but as they came in hordes from south Russia into Iran, then parted to flow east to India and west to Anatolia and Syria, other peoples were caught up and swept along with them. Among the most powerful of these attendant tribes were the people called *Hurrians* (Biblical "Horites"), whose home had been in the the Caucasus. In some cases they followed chiefs who worshiped Aryan gods, as they did to form the state of Mitanni, or were attached to Indo-European tribes. Hurrians mixed with Hittites in both Anatolia and Syria.

The majority of the population of Mitanni, which was formed after the downfall of Mari about 1550 B.C., were Hurrians but their kings worshiped the Sanskrit (Aryan) gods Indra, Varuna, and the Nasatya twins. They bred the finest horses and used the first war chariots in the middle east. A king of Mitanni sent an instructor named

Kikkuli to teach the Hittites the art of training horses, a courtesy his descendants lived to regret. The Hittites carefully recorded and preserved the information in their archives, and used it to build up the most formidable chariot forces of the time. With this chariotry they conquered north Syria, including the state of Mitanni, between 1370 and 1340 B.C.

The Hittites formed a chain of vassal and allied states over north and central Syria, extending from Aleppo and Carchemish in the north to Kadesh, Hamath, and Abina along the Orontes. When the Anatolian-dominated Hittite empire broke up about 1200 B.C., the states of Syria became independent and continued to flourish for several generations. Their culture exhibited a strange mixture of Hittite, Canaanite, and Hurrian elements, but their records were kept in Hittite hieroglyphics. The might of Assyria destroyed them all, one by one, in the ninth and eighth centuries.

ANATOLIA

The Anatolian peninsula (Asia Minor, now modern Turkey) jutted far westward beyond the Syrian coast, and was separated from the north Syrian plain by the Taurus Mountains, which constituted a formidable barrier. Only a few high passes afforded practical land routes between Anatolia and Syria, and the two regions differed greatly in terrain, climate, and resources.

Geography The topography of Anatolia was wild and varied. The bulk of the peninsula consisted of a high plateau, subject to seasonal extremes of temperature and rainfall, and completely encircled by mountains. In a sense it was an extension of the Russian steppe. To the southwest there was no coastal plain, for the mountains dipped to the sea, but farther north along the Aegean, and sharing its climate, the littoral was more hospitable and a plain of varying width watered by winter rain and mountain streams was available for agriculture. Along the Black Sea coast, where the climate was wet and moist, the land was fertile and forests covered the mountain slopes.

The plateau, though giving the appearance of rolling hills pierced by mountain peaks and cut by gorges in which the rivers flowed, actually resembled a great basin and its center was marked by a salt lake. Except for the river valleys, this basin was very dry in summer and more suited to herding than farming. Heavy snows and intense cold characterized the winters, and warm clothing and good shelter were always of concern to the inhabitants.

In addition to the violence of the climate, there were frequent earthquakes. Anatolia—and the Aegean area—has always been subject to severe seismic disturbances, and peoples of the region, ancient and modern, have been forced to adapt their architecture and engineering to the ever-present danger of earthquakes.

Yet in spite of the difficulties of climate, the danger of earthquake, and the limited arable and the rugged terrain, Anatolia was wealthy in resources and attractive to ancient peoples. It was rich in timber and, more important, in metals. Copper, tin, lead, and iron were mined in the mountains; and there were lodes and veins of gold and silver, sometimes separate and sometimes together in a natural mixture called electron. Gold was also panned from certain rivers and streams. Raw and smelted metals, wool, and hides came to be the chief products of Anatolia.

Early Settlement   Settlements arose on the Anatolian plateau by the middle of the seventh millennium, according to James Mellaert. Between 6500 and 4000 B.C. prosperous farmers and stockbreeders built houses decorated with mural paintings and supplied with many comforts. By the fourth millennium Neolithic villages dotted the coasts and islands of Anatolia, and the residents of upland and coastal communities began to use copper tools. Sometime before or about the opening of the fourth millennium barbarians with inferior cultural traditions destroyed many of the western villages, though some survival is indicated in the south by the continuity of the older painted-pottery traditions. Fortification walls were built around the little towns during this millennium.[4] But the Anatolian towns prospered except in the Cilician plain, in the southeast, where they were devastated by unknown enemies about 3000 B.C. Elsewhere, the early Bronze Age developed naturally out of the late Copper Age cultures. Conditions seemed more settled and the several cultures in different parts of Anatolia flourished. By the end of the early Bronze Age, Anatolia was the source from which Assyrians, and probably Mesopotamians and Syrians as well, bought their metal supplies. Urban communities arose as a result of this trade, though agriculture continued to be the basis of economic life.

Troy   The most famous of ancient Anatolian cities was Troy, known through the ages to readers of the *Iliad* and doubly romanticized by Heinrich Schliemann's discovery of its ruins. As a schoolboy in Germany, Schliemann refused to believe that the Homeric story of the Trojan War was a myth. After gaining maturity, he accumulated a fortune and retired from business to devote his time and wealth to prove his faith in Homer. In 1871 he began to dig into the hill of Hissarlik, the traditional site of Troy. He identified several settlements and recovered hoards of jewelry from the site. With the aid of the archaeologist Wilhelm Doerpfeld, he made every effort to identify the Homeric

---

[4]Fortifications were built in much of the Aegean world at this time. The reason is unknown. None of the forts developed into true cities except on the island of Crete.

city, but without the advantage of comparative data Schliemann and Doerpfeld went hopelessly astray. They believed Troy II to have been the city of the *Iliad*, but recent re-excavation by Carl William Blegen has shown that the seventh city on the site was Homeric Troy. Still, mistaken as were his conclusions, Schliemann's investigations in Anatolia and at Mycenae on the Greek mainland were useful, and his dramatic discoveries at both places awakened interest in the archaeology of the Aegean and the middle east.

Troy was founded sometime after 3000 B.C. on the coast of northern Anatolia overlooking the Aegean approach to the Hellespont and the entrance to the Black Sea. It was part of a cultural complex covering the hinterland and several islands as well (Lemnos, Lesbos, Chios, and Emporio). Troy was six times destroyed by fire, earthquake, or conquest before it fell to the Achaeans. Even then, it partly recovered from the sack, but in the disordered times that followed the Dorian migrations the area was abandoned.

The culture of Troy I (*ca.* 2750–2500 B.C.) was more closely connected with the Aegean islands than with the interior of Anatolia. Its first building period showed a small fortified town with houses of rectilinear and megaron style (oblong rooms with front porch), similar to the contemporary island settlements. Troy I was burned, but there was no appreciable interval before it was rebuilt; this was done with no cultural changes, but the new citadel was larger. Troy II had a long history, during which it underwent some seven periods of enlargement and rebuilding. Its end was abrupt and tragic; every house gave evidence of hasty flight by its occupants, and the floors were littered with objects abandoned as their owners fled. The city was burned, though the next levels of rebuilding (Troy III, IV, and V) carry on the cultural traditions of Troy II. Mellaert speculates that the destruction of Troy II might have been due to the Luian invasion in about 2300 B.C. (For Luians, see p. 106). There are no marks of fire in the destruction of Troy V, but with the level known as Troy VI, great changes occurred.

The sixth settlement at Troy shows an entirely different cultural tradition and gives every indication of having been built by a different people (the date is provisionally given at sometime between 1900 and 1800 B.C.). There is every reason to identify the invaders with the peoples then moving into the Greek mainland (Homer's Achaeans). The newcomers were good architects. They reconstructed the little fort and built it into an imposing stronghold. They used the same pottery ("Minyan") as that found on the Greek mainland and all their material culture resembles the early Achaean, but they remained independent of both the Achaeans and the Hittites who entered interior Anatolia. Indeed, the Hittite records are clear that the Troad, which they called *Assuwa*, was never a part of their empire. An earthquake destroyed

Troy VI but the fort and palace were promptly and strongly rebuilt. Mycenaeans from Greece took Troy VII and sacked it between 1270 and 1250 B.C.[5]

THE HITTITE EMPIRE

The Anatolian homeland of the Hittites lay in the hills to the east of the salt lake in the center of the plateau. Their principal cities were dotted along the Halys River, which made a great arc through the hills before turning north to the Black Sea. The peoples already occupying the region called the land *Hatti*, and the Hittites took both the land and the name. "Hittite" means "man of Hatti." A city called *Hattusas* (Turkish "Bogazköy") became the capital of the new state, which became firmly established only after several generations. The invaders did not wipe out the older peoples but became their overlords and formed an elite group in the total population. The written records of the Hittites reveal the diversity of their ethnic origin. No less than nine languages were used: the old Anatolian ("proto-Hittite"), Hurrian, five different Indo-European dialects, Akkadian (for diplomatic correspondence), and Sumerian (for literary reasons). Their material culture was as mixed and varied as their languages.

The period of the Hittite Old Kingdom (*ca.* 1740–*ca.* 1460 B.C.) was an age of internal weakness. Many early Indo-European kingships (as known from the Greeks, Latins, Germans, and even the Medes) were weak, and the Hittite kingship was no exception. The rulers had difficulty controlling their own relatives and their nobles. Not until the reign of a strong king named Telepinus, himself a usurper, was an orderly succession established. His regulations, reinforced by the law code promulgated soon after his death, strengthened the state, and the construction of a fine military organization in succeeding reigns opened the way to empire.

The conquest of Syria began about 1460 with the capture of Aleppo, but advance was slow in the face of strong Egyptian forces and their allies from Mitanni. Circumstances changed under the great Hittite king Suppiluliumas (*ca.* 1375–1335 B.C.). He took Mitanni unexpectedly through Assyria, and profiting by Egyptian weakness under the pharaoh Ikhnaton, pushed south to Abina. By 1370, Suppiluliumas controlled all of north and central Syria. His successors defended the Empire against a revived and strengthened Egypt, and treaties were drawn up

---

[5] Date given by Carl William Blegen (and Herodotus). The traditional Greek date of 1184 B.C. is entirely at odds with the presently known facts of the Dorian invasion of Greece. By 1184 many cities that Homer lists as participants in the Trojan expedition were under attack by Dorians or had already been destroyed.

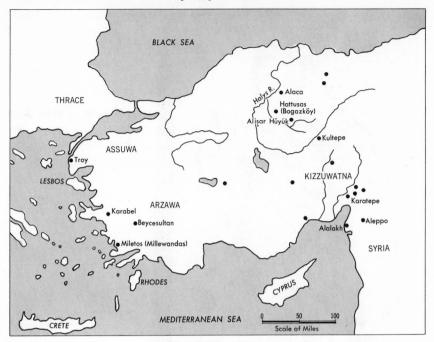

Hittite Anatolia, ca. 1300 B.C.

between the two powers determining the mutual frontier. Ramses II of Egypt broke the treaty sometime after 1290, but was defeated by the Hittite Muwatallis and his allies at Kadesh. The Egyptians escaped destruction and Ramses boasted of victory, but Muwatallis retained Kadesh. In the peace treaty (copies of which exist), signed in 1272 between Ramses and Hattusilis III, a later Hittite king, the Hittites dictated the terms.

Government and Society The Hittite hierarchy was dominated by the king, whose titles were "Great King" and "The Sun." He was never deified in life but "became a god" in death, and his bones and ashes were reverently interred in accordance with an elaborate ritual whose details are preserved in the archives. The king's power was chiefly religious and military, though he occasionally acted as arbitrator in disputes between nobles. In the period of the Empire his religious function came to be even more important, and he was sometimes forced to return to Hattusas in the midst of a military campaign to celebrate a prescribed ritual. The queen was likewise powerful and respected, and was associated with the king in diplomatic correspondence or treaties with foreign states. She too had religious functions and duties.

Royal kinsmen enjoyed great privileges, which they constantly abused, and filled the highest offices in the state. They were appointed

Hittite Warrior (or God) from Bogazköy. (Ankara Museum)

governors over conquered cities or provinces and generals of the army. Below them was a numerous palace bureaucracy and nobles with huge landed estates.

The non-Hittite inhabitants lived in villages under the supervision of Hittite governors. They had their own "Elders," who settled quarrels among the peasants, who made up the bulk of the population, and the craftsmen, called "men of the tool." All citizens, Hittite or non-Hittite, had specific rights under the law code. Slavery existed, and the slave was completely at his master's mercy though he had legal protection against other men and could hold property of his own.

After the formation of the Empire, the state was bound together by a vassal system whose lesser rulers swore solemn oaths of loyalty to one another and to the king at Hattusas. There were also "protectorates," such as Cilicia (Hittite *Kizzuwatna*), and subject kingdoms, such as *Arzawa* (west-central Anatolia), which were ruled by their own kings but had to provide army contingents for the Hittites. These king-

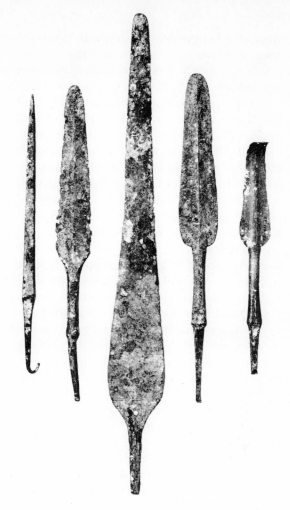

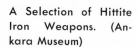

A Selection of Hittite Iron Weapons. (Ankara Museum)

doms were not so reliable as the members of the Empire, and the coastal lands that were only partly subjugated were even less so. Toward the end of the Empire a number of Hittite records describe relations with the king of *Ahhiyawa*, or *Ahhiya*, which is believed to be Achaea, and complaints of Ahhiyawan interference in western Anatolia were frequent. Particular mention is made in this connection with the city (or state) of Millewandas, identified as the Greek Miletos.

Economy Agriculture was the mainstay of the Hittite economy, and much of the law code was concerned with problems related to it. Lists of fields and title deeds, including inventories of estates, provide added information about crops and produce. Animals used for meat or for transportation were the ox, horse, mule, ass, pig, sheep, and goat.

Bees were kept to provide honey for sweets. Grapes, apples, pomegranates, and almonds were used. Barley and emmer wheat were the grains commonly grown for bread and beer, and peas and beans are occasionally mentioned. Wool and flax were produced for clothing.

The metals of the Anatolian highlands were widely exploited, but copper and bronze led in quantity of production. During the second millennium, the Hittites began to smelt iron, but in so small a quantity that it continued to be classed as a precious metal, being five times more valuable than gold and eight times more valuable than silver. A letter exists from an Egyptian ruler begging the Hittite king to send him iron. The request was refused, with the excuse that none was presently available, and indeed there was no large body of craftsmen in the Hittite kingdom skilled in iron-working.

Religion The Hittite gods were composite, drawn from the peoples' varied origins or adopted from their neighbors. Hurrian, Indo-European, and Sumerian divinites were all honored and identified with one another. Out of the mixture, an official pantheon was created. It was headed by the Weather God, who for state purposes was married to the Lady Sun. Below them ranked a number of deities, including the "missing god," Telepinu, the counterpart of the Syrian Adonis and the Egyptian Osiris. All the Hittite gods were shown standing upon or drawn by sacred animals—bulls for the weather god, lions for the sun goddess. Gods were also distinguished in Hittite art by their dress, which was different from that of humans, and by the symbols they carried.

Each god represented some power of nature which had to be propitiated for the welfare of the individual and the state. Particularly interesting was the weather god, called Teshub by the Hurrians. His name in one of the Indo-European dialects (Luian) was written Tarhund, which is in Etruscan Tarchon and Latin Tarquinius. Like the Greek Zeus or the Latin Jupiter, Teshub controlled storms and thunderbolts.

Literature Among the multilingual tablets in the Hittite archives were a number of stories, tales, and myths. Many of them were borrowed from Mesopotamia, but a group of Hurrian and "Hittite" (from which subgroup is not always certain) religious tales are unique. "The God Who Disappeared" explains the alternation of the seasons and why there was a time when nothing grew. Telepinu—or in another version the weather god—was enraged at the wickedness of men and went into hiding, so hurriedly that he put his right boot on his left foot and his left boot on his right foot. All life came quickly to a standstill, and other gods and men had to seek the missing god and lure him back to his duties. An eagle and a bee played a part in finding and returning Telepinu, and divine and human magic was exerted to overcome his anger.

Other tales are "The Snaring of the Dragon" and "The Song of Ullikummi" (or "The Monster of Stone"). Historical legends were also written, though only the "Seige of Urshu" exists in more than a fragmentary state. Many of the Hittite documents are concerned with official matters, but they contain some interesting examples of political pleading, or "justification," on the part of kings. There is very little poetry.

Art and Architecture Hittite art is known chiefly from relief sculpture, though an occasional small statue in the round has survived. Reliefs were executed on limestone cliffs at the open-air religious centers, such as Yazilikaya, or in bas-relief on public buildings and in high relief at ornamental gateways. Gods in human shape, men, and animals are the chief subjects, and they are often well modeled and made to stand out very sharply from the background. Some goddesses are shown in true profile, but normally the men are posed in the Egyptian fashion, with torso in front view and legs and head in profile. In the Syro-Hittite cities winged monsters became popular, and Assyrian styles and techniques influenced sculpture strongly.

Hittite architecture was adopted from the pre-Hittite peoples of Anatolia, though the Hittites contributed ideas of their own in fortifications for defense. Town sites were carefully chosen spots that offered great natural protection. Hattusas was built on a sort of peninsula formed by the intersection of two deep gorges with sheer cliff faces. On the side that permitted easy access rose strong fortifications. Two parallel walls of stone were built with connecting cross walls between them, and the chambers thus formed were filled with rubble. A brick

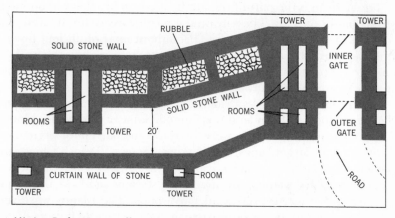

Hittite Defensive Walls. The two lines of solid wall contained rubble-filled "chambers" for extra strength. Towers, with rooms for the guards, were set at intervals along the length of the wall, and flanked the double, inset gate. An outer curtain wall of stone provided additional protection.

superstructure rose above the stonework and rubble to considerable height. The stones of the wall were large and of irregular shape but closely fitted. Approaches, curtain walls, and gateways were cleverly planned to force the visitor to expose his unshielded side to defenders on walls and towers, and a tunnel to permit surprise sorties ran under the wall to a postern gate.

Within the walls were temples and private houses, all with characteristic stone foundations and lower courses of masonry upon which rose brick walls bonded and reinforced at intervals with wooden beams. This type of architecture was well adapted to an area subject to earthquake, as rigidity was decreased by the inserted timbers, and it continued to be used not only in the Hittite Empire but over the rest of Anatolia and most of the Aegean area as well.

The Fall of Hattusas   Hattusilis was followed on the throne by one other great Hittite king, Tudhaliyas IV. He was able to devote most of his attention to religious duties and monuments, and was largely responsible for the gallery of sculptures at Yazilikaya, a few miles from the capital. But soon after 1200 Phrygian invaders, led by kings with the dynastic name Mitas (Greek "Midas"), conquered a weakened Hatti. Another great movement of peoples was in progress, stirred by the entry of the Dorians into Greece and the Aegean. In the words of the pharaoh Merneptah, "the isles were disturbed" and "the peoples of the sea" were cast up on Anatolian and Syrian shores.

THE ISLES OF THE SEA

The Aegean is the part of the Mediterranean Sea that was bounded by Anatolia on the east, Thessaly on the north, Greece on the west, and the island of Crete on the south. Throughout most of ancient times it formed a geographic and cultural unity, as its many islands, the peaks of submerged mountain chains, served as steppingstones to lead peoples from one shore to another.

Geography   Mountains, valleys, and small plains characterized the Aegean lands, so farm land was limited. Some of the smaller islands, of which there were hundreds, were too rocky and barren for permanent habitation, but larger ones like Lesbos, Samos, Delos, Chios and especially Crete offered great advantages to settlers. Crops grew well in the rich valleys watered by mountain streams, and on the slopes were forests of pine, cypress, and hardwoods. The islands were very green. The vine and the olive were native to the area, wild flowers dotted the tall grass in early spring, and geraniums grew to the size of small trees. The climate of the islands was delightful, always moderated by the sea; and though they were subject to sudden storm, rain, and snow in winter, the sky was clear and deeply blue for much of the year. The

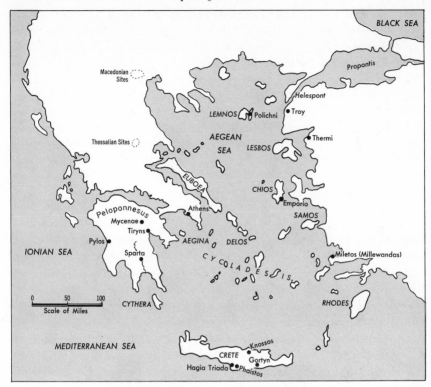

The Aegean Area, ca. 1500–1100 B.C.

sea was equally clear and blue, and the sparkling air brought every object, whether tree or mountain peak, into sharp outline. The landscape and the climate were bracing, stimulating, and beautiful.

The principal drawback to living in the Aegean isles, aside from the limited arable land, lay in the danger from earthquake. Like Anatolia they were subject to frequent, severe shocks which brought down buildings and whole cities, killing or injuring the inhabitants.

Resources were diverse. Timber and stone were plentiful and there were deposits of good clay, but metals were scarce. Some copper and iron were available on mainland Greece, but only Cyprus—which was technically outside the Aegean—had large supplies of copper. Oxen, pigs, sheep, goats, domestic fowl, and wild birds made up the useful animal population. Grains were probably not native to the region but brought in by early settlers. The sea provided some edible fish, squid, and shellfish.

Early Settlement The Neolithic inhabitants of Greece, Thessaly, and the isles of the sea were long-headed Mediterraneans of the same physical type found over North Africa and the middle east, but the cultures of Crete and the islands differed sharply from those of the mainland. For this reason, it is supposed that the islanders came by sea from Anatolia and North Africa, while the settlers in Greece came by land, having learned farming from the Danubian peoples. Whatever their origin, both island and mainland peoples knew agriculture before arrival in their respective homes. They already used pottery and possessed a highly specialized tool tradition. Trusting to the protection of the sea and the absence of other peoples nearby, they built few fortifications before 3000 B.C.

MINOAN CIVILIZATION

Schliemann's discoveries at Troy and Mycenae led directly to recovery of the brilliant, unique civilization of Crete. Guided by Greek legends telling of Minos, the son of Zeus, who had ruled the island, and for whom Daedalus had built a labyrinth to house the Minotaur, Sir Arthur Evans began excavations at Knossos. He traced a long record of growth and progress which began with Neolithic settlements in the fifth millennium and continued with little direct foreign interference until Greeks arrived in the fifteenth century B.C. Total destruction of the great palace at Knossos occurred after little more than a century of Greek occupation. Excavations at other Cretan sites have filled out the total picture and confirmed the general course of historical development.[6]

Crete is a long, narrow island extending a hundred and sixty miles from east to west and ranging from seven and a half to thirty-six miles in its north-south width. The site of Knossos was roughly centered on the northern shore on a spur of land not far from the sea, which could be seen from the palace roof between the intervening hills. In the opposite direction rose Mount Ida, snow-capped the year round. The site was beautiful and had many natural advantages. It had a good water supply, access to the sea, and fertile land for farming. Only twenty miles separated Knossos from Phaistos on the southern coast, and an early road existed between the two centers.

Minoan History   Little is known of the actual events of Cretan history, and its course must be conjectured from archaeological discoveries. Until almost 2000 B.C. there were few fortifications on the island. Life was peaceful, with steady development in agriculture and

---

[6]Archaeological terminology of the Aegean is complicated by the many independent systems used by different excavators. "Minoan," "Helladic," and "Mycenaean" can be roughly equated in their principal divisions of time. More important, here, is to know that Middle Minoan was contemporary with Middle Kingdom Egypt, and Late Minoan with the early Egyptian Empire.

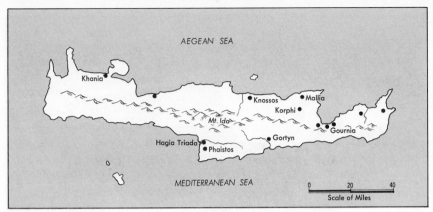

Crete, ca. 1500 B.C.

industry. Trade flourished, especially with Egypt, whence stonewares, ivory, metals, and gem stones were obtained. Cyprus was the source of copper from which the bulk of Cretan tools were made. Fine painted pottery, often decorated with motifs drawn from the sea and its creatures, was manufactured, and this ware, empty or full of wine and oil, was sold abroad.

In the twenty-first or twentieth century B.C. great palaces began to rise at many village sites, but from the beginning the palace of Knossos led in size and splendor. It continued to expand through rebuildings and enlargements over the following centuries. A palace at neighboring Mallia, which sought to rival Knossos in size, was destroyed. On the southern coast Phaistos, whose city and palace were next in size to Knossos, was obliged to accept second place. By 1600 B.C. Knossos dominated Crete, and was connected to other towns and cities by a network of well-built, well-guarded highways with stone bridges and viaducts over streams and bogs.

Meanwhile, beginning soon after 1900, Achaean Greeks established themselves on the Greek mainland. In some places they arrived as violent conquerors; in others peacefully, with no destruction. Like other Indo-Europeans they were bold warriors, users of horses (though they did not ride them) and war chariots, and clever metal smiths in bronze and gold. They made a distinctive pottery called Minyan ware, and fastened their garments with bronze "safety pins." By 1600, the Achaeans were entrenched at a number of fortified sites, among them Aegina, Tiryns, Malthi, and Mycenae. Almost immediately they were subjected to a strong and mounting influence from Crete, which in time affected all Achaean arts and crafts; it is often impossible to be sure whether a given article was made in Greece or Crete.

The Great Staircase, the Palace of Knossos. Restored by Sir Arthur
Evans. (Greek Press and Information Service)

The obvious cultural dominance of Crete over the Greeks lent
support to Thucydides' statement that Minos, the king of Knossos, built
the first sea-empire (*thalassocracy*) over which he maintained control
with his fleet, protecting the sea lanes from pirates and establishing
colonies on many islands. Two Minoan colonies are known through
archaeology, Philakopi on Melos and Ialysus on Rhodes; and several
depots, which were called *minoa*, have been located along the Aegean
coasts. Miletos may have been a Cretan foundation later taken over by
Achaeans. The Theseus legend tells of tribute Athens was forced to pay
Minos—and also makes clear the resentment of the Athenians at paying it.

About 1480 B.C.[7] or a little later the Achaeans attacked Knossos
and conquered it. They established themselves in the great palace,
added a throne room to it, and organized Cretan artisans to work for
them. They modified the Linear A script of Crete to suit the Greek
language, thus creating Linear B which Michael Ventris deciphered, and

[7] This historical reconstruction and the estimated dates follow Sterling Dow. Friedrich
Matz (in the revised *Cambridge Ancient History*) is noncommittal on the subject of a Minoan
empire and Chester G. Starr discards the idea entirely. However, as Dow points out,
neither thereby explains the *minoa*, the colonies, or the Theseus legend—nor is the strong
later Greek tradition taken into account. The situation is further complicated by the
doubts expressed by Palmer and others concerning some of Evans's dating methods.

began to keep extensive records both at Knossos and in the palaces on the mainland. But Achaean residence in Crete was short. About 1400 B.C. Knossos and the other Cretan palaces were plundered and ruthlessly destroyed by fire. Earthquake may have contributed to the damage but the looting and ruin were purposeful and thorough. The palaces were inadequately repaired, in some cases not at all, and the population of Crete declined sharply. Whether the violence resulted from a war between the natives and the Greeks or a vengeful sack and withdrawal by the Achaeans is unknown, but in the succeeding century Mycenae on the mainland emerged as the dominant power of the Aegean.

The Palace of Minos   The palace of Minos at Knossos embodied the brilliant life, art, and culture of the Minoan age. It was a large and exceedingly complex structure of four to five stories so built on sloping ground that the main entrances and the great court, the center of palace life and official activities, were on the third floor. On one side of the central court were the state rooms, the offices, and the storerooms equipped with huge jars—receptacles for the oil, wine, and grain collected as taxes. On the opposite side, spreading downhill, were the domestic and industrial quarters. Here was the royal family's two-story apartment with private staircase and bathrooms with terra-cotta tubs, as well as a schoolroom, an olive press, workrooms, and chapels. A colonnaded staircase led from the lower to the upper levels. The multistoried structure was lighted by a system of "light-wells" and was supplied with running water and a sewerage system that was still in working order when the excavators found it. Around the palace were other buildings: lesser palaces, a theatrical area, or *choros*, such as Homer says Daedalus built for "Ariadne of the flowing tresses," clusters of houses, and in the valley below an inn where visitors could bathe, rest, and refresh themselves.

Government and Society   Lacking any written evidence by the Cretans themselves, a reconstruction of the details of Minoan government is not really possible. But the following speculative account has been developed on the basis of later Greek tradition that is upheld (scantily) by some of Sir Arthur Evans's discoveries and reconstructions.

At the head of the government was the god-king, or priest-king, whose title was Minos (names of individual Cretan kings, such as Rhadamanthos the lawgiver, were known to later Greeks). The palace, or *labyrinthos* (which means place of the double ax), was a shrine as well as a royal residence and administrative center. A bureaucracy collected taxes in kind and kept written records of the royal possessions. Nothing is known of the details of this system or of local government, although there were perhaps royal representatives resident in other Cretan towns. A wealthy, landowning nobility surrounded the king, and mer-

The Throne Room, the Palace of Knossos, Restored. (Greek Press and
Information Service)

chants and craftsmen lived in the palace-dominated cities. The peasants
seem to have been serfs working the lands of king and nobles. Certain
towns, like the later *perioeci* ("dwellers around") of Sparta, may have
been vassal states rather than directly controlled from Knossos.[8]

Social life in the palaces and among the townspeople was active
and brilliant. Court assemblies were held, with music furnished by the
seven-stringed lyre, the flute, and a form of bagpipe. Dancing and
boxing were popular, but the favorite entertainment (according to paintings and other art) was the sport of bull leaping. Athletes, male and
female, met the charging bull, grasped his horns, and flipped over his
back to land on his rump and vault lightly to the ground.

Women participated freely with men in the sports and social functions, and it is possible that Cretan social organization grew from
matrilineal clans. Both sexes dressed richly, the women in short jackets
and long skirts sewn with ruffles and flounces, the men in short, colorful
kilts tightly belted at the waist. Men and women wore long, curled hair,
artfully arranged, and the men were clean shaven. Both affected
extravagant jewelry, wearing armlets, wristlets, anklets, and necklaces.
Women sewed little gold plaques on their dresses, and men hung
inlaid daggers from their belts.

[8]There is evidence that the social system of Sparta reflects that of Crete.

Economy   The type of crops grown in Crete had not changed since earlier times, but surpluses of wine and oil were obviously produced, collected, and stored in the magazines of the palaces with their great *pithoi* (man-sized jars) sunk into the floor. Thence the wine and oil were shipped abroad for sale. Industries that produced goods for home consumption and for export were weaving and dyeing, shoemaking, leatherwork of other types, carpentry, ceramics, stonework, and metallurgy. Metal work was exceedingly fine in design and execution. Short, straight swords and daggers of bronze were cunningly inlaid down the center of the blade with gold, on which natural scenes were engraved. Handles were also of gold, marvelously worked. Copper and bronze vessels were as handsome as the gold-bronze weapons, and Cretan pottery was known everywhere for its fine texture and the beauty of its painted designs.

Cretan ships carried goods in trade over an area that ranged from Egypt and Syria to south Italy and Sicily, where the natives copied Cretan patterns, and encompassed the islands and shores of the Aegean. Cretan goods even reached the Black Sea region. Minoan relations with Egypt were steady and constant during the early empire period, and

Restored Portico, the Palace of Knossos. (Photograph by Ronald P. Legon, reproduced by Frank D. Grande)

Egyptian influence was strong in Crete itself. It is possible that the first harbor works on the island of Pharos were built as a *minoa* to facilitate Minoan-Egyptian trade. Several pharaohs of the Empire boasted of the subjection of Crete and recorded payment of tribute to Egypt, but the claim is seldom believed. Historians have preferred to think that the "tribute" consisted of gifts (and perhaps import duties) freely given by the traders to ensure their welcome in the Two Lands rather than taxes imposed by Egypt on the island.

Art   The Cretans' love of nature, sports, and peaceful pursuits rather than the stern arts of war was reflected in their paintings, which aside from statuettes and small objects make up the surviving master-pieces of Minoan art. Men and women—singly or in gatherings— animals, plants, flowers, sea creatures—such as the octopus and flying fish—were treated impressionistically. The palace walls were covered with paintings in alfresco, which, unlike the realistic but conventional Egyptian murals, were executed freehand in wet plaster. Occasionally the painter, who had to work rapidly, made a spectacular failure but often he caught the very essence of an act or scene: the happy chatter of an audience of women or the lithe grace of a crouching cat stalking a bird. Color was used freely and with no regard for reality. A blue man was legitimate for the Cretan artist if the desired effect was achieved.

Fresco of Dolphins, the Palace of Knossos. (Greek Press and Informa-tion Service)

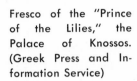

Fresco of the "Prince of the Lilies," the Palace of Knossos. (Greek Press and Information Service)

Statuettes in faïence and ivory reveal the artist's concern with essence rather than reality. The little goddess figures, dressed in flounced skirts but with breasts bare, around whose shoulders and arms snakes twine, capture and display an ideal of feminine beauty and grace. The ivory "bull leapers" catch the lissome human body in twisting, agile motion.

Religion No true temples were erected to Cretan deities but palace and household shrines were common, and caves were frequently considered holy places. There were also open-air shrines. Here were deposited votive objects, though there were no cult statues. These offerings, together with seal engravings, paintings, statuettes, and the reflections in later Greek literature, provide a partial view of religious beliefs. The chief divinity was the goddess whose symbols were the snake, bird (dove?), and column (or tree). She was probably thought to reveal herself in the creatures, and perhaps "appeared" to the worshiper in the pillar. Associated with her was a divine youth to whom bulls were sacrificed. He was sometimes represented as a bull-man (minotaur), by the bull alone or by its horns, and sometimes by the double ax or the huge shield. According to Greek mythology this god died annually and returned again to life.

The most celebrated of the holy places was a cave on Mount Ida, where many offerings were found and where later legend asserts that Minos went once every nine years to consult the gods about the well-being of his kingdom. The Greeks believed that this was the cave in which Zeus had been placed as a newborn infant and in which he immediately grew to maturity, for Zeus acquired some of the attributes and symbols of the Cretan god and may even have taken over part of his myth.

The Cretans believed in immortality and buried their dead sometimes in huge jars, sometimes in elaborately painted sarcophagi. The bodies of important men were placed in caves or chamber tombs hollowed out of the hillsides. Under Achaean rule these tombs were rounded and covered with a false dome; they looked like old-fashioned beehives and are called beehive tombs. Offerings of food and drink were made to the dead, and toys, weapons, vases, jewelry, and other objects appropriate to the age or sex of the dead person were placed in the grave.

Minoan Sarcophagus. Herakleion Museum. (Greek Press and Information Service)

Cretan Pitcher with Design of Squid. (The Brooklyn Museum)

Decline A decline in art and cultural vigor was immediately apparent under Achaean rule during the fifteenth century, but handsome, though static, work was still produced in the arts and crafts. Only remnants of the brilliant civilization survived the destruction of 1400, and before any revival or recovery was possible, the Achaeans returned—if Homer and the archaeologists are to be believed—only to be expelled by the Dorians about 1200 B.C. The Minoan culture was submerged but it continued to exist as an undercurrent, an imperfect memory, among the Cretans and among Ionian and Achaean refugees. Even that slight existence was important to the development of Greek civilization.

MYCENAEAN GREECE

In every phase of early Aegean history, revision of older ideas is taking place in the light of new knowledge—due especially to the additional information available from Linear B texts, new dating methods, and new excavations. The traditional view of "waves" of Indo-Europeans invading or infiltrating the Greek mainland is being modified. It is hardly possible to do more, presently, than point out what the classical Greeks (who called themselves Hellenes) believed about their origins.

Homer called the pre-Dorian Greeks Achaeans, though they consisted of several related tribes speaking different dialects. Some were called Achaeans, others Ionians (from whom the Athenians proudly claimed descent), and still others Aeolians. According to legend each tribe was led by heroes, among whom were Pelops, Heracles, Theseus, and Oedipus. Of the movement south and the blending of the conquerors with the conquered the legend of Pelops may be a vague memory, but the Achaean conquest was thorough and little survived from the preceding culture save Anatolian place names ending in -*nthos*, like Korinthos (Corinth) and Tirynthos (Tiryns), and words with the stem ending -*ss*, like *thalassa* (the sea).

The newcomers speedily adopted Minoan civilization but retained northern elements in housing, dress, and personal fashion. Pitched roofs and central hearths were useful in Greece, which was colder and wetter than Crete, and these features along with heavy fortification walls distinguished Mycenaean from Minoan architecture. Achaean men retained their loosely fitted garments caught together by the fibula (brooch or "safety pin") and refused to shave off their beards. The women were quicker to adopt Cretan dress and hair styling.

Political and social structure can be vaguely discerned from the texts in Linear B. The king, or chief, was called a *wanax* (Greek ἄναξ) and he was assisted by a *lawagetas*, whose exact duties are unknown. The title *basileus* (later Greek for "king") was borne by a lesser magistrate in each small village. Royal relatives and nobles had favored positions and held high office, as in the Hittite kingdom. The *Iliad* indicates that every town had a chief of its own, who served as a member of Agamemnon's council, but the Homeric picture is much later than the Mycenaean hegemony and is not likely to reflect that age with exactitude. The older population of Greece had been reduced to semiserfdom on the land, and war captives were used as household slaves. The gods mentioned in Linear B texts are those of the later Greeks: Zeus, Hera, Athena, and Dionysus.

Mycenae   The most important of Achaean states was Mycenae, a strong fortress on the rim of the Argolid plain. Its ring walls, pierced by the famous Lion Gate, were like those of Hattusas, the Hittite capital, having two parallel stone walls whose intervening space was filled with rubble and included an occasional storage chamber. The masonry was called Cyclopean because awed Greeks of a later age thought only giants could have handled such blocks of stone. The area enclosed was small, just spacious enough for a palace, a few workmen's quarters, and capacious storage magazines built against the wall and within it. A tunnel for sorties ran under the wall to a concealed postern outside. A second tunnel led to a spring. Other Achaean forts, the best preserved of which is neighboring Tiryns, followed the same plan.

In the sixteenth century the palace at Mycenae was decorated in Cretan fashion with alfresco paintings. Other amenities such as baths and drains also appeared to modify castle life, but furnishings can be illustrated only from the tombs. The early kings of Mycenae were buried

The Lion Gate at Mycenae. (Photograph by Ronald P. Legon, reproduced by Frank D. Grande)

in shaft graves arranged in a circle bounded by a wall. The complex resembled the "sacred circle" engraved on the shield of Achilles, described in the *Iliad*. The next dynasty abandoned shaft tombs in favor of enormous beehive structures, whose interiors were hung round with shields. Most of the beehive tombs were robbed, but in the shaft tombs archaeologists have found fortunes in gold jewelry and a small arsenal of fine weapons.

Life in Mycenae followed largely the Minoan fashions. Lords and ladies dressed elaborately and drank wine from handsome gold cups. Youths carried daggers of bronze inlaid with gold and ivory. But unlike the Cretans, great nobles (still bearded) wore plumed helmets of bronze, breastplates, greaves, and body armor and carried figure-eight shields (later replaced by round bucklers) and strong bronze swords.

They rode to war or to the hunt (their principal sport) in two-wheeled chariots drawn by horses.

After the fall of Knossos Mycenae captured much of Crete's trade. Mycenaean products reached Syria, Egypt, and the western Mediterranean, as well as the Aegean islands and coasts. The Minoa and Cretan colonies fell to the Achaeans, and Mycenae brooked no rivals in sea power. Greek legends, such as the story of the Argonauts, may reflect the dangers of a long trading voyage into the Black Sea. The deeds of Heracles, Theseus, and Perseus must already have been sung in the courts of chiefs and nobles.

The culmination of the age was the Trojan War, whose historicity cannot be questioned although the details are lost in the mists of poetic exaggeration. Perhaps Helen did have the "face which launched a thousand ships," though other causes of the war are conceivable. Already Mycenaean settlements (Miletos) occupied the coast of Anatolia, and the citizens of Troy were very like Achaeans themselves. Perhaps the war was part of Mycenae's campaign to subject and control the area, a punitive measure, or a simple looting expedition. Whatever the cause, Troy fell, but her downfall did not long precede that of her conquerors.

THE DORIAN CONQUEST

The Dorian invasions began in the mid-thirteenth century and continued for many years. The hard-pressed Achaeans built a wall across the Isthmus of Corinth in a last-ditch attempt to save the Peloponnesus, but to no avail. Fierce Dorian warriors, armed with iron weapons, took to the sea and by-passed the wall. Pylos was the first Achaean city to be sacked and gutted, but Mycenae's ruin was not long delayed. Rulers and palaces, scribes and records, artisans and wares, all disappeared. The destruction was so complete that the very titles *wanax* and *lawagetas* were erased from the Greek language.

The period that followed the Dorian conquest was a dark age for Greece. By 1223 B.C. the Dorian invaders were pushing into the islands, driving waves of desperate displaced refugees into Anatolia and Syria. A year or two later and again in 1178 and 1175 mixed peoples attacked Egypt by land and sea. Among these were Lycians, Carians, and Ionians who had been driven from their homes. The succeeding centuries were to change greatly the civilizations of the ancient east and of the Aegean world.

5 · The Egyptian Empire

EGYPT DOMINATED THE MIDDLE EAST FOR FIVE
hundred years after the break up of the Hyksos empire. Ambitious pharaohs of the Eighteenth Dynasty, not content with freeing Egypt, moved rapidly north into Syria and south into Nubia.
Success was heady and the great conqueror, Thutmose III, did not
rest until he held sway over dominions extending from the Euphrates
Valley to the fourth cataract of the Nile. As a result Egyptian ideas and
influences molded the societies and arts and crafts of Syria and pene-

Copy of a Wall Painting from an Eighteenth Dynasty Tomb at Thebes, Showing
Musicians Playing at a Banquet. (The Metropolitan Museum of Art)

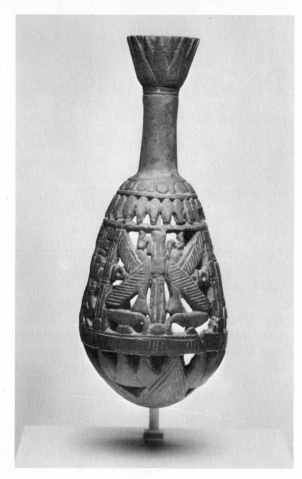

Openwork Glass Vase in Dark Blue, Fourteenth Century B.C. (The Brooklyn Museum)

trated into the depths of equatorial Africa. In return, the Two Lands themselves were molded, changed, and stirred by the ideas and products of the varied peoples with whom they had contact.

THE EIGHTEENTH DYNASTY

Although some Egyptians had accepted Hyksos rule, to later generations the Hyksos became hated foreigners and usurpers. After the princes of the south, the so-called Seventeenth Dynasty, had rebelled in vain, Amosis of Thebes (1570–1545 B.C.), founder of the Eighteenth Dynasty, led the Egyptians to triumph against them. Using war chariots and other weapons borrowed from the Hyksos themselves and rousing the people to a warlike pitch before unknown to Egyptians, Amosis laid siege to Avaris, took it, and followed the retreating enemy into Palestine.

Hatshepsut, Shown as Pharaoh, Offering Jars of Wine to the God Amon, Red Granite. (The Metropolitan Museum of Art, Rogers Fund and contributions from Edward S. Harkness, 1926)

As a result of his victories and those of his immediate successors, kingship was re-established in Egypt with a power, force, and authority never wielded by Middle Kingdom pharaohs. Amosis, in driving out the invader, occupied the Two Lands by right of conquest as a personal royal possession, and Egypt became a military state ruled by a pharaoh, now also an "emperor," who wore a war helmet. He had an effective army equipped with horses and chariots, and was quick to learn the profits to be gained from conquest. Hereditary nobles, if they had survived the Hyksos regime, could offer no effective opposition or hindrance to the pharaoh. The pharaohs of the Eighteenth Dynasty controlled Egypt's man power and resources as did the pharaohs of the Old Kingdom.

Model of the Temple of Queen Hatshepsut at Deir el Bahri, Reconstructed as
It Was in 1480 B.C. (The Metropolitan Museum of Art)

The penetration of Syria was continued by Amosis' successors,
Amenhotep I, Thutmose I, and Thutmose II, but a peaceful interlude
followed under Hatshepsut. This great ruler was not satisfied with remaining a queen, and after the early death of her husband, Thutmose II,
usurped the power from her young son-in-law Thutmose III who had
been crowned pharaoh while still a boy. She ruled Egypt as pharaoh
for several years (*ca.* 1490–1468 B.C.). Her sex was a matter of confusion to many Egyptians for statues and reliefs usually showed her as
a man; only a few revealed her womanhood. She did not pursue campaigns in Syria but turned rather to consolidation, building, and the
peaceful pursuit of trade. She sent an expedition through the Red Sea
to Punt, and it returned successfully with spice trees, gold, and many
other treasures. The departure, return, and the goods exchanged are
all pictured in relief on the walls of her mortuary temple at Deir el-
Bahri.

Hatshepsut's temple was the most beautiful building of the Empire
period. Planned by her architect-minister Senmut, it rose in a series of
broad, colonnaded terraces ascended by ramps, and was backed by the
sheer, towering cliffs of the western valley wall. The site, plan, and
details of decoration make it one of the loveliest buildings in the history
of world architecture.

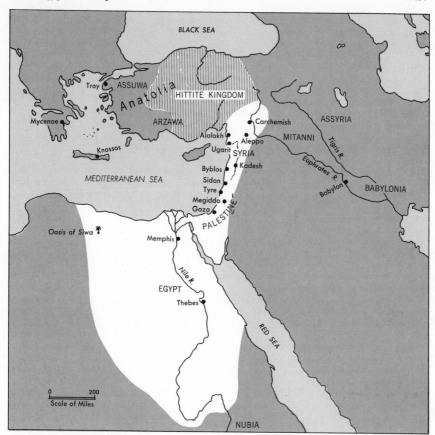

The Egyptian Empire Under Thutmose III, ca. 1437 B.C.

Thutmose III, 1490–1437 B.C.   At Hatshepsut's death Thutmose III expressed his resentment of her domination by ordering her name chiseled out of all inscriptions (workmen's carelessness foiled his purpose) and then renewed the attacks on Syria. He made seventeen campaigns, some by land, some by sea. For the latter he used bases on the Phoenician coast and took men and equipment north by water. All Syria fell to him. The Kassites in Babylon, the Hittites in Asia Minor, and the rulers of Crete sent gifts. On the walls of his chapel in the temple at Karnak Thutmose had records carved of his conquests, pictures of the gold and silver vessels of the tribute, and even portrayals of the strange plants and animals he had come upon in Syria. Four of the obelisks he erected to celebrate his jubilee are still in existence, one each in Constantinople, Rome, London, and New York.

Amenhotep III, 1405–1367 B.C. Thutmose III's successors retained control of the lands of the Syrian empire and added some territory along the upper Nile River near the fourth cataract. When Amenhotep III became pharaoh, the empire was at its greatest extent and power. Diplomatic correspondence on clay tablets, known through the place of discovery as the Tell el 'Amarna letters, shows the prestige and wealth of the pharaoh. The kings of Babylon and Mitanni sent princesses to the royal harem and requested gifts of gold "for gold is as common as dust in thy land." Here is a letter from the king of Karduniaš:

> To Niphururia, king of Eg[ypt], say. Thus saith Burraburiaš, king of Karduniaš, thy brother. I am well. With thee, thy house, thy wives, thy sons, thy land, thy chief men, thy horses, thy chariots, may it be very well. Since my fathers and thy fathers with one another established friendly relations, they sent to one another rich presents, and they refused not one another any good request. Now my brother has sent [only] two minas of gold as a present. But now, if gold is plentiful, send me as much as thy fathers. But if it is scarce, send half of what thy fathers did. Why didst thou send [only] two minas of gold? Now, since my work on the House of God is great, and vigorously have I undertaken its accomplishment, send much gold. And thou, whatsoever thou desirest from my land, write that it may be brought to thee. In the time of Kurigalzu, my father, the Canaanites as one man wrote to him as follows: "Against the border of the land we will go and we will make an invasion, (and wit)h thee we will make an alliance." My father wrote them thus, saying: "Cease making an alliance with me. If you cherish hostility against the king of Egypt, my brother, and wish to ally yourself with another, shall I not come, and shall I not plunder you, for he is in alliance with me?" My father, for thy father's sake, did not listen to them. Now, as to the Assyrians, my subjects, have I not written thee? So is the situation! Why have they come into thy land? If thou lovest me, they should not carry on any business. Let them accomplish nothing. As a present for thee, three minas of beautiful lapislazuli, and five span of horses for five wooden chariots, I have sent thee.[1]

Syrian princes educated at the Egyptian court aped the manners and customs of the conquering rulers. Customhouses were established, and goods from the Aegean, from Asia, and from Punt and Nubia to the south were brought to the markets of Thebes. The ancient harbor discovered submerged off the island of Pharos and well placed at the Canopic mouth of the Nile was probably built at this time.

Wealth made possible great luxury in the houses of the nobles and in their dress and ornaments as well as in the palaces of the pharaohs and the temples of the gods. Across the river from the capital Amenhotep III had a lake constructed in the desert for his royal wife

[1] Reprinted from the book *The Tell el-Amarna Tablets* by Samuel A. B. Mercer by permission of Mr. F. K. Venables and The Macmillan Company of Canada Limited and of Macmillan & Co. Ltd., London. Vol. 1, Letter 9, pp. 29–31.

Copy of a Painted Ceiling from the Palace of Amenhotep III. The bulls' heads and spiral ornament are strongly reminiscent of Cretan designs. (The Metropolitan Museum of Art)

and by it he built her a palace. The paintings in it show Minoan influences and designs.[2] On the edge of the desert he erected for himself a great mortuary temple guarded by two colossal statues. Little of this extravagant array remains except the statues. They are known as the Colossi of Memnon.

The Empire had a pronounced effect on Egyptian thought, art, and religion. In this land where nothing decayed, the power of the past hardly needed the forces of a conservative religion to make itself felt. The methods of agriculture and of industry, the canons of sculpture and of architecture, the subjects of paintings in the tombs and the techniques of such painting, the religious texts and formulas, and the concepts of the gods of Egypt—all had scarcely deviated from the principles laid down in Old Kingdom times. The powerful and wealthy priests of Amon, led by the high priest of the temple of Karnak, were actively opposed to all change, but conquest and active trade brought not only new goods but new ideas. The numerous foreign merchants, artisans, and slaves in Egypt and the Syrian, Hittite, and Babylonian princesses in the royal harem contributed to the ferment of change. The effect of outside influences became patent when under Amenhotep

[2] The sections of painted ceiling from this palace which are in the collection of the Metropolitan Museum of Art in New York might almost have come from Knossos itself.

III a new generation arose imbued with hostility to tradition and a desire for new realism in manners, art, and religion.

Ikhnaton, 1367–1350 B.C. Amenhotep IV, later called Ikhnaton, came to the throne in 1367 B.C. There is a great deal of controversy about this strange person—his physique, ideas, and career. What sort of a person was he and what were his plans? Were his reforms a product of developments in Egypt, supported by older ideas? Were they influenced by Syrian beliefs or were they peculiarly his own? Did he endeavor to establish a true monotheism or was he merely creating a new religion for Egypt? On none of these questions is there any agreement, but apparently he determined to build a new Egypt. The first object of his attack was the priesthood of Amon and the theology that held Egypt in traditional paths. By royal decree he swept away the many gods of Egypt headed by Amon and in their place he set one god, Aten, lord and giver of light and life to the whole world, under the symbol and name of the sun disk. In this he doubtless had the support of the priests of the ancient sun god Re at Heliopolis in the north, ever jealous of Amon. Yet in his concepts, expressed in his own composition, the glorious hymn to Aten, he went far beyond them. The endowments of the temple were transferred to Aten and his priests; the name of Amon

Unfinished Portrait Bust of Ikhnaton. (Staatlichen Museum, Berlin)

was chiseled out of the inscriptions in the temples; and men were forbidden to worship the old gods of the land. The pharaoh changed his own name to Ikhnaton and when opposition became too strong at Thebes, he transferred his capital to a new city, Akhetaton, modern Tell el 'Amarna. There he gathered the supporters of the new regime, both the sincere advocates of reform and those who had been won over by gifts from the treasure of the gods. There Ikhnaton could worship the god he adored, chanting:

> How manifold it is, what thou hast made!
> They are hidden from the face of man.
> O sole god, like whom there is no other!
> Thou didst create the world according to thy desire,
> Whilst thou wert alone:
> All men, cattle and wild beasts,
> Whatever is on earth, going upon its feet,
> And what is on high, flying with its wings.
>
> The countries of Syria and Nubia, the land of Egypt,
> Thou settest every man in his place,
> Thou suppliest their necessities:
> Everyone has his food, and his time of life is reckoned.[3]

In the new capital the pharaoh completely abandoned the old restrictions on the royal office and appeared freely in public with his wife and children. Realistic art was expressed in the decorations of the houses and in Ikhnaton's palace. Busts from a sculptor's workshop in the ruins of the city show that sculpture departed from the old canons. Ikhnaton encouraged not only unconventional sketches but even caricatures of himself. And in many reliefs the sun disk Aten appears, rays ending in kind hands that reach down to earth and extend the emblems of life and power to the pharaoh and his followers.

There is no record of the machinations of the dispossessed priesthood against Ikhnaton. The priests were not powerful enough to overthrow him or to block his reform while he lived, though they doubtless made their influence felt among a people bewildered by the loss of time-honored gods and by the demands of a cult they could not comprehend. But the pharaoh himself played into their hands by his failure to recognize the needs of his kingdom and his empire.

While Ikhnaton was absorbed in the task of remaking Egyptian religion, the Empire was falling to pieces. Uncontrolled officials began an orgy of corruption which resulted in disorder. In northern Syria the Hittite king Suppiluliumas, seeing his opportunity, began a policy

[3] Translated by John A. Wilson in William C. McDermott and Wallace E. Caldwell, *Readings in the History of the Ancient World.* New York: Holt, Rinehart and Winston, Inc., 1951, p. 90.

Portrait Bust of Nefer-
titi, Wife and Sister of
Ikhnaton. (Staatlichen
Museum, Berlin)

of expansion which might not have succeeded in earlier times. Syrian
princes rebelled, and tribes from the grasslands called Khabiru (possibly
among them were the ancestors of the Hebrews) pushed into Syria.[4]
King Rabaddi of Byblos and King Abdikheba of Jersulem sent letter
after letter appealing to Ikhnaton for aid.

> [T]o the king, my lord, say. Thus saith Abdi-Ḥeba, thy servant: At the
> two feet of my lord, the king, seven times and seven times I fall down.
> What have I done to the king, my lord? They slander me [ušâru] to the king,
> the lord: "Abdi-Ḥeba has become faithless to the king, his lord." Behold,
> neither my father nor my mother has put me in this place. The mighty hand
> of the king has led me into the house of my father. Why should I practise
> mischief against the king, the lord? As long as the king, my lord, lives I
> will say to the deputy of the king, [my] lo[rd]: "Why do you love the Ḥabiru,
> and hate the regents?" But therefore am I slandered before the king, my
> lord. Because I say: "The lands of the king, my lord, are lost," therefore am
> I slandered to the king, my lord. But let the king, my lord, know [this]:

[4] Theophilus J. Meek, *Hebrew Origins*. New York: Harper & Row Publishers, 1936,
p. 10.

View of the Antichamber of the Tomb of the Pharaoh Tutankhamon, Partly Cleared, Valley of the Kings, Thebes. A chariot may be seen at the left; two beds, chests, and other objects at the right. (Photograph by Harry Burton, The Metropolitan Museum of Art)

After the king, my lord, had appointed a garrison, Eenhamu took i[t] [al]l . . .

[So] let the king [c]are for his land. [Let] the king [ca]re for his land. [The land]s of the king, the lord, have all deserted. Ilimilku has devastated the whole land of the king. So let the king, the lord, care for his land.[5]

Other desperate letters survive, but the vassals' loyalty was ineffective; the pharaoh would not concern himself with wars and empires while his religion was at stake. When he died, leaving no sons to carry on his uncompleted work, three daughters and their husbands endeavored to rule. It fell to Smenkhkare, the second of the royal consorts, to surrender to the hostile forces. He left Akhetaton, returned to

[5]Reprinted from the book *The Tell el-Amarna Tablets* by Samuel A. B. Mercer by permission of Mr. F. K. Venables and The Macmillan Company of Canada Limited and of Macmillan & Co. Ltd., London. Vol. 2, Letter 286, pp. 707–709.

Thebes, and restored the worship of Amon. This policy was continued by his young successor, Tutankhaten, who changed his name to Tutankhamon. At his early death, Tutankhamon was buried in a small but richly furnished tomb, which was the source of unusual interest at its discovery and excavation in 1922.

The Hittite king Suppiluliumas was puzzled and suspicious when a few years after Ikhnaton's death he received a letter from an Egyptian princess (perhaps the widow of Tutankhamon) asking that one of his sons be sent to Egypt to marry her and become pharaoh. After hesitation and some preliminary investigation, Suppiluliumas was satisfied as to the writer's sincerity and sent a Hittite prince. But before he arrived, the noble Ay had gained control of the Two Lands and the young Hittite was murdered en route. His death brought about a war between Egypt and the Hittites, and ill will continued for some time between the two countries.

The Eighteenth Dynasty came to its end amid confusion, but conservative forces had triumphed. Ay and Harmhab, the next pharaohs, kept peace with Amon. Egypt was not ready for far-reaching religious change. The people, who knew and loved only the old gods, would not take a new religion, however noble, at the pharaoh's com-

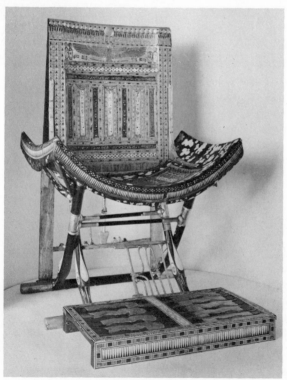

A Chair and Stool from the Tomb of Tutankhamon, Gold and Ebony. (Photograph by Harry Burton, The Metropolitan Museum of Art)

mand, and in the contest between the priests and the pharaoh, the former won. Though Egypt recovered much of the prestige and power it had lost in the last years of the Eighteenth Dynasty, its future held inevitable stagnation and decay under the leadership of a reactionary priesthood.

NINETEENTH AND TWENTIETH DYNASTIES

The pharaohs who established the second period of the Empire were faced with difficult tasks. The administration of Egypt had broken down; southern Syria was in confusion and northern Syria was in the possession of Suppiluliumas, the Hittite emperor who had wiped out the Mitannian allies of Egypt across the Euphrates.

After the collapse of the Eighteenth Dynasty and the short reign of Ay, Harmhab, a general of the army, ruled for thirty-five years and restored order in Egypt. He founded the Nineteenth Dynasty. His successor was Ramses I, who ruled but a short time. His son, Seti I (1309–1291 B.C.) restored some of the earlier greatness of Egypt, defeating the Libyans in the western delta, checking the Hittites, and establishing firm control over southern Syria. Ramses II became pharaoh in 1290 and ruled until 1224 B.C. The length of his reign, the grandeur of his court, the boastfulness of his annals, and the extraordinary extent of his building activities made him a legendary figure for later generations. He fought the Hittites in a battle at Kadesh on the Orontes River where, outmaneuvered and ambushed by them, he and his army were saved by his intrepid courage and the steadiness of the Egyptian troops. A poem in which his deeds were recounted was carved on the walls of his temples in Egypt.

The treaty he made with the Hittite king Hattusilis in 1272 B.C. is of unusual interest because copies of it have survived on Egyptian monuments and in Hittite archives. It provided for peace between the two great powers, for military assistance against internal or external danger, and for the extradition of fugitives from either state.

In Egypt, Ramses II built or enlarged many temples, erected colossal statues of himself in many places, and carved his own name on the works of earlier kings, including those of his father. Under his rule Egypt seemed prosperous and secure, and he boasted one of the largest harems in all history.

The Invasion After the death of Ramses II another storm descended upon Egypt. Tribes from the north invaded Asia Minor and swept the Hittites, perhaps weakened by plague, out of the area. Of the great Hittite Empire, only small Syrian kingdoms remained. The Dorian conquest of Greece and Crete threw the whole Aegean area into confusion. The first warning of trouble came to Egypt during the reign of Merneptah (1224–1214 B.C.), able son of Ramses II, who successfully defended Syria and the delta from "the peoples of the sea." The full deluge of northern tribes fell upon Egypt in the reign of Ramses III (1182–1151 B.C.), second pharaoh of the Twentieth Dynasty and the last great ruler of the Empire. With an army of mercenaries hired from among the invading people themselves, he repelled invasions by land and sea in 1178 and 1175 B.C. Although he lost the Palestinian coast to the Peleset (the Philistines of the Bible), he saved Egypt and its civilization from destruction.

A period of somnolence followed. Ramses III was followed by a line of pharaohs who bore the name Ramses but whose helplessness lost them the respect of the Syrian princes.[6] A family related to the high priests of Amon (with whom they shared the rule of Upper Egypt) took control of Thebes and the south, while the Twenty-first Dynasty ruled the north. Egypt was once more divided. Later, between 945 and 664, Libyan and Ethiopian rulers established themselves as pharaohs.

CIVILIZATION UNDER THE EMPIRE

The military character of the Egyptian Empire produced fundamental changes in the political and social structure of the land. The feudal relationships did not survive the Hyksos period and the military achievements of Eighteenth Dynasty pharaohs, and a centralized government almost as strong as that of the Fourth Dynasty was re-established in the early empire.

Government The pharaohs owed their supreme position to the military triumph of Amosis, but they insisted as of old on their divine parentage and on their god-given right to rule. The walls of the temples were inscribed with pictures and texts to prove their birth as sons of the queen mother and the god Amon-Re. From Amon they received the truth and law by which they ruled, and to him they gave praise for their victories. The formal seclusion of the god-king of olden days was now gone, for as general the pharaoh appeared in public wearing the military helmet and surrounded by his officers and troops. The might and power of the pharaoh are well stated by the great vizier Rekhmire. Speaking of Thutmose III he said:

> What is the king of Upper and Lower Egypt? He is the god by whose dealings one lives, the father and mother of all men, alone by himself without an equal . . . He is the wall in whose shadow Egypt rests . . . .[7]

    [6] Wenamon was an Egyptian who went to Phoenicia somewhere around 1100 B.C. in hopes of buying cedar wood to build a boat for the god Amon. Phoenician rulers robbed and insulted him, with apparently no fear of reprisals from Egypt.
    [7] Henri Frankfort, *Kingship and the Gods.* Chicago: The University of Chicago Press, 1948, p. 47.

The vizier directed the administration, superintended the official cults, acted as viceroy when the pharaoh was absent on campaigns, collected the tribute from the empire, and controlled all foreigners in Egypt. His was the high court of the land. Associated with him was the chief treasurer of the pharaoh. These two made daily reports to each other. A northern vizier was stationed at Heliopolis to watch over the lower kingdom. Under the viziers, officials of the pharaoh governed the nomes, approximately forty-two in number. States of the empire outside of Egypt were ruled by their native princes under the watchful eye of Egyptian residents, assisted by garrisons placed in strategic centers. The sons of these princes were taken to Egypt to be educated in the royal court and trained in loyalty to their suzerain, who dictated their succession to power.

Laws governed the land, though no written code is extant. Local disputes were settled by a board of judges, called a *kenbet*, and the nomarchs were charged with maintaining order. In certain nomes a distinct "chief of police," charged with arresting malefactors and criminals, worked under the nomarch. Appeals were allowed from lower courts to the courts presided over by the viziers. Pharaoh himself was the supreme court, but though the right of appeal was theoretically unlimited, the pharaoh could always refuse to hear a case or return it to a lower court for retrial.

For the settlement of land disputes, as well as for purposes of taxation, the royal scribes kept careful records of all property. Though in theory all Egypt belonged to the pharaoh, citizens possessed land by grant or lease and could transfer property to others freely. Women continued to enjoy equal property rights with men. The officials collected for the pharaoh about one-fifth of the annual produce, made monthly reports of their collections, and paid taxes in gold, silver, cattle, or linen on their own share of the income.

Social Life   The wealth of Egypt in the period of the Empire resulted in a general well-being, reflected in social life and shared by all classes of the population. Women participated equally with men. Great luxury characterized the activities of the official class. An incessant desire for display and for pleasure led Hatshepsut to create a garden, and Amenhotep III a lake, in the desert itself, and caused the great queen to cap her obelisks with gold which, she proudly declared, was measured for that purpose by the bushel. Palaces of the pharaohs and private houses were more spacious and luxurious than in earlier times. Elaborate gowns of fine linen, costly jewelry, jars and boxes of alabaster, and vessels of gold and silver constituted an abundant paraphernalia of wealth. The great men are depicted on the walls of their tombs, like the men of the Old Kingdom, hunting and fishing, enjoying their gardens, or directing their workmen. There are also pictures of mixed

parties with wine, music, and flowers. For the pleasure of such a party
the harpist plays and sings:

> Spend the day merrily, O priest! Put unguent and fine oil together to thy
> nostrils, and garlands, and lotus flowers . . . on the body of thy sister whom
> thou favourest, as she sitteth beside thee. Set music and singing before thy
> face. Cast all evil behind thee, and bethink thee of joy, until that day
> cometh when one reacheth port in the land that loveth silence.[8]

Nor was prosperity confined to the upper class. The scribes grew
in number, in riches, and in pride. An interesting text found in the
papyri illustrates the scribe's ability to calculate the weight of an obelisk,
the number of bricks to be used in building a ramp, and the amount
of food needed for a military expedition to Syria. Other documents
contain instructions to students, model letters, and collections of
maxims, and they display the superiority that the scribes felt over
artisans and farmers.

Economy The expansion of trade which came in the train of
conquest brought prosperity to the merchants and artisans. From Nubia
by way of the Nile came gold and precious stones, ivory, hides, ostrich
feathers, and animals. Hatshepsut renewed the trade down the Red
Sea with Punt, whence came incense, myrrh, ebony, and sweet-scented
woods. A brisk trade with Syria in all sorts of objects accompanied the
conquest of that land. The Egyptian sought particularly, however, wood
and its manufactured products, fish, cattle, horses, and iron. Goods
from Babylon, brought overland, were obtained by the Egyptians in
the Syrian cities. Some of this trade passed on the great road that ran
from the delta across the desert and along the coast to Joppa, Tyre,
Beirut, and Byblos, and inland to the Euphrates; most of it, however,
went by sea from the delta to Phoenician ports. Egyptians maintained
an active trade with the rich centers of Aegean civilization at Knossos
and Mycenae. The Syrian commerce continued even during the period
of decline, as Egyptians still sought to obtain cedars of Lebanon and
other products of the eastern lands.

The furniture, fans, jewelry, boxes, jars, and other objects found in
the tomb of Tutankhamon and in similar deposits testify to the ability of
Egyptian craftsmen to provide the upper classes with articles of luxury
and display. The three nested gold coffins of Tutankhamon in particular are exquisite in their artistry. Such pieces as these attest to the existence of an enterprising and prosperous artisan class at the close of the
Eighteenth Dynasty. Tomb paintings indicate that Syrian and Egyptian
craftsmen worked side by side in the shops. It is interesting to note that a
row of tombs excavated at Thebes indicates that some laborers could
afford fine burials. During the period of decline, however, when Egypt

---

[8]Adolf Erman, *The Literature of the Ancient Egyptians.* Trans. by Aylward M. Blackman.
London: Methuen & Co., Ltd., 1927, p. 252.

Copy of a Wall Painting Showing Egyptians Engaged in Normal Agricultural Occupations. (Photograph by the Egyptian Expedition, The Metropolitan Museum of Art)

was under priestly control, wealth, products, and technical ability suffered together. Methods and designs became crystallized, crafts became hereditary, and caste restrictions prevailed.

Agriculture remained the basis of Egyptian life. The peasants, some free, others half serf, lived and worked as they had in former times. The later generations saw a steady increase in economic bondage as classes in society became stratified. Legal documents indicate, however, that true serfdom did not exist. All contracts for land rentals on a sharecropping basis and all agreements made by native Egyptians for terms of personal service were made for a definite number of years. After the expiration date, the contracts had to be renewed or new ones entered into.

The second period of the Empire saw the formation of a new and powerful group, the mercenary soldiers. As the Egyptians themselves wearied of war or retired to enjoy their booty, the pharaohs hired foreigners to take their places. The army of Ramses III consisted largely of mercenaries drawn from the same tribes with whom he was fighting.

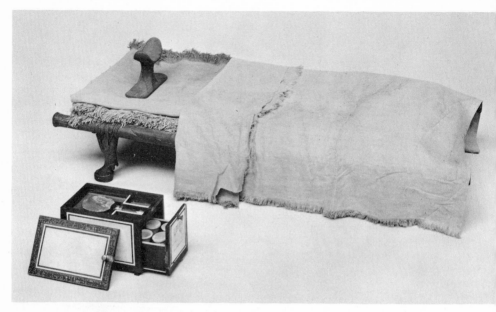

Egyptian Furniture. The bed linens are marked with inked "laundry marks" in hieroglyphics. The box contains a mirror and cosmetic jars. (The Metropolitan Museum of Art)

Great numbers of aliens were brought to Egypt as slaves or allowed to settle in the delta or in Thebes as merchants and artisans. Some even became attendants and officials of the pharaoh. Some scholars believe it was during the Eighteenth Dynasty, rather than during the Hyksos period, that the Hebrew Joseph became a vizier. The thing was not impossible. Passage from one part of the empire to another was easy and frequent, and Khabiru were settled in the grasslands at the edge of the delta. The pharaoh was powerful enough, too, to appoint anyone he chose to high office. But if Joseph was a vizier of the empire, his identity was hidden in records and tomb under an Egyptian name.

The priests slowly but surely became the dominant element in the population. The great conquerors, in return for the victories they attributed to Amon, lavished their riches on his temples and made him rich gifts of land, beef and dairy cattle, and slaves. Next to the pharaoh, Amon was the largest landholder in Egypt. According to the Harris papyrus,[9] at the death of Ramses III Amon possessed 2,756 statues;

[9] The so-called Papyrus Harris is a lengthy document containing the testamentary enactments made by Ramses III on behalf of the temples of Egypt. It is translated in James Henry Breasted, *Ancient Records of Egypt*, IV. Chicago: The University of Chicago Press, 1906, sections 182–396.

86,486 vassals, servants, and slaves; 421,362 head of cattle, large and small; 433 gardens and orchards; 864,168¼ *aroura* of cornland (about 583,313.57 acres); 83 ships; 46 building yards; and 65 cities, townships, or villages, seven of which were in Asia. As a result of this immense wealth, the high priests of Amon were able to direct and finally to overthrow the weak Ramesides. In 1087 B.C. the throne passed to the relations of the high priest, as noted above. They proved even weaker than the last pharaohs of the Twentieth Dynasty, and the period was marked by growing unrest. Tomb robberies, always a problem in Egypt, increased to the point where all dead pharaohs (except Tutankhamon) of the Empire were robbed of their possessions. The ineffectual rulers could do nothing to stop the robberies, and were only able to save the mummies by moving them about from one tomb to another. After each move, a mummy received a fresh tag stating where it had been and where it was going. Some of the mummies when found by an archaeologist bore many such tags.

Religion   Amon, the ram-headed god of Thebes, had been identified with Re during the Middle Kingdom, and he retained this identification in the Empire. The Eighteenth Dynasty pharaohs gave him credit for their victories. It was Amon who rescued Ramses II at Kadesh, and Amon who enabled Ramses III to save Egypt from "the peoples of the sea." "If Amon share my life" became a familiar expression in Upper Egypt. Amon grew famous as a giver of oracles, and it was through this function that the priests gained much power over pharaohs, ministers, and ordinary people. A statue of the god was brought out on certain days and petitioners put questions to it. The "god" nodded his head in reply. By late Rameside times, consulting the oracle became a recognized practice in government.

The great temple of Amon at Karnak was built over a small temple of Middle Kingdom construction. Thutmose I began it, but succeeding pharaohs up to Roman times added to its size. Its avenue of rams, mighty pylons, great courts, colossal statues, and lofty obelisks still exist as reminders of the wealth of the Empire. Most celebrated is the hypostyle (colonnaded) hall, dating from the Twentieth Dynasty. It is a forest of heavy columns with a central nave and side aisles, one of the best preserved examples of the use of clerestory in Egyptian architecture. The completed temple area covered sixty-two acres of ground. The many other buildings that have survived—the beautiful temple of Hatshepsut, the handsome colonnade at Luxor, the temple of Seti I at Abydos, the huge structures of Ramses II at Thebes and Abu-Simbel, and the fortress portico and temple of Ramses III at Medinet Habu— all bear witness to the great achievements of Egyptian architects and royal control of Egyptian labor in the building of houses of eternity for their gods and their pharaohs.

Yet for all his power and wealth, Amon remained an Upper Egyptian divinity. The priests and people of Lower Egypt jealously and stubbornly clung to their own ancient gods. Many people also worshiped the statues of dead pharaohs, or venerated single columns in the temples or the animals sacred to certain gods.

Nearly every Egyptian worshiped the great triad, Isis, Osiris, and Horus. This belief continued to be so powerful that Ikhnaton himself dared not trifle with Osiris, before whom it was believed all men from the highest to the lowest appeared for judgment after death. Priestly technique, however, destroyed the ethical values of Osiris worship. By the magic power of amulets and charms—clay copies of beetles (scarabs) and "eyes of Horus" (symbols of immortality); by figurines called *ushebti* ("answerers") to serve the dead in the future life; and by means of the formulas of the *Book of the Dead,* Osiris himself was deceived and all men secured the blessings of immortal life in the fields of eternity.

Deceased pharaohs, as of old, crossed the "lily lake" to dwell with the sun god and to traverse the upper and underworlds with Re. But the manner of burial underwent a change with the abandonment of pyramids. Thutmose I went into an obscure valley behind the western mountain at Thebes and there had a chamber tomb dug into the cliff, which he vainly hoped would remain concealed and inviolate. Then on the edge of the western desert he built a mortuary temple, where his worship was to be carried on. His example was followed by his successors. Today the valley where these tombs were dug is known as the Valley of the Kings. The tombs consisted of long corridors with many chambers and were adorned with pictures and filled with funerary trappings. All but the tomb of Tutankhamon were plundered by the late Rameside period.

Queens and royal children were buried in another valley to the south. Along the foot of the cliff were clustered the tombs of the nobles, of the scribes, and of the lower classes. They were chamber tombs decorated like the mastabas of the Old Kingdom with scenes from daily life. The hopes to which these people held fast are expressed by the inscription of a nobleman called Intef—and by many texts of a similar type. Intef's inscription reads in part:

> Oh ye that live upon earth . . . if ye love life, and think not on death, . . . so shall ye say: "An offering which the king gives . . . for the *ka* of the hereditary prince . . ."[10]

Conclusion By 1100 B.C. the Egyptian Empire had ceased to exist. Weakened internally by the forces of conservatism and attacked

---

[10]James Henry Breasted, *Ancient Records of Egypt*, II. Chicago: The University of Chicago Press, 1906, section 766.

by strong enemies from outside, the kingdom itself was soon divided. The Egyptians had achieved greatness in government and law, in architecture and art, and in medical science, literature, and religion. As a result of the expansion during the period of the Empire their civilization made a deep impression on the peoples of Syria and of Minoan Crete, and ideas and techniques penetrated far up the Nile into Africa to mold the societies and affect the cultures of equatorial peoples. It might truthfully be said that Egypt's *ka* has lived eternally in the cultures of succeeding peoples.

6 · The Conflict of Empires

THE DECLINE OF THE EGYPTIAN AND THE HITTITE empires, which occurred nearly simultaneously, created a power vacuum in the middle east in which small states were able temporarily to thrive. Several peoples of Syria struggled with one another for space and independence. Among states attaining the greatest political stability and security were Phoenicia, Damascus, Philistia, and Israel. All but Damascus and Phoenicia were founded by newcomers in the area, but each state enjoyed a span of freedom from foreign domination until the rise of new imperialistic powers overwhelmed them. First came Assyria, then a revived Babylon, whose might was contested by a strengthened Egypt, and as climax to the struggle the Persians came to engulf them all.

THE PHOENICIANS

First to reap the benefit of the political situation after the decline of the great empires were the Phoenicians. After the fall of Mycenaean sea power the sea-borne trade of the Mediterranean gradually passed into their hands. The goods they obtained from Egypt or Babylon, or which they made in their own shops, they carried into the Aegean, to the western Mediterranean, and through the Straits of Gibraltar to Cape Verde and the Azores in the Atlantic. They sailed to the Cassiterides (perhaps the Scilly Islands) in the north in search of the tin of Cornwall, and between the eleventh and the eighth centuries they established trading posts at strategic points, such as Utica, Hippo, and Carthage in Africa and Gades (Cadiz) in Spain. Many of these foundations were mere depots, or way stations, on the long sea route to the west, but Carthage grew into a great city that came to dominate the western Mediterranean in the fifth century B.C.

The Phoenicians were famous in antiquity for the skill with which they loaded and navigated their broad-beamed boats. They learned to

144

sail by the stars at night, and the North Star was known as the Phoenicians' star. One company of Phoenicians, under the aegis of a Twenty-sixth Dynasty pharaoh of Egypt, circumnavigated Africa.

Though the extent of their influence over the rising civilization of the Greeks is a matter of controversy, they made their presence felt, and as traders the "black-browed Phoenicians" were well known to the Greeks of the Homeric poems. Eventually Greek merchants displaced them in the Aegean and challenged their power in the west (p. 189).

Tyre was an island secure from attack and equipped with magnificent harbors. It achieved great wealth and prominence, and its ships traversed the known seas. Its woolen goods, dyed with the famous purple, and its glassware were everywhere in demand. The temples of its gods, the palaces of its kings and merchant princes, its workshops and markets, and its throngs of people made it a fascinating city whose only drawback was the odor of the decaying mollusks from which came the dye. A vivid memory of the impression Tyre's greatness made on the contemporary world is recorded in the Book of Ezekiel (chapter 27), which reads like an inventory of world trade.

The Phoenicians' chief gift to the west was the diffusion of the alphabet. The problem of its origin is obscure. Inscriptions found in a temple in the mining region of Sinai and dated variously between 1600 and 1500 B.C. furnish a possible prototype, but inscriptions from Byblos and other north Syrian cities show a trend toward the development of alphabetic scripts, some from hieroglyphics and some from cuneiform antecedents. It seems probable that the Phoenicians, influenced by Egyptian hieratic writing and by earlier attempts at simplified writing in Syria, evolved a system of signs that represented individual consonants, vowel signs being a contribution of the Greeks. By the ninth century the Phoenician alphabet had spread throughout Syria. Adopted and transformed by the Greeks during the eighth or seventh centuries B.C., it has come down to western peoples.

The Phoenicians were the great middlemen of culture. Their civilization reflects Egyptian and Babylonian influences, and what they learned from the older peoples they put to good use in their own work and in the products they carried throughout the Mediterranean.

THE SYRO-HITTITE KINGDOMS

North of the Phoenicians, in the region once dotted with independent city-states and in the territory once controlled by Mitanni, were the Syro-Hittite states, survivors of the Hittite Empire. But their peoples were not all Hittites. These states extended from Carchemish on the Euphrates to Tarsus on the Mediterranean, and inland into the mountains of Asia Minor. Their language was originally a Hittite dialect written in hieroglyphs of their own devising, and it was akin to the language in the Luian documents in the older Hittite archives, but by the tenth or ninth century Aramaic had supplanted it in most of the southern Hittite states. Many reliefs have been found in these cities showing the gods in characteristic dress with conical caps, short gowns, and pointed, upturned shoes. Their kings built palaces with columned porticoes resembling those of later Greek temples, a style enthusiastically adopted by Assyrian architects. The Hittite states prospered greatly from the trade that passed through their lands. For a time, in alliance with Damascus and northern Israel, they held the Assyrians at bay but they fell one by one before the conquerors between 740 and 717 B.C. It was from these people that the name Hittite entered the records of Biblical writers.

PALESTINE AND SOUTHERN SYRIA

The Aramaeans The peace of the rest of Syria was disturbed during the latter half of the second millennium B.C. by the invasions of the Aramaeans, the Philistines, and the Hebrews. The Aramaeans entered the fertile region of Damascus from the Arabian grasslands during the latter half of the second millennium and slowly but completely absorbed or displaced its older inhabitants. They gained control of Damascus in the twelfth century. The city's position at the head of the camel caravan route across the desert to Babylon gave the Aramaeans control over much of the inland trade, and they became the carriers of merchandise between Mesopotamia, Phoenicia, and Egypt. The Damascenes enjoyed independence and prosperity, and their rulers appear as vigorous fighters in the historical books of the Old Testament until they fell to the Assyrians in 732 B.C. Even then loss of freedom did not destroy their commercial pre-eminence. The Aramaic language became the international language of the middle east, and was universally spoken up to the time of Christ. Damascus, though despoiled by many conquerors, has the longest continuous history of any presently inhabited community in the mid-eastern area.

The Philistines The wandering tribes that attacked Egypt in the reign of Ramses III wrought great havoc in Syria. After their defeat in the delta, the Philistines, who had played a major part in the attack, fell back upon Canaan and settled there. They are said by tradition to have come from Caphtor, or Crete, but their pottery, tools, and armor indicate a mixed origin derived from the Aegean (and perhaps Anatolia). Biblical stories[1] refer to customs reminiscent of the Minoan, but their

[1] There is no independent evidence for the Biblical account.

pottery styles copied the Mycenaean, and their art likewise reflects Aegean motives and techniques. The Philistines were a band of mixed refugees displaced from the islands, from Caria, and from Lycia by the Dorian invasions. Iron weapons and a disciplined organization gave them a great advantage over the Canaanites, and they became firmly entrenched on the coast and extended their power over the disunited and barbaric Hebrew tribes of the interior. If the Biblical tradition is trustworthy and the Philistines were forced to depend on mercenaries (for example, David and his young men), they may have been only a caste ruling over the original inhabitants. They were driven back into the narrow coastland after a decisive defeat by David soon after 1000 B.C.

The Coming of the Hebrews (Israelites) During the period of Philistine dominance the land of Canaan passed into the hands of the Israelite tribes of the "Hebrews," who, because of their religious significance, have received a greater share of attention than some of their more powerful neighbors.

Tradition ascribes their ancestry to a patriarch named Abraham who left Ur at about the time of its destruction by the Elamites, moved northwest into the region of the upper Euphrates and thence southwest into Canaan. The character of the story of Abraham and archaeological discoveries in Syria and Palestine combine to indicate that there is a basis of truth in the account. The stories of Isaac, of Jacob or Israel, eponym and hero of the later Israelites, of Joseph and his brethren, of the settlement in Egypt, the oppression, and the exodus are too familiar to require retelling. Internal evidence in the stories, particularly those about Egypt, make it certain that the narrative contains a thread of historical fact.

There can be no doubt that a group of Israelites entered Egypt and settled in the eastern edge of the delta sometime in the second millennium. There the great leader Moses (his name may be Egyptian) arose to lead them out of Egypt. The tribes went first to the peninsula of Sinai and thence to the grasslands of the Negeb (in southern Palestine). During the course of their wanderings Moses taught them the worship of God, to whom he gave the name of Jahoe (Jehovah, or Yahweh), assuring them that this was the god (El) who had watched over and given promises to their fathers, Abraham, Isaac, and Jacob. After the death of Moses, the Israelites began a series of raids into Canaan and eventually gained possession of the land.

The task of fitting these accounts and the records of conquest listed in Joshua and Judges into the framework of known history is exceedingly difficult. During the fourteenth century Egyptian records list attacks by the Khabiru on certain Canaanite cities, but Egypt retained firm control of the region until the death of Ramses II. That pharaoh, however, was building store-cities and forts along Egypt's eastern border, and he may very well have been the pharaoh of the oppression. The exodus may also have taken place in his reign. An inscription from the reign of Merneptah hints that the Khabiru were attacking in Palestine, but Merneptah was having so much trouble driving back "the peoples of the sea" that he could give them little attention. Renewed attacks by "the peoples of the sea" under Ramses III broke Egypt's control over Palestine completely and confined Egypt to its own borders. The Hebrew conquest of Canaan fits into the framework of these known events; a possible date for the exodus is about 1250, for the first conquests somewhere between 1225 and 1200.[2]

The Book of Judges, containing a series of stories of tribal heroes as well as some contemporary poetry such as the Song of Deborah, and the archaeological evidence prove that the conquest of Canaan was difficult and gradual, succeeding first in the mountainous areas while Jerusalem, the plain of Esdraelon, and the coastal strip remained in the hands of the Canaanites. Though the seminomadic tribes clung to their patriarchal and tribal organization, they blended with the older inhabitants, from whom they learned industrial arts and the methods and the religious ceremonies of an agricultural people. The Hebrews received a rude check when they reached the eastern foothills, where the Philistines stopped them, later conquered them, and forbade them the use of iron.

These difficulties forced unity among the tribes and served to keep alive the religion that had been established by Moses. A religious league was organized with its center at Shiloh. Its leaders were the judges, whose deeds are recorded. Under its aegis, the religion took form and content. The Covenant Code (Exodus, chapters 21–23) is dated to this period along with portions of the later codes. Traditions of the patriarchs were also gathered, recited, and handed down — to be written sometime early in the first millennium. The period of the judges was the formative period of Israel.

The United Kingdom   A little before 1000 B.C., because of Hebrew sufferings under Philistine control, Samuel, the last of the great judges, yielded to necessity and brought about the election of Saul of the tribe of Benjamin as king. This able warrior defeated the Philistines and took the plain of Esdraelon from the Canaanites. But Saul suffered from recurring fits of madness, and he broke with Samuel. In the dissensions that followed he was defeated by the Philistines, and afterward committed suicide.

David (ca. 1000–ca. 961 B.C.)   David took over the place and the work of Saul and laid the foundation of the Hebrew kingdom. He took Jerusalem and made it his capital. He defeated the Philistines in the

---

[2] The exodus remains a problem, however. No firm dates are accepted generally, nor is it presently believed that all twelve of the traditional tribes participated in it.

valley of Rephaim, crushing them completely, and soundly chastised tribes crowding in from the east. Under his rule a centralized government was organized over the united land of Israel, and a commercial alliance was made with Hiram, king of Tyre.

Solomon (*ca.* 961–*ca.* 922 B.C.)   David's conquests and wealth were enjoyed by his successor Solomon, son of David's favorite wife, Bathsheba. Solomon established a typical Oriental court with a large harem headed by an Egyptian princess. He organized his kingdom into twelve tribal divisions and levied taxes and task work. In alliance with Tyre he traded across the Mediterranean to Spain and down the Red Sea to Punt. Ezion-geber, his trading city on the Red Sea, has been found at the head of the Gulf of Aqaba. In the district behind it were copper mines and smelters from which much wealth was drawn. Solomon's agents carried on an active trade in horses and their equipment with Egypt and the Syro-Hittite states to the north. With this wealth Solomon built palaces in the capital city, which David had fortified, and with Phoenician aid he built a temple for Yahweh on the summit of a hill in Jerusalem. His commands and judgments gained for him such a reputation for wisdom that later ages attributed to him the wisdom literature in the Bible. But to amass his wealth and carry out his building program, Solomon was forced to tax his people heavily. Corvées of workers were sent off to cut cedars in the mountains of Lebanon. Gangs of men labored in the stone quarries and other gangs worked on palaces and temple under the supervision of Phoenician architects and foremen. Regardless of the needs of the farms and herds, man power was ruthlessly mobilized for these purposes. Too, each district was required to remit produce for the court of the king, for the army, and for the workers. The burden was great and resentment mounted.

Under Solomon's son Rehoboam the kingdom fell apart. Among the ten tribes in the more fertile northern land, intermarriage with the Canaanites and acceptance of their agricultural methods and gods was more thorough than in the south. The greater part of the wealth of the kingdom was in the north, and the people objected to the demands, restrictions, taxes, and labor drafts imposed on them from Jerusalem. The southern area, hilly and less fertile, was occupied for the most part by herdsmen, who were nearer in occupation and in spirit to the original teachings of Moses and who were prone to criticize the devotion of their northern tribesmen to Canaanite gods. When Rehoboam refused to lighten the load on the north, the ten tribes rebelled under the leadership of Jeroboam and established a separate kingdom, whose capital was later located at Samaria.

Development of Hebrew Religion   Many now believe that the worship of Yahweh established by Moses was monotheistic from its beginning. Under Moses' leadership the people made a covenant of loyalty and obedience with Yahweh and in return they believed that He would defend them and care for them. The covenant involved also recognition of God's benefactions and the response of His indebted people. The intensity of this religion, its exclusive character, and the moral inspiration the great lawgiver had embodied in it gave it the power to withstand the strain of the Canaanite influences and made possible its future development. The conviction among the Israelites that Yahweh had promised them Canaan and was fighting for them strengthened them throughout the period of conquest and the wars with the Philistines, and helped to bring about the union of the tribes under the monarchy.

As a result of the conquest the concept of Yahweh suffered transformation. His people, originally shepherds and herdsmen, blended with the Canaanites and became farmers. Instead of accepting the local Baalim (agricultural gods) they continued their worship of Yahweh but assigned to Him the altars in the high places and ascribed to Him the festivals, laws, and practices that fitted their new occupation. Though Yahweh thus conquered the gods of the Canaanites, His worship was henceforth changed, for some of the alien customs crept into His worship. Yet the moral force of His religion was too powerful to allow acceptance of the basest elements of agricultural cults, such as infanticide and religious prostitution.

The formation and prosperity of the monarchy seemed the fulfillment of promise. Nevertheless there was sin in Israel. Many of the people worshiped strange gods and followed forbidden practices. The kings even set up temples to alien gods for their foreign wives. At the same time social and economic evils hostile to the spirit of Yahweh's religion began to appear as the rich and powerful grasped greedily for land, corrupted the courts, and dispossessed the poor. A series of great religious teachers, the prophets, appeared to deal with these offenses. With inspired words they proclaimed the wrath of Yahweh and the inevitability of punishment. In their endeavor to bring the people back to the purity of the religion of Moses they taught Him as a universal God with power over all nature and all nations, and with moral attributes that led Him to demand righteousness and justice.

The Prophets Elijah, the first of the prophets, appeared during the reign of Ahab (*ca.* 869–850 B.C.), ablest ruler of the kingdom of Israel (the northern kingdom). This warrior king secured an alliance with Tyre by marrying Jezebel, a Phoenician princess. He rebuilt and adorned Samaria and fought successfully with the rulers of the kingdom of Judah (the southern kingdom) and with Benhadad of Damascus but he met his match in Elijah. This prophet from the grasslands, horrified at the worship of the Canaanite Baalim, and especially at the establishment by Jezebel of temples to the Tyrian Melqart and Asherah, proclaimed the supremacy of Yahweh over the Israelites, and went so far as to deny any power to the foreign gods. Elisha, the prophet who came after him, aided a usurper Jehu (*ca.* 841 B.C.) in overthrowing the dynasty. Amos (*ca.* 750 B.C.) broadened the concept of God by sounding the note of social and economic justice, predicting punishment for a nation whose leaders "sold the righteous for silver and the poor for a pair of shoes"; and Hosea taught the lesson of the forgiving love of God. These men were teachers in the kingdom of Israel. In 722 B.C. Samaria fell before the Assyrians; its people were carried into captivity and colonists from other lands were settled in their places.

The later prophets arose in the kingdom of Judah. Isaiah (the first)[3] played a dual part as statesman and religious teacher. He was adviser to Hezekiah (*ca.* 701 B.C.), the king who strengthened the walls of Jerusalem, constructed an aqueduct to secure water for the city (it is still in use), and successfully resisted the Assyrian king Sennacherib. Isaiah's religious writings, containing some of the noblest lines ever written, proclaimed the supremacy of God over the whole universe and announced the ultimate coming of a divine kingdom through which justice and goodness would be established in all lands.

Micah, younger contemporary of Isaiah, advanced far beyond current concepts when he denied the necessity for sacrifice and preached "What doth the Lord require of thee but to do justice, to love mercy, and to walk humbly with thy God?" He was followed by an even greater prophet, Jeremiah.

Jeremiah supported a group of reformers called Deuteronomists. To stop the use of Canaanite rites and symbols at local shrines of Yahweh, they worked for abolition of the shrines and concentration of the worship of Yahweh at the Temple in Jerusalem. When a scroll containing rules in conformity with their ideas but believed to be the work of Moses was found in a recess of the Temple by servants of King Josiah (*ca.* 639–608 B.C.) and was accepted by the king, the movement triumphed. Though Jeremiah came from a priestly family that probably lost its position as a result of the reform, he supported the movement, and with burning zeal he inveighed against the economic and social as well as religious evils of his time. He taught the universal power of God over Gentiles as well as over Jews and the consequent unreality of the pagan divinities. To older ideas of national morality he added the great idea of individual responsibility. He saw the impending fall of Jerusalem before Babylon, which he felt was the punishment for sin, and he wept over the nation even when it persecuted him.

Nebuchadrezzar, king of Babylon, took Jerusalem in 598 B.C. He returned in 587 B.C. after a revolt, destroyed the city, and carried the people into captivity.

---

[3] The present Book of Isaiah contains the teachings of more than one man.

The Exile The exile presented a supreme test to the religious leaders of the Hebrews. The people, who had been taught that God could be worshiped only in Jerusalem, asked, "How can we sing the Lord's songs in a strange land?" Ezekiel and the author of the second part of the Book of Isaiah gave definite and magnificent answers to this question. God is omnipresent and omnipotent, they said, and the creator and ruler of the universe, who must be worshiped at all times and in all places. To Ezekiel, however, the chief essential of worship was holiness, which implied obedience to the Law. This idea was put into effect by the community of Hebrews in Babylon, by those who had fled into Egypt, and by those who returned when the Persians allowed the restoration of Jerusalem. Henceforth the Law was the center of Judaism.

Out of the hardships of those troubled times arose the question of why God permits suffering. To this, the post-exilic writer of the Book of Job answered that the ways of God are inscrutable, man is as clay in the hands of a potter, and his only refuge is trust in God. A code of morals of the highest order and based on the Law, a belief in one God who is the creator and ruler of all mankind, and the precept of trusting submission to His will were the great achievements of the Hebrew teachers.

ASSYRIA

During the wars that the Assyrians had waged for centuries against the Babylonians, the Syrians, and the mountain peoples to the north and east, the fiercely independent farmers of this nation became welded into one of the most efficient fighting forces the world had ever seen, almost irresistible under proper leadership. The kings who ruled from the tenth to the seventh centuries B.C. provided such leadership and built the Assyrian Empire.[4]

The Rise of Assyria Assurnasirpal II (884–859 B.C.) vastly increased Assyria's territory. With an army well equipped with iron weapons and brilliantly organized into corps of infantry, chariotry, and engineers and with a ferocity unparalleled in the annals of military history, the Assyrians swept over northern Mesopotamia and Syria and into the nearby mountain lands. Assurnasirpal's achievements were recorded on the buildings that adorned his capital. His successors continued his policies and gained control over Babylonia. The expansion of Assyrian power to the north was temporarily limited by the growth of the empire of the Urartians (the kingdom of Urartu) in the hills around Lake Van, but the Urartians, though they caused the Assyrians constant trouble, could not withstand the superior forces that came against them.

[4]The rise to power began under Assur-dan II (*ca.* 934–912) or earlier. Records are too few to permit a reconstruction of the steps in Assyrian expansion during his reign.

Assyrian Winged Bull from the Palace of Assurnasirpal at Nimrud, ca. 885–860 B.C. (The Metropolitan Museum of Art, gift of John D. Rockefeller, Jr., 1932)

Tiglath-pileser III, 745–727 B.C.   In 745 B.C. Tiglath-pileser III, a usurper, seized the throne of Assur, and under him Assyrian expansion was resumed. He took Damascus in 732, then conquered Babylon, making himself its king, and forced the kingdom of Israel and the kingdom of Judah to pay tribute. He undertook extensive reorganization of imperial administration with the establishment of provinces, governors, garrisons, and the regular collection of tribute. To destroy local feeling, to unify his empire, and to discourage rebellions, he developed a system

An Openwork Ivory Plaque from a Large Group Found at Nimrud, Ninth or Eighth Centuries B.C. Its design, reminiscent of Egyptian styles, inclines some archaeologists to believe it was made by a Phoenician artist. (British Museum)

of mass deportation and colonization. Sargon II (722–705 B.C.), another usurper, brought Assyria still further along the path of empire. The kingdom of Israel had fallen to Shalmaneser V in 722 B.C., just before Sargon's accession, and the ten Israelite tribes in the north had been deported. Under Sargon the last remnants of the Hittites were wiped out and Urartu was defeated. Out of the spoils Sargon built a new capital, Dur Sharrukin.

Sennacherib, 705–681 B.C.   Sennacherib is the best known of the Assyrian rulers. Nineveh, which he made his capital, became synonymous with the Assyrian Empire. He forced Tyre and Sidon to pay tribute, and drove off Egyptian forces sent by Ethiopian kings to the aid of Hezekiah. Sennacherib was recalled from his attack on Jerusalem by a revolt in Babylon, or the siege was ended by a plague that fell upon his army, but he forced the kingdom of Judah to pay tribute nonetheless. He manned boats on the Tigris with Phoenicians and sailed down the river against Elam, and later, in a similar exploit through the inter-river canal into rebel Babylonia, he proceeded in a land attack to destroy Babylon.

The Decline of Assyria   Sennacherib's son Esarhaddon rebuilt Babylon and invaded the Egyptian delta, where he established a native prince, Necho of Sais, as vassal ruler. Assurbanipal (669–627 B.C.), Esarhaddon's successor, was the last great Assyrian ruler, and before he died the empire was falling apart. Assurbanipal collected a huge library

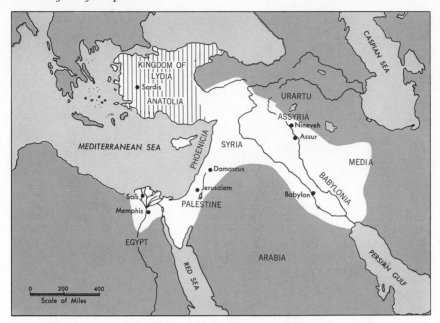

KINGDOM OF
LYDIA
Sardis
ANATOLIA
URARTU
ASSYRIA
Nineveh
Assur
MEDITERRANEAN SEA
PHOENICIA
SYRIA
MEDIA
Damascus
BABYLONIA
Jerusalem
Babylon
Saïs
PALESTINE
Memphis
EGYPT
ARABIA
PERSIAN GULF
RED SEA
CASPIAN SEA
0   200   400
Scale of Miles

The Assyrian Empire at the Accession of Assurbanipal, 669 B.C.

at Nineveh. His own annals are full and extensive, and he set scribes to copying ancient Sumerian and Babylonian texts. Rebellions and wars called him away from such peaceful pursuits. Beginning in 652 war broke out with Elam and a revolt began in Babylon. War was declared also with Gyges of Lydia. For the last twenty-five years of his reign Assurbanipal was forced to fight these and other enemies of the empire. He defeated Babylon but after his death the Chaldeans gained control of it and rebelled again. He almost wiped out the Elamites but was soon confronted with the Medes and other Iranian tribes (possibly forerunners of the Persians) who took their place. He was defeated by Scythian invaders who swept in from the north. In the midst of all this confusion Psamtik I of Egypt, who had been appointed vassal king of the delta (on the death of his father Necho at the hands of the Ethiopian claimant to the throne), freed Egypt from Assyrian control and took Philistia. Assurbanipal was still struggling valiantly against Assyria's many enemies when he died.

His son fell before them. A coalition of Babylonians, Medes, and Persians took Nineveh in 612 B.C. and so ruthlessly destroyed it that its very site was forgotten.

Assyrian Civilization   To the contemporary world the Assyrians were cruel, vengeful warriors "whose arrows were sharp and all their bows bent; the horses' hooves were like flint and their wheels like a whirlwind." The Book of Nahum, the prophet, contains a vivid picture

Ivory Panel Showing an Assyrian Battle Scene, Eighth Century B.C. (The Metropolitan Museum of Art, Fletcher Fund, 1951)

Detail from an Assyrian Relief Showing the Head of a King. (The Brooklyn Museum)

The "Balawat Gates" from the Palace of Shalmaneser III, First Quarter of the Ninth Century B.C. The bronze relief is remarkable in its clarity and detail. (British Museum)

of the fear and hatred the Assyrians inspired among the peoples of Syria. But their importance in history is much greater than their reputation as fighters. They contributed organization to the art of war and to imperial administration. Their army was divided into corps of infantry, chariotry, and engineers, with a well-directed service of supply, in which camels were used for desert warfare. Their empire was divided into provinces with appointed governors and established garrisons. Tribute was collected regularly, and client kingdoms were formed along the frontiers. They exchanged whole populations in certain conquered areas, and to secure better control and easier communication they built a well-planned system of military roads. Later conquerors followed their military example, and the empires of Persia, Macedon, and Rome owed much to the organizing genius of the Assyrians.

The purpose of the Assyrian rulers may have been plunder, but their achievements temporarily brought the entire middle east under

Hunting Scene from the Period of Assurbanipal, ca. 669–626 B.C. Assyrian representation of animals was especially fine. (British Museum)

unified control. When not plagued by rebellions, which were frequent, the imperial system led to increased trade and the growth of wealth and luxury.[5] The practice of mass deportation increased the spread and assimilation of new ideas and customs.

Assyrian triumph was reflected in the life of the people and in the art found in the great capital cities. The wealthy dressed in wool or linen and lived in beautiful houses. The palaces and temples built by the kings were well constructed of brick and stone, and were decorated with monumental gateways, arches, colonnades, and towers. On their walls were carved in brilliant relief pictures and texts that recorded the deeds, often bloodthirsty, of the kings in warfare and hunting. Handsome carved ivory reliefs were made in quantity. Scribes studied and copied Sumerian and Babylonian texts, wrote accounts of the royal campaigns,

[5] Assyrian ivories and other goods were widely traded, and their art styles affected those of peoples inside and outside the empire.

and copied various works of literature composed earlier in Mesopotamia. Astronomers continued the study of the stars, which had been begun long before by the Babylonians, and priests repeated and advanced the Babylonian methods of divination. Assur, warlike sun god, was worshiped as the patron of the kings and the creator of all other gods and men, and Ishtar, Marduk, and the rest of the Mesopotamian divinities were worshiped according to the ancient rites. The kings were representatives of their people before the gods. There are interesting texts describing the "penance" that a certain Assyrian king was required to make to overcome the anger of Assur.

The farmers, who formed the bulk of the population of Assyria, had in the beginning been the source of strength of the country's army. But the empire became extended beyond the military capacity of the Assyrians to control it. Outside powers, too, became stronger, and Assyria fell before the accumulated hatred, greed, and might of its neighbors and former subjects.

THE CHALDEANS IN BABYLON

About forty years before the fall of Assyria Egypt regained its independence under the Twenty-sixth Dynasty, and after the fall of Nineveh the Chaldeans of Babylon began a struggle with the pharaoh for control of the Fertile Crescent. For centuries a new tribe of Semites called Chaldeans had been sifting into Babylonia. They attained ascendancy

A Section of the Mosaic in Enameled Brick That Lined the Sacred Way in Babylon Under Nebuchadrezzar. The background is blue and the lion is brown, white, and yellow. (The Metropolitan Museum of Art, Fletcher Fund, 1931)

The Goddess Ishtar of Babylon Mounted on a Lioness, Neo-Babylonian Period, ca. Seventh Century B.C. Ishtar holds a harp in her right hand, a ring and rod in her left. (The Metropolitan Museum of Art, Rogers Fund, 1957)

there in 626, and it was they who with the Medes and the Persians formed the backbone of the resistance to Assyria. After their king Nabopolassar and his allies had succeeded in capturing Nineveh in 612 B.C., a new Babylonian monarchy was established.

In 605 B.C. Nebuchadrezzar succeeded his father on the throne. His first care was the rebuilding of Babylon with great walls, a ziggurat, palaces, and the famous hanging gardens, so brilliantly described by Herodotus as a ziggurat-like terraced garden, built to please his mountain-born Median queen. Nebuchadrezzar's chief enemy was Egypt, whose control of Syria he challenged. He defeated the armies of Egypt, took Jerusalem, and in 571 B.C. forced Tyre to pay tribute after a thirteen-year siege. Babylon controlled most of Syria and for a brief time enjoyed a period of glory as an imperial capital.

On the death of Nebuchadrezzar a brief interregnum was filled by his son and then by other claimants to the throne. Nabonidus (Nabunaid), a priest, finally came to power. He was an antiquarian and archaeologist, and spent much time collecting texts, foundation stones, ancient statues, and other relics of previous Mesopotamian dynasties. For some unknown reason, he went off to Arabia for eleven years and left his son Belshazzar as regent in Babylon. Neither Nabonidus nor Belshazzar seemed to realize the rising danger from their erstwhile allies, the Medes and the Persians, and Cyrus the Persian took Babylon with no difficulty in 539 B.C.

SAITE EGYPT

Psamtik I of Sais was originally established in power by Assurbanipal (664 B.C.), but he succeeded in escaping Assyrian control and founded the Twenty-sixth Dynasty. Through statesmanship and diplomacy he won Upper Egypt, and with the aid of Greek, Syrian, and Libyan mercenaries captured a strip of the Syrian coast. Necho II, his successor, defeated and killed Josiah of Jerusalem in 608 B.C. and extended Egyptian control to the Euphrates. Driven back by Nebuchadrezzar in 605, Necho gave up his imperial ambitions and turned to domestic affairs. He began to dredge the Wadi Tumilat to open a waterway to the Red Sea, and (according to Herodotus) sent an expedition led by Phoenician navigators to circumnavigate Africa. The voyage was successful, and was completed in three years, the mariners stopping twice to plant and harvest grain on the way.[6]

Psamtik II sent a military force into Nubia, perhaps to prevent a threatened invasion, and broke forever the power of Nubian kings, ending all danger to Egypt from the south. Greek mercenaries, who left inscriptions at Abu Simbel, were used in addition to native troops. Necho II and Psamtik II between them built up a powerful war fleet that was put to good use by the next pharaoh, Apries (Biblical *Hophra*). He broke the peace with Nebuchadrezzar. The Egyptian navy was instrumental in relieving Tyre and helping it to survive a Babylonian siege, but Apries failed miserably in an effort to aid Jerusalem in 587. In 570 B.C. a war against the Greek colony of Cyrene, which ended in an Egyptian defeat, caused his overthrow. He was succeeded by the general Amasis (Amosis II). Amosis II was the last great Saite pharaoh, and under his reign Egypt prospered. Unlike his contemporary Nabonidus,

---

[6] Herodotus doubted the part of the report which brings conviction to modern scholars. He says the navigators claimed "that the sun turned around and rose on the opposite side." G. Posenor, in a well-argued paper, maintains that Necho sent the expedition to celebrate the opening of the canal. In his translation of Darius' canal inscriptions, he notes that only a section, which was again silted up, was reopened by the Persian king. Other scholars think the canal was not completed by Necho, but opened in its entirety by Darius.

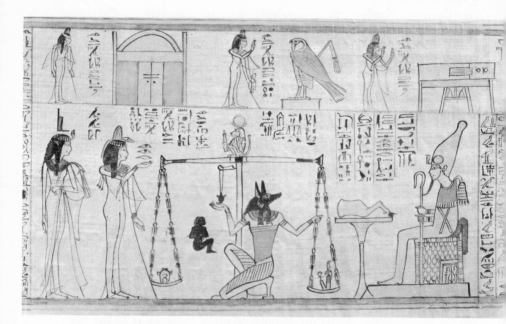

Egyptian Papyrus of the Twenty-first Dynasty, Showing the Judgment Scene Before Osiris. The heart of the deceased is being weighed against the feather of Ma'at (Truth and Justice). (The Metropolitan Museum of Art, Museum Excavations, 1928–1929, and Rogers Fund, 1930)

Amosis was aware of the danger from Persia. He took Cyprus and made a chain of alliances with Lydia, Samos, and other Greek states, and sought a defensive pact with Babylon, but his allies proved shortsighted and weak. One by one they fell to Persia, and Amosis prepared Egypt as best he could to face the danger alone. He died just before the attack came, but his son Psamtik III and the army fought bravely. Unfortunately the admiral of the fleet defected, surrendering without a fight. Egypt fell to the Persian Cambyses in the spring of 525 B.C.

The Legacies of Egypt and Babylon   In Saite Egypt as in Nabonidus' Babylon a spirit of "archaism" was evident. Both of these kingdoms were aware of their great age and were conscious of their glorious pasts. Perhaps confrontation with the "new peoples," the Persians and the Greeks, helped them to this awareness. Egyptian and Babylonian kings, priests, and scribes collected and copied the lore of earlier times. There was much to collect, and much for Persians and Greeks to learn.

Mathematics had advanced spectacularly in both lands, especially geometry and algebra. Babylonians and Egyptians had made use of the theorem for the right-angled triangle, later named for Pythagoras, and

Bronze Cat Wearing a Gold Earring, Late Dynastic Period in Egypt. The cat represents the goddess Bastet. (The Metropolitan Museum of Art, purchase 1958, funds from various donors)

could divide the triangle into equal parts. They could compute the areas of rectangles, the trapezium with parallel sides; and with approximations of pi, they calculated the areas of circles and the volumes of cylinders. The Egyptian approximation of pi was 3.1605 — more accurate than the Babylonian.

In astronomy the Babylonians led. Vast collections of data and observations were available to the priests, who used them for astrological purposes. Eclipses, which were considered dire portents, were studied particularly and sometimes anticipated.

Both peoples had accumulated a store of information on plants, drugs, and other medicinal material. The Egyptian physician was especially scientific, and surgery was advanced in Egypt. In his treatment the surgeon used probes, fire drills for cauterization, absorbent lint, linen swabs, bandages, and splints. Wounds were closed by tape or by stitching, and the Egyptian physician knew how to set bones. He knew that the brain and spinal cord control the nervous system, and he understood something of the function of the heart as the center of a system of distributing vessels; and he had discovered the value of taking the pulse to assist in diagnosis.

Art, architecture, and engineering, too, flourished in Chaldean Babylon and Saite Egypt. Nebuchadrezzar's buildings were extensive and complex. The Sacred Way to the *Ekur* began at the principal city gate. The houses and walls on either side of the Sacred Way, and the *Ekur* wall and its Ishtar Gate[7] were covered with blue tile into which were set, mosaic fashion, rows of colored tile animals marching in procession. The vast ziggurat, whose stages—seven in all—were each tiled in a different color, rose beyond the Ishtar Gate to tower above the city. The royal palace with its gardens lay beside the *Ekur*. The true arch was used in doorways, and there were occasional domed buildings visible above the otherwise flat roofs of the city's sky line.

In Saite Egypt great monuments, temples, and tombs were built, many of them copied from Old Kingdom models. But probably the greatest artistic achievement was in sculpture. Attracted by Old Kingdom styles, Saite sculptors sought, and often realized, realistic and beautiful portraits.

Later peoples were to draw freely from the rich Babylonian and Egyptian stores of experience, invention, knowledge, and technology. The Greek scientific spirit especially benefited from the assembled information, but Persians, Romans, and Arabs too learned from it during the course of many centuries.

ANATOLIA

After the fall of the Hittite state in Anatolia, a succession of powers arose. The Phrygians, whose invasion had destroyed Hattusas, exploited the metallic wealth of the region. They worked iron in quantity, and their wealth in gold gave rise to the Greek story of King Midas and the "Golden Touch." They were crushed by an invasion of Cimmerians in the eighth century B.C.

Lydia The Lydians rose next to take their place as the dominant people in Anatolia. Led by able kings, they secured control of the Greek cities on the coast and of the entire plateau west of the Halys River. They contended with the Medes for possession of the land beyond the river in a war that was brought to a sudden end when in the midst of a battle in 585 B.C. an eclipse of the sun terrified both armies. Thereafter the boundary was fixed at the Halys, and an alliance was formed that lasted until the Median dynasty was overthrown by Cyrus the Persian.

---

[7]Babylon had a temple complex inside a large walled courtyard (*Ekur*) of the same type described earlier for Sumerian cities. The principal gate into the *Ekur* of Babylon was named for the great goddess Ishtar who was especially honored by the Babylonians.

Gold from the streams, wool from the flocks on the hills, and commerce that passed overland from Babylonia through Sardis to the Aegean gave Lydia extraordinary wealth. Herodotus attributes the first coinage of gold to the Lydians. The splendor of their armored chariots and infantry, the high level of Lydian culture, and the fabulous riches of King Croesus, which made his name a byword, are reflected in the poetry of Sappho and in the charming stories of Herodotus. But the period of Lydian supremacy was short-lived.

THE MEDES AND THE PERSIANS

The fall of Nineveh in 612 B.C. and of Babylon in 539 signaled the rise to power of new peoples coming from the plateau of Iran. The Medes and the Persians, Indo-European in origin, secured control of the area under their great king Cyaxares, and took part in the attack on Nineveh. The Medes gained possession of the Assyrian lands north and east of the Tigris, while the closely related tribes of the Persians occupied Elam to the south. Expansion to the west into Asia Minor

Ram (Ibex) of Dark Gray Stone from Persia, Achaemenian Period. (Mr. and Mrs. Alistair Bradley Martin; Guennol Collection, on loan to the Brooklyn Museum)

brought Cyaxares into the conflict with the Lydians which, ending with the eclipse of the sun, fixed the western boundary of his empire at the Halys River.

In 550 B.C. a dynastic revolution took place when Cyrus the Persian deposed his suzerain, Astyages, successor to Cyaxares. The transition to Persian rule, which made no perceptible change in the empire as a whole, brought new force and energy to the direction of affairs and led to renewed expansion in the east, to the subjection of Lydia and the Anatolian Greeks in the west, and to the capture of Babylon. As king of the Medes and Persians, Cyrus became one of the world's great conquerors.

The Conquest of Asia Minor   The first region Cyrus added to his empire was Asia Minor. Misreading the situation, Croesus of Lydia determined on the conquest of the territory east of the Halys River as soon as he heard of the fall of his Median ally Astyages. After a drawn battle with Cyrus, he retired to Sardis and dismissed his allies from Sparta, Egypt, and Samos. Cyrus made a sudden charge on Sardis and caught Croesus unprepared. Using a camel corps, he defeated the Lydian cavalry and took and burned the city in 546 B.C. Croesus was killed, according to a Babylonian record. The Greek states on the coast were speedily added to the Persian Empire (p. 241) after the fall of Sardis.

His western frontier secure, Cyrus made several campaigns to the east, and then in 539 took Babylon and its empire. He allowed the Hebrews who were in captivity in Babylon to return and rebuild Jerusalem. After some vicissitudes the few who took advantage of this permission succeeded in establishing in Palestine a small theocratic state under Persian sovereignty.

Cambyses   Cambyses followed his father as king when Cyrus died fighting in the northeast in 530 B.C. Cambyses invaded Egypt, overthrew the Saite dynasty, and crowned himself pharaoh. After unsuccessful attempts to conquer lands to the south of Egypt, he became insane and died in an accident in 522 B.C. When news of his death reached Persia, a sharp conflict ensued. Darius the Achaemenid emerged victorious and seized the crown. He was to be called by later generations Darius the Great.

Darius the Great, 522–486 B.C.   Darius completed the organization of the Persian Empire. More than twenty large provinces, called satrapies, were established, each under a relative of the king or a Persian noble of high rank. As checks on the power of the provincial governors, or satraps, the king appointed a secretary and a commander of the garrison in each Satrapy as well as inspectors who, as the "eyes and ears of the king," traveled from province to province. Within each satrapy great latitude was allowed with regard to local customs: the

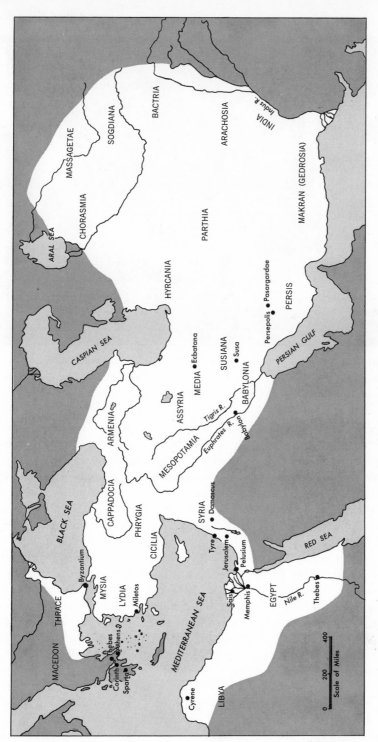

The Persian Empire, ca. 500 B.C.

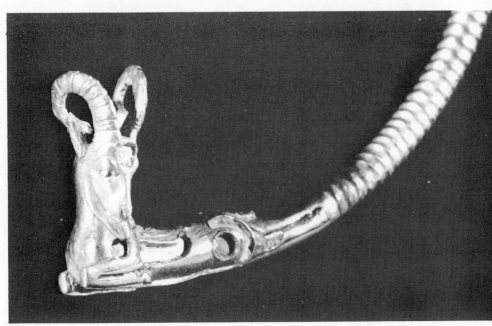

Detail of a Gold Neck Ring from Persia, Achaemenian Period. (Mr. and Mrs. Alistair Bradley Martin; Guennol Collection, on loan to the Brooklyn Museum)

Hebrews were ruled by their priests, and the Greek cities by their tyrants; tribes retained their accustomed organization; and many petty kings were allowed to keep their titles. National law codes were ordered written down for use by Persian governors. Darius himself was king of Babylon and pharaoh of Egypt. The whole empire was bound together by a well-developed system of roads and by couriers who allowed "neither snow, nor rain, nor heat, nor the darkness of night to hinder them in the prompt completion of their allotted tasks."

At the center of Persian imperial government was the king, called "Great King, King of Kings, King of Persia." He was advised by seven councilors, surrounded and assisted by the Persian nobility, and guarded by the Ten Thousand Immortals, the pick of the Persian army. The imperial structure was supported by tribute from the subject peoples paid in kind or coinage. Darius issued gold coins called darics after the king, or archers because they bore the picture of a Persian archer. Some of the satraps also coined silver in the ratio of thirteen to one (silver to gold). All subject states were called upon to furnish the royal army with troops, who were armed and fought in their native fashion. The seaboard peoples such as the Phoenicians, Egyptians, and Greeks supplied the navy.

The Palace of the King   At Persepolis Darius began the construction of a great palace which represented the combination of cultures under the Persians. It was completed by his successors. The architects drew inspiration and workmen from Egypt, Babylon, Assyria, and the Greek cities, and they combined the styles to erect a splendid structure. The palace stood on a huge artificial terrace, to which access was given by a ramp and a royal stairway. Entrance to the terrace was guarded by a gateway faced with lions. The Hall of a Hundred Columns, reminiscent of some of the Egyptian colonnades, provided an audience chamber. King Xerxes later added a hypostyle hall. Behind the hall were gardens and the private suite of the king. The building was plundered and burned by Alexander either by accident or in a fit of rage.

Commerce   All the east from the Mediterranean to the Indus, from Egypt to the Black Sea, was united under the single control of the Persian emperor. The peace that prevailed, the uniformity of weights and measures, and the introduction of coinage fostered the development of trade along the military roads that bound the empire together. Trade flowed freely by land and sea with India and overland with China, and Darius sent an expedition to explore the water route from India to Egypt and another to survey the Mediterranean. In the interest of trade a part of the canal from the Nile to the Red Sea which had silted up was reopened (see note, p. 161). The empire prospered, and

A Section of a Mosaic Wall of Terra Cotta from a Palace in Susa, Achaemenian Period. (The Metropolitan Museum of Art, acquired by exchange, Teheran Museum, 1948)

tribute, fairly proportioned according to the wealth of each area, poured in from its fifty million inhabitants. Darius reinvested much of the income from taxes in the lands from which they were collected, but his successors failed to continue this enlightened policy. Xerxes, Artaxerxes, and their descendants required that gold and silver be sent to Persepolis, where it was melted, molded into bars, and stored in the treasury. Under these rulers dissatisfaction spread over the empire and revolts were frequent. When Alexander took Persepolis, he released a flood of treasure over the world.

Zoroaster   The Persians were, in origin, a vigorous mountain folk who taught their sons to "ride, to shoot the bow, and to speak the truth," and whose highest glory was to serve the king. Their early religion was associated with fire worship, but under Darius the worship of Ahura-Mazda seems to have been established as the official religion. Zoroaster, the great Persian religious teacher, probably lived shortly before the time of Darius. The *Avesta*, the sacred book which developed from his teaching, was composed at a later period, and it is uncertain what parts came from Zoroaster himself. From the older experiences of his people and from his own insight he developed a militant theology of monotheistic character called Zoroastrianism. Ahura-Mazda, god of light, created the world and placed man upon it. He demanded of his followers obedience, morality, and truth. Other gods such as those adored by the Magi, priests of the old religion, or by the Greeks, Hebrews, or Egyptians were his agents or his enemies. Against the forces of darkness and evil, led by Ahriman (the "Lie"), Ahura-Mazda and his worshipers waged a constant war. He promised a reward in paradise to those who died fighting for him, and to the world the ultimate triumph of truth over falsehood. The evil man, the liar and the man who refused to follow Ahura-Mazda, were to be punished eternally after death. Darius the Great, earthly representative of the god, believed that he had received from him a divine mission to practice justice, overthrow injustice, reward friends, punish enemies, and establish law over the lands in the light of Ahura-Mazda. The Persian Empire thus became, under Darius, a state with a divine command.

Darius was an administrator, not a great conqueror, and aside from a few minor campaigns he engaged in no war except with the Greeks. This action and the affairs of his successors are so bound up with Greek history that they can be treated in better perspective while exploring the rise of the Hellenes.

7 · The Rise of the Hellenes

THE GREEKS, WHOSE CLASSICAL ACHIEVEMENT WAS to reach a peak in the fifth and fourth centuries B.C., called themselves Hellenes and their land Hellas. The Hellenic peoples were not confined to the present Greek mainland. They encircled the Aegean Sea and in the eighth century B.C. established colonies around the coast of the Black Sea and on the shores of the western Mediterranean.

The ancient unity of the Aegean which had prevailed during the Mycenaean age was shattered between 1200 and 1100 B.C. by the Dorian invasions. In succeeding centuries, during which historical development is obscure, a new unity was slowly attained. No details of the process can be reconstructed, and even the vague outline of events which can be discerned cannot be accurately placed or timed. Only in the seventh century, when Hellenic unity was already well formed, does the course of events come clearly into view. In the following centuries the articulate and talented Hellenes, who were seekers after civic glory and personal fame, recorded their own history and contributed ideas and principles that form the foundations of western science and thought.

Sources Archaeological sources for the period between 1200 and 700 B.C. provide some clues to life in Hellas, but they are meager indeed. Many scholars reject as unreliable every evidence except the pottery. During some period in this span of time the Homeric epics were composed, and they should be useful in providing a view of early Hellenic customs and institutions, but the epics present more problems than solutions. The question is, what period do they actually describe? The probable answer is so important and yet so puzzling that the Homeric epics must be discussed separately and at some length.

For the period after 700 B.C., and especially from the fifth century on, written sources multiply. Philosophers and historians join the poets in describing Hellenic life and thought. In sheer bulk Oriental

171

records are greater than the Greek, but in contrast to the annals of Babylonia, Assyria, and Egypt, the Greeks wrote true history, setting down clear, closely reasoned and connected narratives of the events of their time seen in the framework of the world as they knew and understood it. The histories of Herodotus, Thucydides, and Xenophon, despite the individual limitations they sometimes reveal, are a hundred times more valuable than the best set of annals. Later historians or biographers, such as Polybius and Plutarch, also are sources of inestimable importance, and every surviving work of Greek literature contributes to a better understanding of Hellenic civilization. Drama is exceptionally revealing of the ways of men and the patterns of life.

Business and legal records are available too. Laws, decrees, proclamations, treaties, and even land boundaries and mortgage records were incised on stone, so great numbers of inscriptions, which epigraphists have copied, studied, and published, are available to amplify and verify the literary histories.

The achievements of Greek architects and sculptors provide their own record, better known to the western world than all the works of eastern art. With the philosophy, poetry, history, and drama, Greek art combines to cast a clear, bright light on classical Hellenic culture.

Geography The geography of the Aegean area, its climate, and its resources have already been described, but more attention should be given to the peculiarities and characteristics of Greece itself. It is a land of contrast, in topography and climate, dominated by sea and mountains and with a widely varying weather pattern from one region to another. Just as the Nile and the Tigris-Euphrates were the centers of their particular cultures, the Aegean Sea was a dominant feature in the history of the Greeks. No place on the Greek peninsula is more than two-days walk from the coast, and the easy navigation permitted by its islands helped to build and maintain Hellenic unity. The Aegean has no tides, but land breezes carried boats in and out of the harbors. The Etesian winds of summer blow all day from the north and northeast to carry ships south, while the counterbreezes of evening send them slowly north again. In ancient times skilled sailors could brave the dangerous westerlies of spring and fall, but stormy winds kept them at home in winter. The sea provided fish (though, because of the scarcity of plant life in the clear waters, fish was not so abundant as might be supposed), squid, shellfish, and salt. The dye-producing mollusks, made famous by the Phoenicians, could also be found in the Aegean.

The Greek mainland is a peninsula, sharply indented by bays. Two of these, extraordinarily deep (the Saronic Gulf and the Gulf of Corinth), penetrate the land from west and east cutting Greece into two parts barely connected by the Isthmus of Corinth. The southern part, shaped like a spread-out human hand, was called the Peloponnesus. In classical times it was dominated by the states of Sparta and Corinth.

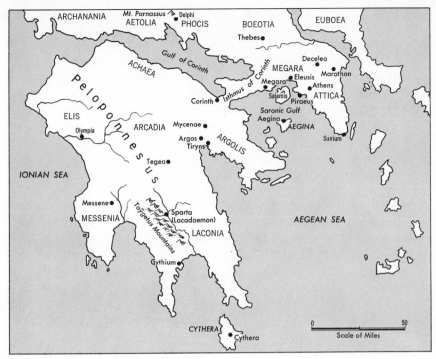

City-States and Regions of the Greek Mainland, ca. 700 B.C.

Four-fifths of Greece is mountainous, leaving little land for farming. In early times the hillsides were forested with pine, fir, beech, and oak, which furnished lumber for shipbuilding and housing and charcoal for fuel, but by the fifth century much of the forest cover was gone, carelessly used by men. Grasslands replaced the woodland, and were used to pasture sheep and goats, which nibbled every green shoot and prevented reforestation. In addition to timber and pasture, the mountains provided metallic resources. Near Sparta, on Mount Taÿgetus, were deposits of iron. Athens was to profit from veins of silver on the Attic peninsula, and elsewhere there were small lodes of gold and copper. The sculptor and builder found whole mountains of marble, and around the bases of the hills were deposits of clay ready for the hand of the potter.

Plant life in Greece varied with the climate and the local water supply. The temperature of the southern and eastern coasts was moderated by the prevailing wind from the sea, and the vine and olive grew well. Inland in the mountains, severely cold winters and hot dry summers permitted little but herding to develop. There were few rivers worthy of the name. None was navigable and most were mountain torrents that flooded in winter and dried up completely in summer, leaving stony beds. But many mountain springs bubbled up from the rocks the year round to water the valleys and small plains and to permit the growth of grains, vegetables, and fruits. In spite of the limited amount of arable land, farming and herding were the principal occupations of the Hellenes, and wars were fought to control the fertile areas. The two-field system of farming (leaving half the land fallow each year) made more severe the natural lack of space. At best there was never enough food in Greece for its population, and many were forced to go abroad or driven to search a livelihood in trade and industry.

Relations with the Outer World   It has been noted that the unity of the Aegean world was shattered by the Dorian invasions, and for some two centuries after then its various parts—the Greek mainland, the islands, and the Anatolian coast—were separated from one another and isolated from the eastern world. According to archaeological evidence contacts were slowly resumed in the ninth century B.C., at first through the Aegean, which strengthened the common linguistic and cultural heritage of the Greeks, and a century later trade was resumed with the east. After the opening of the eighth century the Hellenes participated more and more in international affairs, serving as mercenaries in Oriental armies, traveling to study in Egypt or Syria, competing with the Phoenicians for Mediterranean trade, and establishing colonies to the northeast and west.

THE GREEK MIDDLE AGE

Mycenaean civilization was almost wiped out by the century of turmoil that marked the entry of the Dorians. Pylos was among the first of the great citadels to fall, and refugees from it fled, according to legend, to Athens, leaving behind, among the Linear B tablets in the archive room, records of military assignments which could never be carried out. At about the same time Athens was placed in a state of defense. A wall was hurriedly built to protect the spring on the slopes of the Acropolis, and residents along the line of the wall left in such haste that their dishes were found still in place. Athens was, as tradition states, successful in its defense although the surrounding countryside was ravished, but its prosperity was destroyed. Mycenae, most powerful of the forts, held out for a long time, but by 1100 B.C. the palace and castle lay in ruins. The Greek world fell back upon a more primitive economy and culture. The slow development of the next four and a half centuries forms a period often called the Greek Middle Age.

The population sharply decreased throughout the Greek world, and all evidence indicates that many of the survivors were uprooted from their settled life and forced to subsist as best they could as wanderers or herdsmen in the mountains. Pottery and artifacts were debased

Mycenaean Stirrup Jar
Decorated with Octopi
and Fish, 1200–1125
B.C. (The Metropolitan
Museum of Art, Louisa
Eldridge McBurney Gift
Fund, 1953)

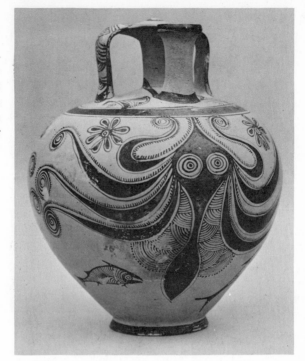

in style and in techniques of manufacture. Linear B was completely forgotten.

Peoples moved from the north to the east and south. Some clans pushed into Thessaly and Boeotia, while others crossed the Gulf of Corinth and settled Elis and the Achaean communities. It was the movement of the Dorians, however, that overwhelmed the rest of the Pelopennesus. They occupied Messenia, Laconia, and Argolis, and took Corinth and Megara in a northward thrust that was stopped only at the Acropolis of Athens. Those who could escaped and began a movement across the Aegean. Attica, overcrowded with refugees, sent out bands of Ionians, who occupied the islands to the east and settled in the central area of the Anatolian littoral. Groups from Thessaly and the north moved in a parallel line to the northern islands, to the Troad, and to the neighboring area called thereafter Aeolis. One band of Achaeans fled and settled in Cyprus. The conquering Dorians followed the fugitives and took Crete, the southern islands, and the lower part of Asia Minor. The central area received not only Ionians but many other groups as well and became the melting pot of the migrations.

This movement east, the repercussions of which were felt throughout the Mediterranean, was made possible by the collapse of the Hittite

Late Mycenaean Cup from Argolis, 1400–1300 B.C. (The Brooklyn Museum)

power. Wandering bands, dislodged from Asia Minor, the islands, or the mainland, overran Syria and fell upon Egypt in the reigns of Merneptah and Ramses III (p. 136). Others went west, one group to be the ancestors of the Etruscans in Italy (p. 381).

The Homeric Question

The only sources of information for the period that followed the invasion of the Dorians are scanty archaeological remains, particularly of pottery, and the Homeric poems, the *Iliad* and the *Odyssey*. A controversy that began in antiquity has raged around the Homeric poems. Who was Homer? When and where did he live? Was there a Homer, or were the poems composed by an evolutionary process or by the gathering together of scattered songs? What civilization do the poems describe? That of the Achaean stage of the Mycenaean period to which the story belongs, or that of Homer's own time during the Middle Age of Greece? These questions cannot be satisfactorily answered. Many competent scholars hold today that Homer lived in southern Aeolis in the eighth century B.C. and that he drew his stories from the songs older bards had brought with them across the sea. From these he created the greatest epics ever composed.

The material civilization — the palaces with their decorations, the great wall of Troy, the gold and silver work — belongs to the Mycenaean period. The political structure and the social and economic life Homer

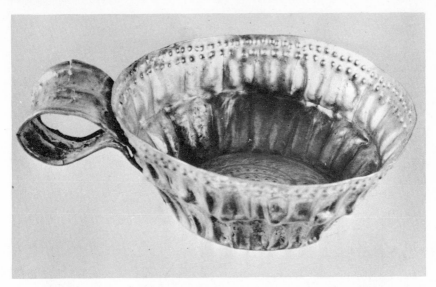

Gold Cup from a Grave at Mycenae. (Greek Press and Information Service)

describes seem to be a reflection of his own experience. Yet there is much confusion, and the lines of division may not be clearly drawn. At times the Homeric heroes go into battle with the huge man-covering shields of the earlier period; again, sometimes in the same scene, they carry the small round shield and wear the complete set of body armor that dates after the Dorian invasion. The men of the Mycenaean age used bronze, but iron weapons and tools that belong to the later period appear in the poems. The *Odyssey* contains the famous line, "The very sight of iron leads men to strife." Though the Homeric kings claimed god-given supremacy, their actual powers were far less than those of the rulers who built the great beehive tombs of Mycenae. More prominent in trade than the seafaring Phaeacians, who belong to the ancient memories, are the "black-browed Phoenicians" who entered the Aegean as merchants after the collapse of Crete and Mycenae. Homeric characters wear loose garments in place of the carefully fitted dresses that appear in the Mycenaean pictures. Finally, Homeric heroes practice cremation of the dead instead of the inhumation characteristic of the earlier period.

The poems likewise disclose a process of transition from a pastoral to an agricultural life such as took place in the period after the migrations. The Homeric heroes are restless warriors who go forth on raids to seize the cattle of neighboring peoples and who are mighty eaters of beef. Yet the similes in the poems and the pictures on the shield of

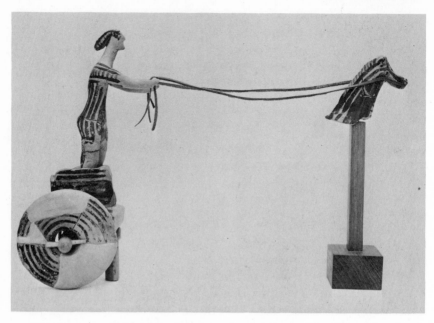

Charioteer and Chariot of Pottery in the Geometric Style. (Greek Press and Information Service)

Achilles portray settled farming communities wherein the slave of a landless man is the sorriest of all humans. The picture of society which may be drawn from the poems thus apparently belongs to the age of the poet, who was himself a keen and sympathetic observer of nature and of humanity.

Homeric Society The society and polity that Homer describes were aristocratic. The great families possessed large estates under patriarchal direction. With Priam in the palace at Troy lived his fifty sons and their wives, his twelve daughters and their husbands. On these estates the nobles did a full share both of direction and of work. Odysseus boasted of his abilities as farmer and craftsman; Penelope spun and wove; and Nausicaä with her attendants did the family washing. Guilds of heralds, prophets, and bards inherited the traditions of earlier times and were welcome guests in the great houses. Lesser men — tenants, serfs, slaves, or hired laborers — tended the herds or worked on the great estates under the watchful eye of the lord of the manor. A few owned farms of their own in the poorer lands. To such a farm Laërtes, father of Odysseus, retired in his old age.

Industry Under the system where each estate sought for self-sufficiency, artisans skilled in many trades were in great demand.

Hephaestus was their heavenly prototype, and they occupied an honorable position. Archaeological discoveries have brought to light the fine geometric pottery they made. The metalworkers learned, probably from Asia Minor, the use of iron, which was soon to produce great changes in the economic and political world.

Trade Trade revived in the ninth century B.C., and Greeks sailed to Syria to buy eastern wares. Shipwrights were singled out for honor. Some of the trade with the east was in the hands of the Phoenicians, but there are many indications of Greek activity, and the stories of the *Odyssey* indicate adventurous exploration of the Mediterranean. Yet trade was hardly differentiated from piracy. "Are you a pirate or do you come as a peaceful merchant?" was the customary greeting to a voyager who had just landed.

Government The king, who was leader in war, chief priest, and judge, was simply the most powerful noble, political heir of the *basileus* who governed a village in the Mycenaean age. His income was derived from his own estates and from the spoils of war. In the distribution of meat, after it had been dedicated to the gods at the sacrifices, he was entitled to a larger share than the others. He made great claims to god-given power, but in reality could not enforce his will. Around him in council gathered the heads of the patriarchal families. They advised him, quarreled with him, and challenged his authority. The monarchy was slowly being transformed into an aristocracy.

The common people, toward whom the aristocratic poet was contemptuous, formed an assembly, but it had little power. When Thersites rose to attack the king, Odysseus with the approval of the mass speedily put him in his place; and when the commoners voted to return home, the nobles vetoed their decision and compelled them to remain. In accordance with ancient traditions, local disputes were settled by the village elders; conditions required nothing more.

Religion Homeric religion was the product of a heroic age. The gods and goddesses were but nobles, supermen and superwomen, who tricked and defeated the will of their king Zeus, as did the nobles of the earth. The very humanness of these divinities, however, was to be an important factor in the later development of Greek religious thought. The virtues of the Homeric age were social rather than religious in their origin—they were family and military virtues rather than divine. The faithful devotion of Penelope and Andromache, the filial loyalty of Nausicaä and Telemachus tell the story of a noble family life. Courage, ability in arms, readiness with words in the council were the greatest glory of man, while cowardice was the worst disgrace. Achilles' choice—a short, vigorous life and everlasting glory—was the expression of the age's ideal.

The Great Goddess Who Was Worshiped Throughout the Aegean (*center*) and Two Figures in Terra Cotta, from Argolis, *ca.* 1250 B.C. (The Brooklyn Museum)

Interstate Relations The sacred ties of guest-friendship bound some family groups together and prevented combat between their members. Otherwise anarchy prevailed save when ameliorated by the laws of religion. The gods protected embassies and heralds, and frowned on treachery, the breaking of oaths, and the use of poisoned weapons. But in this period of piratical raids, war was the natural condition of relationship between groups. Only between organized states could interstate relations exist, and references in Homer and archaeological evidence combine to prove that during the Middle Age such states were developing.

The Polis, or City-State

Four centuries after the Dorian invasion the Greeks began a period of new growth. Settled life in cities came to be the order of the day. Colonies were planted around the seas; industry and commerce, and art and literature developed; and philosophers first dared to question the nature of the universe. Political leaders began the establishment of democratic institutions. In short, it was during this age that the Hellenic world laid the foundation upon which the civilization of its greatest days was to be built.

Growth of the *Polis* The *polis*, or city-state, became during this period and remained for centuries the normal unit of government and the characteristic institution of the Greek world. Except in a few backward regions such as Aetolia, the older tribal organization, the *ethnos*, disappeared entirely or became a feeble bond based upon common worship of an ancestral god. In its place came a number of new organizations based upon locality.

The steps by which this change took place are highly conjectural. The word *polis* would seem to have been applied to the fortress where in Mycenaean times the king and his retainers lived under the protection of the war goddess Athena, guardian of the citadel. Since these fortresses were usually built on those sheer mounds of limestone which rise out of the plains of Greece and lend themselves readily to fortification, the term *acropolis*, meaning high city, was frequently applied to these fortresses, and subsequently to the mounds on which they were built.

With the collapse of Mycenaean culture and the decline in the power of the king, many of these settlements were completely abandoned. Where they did not disappear, the religious element predominated and the *polis* or *acropolis* became primarily the dwelling place of the goddess and the religious center of the community. Here the people of the neighboring villages gathered for religious purposes, and accordingly there developed a local political tie that displaced the older allegiance to the tribe, or *ethnos*. Wherever with the coming of the invaders the older sites were abandoned, new centers of this religious character were developed. It is a striking fact that in most of the states the guardian divinity was a goddess—Athena, Hera, or Artemis—in continuation of the earlier Aegean religious tradition.

Under the protection of the ruling divinity the *polis* became the seat of government and the nobles built their palaces near it. Since the *polis* was fortified, it could be used in time of necessity as a place of refuge from danger. Close at hand a market place developed around which merchants and artisans established their shops and residences. Under favoring circumstances a city in the modern sense of the term would appear. But this was not essential to the idea of the *polis*; in Sparta the people lived scattered in villages over the plain.

If one *polis* was predominant in strength because of the location of its citadel, its religious or commercial pre-eminence, or its numbers, it might reach out and absorb neighboring city-states whose citizens, without moving to the center, would transfer their allegiance to it. Such a *synoecism*, or joining together, took place in Attica, where Athens became the *polis* for all the smaller communities. In Boeotia, by contrast, the small cities remained independent and were united only through the loose ties of a league. Size was no more a criterion of the city-state than was the physical development of a city.

The location of the citadel, which became the religious and political center of the community, was influenced primarily by considerations of defense, of water supply, and of relationship to the plain, rather than of commercial advantages. In fact, for a coastal community an inland location was an advantage as a safeguard against piracy. When commerce expanded, seaport towns grew as an adjunct to the city.

Nature of the *Polis* In the course of these developments the word *polis*, which originally meant citadel, came to be applied to the political entity of the city-state, that is, to the group of people who used the citadel as a common religious, political, and economic center. Special emphasis must be laid on the fact that the city-state was a group, an aggregate of citizens, not a piece of territory. Boundaries were at all times vague and meant but little in an ancient polity. Nor did the natural features, such as mountains, so sought after by modern states, always form the limits of ancient cities; sometimes the limits crossed natural boundaries. Elsewhere, in some of the great plains, several small communities would nestle together undivided by any natural feature but each strong in its allegiance to its own *polis*. As a result pastoral or agricultural rights over hillsides and fields in the borderland between two states were constant causes of disputes.

Membership in the citizen body depended on birth, not on residence in the locality. It could not be obtained except by gift of the community. Conversely, it could not be taken away, even by the destruction of the city itself. Messene was destroyed by Sparta in the seventh century B.C. In 370 B.C. it was rebuilt by Epaminondas, and descendants of the original inhabitants, who had never given up their idea of citizenship, returned.

The older ethnic groups were carried into the organization of the citizen body. In the Ionian states there were four subordinate tribal divisions called *phylae*; in most of the Dorian states there were three. These in turn were separated into *phratries*, brotherhoods of families, which fought and worshiped together and kept the rolls of the citizens.

With this development of the *polis* came the principle that was to remain the fundamental element in all Greek political thought—the right of each city-state, no matter how small, to absolute freedom in the control of its local government and its relations with other states. The city-state was the largest political unit comprehensible to the Greeks. From loyalty to the city-state and desire to serve and glorify it came the idea of democratic liberty as the Greeks understood it, and the great achievements in art and literature which are the glory of Greece. Unfortunately, from these same impulses arose the endless wars that finally wrought the ruin of Hellas and made it an easy prey for Macedon and Rome.

The Aristocracy The development of settled conditions in agriculture and the growth of political organization in the city-state combined to finish a process begun in the Homeric age — the replacement of the Zeus-nurtured king by the aristocracy. It did not take place everywhere at the same time, for kingship survived in Argos until the Persian wars and in Sparta in circumscribed form throughout the classical period. But in most of the states aristocrats who based their power on the land and traced their ancestry to the heroes and the gods assumed control through their council. Names of these aristocrats indicate their position in this pre-eminently agricultural period: Hippobotae, meaning horse raisers, Geomoroi, farmers; Eupatridae, well-fathered. Dreading interference with their possessions, they took away the civil powers of the *basileus* and appointed members of their order to hear cases affecting landownership and later all cases involving ancient customs. In some states they gave the military power of the king to one of their number. Only the religious power was left to the kingship, which then came habitually to be an elective office. In Corinth the royal family was strong enough to keep control in its own group, though the individual kingship disappeared.

The Common People At the same time that saw the growth of the aristocracy the common people were deprived of such rights as they had had in the earlier period. The assembly ceased to meet. The aristocrats, as divinely appointed guardians of the god-given laws, controlled the courts, and though opposition to them was dangerous lest it anger the gods they were nevertheless open to bribes or to influence. Against the land-greedy and corrupt nobility the small farmers had little chance. Many of them sank into tenantry, serfdom, and slavery. Serfdom had certainly existed in Mycenaean times, but it increased and spread under the aristocratic regime. Those peasants who escaped serfdom and slavery were forced into the poorer lands which had formerly lain waste and onto the rocky hillsides, where they terraced and hoarded the soil, planted vineyards or olive orchards, and grew a few vegetables. Others became charcoal burners in the woods or tended herds of sheep or goats on the hillsides. Cattle pasturage declined and the forest began to disappear.

Hesiod The chief source of information for the period after Homer is the poet Hesiod (*ca.* 700 B.C.), author of two didactic poems written in the epic dialect and meter: *Theogony*, or "Descent of the Gods," to instruct men about their divine relations; and *Works and Days*, a book of advice to farmers. His father, he wrote, had fled from poverty in Aeolis to Boeotia where he had occupied a piece of wasteland. Hesiod himself had suffered at the hands of his brother and a venal judge, and his picture of the times was gloomy. The glorious ages of Gold, Silver, and Bronze and of the Heroes had passed, he lamented, and he was living in the Iron Age, when everything was bad and growing worse. "Might shall be right, and one shall sack the other's city." In the beautiful parable of the hawk and the nightingale he portrayed the unjust princes and warned them of the punishment of farseeing Zeus.

He admonished the poor man that his only hope lay in constant, unremitting toil and the avoidance of litigation. The reckless man might unwisely turn to trade and trust himself to the sea, but if he had any wisdom, the poet advised him, he would sail only during the time of the Dog Star. The farmer was at least safe if he worked hard and watched the calendar. To him, Hesiod gave advice as to the methods, the seasons, and the days propitious for his tasks, the hiring of hands, and even about the more serious business of matrimony.

Agriculture   Agricultural methods and the poor quality of the soil combined to make the situation difficult for the small farmer. The crude plow barely broke the soil, and clods had to be crushed laboriously with the hoe. In the absence of proper fertilizer, a two-field system prevailed whereby fields were left fallow in alternate years. To eke out a living, the farmer planted olive trees and vines and sowed the land between the rows of these with grain and vegetables. With the decline of pasturage, meat disappeared from the Greek table save for the great festivals. Cereals, vegetables, and cheese became the chief articles of diet. Olive oil served as butter and as fuel for lamps. The scarcity of produce made prices high and increased the power of the great landowners and the distress of the poor.

8 · Evolution of the Hellenic World

THE LEADERSHIP IN THE MOVEMENTS THAT BROUGHT the Greeks from agricultural self-sufficiency into a full participation in the economic life of the Mediterranean world was assumed by the islands and cities along the seacoast of Asia Minor, of which Mytilene on Lesbos, Chios, Samos, Phocaea, Ephesus, Priene, Miletos, and Halicarnassus were the most important. In these communities, where aristocratic landlords ruled over serfs, the traditions of older times were still strong. The people, vase paintings show, still dressed in the ancient fashions of Mycenae. It was for these people that Homer and his fellow poets sang of past glory in their lays. But the narrowness of their fields and the fact that the strong powers of Phrygia and Lydia in the hinterland made expansion impossible drove them to seek other outlets for the exploitation of their wealth. These they found in the development of trade with the hinterland and with Syria. Phrygia and Lydia loom large in the literature that was produced in Ionia, and the Israelite records contain mention of the "people of Javan," the Ionians who, after their flight across the Aegean, had continued or renewed their mercantile contacts.

The demands of trade produced a revolution in agriculture when the nobles diverted their fields from the growing of foodstuffs to the production of olive oil and wine for export. While this change contributed greatly to the riches and power of the ruling class, it wrought terrific hardship on the poor, many of whom found themselves at once released from serfdom and dispossessed of the land that was their only source of livelihood. Similar developments took place in some of the island cities, particularly in Crete, in Chalcis on Euboea, and in Corinth and Megara on the mainland. An early solution of the problem was found in a movement for colonial expansion.

COLONIAL EXPANSION

Causes   Though the causes of the colonial expansion that took place during the eighth and seventh centuries B.C., were manifold, the basic reasons were agricultural and political. In good seasons the fields of the average state produced hardly enough food to suffice, while a bad year brought on famine conditions in spite of the fact that there was often a superfluity of oil and wine. Families were large, and even the family estates of the nobles were insufficient to support all their members. Where division of estates among heirs was practiced, the farms soon became too small, and when heirs had recourse to litigation, the most influential won. The result was an increasing group of landless, discontented, and therefore troublesome individuals. Political and social factions among the nobility added to the confusion. The Aegean world boiled over. Civil strife broke out in many states, and the defeated were often expelled to add to the list of homeless wanderers. Some went to Egypt, Babylon, and elsewhere, to serve as mercenary warriors; others went forth in bands in search of new lands, to find an *apoikia*, "a home away from home," where they might have land and be farmers.

The desire for commercial expansion and the quest for raw materials and markets for industrial products and the superabundant oil and wine later led to the planting of commercial settlements. Thus the Megarians who had first founded Chalcedon on the Bosporus as an agricultural settlement later established Byzantium on the opposite side of the straits because the site possessed greater commercial advantages. The Black Sea settlements of Miletos, the colonies of Corinth in the west, and the city of Naucratis in Egypt were commercial in origin. Adventurous spirits found an outlet for their exuberance in the new lands. Within the space of two centuries, the Greek world, which came to be called Hellas, had expanded to include most of the littoral of the Mediterranean and Black seas.

Methods   At first the colonial movement was sporadic. Small bands under chosen leaders struck out for themselves and found or seized sites suitable for agricultural colonies. Countless little cities, some of which are known today only by their names and coins, sprang up here and there. In time order came out of chaos. A contemporary religious development had brought the Pythian Apollo of Delphi, god of wanderers, to the fore, and the later colonies set out under the advice of his oracle and the leadership of his priests. The priests, who at first were Cretan, seem to have been extraordinarily well informed as to possible sites and conditions around the seas. When a city determined, for one reason or another, to send out a colony, it first applied to the oracle. On its advice a site was chosen and a leader appointed as founder of the new city. Laws and plans were carefully drawn up in advance.

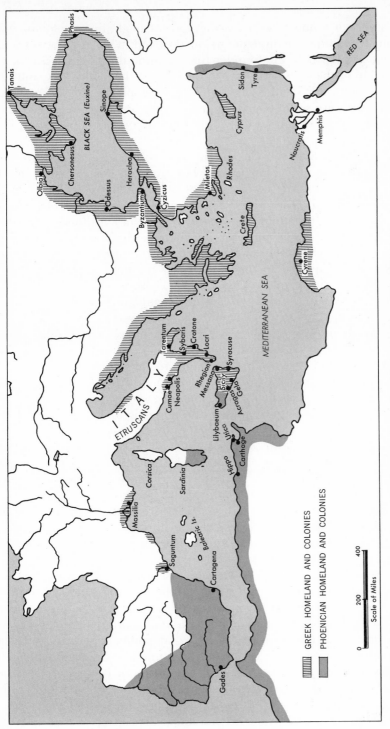

Greek and Phoenician Colonization, 800–600 B.C.

RED SEA

Phasis

Tanais

BLACK SEA (Euxine)

Sinope

Chersonesus

Olbia

Odessus

Heraclea

Byzantium

Cyzicus

Miletos

Rhodes

Crete

Sidon

Tyre

Cyprus

Memphis

Naucratis

Cyrene

MEDITERRANEAN SEA

Tarentum

Sybaris

Crotone

Locri

Rhegion

Messana

Syracuse

Sicily

Gela

Acragas

ITALY

ETRUSCANS

Cumae

Neopolis

Lilybaeum

Utica

Hippo

Carthage

Corsica

Sardinia

Massilia

Balearic Is.

Saguntum

Cartagena

Gades

GREEK HOMELAND AND COLONIES

PHOENICIAN HOMELAND AND COLONIES

Scale of Miles

0   200   400

If sufficient numbers were lacking, the city might invite colonists (men only) from other communities to join the band. When the place of settlement was reached, the founder first set aside the proper area for the worship of the gods according to the cults of the mother city, and then proceeded to divide the land among the people by the casting of lots. The laws were set in operation and the new state was safely launched. The founder, who was usually a member of a noble family, was venerated as a hero.

The New State   Each new city-state was independent. This was a basic principle of the movement. The city-state was entitled to all the privileges of any of the older cities of the Aegean. Its ties with the mother city were, with rare exceptions, close, and based on blood relationship and on community of religious ideas and institutions. Colonists frequently returned home for the great festivals, and in most cases could regain citizenship at home if they so desired. In times of crisis the colony appealed to the mother city for help, as did Syracuse to Corinth in the turmoil of the fourth century. On the other hand, Corcyra, likewise a colony of Corinth, maintained for the mother city an enduring enmity, which resulted in many wars.

Relations between the colonists and the natives usually followed one of two common patterns. In some places the Greeks had to fight for possession, and they would then either reduce the older inhabitants to serfdom or slavery, or drive them back from the coast. In rare instances they failed to make their possession good or permanent. Where they were received peacefully, a quiet intermingling took place, but the culture became Greek. Wherever they went, the colonists endeavored to identify local gods with their own and to find sites connected with the myths and legends of the local gods. The Corinthian settlers of Syracuse were sure that the fountain Arethusa was but the reappearance of the river Alpheus, which came out of Arcadia, flowed by the site of Olympia, and passed through the Mediterranean to greet them in their new home.

Colonizing Cities   Nearly all the important Greek cities except Athens, Aegina, and Thebes took part in the colonial movement. The most prolific, however, were the Asiatic cities, notably Miletos, whose colonists pushed north and east into the Hellespontine and Euxine regions. Megara had a share in the same area and looked to the west as well; Chalcidians from Euboea went north to the promontories along the Macedonian coast and west to Italy. Corinth occupied Corcyra on the route to the west and was the proud mother of Syracuse. Spartans founded colonies on Crete and at Tarentum; Rhodes made settlements in Sicily; and the Achaean cities in the northern Peloponnesus settled thickly in southern Italy. Many colonies throve so well that they added settlements of their own.

The West   According to tradition, Chalcidian Cumae near the Bay of Naples was the earliest colony in the west. Later commercial development caused the settlement of the "New City," Neapolis, or Naples. Rhegion and Zancle, which dominated the straits between Italy and Sicily, Naxos, Catana, and Leontini were also colonies of the Chalcidians.

Southeastern Italy was occupied chiefly by Achaeans. Sybaris, rich in its valley and in its control of an overland route from the Ionian to the Tyrrhenian seas, became famous for its luxury. Crotone was not so fortunate in site but thrived nonetheless, becoming an athletic center and the home of the Pythagorean sect. In the famous rivalry between these two cities, Crotone triumphed. On the other side of the peninsula, Poseidonia, modern Paestum, known today for the ruins of its temples, was Achaean. In addition to these cities, so many small colonies dotted the coast line of southern Italy that the Romans later called it Magna Graecia.

Corinthians under the leadership of Archias, a member of the royal family, first settled on the island of Ortygia and then took possession of the nearby shore to establish Syracuse. That city, because of its harbor and its fertile lands, soon became the leading city in the west. Gela and Acragas on the southeastern coast of Sicily were Rhodian colonies.

A hardy band of Phocaeans pushed further west to found Massilia (Marseilles) near the mouth of the Rhone where it could control the trade with the rich lands of Gaul, and scattered colonies were also founded on the coast of Spain.

The Greeks in the west, however, were checked by the presence and advance of other colonizing powers, the Phoenicians (p. 145) and the Etruscans (p. 381). The Phoenicians had already settled in northern Africa and southern Spain and, in reaction to the Greek movements, began to take possession of western Sicily. In western Italy the Etruscan states were powerful. The Phoenicians and Etruscans were singly and together sufficient to stop further Greek expansion. The Greeks never succeeded in getting possession of the whole of Sicily, and a Phocaean attempt in Corsica in the sixth century B.C. failed because of Etruscan opposition (p. 386).

The North   The most notable achievement in the Aegean Sea was the occupation of its northern littoral. So many Chalcidians poured into the promontories which project to the south that the area was later called the Chalcidice. Olynthus was the best known of their settlements. Potidaea, in the same area, was founded by Corinth. Parians occupied Thasos with its gold mines and pushed over into the Thracian mainland in quest of the same precious metal.

The Thracian tribes seem to have been strong enough to exclude the Greeks from their territory, but there is a different tale for the shores of the Hellespont and Propontis. There are said to have been ninety colonies in these stretches of land. Lesbians founded Sestos; Abydos and Cyzicus, famous for tunny fish, were colonies of Miletos; and Megara colonized first agricultural Chalcedon, and later Byzantium, a commercial city with a brilliant future.

The Black Sea, called Euxine, "well-favored," by the Greeks to soften its temper, had been entered in heroic times when Jason and the Argonauts sought the golden fleece in Colchis, that region of the Caucasus where gold is still taken from the streams by the fleece of sheep. The first colonies of the classical period were Ionian, but these were wiped out by the Cimmerians. After 650 B.C., however, Miletos renewed the effort and founded Sinope, center of naval construction; Trapezus, point of export for the metals of the Caucasus; and Olbia, at the mouth of the Bug River, an export center of fish and grain. The Byzantines established Heraclea in Pontus in the Tauric Chersonese (the Crimea).

The South The southern coast of Asia Minor and the Syrian littoral were too strongly occupied to offer a possible field for Greek expansion. On the Tripolitan coast of Africa a band of Dorians, the majority from the island of Thera, founded Cyrene, source of the drug silphium, much used by ancient doctors.

Egypt Greek colonization in Egypt followed entirely different lines. The Saite monarch Psamtik I (p. 161), learning the military value of the bands of Ionian warriors who raided his shores, employed them as mercenaries. When his wars were successfully completed, he installed them on lands at Daphnae on the Pelusiac branch of the Nile. After an Egyptian defeat at the hands of Cyrene in 570 B.C., a national reaction took place against the Greeks, and Amosis moved them to the Canopic branch of the river and gave them a village called Naucratis. It became a cosmopolitan sort of place. Nine cities had shops and sections in Naucratis, each self-governing under a royal appointee for the whole city. It was obligatory for Greeks going to Egypt to reside there, and it became the chief center of communication between the old and the new civilizations.

Results In the colonial expansion the Greeks and their civilization spread around the shores of the Mediterranean and the Black Sea. Native tribes acquired a veneer of Greek culture from the colonies and offered new opportunities to Greek merchants for the purchase of raw materials and the sale of industrial products. At the same time the mother cities underwent a transformation. The development of their political structure was materially affected by the study of institutions and laws required for the new settlements. Individual landownership in the colonies helped to break down family control of land in the older centers. The demand for home products, the opening of new markets, the increase of knowledge and new ideas about the world, and contact with alien peoples—all brought the Greeks into a consciousness of their own nationality. It was after the colonial movement that the Greeks began to use the words *Hellas* and *Hellenes* to include all Greeks wherever located in order to distinguish themselves from the barbarians.

ECONOMIC GROWTH

The Revival of Industry

The colonial movement was accompanied and followed by extraordinary advances in industry and commerce. Many forces contributed to the revival of industry: importations from Phoenicia, Lydia, and Egypt, coming often by way of Crete and Rhodes, improved local taste and led to increased local demands; colonists sent back home for favored objects; new sources of raw materials were tapped; and specialized craftsmen took the place of "the old village blacksmith." Techniques that had survived from Mycenaean times were revived or expanded, and new methods were developed.

The Ionian cities assumed leadership in the textile industry, and Milesian wool came into general demand. A bountiful supply of sheep in the interior furnished the raw material, while the purple dye secured from mollusks, which was used also by the Phoenicians, gave the woven materials color. Some flax was grown and linen was made, but Egypt remained the chief source of this material.

Pottery Pottery developed as a local industry wherever a sufficient abundance of clay was found. Ionian pottery and a type called by ar-

Dipylon Amphora from Athens, Geometric Style, Eighth Century B.C. (The Metropolitan Museum of Art, Rogers Fund, 1910)

chaeologists proto-Corinthian, whose place of manufacture is not certain, were among the earliest to be exported. In Ionian pottery Mycenaean survivals and Oriental influences dominated. The artists who made and decorated the vases discarded geometric influences and painted, in black on a light slip,[1] figures of birds and human beings, interspersed with rosettes, scrolls, and linear decorations. Proto-Corinthian pottery was more under geometric influence, but at its best the artists produced fine miniature paintings in red or brown on a light-colored clay.

Corinth had a fine supply of clay and for a period was the center of an immense vase industry. Oriental influence was very strong in the portrayal of strange hybrid forms of birds and animals. Figures of warriors and legendary scenes were portrayed with a fine degree of skill. Finally, at the end of the seventh and early part of the sixth centuries B.C. Athenian ware, first black-figured on a red background, and later the finer red-figured on black,[2] displaced all others in the market, particularly in the west. More Athenian vases have been found in Etruria and in the Black Sea region than in the Aegean itself. The distinctive wares of the Greek cities served as "trade marks" to identify the provenance of the wines and oils they contained.

Metallurgy   The presence of local supplies of metals and increased demand, the result of general prosperity, made possible specialization and important advances in the technique of metallurgy. Chalcis became famous for its bronze swords and armor made from the copper of Euboea, and in Lacedaemon the iron of Taÿgetus was used to produce armor and weapons, locks and keys. In the matter of technique, the Greeks learned methods of hollow casting in bronze and discovered an improved process for smelting iron. These advances in conjunction with increased demand led to reduction in the cost of metal armor, so it became possible for the average man to purchase it.

The same influences made themselves felt in other lines of activity. In response to the demands of the growing and flourishing cities, the stoneworkers cut limestone and marble slabs from the quarries and used them for the construction of buildings and statues. The needs of commerce led to developments in shipbuilding, and naval warfare led to invention of the trireme—warships propelled in battle by heavy oars with three men to an oar, which Corinth claimed to have originated. City life brought with it problems in engineering, particularly with regard to water supply. A famous aqueduct was built in Athens, and the

---

[1] Potter's clay in a liquid state used in the casting process and for the decoration of ceramic ware.

[2] The Athenians first painted figures with black paint on the natural red background of the clay. Then they learned to fill in the background and to draw lines with black paint leaving the figures unpainted and red. This made possible a finer development of drawings.

Bronze Ox, Probably Eighth or Seventh Century B.C. (Photograph by Frank D. Grande)

engineers of Samos dug a tunnel through a mountain to bring water to their city.

Methods In spite of the development in techniques and increased demand, industry remained on a small scale. The little family shop was the prevailing unit. There a man worked, assisted by his sons and possibly by an apprentice or two and by such slaves or hired men as he could afford. Chios was the first Greek state to use slaves for industrial work. Slaves from the Black Sea region or the European hinterland were used for the rougher work such as firing the potters' furnaces. But among the slaves were also Greeks who had fallen into slavery for debt or who had been sold as prisoners of war, and Orientals who were highly skilled; these were employed on finer work. Within the shop a spirit of freedom and creative craftsmanship prevailed. The potters had models from which they worked, but of all the thousands of Greek vases in museums no two have been found exactly alike. Many potters were artists who signed their work.

Artisans in the same occupations tended to group themselves in the same quarter of a city and to organize into guilds. They based the form of their association on the family organizations of the nobles. The bronze workers called themselves Chalcidae, or "sons of bronze." They had their patron divinities and their religious activities, and guarded the secrets and regulated the activities of their crafts.

The Revival of Trade

Trade in the Aegean had made a strong recovery during the Middle Age. For a period it was dominated by the Phoenicians, until the Cretan and Ionian cities were strong enough to compete with them. Meanwhile throughout Hellas the need for raw materials and food, together with the natural tendency toward specialization in industrial production, led to the growth of an exchange economy. All the forces that operate to develop trade were at work.

Outcasts became peddlers as they wandered from town to town, and fishermen became merchants. Border markets for local trade appeared at convenient points between neighboring communities. Meetings of religious leagues and the gathering of communities for games or festivals afforded opportunity for the display of products and became fairs. Demand was stimulated, and direct exchange took place between cities through middlemen. Aeginetan professional peddlers went with their mules throughout the Peloponnesus, and wagoners traveled along the sacred ways that led to the great shrines. Broad-beamed sailing vessels were built to carry cargoes, and pentecounters (fifty-oared galleys) and triremes were built in turn to protect them. Anchors, an invention of the seventh century B.C., made sailing safer. Whereas in the time of Hesiod, seafaring was confined to the middle of summer, the skilled sailor of the sixth century B.C. set out in the

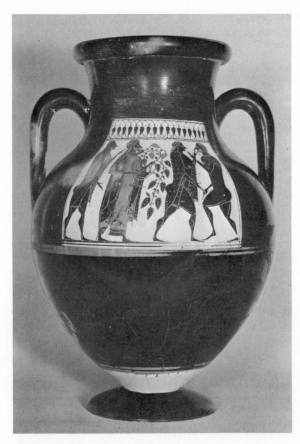

Athenian Amphora, Black Figures on a Red Background, Middle of the Sixth Century B.C. (The Metropolitan Museum of Art, Rogers Fund, 1918)

spring to return in the fall. Safe routes came to be well known and followed. On long trips men trusted themselves out of sight of land and sailed by the sun or at night by the Phoenicians' star. States found it essential to cooperate for the sake of commerce. Harbors were protected by moles; display houses and warehouses were constructed; foreigners were given permission to land and even to remain; seaport towns grew up when the city itself was inland. Men talked of a canal through the Isthmus of Corinth, but it was too great an undertaking. A plank road was constructed, however, over which smaller ships and goods were dragged on rollers.

In primitive societies men passed beyond the crude basis of barter trade when they adopted such standards of exchange as cattle or sheep. The Oriental nations advanced to a still higher point when they began to use established weights of the precious metals to represent value and when the Assyrians in their Ishtars produced the precursors of coined money. Coins, pieces of metal whose weight and fineness are guaranteed by the issuing power and accepted by the users, first appeared in the Greek world in the seventh century B.C.

The earliest attempts at metal coinage were copper or iron spits called obols. Six of them made a handful; in Greek, a drachma. As these metals decreased in value, the obols became mere token coins, useless for large transactions or for trade between states, and the precious metals took over the field. To Asia Minor, either to the Lydians or to the Ionians, belongs the credit for issuing the first true money, when private individuals or the states stamped and guaranteed the weight and quality of pieces of electron, a natural alloy of gold and silver. The Lydians were the first to coin gold and to establish bimetallism on the basis of a ratio of $13\frac{1}{3}$ to 1. Once introduced, coinage spread rapidly. Each city adopted its own standard coin, the drachma or didrachma of a definite weight and fineness, and its own design. The tunny fish stood for Cyzicus, the seal for Phocaea, the tortoise for Aegina, and the owl and the head of Athena for Athens. In general, only silver was coined by the Greeks, though Lydian, and later Persian, gold coins came into use. The varying standards produced much confusion and led to a profitable business in money changing. Most states, however, related their coins to one of two systems, the lighter Euboic and the heavier Aeginetan standards.

Methods Methods of trade were simple. A group of merchants would unite for a voyage, buy up a supply of local products, rent a ship, and set forth. On coming to a port town they would land, lay out their goods for display, and carry on lively bargaining with local purchasers. With the money thus secured they would usually purchase goods that they could sell at home. Similar transactions took place until the original cargo had been sold or the season was over. At home they sold the wares purchased abroad, paid off their debts, and divided the profits.

Such transactions between states brought up the question of rights of aliens in the courts. Because of the Greek conception of the family character of the state and its general exclusion of outsiders who were not born within the family circle, full grant of rights was impossible. Recourse was therefore had to the ancient institution of *proxenia*, hereditary guest friendship. Where before individual families had guest friends, states now had them also. An Athenian family would become guest friends of Corinth. All Corinthians coming to Athens would apply to them for aid in the enforcement of contracts, for representation in the Athenian courts, and for protection. The position was hereditary in the family and was highly regarded as an honor.

During the eighth, seventh, and sixth centuries B.C. the economic character of the Hellenic world was being transformed. In place of small communities ruled by landholding aristocrats there appeared prosperous cities with specialized industries and a flourishing commerce facilitated by the invention of coinage and the establishment of interstate relationships. At the same time the varied commercial activities were spread throughout the Mediterranean and the Black Sea regions by the movement of colonial expansion. In spite of emigration to the colonies, population at home increased. In 600 B.C. Corinth had about 25,000 and Miletos about 30,000 inhabitants, most of whom were artisans or merchants.

POLITICAL CHANGES

Oligarchy Under the multiple economic influences of the times the states underwent startling political changes. The power of the landholding aristocracy suffered a severe blow when, in response to the needs of business, the laws were written down so that all men might know them. With this the laws passed from the domain of the gods and their earthly representatives to the realm of practical affairs and the control of ordinary men. Zaleucus in Locri and Draco in Athens (whose historicity has been questioned) were famous recorders of the law. When the basis of wealth became money instead of land, many men rose from the ranks to riches and were able to demand and secure a share in the government. As a result oligarchies (rule of the few), in which wealth gained from any source rather than from landed estates became the chief requirement for the holding of office, succeeded to political power. The general policy of the oligarchies was the further development of industry and trade, and under such guidance the Ionian cities established their pre-eminence and sent out their commercial colonies.

The oligarchic rulers of Aegina, refraining from entrance into the colonial movement, fostered the manufacture of pottery (which a fine deposit of clay made possible) and the importation and working of metals to such an extent that Aeginetan bronze bowls and caldrons were everywhere in demand. As the trade of Aegina expanded, its coins and weights became a common standard. Aegina was the only western state to participate at Egyptian Naucratis.

In similar fashion the great commercial expansion of Corinth was achieved under the guidance of its oligarchs, a small closely related group of nobles who were called by the name of the old royal family, the Bacchiads. These men, recognizing the trend of events and the value of the location of their city, directed their activities toward commerce. Port towns, built on both sides of the isthmus and connected by a tramway over which goods and even small boats were carried, and colonies like Corcyra and Syracuse gave commercial pre-eminence in the western trade to Corinth.

Timocracy When increased prosperity, cheaper metals, and improved methods of production brought armor within the reach of the average man, most states, following the example of Sparta, organized from among their well-to-do citizens the phalanx (solid body) of heavy-armed infantry. When the newly created infantry realized its power in the state, it was able to secure a share in the government, and the oligarchy yielded to the *timocracy*, the rule of those rich enough to equip themselves with heavy armor. This normally resulted in the formation of an assembly of the well-to-do, with powers of election and legislation, and in the creation of an administrative council drawn from the same body. In many of the states, however, the higher offices were still reserved for the wealthier classes, and the policies of the leaders, like those of the oligarchs, were directed toward expanding industry and commerce. These changes in government did not take place in all states or at one time or in any fixed order, but such was the tendency of the times.

Tyranny In the course of the transition, many crises developed. Quarrels arose between factions of the aristocracy, between the aristocrats and the merchants, between the oligarchs and the artisans. Civil wars were fought with the utmost cruelty, and the survivors of the defeated faction were driven into exile. The poems of Alcaeus and Theognis are filled with the bitterness of spirit of the aristocrats against their successful moneyed rivals. The situation was aggravated by the fact that a shift from a barter to a monetary economy was particularly hard on the debtor class, both farming and industrial. The laws of debt were rigid. The property, the family, and finally the person of the debtor served as forfeits for unpaid loans, with the result that many people were sold into slavery.

The disorders that frequently resulted from these intolerable conditions afforded opportunities in many states for able men to rise to power. Leaders of successful factions, prominent nobles with large bodies of retainers, leaders of the common folk, magistrates, or generals turned their official position or their prestige and power to good account in one state after another, and, seizing the citadel, they made themselves monarchs. Such unconstitutional kings were termed "tyrants" by the Greeks. In some cases they actually became kings; in others elections were held and the constitution continued to function under the supervision of the tyrant. In many states therefore the tyrant occupied much the same position that the political boss holds in a modern American city. The economic basis of the development of tyranny becomes apparent when it is realized that tyranny did not appear in states like Sparta and in Thessaly, which were unaffected by the commercial and industrial changes.

Achievements of the Tyrants Almost invariably the tyrant was a popular champion. The aristocrats were his chief enemies, and he therefore set himself to destroy their power—political, economic, and religious. The leaders of the aristocracy were sent into exile, and in some states their lands were divided up among the peasants. The political powers of the aristocratic council and of the great noble families were thus destroyed. Religion was transformed through the breaking down of some of the older cults and the establishment of new democratic festivals. The tyrant usually paid great attention to the industrial class, which prospered accordingly. His interest in trade led to the planting of commercial colonies and the making of treaties with other states. He sought to glorify himself by becoming a patron of the arts, especially favoring poets, who clustered around him and sang his praises. He beautified his city with fountains, temples, and statuary. In short, the tyrant played an important role in the development of democracy, in industry, trade, and culture.

Nevertheless, the tyrants were always regarded by the Greeks as usurpers. Plots against them were frequent, and many became tyrants in the modern sense of the word. Few were able to establish a dynasty, and almost no tyrannies survived beyond three generations. When they were overthrown, the states became commercial oligarchies or incipient democracies.

Corinth The tyrannies in Corinth and in Sicyon afford noteworthy examples of the policies and achievements of tyrants and of the prestige they secured for themselves and for their states. Quarrels beginning between Corinth and Corcyra resulted in the first recorded naval battle in Greek history, which ruined for the moment Corinthian influence in the west and made it possible for Cypselus, a popular leader, to drive out the Bacchiads (p. 197) and become tyrant. There may be in his triumph some sign of the revolt of the pre-Dorians against the Dorian conquerors. He drove out the nobles, divided the land among the peasants, protected Corinthian commerce, and ruled peaceably for thirty years (657–627 B.C. are the traditional dates). He was succeeded by his son Periander, who was to become the outstanding tyrant of the period, and who completed the work of his father in Corinth. He established a new division of the state into eight territorial tribes. Men without occupation were forbidden to enter the city, and the importation of slaves was stopped, with the result that the artisan class of Corinth was better off than the same class elsewhere. The introduction of a system of coinage and the construction of temples to Apollo and Aphrodite accompanied the other changes. At the festivals of Dionysus, Arion of Lesbos perfected the choral dithyramb, out of which many think the Athenian drama later grew. At this time also the Isthmian games in honor of Poseidon were raised to a new position of importance.

Periander extended the power of Corinth by conquest and colonization and established his fame far beyond the bounds of his city-state. The western end of the Corinthian Gulf came under his control; Corcyra and its colony Epidamnus, on the Epirote coast, which dominated the entrance to the Adriatic and the trade route to the west, were defeated; in the east he founded Potidaea, in the Chalcidice, to secure a source of naval supplies. He established close relations with Athens by a marriage alliance with a noble family. The tyrants of Ionia were his friends, and he corresponded with the kings of Lydia and the Saite rulers of Egypt. So great was his renown that he was asked to arbitrate a dispute between Athens and Mytilene and to arrange a treaty between Lydia and Miletus. Under his rule Corinth reached the height of its power.

Sicyon   A little to the west of Corinth was the city of Sicyon. Rich in the production of grain and olives, it furnished supplies to the neighbering market of Corinth. Its pottery and metal goods supported a growing industrial class. Politically the city was dominated by a Dorian nobility with Argive affiliations. Then the artisans and the peasants, many of whom were becoming serfs, found a leader in Orthagoras, possible a pre-Dorian and said to have been a cook, who became tyrant about 650 B.C., to be succeeded (*ca.* 600 B.C.) by Cleisthenes. Under him the nobles were crushed; the Argive elements in the local religious cults were suppressed; and Sicyon entered and took a leading part in a sacred war waged by Delphi to punish the little town of Crisa for offenses against Apollo. Temples were built and a brilliant school of sculptors established.

Herodotus tells a delightful story about Cleisthenes, who had a lovely daughter, Agariste. He invited young men of noble birth from all Hellas to spend a year at his court so that he might pick her a husband. Among those who came were two Athenians, Hippocleides and Megacles, the Alcmaeonid. The former was the favorite, but at the final party of the year he danced so wildly that Cleisthenes was disgusted, and Megacles was chosen for her. From this union were to come the great Athenians—Cleisthenes, Pericles, and Alcibiades.

After the death of Cleisthenes, the tyranny ended. The nobles regained a moderate portion of their former power and Sicyon sank into the position of a second-rate city.

Interstate Relations   The advancing power of the individual city-states was accompanied by the development of definite interstate relations. Peace under normal conditions came to take the place of the warlike status of earlier times; guest friendships were established; and treaties were made and alliances formed. When directed against the Greeks, piracy was frowned upon. Wars were formally proclaimed by heralds, and prisoners of war came to be held for ransom instead of being sold directly into slavery. Practices such as the use of poisoned arrows or the poisoning of wells were regarded as unethical. The large number of small states of almost equal power made war unprofitable, and the custom of arbitration developed, and was often successful. Appeal was made by the warring states to the oracle of Apollo, to neutral communities, or to prominent individuals such as Periander, tyrant of Corinth, for the settlement of questions at issue.

Amphictyonies   Perhaps the greatest force for the development of interstate law, if not its actual origin, was to be found in the religious leagues called *amphictyonies*, "dwellers around." The tribes or cities near an important shrine customarily united for control of the property of the gods and for direction of the festivals and of the fair that accompanied them. The Ionians met on the island of Delos, as described in the Homeric "Hymn to Apollo." The most famous of the religious leagues, however, was the amphictyony of Delphi. Originally composed of twelve tribes around the shrine of Demeter near Thermopylae, it later moved its chief center to Delphi, seat of the god Apollo, and expanded to take in Athens and the Dorian states of the Peloponnesus. Meetings were held in the fall and spring, and each member sent four representatives to discuss matters and two others to cast the vote. Their primary tasks were the supervision of the shrines and the property of the gods, the issuance of directions to the neighboring states for the repair of the roads leading to the shrine, and the protection of pilgrims from molestation and unjust tolls. If necessary, they declared a sacred war against violators of their rules. More famous, however, are their rules of war: though members were at liberty to war with one another, and the council only occasionally served as a board of arbitration, no member might destroy another member or cut it off from running water, whether in wartime or in peacetime.

In the space of two centuries the Hellenic world advanced from the pastoral stage described by Homer into the ordered political and economic life of the city-states. Industry and commerce had come to take their place beside agriculture, while cattle raising had sunk into the background. The king had yielded place to the aristocrats and they in turn to the tyrant or to the new men of wealth. In some states the first evidences of democratic institutions had begun to appear.

9 · The City-States

THE ANATOLIAN CITIES

The leadership that the rich cities of the islands and the Anatolian coast had assumed in the eighth century B.C. (p. 185) remained in their possession to the end of the sixth. The colonial movement eased the pressure of increasing numbers on the land, and the development of industry and commerce afforded the landless new opportunities for employment. The demand for oil and wine enriched the landholders. Wool from the interior, dye-giving mollusks from the sea, metals from the mountains and the Black Sea region, and a bountiful supply of clay furnished a variety of materials for the artisans. In return for these goods of the homeland in demand among the colonists came ample supplies of food.

Goods carried by the overland route through Lydia to Assyria or by the easy sea voyage to Syria and Egypt brought in return the luxuries and the influences of the Orient. Tourists, merchants, and mercenaries flocked to Egypt, Assyria, and Babylon and returned with new goods and new ideas gained by contact with the ancient cultures of the East. The wealth of Phrygia and Lydia made a deep impression upon writers of literature, and Egyptian, Babylonian, and Persian ideas contributed to the growth of philosophy. Oriental influences, especially from Assyria and Syro-Phoenicia, appear strong in the vase paintings, the architecture, and the sculpture of the Ionians. The trammels of the past were cast aside, and for a brief period the Ionian cities were the torchbearers of Greek civilization.

Strongest among the cities was Miletos, especially celebrated for woolen goods and pottery. Its colonies brought it dominance in the Black Sea trade, and alliances in the west, particularly with Sybaris, gave it a strong hold in Italy. Its activity in Egypt and its treaties with Lydia made it the leader in Oriental commerce, and its wise men caused it to be the leader in intellectual advances. Ephesus, famed for its temple

201

of Artemis, Mytilene with its poets and its lawgiver Pittacus, and later Samos under its tyrant Polycrates were in the second rank.

Internal weaknesses were to prove the ruin of Ionia. In almost every city there was civil strife between aristocrats and commoners, oligarchs and democrats. Tyrants seized the power and were overthrown; reprisals were fearful and hatreds undying. The poems of Alcaeus burn with an unquenchable hatred for political enemies. A fierce clinging to the idea of local independence and a desire to dominate neighbors made unity impossible, so that wars between the states were frequent.

An eighth century B.C. invasion of Cimmerians was repelled, but before the organized forces of Lydia, the discordant cities were powerless. In the latter half of the seventh century the kings of Lydia conquered the smaller cities and made a treaty of alliance with Miletos. In the next century Croesus (*ca.* 560–546 B.C.), most celebrated of these rulers, sought to strengthen his position by securing cultural leadership as well as political domination. He invited the wise men of the Aegean to his court, made presents to the Greek shrines, and sought advice from Apollo of Delphi. The pre-eminence of his position in Greek story and the tales of his activities and wealth told by Herodotus witness to the success of his program.

After the Persian conquest of Lydia (p. 166) the Greeks of Anatolia passed into the hands of the victors. Cyrus had made advances to the cities to secure their aid against his Lydian enemy, but they had remained loyal to Croesus. Accordingly, after the capture of Sardis the Persian king refused to grant them favorable terms. Only Miletos was permitted an alliance; the other cities were reduced by armed force, and placed under the rule of local tyrants and under the supervision of provincial governors in the interior.

Polycrates The fall of the Ionian cities on the mainland offered an opportunity that Polycrates, tyrant of the island of Samos, quickly turned to his advantage. He built a great fleet, suppressed all piracy save his own, and brought many islands under his sway. He entered into close political relations with Amosis, king of Egypt, and then with the Persian enemies of the Egyptian king. Although Samian exiles with Spartan aid attempted to break his power, they failed. Polycrates enlarged and beautified the city of Samos. A tunnel was dug through the mountain to bring water to the city; a great temple was erected to the goddess Hera; and a mole was constructed to protect the harbor. Anacreon and many other poets and artists came to his court. Herodotus tells many stories about this man whose wealth, power, and arrogance made a deep impression on his contemporaries. He finally fell victim to his own greed and to Persian treachery; when he crossed to the mainland to consult with the Persian governor about the division of a treasure, he was killed and his body crucified, and Samos was added to the Persian Empire.

The Persian conquest increased for a brief period the economic prosperity of the Anatolian and island cities. The roads that led into the interior were open to them as subjects of the empire, and their industrial and artistic products were sought in the new capitals of the empire. Their soldiers and sailors received occupation in the forces of the Persian kings. Greeks leaders and wise men were welcomed at the court; Darius' personal physician was a Greek, Democedes of Crotone; and the influence of Persian thought may be seen in the history of Greek philosophy. Yet the cities chafed under the yoke, and their effort at revolt resulted in a disaster to themselves which ended their period of leadership and helped to involve the rest of the Hellenic world in war with the Persian Empire.

SPARTA

The leading cities of the mainland during the eighth and seventh centuries were Corinth, Megara (p. 188), and Sparta, all of which took part in colonization. But Sparta followed an imperialistic policy that was to make it unique among Greek states.

The early history of Sparta paralleled that of other Dorian states. The first Dorian conquerors took the hills from Mycenaeans and settled in four villages west of the river Eurotas soon after 1200 B.C. They were strong enough by 1100 to send colonists to the islands of Melos and Crete, where they colonized Lyttos and Gortyn. From the tenth century on the Spartans were living a settled life with no sign of Mycenaean influence. No reliable "history" of Sparta is possible before the eighth century, and even then the facts are obscure and a detailed reconstruction is impossible.

Lacedaemon The traveler from Argos crosses the Parnon range into the foothills of the Arcadian mountains and then goes south until the road drops with comparative swiftness into a low-lying plain, between Mount Parnon on the left and the Taÿgetus range on the right. Down the center winds the Eurotas, giving water to the rich bottomlands of "hollow Lacedaemon." As the valley approaches the sea, the mountains converge until finally the river cuts its way through a narrow gorge. Beyond lies a marshy plain with an inhospitable coast open to wide stretches of the Mediterranean and flanked on either side by capes dangerous to round. Only the island of Cythera gives shelter to the mariner. The Parnon range cuts the valley off from the sea in the east. The inhabitants of Lacedaemon, as a result, were naturally farmers rather than merchants.

Early History   In the eighth century B.C. the Spartans were in contact with Anatolia and Crete through their colonies. The relationship with Crete was close enough to cause Sparta to share in the brilliant revival experienced by that island as trade between it, the Syrian coast, and Egypt was renewed. The Cretans traded in turn with the Greek cities on other islands, with Anatolia, and with the mainland. Cretan priests even came to the mainland to found the Delphic Oracle. Sparta was one of the Oracle's staunchest supporters because of the traditional and hereditary connection, and Spartans were frequent petitioners at the shrine.

The Rise of Sparta   Also in the eighth century B.C. Sparta took the village of Amyclae and expanded into the lower valley of the Eurotas. The new village took its place as one of the five *oboi*, or divisions, of the Spartan state. The *oboi* organization replaced the older tribal units and became the basis for a new political and military organization. A common religious and political center was developed to unify this unusual *polis*, or city-state.

The conquered land in the valley was called civic land and was divided up among the citizens in lots that descended regularly to the oldest son. A few nobles received larger shares than the rest. Hunger for land with increasing population in the restricted area drove the Spartans in the late eighth and early seventh centuries B.C. over the Taÿgetus range into Messenia. There they found a mixture of Achaeans and Dorians, who put up a vigorous resistance that centered around Mount Ithome. According to tradition, the struggle lasted nineteen years before the Messenians were defeated. Some escaped and found refuge at Zancle in Sicily, henceforth known as Messana; the rest were reduced to serfdom. Their lands were divided up into lots and given to the Spartan families. Around the civic lands so acquired and distributed, the Spartans conquered or colonized a series of towns which possessed local independence and whose citizens were known as the *perioeci*.

Early Culture   In the early revival of culture Sparta played a prominent part. The iron mines of the Taÿgetus range and a bountiful supply of clay led to a prosperous development of industry in the various towns. In spite of the natural handicaps commercial relations were established with the outer world, and Sparta came into close touch with Sardis and with Samos. Many exquisite ivories, implying trade with Assyria and Egypt and showing distinct Oriental influences in their carving, have been found by the excavators. The city built a fine council hall, a magnificient temple to Artemis Orthia, and a temple of wood covered with brass plates to "Athena of the Brazen House." Sculptors of reputation carved in wood and stone. Festivals attracted men from all over the Greek world. Terpander of Lesbos and Thaletas of Crete introduced the seven-string lyre and the choral dance. Alcman, said to have come from Sardis but more probably a native Spartan, wrote beautiful odes for the maidens to sing in their processions. Sparta was well on its way to cultural leadership in the west when its cultural advance was suddenly halted.

The Messenian Revolt About 650 B.C. the Messenian serfs revolted under the leadership of their hero Aristomenes. Ithome, fortified again, held out for twenty years. At the crisis, Tyrtaeus, the last Spartan poet of merit, appeared. With vigorous war songs he restored Spartan courage, and as their general he led the Spartans to victory. When the war produced a political and economic crisis in Sparta, he allayed the incipient civil strife with a brilliant poem, "Eunomia." A band of malcontents left to found Tarentum in Italy, and order was temporarily restored.

But the conquest of Messenia did not satisfy the land hunger of many Spartans, nor did the new colony drain off all malcontents, for the new conquests were unequally shared. Continuing internal strife produced the reformer Lycurgus who, with the aid of the two kings, promulgated a constitution given him by the Delphic Oracle. Called the Great Rhetra, this constitution established the *gerousia*, a council of thirty, and the *apella*, an assembly of citizens which was to hear and vote on matters important to the people. During the Messenian wars a magistrate had been chosen from each of the five *oboi* to substitute for the kings while they were absent on campaign. These officials, the *ephors*, were retained in the constitution to function as executives of the villages and assistants to the kings.

Lycurgus' reforms, if they were meant to give more voice to the ordinary Spartan, were soon nullified. A clause was added to the Great Rhetra which permitted the ephors and *gerousia* to "decline to entertain" any "crooked proposal" of the *apella*. The kings, too, lost power in the seventh and sixth centuries. The ephorate was made elective and these magistrates superseded the kings as the executives of the state. The kings were reduced to membership on the *gerousia* and to acting as commanders-in-chief of the Spartan army. They could even be impeached by the ephors, if suitable omens were observed.

Still, Sparta's evolution into an armed camp was slow. Industry and trade continued to flourish until after 550 B.C., when the Athenians and other traders began capturing the Spartan markets. As their economy declined, the Spartans became more isolated in thought and more rigid in their social and political life. But the classic picture of the hide-bound Spartan state belongs to the fifth and fourth centuries. Sparta's society and institutions in this later period can be explored in detail.

The Helots At the bottom of the social ladder were the helots, who were owned by the state and who could not be sold, transferred, or freed except by its action. They were assigned to the lands of the Spartans and were ordered to pay the owners a fixed quota each year,

the balance accruing to themselves. Improvement of the land was therefore to their advantage, and some became fairly prosperous. Some were
called to attend the Spartans on their campaigns, and others served as
light-armed troops in the army. In return for meritorious service they
might be freed by the state and even given an inferior form of citizenship.

    For the most part, however, the helots had few real rights. The
state watched them jealously; young men in training for the army
were sent out to spy on them; any helot who appeared dangerous
might be slain forthwith, and in times of danger whole companies were
led off and massacred. The treatment they received tended to degrade
them in mind and body. It is said that the Spartans compelled them to
become drunk so that the citizen youth might be impressed with the
bestiality of drunkenness. The helots greatly outnumbered the Spartans,
and the constant fear of revolt kept the Spartan army always on the alert
and for a long period always near home.

    The *Perioeci* The *perioeci*, or "dwellers around," occupied a
more favorable position. They were at least citizens of their own communities, where under Spartan supervision they governed themselves,
although their foreign relations were entirely under Spartan control.
They paid tribute to Sparta, served as heavy-armed troops in the army,
and were employed to prevent helots from escaping. Most of the land
in their communities belonged to Spartans, but, as Spartans abandoned
it after 550 B.C., they devoted themselves to industry, particularly to
the manufacture of iron products and of woolen goods, the dye for
which came from Cythera. Their locks and keys were renowned
throughout the Greek world. Not subject to Spartan restrictions, many
of them became wealthy. The Spartan expulsion of foreigners, which
did not affect them, gave them a monopoly of the local market. As a
result, they were for the most part loyal to Sparta, even in the days of
her decadence.

    The Spartans Ruling over these subject peoples were the citizens
of Sparta, who called themselves equals, though actually divided into
nobles and commons. Both classes, however, passed through the same
system of training and were subject to the same rules.

    The first requisite to citizenship was Spartan parentage on both
sides. Immediately after birth a child was presented to the elders, who
decided whether or not it should be reared. If deformed or evidently
a weakling, it was exposed on the slopes of the mountains. To the
age of seven the boys remained under the control of the mothers and
nurses, but thereafter they were brought up by the state. They were
formed into companies and slept in barracks, where their only bed
was a bundle of reeds gathered by themselves; they were restricted to
one coverlet and one garment. Their time was spent in continual drill-

ing and exercising, each company being under the direction of a youth of over twenty. Given but scant meals, they were supposed to augment them by theft. If they were caught stealing, they were severely punished for being so clumsy as to be detected. Thus they were taught endurance under hardship, skill in foraging, and expertness in military tactics. At the festival of Artemis Orthia, an ancient religious rite of flogging was developed into a test of endurance. The boys learned to read, write, and do simple sums, and they were given passages to recite from Homer and the war songs of Tyrtaeus and other poets. Dancing and music were stressed. The elder citizens regarded it as their special task to supervise the boys, and they chastised them for the slightest infraction of the rules.

At the age of twenty the young men were enrolled in mess clubs, which were lifelong associations. Membership in the clubs depended to some extent on residence. Votes were taken, and a single adverse vote threw the youth off the citizen rolls. They were supposed to marry, but were forbidden to see their wives save by stealth; and their enemies insisted there were Spartans with children who had never seen their wives by daylight.

At the age of thirty, according to Xenophon, the men in good standing, the equals, received citizenship. Henceforth they might live at home and vote in the assembly. They were, however, required to eat the evening meal always at the public tables, where the chief dish was the famous black broth that none but a Spartan would eat. They did not engage in any industry, not even supervision of their family estates. They had to be eternally ready for the call to war and hence could not leave the neighborhood of Sparta save by order or special permission. Their days were spent in exercise or drill. Only on the march were the rules relaxed, and it has been said that for the Spartans war was a relief from the horrors of peace. At the age of sixty the men were released from the system and allowed to live at home and in peace. They spent their remaining years in supervising the youths.

The income of the Spartans depended entirely upon payments in kind from the helots on their lands. Not only did all forms of economic activity come to be forbidden to them but trade and industry were effectively checked by the monetary situation. Since the monetary system had developed before the appearance of gold and silver coinage, the law still restricted the Spartans to the use of the iron money of earlier times; in fact even possession of the precious metals was forbidden. After the appearance of gold and silver coins, the worthlessness of the Spartan iron coins reduced exchange practically to a barter basis.

From such income as the Spartan received, he was required to make a contribution to the expense of the public meals, failure to comply resulting in the loss of civic rights. Though the land passed regularly into the hands of the eldest son, it was regarded as a family possession; and if it were sufficiently large, contributions were provided for the younger sons as well. Women could inherit in default of male heirs, and marriages with Spartan heiresses or adoptions into heirless families provided for some. Otherwise they lost their standing as citizens. Because of these conditions there was a distinct tendency among the Spartans to restrict the size of their families. Not only failure to make their contribution but defeat in the vote in the clubs, infraction of the training rules, or cowardice in war resulted in the loss of citizenship. Thus there appeared in Sparta a class of "inferiors" whose status was ill-defined. The inferiors added to the dangers surrounding the citizen body.

By the Second Messenian War (*ca.* 650 B.C.) the phalanx was developed in which the heavy-armed hoplite was used to the fullest advantage. The hoplite wore helmet, breastplate, and greaves, protected himself with a round shield, and carried sword and lance. Men marched in solid formation, shoulder to shoulder, and in files of varying depths, usually of eight men. Cohesion and weight gave this phalanx force. Through their training the Spartans gained not only unity but a facility in maneuvers that made their phalanx superior to those of the Greek states who copied their organization but not their discipline.

The girls remained at home, but they passed through a series of physical exercises and competitions calculated to make them what the state desired them to be—fit mothers of soldiers. They, too, were taught the meaning of Spartan discipline. The Spartan mother's instruction to her son was "come back with your shield or on it." After a terrible defeat, those whose sons had been killed adorned themselves with garlands while the mothers of the survivors put on mourning.

The Spartan system produced a race of hardy and skillful warriors. For a period their athletic exercises made them leaders in the games, but when men from other states began to specialize, they lost their pre-eminence. Their courage in warfare and their simplicity in life won for them the admiration of later ages. Sparta needed no walls save its sons. On the other hand, Spartans were ignorant, narrow in mind and character, venal and untrustworthy away from home, and knew no means of control save the force of arms.

The greatest danger to the Spartan oligarchic system was in the decline of the equals. Losses in war, the tendency to restrict the number of sons to one, the union of family possessions through marriage, and the rigidity of the rules produced a steady decrease in the population. In 500 B.C. the Spartans could put an army of eight thousand citizens in the field; two centuries later their numbers had dwindled to a few hundred.

Government   The Spartan government of the fifth and fourth centuries B.C. has been called a *gerontocracy*, or government of old men, because its chief magistrates, and particularly the council, were ordinarily chosen from men past sixty who had completed their military requirements.

The ephors, or overseers, were elected annually, one from each of the five *oboi*, and served as the executive board of the state. They supervised the youths, enforced the laws, and watched over the kings, the citizens, the helots, and the *perioeci*. They could order the deaths of members of the latter two classes without trial. They called and presided over the *gerousia* and the *apella*, introduced measures before either body, and dismissed the sessions. They had final judicial power over civil cases. Two of their number accompanied the kings on military campaigns and took note of royal orders and actions. The ephors could not interfere during a campaign, but could fine the king on his return to Sparta or even force him to abdicate.

Sparta's two kings had at one time enjoyed supreme power, though one of the royal houses was considered junior to the other. Kingship did not necessarily descend to the eldest son in either family, but if a king of the Eurypontid line died, another male of the same family was elected king by the *apella*. The same procedure applied to the Agiad family. Ordinarily a king served for life—unless deposed by the ephors. In the fifth century and afterward the Spartan kings were restricted to three functions: they were priests of Zeus, commanders of the armies, and members of the *gerousia*. A king had a measure of power only outside Sparta, when commanding an army.

The *gerousia*, in addition to the kings, consisted of twenty-eight men over sixty years of age. Members were chosen by acclamation in the *apella* and served for life. The *gerousia* was the real power in the state. It prepared all measures for submission to the *apella*, and could, if it desired, veto the latter's action. It received and sent ambassadors, tried criminal cases affecting the citizens, assisted the ephors in training the youth and supervising the citizens, and passed on the right of any child born in Sparta to live.

The *apella* was made up of all Spartan citizens over thirty in full possession of civic rights. A passive body without initiative, it acted only on measures submitted to it by the *gerousia* and it elected the ephors.

The Peloponnesian League   In the early sixth century B.C. the Spartans started again on a career of conquest. Argos was their first enemy. This city, which had taken the territory and the place of Mycenae, had enjoyed a brief spell of power shortly after 700 B.C. through its king Pheidon. He conquered the neighboring states and extended the Aeginetan system of weights and measures throughout the Peloponnesus, but he failed in an attempt to consolidate his power by securing presidency of the Olympic games. Under his weak successors the city rapidly declined. The Spartans defeated Argos and took from it Cynuria on the Aegean coast and Cythera. When after this success they tried to overcome the Arcadian cities of Tegea and Mantinea, they failed, and their failure resulted in a shift of policy.

In place of further conquest the Spartans began to effect a system of alliances which resulted by 505 B.C. in the creation of the Peloponnesian League, into which were brought all the states of the Peloponnesus save Argos and the little Achaean cities on the northern coast. Corinth, prosperous under the rule of its merchants, who had secured control after the death of Periander (p. 199), and Megara, to which a favorable position on the isthmus and colonies in both the east and the west had brought wealth, were both included. The first recorded action of the league was an invasion of Attica under the command of King Cleomenes (p. 220). The attempt failed and the party of Cleisthenes expelled the Lacedaemonians.

NORTHERN GREECE

Northern Greece, divided by the mountains into a series of little pockets, contained a number of tribes and states that played no role in the early history of ancient Greece. Epirus and the western areas were still in a state of barbarism in the sixth century B.C. The only important place in Epirus was Dodona, in which there was an oracle where Zeus gave advice to men through the rustling of oak leaves. Phocis gained its only renown from the presence of Delphi. The rich plain of Thessaly supported a number of horse-raising nobles who lived by the work of their serfs. Boeotia was of greater importance. This fertile plain was occupied and prosperous in the Mycenaean age. During the time of the Dorian invasion, there was a fresh incursion of invaders, the Boeotians. Thereafter a number of small cities developed in the region, but no one was strong enough to compel them to unite, nor was there sufficient economic or military incentive.

Thebes, situated at the crossroads where the ways parted to go to Delphi, to the isthmus, and to Athens, became the largest community and the center of the league, which held the cities loosely together. The southern cities of the plain protected themselves from Thebes by maintaining close connections with Athens. The region was agricultural, and the Boeotians were celebrated in ancient literature as stupid farmers. Nevertheless they produced Hesiod in the eighth century B.C.; Corinna, a poetess whose works have not survived; and her contemporary, the great Pindar, at the end of the sixth.

The Charioteer of Delphi. This bronze statue commemorated a victory in the chariot races by the tyrant of Gela. It was dedicated at Delphi in 474 B.C. (Greek Press and Information Service)

The cities of Chalcis and Eretria on the island of Euboea are worthy of mention in passing. Their colonies in the west and in the northern Aegean and the renown of their metal products raised them in the eighth century to high rank. Shortly after 700 B.C. they waged a famous civil war over the Lelantine plain which lay between them, a war that involved most of the commercial states in the Aegean. However, they later lost their position in the west to Corinth, and in the east to Athens.

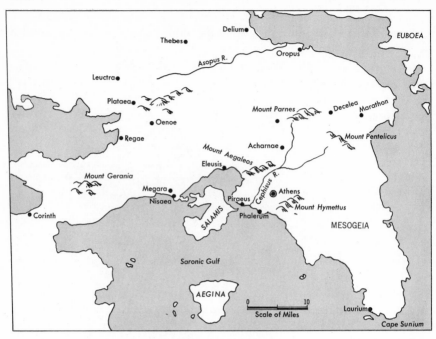

Attica, ca. 500 B.C.

ATHENS

Attica   Attica is like a promontory jutting out into the Aegean. It is a mountainous land about one thousand square miles in area. About one-fourth is arable, and the arable land is for the most part divided among the four plains—Marathon, Eleusis, the Mesogeia, and Athens. The hills produced wood for charcoal; the plains, grains and olives; the slopes of Hymettus, flowers for honey. Pentelicus was a mountain of pure white marble; silver and lead were mined at Laurium; and the clay deposit for pottery in Attica was the finest in the Greek world.

The Synoecism   Among the many small cities that Attica once contained, Athens was naturally pre-eminent. Its plain was the largest and richest and contained the best clay. It was protected by ridges through which there were openings to the other valleys, and it commanded Pentelicus and Laurium. Moreover, the Acropolis was the strongest center of defense in the entire region. The wide, sweeping bay of Phalerum was well suited for the merchant of early times who pulled his boat up on the shore. Hard by, the little promontory of Peiraeus furnished landlocked harbors that needed little improvement to be adapted to the use of larger boats and warships when they appeared. It was almost inevitable that the land should be united under the leadership of Athens.

Though tradition ascribed the synoecism, or union, to Theseus, memories of later wars between the cities indicate that it was a gradual process not completed until the eighth century B.C., although local feeling survived into the sixth century B.C. At whatever time the process took place, it is evident that most of the people remained in their villages, while the nobles, moving to Athens for political and social reasons, tended to center their possessions in the plain around the city. At the same time Athens recognized the local religious customs of the villages of Attica, raised some to the level of state festivals, and bound many others closely to the divinities of the city. In this way the whole area was knit closely into the city-state of Athens.

The people of Athens claimed that their ancestors had always lived in the land. This simply indicates that Attica never suffered violent invasion. It was first inhabited by men of Aegean stock. During the early Mycenaean period it received as immigrants a branch of the Achaean group called the old Ionians. A palace rose on the Acropolis, which was fortified by walls of heavy stones, remains of which are still to be seen. In many places in Attica beehive tombs of the period are found. The Dorians did not take Athens, but during their invasion of the Peloponnesus it was a haven for those who fled from their homes. From it men moved into the islands and across the Aegean Sea to the area later called Ionia.

The Dipylon Age, *ca.*1000 B.C. The age that followed 1200 B.C. in Athens is best known for the fine funerary pottery found near the Dipylon gate of the later walls; it is geometric in style and bears pictures of men on horseback, in chariots, and going to sea in warships. During this period Athens was ruled by kings. They were assisted by treasurers, whose name, *colacretae* (butchers), recalled the time when their income consisted largely of a share of the booty in war and of the sacrifices at festivals. Around the king in council gathered the heads of the noble families, and there was probably an assembly of the people.

Before their entrance into Attica the Ionians had been divided into four tribes. This subdivision was kept, and the tribes became territorial divisions of the *polis*. Smaller organizations of a military, social, and religious nature were the phratries, or brotherhoods, groups of families that claimed common descent and were accustomed to worship their common ancestors and fight together in war. Since such groups would naturally cling together in the settlement of the land, the phratries were also, in a measure, territorial. They kept lists of their members, recognized the legitimacy of children, preserved the citizen rolls, and took care of their mutual interests in court.

The landowning nobles, who called themselves Eupatridae, "well-fathered," were divided into family groups, called *genē*, with strong feelings of relationship. These groups were primarily religious organizations meeting for the worship of the family gods and ancestors, but they acquired much social power and control over family lands and customs. There was a great deal of rivalry between some of them. In the small valleys and on the hillsides dwelt the independent small-farming class or *georgoi*. The artisans, merchants, and fishermen were grouped as *demiurgoi*, "public workers."

The Aristocracy   With the unification and development of the city, the power of the king declined. First the nobles chose one of their number to be *polemarch*, commander of the army. Later another official called an *archon* was added to stand guard over property rights. The kingship was left with merely religious power; and it was changed into an office to which at first members of the royal family, the Medontidae, were elected for life, then for ten years, and finally, in 683 B.C., it was made an annual office for which all nobles were eligible. The archon thereupon became the chief civil magistrate.

With the development of commerce and the expansion of the state during the seventh century B.C. more judges were needed, and six *thesmothetae*, "guardians of the established customs," were elected annually. These men were chosen and advised by the council of nobles. The council met in the market place for ordinary deliberations, but when it assembled as a murder court, it convened on the hill of the Areopagus near the shrine of the Furies. Hence it was called the Council of Areopagus. It exercised the same general supervision of the citizens as did the *gerousia* in Sparta.

The army was composed of the four tribal regiments commanded by the *phylobasileis*, or tribe kings, who were nobles.

Military and financial exigencies during the seventh century B.C. led to a redivision of the people into census classes according to their wealth and according to the stage of development of timocratic government in Athens. Those whose estates were large enough to enable them to keep horses were called *hippeis*, "knights." They were probably all nobles, and served as officers in the state and army, furnishing such cavalry as the state possessed. The commoners whose farms were worked by oxen were called *zeugitae* "teamsters." They served in the infantry. The rest—laborers, renters, and artisans—were called *thetes*. At about the same time and for the same reasons the state was divided into forty-eight local units called *naucraries*, whose purpose was to collect funds to provide horsemen for the army and ships for the nascent fleet.

These political movements were the result of a gradual economic awakening that followed the economic revolution of the eighth and

Archaic Horses in the Acropolis Museum. (Greek Press and Information Service)

seventh centuries B.C. For a long time Athens had made but little progress. Land was limited and industry undeveloped or purely local. Aegina, Corinth, Megara, and Chalcis dominated the commercial field. The Athenian nobles, however, grasping for land and striving for wealth, followed the example of the Ionians in the production of oil and wine and sold their produce at famine prices. They entered into commercial activities, took Salamis from Megara, and founded Sigeum on the Hellespont to secure a share in the Black Sea trade. The last act led to a war with Mytilene on the island of Lesbos, which was settled in favor of the Athenians by the arbitral decision of Periander of Corinth.

The cost of the wars and the rise in prices attendant upon the growth of vines and olive trees in place of grain bore heavily on the lower classes. Many of the farmers of *zeugitae* census labored under heavy mortgages or if they failed to pay lost their lands and were reduced to the status of *hectemoroi*, "sixth parters," or tenants who paid the sixth part of their produce as rent.[1] Members of the thete class who failed to make their payments of rent or loans were sold into slavery for debt. The popular discontent that arose from these practices made Athens ripe for tyranny or reform.

Cylon   In the strife for power and wealth, factions arose among the nobles and feuds among the great families. One young noble, Cylon,

[1] It is not certain whether the *hectemoroi* paid a rent of one-sixth or of five-sixths.

married the daughter of Theagenes, tyrant of Megara, and with the latter's assistance tried to become tyrant of Athens in 632 or 628 B.C. His failure was due chiefly to the opposition of the Alcmaeonid family, headed by Megacles. This nobleman, however, committed the error of putting some of his enemies to death in a sacrilegious manner, whereupon he and his family were accursed and exiled, and his descendants never fully escaped from the curse.

Draco Commercial development, legal confusion, and such feuds as that between the followers of Megacles and Cylon made a clearer conception of the laws necessary. Elsewhere, under the influence of Apollo of Delphi, laws were being written down during this period, and in 621 B.C. Draco was elected *thesmothete* with powers and instructions to record the ancestral customs. Little of his code has survived save an undeserved reputation for severity. This was due chiefly to the fact that the theft of food, which was scarce in Attica, received the death penalty. The Draconian laws of homicide, however, were exceedingly enlightened, probably because of Delphic influence, and survived into later times. The various kinds of murder were defined and proper penalties were affixed; rites of purification were established for accidental or justifiable homicide, and the killer was protected from the vengeance of the dead man's kin.

While the recording of the law secured a more balanced justice, it did not correct the fundamental economic evils of the period. Through debt or dispossession the peasants were steadily losing their lands and becoming serfs or slaves. The situation was aggravated for the debtor class by the scarcity of food, the introduction of coinage, and the high rates of interest. As a result the army was ruined. Civil strife broke out, and in the confusion Mytilene took over the Hellespontine settlement, and Megara regained Salamis. The aristocrats turned back to a repressive agricultural policy and forbade anyone to mention Salamis.

Solon In the crisis the first of the city's statesmen, Solon—poet, general, and lawgiver—came into prominence. With his poems he stirred the Athenians to victory over Megara. He, like Tyrtaeus, wrote poems on the civil situation, and in 594 B.C. he was elected chief archon with plenary power. The reforms he carried through were the first step toward Athenian greatness, and they deserve careful attention.

In his attempt to solve the economic problems, he canceled all debts secured by the land or by the person of the debtor. Those who had been enslaved for debt were freed; those who had been sold outside of Attica were redeemed by the state, and slavery for debt was henceforth forbidden. This much Solon did for the peasantry. Over the fields already in the hands of the nobles he had no power, and he refused to take the revolutionary steps necessary to redivide the land. However, he did much to aid the poor, especially by forbidding the exportation of foodstuffs and by encouraging the production of olive oil, "nurturer of children." To develop Athenian industry, he gave citizenship to aliens who would settle in Athens as skilled craftsmen. Tradition says that he provided that every man must teach his son a trade, or the son would be exempted from supporting his father in old age. He established a coinage system on the Euboic standard; this freed Athens from Aeginetan influence and brought it into line with Corinth and Chalcis, and created a mild and healthy inflation.

Solon's reforms increased the power of the individual over the family by giving the property owner the right to will his land in default of direct heirs, and by providing that any citizen might go to the legal assistance of another, regardless of family or phratry.

In the constitutional field Solon was equally moderate, but he prepared the way for the later democracy. He clearly defined the census classes. To the first belonged the very rich whose estates produced five hundred measures of grain or oil. A few special privileges and duties were reserved to them. The second class, the three-hundred-bushel men, called *hippeis*, "knights," served in the cavalry. From these classes the higher officers were chosen. The two-hundred-bushel men, *zeugitae*, chiefly small farmers, served as hoplites in the army and as members of a new council he created. The landless and poor, still called *thetes*, gained the vital right of membership in the assembly and the court. The most important result of Solon's definition of the classes was the possibility that a prosperous man might rise to greater power, regardless of his origin.

The archons and thesmothetae (usually called the nine archons) were henceforth elected by the assembly, and when their term was ended they became members of the Council of the Areopagus. Although this body had lost its deliberative and administrative powers, great honor was paid to it, nevertheless, as the ancient murder court and as guardian of the laws and customs. A new *boule* (council) of four hundred was established, one hundred from each tribe chosen by lot from the first three census classes, which supervised the administration and prepared measures for submission to the assembly. To the latter body, called the *ecclesia*, all classes were admitted. It passed on measures submitted to it by the council and elected the magistrates. Solon added a new institution which was to be the cornerstone of the democracy, the *heliaea*, or popular supreme court. To it all citizens over thirty were eligible. Its members might hear appeals from the magistrates and compel the officers to render an accounting of their administration.

Peisistratus Although Solon's reforms tided over the crisis, they did not end the political and economic struggles. After he left Athens, hated as a moderate by both sides, factional strife broke out afresh

An Archaic Kore Now
in the Acropolis Mu-
seum. (Greek Press and
Information Service)

along social and, to some extent, local lines. The aristocratic landowners of the Plain, led by Lycurgus and Miltiades, found vigorous rivals in the merchants, artisans, and fishermen of the Shore. The Alcmaeonid, Megacles, who had married Agariste of Sicyon, came to the head of the latter party, an indication of the future policy of that family. The small farmers, charcoal burners, and miners of the back country, the Hill, were organized and led by a young noble, Peisistratus, who had given evidence of great ability in a war with Megara. The rivalry was so keen that in some years no archons could be elected. Finally, in 560 B.C., Peisistratus won and made himself tyrant. A hostile combination drove him out; but a marriage alliance with Megacles gave him the support of the Shore and he returned. Expelled again, he went north, gained control of silver mines in Thrace, and returned with mercenaries. Thereafter he ruled peacefully until 527 B.C., when he was succeeded by his son Hippias assisted by Hipparchus, the latter's brother.

Work of the Tyrants The tyrants carried on the work begun by Solon. Since most of the nobles were in exile, their lands were confiscated. It was distributed among the peasantry, who were assisted in the development of olive orchards. With this came prosperity to the farming class. Ionian artisans and artists were encouraged to settle in Athens and ply their trades. Coincident with the increase in the supply of olive oil was the production of the fine black-figured pottery, followed before the end of the tyranny by the beautiful red-figured ware. Many of the painters signed their names to their work, names which, in some cases, indicate the appearance of alien craftsmen.

A peristyle was built around the temple of Athena, and a temple to Olympian Zeus was started on a grand scale. The great Panathenaean games held every four years and the Eleusinian mysteries were raised to national importance. The city festival in honor of the rural Dionysus was instituted, and Thespis won the first recorded prize in the drama. In the reign of Hippias, Anacreon and other poets visited Athens. Fine statues of maidens, *korai*, Ionian in style, were set up on the Acropolis. The tyrants settled additional colonies on the Hellespont, one under the leadership of Miltiades. Friendly relations were cultivated with the neighboring states, and Athens prospered. The tyrants did not interfere with the working of the Solonian constitution beyond seeing that their

The Calf-bearer, Late Archaic, ca. 570 B.C. Acropolis Museum. (Greek Press and Information Service)

partisans were elected to the offices of state and maintaining a rigid control over finance.

In 514 B.C. a private quarrel led to a conspiracy and the murder of Hipparchus. The movement failed; the leaders, Harmodius and Aristogeiton, were killed, and Hippias was driven to violence to defend himself. The ultimate result, however, was his overthrow. The Alcmaeonid family, which had been exiled during the previous disturbances, drove Hippias out of Athens. They were aided by the Spartans, who were urged into this interference by the Delphic Oracle. The Alcmaeonids had generously rebuilt Apollo's temple and the god, or his minions, took this means to repay them. The Spartan Cleomenes hoped to add Athens to the Peloponnesian League (p. 210), but Isagoras whom he supported lost in the ensuing struggle for control of Athens, and the Spartans were expelled.

The tyrants contributed much to the development of Athens. By the confiscation and redivision of lands they dealt a death blow to the power of the aristocracy and established a vigorous and prosperous peasantry. Commerce and industry advanced and the cornerstone of the structure of Athenian arts and letters was laid. The prosperity their rule brought to the city caused many people to desire their restoration. Nevertheless the unconstitutional character of the tyrannical position, the collection of direct taxes inconsistent with the Greek idea of freedom, the use of mercenaries to overawe the citizens and to maintain their power, and the violence of the last years of Hippias—all combined to create in patriotic Athenians a hatred of tyranny which made restoration of the Peisistratids impossible. To such a pitch did this hatred develop that the tyrannicides Harmodius and Aristogeiton, who had led the revolt, were celebrated as national heroes.

Cleisthenes   The nobles, led by Isagoras, regained control in Athens and to make their political position safe began to strike off the rolls all who did not belong to the ancient phratries and had been made citizens by Solon and Peisistratus. Cleisthenes, the Alcmaeonid leader, defeated Isagoras in 508 B.C. in a victory notable in that it led to a reorganization of Athens and to the further development of the democracy. He retained power until 505, when his new constitution went into effect.

The problems Cleisthenes endeavored to solve were threefold: first, he sought to bring to an end the local rivalries between the Plain, the Shore, and the Hill that had caused so much trouble during earlier generations; second, he wished to break the political power of the great families of the aristocracy, which they exercised through their influence over the peasantry, and to make secure the citizenship grants that had been attacked; third, he planned to prevent such party rivalries as had made possible the rise of Peisistratus and his own strife with Isagoras.

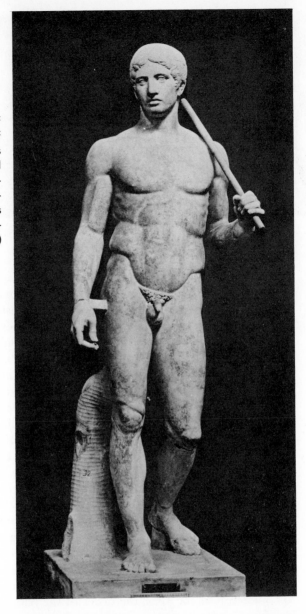

Reproduction (Cast) of the Roman Copy of Polyclitus' Doryphorus (Spear-bearer), Second Half of the Fifth Century B.C. Found at Pompeii, now in the Naples Museum. (The Metropolitan Museum of Art)

Cleisthenes took as the basic unit for the Athenian state the demes, or villages, which were scattered over Attica, and so as to have units in Athens corresponding to them he divided the city into several wards. Each deme was given a local organization with a demarch at its head to conduct local government and to keep the roll of the citizens. All free residents of Attica were included on this roll, with the result that the

Base of a Statue Showing Wrestlers in Relief, About 510 B.C. (Greek Press and Information Service)

power of the great families and of the ancient *gene* over the citizen body was forever shattered. In typical Greek fashion, however, a man so enrolled remained a member of his deme, even though he might later move to another; and in the local assemblies of these demes the Athenians received fundamental training in self-government. The demes, over one hundred in number, were combined into thirty organizations called *trittyes*, or thirds. These *trittyes*, approximately equal in population, were combined to form ten tribes, each containing sections of the parties of the Plain, the Shore, and the Hill. Thus local factionalism was made impossible, and the influence of the nobles over the people in their districts became of little avail. The tribes later served as the basis for military and financial levies. Each had a definite political and religious organization, the latter centering around one of the heroes of Athens.

The *boule* was perforce reorganized. Each tribe chose by lot from the whole body of its citizens fifty men, roughly apportioned among the demes according to their size. The council was thus increased to five hundred. Since such a body was unwieldy in administrative affairs, the fifty men from each tribe were constituted as an executive committee for one-tenth of the year, the order of the tribes being determined by lot. These committeemen were termed *prytaneis* and the term of their service a *prytany*. They lived at state expense in the council house, and some of their number were required to be always on hand. They dealt directly with ordinary routine matters. More important measures they submitted to the whole *boule*, and in anything that required general action they drew up a bill for submission to the *ecclesia*.

The Theater at Epidaurus with a Modern Audience Watching an Ancient Greek Tragedy. This is the only Greek theater left with the circular orchestra in its original form. (Greek Press and Information Service)

The magistrates who were collectively called "the nine archons" were retained and elected from the upper three classes. Each had a specific duty. For example, the king-archon was in charge of religious festivals, the polemarch concerned himself with the army and its supplies, and the treasury archon (who had to be chosen from the wealthiest class) was in charge of state funds, the budget, and the expenditures.

Ten generals (*strategoi*) were elected to supplement these magistracies, one from each of the ten new tribes. This unusual and artificial tribal division served a military and political purpose. Each tribe called up troops, and originally each tribe elected its *strategos*. In later years the board of *strategoi* were to exchange places with the archons and become the executive board of Athens. By that time the office was open to any citizen who owned land in Attica, no matter what his tribe, on the basis of an annual election by the people, and he could be re-elected indefinitely.

To prevent further civil strife, Cleisthenes is said to have instituted the peculiar custom known as ostracism. Once a year a vote was taken. The issue had to be important enough to bring out six thousand votes, a number apparently considered as comprising a quorum of the voting population and much greater than the size of any ordinary assembly. The voters wrote the name of any man they considered dangerous to the state on a potsherd, or *ostracon*. The man against whom the plurality of votes was cast was sent into honorable exile for ten years without confiscation of property. As a matter of fact, this powerful weapon was seldom employed except in the period after the battle of Marathon (p. 245).

The democracy was, however, not yet fully established. Many of the higher offices were still restricted to the upper classes; in others the poor could not afford to serve without pay. Conservative forces were strong in the Areopagus, which continued as a powerful body in the state. But the new arrangement of demes and tribes brought to an end the strife of the sections; the institution of ostracism served as an effective check against party divisions that might prove dangerous to peace; and the general right of participation in deme affairs, in the *ecclesia*, and in the *boule* laid the foundations of the later democracy.

Although civil strife had ended, Cleisthenes was forced to defend himself from outsiders, when Cleomenes, hoping to restore Isagoras' party, led an army of the Peloponnesian League into Attica, and Thebes and Chalcis sought the opportunity to crush the rising power of Athens. Athens even appealed to Persia for aid in this emergency. But dissension

The Temple of Poseidon at Paestum. This temple in the Doric style is the best preserved of all Greek temples. (Photograph by Mary Francis Gyles, reproduced by Frank D. Grande)

between Cleomenes and the other league forces sent the Peloponnesians home, and the other cities were decisively defeated.

Cleisthenes had, in fact, completed the work of the century of reform. The power of the aristocracy had been broken; moreover, new political powers and the control over their leaders provided by the *heliaea* and the institution of ostracism rendered the peasantry and the industrial and commercial classes in the city secure in their position. With the bases of friction removed, popular discontent was brought to an end, and Athens was ready to forge ahead.

Conclusion By 500 B.C. Sparta, strengthened by its army and its league, and Athens, united and content save for a group of sympathizers with the exiled tyrants, had emerged as powerful states ready to meet the coming struggle with Persia.

10 · The Greek Renaissance

HE POLITICAL AND ECONOMIC PROCESSES OF THE
period 800–500 B.C. were accompanied and affected by a corresponding development in religion, art, literature, and thought—
the Greek Renaissance. All the cultural phases of life, developing
or being transformed to meet the growing needs of the people, felt
the new influences—the rising power of the city-state, the greater importance of the lower and middle classes, and the increase of knowledge
produced by the colonial movement and by trade and contact with
Oriental civilizations.

RELIGION

It has been said that Greek religion existed to make men at home in
the world. This religion penetrated every part of life and filled all that
it touched with spiritual power. All nature was divine. Spirits lived in the
trees and the flowers, in the springs, the streams, and the sea. The sky,
sun, moon, and stars, the light breezes of morning and evening, the
winds and the thundercloud—all told men of their divine elements.
Similarly, all of the daily acts of man—his work and his play—had
religious significance. The family, as its members gathered about the
sacred hearth fire, while the ancestors hovered in spirit around, was
conscious of its supernatural protectors. At the larger political and
social gatherings the gods were always present.

To these spirits, great and small, men turned for companionship
in their joy and for comfort in their sorrow. The evil spirits that existed
and brought fear to the hearts of men were given pleasant names or
beautiful forms to avert their wrath. Fear was banished by beauty,
and love for the gods and pleasure in their worship became the central
theme of Greek religion. Men felt comfortable enough with their gods
to strike "bargains" with them, paying the spirit for its assistance in daily
needs or emergencies.

The Gods of Olympus   Certain divinities were universal. These, connected with the larger aspects of nature and of life, were recognized as the great gods, the dwellers on Olympus. Zeus was in origin the sky god of the Indo-Europeans, wielder of the thunderbolt, sender of rain, king and father of gods and men. Hera, his wife, was the queenly embodiment of wife and mother. Athena, virgin goddess, was protectress of the king and of the citadel, leader in organized, intelligent warfare; and later, in Athens, she was to become the embodiment of wisdom. Poseidon, dwelling in the midst of the sea, was the god of the waters, sender of earthquakes and at the same time giver of horses to men. Demeter was the earth herself, giver of grain. Apollo, god of the sun and of light, leader and protector of wanderers, god of healing, prophecy, and song, adviser of youth, became the personification of the Greek character with its intelligence and its sense of order. Artemis, the huntress, sister of Apollo, was goddess of the moon and of the woods, and watcher over the animals. Dionysus was god of spring, of wine, of divine ecstasy. Aphrodite, said to have been born of the sea foam, was the goddess of the mystery of life and of reproduction; she later became the goddess of perfect physical beauty. Ares was the spirit of combat. Hephaestus, smith of the gods, was worshiped by artisans. Hades, brother of Zeus, was ruler of the underworld.

Local Gods   Besides these great divinities were countless local deities worshiped at small shrines. In time many of them became identified with the great gods, and the name of the little god then survived as an adjective attached to the greater name. Thus at the shrine of Hyakinthos, Apollo absorbed the attributes of the pre-Hellenic divinity and was called Apollo Hyakinthos. At the same time, in appealing to a deity for aid of a special sort, men attached to his name an adjective befitting the request and, as it were, thus created a special divinity for a special task. To illustrate, Athena was worshiped in Athens as Athena Polias, guardian of the city, as Athena Ergane, patroness of artisans, as Athena Hygeia, giver of health, and as Athena Parthenos, the virgin, who was also goddess of wisdom. Technically, as a matter of cult practice, each Athena was a separate goddess worshiped only in that aspect; yet through all there flowed the realization of the unity of Athena herself.

This process of identification and separation led to a wide diversity in the characteristics of each divinity and to a very considerable overlapping of godlike functions from one place to another, a confusion increased by early combinations of northern and Minoan divinities. Thus the virgin huntress, Artemis, was blended with the old mother goddess of the Mediterranean to become the famous "Many-breasted Artemis of the Ephesians."

Heroes   Of lower order than the gods were the heroes, spirits of the great dead who continued to protect the interests they had served in life. Groups worshiped as their ancestors the leaders of the epic period. Cities venerated their founders. Shrines called *heroa* were erected, rituals were developed, and every honor was paid to these demigods.

Beyond the gods lay something the Greeks called *Moira*, fate, a power to which the gods themselves were subject, a law created by them but by which they were bound. In close relationship to it was *Nemesis*, the personified jealousy of the gods, which pursued and destroyed the man who was too successful or who aimed too high.

Divination   Like the Orientals, the Greeks sought to know the will of the gods and to peer into the future. From the East they learned divination by examining the liver or entrails of animals. They watched the action of the sacrificial animals or that of the fire on the altar. They observed the flights of birds, regarded as the messengers of Zeus, and they believed in all sorts of accidental omens. In addition to these avenues of approach, men asked advice of the gods directly at one of the many oracles. The most famous of these were at Dodona and at Delphi. Zeus spoke to men at Dodona through the rustling of oak leaves, and at Delphi Apollo made known his will through the wild utterances of a priestess in ecstasy. Here the good sense of the Greeks recognized the right of the god to give deceptive advice, which might lead men to fated ruin, or to give to presuming questions about the future those ambiguous answers that have given meaning to the modern phrase "oracular utterance."

The Greeks of the early period took but little interest in a future life. The shades of the dead dwelt in colorless form, flitting about in a place so dreary that, according to Homer, Achilles would rather have been slave to a landless man than king of the dead.

Mythology   To explain their religious experiences and their rituals, the Greeks told many stories, products of a childlike but rich imagination, yet not essential to religious worship. Our pictures of the gods are derived from these. The wide diversity of functions of individual gods, the essentially local character of the worship, and the absence of any authoritative pronouncement made dogmatism in matters of belief impossible. So long as local acts of worship were performed according to ancestral tradition, gods and men were satisfied. To secure such performances was the function of the priest. Because priesthoods were hereditary in great families or were elective, and because few men devoted themselves exclusively to the service of the gods, freedom of belief was preserved. Greek religion was not an individual matter but a concern of a group—family, genos, tribe, or city. Activity in the service of the group and its gods was the greatest virtue, and self-seeking arrogance the greatest vice.

Ritual   The sole essential to worship was an altar in the open air and a ritual prescribed by ancestral tradition. Prayer, hymns, choruses, processions, and sacrifices—all were employed to win the favor of the gods. In one form of sacrifice the animals were butchered and the meat was cooked and passed out to the worshipers, while the entrails were placed on the altar and burned. Thus the god and his worshipers sat down to a common feast. In certain other sacrifices, particularly those to the earth divinities, the animals were burned entire for the propitiation of the gods.

Growth of Greek Religion There are many indications in myth and in religious language and customs that a large number of the Greek gods were once associated with animals or birds, or inanimate objects. With the development of mythology, however, they emerged from these crude beginnings and assumed the forms of men and women, a religious conception called anthropomorphism. This process was completed by Homer and Hesiod. In the *Iliad* and the *Odyssey*, poems of universal significance to all Hellenes, Zeus and his court appear in human form, as supremely beautiful and powerful men and women with personalities of their own and living human lives. The poet brought the gods very near to man and taught in marvelous guise "the humanity of God and the divinity of man," but by thus limiting the gods in time and place, he weakened them at the same time for their real service to mankind. In a later generation Hesiod endeavored to bring order into mythological confusion when in *Theogony* he arranged the gods in a genealogical table. Then in *Works and Days*, in which he laid emphasis upon the moral character of the gods, he warned the princes that Zeus would punish them for their corruption and injustice.

With the development of the city-states the gods were so woven into the political and social structure that they became the protectors and heavenly rulers of the communities. Devotion and service to them was implied in loyalty to the *polis*, and the performance of religious ceremonies to secure their favor was a matter of prime concern to the officials of the state.

Apollo During the period of colonization Apollo of Delphi became a divinity of wide power and significance. Appeals came to his oracle from all parts of the Hellenic world and on all sorts of problems, and his answers were invariably in accordance with traditional usage and reasonable interpretation. His priests directed the course of colonization and settled territorial disputes between cities. States consulted his priests in writing down their laws, and the priests' influence is seen in the definition of the kinds of murder and the appropriate treatment. The priests developed rites of purification, some of which may have had Minoan origins, to salve the troubled conscience of the evildoer. Although this was a legalistic service, it was essentially a ritualistic legalism that did not reach far into the moral realm or subjugate human life to rules. Only through Apollo's fundamental pronouncements to men, "nothing to excess" and "know thyself," did his priests lay down principles that were later to be transformed into ethical systems. Arrogance and self-seeking were still, in the eyes of Apollo, the greatest crime against the gods.

A new development in religion took place as the result of the social and economic difficulties of the seventh and sixth centuries B.C., for when the old gods whose cults were under aristocratic control failed to answer the needs of the poor and the oppressed, emotional and individualistic religions took their place.

Dionysus In the forefront of the new rites was the worship of the god Dionysus, whose cult had been in existence since Mycenaean times. He was a typical nature divinity who died and was brought back to life again. His worshipers roamed the mountain tops in wild revels, and sought union with the god in ecstasy. In the sixth century one phase of his worship crystallized in the Orphic sect, which took its name from the mythical minstrel, Orpheus. The leaders of this group developed rituals, dogmas, and rules of life, and they believed in the transmigration of souls. To the initiate they promised release from the wheel of life and eternal bliss as a reward for the sufferings of this world. This cult was especially favored by the tyrants, and had it been universally successful it would have meant the development of a priesthood and an authoritative dogma among the Greeks.

In Athens the tyrants began the development of the festivals of Dionysus at which dramatic contests were held in honor of the god. At Eleusis the addition of Dionysus to the ancient cult of Demeter and her daughter, Persephone, resulted in a religion, called the Eleusinian Mysteries (p. 286), of high emotional content. The ceremonies were open to all Hellenes. After a sacred procession and sacrifice and the initiation of newcomers, a "passion play," based on the myth of Hades' theft of Persephone, was presented in deepest secrecy. The *mystai*, or initiates, were assured of a blessed immortality, happier than the lot promised by the older beliefs.

GAMES

One of the most striking features of the Greek religious festivals was the idea of competition. There were contests of skill and speed in athletics, in poetry, music, choral dancing, and dramas. In some festivals men presented the products of their skill for awards. At one festival of Demeter, a prize was given to the mother of the best baby; at another the man who could stand longest on one foot on an inflated greased hide did honor to Dionysus; and in Megara there was even a contest in kissing.

Of all these contests the most famous were the athletic. Their origin may be found in funeral games held in honor of some deceased hero, but in any case they were a natural product of the outdoor life of the Greeks. Almost every state had its local games, but four attained the rank of national meets: the Olympic games, held every four years at the shrine of Zeus at Olympia in Elis; the Pythian games, held every four years at Delphi, where Apollo was patron and where therefore the original contests were musical; the Isthmian and the Nemean games, biennial affairs, both in the neighborhood of Corinth and performed in honor of Poseidon and Zeus, respectively. The Olympic games attained such prestige that later historians used the Olympiads as a system of dating.

The first Olympiad of record began in 776 B.C., though the legendary date for the origin of the games is much earlier. The fully developed program included elaborate religious ceremonies, athletic contests, and chariot races. Before multitudes assembled from all the Hellenic world the greatest runners contested barefoot in the dash the length of the stadium (about two hundred yards), in the double course, in a race of about three miles, and in a race in armor; athletes threw the discus and the javelin; and strong men matched their strength in wrestling, boxing, and a combination of the two called *pankration*. The *pentathlon*, greatly esteemed, was a combination of the single and double course, discus and javelin throwing, and wrestling. Victory in the chariot race was especially sought after by men of wealth. There were contests for boys, mule races, and other events. To enter, contestants had to prove to the governors their Greek parentage and had to train for at least one month at Olympia under their supervision. The prize was but a wreath of olive, but the victor found his real reward when he returned home a hero.

The festival truce became a religious duty for all Hellenic cities. Heralds proclaimed the season to all; hostilities were laid aside; embassies to the games might pass through hostile territory in perfect safety under the protection of the god. The greatest disgrace, exclusion from the games, was visited as a punishment upon anyone who offended against the truce. At Olympia the leading men of every state foregathered. Views were exchanged, differences were harmonized, agreements were consummated and tablets recording them were set up in the shrine to ensure their fulfillment. Matters of interest to all Greeks were announced and discussed. Following close on the diplomat came the trader with his wares. Booths were set up and goods exchanged. The foundations for commerce between cities were laid here in the creation of demand for products.

Pheidon, an early king of Argos, saw in the games an opportunity for the unification of Greece under his influence and endeavored to secure domination over them. The rising power of Sparta drove him back, and never again was any man so presumptuous. Though Sparta

had aspirations of the same sort, the little state of Elis guarded its prerogatives so carefully and fostered the public opinion of the Greeks so
zealously that Sparta itself was not able to escape the penalty when it
violated the sacred truce.

ARCHITECTURE

Anthropomorphism in religion and the development of the civic
communities played most important roles in the development of architecture. Where caves and groves, courtyard altars and household shrines
had sufficed in Minoan and Achaean times, the gods of the city-states
needed houses in which to live. The builders turned naturally to the
fine dwellings they knew. Some of the older divinities were housed in
primitive round huts, made of wood or stone, but developed and elaborated. For the temples of the others, men used as models the megara
that had formerly been the dwellings of the kings. The simplest form
consisted of a single room, in front of which was a porch supported
either by square piers terminating the side walls, with columns intervening, or by a row of columns called the *prostyle*. Later, rear porches
and sometimes additional rooms were added, and in the interest of
beauty a series of columns called the *peristyle* was carried around the
whole building. Within, the ceiling was supported by rows of columns,
normally two in number.

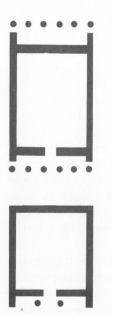
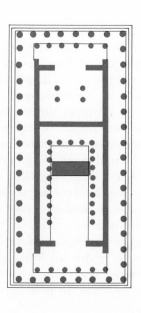

Greek Temple Plans.
The earliest temples
were small, one-roomed
structures with a front
porch whose roof was
supported by two col-
umns *(in antis)*. Later,
a porch was added on
the back for a bal-
anced appearance. The
last step was to extend
the porch, supported
by a colonnade, all
around the building.
The usual temple con-
tinued to have only
one room. The Par-
thenon, shown at right,
was unusual in having
two; the larger was the
temple, the smaller the
Athenian treasury.

While the plan of the building was essentially native and while many of its later features show its development locally and directly from wood into stone, there can be no doubt that the architects drew upon the traditions of the great builders of Aegean times and the experiences of the Orientals — Egyptian, Babylonian, and Hittite. Out of these, in varying proportions and in accordance with local demands and ideas, two distinct orders of architecture were developed: the Doric, chiefly in the Peloponnesus and in the west, and the Ionic, in the east.

The chief features of the Doric order, on which Egyptian (and perhaps Minoan) influence was strong,[1] were strength and simplicity. The column rested directly without base on the top step and was surmounted by a simple capital of two blocks: the first saucerlike; the second, the abacus, flat. Above the architrave (the row of flat blocks connecting the columns), which was undecorated, was the frieze. It consisted of two alternating parts: the *triglyphs*, three scuptured projections, originally the sheathed ends of beams; and the *metopes*, square spaces between the triglyphs, at first filled with paintings or with stucco figures and later with relief sculpture in stone.

The Ionic order was more ornate, and it developed, fittingly, in the wealthy cities of Asia Minor under Babylonian, Hittite, or Egyptian influence. A base consisting of a series of convex and concave surfaces gave elaboration and height to the columns, which were themselves of slimmer proportion than the Doric. The capital, originally modeled on a palm frond, was transformed in stone into the *volute*, or scroll, which became characteristic of the Ionic order. The later Corinthian style was developed from the Ionic by the substitution of a more ornate and loftier capital produced by the carving of acanthus leaves in stone. The architrave was divided into two or three members called *fasciae*. The frieze above was a plain band of stone which when decorated by sculpture presented a unified picture across or along the building.

From the beginning the Greek architects sought after grace and proportion as the chief elements of beauty. With keen aesthetic sense they carved grooves, or flutes, in their columns, and gave to the columns themselves a gentle swelling curve called *entasis*, which overcame the optical illusion that makes two straight, parallel lines seem to curve inward. They experimented with the length and breadth of buildings and with the height and diameter of columns, in search of the most artistic relationship. Many of the earlier buildings were too long or too broad, and their columns too heavy. In the best period the peristyle established the proportions of the building, the side rows containing one more than twice as many columns as the end. At the same time the

---

[1] The pyramid temple complex of Zoser was known to the Greeks in this period, and there is every reason to believe its colonnades influenced Greek architecture and the Doric order in particular.

Greek Styles of Architecture. In the classic period, temples and other public buildings were decorated in one of the two styles shown. The Doric originated on the Greek mainland, and was used widely in Greece and among the Greek colonists in Italy and Sicily. The graceful, more ornate Ionic style was developed along the coast of Asia Minor and on the Ionian islands. It was used in Athens for the Temple of Athena Nike and the Erechtheum. The Doric Parthenon had Ionic features. In the Hellenistic period the Ionic style became the basis for the Corinthian style. The Corinthian differed from the Ionic chiefly in the capital of the column, where an acanthus-leaf design replaced the scroll.

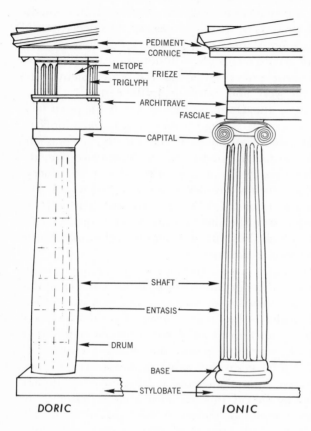

DORIC   IONIC

shaft of the Doric column was in height five and one-half times its diameter, and the lighter Ionic had the ratio of eight or nine to one. Rarely, the architect secured a different but interesting effect by the use of human figures in place of columns.

The temples of the early period were products of experimentation. The oldest temple known from its remains is that of Hera at Olympia. Originally built of wood, probably in the seventh century B.C., its first columns as they decayed were replaced by stone according to the best technique of replacement at the time. As a result, those that have survived show diversity in proportion, in number of flutes, and in forms of capitals. The temple of Apollo at Corinth and many of the structures which have survived in Sicily and southern Italy illustrate in their heaviness or their lack of proportion the failures of the early architects, but at the same time they reveal, in spite of their defects, the ideals that animated the builders and that resulted in the perfection attained by their greater successors in the fifth century B.C.

SCULPTURE

Sculpture, like architecture, was a product of Greek religion, of the need for cult statues of the divinities and of the desire to decorate the temples with figures in relief. The games also inspired the idea of making statues of the victors, the athletes themselves serving as models. Although the first statues were of wood, the artists, probably under strong Egyptian influence, learned to use limestone, then marble, and finally bronze. In Ionia, doubtless as a result of the dominance of the mother goddess in religion, great attention was paid to female figures and to the arrangement of hair and draperies. Male figures were often effeminate. On the mainland, however, where the athletic influence was strong, nude, virile male figures predominated.

The early statues were stiff and ill-proportioned and were posed like the Egyptian, with one foot forward, hands and arms rigidly beside the body, face forward, and eyes staring straight ahead. The artists had to learn for themselves the proportions of the human body, the proper position of the eyes and the ears on the head, the relative length of legs and arms. In addition the artists had to acquire techniques in working the material necessary to give adequate representation of human hair and flesh, of the texture of draperies and the suggestion of the human figure beneath. In relief sculptures on frieze or pediment, there arose problems of composition, of the relative height of figures, and of the representation of movement; but in the solution of all these difficulties the artists were inspired by an aesthetic ideal. Furthermore, their experiences in athletics and religion gave the Hellenes a concept of the divinity of human beauty. Their efforts to represent this in stone gave the crude statues of the archaic era a freshness and glory that transcend the sculptor's errors. The knowledge of anatomy and the mastery of technique which the early artists slowly acquired prepared the way for the finer works of later generations.

LITERATURE

The varied influences of the political and economic changes of the age were reflected in the literature and the thought as well as the religion of the period. Epic poetry, in which the poet was but the teller of a story, was essentially the product of the heroic age. Though in later centuries men still turned to Homer for delight and inspiration and though many lesser epics of which we possess but fragments were written in Ionia in the seventh century B.C., the epic no longer suited the temper of men, and so yielded place to new literary forms.

Hesiod's poems, though written in the epic meter, marked the first departure from the older style, since in his passion for justice for the oppressed of the land he burst the bonds of tradition and expressed himself vigorously on current social and economic problems. But even the meter was unsuited to the new age of city-state life, of party strife, and of nascent individualism. New subjects and new emotions demanded new vehicles of expression. So in meters varied to suit the subject, poets sang the praises of their states or their party leaders and vilified their opponents. They praised victorious athletes, and wrote of love and wine and nature; or in sterner tone they rallied their countrymen to the defense of native land against present foes. Some composed choral hymns for youths and maidens to sing in concert in honor of the gods, or battle songs to rouse the warriors, who sang them with martial fervor.

Under the impetus of the times religious leaders asking new questions and making new demands upon the gods developed an emotional religion (p. 286). Thinkers, drinking deep of the ancient learning of the East and discovering themselves as individuals in a great universe, began to ask questions of how and why, and established Greek philosophy.

The leadership in all these intellectual movements came naturally from the Anatolian cities, where political and economic forces were most active and where the contact with Oriental culture was closest. Nevertheless the poets, religious leaders, and philosophers filled a pressing need in this age of ferment and found a ready welcome wherever they went. In many circles their presence was earnestly solicited. Speaking a language that all could understand, they became, like the great poets of the epic age, the common property of all Greeks and an added bond of union among them.

The adoption of the Phoenician alphabet and the availability of papyrus from Egypt played an important part in the development of Greek literature. The Linear B script was abandoned during the Dark Ages, when writing itself almost disappeared. By the seventh century the Phoenician alphabet had reached the Greeks and the signs were adapted so that vowels, not written in the Semitic original, could be written in Greek. There were for a time a number of varying alphabets used in different parts of the Hellenic world, but the basic elements were the same. The Ionic alphabet was officially adopted in Athens in 403 B.C. and became standardized there. Early inscriptions were on stone or clay. One of the oldest specimens of Greek writing known is that of some Greek mercenaries who went far up the Nile with Psamtik II and were the first of a long line of tourists to scratch their names on Egyptian monuments. Lists of officials, laws, and treaties were recorded on wooden tablets or on stone, or, later, were cast in bronze. Trade with Egypt brought in papyrus, and written literature became possible. Parchment provided a second convenient writing material.

The first personality to stand out vividly in the new literature was Archilochus (fl. *ca.* 650 B.C.), who developed the iambic satire. Born in Paros, he had an unfortunate love affair there. His verses are said to have driven the young lady and her family to commit suicide, whereupon he was forced to leave home and went as a colonist to Thasos. From there he moved on to become a restless mercenary warrior. In describing himself as a soldier and a poet, he said, "I am the servant of the lord Enyalios, and I am skilled in the lovely gift of the Muses." He wrote religious poems, satirical fables, and a long series of personal poems varying in subject from wine to shipwreck. The literary importance of his work rests on the fact that he was the first Greek to use the poetic medium to express himself as an individual. In so doing he broke the bonds of the older meter and created new standards. Lyric poetry was born. His philosophy of life was typical of the age:

> Endure, endure my soul, disquieted by griefs beyond remedy and setting thy breast against the foe, hold thy ground, taking thy stand firm and close amid the spears of the enemy. If thou conquerest, exult not openly, and if thou art conquered, lie not down in thy house and mourn. Rejoice in that which is meet for rejoicing and grieve not overmuch at calamities, but learn what condition prevails among men.[2]

Alcaeus of Mytilene in Lesbos is the best proponent of the era of adventure and political strife which ushered in the sixth century. A noble, a politician, a soldier, a traveler, a *bon vivant*, he is the product of Mytilene at the height of its greatest splendor. He took part in wars, was driven into exile by the democratic tyrant, and visited Egypt. His songs were of war, of party strife, of love, of wine, and of spring.

Sappho, contemporary of Alcaeus, was a product of the happy freedom and wealth of the social life of Mytilene. She stands supreme among the poetesses of love.

> The fairest thing in all the world some say is a host of horsemen, and some a host of foot, and some again a navy of ships; but to me, 'tis the heart's beloved . . . one of whom I would rather the sweet sound of her footfall and the sight of the brightness of her beaming face than all the chariots and armored footmen of Lydia.[3]

Erotic poetry reached its culmination in this century in the work of Anacreon of Teos. His life was typical of the age. Driven from Teos by local disturbances, he settled at Abdera in Thrace, where he took

---

[2] Wallace E. Caldwell, *Hellenic Conceptions of Peace.* New York: Columbia University Press, 1919, p. 53.

[3] G. W. Botsford and E. G. Sihler, *Hellenic Civilization.* New York: Columbia University Press, 1915, p. 197.

part in wars with the native Thracians. After his poetry became famous, he spent many years in the court of Polycrates of Samos, piratical despot and adventurer. From there he went to the court of Hippias at Athens. Amid scenes of splendor and glory he clung to the golden mean, envying neither pomp nor power nor wealth, but desiring tranquillity and happiness above all. Eros and Dionysus were his most loved divinities. In an epigram he described war as evil, for it took away the bravest of the city's youth and left the coward in their place. The odes of these poets were meant to be sung as solos to the accompaniment of the lyre.

Other poets, such as Alcman at Sparta, wrote choral songs to be sung in procession by youths or maidens, or dithyrambs to be performed by the chorus at the festival of Dionysus.

Another form of verse was the elegiac couplet, consisting of alternate lines, the first with six feet and the second, because of a caesura, seeming to have five. Such poems were especially adapted to recitation and were used as war songs or for political purposes. Among the poets who used this measure were Tyrtaeus, general in Sparta, who wrote a stirring war song to encourage his followers and another poem called "Eunomia" (meaning good laws well obeyed), to allay incipient civil strife; Solon, who used his verse to set his political ideas before the Athenians; and Theognis of Megara, a poet of the aristocracy who wrote verses as instructions to his younger friends. Theognis bitterly attacked the democratic leaders and tyrants, the power of money over birth, and the tendency to marry out of class in the interests of wealth; the "good" were the aristocrats, and the "evil" were the base-born.

The greatest of the lyric poets was Pindar (520?–441 B.C.), a Theban. So great was he that his contemporaries regarded him as a special favorite of Apollo, god of song, and reserved a seat for him in the temple at Delphi. Of his many poems on varied subjects, chance has preserved, aside from a few fragments, only his songs of praise of the victors in the national games. In these he praised not so much the individual as the city and its noble leaders. Throughout his poems runs the common theme of the greatness of nobility, of its duty and privilege of service to the state and to the gods, and of the glories of its achievements. His thought is colored by a deep religious feeling founded on Orphism. Though he lived in the next generation, his work and his ideas are the product and the culmination of the forces of the sixth century B.C.

PHILOSOPHY

The intelligence of men directed their eyes to natural causes, and they dared to examine the world in an endeavor to explain its origin, its form, and its purpose. Greek philosophy began in the sixth century B.C. with a bold attempt to reduce the universe itself to a simple principle. The most powerful element in the thinking of the time was the idea of descent, doubtless derived from Hesiod, who in his *Theogony* had attempted to explain the genealogy of the gods themselves in their descent from the first divinities. But though the Orphists clung to his ideas, contact with other lands and with other ideas had weakened, for many intelligent men, the structure of Hesiod's theology. Herodotus (II, 143) recounts the experience of Hecataeus of Miletos in Egypt. When discoursing of his genealogy at Thebes, Hecataeus declared that a god was his sixteenth ancestor, the priests of Amon showed him three hundred and forty-five statues of priests, each of whom they claimed was the son of the man before him, and denied that any man was ever born of a god. It is little wonder that after such an experience Hecataeus wrote, "The stories of the Greeks appear to me to be altogether foolish."

The first man to attempt a new explanation of the world was Thales (*ca.* 585 B.C.), general, statesman, and philosopher of Miletos, who declared that all things were descended from a first principle, water. He described the earth as a flat disk floating on water. He is said to have predicted the eclipse of 585 B.C. (using the Babylonian method) and from his ability as a meteorologist to have made a fortune out of a speculation in the olive crop. His search for a materialistic answer to the question of origins was continued by his successors, Anaximander and Anaximenes. Anaximander, who probably composed the first Greek book written in prose, denied the presence of any original matter save "the boundless" from which matter was separated by motion in the form of opposites, like hot and cold, wet and dry. In the pursuit of his studies about the world he made the first Greek map. Anaximenes, returning to Thales' concept, identified origin with air, from which all things are made by the processes of rarefaction and condensation.

> In a word the Milesians had drawn the outlines of the theory of matter in the physicists' sense of the word, and these outlines still survive in a recognizable form in our text-books. That . . . is the central thing in the system, and that is why it is reckoned as the beginning of philosophy. It is the earliest answer to the question, "What is reality?"[4]

The philosophic studies begun by these men were continued in the last part of the sixth century B.C. by two Ionians, Xenophanes and Pythagoras, who fled in exile to the west. Xenophanes devoted his writings chiefly to religious and social problems. He declared the existence of one god, the earth, the beginning and end of all things.

[4] John Burnet, *Greek Philosophy Part I: Thales to Plato.* London: Macmillan & Co., Ltd., 1914, pp. 27–28.

But mortals fancy gods are born and wear clothes, and have voice and form like themselves. Yet if oxen and lions had hands, and could paint with their hands, and fashion images, as men do, they would make the pictures and images of the gods in their own likeness; horses would make them like horses, oxen like oxen.[5]

He attacked the luxury of Ionian life and bitterly condemned those who praised and rewarded victorious athletes but ignored the wisemen. "For our wisdom is better than the strength of horses and men."

Pythagoras of Samos, after travels and study in Egypt, settled at Crotone in Italy. Here he developed his famous explanation of the order of the universe in mathematics, the science of numbers. He laid emphasis upon chord and discord, harmony and its lack, and the proper balance of all things. His school developed under Orphist influence to become a religious sect, the members of which were essentially ascetic, living by rules laid down for every phase of life. His doctrines gave great impetus to the study of mathematics and made important contributions to medicine.

The beginnings of historical studies and of human geography were counterparts of Ionian philosophy. History, however, sprang out of the desire of the leaders of the day to prove their descent from the heroes of the traditional past. Hence the first historians were really genealogists, who endeavored from myth and tradition to discover the ancestry of, and to work out lines of descent for, their contemporaries. Their conclusions were recorded in prose. Critical acumen caused them to rationalize or to explain the myths, although the influence of the past prevented any denial of their truth.

The leader of these early prose writers was Hecataeus of Miletos, who was also the first geographer. Anaximander had made a map, and on the basis of it Hecataeus, who had traveled throughout the Mediterranean and Black seas, in Persia, and in Egypt, composed a description of the lands and peoples he had seen, together with some account of their past history.

Like the artists and the architects, philosophers and scientists during the sixth century b.c. inaugurated processes and methods which through awakened interest continued to advance men's ability and knowledge until they reached fruition in the greatest works of the Greek intellect.

[5] Charles M. Bakewell, *Source Book of Ancient Philosophy.* New York: Charles Scribner's Sons, 1939, p. 8.

II · The Persian Wars

THE GREAT WAR BETWEEN THE GREEKS AND THE Persians took place during the first years of the fifth century B.C. It was a contest memorable in itself and a prelude to nearly two centuries of struggle ending only in the later years of the fourth century B.C. when Alexander the Great destroyed the Persian Empire.

As an aftermath to the conquest of Lydia Cyrus had added the Anatolian Greeks to his empire, placing them under the rule of local tyrants supervised by the satraps of the provinces. This conquest and the resultant development of trade led inevitably to relations with cities on the other side of the Aegean and with the Greek colonies scattered around the Mediterranean. But trade was not the only connection maintained by the cities of Ionia with other Greek states. When rebellions were planned against Persia, the Ionians sought and received aid from Athens and other mainland states. This hostile action made Darius the Great (p. 166) determine on a conquest of the Greek mainland. Disunity and intrigue among the Greeks made the task appear easy: the Alcmaeonid party in Athens had appealed to Persia for aid against the Peloponnesians, and Hippias, deposed tyrant of Athens, and Demaratus, exiled king of Sparta, sought refuge and restoration from the Persians. Accordingly Darius, undoubtedly planning conquest, sent a fleet guided by his physician Democedes (who deserted at Crotone) to make a survey of the Mediterranean.

Expedition Across the Danube As a first step Darius invaded Europe in 512 B.C. and marched north across the Danube to protect his rear against the Scythians of southwest Russia. Here he met with some success while his generals completed the conquest of Thrace. Ionian Greeks who took part in the expedition stood guard at the bridge of boats across the Danube.

The Ionian Revolt Shortly after Darius' return the Ionian revolt broke out. The plots of Aristagoras, tyrant of Miletos, precipitated the movement, and the cities of Asia Minor, constantly fretting under

241

Persian rule, eagerly cooperated. Aristagoras himself went across the Aegean in search of help. Sparta refused because Susa was too far away, but Athens and Eretria sent ships and men. The Greek army won an initial victory, captured Sardis and burned it. On their way home the Greeks were overtaken by the Persian forces and defeated, whereupon the Athenians withdrew. Persian success followed dissension in the Greek alliance. The Ionian fleet was defeated and destroyed off Lade, near Miletos, and one after another the cities were retaken until in 494 B.C. Miletos fell and was destroyed. Darius established democratic governments in place of the tyrants who had proved treacherous, and then proceeded with his original plans.

The Persian Advance   In 492 B.C. Mardonius, son-in-law of the Persian king, started a campaign against the Greeks with a combined land and naval expedition along the coast of Thrace. Thracian tribes defeated the Persian army, and the fleet, caught in a storm off Mount Athos, was wrecked. This failure resulted in a change of plan: Darius determined to abandon the land route and strike directly across the Aegean. He sent envoys to demand earth and water, tokens of submission, from the Greek cities. Many of the islands and mainland communities yielded, but the Athenians threw the envoys into a pit, and the Spartans dropped them into a well. These violations of the sanctity of ambassadors were a recognition of the inevitability of the struggle. In 490 B.C. Datis and Artaphernes, accompanied by the Athenian Hippias, led a force by sea against Athens. Naxos and Delos were captured en route, Eretia was taken and destroyed, and a portion of the army was landed at Marathon on the coast of Attica.

Preparations of the Athenians   The situation in Athens was critical. The city had prospered under the Peisistratid tyranny, and the Areopagus had been filled with followers of the tyrants. A strong party could therefore be counted on to aid the Persians for the return of Hippias. The Alcmaeonid successors of Cleisthenes were under suspicion because of the earlier appeal to Persia for aid against the Spartans (p. 241). Balancing these forces was the patriotic faction led by Aristides and Themistocles, the men who had been responsible for Athenian participation in the Ionian revolt. The failure and return of the army threw the balance against them. When the dramatic poet Phrynichus, probably inspired and supported by Themistocles, produced a tragedy, *The Fall of Miletos*, the Athenian people fined him "for reminding them of their sorrows." The play secured its desired effect, however, and Themistocles was elected archon for 493–492 B.C. He used his year to good advantage by fortifying the natural harbor of Peiraeus and beginning the development of the Athenian navy.

When the Persians came in 490 B.C., the city was determined upon resistance, though its neighbors, Thebes and Chalcis, were openly

Persian Drinking Horn (Rhyton) of Gold from the Achaemenian Period. (The Metropolitan Museum of Art, Dick Fund, 1954)

hostile to Athens, and only Spartan intervention prevented Aegina from surrendering its important naval base to the Persians. Pheidippides ran to Sparta, one hundred and fifty miles in two days, to seek aid, but the Spartans were delayed by a religious festival and arrived too late to be of any assistance. Fortune favored the Athenians, however, by providing them with Miltiades. He had gained experience fighting the Persians at Chersonese, an Athenian colony on the Hellespont. In a close vote among the generals, he was given command. Callimachus, the polemarch, cast the deciding ballot.

Marathon Information about the famous struggle at Marathon is scanty and confused. Apparently the Persian plan called for a division of forces. One portion of their army was to march upon Athens from Marathon while the other was to be landed at Phalerum. Traitors could then be relied on to open the gates. The Athenian army, aided by a small force from Plataea, occupied a strong position in the hills above the plain of Marathon and awaited developments. When the Persian fleet and army began to move, Miltiades waited until the enemy was well in front of him and then gave the order to charge. When his forces arrived within bowshot, they advanced at the double quick; consequently the phalanx came to close quarters before the Persian arrows could do great damage. There the heavy-armed troops, fighting in close formation, proved their superiority over the lightly equipped Persians. The battle was hotly contested, but the Persians were beaten and driven back to their ships. During the night after the battle the Athenians marched back to Athens, so when the Persian fleet appeared off Phalerum the next morning it was confronted by the waiting Athenian army. Not willing to risk another engagement, the Persians turned their ships around and sailed back across the Aegean. The Spartan forces, arriving too late to be of help, merely surveyed the scene of battle, complimented the Athenians, and returned to Sparta.

Xerxes' Plans   To the Persians Marathon was only a temporary check. Darius prepared to invade Greece again but he died in 485 B.C. It was not until 480 B.C. that his successor, Xerxes, completed his plans. Once more the Persians prepared with care and forethought for a combined land and naval attack along the lines of the first expedition. Supplies were gathered at convenient places across Thrace and Macedonia. A canal was cut behind Mount Athos. All Persian subjects were called upon to send contingents, and a fine fleet of Phoenician, Carian, and Ionian Greek ships was gathered.

Herodotus' stories of the extraordinary size and diversity of the Persian army, which drank rivers dry and ate districts barren on the march, are in a measure indicative of what the Greeks believed was coming against them. Small wonder that weaker states trembled and went over to the Persian side, while even Apollo of Delphi wavered. Athenians seeking advice from Apollo were driven from the temple with fearful imprecations of impending doom. They returned as suppliants on the advice of a Delphic priest and finally secured an answer that may have been inspired by Themistocles:

Pallas has not been able to soften the lord of Olympus,
Though she has often prayed him, and urged him with excellent counsel.
Yet once more I address thee in words than adamant firmer.
When the foe shall have taken whatever the limit of Cecrops
Holds within it, and all that divine Cithaeron shelters,
Then far-seeing Zeus grants this to the prayers of Athena,—
Safe shall the wooden wall continue for thee and thy children.
Wait not the tramp of the horse, nor the footman mightily moving
Over the land, but turn your back to the foe and retire ye.
Yet shall a day arrive when ye shall meet him in battle.
Holy Salamis, thou shalt destroy the offspring of women,
When men scatter the seed, or when they gather the harvest.[1]

Triumph of Themistocles   In the ten year interval since Marathon the Greeks had not been idle. The Athenians had cleaned house by exiling the tyrant and the Alcmaeonid leaders. In 487 B.C. a law was passed which provided for the election of archons by lot. This democratic reform curtailed the office, and the leadership of the state passed into the hands of the board of generals, one of whom was henceforth

[1] Herodotus, *History*. Trans. by George Rawlinson. New York: Tandy-Thomas Co., 1909, 7. 141.

chosen as commander-in-chief. At the same time the opening of a new vein of silver in the state-owned mines at Laurium gave the city a surplus of wealth. Aristides, the conservative leader, proposed to divide it among the citizens in order to increase the numbers of the *zeugitae* and thus strengthen the army. Themistocles, however, with a truer vision of the future, urged the building of a great fleet, ostensibly for the war that was being waged with Aegina, actually for the impending conflict with Persia. After a period of discussion recourse was had, in 483 B.C., to ostracism. In the test vote Themistocles won and Aristides was ostracized. Freed of his chief rival and opponent, Themistocles was able to secure his own election as general and execute his program. When the Persian forces appeared, Athens, under his leadership, was ready to meet them on the sea.

Campaign of Thermopylae In 481 B.C. a conference was held at Corinth for the organization of a Hellenic league. The new league proved to be little more than an extension of the Peloponnesian League, but it put an end to such local wars as that between Athens and Aegina. On the motion of Themistocles the command of both land and sea forces was entrusted to Sparta. The Spartans advised the abandonment of the north and the fortification of the isthmus, but Athenian pressure drove them unwillingly to a different plan: defense of the northern passes.

After making a futile attempt to stop the Persians at Tempe, the Greek army took its stand at Thermopylae, the fleet at Artemisium protecting its rear. Sparta had sent an advance force of three hundred Spartans and twenty-one hundred helots under King Leonidas. These with allies, who brought their number up to six thousand, held the Persians at bay until a traitor showed the Persians a pass through the hills. Leonidas dispatched his allies to the south, probably to stop the enemy as they came down from the hills. Then with his Spartans and a few Thespians and a Theban force of doubtful loyalty he endeavored to hold his position rather than retreat before the enemy. It was a magnificent gesture, perhaps the finest product of the Spartan system. The allies failed to check the encircling movement and Leonidas was trapped. The Thebans deserted, and of the Thespians there is no further mention, but the Spartans fought to the last. Simonides wrote their epitaph:

> Go, stranger, to the Spartans tell,
> That here, obedient to their laws, we fell.[2]

Salamis The fleet had been successful in checking the Persian advance, but when news of the fall of the pass came, the fleet fell back into the bay of Salamis, across from Athens. As the Persian army ad-

[2] Herodotus, *History*. Trans. by George Rawlinson. New York: Tandy-Thomas Co., 1909, 7. 228.

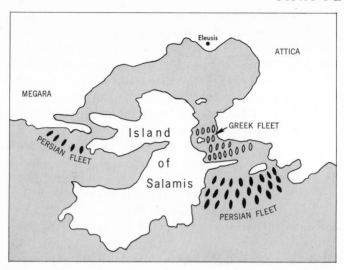

Fleet Positions at the Opening of the Battle of Salamis, 480 B.C.

vanced, Thebes openly went over to the Persian side, and only a timely earthquake saved Delphi from plunder and destruction. Since the oracle had advised the Athenians to trust to the wooden walls, which Themistocles interpreted to mean the fleet, the population of Attica was removed to Salamis and Troezen.[3] Athens fell and was sacked. Again dissension appeared in the Greek camp as the Spartans once more urged withdrawal to the isthmus. It required a combination of argument and trickery on the part of Themistocles (in which he was aided by Aristides, who had been recalled from exile) to force a stand and thus bring about the battle. But when it came, the Greeks laid aside their differences to win. The clever planning of Themistocles trapped the Persians in the narrow strait between Salamis and Attica, and the victory was decisive. After the battle a vote was taken among the Greek captains as to who did the most to win the victory. Each captain received one vote (his own) for first place, but Themistocles was the unanimous choice for second place.

Plataea After the battle Xerxes, fearful for his bridge over the Hellespont, sent his fleet back across the Aegean while he himself returned the way he had come. He left Mardonius with a powerful army in Thessaly, however, to complete the conquest. The next winter Mardonius offered favorable terms to the Athenians if they would join him, but the memory of Marathon endured, and they refused. When the Spartans again proposed defense of the isthmus, the Athe-

[3]An inscription discovered at Troezen commemorates this event.

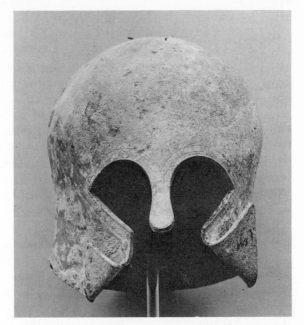

Greek Corinthian-type
Helmet of Bronze from
the Fifth Century B.C.
Found at Olympia. (The
Metropolitan Museum
of Art, Rogers Fund,
1907)

nians forced action from them with a threat to withdraw from Greece
and establish a colony in the west. After the usual argument, during
which Attica was again invaded, the Spartan army advanced into Boeotia
under Pausanias, regent for the young son of Leonidas. The battle
took place on hilly ground near Plataea, where the Persian cavalry
proved ineffective and the Spartan phalanx established its superiority.
At the same time the Persian fleet and a military contingent were
destroyed by the Greeks at Mycale near Miletos. The Persian invasion
had come to an end.

THE WEST

While the Greeks in the Aegean were dealing with the Persian
challenge, their colonies in the west, some of which had become large
and flourishing cities, were likewise faced with an attack, by the Phoenician power of Carthage.

Sybaris During the seventh and sixth centuries B.C. the Greek
cities in Sicily and southern Italy had shared in the development of
trade, industry, and culture. For a period Achaean Sybaris was the
leading city in Italy. Its rich valley provided abundant resources and
commercial relations with Miletos brought wealth from the East. A
pass over the Apennines to the west and its colony Poseidonia, on the

shore of the Tyrrhenian Sea, gave it control over the rich trade with the Greeks and the Etruscans of western Italy. Later moralists told many tales of the wealth and luxury of this city, where inventive cooks were given prizes and men slept on beds of rose leaves.

Crotone Crotone immediately to the south, had a different history. Not given to luxury, it produced a series of famous athletes including the great Milo, who was six times victor in wrestling at the Olympic games. Pythagoras settled there, and his followers became prominent in the government of the city. In 510 B.C. a war broke out between Sybaris and Crotone in which the Sybarites were defeated. Their city was taken and destroyed, and its site placed under a curse.

Locri The little town of Locri is worthy of mention because it produced Zaleucus, the first Greek to write down the laws. The traditional date is 664 B.C. The Locrian code was even more severe than the later laws of Draco. A curious provision was added that any citizen who wished to propose a change in the laws must appear with a rope around his neck to be used if the people rejected his proposal. Locri thus became renowned for its conservatism in law.

Other Cities Though the Spartan colony of Tarentum possessed the best harbor in eastern Italy, it was not yet of much importance. The Straits of Messana were under the control of Rhegion, which at the end of the sixth century B.C. was governed by a tyrant, Anaxilaus. The town of Zancle on the Sicilian side was a subject of contention between Rhegion and Syracuse. After a series of vicissitudes, it was finally occupied by fugitive Messenians, settled there by Anaxilaus, and its name changed to Messana.

Cities of Sicily Of the Sicilian cities, Acragas and Gela were for a period the most powerful, but they were soon eclipsed by Syracuse. Acragas was ruled in the middle of the sixth century B.C. by a tyrant, Phalaris, who is said to have dealt with his enemies by roasting them in a brazen bull. Gela was governed by a series of tyrants who extended its power until in 492 B.C. Gelon, commander of the cavalry, made himself ruler. This able leader took advantage of local troubles in Syracuse in 485 B.C. to make himself ruler of that city also. From this date begins the greatness of Syracuse. Gelon enlarged it by bringing in peoples from neighboring towns. Around the city he built a great wall. Then in alliance with Theron of Acragas he moved toward the conquest of the other cities of Sicily. This aggrandizement alarmed Anaxilaus of Messana and the Carthaginians, and conflict began when Theron seized Himera to the north.

Carthage The chief rivals of the Greeks in the western Mediterranean were the Phoenicians. Carthage had been founded by Elissa, princess of Tyre, about 825 B.C. Because of its harbor and fertile valley it had soon become the most important of the Phoenician cities in the west and had acquired leadership over the settlements in Africa, Sicily, and Spain. The Carthaginians made treaties with communities around the shores of the western Mediterranean, securing for themselves exclusive rights to the sea-borne commerce. Affairs were directed by a council of oligarchs with two *suffetes* (judges) as the chief magistrates. In the classical period command of the army was vested in hereditary generals of the family of Mago. Cambyses had been blocked in his intention to conquer the city when the Phoenician fleet refused to sail against their kinsmen. According to tradition, the Carthaginian expedition to Sicily was inspired by Xerxes. Whether there is truth in this story or not, there was ample reason in Sicily for Carthage's alarm at the advancing power of the Greek tyrants, which threatened its control over its own possessions in the northern and western sections of the island.

Himera A large Carthaginian force, dispatched in response to appeals for aid from both Phoenicians and Greeks, trapped Theron within the walls of Himera, and Gelon advanced to the aid of his ally. The Greeks claimed that the decisive battle was fought on the same day as the conflict at Salamis. Gelon and Theron won the day, and the Carthaginian menace in the West was checked. Gelon was succeeded in Syracuse by his brother Hiero, who completed the triumph of Syracuse by defeating a fleet of Etruscans off Cumae in 474 B.C. To his brilliant court came the poets Pindar, Simonides, Bacchylides, and Aeschylus, and the philosopher Xenophanes. After his death the tyranny was overthrown, and a period of confusion followed.

Acragas, too, profited from the victory at Himera, for the prisoners of war became public and private slaves. With the wealth gained from the spoils and the labor of these slaves, Theron adorned his city with a series of magnificent temples, many of which are still standing.

Conclusion In the east and in the west the Hellenic states had successfully repelled their enemies, although to the Persians and the Carthaginians the defeats meant little more than a check to further expansion. Continuing wealthy and powerful, Carthage remained a constant menace to the western Greeks. Though the Persian plans for conquest and control of the Aegean had failed, and though this failure was soon followed by loss of the Greek cities of Asia, still the power of the Persian kings suffered little and they continued to exert a powerful influence over Greek politics through the fourth century.

For the Greeks, however, the victories had extraordinary significance. During the sixth century B.C. confidence in the justice of the gods and in the moral order of the universe had waned, and an individualism that had found expression in religion and in philosophy had become dominant. Then in the test of war the citizen armies of the city-states, animated by a courage based on patriotic devotion, had won a notable triumph against overwhelming odds. It seemed as if the gods themselves had overthrown the arrogant might of Persia. Individual doubt yielded to a sublime confidence in man's power as a citizen, under the guidance of the gods of the state, to achieve all that was humanly possible. Freed from the threat of oppression and inspired by their victories, the Athenians especially were ready to advance to the full flowering of their genius.

12 · The Greatness and Fall of Athens

THE YEARS THAT FOLLOWED THE DEFEAT OF THE Oriental invasions formed one of the most brilliant periods in the history of mankind. The first generation, from 479–461 B.C., was an era of transition during which Athens, inspired by the memories of Marathon and Salamis and strengthened by its great fleet, rapidly rose to leadership in the maritime activities of Hellas. The Greek cities in Asia were freed; the Persians and their Phoenician subjects were completely driven out of the Aegean; and into the hands of the Athenians passed the trade that had belonged to Miletos before its fall in 494 B.C. or to the Phoenician merchants. The advance toward democracy in Athens begun by Solon and Cleisthenes was completed, and the first steps were taken to rebuild and beautify the city. Art, literature, and philosophy continued the development of the earlier centuries. Then, under the guidance of Pericles (461–431 B.C.), Athens became the economic and cultural center of Hellas. Its wealth and its artistic and intellectual achievements attracted to it the elite of the Hellenic world. But its very pre-eminence aroused jealousy, and its ambitions for expansion brought fear to the hearts of the Corinthians and the Spartans. The result of this jealousy and fear was the Peloponnesian War, which lasted from 431 to 404 B.C. and ended with the collapse of Athens.

THE PERIOD OF TRANSITION

Throughout the period of transition two problems were pressing for solution: the future of Hellenic unity and the question of the political control of the agricultural and the urban elements within the states.

The Growth of Unity The events of the Persians Wars had brought sharply to the fore the hope of a possible unification of the Hellenic world on a federal basis. The seventh and sixth centuries B.C.

251

had seen the rise of great numbers of small city-states, each clinging fiercely to its right of absolute freedom. Not even the threat of Persia had been sufficient to force the Ionians to unite. However, the logic of events had been against them. On the mainland in the Peloponnesian League Sparta had risen to power over the small states of that area. Athens had united the land of Attica, had repelled its immediate neighbors, and under the guidance of Themistocles had prepared for eventual leadership at sea. The Ionian revolt had brought the states of Asia Minor together, at least temporarily. Finally, in 481 B.C. the Hellenic League had united the patriotic states of the peninsula under the command of Sparta and was soon to expand by taking in the states freed from Persian control. The victory itself had served to bring into sharp contrast Greek and non-Greek, and to give impetus to the spiritual unity of Hellas.

Though the principle of particularism remained to plague the statesmen and in the end to bring the cities to ruin, it seemed at the moment of victory as if the internecine wars of the Greeks might be ended and the eventual union of Hellas on a federal basis accomplished. Unfortunately, the past left other legacies that made this an idle dream, as the ever-increasing rivalry between Athens and Sparta wrecked all hopes of such an accomplishment.

New Parties   The economic and social movements of the preceding centuries, reflected in the political development, had created in most states two factions. The first, a conservative party, was made up of the old aristocratic families, who had opened their ranks to absorb the most successful of the commoners and, in union with them, clung to the ideals of aristocratic government. It was an aristocracy that prided itself on excellence, on achievement, and on intelligence. The land remained essentially its basis, and its strongest supporters were among the peasants, for whom the great names still had appeal. In Sparta the ruling class supported this oligarchic party. The leaders of this group in Athens were Aristides and Cimon, son of Miltiades. The lyric poet, Pindar (p. 238), and the Athenian dramatist, Aeschylus (p. 302), were its chief literary representatives. Added to the lofty position of these aristocrats was the patriotic memory of their heroic leadership in the war with Persia.

Commerce and industry, however, had resulted in the creation of an urban party of decidedly radical tendencies made up of men who looked to a domestic program of democracy and to a foreign policy of expansion. The time had not yet come when this group would develop its own leaders, but aristocrats were not lacking to follow in the path of the Athenian Cleisthenes and to set themselves at the head of the popular elements. Themistocles of Athens, himself a "new" man without the background of a great family, and Pausanias of Sparta planned for a new era. One concept dominated the minds of both parties and became an essential element of the new age—the idea that the basis of the state was law which knew not position, privilege, nor individuals.

Spartan Leadership   The Spartans had proved their right to military leadership in the Hellenic League. But Sparta was not fitted for solution of the problems which that body faced. The task of freeing the Asiatic Greeks and keeping Persia out of the Aegean was essentially a naval one. It required leaders who would be resourceful, adaptable, and tactful. Such men the Spartan system did not produce; its leaders knew no argument but force, and to their narrow viewpoint and natural arrogance was added a lack of interest in affairs outside the Peloponnesus. Problems at home were pressing: the number of Spartans had begun to decline, the perioeci were at best of doubtful value, and the helots were a positive menace. Sending large forces to the other side of the Aegean would be attended with serious dangers of revolt at home. Further, the conservative Spartans might well have feared what events proved: that individual Spartans were not to be trusted away from home when exposed to foreign wealth and foreign ideas. There was a considerable party favorably inclined to Athens and willing to leave matters to that city, confident in its friendship and loyalty.

Pausanias   As it happened, Spartan command failed lamentably. Pausanias, leading an allied fleet into Persian waters in 478 B.C., gained some success in Cyprus, then wheeled around and took Byzantium. But success went to his head. He had already been treating the allies with arrogant cruelty, and presently he entered into intrigues with Persia and set himself up to rule in almost Persian style, enjoying to the full his newly gained power and wealth. On the representation of the allies, he was recalled home, where he put his new ideas to work by planning a revolution, the freeing of the helots, and the modernizing of Sparta. After his plot became known, the ephors hesitated for a time to touch the hero of Plataea. When he fled to the shrine of Athena for protection, however, with Athenian consent they walled him in and left him to die of starvation, releasing him only when he was on the point of death lest he pollute the shrine.

The Rise of Athens   The naval leadership of the League then passed to Athens, which was pre-eminently fitted to undertake it. At the end of the war Themistocles was the hero of the hour. Wherever he went he was acclaimed, and states invited him to arbitrate their disputes. Under his leadership Athens speedily regained all that the war had cost it and added to itself fresh laurels. Houses and temples were quickly, though for a time rudely, reconstructed. Despite the opposition of Sparta, a wall was built around the city, and the Peiraeus was fortified as a naval base. In the country the Areopagus supervised the reconstruction of farms and the renewal and extension of olive orchards and vineyards. Trade connections were re-established with the Italian cities, with the Etruscans, and with the Black Sea region, and the friendship of the Ionian cities was cultivated.

Party struggles in Athens between the more conservative forces, led by Aristides and Cimon and supported by the aristocratic families and by the farming class, and the growing industrial and commercial groups in the city, whose champion was Themistocles, resulted in victory for the former. Themistocles, whose pride and austerity had given offense, was ostracized. Later he was implicated in the plot of Pausanias, and when recalled to Athens for trial fled to Persia where, according to tradition, he ended his life by poison to escape compliance with an order to lead an attack against Hellas. His remains were later brought back to Athens, and Thucydides, the Athenian historian, recognizing the greatness of the man, wrote a panegyric on him.

The needs of Athens made it evident that the work Themistocles had begun could not end. Though for a period the Areopagus was once more in power as a guiding force, and Athens was led by Aristides and Cimon, their policies were perforce but a continuation and completion of the program of Themistocles.

Cimon was a typical product of his time and class. Handsome, vigorous, aristocratic to the core, he had the ability to meet all men on a friendly footing and was personally very popular. As a naval commander he was without rival, laying the foundations upon which rested the greatness of Athens in the next generation.

The Confederacy of Delos   The first step in the rise of Athens came with the organization of the Confederacy of Delos, the brain child of Themistocles and the work of Aristides. A series of offensive and defensive alliances was concluded between Athens and the maritime states, according to which a fleet was to be provided to protect the Aegean from Persia. Those states that were able constructed ships; others paid contributions to the common treasury, out of which expenses were to be met. The old Ionian shrine of Apollo on the island of Delos was made the center of the Confederacy. The money was deposited in the temple in the care of its priests, and a congress of deputies met regularly under Athenian presidency. The commander of the fleet was to be an Athenian, and to this office Cimon was appointed. Under his leadership the rest of the Asiatic Greek states were liberated, and in a battle fought near the mouth of the Eurymedon River in 468 B.C. the Persian fleet and army were routed.

The Aegean was freed for the time from the Persian menace. Some of the smaller states thereupon failed to make their payments, which seemed vexatious and unnecessary, but the fleet of the Confederacy compelled them to continue. In 468 B.C. Naxos, and shortly thereafter Thasos, tried to secede. Force was used, and the two cities were not only compelled to surrender but to enter into a treaty that involved political subjection to Athens. The first steps were thus taken in the transformation of the Confederacy into an Athenian empire.

The Helot Revolt In 464 B.C., after an earthquake, the helots revolted in Sparta. Ithome was again fortified, and Sparta itself only just saved. In 462 B.C., after failing to put down the revolt, the Spartans appealed to their allies, and particularly to the Athenians, for assistance. Cimon favored their request, since the policy of his party had been established on the principle of Hellenic unity, and he carried the day. But the victory proved fatal to him. The Athenian forces failed to do all that was expected of them and friction developed. The Spartans finally requested them to return home, and subdued the helots without Athenian assistance. Cimon returned, only to be ostracized. Meanwhile a new party had arisen in Athens. The younger generation was restless under the supervision of an Areopagus composed increasingly of mediocre men who were chosen by lot as archons. After the passing of Themistocles and the death of Aristides, the radical group found a leader in Ephialtes, and after his assassination in Pericles. They first attacked and destroyed the power of the Areopagus and then accomplished the overthrow of Cimon. In 461 B.C., the age of Pericles began.

THE AGE OF PERICLES

Triumph of the Democracy The victory Ephialtes and Pericles won over Cimon in 461 B.C. marked the completion of the work of Solon, Peisistratus, Cleisthenes, and Themistocles. Athens had been transformed from a small agricultural state into a flourishing commercial and industrial city possessing a powerful fleet and heading a maritime confederacy. As if in recognition of this transformation, the final steps were taken in democratizing the constitution. The powers of administrative supervision held by the conservative Council of the Areopagus were transferred to the democratic *boule* (council) of five hundred, and the judicial functions of the Areopagus, except for the trial of homicides, were given to the *heliaea*, or popular supreme court. To enable the *heliaea* to carry out its newly acquired tasks, it was established as a yearly panel and divided for the trial of cases into a number of juries. Finally, to permit all men, whatever their means, to serve the state, the principle of payment for public service was introduced. The shopkeepers or laborers in the city who served as oarsmen in the fleet thus won a share in the government of Athens along with the aristocrats and the farmers.

Athenian Imperialism The democratic party and its leader, Pericles, were firmly imperialistic, determined to secure for Athens leadership in the Hellenic world and control over Greek trade. As the first step in this program the Long Walls were constructed from Athens to Peiraeus, a distance of about four and a half miles. These parallel walls, five hundred and fifty feet apart, protected Athenian communications with the overseas sources of its grain supply. So long as the fleet controlled the sea, Athens could not be starved into surrender.

The problem of the supply of grain was of supreme importance to the Hellenic cities. While in all the states agriculture was the basis of economic life, it was so given over to the culture of the olive and the vine that few states produced enough food to provide for their people. The chief sources of grain were the Black Sea region, Egypt, and the rich fields of Italy and Sicily. Athens was able to regulate the Black Sea trade through colonies on the Thracian Chersonese and Byzantium on the straits of the Bosporus, which was in the Confederacy of Delos. Control over trade with Egypt and the west would not only make the Athenians secure but would give them an effective strangle hold on the balance of the Aegean world. The only enemy they needed to fear was Sparta. Accordingly Pericles planned the development of a strong league on the Greek mainland, which might effectively challenge Sparta's Peloponnesian League, and the adoption of measures that would establish Athenian control over the sources of grain supply.

The Land Empire   To secure an outpost against Sparta, Pericles made an alliance with Argos, which had abolished its monarchy and established a democratic constitution. When Megara seceded from the Peloponnesian League and entered into alliance with Athens, the Athenians gained not only control over the isthmus but a foothold on the Corinthian Gulf. Thessaly was also brought into the alliance. Sparta countered by sending an army into Boeotia to strengthen the power of Thebes and to re-establish the Boeotian League, which had been destroyed by the defection of Thebes to the Persians. Though this army won a victory over the Athenians at Tanagra in 457 B.C., it failed to accomplish its purpose. When it returned to Sparta after the battle, the Athenians easily defeated the Thebans and drew Boeotia, Phocis, and Locris into the League.

The Western Trade   Athens fortified the position it had gained on the Corinthian Gulf by building walls across the isthmus connecting the seaports of Megara on either side. The Achaean cities on the southern shores of the gulf joined with Athens and the Messenian helots, who after their revolt had been allowed to leave the Peloponnesus. They were settled at Naupactus (459 B.C.) near the mouth of the gulf on the northern shore under Athenian protection. The Gulf of Corinth thus passed into the control of Athens, Corinth was bottled up, and Athens dominated the western trade.

Aegina   At the same time Aegina, most dangerous enemy of Athenian commerce because of its location in the Saronic Gulf, was overcome. The Aeginetans had vainly struggled against the loss of their commercial pre-eminence to the mainland city. An earlier war between the two had been brought to an end by the invasion of Xerxes. In 457 B.C. an Athenian force was landed on the island, and the following year the city surrendered, tore down its walls, and entered the Confederacy of Delos.

Egypt   Not content with all of these undertakings, Pericles continued to prosecute the war against Persia with a vigorous campaign in Cyprus. A revolt that broke out in Egypt against Artaxerxes, son of Xerxes, gave him an opportunity to strike a deadly blow at the Persian king and to secure for Athens possession of the rich Egyptian trade. Accordingly a fleet was dispatched to carry aid to the rebels. In this, however, Athens met its first reverse. In 454 B.C. a Persian army put down the revolt and destroyed the Athenian fleet, along with fifty ships which came too late as a reinforcement.

The End of the Persian Wars   This blow to Athenian power and pride was serious. When fear arose that the weakening of the fleet might result in a renewed Persian attack on the Aegean, the treasury of the Confederacy was moved from Delos to Athens, and Cimon was brought back into power to handle the Persian menace. In 450 B.C. he negotiated a five years' truce with Sparta, and the following year he led an expedition against Persia. On the island of Cyprus, though Cimon died shortly before the battle, his forces won a victory over the Persians. Thus ended the Persian Wars. An Athenian, Callias, negotiated an oral agreement with Susa whereby each agreed to leave the other alone. The Persian kings, however, never formally recognized the loss of their Greek possessions in Asia Minor.

The Thirty Years' Peace   The failure of the Egyptian venture was followed by disaster at home. The defeat of an Athenian force in 447 B.C. at Coronea in Boeotia resulted in the loss of Boeotia, Phocis, and Locris. The same year Megara and Chalcis revolted and a Spartan army invaded Attica. Pericles acted with great promptness. The Spartan king was persuaded, possibly by bribes, to withdraw; Megara was allowed to return to the Peloponnesian League; but the Chalcidian revolt was crushed. Athens had overtaxed its human resources, and the great dream of power had come to an end. In 445 B.C. a thirty years' peace was negotiated with Sparta on the basis of the *status quo*. Of its continental allies, Athens kept only Plataea and Naupactus; Sparta was recognized as supreme on land; Athens, on sea. Aegina and the other island states remained allied with Athens. Neither side was to interfere with the other, and all disputes were to be settled by arbitration. Consolidation of the maritime empire, the possession of Athens under the treaty, was Pericles' next task.

The Athenian Empire   The Confederacy of Delos had been organized originally as a union of free states for defense against Persia to which some members contributed ships and others money. The sub-

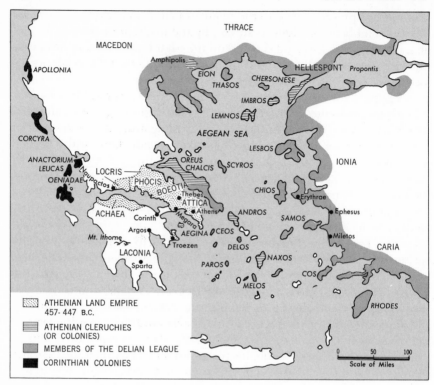

THRACE

MACEDON

APOLLONIA

Amphipolis

EION
THASOS
CHERSONESE

HELLESPONT   Propontis

IMBROS

LEMNOS

CORCYRA

AEGEAN SEA

LESBOS

IONIA

ANACTORIUM
LEUCAS
OENIADAE

LOCRIS
PHOCIS
BOEOTIA
Thebes
ATTICA
Athens

OREUS
CHALCIS

SCYROS

ACHAEA   Corinth
Argos
Mt. Ithome

Megara
AEGINA   CEOS
Troezen

ANDROS

CHIOS

Erythrae

Ephesus

SAMOS

Miletos

CARIA

LACONIA
Sparta

PAROS

DELOS

NAXOS

COS

MELOS

RHODES

☒ ATHENIAN LAND EMPIRE
    457- 447 B.C.

≣ ATHENIAN CLERUCHIES
    (OR COLONIES)

▨ MEMBERS OF THE DELIAN LEAGUE

■ CORINTHIAN COLONIES

0   50   100
Scale of Miles

The Athenian Empire, 457–447 B.C.

jection of Naxos and Thasos by Athens when they revolted began the
transformation of the League into an empire. The transfer of the
treasury to Athens in 454 B.C., dictated by fear of Persia and proposed
by Samos, strengthened Athenian control. Gradually in the following
years the smaller states were reduced to a subject status, until only
Chios, Lesbos, and Samos were left independent. In 440–439 B.C.
Samos revolted and was compelled to submit. The council of the League
ceased to meet, and henceforth the affairs of the empire were directed
by the Athenian Assembly. Pallas Athena replaced the Ionian Apollo
of Delos as the guardian divinity of the empire and the recipient of its
treasures. The surplus of imperial funds was used in beautifying
Athens for the glorification of the goddess.

Organization of the Empire   A new organization was developed
after 445 B.C., partly through treaties with individual states and partly
by Athenian legislative enactments. In the city-states secured by treaty,
Athens supported democratic governments, while those cities that had
revolted received charters prescribing their constitutions. In 442 B.C.
a commission divided the empire into five districts for purposes of administration. The amount of tribute was fixed by Athenian officials

every four years, but appeals from their decision might be carried to the Athenian juries. Cases at law involving capital punishment or loss of citizenship and suits involving large sums had to be taken to Athens to be tried before the Athenian law courts. The rights of independent coinage and the use of local weights and measures were likewise restricted.

Cleruchies So that Athens might hold the empire securely, it placed military posts in strategic towns, and settled groups of Athenian citizens on confiscated lands in the empire. Such settlements were called *cleruchies*; the settlers retained their full rights in Athens and served, like the Roman colonies (p. 399), as permanent garrisons to overawe and Atticize the subject states.

The Black Sea After the reorganization of the empire had been completed, Pericles determined upon its extension into the Black Sea region in order to ensure and extend Athenian control of this chief source of food for the city. Accordingly he voyaged around its shores with a magnificent fleet, settled colonies in the region, brought the Greek cities into the empire, and made alliances with the native princes, particularly in the Crimea. He thus brought the rich trade of that region into Athenian hands and at the same time began the process of Hellenizing the peoples of southern Russia.

Results of Imperialism The empire brought many benefits to the Aegean world. Within it were peace, uniform coins, weights and measures, consistency in law, and freedom from piracy. Abroad, peace with Persia made possible trade with Egypt, with the Mesopotamian lands, and even with India. Control of the Black Sea area brought to Athens fish of that sea and of the Propontis, the metals, timbers, and other commodities of its shores, the grain of Russia, and, by means of the route over the Urals, the products of central Asia and of China. Trade relations were established with the non-Dorian cities of the west, as far as Massilia. Athens, itself, center of commerce, obtained bountiful quantities of food and the wealth derived from tribute and from commercial profits which made possible the great culture of the age.

On the other hand, the imperial system was attended by evils. There was a complete lack of representation for lesser states of the empire. Athenian interference in local affairs of the Aegean and its complete control over the foreign relations of the cities offended the basic Greek idea of the right of each city-state to freedom and autonomy. Oligarchs everywhere opposed the empire, and even the democrats who benefited most were discontented. Public opinion in the Hellenic world ran high against Athens, and opposition to the Periclean program was not lacking even in Athens itself. The conservative party, led by Thucydides, son of Melesias, charged Pericles with treason to Hellas, tyranny over the allies, and mismanagement of the funds of the empire. In the test vote in 442 B.C. Pericles won and Thucydides was ostracized.

THE PELOPONNESIAN WAR

Causes The Athenian empire was the fundamental element in the situation out of which came the struggle between Athens and Sparta known as the Peloponnesian War. Corinth, fearing the loss of trade, and well aware of the menace of Athenian control over the western sources of food, and Sparta, jealous of Athenian power, were ready to retaliate at the first sign of renewed Athenian aggression. A series of incidents brought the states to war.

In 435 B.C., Corcyra, at the mouth of the Adriatic, was at war with Corinth and offered alliance to the Athenians. The offer was cordially accepted, and Corinth was defeated. A second blow at the Peloponnesians was struck (probably in 432 B.C.) by the Athenian decree that excluded Megarians from all markets of the empire. This meant to them financial ruin and starvation, and it served as a warning to any other state that might block the path of the Athenians. A third action involved Athenian use of force against Potidaea, which had refused to expel its Corinthian magistrates.

The Corinthians, fully aroused, appealed to Sparta to act in its traditional role as the defender of Hellenic liberty. To the Athenian offer of arbitration, made according to the treaty, the Spartans answered, "The honor of Sparta demands war." In the assembly of the Peloponnesian League which voted for war, the keynote was sounded: "We are fighting for the liberty of Hellas." Arbitration as a means of preventing war had failed in the crucial test. The real cause of the war, the Athenian empire and all it implied economically and politically, was not a problem that could be resolved by arbitration. In 431 B.C. hostilities began.

The Contestants A land power and a sea power fought for control in Hellas. Athens, through its strong fleet, controlled the sea. Its treasury possessed an enormous reserve fund for carrying on a maritime war, and its Long Walls protected it by land so that siege would avail nothing. Sparta was superior on land, but it lacked both a fleet and the money by which to acquire one. Pericles' plan for the war was clear. When the Spartans invaded Attica, the Athenians were to withdraw within the city where, refusing to engage in combat on land, they could be fed by the fleet; in retaliation the Athenian fleet would harass the Peloponnesian coasts and fight with Corinth for control of the western trade.

The Plague In the first year of the war the Spartan king, Archidamus, invaded Attica and destroyed crops and buildings while the Athenian fleet, as planned, menaced the Peloponnesus. But in the second year the Periclean strategy was wrecked by an unforeseen catastrophe. A plague broke out in Athens. Because of the crowded conditions of the city and the general lack of sanitation, it spread rapidly and destroyed almost a third of the population. In the attendant confusion, the people suspended Pericles from office and fined him, then reversing their action, they re-elected him general. In the next year, however, he died of the disease. His place as leader of the people fell to members of the artisan class: Cleon, the tanner, and Hyperbolus, the lampmaker. Though a strong, predominantly agricultural party called for peace, the war continued.

The Archidamian War After the plague had subsided, the Spartans continued their yearly invasion of Attica, and in 427 B.C. they gained substantial success in the capture of the Athenian ally, Plataea. On the other hand, the Athenian cause also prospered. A revolt of Lesbos in 428–427 B.C. was rigorously suppressed. The fleet under Phormio won several brilliant victories around the mouth of the Corinthian Gulf, and an Athenian army secured control of its northern shore. Then in 425 B.C., by an unexpected victory, the Athenians gained possession of Pylos on the west coast of the Peloponnesus and took captive one hundred and ten Spartan soldiers. When Sparta offered terms of peace, Athens, led by Cleon, refused.

Confident of ultimate triumph in the war and over the opposition of the peace party, Cleon doubled the tribute upon the cities of the empire to secure funds for the prosecution of the struggle with Sparta. Though this financial measure increased the immediate resources of the city, it brought hardships to the allies and increased their hostility, which later led to their revolt. Finally Brasidas, the sole outstanding Spartan of the war, found the Achilles' heel of the Athenian empire when he led his forces to the capture of Amphipolis in Thrace. Cleon went to meet him, and in the ensuing battle both were killed. Thereafter the peace parties prevailed in both cities, and in 421 B.C. the Peace of Nicias provided for the restoration of all lands and prisoners and for an alliance between Athens and Sparta. This brought to an end the ten-year period known as the Archidamian War, which had brought victory to neither side. Athens had lost prestige, and Sparta's Peloponnesian League was dissolved. Sparta could not even compel its erstwhile allies to carry out the terms of the peace. Into this unsatisfactory situation a new element was injected in the person of Alcibiades.

Expedition Against Syracuse To the leadership of Athens came Alcibiades, the youthful nephew of Pericles. Brilliant and popular, but unstable, vain, and self-seeking, he proposed to restore Athenian supremacy by an alliance with Argos and by expansion overseas. The Argive alliance involved Athens in a disastrous conflict in the Peloponnesus between Argos and Sparta which ended with a Spartan victory at Mantinea and restoration of the Peloponnesian League. Alcibiades' maritime scheme, however, called for the capture of Syracuse and formation of a western branch of the empire. In 415 B.C. a great fleet started for the west with high hopes and with every chance of success. It had not yet reached Syracuse when Alcibiades was recalled to stand trial on a charge of impiety. The night before the expedition sailed, a band of roisterers had mutilated the busts of Hermes (*hermae*) which stood before the doorways of Athenian houses, and Alcibiades was accused by his enemies of the sacrilege. Instead of returning, he fled to Sparta, where he disclosed the Athenian plans.

The Spartans sent aid to Syracuse and prepared to renew the war with vigor. The Athenian fleet was grossly mismanaged; one commander, Lamachus, a professional soldier, was killed; another, Nicias, a conservative who had opposed the expedition, proved utterly incompetent. A fleet, sent as reinforcement in 413 B.C. under an able commander, Demosthenes, found Syracuse ready for an attack, and the offensive therefore failed. When Demosthenes proposed to return, Nicias refused to leave because of an eclipse of the moon. An engagement followed; the fleet was defeated and blockaded in the harbor. The Athenians then attempted to retreat by land, but after fearful sufferings, they were forced to surrender to the Syracusans. Their generals were killed, and the men, imprisoned in stone quarries, suffered even greater agonies. Eventually the survivors were sold into slavery. The Athenian fleet and the flower of the Athenian army had been destroyed.

The Decelean War The position of the Athenians was critical in the extreme. They had lost a fleet and a large army, and the city and empire were in grave danger. Sparta, on the advice of Alcibiades, seized and fortified the stronghold, Decelea, in Attica, so that the Athenian farmers were obliged to remain within the walls of Athens. At the same time Sparta approached the Persians seeking financial aid and the assistance of a Phoenician fleet. At the price of the Greek cities in Asia Minor, which the Spartans surrendered to him, the Persian king promised and sent aid.

In the face of these difficulties the Athenians rallied and determined to defend themselves with vigor. To hold the empire and yet obtain funds, they abolished the tribute collections and levied a five per cent import and export duty throughout the empire. To secure effective administration, they elected a board of ten men as a committee of public safety to direct the affairs of the state. Political revolution followed when a coalition of the clubs of wealthy men, led by Peisander and Antiphon, terrorized the people into the acceptance of an oligarchic government in Athens. A council of four hundred drawn from the clubs was established to manage the state, and a definitive constitution was drawn up. The oligarchs hoped to alienate Persia from Sparta through the intrigues of Alcibiades, who wanted to return to Athens and who therefore promised to help them. By securing Persian support the oligarchs expected to bring the war to an end.

Alcibiades failed to keep his promise, and Persia remained on the side of Sparta. The Four Hundred proved incompetent in the direction of the war. Splitting into factions, this council was then overthrown by the moderates, who had the support of the army.

Full democracy was restored in 410 B.C. after Alcibiades, who had been recalled by the Athenians, won a brilliant victory off Cyzicus. This battle renewed the courage of the Athenians and restored Athenian access to the Hellespont and Black Sea. Athens therefore refused a Spartan offer of peace, though most of the subjects of the empire had revolted. Samos remained loyal, and from it as a base the Athenian army and navy carried on the war. Alcibiades was banished again when one of his subordinates, disobeying orders, was defeated at Notium in 407 B.C.

The following year, however, the fleet won the battle of Arginusae. In the last stages of this battle a storm arose and, to save the fleet, the Athenian commanders made no attempt to rescue the sailors whose ships were lost in the battle. This failure, in spite of their victory, caused their trial and execution in Athens.

Aegospotami After Arginusae the tide turned once more in favor of the Spartans. They had found an able commander in Lysander, an unscrupulous, ambitious, but competent man, who drew to his aid Cyrus, son of the Persian king and satrap of Sardis. With Persian money and a large fleet Lysander attacked the Hellespont, route of Athenian supplies. There, in 405 B.C., he made such a surprise attack on the Athenian fleet at Aegospotami while the men were seeking food on shore, that only the admiral, Conon, and a few ships escaped. It was the final disaster for Athens. The Spartans laid siege to the city, and in 404 B.C. Athens capitulated. The Long Walls were torn down to the music of flutes, as the Athenians gave up their fleet, their democracy, and their claims to empire. Amid great rejoicing over the fall of Athenian power the freedom of Hellas was proclaimed.

Results of the War "The Peloponnesian War," said the historian Thucydides, "was a protracted struggle and attended by calamities such as Hellas had never known within a like period of time. Never were so many cities captured and depopulated—some by barbarians, others by Hellenes themselves fighting against one another. . . . Never were exile and slaughter more frequent, whether in war or in civil strife. . . . There were earthquakes unparalleled in their extent and fury, and eclipses of the sun more numerous than are known to have happened in any former age; there were also in some places droughts causing famines and, lastly, the plague, which did immense harm and destroyed numbers of people."[1]

[1] G. W. Botsford and E. G. Sihler, *Hellenic Civilization.* New York: Columbia University Press, 1915, p. 28.

Truly the war had wrought havoc in the Greek world. In many of the cities factions engaged in party strife. Megara had been completely ruined by the Athenian policy of exclusion and by the annual raids during the first part of the war. The Ionian cities had fallen back into the power of Persia. The island states passed under the control of Sparta, and with the collapse of Athens their markets were ruined.

To Sparta, the triumph was of little real value because of its lack of interest in trade or in mobile wealth. Thebes was the chief beneficiary. The Thebans had grown wealthy from their raids into the north of Attica. Moreover they purchased at a low price the goods captured by their Spartan allies. They had also gained a military experience that was to stand them in good stead during the next century.

The freedom of Hellas won by the Spartans proved to be a delusion. In place of Athenian control Spartan military hegemony now interposed its iron hand. Lysander, eager to secure power and glory for himself as well as for Sparta, saw to it that Spartan influence was established among the former allies of Athens. The democratic leaders who were favorable to Athens were driven out, and decarchies, boards of ten men, were put in control of the states. To keep them in power, Lacedaemonian garrisons under helot commanders, called *harmosts*, were placed in some of the cities. The result was "plunder, oppression and murder." Spartan power was based on military force and it would endure, therefore, only so long as Sparta was supreme on land and on sea.

In Athens a board of thirty Athenian oligarchs was established as the ruling power. These Thirty Tyrants, led by Critias and supported by Spartan troops, held Athens in complete subjection and entered upon a policy of terrorism and corruption until in 403 B.C. the democracy was restored after a popular revolt. The great days of Athens were over. It had failed to unite the Greeks and in its failure had fallen miserably. Yet during the generations of its power it had lighted torches of democratic liberty and cultural ideals that still burn brightly.

13 · Athens in the Days
of Its Glory

P ERICLES, IN HIS FUNERAL ORATION, TOLD THE
Athenians: "I say that Athens is the school of Hellas and that
the individual Athenian in his own person seems to have the
power of adapting himself to the most varied forms of action
with the utmost versatility and grace."[1]

In the generations from Marathon to Aegospotami Athens occupied
the stage of Greek history. Its democratic government, economic
activities, buildings and works of art, literary productions, and scholars—
all made it the focal point of Hellenic civilization. Artists, philosophers,
scientists, and enterprising men of business from other parts of the
Greek world flocked to it to share in its wealth and glories. Athenian
democracy and Greek democracy, Athenian culture and Greek culture,
came to be synonymous.

Historians have long debated the explanation of its greatness. Was
it mere chance that there appeared so many great men in one city
in the same period? Was Athenian culture the product of a small
leisure class supported by slave labor? Or was it rather an achievement
in which every resident of Athens—citizen, alien, and slave—had a part
and to which the Hellenic world contributed of its best? The answer
to these questions must be sought in a survey of the institutions, the
people, and the achievements of the city.

THE DEMOCRACY

"It is true that we are called a democracy, for the administration is
in the hands of the many and not of the few. But while the law secures
equal justice to all alike in their private disputes, the claim of excellence

[1] This and the following quotations of the words of Pericles are from the funeral
oration in Thucydides, *History of the Peloponnesian War*, 2. 35–36. Trans. in G. W. Botsford
and E. G. Sihler, *Hellenic Civilization*. New York: Columbia University Press, 1915, pp.
239–246.

is also recognized; and when a citizen is in any way distinguished, he is preferred to the public service, not as a matter of privilege, but as the reward of merit. Neither is poverty a bar, but a man may benefit his country whatever be the obscurity of his condition. . . . An Athenian citizen does not neglect the state because he takes care of his own household; and even those of us who are engaged in business have a very fair idea of politics. We alone regard a man who takes no interest in public affairs, not as a harmless, but as a useless character; and if few of us are originators, we are all sound judges of a policy." With these words Pericles gave utterance to his ideal for Athenian democracy. The organization of the state at least made possible its attainment. Without any material change in structure, the political constitution of Athens had broadened and deepened since the reforms of Cleisthenes.

The Population Accurate information about the population of Attica and its distribution is lacking. The most recent estimates, based upon such scraps of information as are available, indicate a total in 431 B.C. of about 315,500, consisting of 172,000 citizens, 28,500 resident aliens, known as *metics*, and 115,000 slaves. According to the same compilation, 60,000 citizens, about one-third of the total, together with 25,000 aliens and 70,000 slaves, lived in the city and the port town, giving the urban area a population of 155,000. Of the approximate number of 43,000 male citizens, 25,000 were rich enough to buy armor, and about 18,000 belonged to the *thetes*.[2]

Athenian Citizenship An Athenian citizen was the child of Athenian parents. In earlier periods marriages of Athenian men with foreign women had been regarded as legal. But the greatness of Athens, the high value of citizenship in an imperial city, and the desire to keep Athenian blood pure caused Pericles to propose a law in 451 B.C. which declared the children of mixed marriages ineligible for citizenship. It is interesting to note that had this law been in effect earlier, Pericles himself would not have been an Athenian citizen, since his great-grandmother was Agariste of Sicyon. Tombstone inscriptions and later attempts at purification of the citizen lists indicate that this law was not strictly enforced.

The Census Classes The Athenian constitution retained among its legacies from the past the four census classes of Solon's laws (p. 217): five-hundred-bushel men, *hippeis* (knights), *zeugitae*, and *thetes*, an apparent though not actual contradiction of the democratic ideal. Only a few financial offices were still restricted to the upper classes, the five-hundred-bushel men and the knights. The archonship, however, was

---

[2] These estimates are taken from A. W. Gomme, *The Population of Athens in the Fifth and Fourth Centuries B.C.* Oxford: University of Glasgow Publication, 1933, *passim*, who frankly recognizes the uncertainty of the figures. It seems likely that the number of slaves is much too large.

opened to the third class, the *zeugitae*, and the officials actually made no objection when the lot fell upon a citizen classified as a *thete*. The classes served as a convenient means whereby the state might exact financial and military services according to the ability of each man to render them. At the same time the measure of classification shifted from the bushel to the drachma. This made it possible, in the era of prosperity, for a member of the lowest class, the *thetes*, to rise to the highest if he prospered in business. In the major political activities of the citizens — in the deme, council, and assembly — the classes played no part.

The Deme   The deme was the local unit of government and provided for the registration of voters. Its members held meetings, elected local officials, dealt with local business, kept the list of citizens, provided for the necessary nominations for state office, and gained in all this a fundamental training in self-government. Each deme had its local divinities and heroes, whom the demesmen worshiped in local festivals. So satisfying were these political and religious experiences that many a country demesman never felt the urge to go beyond them to participate in the larger affairs of the city. To all, the deme was the first object of affection. One of the most beautiful passages in the plays of Sophocles was written in praise of his own deme, the Deme of Colonus. Every Athenian was known by the name of the deme to which he belonged.

There is a danger here, however, of reading into the situation a modern concept of territorial division. The deme, though originally a piece of territory, was politically a group of people, not an area of ground. Membership was gained by inheritance, not by residence. If the demesman moved, he still belonged to his ancestral deme, and in fact paid a small fee to the deme in which he took up his residence for the privilege of living there.

The Tribes   The demes were united in the artificial and, for the most part, spiritless *trittyes* (thirds) and through these into the ten tribes. Each tribe took its name from a hero of Athens and celebrated a festival in his honor. Each had its assembly which chose its leaders and dealt with tribal affairs. Through the tribes war taxes were apportioned and levies made for the army. Men marched into war in the tribal regiment, and tribes set up tablets in honor of their heroic dead. Though these tribes were political creations and had none of the binding force of tradition possessed by kinship groups, their responsibilities to the state gave them such life, importance, and solidarity that when an individual was injured men said a whole tenth of the state suffered with him.

The Boule, or Council, of Five Hundred   Fifty men from each tribe, apportioned among the demes according to their size, were chosen to serve in the *boule*, or council, of five hundred. The payment of a drachma a day, introduced by Pericles, made it possible for any citizen to serve the state as a councilor. Since no man could serve more than twice, it is fairly safe to assume that any man who had the slightest inclination to public service could at some time hold this office and obtain actual experience in governmental administration. Each tribal group of fifty served as an executive committee, or *prytaneis*, for the whole council for a tenth of the year, a *prytany*.

The *prytaneis* lived in the council house during the prytany and some of their number had to be always on duty. One of them was chosen by lot to preside over the council and the assembly. The executive committee dealt with routine matters and with emergencies, reporting daily to the whole council, whose agenda it prepared. The council received and acted upon these reports in its daily meeting. In unimportant matters of state administration it could pass decrees binding upon the people for a year. In all matters of importance it discussed and prepared bills for submission to the people.

In itself a sort of executive committee for the Athenian citizen body, the council's duties were many and various. It examined the qualifications of the magistrates and of the new council to see that no persons unworthy or unqualified by law were chosen. It supervised the execution of the decrees of the people, the management of public property, the collection and expenditure of public moneys, the erection of public works, and the condition of the army and navy. After the downfall of the Areopagus, it assumed guardianship of the constitution and of that moral discipline which the ancient states always felt necessary. The councilors thus had manifold opportunities to learn the problems and the aims of statecraft.

The Assembly   All male citizens over eighteen belonged to the *ecclesia*, or assembly, the number present at any meeting depending upon the degree of public interest at the moment. The laws required that the assembly meet at least four times a prytany and whenever summoned by the council. At the first regular meeting of each prytany, it received the reports of the magistrates and provided for their recall and trial if these were deemed unsatisfactory. The same meeting dealt with questions of grain supply and defense. Under the presidency of one of the *prytaneis*, chosen by lot, the assembly debated freely and approved or rejected measures presented to it by the council. The magistrates, particularly the generals, addressed it; after them precedence was given according to age and service. But anyone could move to amend or initiate legislation. All new proposals were referred to the council for consideration and report; however, each individual was held responsible for his proposals. Even though the people passed his bill, if within the year it was thought to be unconstitutional or detrimental to the best interests of Athens, a "writ of illegality" was brought against him and his decree. If the court where the writ was presented gave adverse decision, the decree was set aside and the proposer punished. After a bill had been in effect a year the people as a whole assumed responsibility for it.

Laws   Measures thus passed by the people were called *psephismata*, administrative decrees. The laws, *nomoi*, dealt with fundamental constitutional questions, and the council, the assembly, and the magistrates were all subject to them. For these laws a special procedure was adopted, probably during the period of the Peloponnesian War. In the first prytany of the year the thesmothetae reviewed the existing laws before the people. If they found any obsolete or in need of change, they presented their recommendations. At the same time any private citizen who desired to do so might propose amendments. After discussion in the fourth session of the prytany the people provided for the drafting and pay of a large jury, the members of which were called *nomothetae*. When this jury met, the laws under discussion were put on trial as if they were persons. Those who proposed changes were the prosecutors, while five advocates appointed by the people acted as defenders. The majority decision of the jury determined the law.

The Magistrates   While the structure of the magistracies had not been changed since Cleisthenes, they had been considerably democratized by the development of sortition (choice by lot), the introduction of payment for public service, and the great increase in the number of those serving the state in official capacity.

The Archons   The nine archons and their secretary were chosen by lot, originally from five hundred candidates of the first three census classes nominated by the demes, and later from one hundred presented by the tribes but in such a way that there would be one from each tribe. Those chosen had to prove to the council that they had the requisite means for their census class, that their ancestors had been Athenians for three generations, that they worshiped the traditional Zeus of the Household and Paternal Apollo, and that they had fulfilled their duties to the state and to their parents. During their year of office they received four obols a day, and after it, ineligible for re-election, they became life members of the Council of the Areopagus.

The archons, formerly so powerful, had become merely religious officials and clerks for the law courts after the law of 487 B.C., which, by providing for the choice of archons by lot, had brought mediocre men into office and transferred direction of the state to the generals. The chief archon dealt with cases involving family matters and the protection of widows and orphans, and presided over the Great Dionysia. The king archon had jurisdiction over religious cases and conducted the Mysteries and other festivals; his wife was united in ritual marriage to the god Dionysus. The polemarch had the direction of all cases involving foreigners and of certain rites connected with war. The six thesmothetae guarded the laws, and prepared all other cases for trial by the courts.

The Generals   Executive direction of the state was in the hands of ten generals, *strategoi*, who were elected by the assembly, at first one from each tribe, but eventually from the entire citizen body without reference to tribes. The only qualifications were Athenian citizenship and the possession of land in Attica. They were apparently unpaid save when on active military service in time of war. They could be re-elected, and it was this office that Pericles held for over thirty years. While all ten were theoretically equal, except as the people assigned special duties to them, it was inevitable that the one among them who had the most forceful personality or the greatest experience, or was the best orator, should gain ascendancy over the others and act as their spokesman. This is what occurred in the case of Pericles, and he was at times called *autocrator*, or absolute master, in consequence. The *strategoi* were commanders-in-chief of the army and navy, looked after the defenses of the city, and dealt with its foreign relations. They recommended measures to the council and asked it to call meetings of the assembly. Thus they were the executives of the state and the directors of its public policy. Although accustomed to follow their recommendations, the people kept sharp watch over the generals at all times.

Lesser Officials   Besides the officials just mentioned, there were a host of others of all kinds, regular and special, most of them being paid for their services. A few of the financial officials were elected; the remainder were chosen by lot and usually in boards of ten. Only members of the first two census classes could hold financial offices. Some of the other positions were restricted to the *zeugitae* class, but most of them were open to all the people. Nominations were usually made by the demes or the tribes. There were receivers of revenue, treasurers, and auditors, and supervisors of the grain supply, of the water supply, of the market place, of the roads, and of the religious functions. For special tasks, such as supervision of the erection of public buildings like the Parthenon and the handling of emergencies that required unusual attention, temporary committees of ten were established by public enactment. Aristotle says that there were normally seven hundred citizens in the service of the state in these capacities, besides a large number engaged abroad in the affairs of the empire.

Athenian Law Courts   The stronghold of the democracy, perhaps the most distinctive feature of the Athenian government, was the jury system developed by Pericles out of Solon's *heliaea*, or popular supreme court. Every year six thousand jurors, called *dicasts*, were selected by lot from all those over thirty years of age who wished to be enrolled. These jurors were divided by lot into large sections. Later, though perhaps not in the time of Pericles, they ordinarily were divided into groups containing from two hundred and one to one thousand and one men, called *dicasteria*. The number depended upon the importance of the case. All cases that could not be settled by arbitrators were submitted to the dicasts. The jurors took an oath to judge the case before them in accordance with the laws and statutes of Athens, and received one (later, three) obols for each day of service.

The procedure in law suits was fairly simple. Civil cases were first submitted to a man over sixty who served as arbitrator. If his decision did not satisfy, an appeal was carried to a jury. Criminal cases went directly to the court. The plaintiff, who in public cases would be a magistrate or an advocate appointed by the people, entered a charge with the proper official, who was in ordinary cases at law one of the thesmothetae. After the defendant was notified, a preliminary hearing was held. Plaintiff and defendant then submitted briefs containing statements of the charge and denials thereof, citation of the laws involved, and evidence in the form of depositions. If the magistrate deemed the charge unsustained, the case was dismissed. If the magistrate sustained the charge, after appropriate oaths had been given by the litigants, the briefs were sealed in an urn. On the day appointed for trial, the case was assigned to a jury. The magistrate who presided opened the urn and read the statements. Conducting their own cases, the plaintiff and defendant then addressed the jury. Witnesses might be called on for evidence, and special pleaders might be drawn in. If the special pleader were a fine speaker and popular, the jury would probably applaud. Appeals were frequently made to past services, to patriotic feeling, to family sentiment, and to all the foibles and prejudices of the jury.

After the case was presented, the jurors cast their votes, and a majority decided the case. If a penalty was involved, a verdict of guilty was followed by a second action. Plaintiff and defendant submitted alternate verdicts, and in a second ballot the jury chose between them. Public penalties were enforced by the magistrates. The settlement of private claims was left to the individuals involved, which sometimes necessitated further legal action.

Finances Though more orderly than in most of the other Greek states, the financial system of Athens was still decidedly irregular from the modern point of view. The aversion all Greeks felt for direct taxation as unbefitting the character of freemen made it impossible for the state to collect any such regular source of income. But it owned a great many properties in the form of public buildings, olive orchards, pastures, and mines, from all of which rental was derived. The most important, the mines at Laurium, were leased to contractors who paid yearly a rather large and fixed amount, and possibly also a tax on the annual production. The treasury derived occasional income from the sale at auction of houses and movable property that came into the poses-sion of the state by confiscation. Port and market dues, an import and export tax of two per cent ad valorem, sales taxes, court fees and fines, and a tax collected from all resident aliens amounted to a substantial sum. The rich were called upon regularly in turn to perform liturgies, special tasks that required them to provide out of their own means for certain expenses of the fleet and of the religious festivals. In wartime the *eisphora*, a special war tax on capital, was levied on the tribes as needed and collected from the citizens according to the valuation of their property. The greatest source of income during this period was, of course, the tribute from the subject states of the empire.

Out of these funds the expenses of the government were met, the magistrates and the jurors paid, the army and the navy maintained, religious festivals held, public works erected, gifts of honor made, the orphans of citizens slain in war and invalid soldiers supported, and, at times, the poor assisted. The surplus was added to the treasuries of the gods as the people directed.

The Athenians recognized the importance of proper control of finance. The financial officials, always men of wealth, were elected, not chosen by lot, and often for long terms of office. Each year the council prepared a budget of the needs of the state; on its advice the assembly specified the distribution of moneys, and efforts were made to devise means of raising the necessary funds. It was understood that court fees and fines should be diverted to the payment of the jurors, and that the first charges upon the imperial revenues were the fleet and the maintenance of a war chest. The latter was entrusted to the temple of Athena as a reserve for emergencies. At the outbreak of the Peloponnesian War it amounted to six thousand talents. Yet the haphazard character of financial control and the general reliance upon irregular or external sources of income made it possible for Gladstone to say without exaggeration, "Athens perished because of its poor public finance."[3]

The Army   The army was composed of the able-bodied citizens of Athens. The tribal military commander of each tribe kept for it the muster roll, or list of all citizens from the ages of eighteen to sixty of *zeugitae* census or above arranged according to the years of their enrollment. Resident aliens (p. 277) were enrolled on these lists through the deme in which they resided. The wealthy who belonged to the first two census classes and could not show physical disability were called out for the cavalry. They and their horses were carefully examined each year by the council. If accepted, each knight was given an allowance for the upkeep of his horse, and received special training in horsemanship and cavalry maneuvers. To be a member of the knights

---

[3] Quoted in Andreas M. Andreades, *A History of Greek Public Finance.* Trans. by Carroll N. Brown. Cambridge, Mass.: Harvard University Press, 1933, p. 207.

was a great honor. The knights formed a corporation with special privileges, and appeared in public processions, notably the Panathenaea.
At the outbreak of the Peloponnesian War there were about one
thousand knights in the army.

All others were liable to military service in the infantry as hoplites,
heavy-armed warriors. At the age of eighteen, when the youths were
first enrolled, they took the oath of service and entered upon a two-year
period of training. During the first year they were instructed in gym-
nastics and in the handling of weapons. At the end of the year the
state presented them with a spear and a shield, and they donned
the hat and cloak that were their marks of distinction. For the second
year they garrisoned the fortresses of Attica and were drilled in field
tactics. They were not called out for active service but, with the older
men, formed the line of home defense. From the age of twenty to fifty
they were liable to service or call as the people might direct. At times of
crisis the entire army could be called out. In 431 B.C. this meant an
effective force of twenty-five thousand men. The hoplite's equipment,
which he furnished himself, consisted of shield, helmet, breastplate,
greaves, sword, and spear. Only the orphans of men slain in battle received from the state their panoply, or full set of armor. Each warrior
carried with him three days' provisions, and received a drachma a day
for himself and one for his servant. The *thetes* were called upon for
service as light-armed troops and as bowmen.

The troops were enrolled in tribal regiments, but the commanding
officers reorganized them into field battalions according to necessity.
Although the Athenian phalanx was no match for the highly trained
Spartans, with the tradition of Marathon behind it, it acquitted itself
respectably. Contemporaries credited it with special aptitude in the
siege and capture of fortified places.

The Navy The glory of Athens lay in the fleet, which it owed to
Themistocles and Cimon. In 431 B.C. the fleet consisted of three hundred triremes, (p. 260), ships of the line, and a reserve of one hundred
select ships for the defense of Peiraeus. At the beginning of each year
the state picked certain men of the first census class as *trierarchs*, or commanders of triremes. To each of the trierarchs the state furnished a ship,
together with a supply of canvas and rigging. The trierarch purchased
the remainder of the equipment necessary and engaged the crew.
Usually ten hoplites were picked as marines. A number of skilled sea-
men and mariners were also chosen to direct the sailing of the ship.
Finally, there were the oarsmen, sixty for the upper row and fifty-four
for each of the two lower rows. These were recruited from the *thetes*,
from the resident aliens, and from the citizens of the allied states. All
were paid by the state, the upper row of oarsmen, usually all citizens,
receiving somewhat more than the others. The trierarch might hire the

captain or assume command himself, the latter usually being the case. It was a notable chance for a citizen of wealth to distinguish himself in the public service. A golden crown was offered as a prize to the trierarch whose ship was the first ready to sail, and meritorious service in war was certain to receive proper recognition. On the other hand, it was recognized at the same time that the use of *thetes* in the fleet was the surest foundation and safeguard of the democracy, since it assured to that class political rights, just as service in the infantry had earlier given similar power to the heavy-armed warriors of the middle class (p. 197).

Democracy in Athens   If the right of every citizen, whatever his rank or means, to participate in political decisions and in the direction of the state, and the obligation of every citizen to serve the state with money and in person according to his wealth and ability constitute a democracy, then Athens was democratic. The charge is often made, however, that the Athenian citizen body constituted a small, privileged group ruling over a large number of foreigners and slaves resident in Athens who could not acquire citizenship, and that Athens was therefore not a true democracy. From the modern point of view this contention is valid, but it is one the ancient Greek would hardly have understood. Citizenship was a natural right acquired by inheritance and protected by ancestral divinities. Residence in a city, therefore, no more made one a citizen than the renting of a room today makes one a member of the family of the house.

The foreigners were citizens of their own communities who were residing in Athens by their own choice and under no constraint to remain there. Since they could not worship the ancestral gods of the Athenians, they could not hope to participate in the activities that were under the protection of the gods unless the state, in return for services rendered, granted them those rights by an act equivalent to adoption.

Slavery was a recognized institution. In the Greek view, slaves were inferior subjects, and any thought of allowing them participation in politics was absurd. Athens, governed by its body of citizens, the *demos*, as the Athenians called it, was, by the standards of the ancient Greeks, a democracy.

THE PEOPLE AND THEIR OCCUPATIONS

The Athenian citizen body, with its varied groups and classes—the fishermen of the seacoast, the merchants and artisans of the city, the farmers of the plains and valleys, and the herdsmen and woodsmen on the mountainsides—presented almost a cross section of the Greek peoples and brought to bear upon the life of the city a wide diversity of experiences and ideas. In addition, the large group of aliens and slaves, Greek, Oriental, and barbarian drawn from every corner of the ancient world, made its own contributions to Athenian civilization.

The Peasantry In the villages scattered over the land lived a sturdy peasantry, in the Periclean Age fairly prosperous and contented. They made their living in various ways. On the hillsides they raised goats and cattle, or they cut and dressed wood, or made it into charcoal. They kept bees and found a ready market for honey. They terraced the hillsides and planted vineyards. In the valleys they tended olive orchards and raised grain between the rows of trees. They still employed primitive implements and the two-field system. Near the city, truck gardens of vegetables, fruits, and flowers provided excellent sources of livelihood.

The assemblies and offices in the demes and the local religious festivals, particularly those in honor of Dionysus, furnished the peasantry with sufficient opportunities for political and religious expression. Most of them were wealthy enough to belong to the *zeugitae* class, and they formed the main body of hoplites in the army. Content with their village life, they seldom went to the city, save when political or military requirements demanded, or perhaps when the great festivals were held. Aristophanes, the comic poet, who knew and loved them, represents them as bewildered by the noise and confusion in the city, thoroughly unhappy until they found themselves back on their native hillsides. Naturally conservative, they were a steadying influence in the Athenian assembly on the rare occasions when they made their presence count.

The Aristocracy Most of the aristocrats who had maintained ancestral estates in the plain lived on them in fine villas and operated their estates with the help of tenant farmers, hired laborers, or slaves. Others moved to the city and left their farms in charge of stewards. These estates would not be considered large in modern times since the largest of which we know was sixty-four acres. Agricultural slavery was apparently unprofitable and not practiced except on the larger estates, though the small farmer frequently hired slaves in the rush seasons.

Many of the aristocratic class, like Pericles and Nicias, rejoiced in the glory of Athens and were proud to serve it with their wealth and their abilities. Others despised the democracy, and fought the policies of Pericles in state and empire. These were temporarily demoralized by the ostracism of Thucydides, son of Melesias, but they vigorously renewed their activities during the Peloponnesian War, which they opposed. In the early days of the war their motto was "business as usual," and they built for themselves fine houses in the city, adorned with tapestries, carpets, and mural paintings. The Decelean War bore heavily upon them, however. Their country estates were ruined; twenty thousand slaves (most of whom were employed in industry) escaped, and the burdens of the trierarchy increased.

Blaming their troubles upon the democracy, they withdrew from active participation in politics to avoid contact with *hoi polloi* (the masses). In their social clubs they discussed ideal oligarchic constitutions and planned the overthrow of the democracy. Their attempt to accomplish this, however, in setting up the Four Hundred and in writing the definitive constitution was a complete failure. The establishment of the Thirty later restored them to power for a brief and inglorious period.

For the most part the education of the aristocrats turned them against the traditional religion. One club burlesqued the Mysteries and brought severe penalties upon its members. Another, or possibly the same, was probably responsible for the mutilation of the Hermae. Critias, a leader among them, went so far as to declare that religion was merely a device developed by clever men to control the rest. Others, such as Nicias, who refused to move during an eclipse of the moon, clung to a strict obedience to old customs and superstitions.

The Common People   The commoners earned their livelihood in all the variety of ways known to a big city. Some were farmers who lived in town and went out by day to work their nearby farms. Herdsmen led their sheep and goats out to pasturage and back into the city by night; the walls of the gates that are still standing were worn smooth by the wool of the herds. Many owned or rented houses in the city and in them plied their trades as blacksmiths, carpenters, potters, weavers, dyers, tanners, cobblers, retail dealers, or schoolteachers. Others worked as stonecutters or masons on private buildings and public works. Still others were day laborers, porters, and the like. Some engaged in the wholesale trade, though that was left in part to the resident aliens. The more prosperous gained knightly or *zeugitae* census rank. Many were employed by the state in all sorts of capacities. Older men particularly delighted in the excitement and the pay gained from service on the juries.

Pericles decreased the number of landless by settling some six thousand in the cleruchies throughout the empire. When the suffering of the poor became intense during the last period of the war, the state provided them with a dole of two obols a day and began a program of public works to provide them with employment. Ordinarily they made up the bulk of the assembly, and for years they followed Pericles implicitly. But under the stress of war they became restless and excitable, easily roused to high pitches of enthusiasm by a Cleon or Cleophon, and as easily depressed by news of disaster. Their treatment of Pericles during the plague was an example of their fickleness. After the overthrow of Mytilene they voted, on the advice of Cleon, to put all male citizens to death and sent a trireme to carry the order to the army.

The next morning they reversed their decision and issued a new command for the execution of the leaders only. A second trireme set out amid great excitment and arrived only just in time to save the people.

In 416 B.C. the people again showed their bitterness when the little Dorian island of Melos, an important harbor on the route to Egypt, refused to submit to Athens on demand. When it was taken, all men of military age were put to death and the rest of the people sold into slavery. Similar action under stress was revealed by the treatment of the generals after Arginusae (p. 263). Yet, except for these incidents, they bore well the sufferings of the war and fought to the end with undaunted courage.

The Metics   Business opportunities attracted numerous aliens to Athens, and the state, following the policy begun by Solon, was hospitable to them in most respects. They were not allowed to own land in Attica and they could not obtain citizenship, save by special grant, as indeed many did as a reward for meritorious service. They had to have an Athenian patron to represent them in the law courts and had to pay a small tax for the privilege of living in Attica, where they were called *metoikoi*, or metics ("dwellers with"). Apart from these restrictions, there was little to differentiate the metics from the citizen body. Many of them found prosperity in Athens and proved as loyal as the citizens. They were proud to serve with their money in the performance of liturgies and with their strength and lives in the army and the fleet. The wealthy metics were received freely in Athenian society, save for the restrictions on marriage between citizens and foreigners. The occupations of these aliens were as varied as the interests of the city. They engaged in foreign commerce in Peiraeus; handled money-changing tables, which eventually developed into banks; and participated in all industries, excelling in textile, pottery, and metal working. They worked side by side with citizens and slaves in the shops and quarries and on the public works. In contradiction to the traditional view, there is reason to believe that they by no means monopolized either wholesale trade or any of the industries to the complete exclusion of the citizens.

In addition to the metics there must have been many foreigners, merchants, teachers, and tourists who, coming to the city as transients, were not enrolled as resident foreigners but helped to swell the numbers of its population.

The Slaves   Slaves, who were being pressed into ever-increasing uses, constituted the lowest class of the population. Most of the work of the better class household was done by them under the supervision of the mistress. They did the cooking, cleaning, spinning, and weaving. Old slaves accompanied the boys to school as *paidagogoi* ("leaders of the boys") and had general supervision over their behavior. Others acted as guards to the mistress or her daughters when they went out into the city. A trusted slave served as private secretary or steward to the master. Pericles, for example, turned over his entire family estate to a slave steward to manage.

Except on the lands of the rich, there was little, if any, agricultural slavery. Agriculture was on too small and intensive a scale for it to pay.

In the city, however, slavery was everywhere present. In the potters' shops slaves tended the furnaces and elsewhere did much of the rough work normally done by unskilled labor. In most occupations skilled slaves who had learned their trades before slavery overtook them, or who were trained by their masters, worked side by side with their master and with free citizens and aliens. Some of them managed retail or manufacturing shops of their own or belonging to their masters and paid a share of the proceeds to their owner.

The state owned slaves who worked on the roads, in the dockyards, in the mint, and on public buildings. The Scythian archers who formed the police of Athens, the executioner and his staff, the inspectors of weights and measures, and many of the heralds and clerks were the property of the demos. The lowest class of slaves worked in the mines at Laurium.

Many men of wealth invested in slaves, whom they rented out by the day to the mine contractors, to the state, or to business. There was a recognized place in the market where those who wished to hire slaves for unskilled labor might find them. In this fashion, Athens took care of the problem of casual labor.[4]

The sources of slaves were many and varied. Piratical raids were made on the barbarians around the shores of the Mediterranean and the Black Sea; prisoners of war who could not find means of ransom were regularly sold into slavery; dealers gathered up unwanted children who had been exposed to die by their parents and raised them for service. In some states parents were permitted to sell superfluous offspring, and men were still sold into slavery for debt. Of course, there were also some children born into slavery, although the breeding of slaves was rare because it was unprofitable. As a result of these varied sources, there was a wide diversity in skill, intelligence, and race among the servile population. Comparatively few slaves were Greeks.

The lot of the slaves in Athens was not entirely bad. In the mines they undoubtedly suffered hardships, but in the city the master's own interest and the law intervened to protect them. New household slaves were received with showers of confetti and came under the protection

---

[4] Gomme (*op. cit.*) estimates that thirty-five thousand industrial slaves, one-third of the total number of slaves, and the same number of domestic slaves were in the city, leaving another third for the domestic and agricultural slaves in the country. Excavations at Laurium indicate that many of the slaves used there may have been children. The mine passages were often too small for the admission of an adult.

of the family divinities. The shop owner strove to protect his investment, and skilled slaves found the same opportunities for self-expression as the free laborer and without many of the latter's worries. Most slaves received a small share of the proceeds of their labor and, particularly those who worked for hire or managed shops, were able to amass enough to purchase their freedom and secure recognition as resident aliens. Slaves were protected from murder by law. If the master's treatment was outrageous, the servant might appeal to the magistrates for protection and receive it. Such license was permitted the slaves in the streets that the conservatives complained of it.

Slaves and Citizens Slaves were never so numerous, so widely owned, or so generally used as to justify the modern idea that Athenian civilization consisted of a small leisure class resting upon slave labor while the bulk of the citizen population was supported by the state. The major portion of the work of Athens was done by its citizen body. Because of the restrictions on repetition of offices, state support was at best a meager and intermittent source of income and, except in wartime, was directed not at charitable relief but at making possible active participation of all citizens in public affairs. There is further ample evidence in the writings of the period that the later philosophic contempt for work was not shared by the people as a whole. Indolence was frowned upon, for the law still required every man to teach his son a trade. "To own to poverty," said Pericles, "with us is no disgrace; the true disgrace is in doing nothing to avoid it."

Industry Industrial and commercial methods had not changed materially since the earlier period. Some wealthy men might own large establishments with as many as twenty or twenty-five workers, but, as in the earlier period, the personnel of the average shop comprised the owner, his family, an apprentice or two, and one or two slaves, perhaps, to do the rougher work. Specialization, however, had become the general practice. Not only was there a sharp line between crafts, but in most cases there were specialists within the craft who centered their activities on one phase of the work. Thus one shop would be devoted to making tunics and another, cloaks. Within the shop the different tasks were parceled out, though there was not so high a degree of specialization as in the modern factory. Many articles were made to order, and sometimes the purchaser even furnished the raw material. But the increasing demands of trade led naturally to a larger supply of goods on hand for sale to the consumer, to retailers, or for export.

Athenian pottery, found wherever Athenian trade went and especially in the Black Sea region and in Italy, where it was in great demand among the Etruscans, is the best surviving witness of an industry that flourished by production not on order but for export. The fine quality and beautiful decoration of this pottery likewise give evidence of the skill and aesthetic perceptions of the artisans of Athens.

Commerce In trade as in industry an increase in volume and a tendency toward specialization were the chief features that distinguished this period from the earlier ones. Peddlers still went about the countryside, and Megarians and Boeotians traveled by land to the nearby Athenian market. Some merchants followed the great roads to Delphi and Olympia to participate in the fairs that accompanied the festivals. Most of the traffic, however, followed the sea. Boats had been improved, and knowledge of navigation and of routes had increased. Consequently, the season for shipping had been extended somewhat and the traveling time shortened. But in stormy weather, as before, shipping was at a standstill. During the season boats went to the Black Sea, to Syria, to Egypt, and to the west, carrying Athenian pottery and other manufactures, wine, and oil. From these regions they returned with slaves, grain, drugs, tapestries, linen, papyrus, and the myriad products of the lands they had visited.

The state zealously fostered this trade. The peace with Persia, Pericles' expedition to the Black Sea, the constant activities of Athenian agents in Egypt and in Italy, the work of the navy both in suppressing piracy and in opening new markets, and a widespread network of commercial treaties within and without the empire made Athens the focal center of Mediterranean trade. The wise policy of the state in firmly maintaining the value of Athenian coins, known as owls, and securing their acceptance throughout the civilized world greatly facilitated the commercial transactions of the Athenians.

The major public interest was in the grain trade, vitally necessary to the Athenians and a major cause of Athens' wars. Not only did the state take measures to control or develop the sources of supply, but it passed regulatory laws. All grain ships over which Athens had control were compelled to stop at Peiraeus, and two-thirds of all the grain they carried had to be sold in Athens. The other third could be exported only after local needs were satisfied. On occasion officials took vigorous action to prevent the merchants from cornering the market or unduly elevating the price of grain. Trade in lumber, needed greatly for shipping and the navy, was subject to similar regulations.

The financial system developed to meet the needs of trade. Men of wealth invested their money in loans on shipping or in other commercial ventures at rates of interest depending upon the risk involved. Commercial banking carried on by the money-changers, however, was just beginning at the end of the period.

The Agora The *agora*, or market place, center of all economic activities, hummed with life. There the businessmen held their conferences; the money-changers set up their tables; the farmers sold their produce and the hucksters, their vegetables, flowers, or fish; the artisans displayed their handicraft and the merchants, their goods from home and abroad. The cries of the salesmen bewildered the country-men who came into the city to make their purchases, while the Athenians and their friends were all busy at the congenial tasks of working, bargaining, and making money.

PRIVATE LIFE

Education   The training that men and women received and the part they played in life depended, of course, on their social and economic status. On the seventh or tenth day after the birth of a son in an Athenian family he received his name, and at the following celebration of the *Apaturia*, an ancestral festival of Zeus and Athena, his name was enrolled by the phratry if the family record was clear, and his citizenship was thus acknowledged and assured. Then until his seventh year he and his sisters remained under the care of his mother and nurse. Spartan women, it may be noted, were particularly sought after in Athens as nurses. After that the lives of brother and sister followed different lines.

If the family means were scant, the boy received instruction in reading, writing, and arithmetic in some inexpensive little school the family could afford. He learned his trade in his father's shop or was apprenticed to another, and received the rest of his education in the streets of the village or the city.

Wealthier Athenians assigned the care of their sons to elderly slaves, the *paidagogoi* who accompanied them to and from school and who apparently watched over them during school hours. It was the pedagog's task to see that the young men behaved fittingly in school and at play, and learned to arrange their clothes properly and to walk in the streets with easy rhythmic stride and proper demeanor, yielding place deferentially to their elders.

Schools for the most part were taught by poorly paid and generally despised men of inferior class who eked out their living from tuition fees. There were no public schools, but the state paid for the education of the sons of citizens who had fallen in battle. After instruction was given in the elementary subjects, the boys were taught poetry, singing, and the art of playing on the lyre. The poems of Homer and the other epic writers, of Solon, of Theognis, and of Pindar were memorized to teach lessons of high morals and patriotism from the deeds of past heroes and to inculcate into the youth by means of recital that rhythmical speech which befitted a gentleman. The boy learned also to accompany himself on the lyre so that later he might entertain guests with song and music as an Athenian gentleman should. This whole division of education was called music.

In the afternoons the boy went to the exercise grounds and there engaged in a variety of athletic sports to develop his physique. He learned to swim, and in his playtime enjoyed games of tag, ball, blindman's buff, marbles, and the other games of childhood. This continued until about his sixteenth year. Then, in the latter part of the fifth century, if his father could afford it, the boy, in order to learn rhetoric, argument, and "all the knowledge necessary for a statesman," went to one of the new teachers called Sophists who were beginning to appear in the city, or he might attach himself informally to a philosopher like Socrates. On his eighteenth birthday he was enrolled on the list of citizens in his deme and became legally a man and a full citizen of Athens. The state then called him to arms, and for two years he served as an *ephebos*, learning the military art. His education, however, was not yet at an end. For in the discussions in the market places and in the barber-shop clubs, in the assembly and on the jury, in the dramatic festivals, either as participant or as spectator, and at the evening banquets, he learned all that men were thinking in the world.

Athenian Women In the meantime his sister had remained at home under the tutelage of her mother and her nurse, learning to spin and weave, to cook, manage the household stores, and direct the servants. Such housewifely accomplishments formed the main body of her education. She might and presumably did learn to read and write. While still quite young, she was usually married to a man much older than herself. The marriage was arranged by her parents, frequently through the medium of a professional matchmaker and with due regard to financial considerations. In spite of this, many marriages resulted, as the inscriptions show, in real tenderness and affection. The bride's dowry remained her possession and was restored to her in case of divorce. Social custom confined her to the women's quarters in the house, and she went abroad only when accompanied by a male member of her family or by a slave. At banquets, when her husband brought guests to the house, she did not appear. "Not to be talked about either for good or evil" was set forth by Pericles as the ideal of womanhood. The state assumed wardship of an heiress, and family property considerations dictated the idea that she should marry the nearest of kin among her male relatives outside of her immediate family.

In practice these customs did not result at all times in the rigid seclusion of women, a subject that has been given far too much emphasis by modern writers. Women played a prominent part in the Panathenaic festival. They were present at the festivals in honor of Dionysus and at the Eleusinian Mysteries. They had, as well, their peculiar religious observances, to which women alone were admitted. They visited their women friends and were visited in turn. Their education and influence in the home and in public life depended largely upon their personalities. The wife and the sister of Cimon, for example, wielded powerful political influence. The noble women depicted by the dramatists had their prototypes in real women of the day. The writings of Plato and the comedies of Aristophanes indicate a widespread discussion of woman's place and position in Athenian society; in the *Ecclesiazusae* Aristophanes even goes so far as to represent the women as taking over the government. None of the restrictions noted above applied to women of the lower classes, who were driven by economic necessity to work on the farms, in the shops, in the booths of the market place and elsewhere as opportunity might arise.

The law of citizenship made the status of women of the metic class somewhat different. Public opinion allowed greater freedom to them, although in the ordinary course of affairs their behavior could not have been materially different. Tradition has ascribed to them, however, superior intellectual training.

Aspasia The most famous of the women of metic class was Aspasia, a Melesian woman, well educated and of remarkable personality, who came to Athens probably to set up a school of rhetoric. Her mental ability and personal charm rapidly drew around her the intellectual elite of her day. Socrates paid tribute to what he learned from her, and Pericles fell in love with her. Unhappily married, Pericles divorced his wife, found another husband for her, and then, in violation of the law, married Aspasia. Their children, however, were later legitimized by the Athenian people. Aspasia's influence on Pericles and on the group of men around him was extraordinary. To her house also came many of the women of Athens, and she apparently combined sage counsel on wifehood with an attempt to secure more education and greater freedom for Athenian women. Her activities and influence aroused great opposition among the conservatives of both sexes, and foul charges were made against her by the comic poets. Prosecuted on a charge of impiety, she was acquitted after an impassioned plea to the jury by Pericles himself.

Hetaerae Women of the poorer class of citizens and many of the metic class formed a group called *hetaerae* ("companions") who made their living in the service of their goddess, Aphrodite. Some were flower, flute, or dancing girls, in demand for entertainments. Others, ranging from ordinary courtesans to educated ladies who perhaps modeled themselves after Aspasia, were beautiful women who were successful in their ambition to become mistresses of men of wealth and position.

Dwellings Built of sun-dried brick covered with stucco or lime and with a flat roof of clay tiles, the houses in which the residents of Athens lived were simple in the extreme. There was frequently a second story, usually the women's quarters. The floors were of hard-packed earth or of cement, and except perhaps for the houses of the very rich, the interiors were undecorated. The rooms opened off the inner court, which was the dominant feature of the house and the very center of family life. In it stood the altar of Zeus of the Household and the statue of Paternal Apollo. There was not much furniture—couches, used for reclining at meals as well as for resting, chairs, stools, light tables, and storage chests. Light was provided at night by torches or lamps. Braziers filled with coals and ashes furnished heat in cold weather. Implements were made of pottery, bronze, or iron. Rain water was collected in cisterns, and drinking water was carried into the house from springs.

Clothing   Clothing likewise was simple. A tunic for ordinary wear and a gown and sandals for public appearance were the basic elements of dress for both sexes. The wealthier citizens wore colored gowns, and the ladies spent much time in the graceful arrangement of draperies for which they were renowned in their day and of which there is ample evidence in the sculptured monuments.

The Social Day   The Athenians could never understand the solitary man who withdrew into his study to ponder. They considered houses primarily as places for sleeping and eating, to be lived in only when the weather was inclement.

Athenian life was intensely social and out of doors. For the men, social life centered in the market place and in the exercise grounds; for the women, it centered in the courtyard. The citizen of wealth, after a light breakfast, would normally spend his morning marketing, supervising his financial interests, and greeting his friends and business acquaintances in the market place. About noon, a hearty lunch was served in the portico of the courtyard. He would devote the afternoon to exercise in one of the *palaestrae* (exercise grounds), or perhaps to some less strenuous sport like checkers, or to walks and conversation with his friends. In the late afternoon he bathed in one of the public bath houses.

The Symposium   Dinner was served early. If there were no guests, the family ate together, but if guests were present, as was frequently the case, the women and children retired. Invitations were informal, and an invited guest would often casually bring a friend along with him. After the serving of the food followed the symposium, the chief feature of the dinner. The bowl was brought in, a libation poured, and a ruler of drinking was chosen. His first duty was to supervise the mixing of water with the wine, usually in the proportions of two of water to one of wine. Then the cups were passed around and the drinking and entertainment began. Flute or dancing girls or other professional entertainers might be brought in; the lyre might be passed around and each guest called upon to perform; or the leader might set some topic, light or serious, for general discussion. The conversation might even run along decidedly serious lines, as is recorded in Plato's *Symposium*.

When the entertainment was over or the discussion at an end, the slaves lighted their masters home, and the day was over. The disputants in Plato's dialogue continued their arguments so long that morning found all the guests save Socrates asleep around the table.

Clubs The wealthy men of Athens belonged to social clubs in which their activities centered and which played an important part in political and legal affairs. Comparable social groupings were not lacking among the poorer citizens and the resident aliens. While we do not hear much of the guilds of commerce or industry which had been licensed by Solon, they undoubtedly existed. The shops themselves were social centers, not only for the people who worked in them but for idlers and shoppers. Socrates frequented the stoneworkers', the armorers', and the saddlers' shops, where he could always find an audience. Blacksmiths' forges and barber shops frequently served as clubs. The demesman from the country who came to town made his headquarters at a favorite shop where he could find fellow demesmen. On feast days, all those in the shop, even the slaves, partook together of a sacred meal for which the employer paid. There were also numerous religious associations, which brought together all classes of the peoples. The palaestrae, or gymnasiums, and baths were open to all citizens, and the Cynosarges, one of the palaestrae, was open to aliens as well.

RELIGION

The element of religion permeated all phases of Athenian life. The Athenian people were intensely religious, at least as far as cult was concerned. Every deme had its local divinities and its local hero in whose honor there were festivals, some of which became of state importance. The way in which the local religious cults had been reorganized by the state and bound to the central religious activities in Athens accounted in large part for the successful unification of Attica. The family upheld religious unity based on its gods and ancestors, to whom due reverence was paid at meal times, on leaving and returning home, and on festal occasions. The nobles perpetuated the religious features of their gentile[5] organizations (p. 228) after their political significance was lost. The groups of workmen in the various crafts had their special patrons among the gods and the demigods. There were also special festivals for the women. Young girls enjoyed the festival of Artemis Brauronia, in which chosen ones of their number played the parts of bears. Later, as married women, they celebrated the *Thesmophoria* in honor of Demeter as founder of political life, patroness of marriage, and giver of children.

---

[5] The family organization which the Greeks called *genos*, pl. *genē*.

Festivals   The series of state festivals held at different times consumed from sixty to seventy days of the year. There were festivals in honor of Theseus and of the heroes of Marathon and Salamis; the *Epitaphia*, when sacrifices were offered to the ancestral heroes and the annual oration was delivered in honor of Athenian citizens who had died in service during the year; the *Synoecia*, when the union of Attica was celebrated; the *Oschophoria*, when boys carried grapes and chanted while others raced from a temple of Dionysus to that of Athena at Phalerum; the *Apaturia*, where the phratries honored Zeus and Athena. The greatest of the festivals were in honor of Dionysus, Demeter, and Athena. In early spring came the *Anthesteria*, a Dionysiac festival in which the slaves took part. During the winter the rural *Dionysia* were celebrated in the country demes with buffoonery and dances. Out of them grew two city festivals, the *Lenaean, or Lesser, Dionysia* and the *City, or Greater, Dionysia.* The *Greater Dionysia* was attended not only by Athenians but by all residents of Attica, by delegations from the cities of the empire, and by a host of visitors. After a procession and a feast of wild rejoicing, there followed four days devoted to the performance of tragedies and comedies in competition. The great dramatic productions that are a lasting memorial of the age come from this festival. In the presence of the assembled multitude the sons of those fallen in war, on their attainment of manhood, received from the state the panoply of arms. A charge of two obols was made for attendance at the dramatic festival, but so that all might worship the god, the state furnished the poor with the price of the tickets.

The Eleusinian Mysteries   The great festival in honor of Demeter was the celebration of the mysteries of Eleusis after the harvest. Participants had prepared by a purification during the winter. Then in the fall ambassadors were sent forth to proclaim a sacred truce in an attempt to make the feast as panhellenic as the great games. As usual, it began with a procession. Then after the king archon had pronounced the sacred formula that excluded the unclean, notably those branded with infamy or stained with crime, the celebrants marched to the sea with their sacrificial white pigs, purifying themselves and their sacrifices in the salt waters. The following two days were consumed with the sacrifices after which took place the procession to Eleusis, the secret rites of initiation, and probably the performance of a sacred drama dealing with the story of Demeter and Persephone. Out of the symbolism of seed planting and harvest—the loss of Persephone and her return—the *mystai* learned something of the meaning of life and achieved a hope of something better in the life to come.

The Panathenaea   The greatest of all the festivals, however, was the Panathenaea. Celebrated annually in honor of Athena, it was held with especial magnificence in the third year of every Olympiad, when it attained almost as much renown as the great national games. The series of contests included athletic sports for boys and men, torch races, and a regatta. The prize for the winner consisted of a jar decorated with a figure of Athena and a picture of the event, and containing oil from the olives of the sacred olive trees. The central feature of the festival was the great procession, when priests, cavalry, sacrificial animals, and all the people conducted to the old temple of Athena Polias the maidens bearing a *peplos*, or cloak, which they had woven and decorated appropriately. Phidias' famous frieze on the Parthenon was a picture of the Panathenaic procession.

Athenian Tolerance It is to be noted that this religious activity was essentially a matter of cult performance, not of dogmatic belief. There were few professional priests. The chief archon and the king archon had supervision over many religious ceremonies, but the Eleusinian Mysteries were in the hands of the Eumolpid family; the worship of Athena and Erechtheus was conducted by the Butadae. Other priests were elected for life or for a term. Most of them engaged in their usual occupations, save for the period of the festival. Their chief task was to see that the ceremonies were properly performed, not to direct the worshipers how to behave or what to believe. Only in the Mysteries was there a moral element. Men might believe and say what they chose, so long as they did not become dangerous to the state through blasphemy or interference with the cult. Even then the people were tolerant, save in time of emotional stress. The philosopher Anaxagoras was regarded with suspicion because he said that the sun and the moon were not gods, but when he was banished, it was for political reasons. The execution of Socrates was likewise the result of politics rather than of intolerance.

The true center of the Athenian's religion was Athens itself, of which the goddess Athena was the personification. "I would have you," said Pericles, "fix your eyes upon the greatness of Athens until you become filled with the love of her." The city was replete with reminders of the achievements of its citizens, statues of the great men of the past, pictures of Marathon on the Painted Porch, inscriptions written on tablets set up on the Acropolis. Above all, in the minds of men there was a sure sense of the stability of law and of the wisdom sprung with Athena from the head of Zeus. The devotion thus aroused, the desire to serve Athens loyally and fully, was the basis of the inspiration that produced the works of art and letters that make the age one of the high points of human history.

Competition Through all activities, social, economic, and religious, ran the element of competition—competition in business, within the shop and between men of the same craft; in the market place and in the wider market where Athenian goods traveled; at social affairs where the guests vied with one another in playing or singing; in athletics, in the palaestra or at the games; in music; in choral dancing; in the writing and production of plays; in the Athenian law courts; and in politics. The competitive spirit penetrated every phase of Athenian life, and noteworthy service in any respect was likely to receive recognition. For the citizen it meant honor and office; for the metic it might mean the reward of citizenship, for the slave, freedom.

Since such competition necessarily contributed to the development of technique, the artisan improved his craft, the merchant his skill in business dealings, the mariner his knowledge of navigation. Dramatists studied the technique of the drama; young men aspiring to be orators or leaders of the people studied rhetoric under professional teachers; and the battle of wits in the agora and palaestra produced that master of dialectic—Socrates.

There was thus ample opportunity for every man to express himself freely and fully as an individual and as a member of a group, and to gain therewith such recognition as he had earned in whatever capacity or station of life he found himself. The use of the technique the individual had mastered in competing for glory in the group to which he belonged resulted in a condition of competitive cooperation most favorable to the development of the creative spirit from which came the great achievements of the Athenians.

14 · Athenian Culture

IN FULFILLMENT OF THEIR DESIRE TO BEAUTIFY THE
city, to serve the gods, and to glorify the state, yet at the same time
to gain individual pre-eminence, the Athenians of the great age
made noteworthy contributions to three fields of culture — art, literature, and philosophy. The buildings and the statues they erected, together with the works of their great painters, made Athens the artistic
center of the Hellenic world. The drama was an Athenian creation. To
the city came scientists, philosophers, and teachers. In Athens the art and
the science of history were begun, and its own citizen, Socrates, established the study of ethics. In all these fields of artistic and intellectual
endeavor great names appear and productions that have served as
models for later ages have survived.

ART

Architecture

One of the first tasks that faced the Athenians after the Persian
Wars was the rebuilding of Athens into a city worthy of its wealth and
the glory of its empire. The Persians had sacked it, broken its statuary,
destroyed its temples. The hastily constructed private houses built
when the Athenians returned to their homes were simple and without
ostentation. Not until the period of the Peloponnesian War did the
wealthy begin to erect luxurious residences for themselves. Hitherto the
wealth and genius of Athens had been devoted to public buildings and
temples. To understand the general plan it is necessary to have a conception to the topography of Athens.

The center of Athenian devotion was the Acropolis, a rocky
mound that rises 512 feet above the plain. Its slopes are so steep that
it can be approached only on the west side. The residence of the kings
and the chief stronghold in Mycenaean times, it was later the site of
many temples and statues. On its southern slope was a shrine of

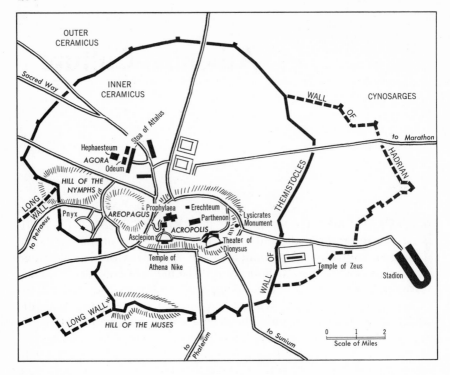

The City of Athens, ca. 407 B.C.

Asclepius, god of healing, and at its base were the theater of Dionysus and several handsome monuments. The hill of the Areopagus, where the famous council met as a homicide court, lies close to it on the west. Its name, traditionally derived from Ares, was more probably taken from the *Arai*, or *Eumenides*, spirits of punishment, whose shrine was on its northern slope. A low valley, the market place of early times, separated the Areopagus on the west from the Pnyx, where the assembly held its meetings. North of these hills was the agora, business center of classical Athens. Beyond it lay the inner Ceramicus, the potters' quarter, which derived its name from the production of ceramics. The dwellings of the Athenians crowded around the Acropolis and spread out to the north and west.

The famous wall of Themistocles, about five miles in circumference, enclosed the city. On the south it ran close to the Acropolis. Outside the wall ran the Ilissus River, above whose banks rose the temple of Olympian Zeus, begun by the tyrants but destined not to be completed until the time of the Roman emperor Hadrian. Where the wall adjoined the potters' quarter stood a great double entrance, the Dipylon Gate. Beside it was a smaller opening through which flowed the Eridanus, a small stream that rose in the barren hill of Lycabettus to the northeast and traversed the city. In the outer Ceramicus, beyond the Dipylon Gate, was the Athenian cemetery, where many noble monuments have been found. From there the roads led west to Eleusis and southwest to Peiraeus. The Academy, favorite grove and exercise ground of the Athenians, was slightly northwest of the gate. Other gates were located at convenient places in the wall, with roads leading to various places in Attica.

Cimon began the task of rebuilding the city. He constructed a retaining wall around the Acropolis and laid the foundations for a temple to Athena. Pericles continued the work of Themistocles and Cimon.

Peiraeus Themistocles had fortified Peiraeus and made it the port of Athens in place of Phalerum. To reconstruct Peiraeus, Pericles hired an expert, Hippodamus of Miletos, who laid out the streets of the town at right angles and built huge dockyards for ships and storage houses and display rooms for the local trade. Then Pericles connected Peiraeus with Athens by the Long Walls.

The City In Athens itself *stoae*, or porticoes, one of which has been restored, and administration buildings were erected around the agora, and on a slight hill above it was built a beautiful Doric temple, still standing, dedicated probably to Hephaestus, though today it is wrongly called the Theseum. The theater did not receive its stone seats and other improvements until the fourth century B.C. Until that time the spectators at the plays sat on wooden benches or on the grass. East of the theater at the foot of the Acropolis, Pericles built for the Panathenaic contests a round music hall, the Odeum. Its roof was said to have been made of the masts and yards of the Persian ships taken after Salamis and to have been conical in imitation of Xerxes' tent. No remains of it have survived.

The Acropolis Pericles approved a new and comprehensive plan for the adornment of the Acropolis. The Sacred Way started at the Dipylon Gate, passed through the agora, and wound up the steep western approach to the ancient citadel. As it entered the Acropolis area it passed through a monumental gateway of marble, the Propylaea. On the western façade of this structure stood a Doric porch flanked by a small wing on the left which was used as a picture gallery. The road passed through the porch, between rows of Ionic columns with steps on either side, which served to introduce the traveler to the sacred area. The Propylaea formed a stately and superb entrance to the domain of Athena. Mnesicles was the architect.

Athena Nike The right wing of the Propylaea could not be built to balance the left because the space belonged to Athena, the goddess of victory. On a bastion in this space, therefore, rose a beautiful

Model of the Acropolis Looking to the Northwest. The theater of Dionysus on the lower slope is seen in the foreground with the Parthenon standing high above. Beyond the Parthenon is the Erechtheum. To the left, on the lower slope, is the Aesclepium. The temple of Athena Nike and the Propylaea are out of sight beyond the Parthenon. (The Metropolitan Museum of Art)

View of the Temple of Athena Nike (right) and the Propylaea. The only entrance to the top of the Acropolis is by means of the steps between the two buttresses, shown here, and through the colonnade of the Propylaea. (Photograph by Ronald P. Legon, reproduced by Frank D. Grande)

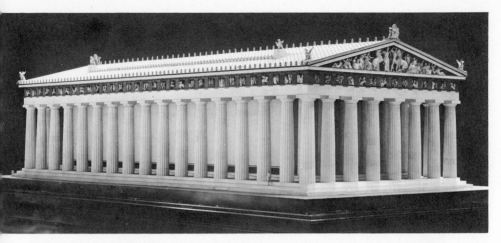

Model of the Parthenon as It Looked Soon After Its Completion in the Last Half of the Fifth Century B.C. (The Metropolitan Museum of Art, purchase 1890, Levi Hale Willard Bequest)

little temple, Ionic in style, with a frieze portraying events of the Persian Wars. Around the bastion was later erected a balustrade with panels of "Victories," of which the beautiful "Victory Adjusting Her Sandal" survives.

Athena Promachos As the Sacred Way left the Propylaea, it passed Phidias' great bronze statue of Athena Promachos, and then with lesser shrines along its route it curved to the eastern entrance of the Parthenon, the greatest glory of Greek architecture.

The Parthenon In 447 B.C. a board was appointed to engage architects and supervise the erection of a temple to Athena Parthenos. Callicrates and Ictinus were the architects chosen, with the sculptor Phidias and the painter Polygnotus as advisers. Built of Pentelic marble, the Parthenon was perfect in its proportions. Around the outside of the structure ran a peristyle of Doric columns thirty-four feet in height, eight on each end and seventeen on the sides, counting the corner columns twice. At each end within the peristyle was a prostyle of six columns. The entablature was Doric, and the pediment rose to a graceful angle so that the total height of the building from ground to ridgepole was sixty-five feet. To achieve grace and life, a slight convex curve was given to all prominent lines.

The interior was divided into two rooms. At the west end was a room forty-three feet long and sixty-three feet wide, its ceiling supported by four Ionic columns. This was originally called the Parthenon before the name was applied to the whole building. It faced the Propylaea and the business section of the city, and was used as the treasury of

A section of the Ionic Frieze from the Parthenon Showing Two Youths on Horseback. (British Museum)

Athena. The main room, called the *naos*, or shrine, was of the same width and one hundred Attic feet (about ninety-eight feet) in length. It was divided into two side aisles and a nave by two rows of short Doric columns. On these rested an architrave, and above it another row of columns supported the ceiling, which was coffered. The interior was lighted only by the opening of the great doors. Within the naos stood the gold and ivory statue of Athena Parthenos by Phidias.

The building was adorned with sculptures carved under the directing genius of Phidias, their subjects taken from the legendary history of Attica. The metopes were single pictures of strife between Lapiths and centaurs, Greeks and Amazons, gods and giants. The eastern pediment dealt with the birth of Athena from the head of Zeus, the western with the strife between Athena and Poseidon for possession of the city. Around the temple walls inside the peristyle ran an Ionic frieze representing the Panathenaic procession.

The architects' plans and Phidias' designs for the sculptures were executed, not by slaves driven to their tasks, but by citizens, metics, and slaves working side by side — men who had learned their technique in the quarries and in stonemasons' shops of Athens and who, to the glory of Athena, polished the stones so that when put together they seemed to have been placed there by nature. Years after, Plutarch wrote, "There is a sort of bloom of newness upon those works preserving them from the touch of time as if they had some perennial

One of the Caryatids (Maidens) from the Porch of the Maidens on the Erechteum. (Photograph by Mary Francis Gyles, reproduced by Frank D. Grande)

spirit and undying vitality mingled in the composition of them." Even today the Parthenon, though shattered, is not a ruin but a glorious monument.

The Erechtheum During the Peloponnesian War the Athenians built the Erechtheum in fulfillment of a religious duty to the ancient divinities of Athens. The edifice was started about 421 B.C. and finished about 407 B.C. It was the joint shrine of Athena Polias, guardian of the citadel, and of the mythical king, Erechtheus. It was built on two levels; on the upper level to the east the shrine of Athena was faced by an Ionic porch; on the lower level a porch with six lofty Ionic columns was erected on the northern side because to the west, where the porch would normally have been, stood the sacred olive tree of Athena. A hole was left in the roof of this porch so that the sun might fall on the fissure in the

The Treasury of the Athenians at Delphi. (Photograph by Ronald P. Legon, reproduced by Frank D. Grande)

rock which, it was said, Poseidon had made with his trident.[1] On the southern upper level and to the rear corner of the building was the beautiful Porch of the Maidens, the Caryatids. These maidens bore on their heads a representation of a chest which contained objects used at the festivals of Erechtheus. With consummate grace sculptured human beings thus served as columns. The final result was a building that ranks next to the Parthenon as one of the most perfect pieces of Greek architecture.

In addition to these temples there were on the Acropolis record houses, small shrines, and many statues of famous men, along with stone tablets inscribed with laws, treaties, and honorary decrees.

Sculpture

In sculpture as in architecture the artists of the fifth century B.C. approached closely to classical perfection in the portrayal of the human form and in the expression in marble of human ideals and aspirations.

The Age of Transition During the period of the Persian Wars artists were mastering the techniques both of the Doric school of ath-

---

[1] In early times, according to the myth, Poseidon and Athena had contested for possession of the city. Poseidon brought forth a spring on the Acropolis by striking the rock with his trident, but Athena won the victory by causing the sacred olive tree to grow. Marks resembling those of a trident in the rock are still plainly to be seen.

Poseidon (or Zeus). Life-size bronze statue now in the National Museum at Athens. (Greek Press and Information Service)

letic sculpture and of the soft, voluptuous Ionian carving of draped statuary, so they became competent to handle both the figure and the drapery with equal skill. Prolonged study had given them sufficient knowledge of anatomy and proportion to enable them to avoid the errors of earlier times, and mastery of their material made possible a departure from the law of frontality and a presentation of the subject with freedom and grace. Nevertheless, during the age of transition a certain stiffness remained. This stiffness, combined with failure to represent the hair naturally or the expression of the face, as well as a hardness of finish in the marble, caused the statues of the period to be described as "severe" in style. The pediments and metopes of the temple of Zeus at Olympia and of Aphaia on the island of Aegina illustrate the characteristics of the period. The statues of Harmodius and Aristogeiton at Athens, though powerful in execution and vigorous in pose, are nevertheless hard in muscular treatment and incompetent in the treatment of hair and facial expression.

The finest surviving product of the artists of the severe style is the bronze Charioteer of Delphi, made early in the fifth century. Originally part of a group of which only fragments survive, and pos-

Reproduction (Cast) of Myron's Discobulus (Discus-thrower). Restoration based on the statue in the Vatican and the head in the Lancelotti Palace, Rome. (The Metropolitan Museum of Art)

sibly the work of the Athenian Calamis, the youthful charioteer stands erect, strong, and dignified. The modeling of the hair shows ability and freedom, the face is serene, the garments drop from the shoulders in folds like the flutes on a column, and in this piece "exquisite workmanship is combined with accurate observation of nature and great dignity of conception."[2]

The Great Age   Three fifth-century Greeks—Myron, Phidias, and Polyclitus—represent the fulfillment of the promise of the work of earlier sculptors. Myron, an Athenian, oldest of the three, became famous for his statues of animals and of athletes looking as if they had been frozen while in motion. The ancients claimed that his bronze cow was so lifelike that living cattle gathered around it. His Discobolus, or Discus Thrower, has survived in Roman copies; the details of position are carefully studied; the expression of physical power in the athlete

[2] Harold N. Fowler and James R. Wheeler, *Handbook of Greek Archaeology.* New York: American Book Company, 1909, p. 221.

is superb, but his face is without any expression of the intensity of his action.

Phidias, younger contemporary of Myron, was renowned for the beauty and the idealism of his statues. He planned and supervised the execution of the sculptures of the Parthenon, and his Panathenaic frieze ranks supreme among works in relief. His two most famous works were gold and ivory statues of Athena Parthenos and of Zeus at Olympia. To these he was able to impart such religious feeling that he was said to have added something to traditional religion.

Polyclitus, the Argive, third of the masters, endeavored to reduce the treatment of the human body to a canon of measure and thereby to produce statues of ideally beautiful men and women, and he was even more noted than Myron for capturing the effect of arrested motion. The Doryphorus, or Youth with Spear, the Diadumenus, or Youth Tying Band about Head, and the Amazon, which survive in marble copies of the original bronze, represent his achievements.

Painting

All our information about the art of painting, which developed by the side of sculpture, is drawn from descriptions of great works or from vase decorations that imitated them. Painters of the archaic period had paid great attention to beauty of line, but their pictures were flat and severe in style and limited in the main to three colors—black, red, and white—with only occasional uses of yellow.

The need for decoration of the new buildings in Athens and the inspiration of the age led to great achievements. In Athens there were two native artists, Micon and Panaenus, the brother of Phidias, and to the city came Polygnotus of Thasos, who was the greatest painter of the period. These men covered the walls of the Painted Porch, of the Picture Gallery of the Propylaea, and of many other buildings. Polygnotus used four colors by adding yellow to his palette and gained further values by mixing. He was able to represent emotion by skillful drawing and, avoiding flatness, he gained a sense of perspective (though not a real perspective) by arranging his figures on different levels on the walls. The figures, furthermore, were carefully posed and arranged in groups placed with symmetry and dramatic contrast. Polygnotus was a master at representation of "transparent wind-blown drapery." His poses and drapery influenced contemporary sculpture, and the vase painters imitated his composition. Aristotle praised the ideal character of his portraits and the "moral uplift" of his paintings; in this Polygnotus was a fitting counterpart to the sculptor Phidias.

These artists, masters of technique, expressed in stone, in metal, or in color the same confidence in the ability of men, the same devotion to the gods, and the same search after perfect beauty that inspired the architects and the men of letters.

Athenian Amphora, Black-figured Ware, ca. 540 B.C. (The Metropolitan Museum of Art, Rogers Fund, 1917)

Athenian Calyx-krater, Red-figured Ware, Early Fifth Century B.C. (The Metropolitan Museum of Art, bequest of Edward C. Moore, 1891)

LITERATURE

The Drama

By tradition drama, like architecture, was the product of religion. In the first centuries of Athenian history it had been the custom for men dressed as satyrs, followers of the god Dionysus, to sing choruses in honor of the god at his festivals in the country. In 534 B.C. Peisistratus established the festivals in the city with competition between choruses. Aristotle says that Thespis changed the choral performance into a play by introducing an actor who took various parts in turn and carried on a dialogue with the leader of the chorus. Aeschylus added a second actor and made the chorus subordinate to the dialogue. Sophocles completed this process of development by adding a third actor. The number of parts in the play, though always small, was not fixed, because each actor played several roles, but there could never be more than three on the stage at the same time.

The Contest in Tragedy   Three poets were chosen by the chief archon to present plays at the Greater Dionysia. Each composed four plays and the music to accompany them. Originally the first three, a trilogy, dealt with a single theme; later, the poets were allowed to write on three different subjects. The fourth was usually a "satyr" play in honor of Dionysus. To each poet the archon assigned a wealthy man as *choregos*, who paid the expenses for the hired actors and chorus. The last three days of the festival were devoted to the performances. Judges, selected with great care, awarded prizes to the best *choregos*, the best poet, and later to the best actor.

Tragedy   The orgin of the word *tragedy* is unknown, though it may have come from a word meaning goat song. Greek tragedy, springing from the worship of Dionysus and always performed at his festivals, partook of the nature of a religious ritual. This fact colored both its form and its choice of subjects. Essentially musical, it was always composed in verse, and the chorus with which it began remained a fixed element in the performance even after it ceased to play an important part in the action. It must be remembered further that the plays were produced in competition and that the judges, already familiar with the story, doubtless based their opinions on the language, the rhythm of the verse, and the interpretation of the action. The use of masks and heavy costumes made facial expressions and rapid or violent action impossible and accordingly influenced the work of both playwrights and actors by laying emphasis upon the speeches of the characters and the lyrics of the chorus.

The dramatists established, though they did not always respect, the three famous unities: interest, essential to any great drama; time, made advisable though not absolutely necessary by the fact that choral songs were the only interludes between episodes; and place, enforced by the impossibility of much scene shifting and the continual presence of the chorus.

The cults of the heroes vitally influenced the development of the drama, and most of the subjects were drawn from the great mass of legendary material of the heroic age. They dealt with gods or with great personages, and usually with grand themes of struggle and suffering. The dramatists used the traditional stories as vehicles for the discussion of the great ethical and social problems of their own day. Men saw portrayed in the plays the deepest feelings and passions of the human heart. The emotions of admiration, pity, terror, and sympathy which they awakened in the audience produced, said Aristotle, a catharsis, which may be defined as a purification of the emotions, though its exact meaning has long been the subject of discussion among literary critics.

Aeschylus (525–456 B.C.**)** Of the many tragic poets, three — Aeschylus, Sophocles, and Euripides — were regarded as supreme. Their most popular works were often performed in later times, and some have come down to us. Aeschylus belonged to the generation of the Persian Wars. A native of Eleusis, of an old Eupatrid family, educated, as befitted a noble, in athletics, in music, and in Homer, he was a follower of Cimon in his conservatism at home and Panhellenism abroad. He fought at Marathon and was prouder of this than of his contributions to the literary world. In his plays, seven of which are extant, he portrayed the spirit of his times.

In his trilogy dealing with the story of Prometheus, who had brought civilization to men against the orders of Zeus, employing majestic language he attacks the problem of eternal justice. Only *Prometheus Bound*, one of the three plays, has survived. In it he seems to suggest as a solution for human struggles the concept that through the intelligent making and application of the laws of heaven justice must and will prevail. In three plays that deal with the fate of the house of Agamemnon the same idea appears in a story of men. Agamemnon falls because of his crimes. Clytemnaestra cannot escape her fate, nor can Orestes avoid the consequence of his matricide. Not even the purificatory rites of Apollo can save him until, through Athena and the ordered channels of the law, release from suffering is obtained from the Court of the Areopagus. In the last of these three plays a protest may be seen against the radical assaults on the powers of the Areopagus (p. 255). In *The Persians*, and its accompanying plays (now lost), Aeschylus deals sympathetically with the punishment of Xerxes for the overweening arrogance that led him to his assaults not only on the Greeks but on their gods.

Aeschylus was confident of the justice of the gods, of the soundness of a moral order founded on intelligence, and of the right of the intelligent noble to rule. He died in Gela in Sicily in 456 B.C., and his place in Athens was taken by Sophocles.

Sophocles (*ca.* 496–406 B.C.) Sophocles developed the technique of dramatic composition on which he is said to have written a treatise. One of his plays, *Oedipus Tyrannus*, was designated by Aristotle as the perfect tragedy. Of the many plays he composed, seven have survived. The greatest of these are three drawn from the Theban story of Oedipus, *Oedipus Tyrannus*, *Antigone*, and *Oedipus at Colonus*, the last having been produced in 401 B.C. after his death. The plays are motivated by the same forces that produced the Parthenon, and although they exhibit less majesty than do the plays of Aeschylus, they have greater serenity and more perfect symmetry.

Sophocles himself, of good family and of some wealth, was distinctly a product of Periclean Athens. As a boy he led the chorus that celebrated the victory of Salamis. He grew to manhood in the days of Aristides and Cimon and, as befitted a true citizen, he served the state in official capacity. His political insight, his fine knowledge of human psychology, his nobility of character, and his supreme courage and confidence in the city and in the eternal justice of the gods must have been drawn from the life of the city around him and in which he participated. The noblest expression of the Periclean spirit is in a chorus of *Antigone*:

> Wonders are many, and none is more wonderful than man; the power that crosses the white sea, driven by the stormy south wind, making a path under surges that threaten to engulf him; and Earth, the eldest of the gods, the immortal, the unwearied, doth he wear, turning the soil with the offspring of horses, as the ploughs go to and fro from year to year.
>
> And the light-hearted race of birds, and the tribes of savage beasts, and the sea-brood of the deep, he snares in the meshes of his woven toils, he leads captive, man excellent in wit. And he masters by his art the beast whose lair is in the wilds, who roams the hills; he tames the horse of shaggy mane, he puts the yoke upon its neck, he tames the tireless mountain bull.
>
> And speech and swift-winged thought and all the moods that mold a state hath he taught himself; and how to flee the arrows of the frost when 'tis hard lodging under the clear sky, and the arrows of the rushing rain; yea, he hath resource for all; without resource he meets nothing that must come; only against Death shall he call for aid in vain; but from baffling maladies he hath devised escapes.
>
> Cunning beyond fancy's dream is the fertile skill which brings him now to evil, now to good. When he honors the laws of the land and that justice which he hath sworn by the gods to uphold, proudly stands his city; no city hath he who for his rashness dwells with sin. Never may he share my hearth, never think my thoughts, who doth these things![3]

[3] G. W. Botsford and E. G. Sihler, *Hellenic Civilization*. New York: Columbia University Press, 1915, p. 328.

Euripides (480–406 B.C.)   Euripides, the third of the great tragic writers, was the least successful in competitions but the most popular in later generations. Eighteen of his tragedies and a satyr play, *Cyclops*, have come down to us. Many of his plays were composed during the Peloponnesian War, and they therefore reveal the stress of wartime. Deeply interested in men and in their problems, he was ever the spokesman of the poor, the humble, and the oppressed. Though at first he championed the cause of Athens against Sparta, his later plays protest against war and portray its horrors.

> O miserable mortals, why do ye get yourselves spears and deal out death upon each other? Stop and withdraw from these toils. Peaceful, 'mid the peaceful, guard your towns. Short is your span of life. Best then to pass through it as gently as may be, not worn by burdens.[4]

The Trojan Woman, a picture of the sufferings of women in war, is thought to have been composed as a protest against the Athenian treatment of Melos. In *Medea* Euripides sets forth in most poignant language the feelings of wronged womankind. He brings the gods down to earth and discusses their actions in the light of human reason. He criticizes them for allowing evil on earth and for their failure to sustain the moral order. In the last analysis he reduces them to psychological forces. Then in his old age he wrote *Bacchae*, a perfect Dionysiac tragedy. Some modern critics regard it merely as an attempt to display his dramatic artistry; others believe that he found in mystical religion the answer to the problems that had beset him. Professor Glover of Cambridge described it as "the play of all his plays where men find most the note of freedom and escape—escape from the sea and its storms, the haven reached and toil ended."[5]

Although not so great a poet as Sophocles, Euripides was an expert dramatic technician, a scholar who devoted his life to the writing of plays, not a citizen to whom playwriting was incidental. In his desire to express himself he departed from classical standards, introducing befitting costumes and using varied meters for effect. These changes, along with his ideas, offended the conservatives of his day, and Aristophanes made mock of him. Yet Euripides was much admired. It was said that after the disaster in Sicily in 413 B.C. the Syracusans set free all Athenians who could recite for them verses from Euripides.

Comedy   On the afternoons of the days of the dramatic contest, comedies were produced, likewise in competition. The first contest was held in 488 B.C. Comedy seems to have resulted as a combination of the vulgar buffoonery of the country festivals and of farces that had developed at Megara. Because of its origin and development, comedy

---

[4] Euripides, *Suppliants*, lines 949–954.
[5] T. R. Glover, *From Pericles to Philip*. London: Methuen & Co., Ltd., 1926, p. 139.

was free from the strict requirements of tragedy and gave free rein to caricature and ridicule; its imagery was often sexual. Even the gods were treated with a license that at times seems blasphemous. Its subjects, however, were drawn mostly from the passing scene, and it played much the same part that the cartoon and the newspaper column play today.

Aristophanes (*ca.* 450–385 B.C.) The greatest of the writers of comedy was Aristophanes. His major work was done during the Peloponnesian War, though he continued to write well into the fourth century B.C. He was a conservative democrat, hostile to the passions of the city mob, to the war, and to those he held responsible for it, as well as to the new learning and its exponents (p. 309). All that he disliked he held up to ridicule in his plays with a courage that at times verged on daring. His imagination was vivid, his sense of the comic, inimitable, and his ability to puncture pretense by a cartoon of words is unequaled in literature. With ribald license, impossible in the modern theater, with daring boldness, and yet with deep feeling for the realities of life, he attacked the leaders of the Athenians, the whims and foibles of the people, and sham or corruption wherever he saw it.

He loved the simple farmers of the Attic countryside and admired the old gods and the old manners. He charged Pericles and Aspasia with causing the war, and the professional soldiers and self-seeking demagogues with continuing it. He held up Cleon to especial scorn. In a beautiful play *The Peace* he portrayed the rejoicing of the Greeks over the Peace of Nicias. Later, when war was renewed, he wrote *Lysistrata*, an amusing and ribald representation of an attempt of the women to end the war, a play filled with an all-embracing spirit of panhellenism. He made fun of the Athenian jurors in *The Wasps*; he played with the ideal states of the oligarchs in *The Birds*, in which the birds create a new state, called "Cloud-Cuckoo Land." He criticized Socrates and the new learning in *The Clouds*. One of his most celebrated plays is *The Frogs*, a remarkable piece of literary criticism containing a savage attack on Euripides. Some of his lyrics, notably in *The Frogs* and *The Birds*, are among the most beautiful in any language.

History

History as a branch of literature and a scientific study distinct from the genealogical or geographical compositions of the earlier Ionians, and like drama a contribution of fifth-century Greece, began with the writings of Herodotus, the "Father of History," and Thucydides, the first "scientific historian."

Herodotus (*ca.* 484–*ca.* 425 B.C.) Born in Halicarnassus in Asia Minor, Herodotus was early involved in political troubles and set forth upon a series of travels which carried him to Egypt, Babylon, the Black Sea region, and Italy, but his second home was Athens from which he drew his inspiration. He wrote a history (the Greek word means inquiry) of the Persian Wars that "time may not obliterate the great and marvelous deeds of the Hellenes and the Barbarians and especially that the causes for which they waged war with one another may not be forgotten." He envisaged the war as an episode in the conflict between East and West. Accordingly, he traced the background of these struggles in the sixth century B.C., proceeded to a description of the lands that were in the Persian Empire, and wrote an account of the war itself. While somewhat credulous, he was eminently fair-minded. He felt it his duty to inquire and then to report what he learned, whether he believed it or not. When opinions conflicted, he presented them all. He was an inimitable storyteller, and the greatest charm of his book is to be found in the many digressions when he tells a story.

Though freed by the enlightenment of his generation from much of the supernaturalism of his predecessors, he believed firmly in the justice of the gods and paid due respect to the gods of other lands. But above all he believed in the happiness of the individual as a citizen, an individual not so arrogant as to offend the deity and bring down vengeance upon himself, but mindful of the gods and of the limitations they placed on all human achievements. His ideal of human happiness is best illustrated by the story he tells of Solon's visit to Croesus. When Croesus asked Solon whom he deemed to be the happiest of men, Solon replied, "Tellus of Athens . . . because he lived in a well-governed commonwealth and had sons who were virtuous and good; and he saw children born to them all and all surviving; in the next place, when he had lived as happily as the condition of human affairs will permit, he ended his life in a glorious manner; for coming to the assistance of the Athenians in a battle with their neighbors near Eleusis, he put the enemy to flight and died nobly. The Athenians buried him at the public charge in the place where he fell and honored him greatly."[6]

Thucydides (*ca.* 460–*ca.* 395 B.C.) Thucydides,[7] the Athenian, who recorded the history of the Peloponnesian War began to write, he said, at its very beginning because he felt it was going to be great and memorable above all wars. His own part in the struggle ended with his exile in 424 B.C. after a defeat in Thrace for which, as general, he was held responsible, and he was thus enabled to devote himself to the gathering of the materials. In performing this task, he became the founder of scientific history. He visited and studied the scenes of events, talked with eyewitnesses, copied documents, and used all available evidence to reach conclusions and to be able to state what actually happened.

In the treatment of events and personalities he showed for the most part an admirable balance, except perhaps in the case of Cleon,

---

[6] Herodotus, *Histories*, 1. 30.

[7] Not to be confused with the conservative leader who was also named Thucydides; see p. 259.

against whom he was prejudiced. Interested in the problem of causation and with a mind freed from superstition by his education, he brushed aside traditional views. Earthquakes and eclipses were to him not divine portents but natural phenomena. He disregarded oracles and omens of supernatural interference and found his causes in the actions of man and in the relation of events. He failed, however, to emphasize sufficiently those underlying social and economic elements in history upon which present-day historians lay such stress. His comments on the actions of people under strain of war are nevertheless full of wise observations.

In one respect he disregarded modern canons. Instead of merely reporting speeches, he wrote them out in full in his own words. He acknowledged this practice frankly: "As to the speeches which were made either before or during the war, it was hard for me and for others to recollect the exact words. I have therefore put into the mouth of each speaker the sentiments appropriate to the occasion, expressed as I thought he would express them, while at the same time I endeavored, as nearly as I could, to give the general purport of what was actually said."[8] Many of these speeches presented Thucydides' analysis of a situation with arguments pro and con. Notable in this respect was the dialogue between the Melians and the Athenians before the destruction of Melos.

History to Thucydides was primarily a useful subject. "Very likely the strict historical character of my narrative may be disappointing to the ear. [Ancient books were written to be read aloud.] But if he who desires to have before his eyes a true picture of the events which have happened, and of the like events which may be expected to happen hereafter in the order of human affairs, shall pronounce what I have written to be useful, then I shall be satisfied. My history is a possession forever, not a prize composition to be heard and forgotten."[9]

He was not only a master of scientific history but of a literary style that showed a keen sense of dramatic values. His descriptions of the plague in Athens and of the retreat from Syracuse are marvels of exposition. Some critics think that the book was composed as a prose tragedy under the spell of the great dramatists. Certainly his subject was worthy of such treatment.

His book comes to an abrupt end in 411 B.C.; why, no one knows. He outlived the greatness of Athens, but probably he did not live to finish his account of the downfall of the city he had helped to render immortal.

---

[8] Thucydides, *History of the Peloponnesian War*, 1. 22. Trans. in G. W. Botsford and E. G. Sihler, *Hellenic Civilization*. New York: Columbia University Press, 1915, p. 29.

[9] Thucydides, *History of the Peloponnesian War*, 1. 23. Trans. in G. W. Botsford and E. G. Sihler, *Hellenic Civilization*, p. 28.

Science and Philosophy

Under the inspiration of the same stimuli that had led to the works of art and literature, great advances were made in medicine, philosophy, and education.

Greek men of medicine took the first steps in freeing their practice from the age-old domination of magic and in establishing it as a science. Greeks who wished to be cured of their diseases were accustomed to rely on charms or to visit the shrines of Asclepius, god of healing. They passed a night in the shrine, slept and dreamed. In accordance with their dreams the priests prescribed for them, and it was inevitable that the priests would acquire by experience a considerable knowledge of drugs and of the treatment of disease. There were doctors, too, such as Democedes of Crotone, physician to Darius, who knew much about medicine and probably learned what Babylonia and Egypt had to teach them. Yet magic prevailed until the appearance of Hippocrates of Cos. On the island of Cos stood the most celebrated temple of Asclepius, and its priests were regarded as the most skillful in Hellas.

Hippocrates, by birth a member of the priestly class, studied in the temple of Asclepius and went to Egypt for further instruction. Thus equipped he became a great physician, the founder of scientific medicine and of medical ethics. He abandoned the superstitions of the shrines and laid down in his teachings and writings the principles of natural causes and natural cures of disease. He noted the effects of climates and seasons. While many of his theories have long been discarded, by insisting that scientific observation and experience are the only sure bases for the practice of the art, he laid the foundations upon which modern medicine rests. The Hippocratic oath, administered to students of medicine in ancient times and still taken by graduates of many medical schools today, expresses the highest ideals of the medical profession. There exists today a great body of medical writings composed by him and his followers.

Throughout the fifth century B.C. the philosophers continued their attempts to answer the questions raised by Thales and his successors (p. 239). Heraclitus of Ephesus, who lived during the first half of the fifth century B.C., in his search for reality was impressed by the fact of constant change—"Everything flows; nothing abides." The never-ending strife between opposites he expressed by the statement, "War is the father of all things." Yet amid this flux and strife there is a balance, a regular alternation as of day and night, which implied to him justice and reason in the universe. Accordingly he postulated a world-soul symbolized by fire, which he called *logos*, the Word, a mysterious power which few can understand but which rules the universe.

Parmenides and Zeno (fl. 475 B.C.) of Elea in Italy opposed the views of their contemporary Heraclitus with famous arguments to prove creation and motion impossible. Creation is impossible because "from nothing, nothing comes"; motion implies empty space, which being nothing cannot exist. Further, Zeno endeavored to prove mathematically that Achilles could not catch the tortoise, because whenever he reached the place the tortoise had been, it had moved on. Thus the only reality, the firm principle of the universe, is unchanging stability.

Other men sought a way out of the impasse created by this divergence of views between Heraclitus and the Eleatics. Empedocles of Acragas (495–435 B.C.) described a world made up of four elements — earth, air, fire, and water — combined and separated by opposing forces, love and hate, which thus produced substance and change, life and death. His idea of the four elements, accepted by Aristotle, remained the basic theory of the universe until modern times.

Leucippus and Democritus (*ca.* 460–350 B.C.), refusing to accept the limitation of substance to four elements, conceived the thought of a universe of limitless particles, which they called atoms, moving through empty space and united and separated by a physical force, called gravitation. This atomic theory, rejected by the contemporaries of its creators as mechanical and atheistic, became the cornerstone of modern science.

Anaxagoras of Clazomenae (*ca.* 500–*ca.* 428 B.C.), who came to Athens and was a friend of Pericles, accepted the concept of many elements, which he called seeds, but he substituted for gravitation or for the strife of opposites a divine intelligence, *nous*, which directs all things. In his study of the world he reached the conclusion that the sun was not a god, but a mass of molten metal, somewhat larger than the Peloponnesus. He was banished from Athens on the charge of atheism, but his exile was really the result of a political attack on Pericles.

These men with their never-ending discussions of the material of which the world is made, of the problems of motion and change, and of the motivating power that controls it all, presented theories from which the great philosophers of later centuries drew and which therefore have materially affected philosophic thought down to our times.

The Sophists While these philosophers were boldly endeavoring to understand the universe, other thinkers, directing their attention to the problem of man in society, advanced the work of education. These teachers, called Sophists, "men of wisdom," arose to meet new needs created by life in the city-state. Those who wished to serve the democracy or appear before the law courts needed not only training to enable them to speak in public but education to acquire political wisdom. Accordingly, a group of teachers arose who taught men how to speak and instructed them in the practical workings of government and society. In their work they established the studies of grammar and rhetoric and began those examinations into the practices of men in society which have resulted in our modern social sciences — political science, economics, and sociology. In education their doctrine was essentially utilitarian. Before them was a definite goal and only those studies — among them, history — which contributed to that end were worth investigating. They denied the value of philosophic speculations on the universe.

The Sophists professed to make their students better, yet the training they gave in argumentation laid them open to the charge of training in cleverness rather than in virtue. Their opponents claimed that they taught the youth "to prove that black was white and to make the worse appear the better cause." The democrats suspected them because most of their students were drawn from the wealthy class, which affected to despise the many. The aristocratic Plato condemned them for their ideas and because they accepted pay for their teaching. In spite of these charges against them, however, as the Sophists traveled from city to city to give instructions, they were eagerly sought after by ambitious youths. Leaders among them were Protagoras (*ca.* 490–415 B.C.) of Abdera in Thrace and Gorgias (*ca.* 480–395 B.C.) of Leontini in Sicily, both of whom taught in Athens.

Because the ultimate aim of Sophist teaching was individual success, the inevitable content of their thought was the place of the individual in the world. Consideration of this question made them skeptical of the established traditions of the gods and of the state, and of the standards of human behavior. In their teaching of ethics they laid emphasis on things that are practical, possible, and contributory to success, rather than those that are just or right in an absolute sense. The standard they set up was the good of the individual. "Man," said Protagoras, meaning each individual for himself, "is the measure of all things; of things that are, that they are; of things that are not, that they are not."[10] The acceptance of this concept meant the end of the Periclean ideal of man, the citizen, under the gods.

Socrates (469–399 B.C.)   The greatest intellectual figure of fifth-century Athens was the philosopher Socrates. It is hard to penetrate through the jibes of Aristophanes, the memoirs of Xenophon (p. 329), and the dialogues of Plato (p. 332) to Socrates' own thought, for he wrote nothing himself. But of his dominant position in the history of thought there can be little doubt.

Born in a family of restricted means, he was trained in his father's shop as a stonecutter, a trade he later neglected in order to spend his time arguing in the shops and the market place of Athens and wherever loiterers gathered. From such myriad conversations with all ranks of people he gathered the major portion of his education, the fundamental element of which was recognition of the principle that the admission of

[10] Charles M. Bakewell, *Source Book of Ancient Philosophy.* New York: Charles Scribner's Sons, 1939, p. 67.

ignorance is the foundation of true knowledge. When a friend came back from the temple of Apollo at Delphi with the words of the oracle proclaiming Socrates as the wisest of men, he took the words as an order from the god to search after the truth and impart it to his fellow men. In that search he was indefatigable. His method was dialectic, that is, question and answer, argument in the analysis of a statement to find out what was true. He put aside the disputes in which the earlier philosophers were engaged as to the nature of the universe, to turn to questions that dealt with men's relations with one another. He tried to discover what is true, noble, just, and pious. He was therefore the founder of the study of ethics. He felt that the Sophists were superficial and were engaged in training men for success rather than for character.

He believed in the gods, as ever-present and all-knowing. He performed with true piety all the traditional forms, though he was not interested in the Mysteries, and he felt himself especially guided by a *daemon*, or guardian spirit. Socrates' early manhood occurred in the age of Pericles, and he learned then to believe in the state and in the fulfillment of the individual therein. He served Athens loyally in the army and in the council. So fond of the city was he that he could scarcely be tempted out of it. He strove to train intelligent men who would serve it and direct its course along lines of reason. He taught the beauty of the family and the dignity of labor.

Intensely social, he was always the center of a throng of men. Youths trooped at his heels to learn from him and to watch him break down the arguments of a man who was overcertain of his opinion. Notable among his followers were the young Alcibiades, Critias, and many future leaders of the intellectual group at Athens. Naturally he aroused many enemies, and, because he used the dialectic method in teaching, he was confused with the Sophists. In his old age he was made the victim of the reaction that followed the Peloponnesian War, and was accused of denying the gods and of corrupting the youth of Athens. The defense he made, as reported by Plato, is a masterly exposition of his whole career and purpose, one of the greatest of all documents. In the passion of the hour the jury condemned him. He was offered a chance to escape the penalty. This but gave him an opportunity to explain his attitude toward the laws of the state. Then after a discussion of immortality, in which he believed, he drank the hemlock.

Epilogue For a brief period not only did all the forces of the Greek world focus upon Athens, but goods, men, and ideas from all parts of the civilized world concentrated there, where they found a citizen body, varied, versatile, and receptive. The result was the age of Pericles.

In his character, Pericles was a symbol of the spirit of the age, as he was its leader. His career is an epilogue of the achievements of his generation. His father Xanthippus came of an old, priestly family renowned for its services to the state. His mother was Agariste, descendant of Megacles, the Alcmaeonid, and Agariste of Sicyon, and the niece of the lawgiver Cleisthenes. Pericles' education was the best the time could provide, and the artists, literary men, and philosophers of Athens were his friends and constant companions. His influence was the inspiration of the architects and sculptors of the Parthenon. Turning his property over to a slave to manage, he entered the service of the state and became its directing genius.

A majestic speaker, he swayed the assembly and so dominated the policies of Athens that its actions are spoken of as his own. At the end of the first year of the Peloponnesian War he delivered a funeral oration in honor of those who had fallen during the year. It was a panegyric on the age and the supreme expression of the statesman's ideals for his city. He described the institutions and customs of the Athenians and proudly declared that "Athens is the school of Hellas." He recounted the glories of the empire and the achievements of the city. "For we have opened every land and every sea to our arms and have everywhere planted eternal memorials of our friendship and our enmity." He called all citizens to the service of the city. The glory of Athens was the glory of its citizens. He praised the city rather than the men who had fallen, because "in magnifying the city," he said, "I have magnified them and men like them whose virtues have made her glorious." Pericles died of the plague in the third year of the war.

The Peloponnesian War deprived Athens of its wealth and power, and weakened the allegiance of its citizens. Yet the city had sufficient vitality in the next generation to revive and to make new contributions to the culture of the world. But the bloom of the classical age had passed. In comparison with it, the story of the next century, the fourth B.C., is dreary.

15 · The Fourth Century

THE FOURTH CENTURY B.C. WAS A CONFUSED AGE, and it is difficult to follow its various ramifications as one state after another endeavored to gain advantage or to rise to power. The fall of Athens left Sparta supreme in the Aegean world, and the first attempts of Athens and of Thebes and Corinth, erstwhile allies of Sparta, to rehabilitate or to strengthen themselves were suppressed by Sparta with Persian aid. In its second effort Athens was successful in achieving again maritime leadership, only to find that Thebes, under its great commander Epaminondas, had been able to crush Sparta and establish itself as a great and leading power. Several smaller states, struggling to establish a balance between the powers, had made unsuccessful attempts at federation, but the Theban failure after the death of Epaminondas left Greece disorganized and dismayed, and an easy prey to the able and wily king of Macedon with whose victory the period closed. The period was marked also by the frequent involvement of Greek states in Egypt's struggle for freedom from Persia.

THE PERIOD OF SPARTAN POWER

The opening events of the fourth century B.C. proved that the Peloponnesian War, which was to have accomplished so much, had actually settled nothing. In 404 B.C. Athens seemed to be safely in Spartan power under the rule of the Thirty Tyrants. Sparta had feared too much the growing power of Thebes, as well as the condemnation of all the Hellenes, to allow the city to be destroyed. But the Spartan tyranny was soon overthrown, and with Persian assistance Athens rose again, rebuilt its walls, and became once more an aspirant to power, the rallying center for all democrats against oligarchic Sparta.

Other cities in addition were ready to challenge the leadership of the Dorian state. Corinth had suffered greatly from the war and had received none of the expected benefits. Thebes, on the other hand, had

313

profited from the misfortunes of Athens. Its population had grown through an influx of refugees and fugitive slaves, many of whom were highly skilled. Its wealth had been increased by the spoils of the victory, and its control over the other Boeotian cities, lost at the time of the Persian Wars, had been renewed. Like Corinth, however, it was dissatisfied with Sparta's attitude at the end of the war and with its share of the booty. Both cities were ready to cause trouble.

Persia at the opening of the fourth century was wealthy and vigorous. The king and his satraps had learned the power of money in the Greek states; they were ready to use it to regain control over the Asiatic cities and to prevent any Hellenic power from becoming strong enough to resist a Persian return to the Aegean. The Persians had helped Sparta break the Athenian empire and were now equally willing to assist Athens in weakening Sparta if that city became aggressive.

Against this array of hostility the Spartans could oppose only military force and the self-interest of a few oligarchs. With no commercial activity and no interest in trade, Sparta could never be the economic center of the Aegean world as Athens had been, giving vitality to the Athenian empire. Its power would last only as long as it was supreme on land and sea.

An additional element that served to hinder conditions of peace was the great number of men available for mercenary service. In earlier times though Greeks had served for pay in the armies of Egypt and Babylon, or as hired bodyguards for tyrants, the defense of the cities had been entrusted to its citizens. The Persian king and his satraps had found it advantageous, in their wars of the fifth century, to hire Greeks; and Sparta had made use of Arcadians in the overseas campaigns of the Decelean War. Mercenary service developed so rapidly during the fourth century, however, that by the end of the period professional soldiers had almost displaced the citizens in the armies of the Greeks, Persians, and Egyptians. Several reasons account for this. The end of the Peloponnesian War had let loose a large number of men whose careers had been devoted entirely to fighting and who were eager for further service. Other men driven from their homes by the strife of the war period wandered with their families in search of employment. The number of those displaced was constantly augmented by the civil troubles of the fourth century, by economic distress in the cities, and by an overflow from the agricultural regions of Arcadia and Aetolia. In early times such men had gone out to found colonies. But the available land had now been occupied, so that mercenary service provided the only outlet. All states made use of hired troops. In the Persian armies that offered resistance to Alexander the Great, for example, were many thousands of Greek mercenaries. The presence of unemployed men eager for hire, ready to serve any state that would pay them and to plunder friend or foe with equal alacrity, made it easier for the citizens of the states to vote for war without peril to themselves. This, too, contributed to the confusion of the century.

THE ANABASIS OF THE TEN THOUSAND

The history of the period is tangled with rivalries, intrigues, and wars. It opened with an episode of minor importance but of great significance and of even greater interest. The interest results from the fact that the event was recorded by Xenophon in his *Anabasis*, the first textbook in Greek for generations of students. Darius II, king of Persia who died in 404 B.C., was succeeded by his eldest son Artaxerxes II. Cyrus, younger and favorite son, challenged his brother's right to the throne. As satrap in Sardis during the Peloponnesian War, Cyrus had come into close contact with the Greeks and knew their conditions and their abilities. To put himself on the throne, he therefore hired a band of some thirteen thousand mercenaries, mostly veterans of the Peloponnesian War, under a Spartan commander. With these and a large number of Asiatic supporters he advanced into Mesopotamia in 401 B.C. In a decisive battle at Cunaxa, the Greeks were victorious, but at the moment of victory Cyrus was killed. Shortly thereafter the Greek commanders were treacherously slain by the Persians.

The army, though victorious, was disorganized by the loss of its leaders and in a desperate plight in the heart of the enemy's country. Never did Greek training better justify itself. The soldiers organized themselves into a city-state without a city, drew up laws, elected generals (among them the Athenian Xenophon), and scrupulously obeyed them. With Xenophon as the directing genius, this reorganized band, now numbering about ten thousand, marched north across the mountains to the Euxine Sea, and after much discussion of their future course entered the service of Sparta and disappeared from history. They had exposed the weakness of Persia and proved the political ability of the Hellenes. Thereafter Isocrates and other leaders of Greek thought clamored for a war against Persia to furnish occupation and lands for the restless element among the Greeks. Throughout the century many Greeks drifted into Persia and some even enlisted in the Persian armies.

Lysander At the end of the war with Athens, Sparta had endeavored to establish a Spartan empire by setting up the Thirty Tyrants in Athens and the decarchies in the maritime states, all supported by Lacedaemonian garrisons. The Asiatic cities had been surrendered to Persia. The guiding spirit in these actions was Lysander. Son of a Spartan father and helot mother, this man of genius planned to use the wealth and position he had attained to make himself king of Sparta. The Spartan magistrates, suspicious of his designs, removed him from office. At the same time the Thirty were overthrown by the Athenians, and many of the decarchies and garrisons were expelled from the allied states. Still Lysander did not give up hope. He intrigued in Sparta and tried to get the oracles of the gods to help him. Though he failed, he still retained great influence over the Spartan people.

The War in Asia Minor   Then, because of its participation in the expedition of Cyrus, Sparta became involved in a war with Persia. When an appeal for help came from Ionia, the Spartans sent forces to free the cities from the Persian satraps. In 396 B.C. Agesilaus, king of Sparta, was sent to take command. Agesilaus, though lame, had become king through Lysander's influence and through him Lysander had hoped to regain his position. But again Lysander was disappointed, for the king was independent and vigorous. Lysander, finding his advice disregarded, withdrew and was shortly after killed in a skirmish with the Athenians. Agesilaus, however, had succeeded in liberating most of the Asiatic states by the time events in Greece called him home.

The Corinthian War, 395–387 B.C.   The enemies of Sparta had found common cause and had united to wage war once again for the freedom of Hellas. Athens, Thebes, Corinth, Argos, and many of the islands formed a league, and in 395 B.C. the Corinthian War began. Sparta's only ally was Egypt, which had freed itself from Persian control in 404 B.C. Nepherites, the pharaoh, sent Sparta grain, money, and a hundred ships. In 394 B.C. Conon, an Athenian, now admiral of the Persian fleet, won a victory off Cnidus which destroyed the Spartan and Egyptian fleets, and then, with Persian money, aided in rebuilding the Long Walls of Athens. Persia knew well how to prevent united action among the Greeks. Athens, once again able to lift its head and to hope for a renewal of wealth and empire, refused to follow the lead of Sparta and began the formation of a new league among the islanders.

THE KING'S PEACE, 387–386 B.C.

In spite of the naval defeat Agesilaus was able with difficulty to maintain Spartan supremacy on land, and the allies could make little headway. When the tide turned against Sparta, that city appealed to Persia. It was not to the interest of the Great King to allow Sparta to be crushed and the Athenians to return to power. In addition, the Lacedaemonians, abandoning their Egyptian ally, were willing to pay his price for support—to allow him once more possession of the Asiatic cities. Once his financial aid was withdrawn from Athens and its allies, they could do nothing but accept Persian terms. A conference met at Sardis in 387–386 B.C. from which this proclamation, known as the King's Peace, was made.

King Artaxerxes deems it right that the cities of Asia with the islands of Clazomenae and Cyprus should belong to himself. The remaining cities, small and great, he wishes to leave independent with the exception of Lemnos, Imbros, and Scyros, which three as formerly are to belong to Athens. Should any of the parties concerned not accept this peace, I, Artaxerxes, together with those who share my views, will wage war against him or them by land and sea, with ships and with money.[1]

To the familiar terms of freedom and autonomy, a new principle had been added—the armed enforcement of peace. With the exception of the shameful surrender of the Asiatic cities, and the leaving of Egypt open to certain Persian attack, the peace seemed eminently fair and just. Yet it brought untold confusion. By the terms of the treaty, which set all small states free, the Athenian maritime alliance was broken and the naval power of Athens was so shattered that pirates once more ruled the seas. The Boeotian League was likewise disbanded and the hopes of the Thebans were crushed. The wealth of Corinth had been destroyed by the war.

Only Sparta gained. The principles of military power for which it stood had been vindicated in fact if not in word. It was generally understood that Sparta was to enforce the peace with Persian backing. Its power in the Peloponnesus was not broken by the peace and there was none that might gainsay Sparta, none to protect the weaker states or even the peace itself against the city. Autonomy was easily translated to mean rule by the friends of Sparta. Decarchies were once again set up, and there followed a new series of revolutions. Exiles again wandered in armed mercenary bands and menaced life and property throughout the land. The orator Isocrates declared that more cities were taken during the period of the peace than before the treaty had been concluded. But an undeclared war continued, revolving about Egypt. The pharaohs hired thousands of Greek mercenaries to resist Persian attempts at reconquest. Many of these mercenaries were provided with the tacit approval of Greek governments, as in the case of the Athenians led by Chabrias. He was, however, recalled on Persian demand.

Sparta itself broke the peace. To punish Mantinea for disaffection, it crushed and destroyed that city. Then a Spartan commander on his way to the Chalcidice seized the citadel of Thebes. When he was tried at Sparta for this infraction of the peace, Agesilaus defended him on the ground that he had acted for the best interests of the state, and he escaped with a fine, while Sparta kept the citadel.

The Olynthian League   To the north a group of states were offering a new solution to the problem of peace and unity. Olynthus in the

[1] Xenophon, *Hellanica*, 5. 1.31. Trans. by H. G. Dakyns. *Selections from Ancient Greek Historians in English.* Ed. by Royal C. Nemiah. New York: Charles Scribner's Sons, 1939.

Chalcidice had become the center of a federal union. Citizens in each
state of the league were given full rights of citizenship in every other
state and were thus held together by a common interest. Even those
who had been forced into the organization soon lost their local interests
in the welfare of the whole league. The character of this federal union
was unprecedented and important. Not interfering with local affairs and
bringing no states into subjection, the league did not offend the traditional Greek spirit of local independence. Instead, it created a higher
loyalty and provided a program for the enduring unification of the
fiercely proud cities of the Aegean. Its growing power was naturally
regarded as a menace by its neighbors, including Macedon, and by the
Spartans. Federalism had no place in a world ruled by Sparta. When
the Olynthian union had been destroyed by Sparta in a short war
(379 B.C.), Spartan power had reached its climax. Agesilaus had attained
his goal.

Second Athenian Confederacy Athenian resistance to Spartan
supremacy, both natural and inevitable, was once more made possible
by formation of the Second Athenian Confederacy in 378–377 B.C.
When the decarchies were overthrown after the fall of Lysander, the
maritime states had naturally gravitated to Athens for commercial
reasons. The first attempts at alliance were broken up by the King's
Peace. In the confederacy of 378–377 every care was taken to avoid a
breach of the peace and to prevent a recurrence of the abuses that had
changed the Confederacy of Delos into an empire (pp. 257–258). No
state was forced to join, and each treaty provided for local freedom and
autonomy. The assembly of the allies met without Athenian interference and only required the sanction of the Athenian assembly for
action. No tribute was collected, but ships and money were to be contributed when needed. The purpose of the league was defense against
Sparta.

The Liberation of Thebes, 379–378 B.C. Thebes, meanwhile, had
been freed from its Spartan garrison. A band of exiles led by Pelopidas
had crept back into the city. Disguised as girls, they were brought to a
dinner given for the Spartan officers, whom they promptly killed. The
garrison thereupon withdrew. The clever Epaminondas and his friend
Pelopidas guided Thebes along the path that led to power in the
Hellenic world. As a first step the Boeotian League was reorganized.
Then, in alliance with Athens, Thebes declared war against Sparta for
the freedom of Hellas.

War with Sparta, 378–371 B.C. Though the allies outmatched
Sparta in strength, they were unable to agree on concerted action.
Thebes, as a matter of fact, left the conduct of the war to Athens and
devoted itself to increasing its own power in Boeotia and Phocis. Athens,
alarmed at these activities of its neighbor, endeavored to secure peace.

The Peace Conference of 371 B.C.   To this end a congress was
called to meet in Sparta in 371 B.C. All the major states of Hellas, and
Persia as well, were represented at the meeting. It was recognized in the
discussion that the chief difficulty lay in the governmental differences
between Athens and Sparta. In every small state in Greece, the democratic party looked to Athens for support, while the oligarchic looked
to Sparta. Alliances followed the will of the party in power, and party
strife led to appeals to Sparta and to Athens from both sides. Thus the
two leading states became involved in war with each other. It was agreed
that the only solution lay in open friendship between the two powers and
in an agreement not to interfere in local disputes. To achieve this, the
peace provided that all governors should be withdrawn, that each state
should be left free to choose its own form of government and its own
alliances, and that both naval and military forces should be disbanded.
Furthermore, "if any state transgressed these stipulations, it lay at the
option of any power whatsoever to aid the states so injured, while conversely, to bring such aid was not compulsory on any power against its
will."[2] The last provision proved to be the weak link in the chain.

The success of the plan involved the end of the growing power of
Thebes. Athens and Sparta would allow no rival. Epaminondas, the
Theban representative, was ordered by the congress to sign for Thebes
only and to allow the other Boeotians to sign for themselves. This
meant the disintegration of the Boeotian League. Rather than yield to
what they regarded as virtual destruction, the Thebans withdrew from
the conference, and their state was consequently excluded from the
treaty. Sparta thereupon took up the burden of enforcing the peace
against Thebes. One Spartan opposed this action before the assembly
and made a remarkable suggestion. He proposed that the army should
be recalled and disbanded according to the treaty; that contributions
should then be placed at Delphi; then if any violated the peace or the
independence of the states all others could be invited in and funds
would be at hand. The sanction of heaven and the enforcement of the
peace would thus be secured with the least annoyance to the states.
"But the assembly on hearing these words agreed that this man was
talking nonsense."[3]

Leuctra, 371 B.C.   A Spartan army met the Thebans at Leuctra in
Boeotia. Epaminondas, in command of the Theban forces, proved himself a military genius. He made his left wing unusually heavy and arranged his center and right *en échelon*. While the Spartans were rallying
to stop the charge of the wing, he sent his center and right against them

---

[2] Xenophon, *Hellanica*, 6. 3. 20. Trans. by H. G. Dakyns. *Selections from Ancient Greek
Historians in English.* New York: Charles Scribner's Sons, 1939.

[3] Xenophon, *Hellanica*, 6. 4. 2. Trans. by H. G. Dakyns. *Selections from Ancient Greek
Historians in English.* New York: Charles Scribner's Sons, 1939.

successively. The Spartan phalanx was crushed for the first time in Hellenic history, and Spartan prestige was irrevocably destroyed. With it went all the bright hopes of the peace conference.

Theban Hegemony, 371–362 B.C.   Leuctra was followed by a brief period of Theban hegemony. Epaminondas at once invaded the Peloponnesus and even entered Lacedaemon. Though he approached so near Sparta that the people could see his campfires, he did not venture to attack the city, for such an attack would mean a battle to the death. Instead he crossed over into Messenia and freed the helots there. Messene was rebuilt and fortified, and descendants of its ancient citizens returned from Messana in Sicily and from Naupactus. Then he organized a league among the Arcadians to keep watch over Sparta and persuaded them to found a capital city called Megalopolis, "The Great City." At the same time he was endeavoring to conquer Thessaly, build a fleet, break the Athenian Confederacy, and secure control over the sea.

Since Epaminondas recognized that his army and navy were not strong enough to accomplish all he desired, with the assistance of Persia he tried to secure recognition of the Theban position. Conferences were held at Delphi, at Susa, and at Thebes, but without securing this recognition.

Mantinea, 362 B.C.   At first Athens made use of the fall of Sparta to increase its own powers by bringing into alliance with itself many of the smaller states that had been allies of Sparta. Then, alarmed by Theban policies, Athens rallied to the assistance of Sparta. A great army, including even a contingent from Syracuse, was gathered in the Peloponnesus. Epaminondas met it at Mantinea in 362 B.C. In this battle the Thebans were victorious, but Epaminondas was mortally wounded. With his death the period of Theban hegemony ended. Pelopidas had been killed in Thessaly, and with these two men gone Thebes was stripped of great leaders. The battle that was to have decided the fate of Hellas resulted in general chaos. A meeting was held and a peace was made "so that," in the words of the treaty which has survived in an inscription, "putting aside the war against each other, each should make his own city as great and prosperous as possible and shall remain useful to friends and strong." Sparta remained aloof from this treaty because she steadfastly refused to recognize the loss of Messenia.

A side result of this treaty brought an interesting cooperation among Athens, Sparta, and Egypt. The pharaoh Tachos had formed the grand design (also advocated by many Greeks) to attack Persia by an invasion through Palestine and Syria. Agesilaus of Sparta, although eighty years old, accepted the proposal eagerly, while Athens with equal enthusiasm dispatched Chabrias and ten thousand mercenaries. The Greek leaders quarreled bitterly but the real cause of failure was a rebellion in Egypt. Tachos had made the mistake of confiscating temple properties to finance his expedition and the complaints of the priests roused the people against him. Tachos' nephew took the Egyptian throne but had perforce to abandon the attack on Persia. Agesilaus stayed to settle the new pharaoh securely, then died on his way back to Sparta.

The Social War In the meantime the Second Athenian Confederacy, from which so much had been expected, had fallen on difficult times. The Athenians had departed from their lofty resolves. They had failed to protect the allies properly and had spent the money of the league for their own purposes. Some of the states had been reduced to subjection, and others had been plundered by the mercenary soldiers who were hired to defend them. In 357 B.C. several of the islands, led by Chios, Rhodes, and the city of Byzantium and supported by Mausolus, king of Caria, revolted. Persia interfered; the Athenians were compelled to recognize the independence of the seceders; and within a year the confederacy collapsed entirely. Because of the shortsighted, self-seeking policy of Athens, the last experiment in Hellenic unification during the days of Greek freedom had failed. All the powers had passed — Athenian, Spartan, Olynthian, Theban, and Athenian again. There was no power strong enough to lead, no city willing to follow. When peace and unity came to the Hellenic world, it was enforced from without.

THE WEST

Dionysius of Syracuse The history of the western Greeks during the fourth century B.C. was dominated by the achievements of Dionysius, tyrant of Syracuse. After the time of Gelon and Hiero (p. 249) the western Greeks had played little active part in the development of Hellas. They had produced brilliant thinkers and teachers, but most of these had gravitated to Athens. Trade with the Etruscan cities of Italy, with Rome, and with Gaul, was brisk, and Syracuse became, perhaps, the richest of the Greek cities. The Athenian attempt to secure control over this trade had failed. After the defeat of the Athenians the Syracusans under a democracy had aided Sparta in the war in the Aegean. But the Carthaginians, who were watching Syracusan progress with jealous eyes, interfered and declared war.

When the city's generals failed to cope with the Carthaginian armies, a young clerk, Dionysius, grasped his opportunity. By attacking the generals he secured his own election, and then by a series of brilliant strokes made himself tyrant of Syracuse in 405 B.C., remaining in power until his death in 367 B.C. He fought several wars with Carthage with varying success but was never able to drive the Phoenicians out of

Sicily. He succeeded, however, in bringing all western Hellas under his control and in extending his interest into the Adriatic. He kept an eye on the Aegean and entered into intimate relationship with Sparta. By the practices of enslavement of the population of entire cities, of mass ransom, and of the seizure of booty he introduced to ancient warfare methods whereby the enemy paid for his wars—methods that his successors in Sicily, and the Romans as well, followed most readily. Noteworthy contributions were made by Dionysius to the art of warfare when he introduced larger warships with five rowers on each oar and huge catapults for use as siege engines. With the walls and fortresses he built Syracuse became the most strongly fortified city in the Mediterranean. Many famous stories are told of this tyrant, among them the familiar one of Damon and Pythias.

Timoleon After Dionysius' death the contests between his weakling son and his son-in-law produced confusion among the Greeks and enabled Carthage to recover lost territory. In despair the Syracusans appealed to their mother city, Corinth, for aid in 344 B.C., and Corinth sent them Timoleon. This able man drove out the tyrants and defeated the Carthaginians. He restored democracies in all of the Greek states and organized a federation to keep peace in Sicily. His work accomplished, the liberator gave up his power and spent the rest of his life in great honor as a private citizen of Syracuse.

THE RISE OF MACEDON

To the north of Greece, in a valley above modern Salonika, lay Pella, capital of the kingdom of Macedon. Macedon, which consisted of several river valleys separated by mountains, was inhabited by warlike tribes of land-holding nobles and peasants, shepherds, and hunters, who spoke a Greek dialect. Though the Macedonian kings claimed descent from Heracles, the cultured Greeks to the south regarded them as barbarians. Their early history was filled with wars for supremacy carried on among the chieftains in the valleys. A king called Alexander had gained control shortly after 500 B.C. He participated in the defeat of Macedon in the first Persian expedition, and perforce went over to the side of Xerxes, though he continued to pose as a friend and adviser to the patriotic Greeks. After the retreat of the Persians he cultivated the friendship of the Greeks and took part in Greek festivals. Perdiccas (*ca.* 455–413 B.C.), cunning and unscrupulous king of Macedon, was at the same time friend and enemy of the Athenians, who controlled his outlets to the sea and who purchased lumber from him for their ships. During the Peloponnesian War he veered from one side to the other as the fortunes of war shifted. Archelaus, who succeeded him in power, made Pella his capital, and by building cities and roads and inviting poets and artists to his kingdom endeavored to introduce Greek culture in his court.

Philip II, 359–336 B.C.   After a period of disorder in the first half of the fourth century Philip II seized the throne in 359 B.C. He had a shrewd mind, remarkable foresight, and a genius for organization. Held as a hostage in Thebes during his youth, he learned military science from Epaminondas and gained a clear conception of the weaknesses of Greece and an understanding of how these might be used to his advantage. It was his ambition to raise himself with his people to a controlling place in the Hellenic world.

Philip's first task was the organization of his own kingdom. He ruthlessly crushed all opposition, welded the tribes firmly together, and brought the Paeonians and Illyrians in the west into subjection. He trained the peasants in the newest methods of warfare and organized them in the famous Macedonian phalanx, a solid body of infantry armed with long pikes which presented to the foe a bristling wall of spears. The cavalry, drawn from the nobility, traditional force of the Macedonian army and bound closely to the king as his "companions," was developed into an offensive weapon of tremendous power and employed for flank attacks on opposing forces. With every man in the kingdom assigned to his place and supplies of money and munitions gathered, the entire nation was placed on a wartime basis.

Philip solved the problem of foreign relations with the same efficiency. Spies in his employ were everywhere, and he took precautions to secure friends in many of the cities and to prevent a coalition of Greeks against him. He disbursed gold freely among the venal; for some, the flattery of friendship sufficed; he won others over by promises of support in local politics or in petty wars; exhibitions of power won the fearful; and a few able leaders, notably the Athenian Isocrates (p. 330), followed Philip from the conviction that under his leadership peace might be achieved in Hellas. Before the final conflict began, there was a strong Macedonian party in every city of Greece, and some cities had declared themselves Philip's friends.

The Sacred War   Two conditions were needed to establish Philip's place in the sun of the Aegean world: (1) recognition of his position as a leading power by the Greeks so that he might dominate their councils; and (2) his supremacy over the stretch of seacoast reaching from the Chalcidice to Byzantium so that he might control the rich gold mines of Thrace and secure a vantage point against the naval power of Athens. A heritage from the past gave him the first. An old quarrel between Thebes and Phocis led to strife when the Amphictyonic Council accused the Phocians of trespass at Delphi and under the influence of Thebes declared a sacred war. The Phocians retaliated by seizing the treasure of the temple and hiring a large force of mercenaries. Thebes appealed to Philip for aid (356 B.C.). At the moment he was busy in the north, but in 346 B.C. he marched south and devastated the land of Phocis. He was given the two Phocian votes in the Amphictyonic Council and was elected president of the Pythian games. His place in Hellas was thus recognized and his prestige tremendously enhanced.

The War with Athens 357–346 B.C.   In the meantime Philip had devoted all of his means to the conquest of the Thracian seacoast. Clever trickery, bribes, and quick action brought him such gains that Athens declared war in 357 B.C. But the Athenians were not sufficiently aware of the menace to take aggressive action. One Athenian saw Philip's purposes and realized the threat. In 351 B.C. Demosthenes, the orator, made a vigorous attack on Philip in a speech known as the First Philippic, and endeavored in vain to arouse the Athenians. In 349 B.C. the Macedonians fell upon Olynthus and its neighbors. Though Demosthenes pleaded with the Athenians in his Olynthiac orations, little help was sent, and the cities were taken. Many of them were destroyed, their inhabitants killed or sold into slavery. By this victory Philip took a giant step in his rise to power. In 346 B.C. Athens made a peace with him which recognized his conquests and left him free to punish the Phocians.

Philippics   Demosthenes, realizing the necessity for peace, took part in the embassy that made it. But on his return to Athens he made a series of orations against Philip. So brilliant and so fierce were these speeches that invective orations ever since that time have been called Philippics. The fire of his eloquence aroused the people to momentary enthusiasm, but the spirit of earlier ages was lacking. They voted for war and large expeditions, and then failed to contribute money or to enlist. The small fleets and armies of mercenaries that Athens dispatched against Philip were often left unpaid. Not until Philip had advanced to the Bosporus and had threatened the Athenian food supply from the Black Sea was decisive action taken. Then a strong fleet was sent and Philip was driven back from the walls of Byzantium.

Chaeronea, 338 B.C.   Athenian power alone blocked Philip's path to empire. On the pretext of a sacred war against the little town of Amphissa near Delphi he marched south into Greece. Desmosthenes rallied his countrymen and secured alliances with Thebes and a number of smaller states. The battle was fought at Chaeronea in northern Boeotia, in 338 B.C., where the citizen levies of Athens and Thebes were no match for the trained army of the Macedonian king. The deciding stroke, however, was the cavalry charge led by Philip's son, the youthful Alexander.

The Hellenic League   After Chaeronea, Philip held a congress at Corinth and organized the Hellenic League of mainland and island states, from which Sparta, pitifully weak but stubbornly defiant, alone remained aloof. Peace and order were to be established and maintained among the Greek states. Each state was to be independent, self-governing, released from the fear of encroachment or interference by other cities, and free to sail the seas as it chose. All attempts at revolution, the overthrowing of constitutions, executions or banishments contrary to law, forcible return of exiles, confiscations of property, abolition of debts, or emancipation of slaves for revolutionary purposes were strictly forbidden. Philip thus endeavored, by the terms of the treaty and the threat of reprisal, to bring to an end the political and economic unrest that had caused so much trouble during the preceding period. An offensive and defensive alliance with Macedon provided the basis for a combination under Philip's command for a war against Persia which was to secure Hellenic unity and provide room for the settlement of the poor and the exiles. Already the March of the Ten Thousand had proved a successful invasion of Persia possible; Agesilaus had tried twice to bring it about, and the orators, particularly Isocrates, had pleaded for it with fervor. An important and natural ally had, too, been lost when Egypt was reconquered by the Persians in 345 B.C. The Macedonians and Greeks would have to depend on their own resources. In 336 B.C., when all was ready, Philip was assassinated at the instigation, it was rumored, of his wife Olympias. The accession of his son Alexander ushered in a new age.

SPARTA AND ATHENS IN THE FOURTH CENTURY B.C.

Sparta

Attempts at Reform Though Sparta was in a position of power during half of the fourth century B.C., its domestic history is one of decline. The treasure Lysander had gathered and the tribute Sparta had received from subject states were of no value to the simple agricultural city. Individual Spartans returned home wealthy, in violation of the law, but they could profit little from their wealth. Most of the money of private citizens was deposited in Arcadia and was lost after Leuctra. Furthermore, under the stress of war and of service overseas, many Spartans were reduced to the rank of inferiors. Lysander's plans for revolution failed, and a conspiracy organized by an inferior, Cinadon, in 398 B.C., was discovered and blocked. Conservative action by the council ended all thought of giving citizenship to inferiors, helots, or perioeci.

The Decline of the Spartans The freeing of Messenia ruined many Spartans, and the disasters at Leuctra and Mantinea resulted in a severe loss in man power. A decline in the birth rate and the accumulation of land by Spartan heiresses, of which Aristotle speaks, were additional causes of decline. At the end of the period the Spartans in service numbered only seven hundred. Yet Sparta proudly refused to make peace or to join Philip's Hellenic League. The fall of Sparta and the breakup of the Peloponnesian League were disasters of the greatest moment, for they not only destroyed the structure that had been the military backbone of Hellas but made the Macedonian conquest sure and comparatively easy.

Athens

Political Recovery The story of Athens during this period is one of political recovery and economic prosperity. In 404 B.C. Athens found itself ruined by the loss of markets and slaves and by the destruction of the olive orchards. Politically it was under the cruel authority of the Thirty Tyrants. But Athens had too much vitality to remain in this position long. A band of democrats, led by Thrasybulus, seized Peiraeus, defeated the Thirty, and restored the democracy. After the leading oligarch Critias had been killed, a general amnesty was proclaimed. But Socrates paid the penalty for the sins of some of his students. Henceforth oligarchy was unthinkable in Athens, and the democracy was strengthened by a series of reforms. A code of laws begun in 411 B.C. was completed. To prevent bribery and the use of undue influence, minor changes were made in the administration and in the court system. For the purpose of official records the Ionian alphabet was adopted, a measure of great importance for the modern study of Athenian inscriptions.

State Aid to the Poor Advancing concepts of democracy demanded that the state provide for its poor, whose numbers had increased greatly due to the decline in employment during the economic crisis entailed by the Peloponnesian War and the loss of the empire. The general rise in prices which took place during the fourth century was a heavy burden to the poor. Yet as Athenian citizens, they were felt to be entitled to participation in the political and religious activities of the city and to share in its wealth. During the later years of the Peloponnesian War a dole of two obols had been distributed among the very poor, and in the fourth century B.C. pensions were provided for indigent cripples. To secure political rights for the laboring class, pay was introduced for attendance upon the assembly, at first one obol, later three. To give them a share in the religious festivals, Eubulus secured the passage of a law which provided that the surplus income of the state be paid into the so-called theoric fund, from which two obols a day were drawn to buy tickets to the dramatic festivals for the poor. It was with the greatest difficulty that Demosthenes persuaded the people to stop this practice and devote all the means of the state to the prosecution of the war against Philip.

Finance The increased costs of government inherent in these policies and the cost of the fourth-century wars bore heavily upon a treasury that had lost its chief source of income—tribute from the empire. To enable the state to meet its expenses recourse was had with startling frequency to the emergency capital tax, the *eisphora* (p. 272). To render collections simpler, after 378 B.C. the people were enrolled in associations called *symmories*, each of which was responsible for its share of the total amount. After 362 B.C. the three hundred richest citizens were called upon to advance the sum levied as a new form of liturgy (p. 272), to be reimbursed by later collections from the *symmories*. The burden of the trierarchy had become so great that similar associations were formed, each to finance a trireme. Some wealthy individuals, however, still earned repute by assuming the expense of outfitting boats. In this period the political leader of the state needed above all to be a financier.

Professional Commanders Perhaps the most striking political change in Athens was in the conduct of foreign affairs. With the development of mercenary forces warfare by land and sea had become more technical. As a result the office of general in Athens became purely political and administrative, while the commanders of the army were professionals hired for the war. In Iphicrates, who once succeeded in destroying a Spartan heavy-armed troop with a light-armed but well-trained force, the Athenians possessed a military leader of great skill. They also were fortunate in having brilliant admirals like Conon and Timotheus.

The Informers Both their experience with the oligarchy of the Thirty Tyrants and the attitude of the conservative rich made the demos suspicious of their leaders and of men of wealth. After the restoration of the democracy we hear, accordingly, of many impeachments and trials and of professional informers who lived by blackmail. There is, however, surprisingly little evidence of convictions or of wealthy families ruined by unjust persecutions. Indeed, the stability of the Athenian people in their choice of, and obedience to, their leaders in this age was notable. Though, like Plato, many of the conservatives withdrew from politics, the democracy was well served by a number of able administrators, particularly by such men as Thrasybulus, Eubulus, and Demosthenes.

Economic Revival Economic prosperity soon returned to Athens. Farming never quite recovered its earlier pre-eminence after the despoliation of the fields and orchards during the Peloponnesian War. The statistics that are available indicate a distinct movement from the country demes to the city. Men of wealth acquired larger estates on which they began to introduce a three-field system and capitalistic methods of agriculture.

Athenian commerce, however, revived rapidly as the maritime states returned, out of economic necessity, to their former allegiance. Trade with the peoples on the shores of the Black Sea flourished, especially with the cities and tribes of southern Russia. The reason for this was the importance of the region to the Athenian grain supply. As in the age of Pericles, treaties were made with the kings of the region, and their good will was so zealously fostered that many sent their sons to Athens to be educated and at times made presents of grain to the citizens of Athens. Egypt had also furnished grain, on occasion, to pay for Athenian aid against Persia.

The development of banks assisted the growth of commerce. The money-changers first began to accept deposits of money and valuables without interest for safekeeping. Since their occupation involved the care of large sums anyway, they were able to render this service. The next step was the payment of sums on order to creditors of the depositor and the transfer of credits on their books from one customer to another. Finally, they were able to arrange for the transfer of credits between financial centers. The money deposited with them they lent on interest to the state or to businessmen for commercial transactions. Careful bookkeeping (usually done by slaves) and an impeccable reputation for probity were the prime essentials for the successful banker. The best known was Pasion, a former slave, described by Demosthenes. He had unlimited credit throughout eastern Hellas, and for his services to the state he received Athenian citizenship.

An increase in the quantity of money due to the opening of temple treasures by loan or confiscation, to the circulation of large amounts of Persian coins, and to the working of the Thracian mines by Philip led to an increase in prices that bore heavily on the working class. Industry had increased as trade increased, but there was a tendency for larger establishments to employ slave labor exclusively. As a result, though wages rose, they did not increase as much as did the cost of living. The industrial class on the whole was less prosperous than it had been in the age of Pericles, and the state was forced to come to the aid of the very poor.

LITERATURE

The varied political and social interests of the age were reflected in literature, poetry yielding place to prose as the principal form of composition, and individualism, developing under the influence of sophistic education, replaced civic devotion as the inspiration of thought. Athenians of the better class, who could afford the new education, came to pride themselves on the culture and refinement thus achieved and tried to appear as an aristocracy of intelligence. Many of them withdrew from active participation in Athenian politics and spent their time in discussions of philosophic problems after the manner of Socrates.

Others, however, continued in the service of the people and wrote or spoke primarily for them. The full development of the democracy and of the law courts made a high degree of training essential for the man who would take an active part in the life of the city, and from such highly trained men sprang the full flower of Athenian oratory. Still others, under the spell of Thucydides, wrote histories. In spite of the loss of political pre-eminence, Athens remained the center of intellectual activity for the Hellenic world, and the leading Greeks of the century came to its schools as teachers and students.

Poetry The fourth century B.C. witnessed the end of Athenian poetry. Tragedies were still composed, but of such little originality or value compared with those of the great masters that none has survived. Aristophanes lived into the period, but he left politics alone and wrote on social issues. He made fun of women and their pretensions to power, and in the play *Wealth* (*Plutus*) he disclosed what would happen if the blind god of wealth were made to see and visited men according to their deserts. After Aristophanes' time manners and customs became the subjects of comedy.

Prose Written prose, made possible by an increased supply of papyrus from Egypt and by the development of methods for the publication and distribution of books and pamphlets, became the form of literature characteristic of the period. Minds trained in science and in correct habits of speech and composition found it a more exact means of expression than poetry.

Xenophon (*ca.* 430–*ca.* 350 B.C.) The first writer of the new age was Xenophon, an Athenian and a pupil of Socrates, whose memoirs he later wrote. Quitting Athens after the re-establishment of the democracy, he took a leading part in the expedition of Cyrus (p. 315). The *Anabasis*, which he wrote as a record of this trip, is considered one of the outstanding works in the realm of military history. Unable to return to Athens after the expedition because of a sentence of exile (for an unknown reason), he spent the greater part of his life in the Peloponnesus, where he occupied his time in the composition of many works. His writings show the varied interests he acquired from his teacher — history, education, household management, public finance, politics, and military affairs. His large historical work, *Hellenica*, a continuation of the books of Thucydides, carries Greek history down to 362 B.C. It is a simple, direct tale, more the work of a journalist than a historian, for he had little understanding of causes or of results and no sense of the underlying forces of history. His work reveals the influence of the Spartan point of view; for example, in deference to the feelings of his Spartan friends he left out all mention of the loss of Messene, whose independence Sparta never recognized. His style is clear and entertaining, and he is at his best in the portrayal of personalities. In his devotion to the ideal of the city-state as an institution for the increase of virtue among its members and his belief in education as the only true title to public service, he represents the best features of his class and time.

Oratory With the exception of Xenophon, the writers of the age tended to specialize in one of the three branches of prose writing — oratory, history, or philosophy. The first was the ultimate product of Greek democracy. The frequent necessity of appearance before the law courts, the increasing use of advocates, and the opportunities for expression in the public assemblies and before the throngs gathered at the great festivals gave rise to a great school of rhetoricians. Leading orators addressed the Olympic visitors or swayed the multitude in the assembly. Professional speech writers wrote pleas for the litigants to deliver before the courts and on occasion, and to the delight of the jury, appeared themselves.

Lysias (*ca.* 440–*ca.* 380 B.C.) Lysias, the first professional orator, was the son of the Syracusan Cephalus, who had come to Athens and grown wealthy as a manufacturer of armor. After he lost his property at the time of the Thirty, Lysias supported himself by writing speeches for others to deliver. His rhetoric was unadorned; his language, that of everyday life. Contemporary with him was the Chalcidian Isaeus, a resident of Athens, who applied his intellect to speeches dealing with cases of private law. The orations which these men wrote are valuable sources of information about Athenian law and social practice.

Isocrates (436–338 B.C.) The most influential teacher of rhetoric was an Athenian, Isocrates. He had studied under the great Sophist leaders of the Peloponnesian War period and about 390 B.C. set himself up as a teacher of practical wisdom. He wrote speeches as pamphlets to be read by other men, but he delivered none himself. He devoted the genius of his mind to solving the problems of the Hellenic world. At first he offered a program of federation in *Panegyricus*, a speech to be delivered at Olympia in 380 B.C., in which he advised the union of all Greece, nominally under the leadership of Athens and Sparta, for war against Persia. Actually the burden of the speech was the right of Athens to command and the unfitness of Sparta. The speech was not without its effect on the formation of the Second Athenian Confederacy. He reiterated the same theme in a series of later pamphlets which culminated in the *Panathenaicus*, in 339 B.C., in which he reviewed the past glories of Athens. Because he despaired of finding a leader in Athens, he appealed without success to a number of outstanding men throughout Hellas. Finally, he called upon Philip to organize a friendly alliance of all Greeks, to call a council in which the Greeks might deliberate under his presidency, and to lead them against Persia. His letter undoubtedly influenced the deliberations of the congress at Corinth which followed the battle of Chaeronea.

In the composition of his speeches Isocrates sought after musical rhythm and the balanced period; he is said to have spent ten years on the composition of *Panegyricus*. His rules of style became the basis for later generations of orators and writers. He gained great fame also as a teacher, for from his school went orators, historians, statesmen, and generals to carry his influence with them throughout the Hellenic world.

Demosthenes (384–322 B.C.) Athenian oratory reached its culmination in the speeches of Demosthenes. Deprived of inherited wealth by dishonest guardians, he trained himself in his youth in order to appear in the law courts against them. At the same time he secured a means of livelihood as a writer of speeches. Many stories are told of his assiduity. Practicing long hours, he steeped himself in the style of Thucydides. As a result, he became the most popular speaker in the law courts. He used his talents to serve the public interest, and among his many political speeches the most famous were the Philippics. Following the battle of Chaeronea he was voted a golden crown for his services to Athens. Charges were brought against the proposer of his award, and Demosthenes defended his friend in a debate with his great opponent, Aeschines. This speech, "On the Crown," is considered, from the point of effective argument and organization, the greatest of all pieces of oratory.

Estimates vary as to the value of Demosthenes' service as a statesman. To many he appears as the last champion of the free *polis* and of Greek democracy, fighting a valiant battle against overwhelming odds. Others have regarded him as a weak opponent of the progressive force of history. Nevertheless, the unquestioned courage of his stand against Philip has nearly always aroused the historian's admiration.

Demosthenes' rival, Aeschines, the professional speech writer Hypereides, and the statesman Lycurgus are also worthy of mention as able writers and makers of speeches.

History After Xenophon, and under the influence of Isocrates, history turned to rhetoric and to the search for exact information. Ephorus of Cyme, in Asia Minor, wrote in rhetorical style a universal history. In the same manner Theopompus of Chios continued Thucydides' work and wrote an account of the career of Philip. On the other hand, a group of chroniclers, of whom the greatest was Androtion, examined the past of Athens in great detail, discovering and systematizing the facts in works called *Atthides*. Of all these writings but few fragments survive.

PHILOSOPHY

Plato (*ca.* 428–347 B.C.**)**   In the intellectual history of Europe two men, Plato and Aristotle, almost certainly rule supreme. Plato, a follower of Socrates, devoted himself first to recording the words of his master in a series of dialogues and in the celebrated *Apology of Socrates.* Later he established a school in the Grove of Academus, where he and his students discussed and developed philosophic concepts. His educational practice in his school, based on the theory that all knowledge is innate in man, adhered to the question-and-answer method, rather than lecturing, because this method draws out information already known and develops the power of clear and rational thought. As a youth Plato had wanted to write drama, and in a sense he did, recording his ideas in dialogues, with Socrates always as the chief speaker. He presented a wide discussion in the philosophic field rather than any fixed system. "The object of our discussion," said Socrates to Philebus, "is not that my words may triumph over yours, nor that yours may gain the victory over mine, but that between us, we may discover the most perfect truth."

In this search for truth, intellectual freedom was for Plato the first necessity. Whenever in later history the minds of men have revolted against the bonds of authority, they have returned in spirit to Plato. His own search led him to the theory of "ideas," that is, the reality of the universal concept, or ideal, of which actual objects are but shadows.

In *The Republic,* his most famous work, Plato first discusses justice, and then works out in detail his conception of the ideal state. The concept of the republic is based on the idea that the city-state is the best institution to achieve the perfection of man. Plato's state of about five thousand citizens is small enough to allow all to participate in its activities, and to be self-sufficient politically, socially, and economically, at the same time maintaining "the moral character of the state" and the code of social ethics which he emphasized. Since the state is to be governed according to a system of social ethics, its members should be subordinated as individuals to occupy that place in society where they can best serve for the good of all. Accordingly, the mass of the people should provide industry, the warrior class defense; and the intelligent, by virtue of their special training and comprehension of realities, should rule. He was actually endeavoring to combine the best features of the intellectual freedom of Athens with a system of control, derived in part from an appreciative study of Spartan institutions, which would render impossible the excesses of Athenian democracy.

Plato's thought has been described as vague and indefinite, with no sound explanation of the origin or nature of evil. Yet its influence was so great that ever since his time idealism, in one form or another, has been the basis of one of the major philosophic schools, and in certain political and scientific thinkers of the present generation there may be seen a trend in the same direction.

The dialogues are masterpieces of dramatic form. Each has its setting from which the discussion flows naturally toward the chosen topic. The language is poetry without meter or rhyme. It is the high-water mark of Attic prose.

Aristotle (384–322 B.C.) Aristotle, too, stands like a colossus in the intellectual world. He was born of a Chalcidian family in Stagira in Macedon in 384 B.C. His father was a doctor, and Aristotle grew up in a scientific tradition and atmosphere. For twenty years he studied under Plato in the Academy. From there he was called to Pella to be tutor to the youthful Alexander. In 335 or 334 B.C. he established his school in a garden called the Lyceum in Athens, where he strolled as he discussed philosophic problems with his students. Because of this custom of walking, his followers became known as the Peripatetics (walkers-around). After the death of Alexander in 323 B.C. he fled from Athens to Chalcis, where he died the following year.

He took for his subject the whole domain of knowledge, and he wrote books dealing with every branch of knowledge. In his lectures and his books he laid the foundations of scientific method and established the principles and the divisions of knowledge. The first step in his method was the study of knowledge already acquired. For this he collected the books of his predecessors and organized the first Greek library, the inspiration and model for the great libraries of Alexandria and Pergamum. The second step was observation and study. He and his students observed the actions of plants, animals, and heavenly bodies. To understand politics, he studied and wrote the constitutional history of one hundred and fifty-eight Greek states. Of these compositions, only the constitution of the Athenians is in existence. Recovered from papyri in Egypt fifty years ago, it is almost, though not entirely, complete. From facts gathered by these processes he arrived at general conclusions inductively, and then by deduction applied his results to individual cases. In so doing he made use of his greatest contribution to knowledge, the creation of formal logic. He said, however, "We must not accept a general principle from logic only, but must prove its application to each part, for it is in facts that we must seek general principles and these must always accord with facts."

He divided philosophy, or knowledge, into three groups according to purpose and further subdivided these groups into subjects. Within these subjects he established the categories of genera and species. The departments of our modern universities go back historically to the Aristotelian classification.

In the realm of philosophic theory he accepted the reality of the Platonic ideal but denied its separate existence. He defined the universal as that which a number of individual objects have in common but which exists in the individual object only. Every object, he taught, is composed of the four elements—earth, air, fire, and water—and has four causes—material, formal, efficient, and final, or purposive. He held motion on earth to be rectilinear, therefore broken and productive of change; in the heavens, circular and therefore unending and perfect. He believed that throughout the universe is God, the efficient and final cause of all, Himself immovable who causes all else to move.

In the realm of human behavior Aristotle treated ethics as a social and political problem rather than as an individual one. The determining principle of virtue is the "golden mean," or balance, which is based on reason and discoverable by intelligence.

In his political writings Aristotle showed himself a firm believer in the Greek city-state, but he maintained with Plato the idea that to secure the greatest good for all the state should be carefully regulated by law based on intelligence. He classified governments into monarchy, aristocracy, and "commonwealth," and condemned the perversion of these into tyranny, oligarchy, and democracy, or rule of the majority, since these sought chiefly the good of an individual or of a group, and not the good of the whole state. He dealt similarly with the creative arts, particularly poetry.

During his lifetime he composed many books on a wide variety of subjects. He was many years in writing some of these, and a few, like his *Politics*, remained unfinished at his death. Fortunately they were preserved, to dominate the learning of the medieval universities and to form the background of modern education. Continuing his work, his students collected libraries, made scientific investigations, and wrote treatises.

ART

Architecture The growing individualism and democratic trend of the age reflected in oratory appeared no less clearly in the architecture and art of the period. Also apparent were influences acquired from increased contacts with the East. In architecture the luxuriant Corinthian capital is characteristic of the wealth and freedom from restraint which prevailed. Few noteworthy temples were constructed; cities began to build instead stadia and theaters of stone. The stone theater at Athens was completed about 340 B.C. by Lycurgus. A little later a majestic hall, the Telesterion, similar in style to the Egyptian hypostyle halls, was erected at Eleusis for the performance of the Mysteries. The most renowned structure, however, of the Hellenic world was the Mausoleum (*ca.* 350 B.C.), a tremendous creation to

Hermes Holding the Infant Dionysus by Praxiteles. Olympia Museum. (Greek Press and Information Service)

serve as a tomb for Mausolus, king of Caria, and his wife Artemisia. It was decorated with reliefs by the sculptor Scopas.

Sculpture Sculpture, too, showed a lessening of restraint. Scopas is renowned for the intensity of the emotion his figures displayed. Praxiteles (fl. 360 B.C.), the greatest of all masters of the chisel, produced a series of beautiful portraits of divinities. His statue of Hermes, found among the ruins of Olympia, represents the youthful divinity in a moment of relaxation holding the infant Dionysus on his arm. On the face of the god transient human emotion is expressed rather than divine idealism. The marble has the texture of flesh; the god has become a supremely beautiful mortal. The same concept of divinity appears in the Aphrodite, which survives in a copy known as the Cnidian

Reproduction (Cast) of a Roman Copy of the Aphrodite of Cnidos by Praxiteles. Original in Glyptothek, Munich. (The Metropolitan Museum of Art)

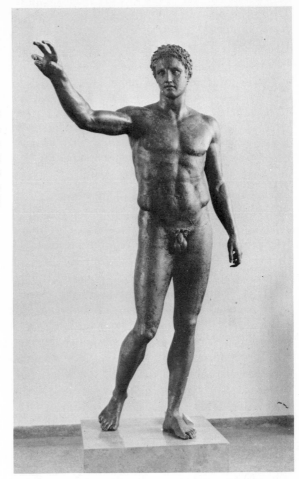

The Ephebus (Youth) from Anticythera. A larger than life-size bronze statue dating from 340 B.C. This statue was found in the sea. (Greek Press and Information Service)

Aphrodite, and in the Satyr, immortalized by Hawthorne in "The Marble Faun." It is possible that the later Aphrodite of Melos (Venus of Milo) was produced by followers of his school. Praxiteles' statues are slenderer and more graceful than those of Polyclitus. Lysippus (fl. 335 B.C.) was a worker in bronze whose Apoxyomenus (Youth Scraping Himself with a Strigil) has survived in a marble copy.

Painting Greek painting of the classical period reached its peak with the works of Zeuxis (fl. 425 B.C.), Parrhasius (fl. 375 B.C.), and Apelles (fl. 335 B.C.). These artists used the same four colors that Polygnotus used, but they advanced the technique of mixing and they also learned the use and value of shadow and gained in knowledge of perspective. They were cosmopolitans and temperamental. Parrhasius signed himself "a friend of pleasure, but one who respects virtue, . . . the first of the Greeks in art." Zeuxis is said to have died from laughing at one of his own paintings. Pliny, the Elder, recounts this story of the two painters.

> The story runs that Parrhasius and Zeuxis entered into competition, Zeuxis exhibiting a picture of some grapes so true to nature that the birds flew up to the wall of the stage. Parrhasius then displayed a picture of a linen curtain realistic to such a degree that Zeuxis, elated by the verdict of the birds, cried out that now at last his rival must draw the curtain and show his picture. On discovering the mistake he surrendered the prize to Parrhasius, admitting candidly that he had deceived the birds, while Parrhasius had deluded himself, a painter.[4]

Apelles, the greatest of all classical painters, was a master of the use of light and dark and of illusion. According to Pliny, he "painted for twenty talents, in the temple of Artemis at Ephesus, a portrait of Alexander holding a thunderbolt. The fingers seem to stand out and the thunderbolt to project from the picture. The reader should remember that all this was done with four colors. . . . Skilled judges of painting prefer among all his works his equestrian portrait of Antigonus and his Artemis amid a band of girls offering sacrifice, a painting thought to have excelled the lines of Homer that describe the same scene. Further, he painted the unpaintable, thunder, for example, lightning, and thunderbolts."[5] His most celebrated painting, Aphrodite Arising from the Sea, was praised for its flesh tones, the beauty of figure, the rendering of waves and sea foam. Of the wonders of this art we have a few memories surviving in mosaics and frescoes of later periods.

Conclusion The classical history of Greece comes to an end with the battle of Chaeronea in 338 B.C. Alexander the Great, son of Philip II, created by his campaigns a new world in which there was no room for Athenian democracy or the free city-state. Greeks of genius made many more contributions to civilization in the later periods, but the mainspring of their efforts had changed. The old order of things had passed, and the age of the city-state had come to an end. With eyes blinded by local patriotism the Greeks had refused to look beyond the borders of their own communities save with the greed of conquest or the fear of subjection. The city-state was too small a unit to control effectively the forces and movements resulting from economic expansion. Instead of combining politically, the cities wasted their substance and impoverished their people by continual wars. Their failure to work out an intelligent, or even possible, plan of peace and union made the Macedonian conquest easy, and unification came, not as a voluntary and progressive

---

[4] Pliny, *Natural History*, 35. 36. 65–66. Trans. in G. W. Botsford and E. G. Sihler, *Hellenic Civilization*. New York: Columbia University Press, 1915.

[5] Pliny, *Natural History*, 35. 36. 92 and 96. Trans. in G. W. Botsford and E. G. Sihler, *Hellenic Civilization*.

A Small Bust Believed To Be a Portrait of Alexander the Great. It was found in Egypt. (The Brooklyn Museum)

measure, but at the order of a conqueror and as a burden of oppression. Whatever its weaknesses, the city-state taught the world lessons that it has never forgotten. The Hellenes contributed the ideals of political and intellectual liberty, standards of perfection in literature and art, the inquiring mind and the instructive tongue, the example of men who first dared to look frankly at the universe and with open minds to question it and their place in it. In *Philebus*, the same dialogue as is quoted above, Plato sums up the quest of the Greek spirit. "If we may not approach the Good with the aid of one idea, then let us overtake it with three—beauty, proportion, and truth."

16 · The Hellenistic Age

THE ASCENDANCY OF MACEDON AFTER CHAERONEA, and particularly the conquests of Alexander, profoundly changed the fundamentals of life for millions of people—Greeks and "barbarians" alike. For Alexander did more than overthrow the Persian kings. He took over their empire and expanded it with the addition of Macedon and Greece. Greeks, Syrians, Jews, Egyptians, Babylonians, Persians, and Indians were brought into new contact during his short reign and after it. Alexander's successors continued to spread Greeks and Macedonians over the middle east, and the varying streams of eastern culture mingled with the Greek. Under the influence of this fusion, the civilizations of the Greeks, the Asiatics, and the Egyptians were transformed. The cultures that developed are termed Hellenistic, and the period that is characterized by them is called the Hellenistic age. While Hellenistic culture had an important influence on Rome and survived as the basis of Eastern civilization under the Roman Empire, the Hellenistic period itself may be considered as ending with the Roman conquest of Egypt in 31 B.C.

SOURCES

Histories The age is of fundamental importance in world history, since it was the Hellenistic and not the Hellenic culture which influenced the Romans and which they transformed and transmitted to the Western world. Our knowledge of the Hellenistic culture, however, is very fragmentary. Alexander kept a daily journal of his campaigns and took historians with him to record his achievements. Many of his generals wrote memoirs. Later historians wrote of his successors, the wars they waged, and the kingdoms they founded. All these records are lost save for scattered fragments. For Alexander's life we are dependent upon writers of the Roman Empire: a rhetorician, Curtius

340

Rufus, who lived in the first century A.D.; the biographer Plutarch; and Arrian, an officer of Hadrian, who wrote the *Anabasis of Alexander.* On Alexander's successors, there is the work of Diodorus, the Sicilian, who composed his *Library of History* around the middle of the first century B.C., and the brief summaries of late Roman writers who made epitomes, or abridgments, of classical works. There is fuller information about the Greek cities and leagues, because Polybius included, in his account of the Roman conquest, their history during the period of Rome's entrance into the Mediterranean scene. Some pieces of literature, particularly the work of the poets, and some records of the achievements of the men of science have withstood the ravages of time and are of use to the historian. Inscriptions and coins help to fill the gaps.

The Papyri Greek papyri recently discovered in Egypt are sources of great value. In mummy wrappings and in the dust heaps of the ancient villages of Egypt archaeologists have found thousands of papyri, some written in demotic and others in Greek for the Greek dwellers in the land of the Ptolemies. Lost books of the classical period, such as poems of Bacchylides and of Alcaeus, long sections of some plays of Menander, and Aristotle's *Constitution of the Athenians*, have been recovered. Fragments of histories have been found. Most numerous and important are papers that deal with public and private live — official documents, laws, royal decrees and appointments, letters, and business and household accounts. These have slowly unfolded the life of Egypt in the Greek and Roman periods. The discovery of papyri and inscriptions has furnished such a wealth of new material that even the lives of individuals, the management of private estates, and the business life, national and international, can be accurately described. The Hellenistic age was one of change and great achievement in economics, politics, and culture.

ALEXANDER THE GREAT

Youth The Hellenistic age was ushered in by the campaigns of Alexander the Great. Many tales are told of the youth of this brilliant son of Philip II and his Epirote wife, Olympias. Like his father, Alexander possessed shrewdness and an ability at cold calculation, and like his mother, a vivid, glowing, romantic imagination. His tutor, the great Aristotle, trained his mind and imbued him with a wholesome regard for Greek culture. Homer was his boyhood god, and he longed for such a poet to sing his praises and for fame for himself equal to that of Achilles. He displayed his mettle as a warrior when at the age of eighteen he led the victorious cavalry charge at Chaeronea in 338 B.C. He was but twenty when his father's death put him in power and left him to expand and execute his father's plans. Philip had probably planned the conquest of only Asia Minor; Alexander enlarged the program until he reached distant India.

Early Conquests   The joy of the Greeks at their seeming liberation by the death of Philip and the accession to the throne of a boy of twenty was short-lived indeed. Alexander set his house in Macedon in order, and when Thebes, led on by a false rumor of his death, revolted, he swept down on that city and ruthlessly destroyed it. By contrast he was inexplicably gentle with Athens, even though it had supported Thebes.

In the spring of 334 B.C. Alexander began his campaign with the invasion of Asia Minor. A daring charge across the Granicus River gained him a victory over a Persian force hastily assembled. He spent the rest of the year freeing the Greek cities of Asia Minor from Persia and securing control over the interior of Anatolia. The battle of Issus (333 B.C.) in Cilicia resulted in the destruction of the first large Persian army and gained him entry into Syria. A series of sieges and assaults reduced the coast cities. The siege of Tyre, which lasted seven months, was the most famous of these conquests. The climax of the campaign was Alexander's coronation in Egypt, to which he had been invited by the natives eager to be freed from Persia. He was crowned pharaoh in Memphis, then marched down the Nile and founded the great city of Alexandria, destined to supplant both Tyre and Athens as a commercial center. From Alexandria he took a dangerous trip into the Libyan Desert to the shrine of Zeus Amon in the oasis of Siwa. There the priests hailed him as the son of the god Amon, to the amazement of the Greek world.

Conquest of the East   Having gained control of the western fringes of the Persian empire, with the seacoast safely in his hands, Egypt under his control, and the rear of his army protected, Alexander advanced to destroy Persia itself and to become King of Kings. In 331 B.C. he defeated the Persian host at Arbela on the royal road from Sardis to Susa. Darius III fled and was later assassinated by a cousin. Alexander took Babylon, Susa, and Persepolis, and the great wealth of the Persian rulers fell into his hands. As if in token of the ending of Achaemenid rule, the royal palace at Persepolis was burned accidentally. Alexander turned next to the mountains and subdued the satrapies and monarchies as far as the Caspian Sea. Then he marched south into India, where he crossed the Indus and defeated the great king Porus. When his troops refused to go farther south with him, he turned back and followed the Indus to its mouth. From there he dispatched a fleet to seek and study the water route to the Persian Gulf and the mouths of the rivers, while he himself led the army through the Gedrosian Desert to Susa and Babylon.

Safe in Babylon he began to regulate the organization of his vast dominions and to plan the conquest of Carthage and the West. But the hardships of his campaigns and a wound he had received had weakened him, and in 323 B.C. he died suddenly — perhaps of pneumonia.

ALEXANDER'S EMPIRE

Alexander, God Before his death Alexander had begun the organization of his conquests and had revealed in part the conception he held. The civilized world was to be united into one vast empire of which he, Alexander, was to be the divine ruler. In Egypt, he was pharaoh, son of Amon-Re; in Persia, he had acceded to the god-given authority of the great kings. He demanded of the Greek city-states that they list him among the gods, possibly, as has been suggested, so that he might control them without violation of the Greek tradition of political autonomy. He demanded of his followers the honors due a god, particularly prostration on entering his presence. To the Persians such obeisance presented no difficulties, and the Greek cities accepted the idea with equanimity, but Alexander's generals were not so happy. Several of his best friends and advisers offended Alexander because of it and were killed as a result.

In this manner the concept of the god-king was introduced to the Hellenic world. How much Alexander's action owed to Egyptian and Oriental precedents, how much to Greek hero worship, and how much to contemporary philosophical ideas can hardly be determined. For some years the Anatolian Greeks had been paying divine honors as a compliment to such men as Lysander, and Alexander's claim may have seemed merely a further extension of such honors. The god-king idea, however, became a powerful force in both politics and religion in the Hellenistic world and a predominant unifying element in the Roman Empire.

Unity of Empire Ultimate unification of the empire was to be achieved by the combination of Macedonians, Greeks, and Persians in one race. Alexander himself had married Roxana, a Bactrian princess. Several of his generals followed his example, and ten thousand of his soldiers took Asiatic wives.

To achieve the mixture Alexander founded Greek cities in all sections of his empire from Egypt to India, the most famous of them being Alexandria in Egypt. This act served to provide an outlet for the surplus population of the motherland, but as Hellenizing forces the cities were a failure. In charge of the satrapies Alexander appointed Persians, along

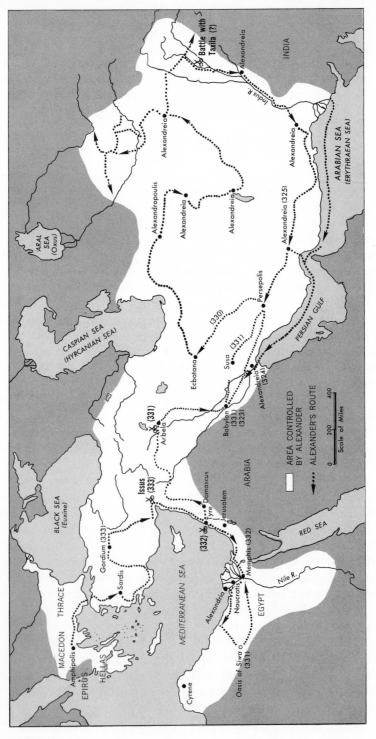

Alexander's Empire, 323 B.C.

with Greeks and Macedonians, reserving military command to the Macedonians. This scheme also was unsuccessful, and the Persians were replaced by Alexander's men. When thirty thousand Persian youths were equipped and trained for the army in the Macedonian fashion, the Macedonian veterans mutinied. Special honors were given to placate them, and the use of native troops was abandoned after Alexander's death.

The confusion following Alexander's untimely death and the subsequent division of his empire among his generals brought about the ultimate ruin of his grandiose plans.

None of Alexander's measures had been able to produce complete unification — political, racial, or cultural. The amount of fusion which took place varied greatly between the major divisions of Egypt, Syria, and Mesopotamia. In Egypt and Syria, where there were large numbers of Greeks, Hellenic culture combined with native ideas and customs, especially in religion. There was, moreover, some intermarriage among the peoples, particularly among the lower classes. But in Mesopotamia and its hinterland Greek influence was slight, and although the later Parthian rulers (p. 352) assumed a veneer of Hellenistic culture, the Greeks themselves were rapidly swallowed up in the vortex of other peoples.

The Wars of Succession The fifty years that followed Alexander's death were filled with the utmost confusion. There were intrigues and wars in which Olympias, mother of Alexander, Cleopatra, his sister, and other women had a share, along with his generals, and after them their sons. At first attempts were made to preserve unity under regents for the posthumous son of Alexander and Roxana and for Alexander's half-witted brother, Philip Arrhidaeus. After the failure of these regencies, Antigonus, the One-eyed, made a brilliant attempt to secure control over the empire. In the course of his wars the famous siege of Rhodes by his son Demetrius, the City-taker, occurred. The other generals combined against Antigonus, and he was defeated and killed at the battle of Ipsus in 301 B.C. Seleucus, cavalry commander under Alexander, tried to unite Asia and Macedon, but he was killed by the son of Ptolemy almost at the moment of victory. When the wars finally dragged to an end, the empire had fallen into three great kingdoms, Egypt under the Ptolemies, Asia under the successors of Seleucus, and Macedon under the descendants of Antigonus, as well as a number of smaller states kept alive by the rivalries of the great powers. Egypt and Asia contended for the control of Syria; Asia and Macedon were rivals in Asia Minor and Thrace; Macedon and Egypt endeavored to maintain control of the Aegean. This three-cornered struggle continued until Rome entered the field and became master of all.

A SURVEY OF THE HELLENISTIC WORLD

Athens   A survey of the Hellenistic states reveals the extent and the character of the world into which Rome was to enter. We may properly begin with Athens and the Greek motherland. From Philip after Chaeronea and from Alexander after the destruction of Thebes, Athens had received the signal favor of immunity from interference. Alexander was even constrained into withdrawing his demand for the surrender of the anti-Macedonian leaders. If this favor was due to his desire for the assistance of the Athenian fleet, it was rendered in vain.

Throughout Alexander's life, the city remained prosperous but quiescent. The pro-Macedonian Phocion, a man renowned for his probity, took the place of Demosthenes as a leader of policies. Lycurgus, orator and financier of great ability, was in charge of finances. Under his direction the finances were well handled and public buildings, docks, and arsenals were maintained and improved. Yet the aging Demosthenes remained active. Against his rival, Aeschines, he defended his anti-Macedonian policies ably in the great oration on the crown. When Harpalus, one of Alexander's treasurers who had embezzled and fled, came to Athens with funds to stir up a revolt, he was stopped and his funds were seized by the Athenian government. Demosthenes, accused of accepting bribes, was tried, found guilty, and heavily fined by the Council of the Areopagus. There is still doubt, however, of his guilt; he may have been the victim of political trickery. Nevertheless he fled into exile, where he remained until the death of Alexander brought him back to Athens.

A coalition of the Greek states was formed and a war for independence, known as the Lamian War (323–322 B.C.), was started against Antipater, regent in Macedon. At first the Athenian general Leosthenes was victorious, and Antipater was bottled up in Lamia. The death of Leosthenes, however, wrecked Athenian hopes. The Greeks were defeated at Crannon, and Antipater descended upon Athens. The anti-Macedonian leaders were put to death; Demosthenes took poison to avoid capture. The constitution was revised in favor of the well-to-do, and Athenian democracy was finished. A Macedonian garrison was stationed on the hill of Munychia. From 317 to 307 B.C. the city was ably controlled by the philosopher Demetrius of Phalerum. In 307 B.C. it passed into the hands of Demetrius, the City-taker, who was hailed by the Athenians as a liberator. For the succeeding generation Athens was the spoil of the wars of the generals until, after the Chremonidean War (266–262 B.C.), a last attempt at freedom, it passed into the power of Macedon. With that, the great political history of Athens came to an end.

Sparta   Meanwhile Sparta had fallen upon evil days. The loss of man power in the battles of Leuctra and Mantinea, as well as the decline of military prestige, had been a serious matter to the state. When Epaminondas freed Messene, many Spartans were deprived of the means whereby they made their contributions to the public tables. The number of Spartans declined until there were but seven hundred in full possession of civic rights. Still Sparta refused to join the Hellenic League under Philip and Alexander.

After a brief and unsuccessful revolt in 331 B.C. Sparta sank into weakness, and the ancient system of training was neglected. Then in 244 B.C. Agis IV, the king (p. 361), advanced a program of reforms to re-establish the city's ancient glory. The land was to be redivided; some of the perioeci were to be enfranchised; and the ancient Lycurgan discipline was to be enforced once more. The program failed when Agis was put to death in 241 B.C. for treason.

His son-in-law, Cleomenes, was more successful. By the use of vigorous methods and supported by mercenary troops, Cleomenes carried the reform movement through in 226 B.C. When he endeavored to restore Spartan power in the Peloponnesus, however, he found opposition in Aratus, general of the Achaean League, who rather than yield appealed to Macedon for help. In 222 B.C. Antigonus Doson defeated Cleomenes in the battle of Sellasia. The Spartan fled to Egypt, and the old regime was restored. In 207 B.C. revolution broke out again under the leadership of Nabis, who made himself tyrant, robbed the well-to-do, abolished debts, redistributed the land, and freed many of the helots. After his death his work was undone by the leaders of the Achaean League, and Spartan history ended in the utter ruin of the community.

The Aetolian League   The real power in Greece during the Hellenistic age was in the hands of the Aetolian and Achaean leagues. The Aetolians had been a backward folk during the classical period of Greek history, organized in tribes and living in scattered villages in northwestern Greece. In the latter part of the fourth century B.C., however, they emerged with a well-developed federal union of city-states, among which there was potential exchange of citizenship. Each year two assemblies of the league were held in which all citizens of the member states might participate.

These assemblies, which voted on questions of peace and war and elected officials, possessed real power of control over the affairs of the league. A council of one thousand was established, with membership distributed among the cities in accordance with the number of troops furnished to the army. From this body an executive committee of thirty was chosen. At the head was a general, assisted by a hipparch, a secretary, and seven financial stewards. The cities were independent in local affairs, but the central government maintained full control over foreign affairs, wars, alliances, command of the army, and direction of such matters as the uniformity of weights, measures, and coinage. As new cities were added, they were given full rights of citizenship with the old. This created a powerful and well-knit group. The league extended to the east, secured control over Delphi, gained great prestige by the defeat of a Gallic raid, and finally, in alliance with Macedon, controlled northern Greece from sea to sea.

The Achaean League   The Achaean League was an ancient body composed of the little and insignificant states along the southern shore of the Gulf of Corinth. Its organization was similar to that of the Aetolian League: an assembly of all citizens over thirty years of age met once a year; the cities were represented in a council according to their population; a general who could be re-elected to office only every other year was the chief executive; a board of ten advised the general. As in the Aetolian League, the central government controlled external relations and the uniformity of standards within the cities. To this the league added the idea of the guarantee of a stable government which would provide security for its wealthy citizens and prevent economic and political revolution.

The league became important when, in 251 B.C., Aratus led his city, Sicyon, to membership and became the dominating force in the organization. He was elected to office every other year, with friends whom he could control as generals during the alternate years. Under his guidance the league expanded to take in Corinth, Arcadia, and eventually the whole northern Peloponnesus. Its conservative leaders were shocked and frightened by the social program of Agis and Cleomenes, and when, in addition, Cleomenes blocked Aratus' path to power, the latter laid aside his consistent policy of resistance to Macedon, invited Antigonus to end the Spartan menace, and surrendered control of the Peloponnesus to him.

Macedon   Nowhere was there worse confusion in the years following Alexander's death than in Macedon, as one general after another endeavored to secure the throne of the victorious state. It was occupied by many adventurers, among them Pyrrhus of Epirus (homeland of Alexander's mother) and Ptolemy Ceraunus. In the midst of the disorder there appeared a horde of Gauls similar to the band that had raided Rome a century before. They plundered Delphi and killed one of the holders of the Macedonian throne. In 277 B.C. Antigonus Gonatas, son of Demetrius and grandson of the great Antigonus, defeated them and by his victory secured control over Macedon. From then until the Roman conquest he and his descendants, called Antigonids, were kings in Macedon. They achieved and maintained control over Greece and in the Aegean defeated the Ptolemies in naval battles.

Macedon was a strong military monarchy of some four million sturdy peasants. The rulers were generals who were recognized as kings by consent of the army. Unlike Alexander and the rulers of Egypt and Asia, they made no pretense to divinity; indeed they would have been unsuccessful had they sought to achieve such recognition. The state was financed by income from the royal domains, the forests, the mines, and from duties and tribute. Ultimately, it allowed itself to become involved in the affairs of Rome and paid the penalty of defeat.

Pergamum For a brief period Thrace and western Anatolia were controlled by Lysimachus, who was defeated and killed by Seleucus at Corupedium in 281 B.C. Seleucus in turn was assassinated, and Thrace then became the property of Macedon. Western Anatolia passed into the hands of Philetaerus, secretary of Lysimachus, who had gone over to Seleucus with the treasure of Lysimachus. Philetaerus was allowed to establish himself as a petty ruler in Pergamum, and he extended his power by judicious use of the treasure. His nephew and successor, Eumenes, defended himself successfully against the son of Seleucus. Attalus I, who followed, defeated a group of Gauls that had penetrated Asia Minor, and in memory of his victory he commissioned the well-known statues of the Gauls.

The kings of Pergamum claimed divinity while posing as democratic rulers. Their government has been called an organized machine for the accumulation of wealth. Scientific agriculture was practiced on the royal domains, and the manufacture of textiles and the production of pitch from the highland forests prospered under royal direction. To break the monopoly of writing materials which Egyptian papyri enjoyed, the preparation of sheep skins into *pergamentum* (parchment) was developed into a large-scale business. The city of Pergamum, famous for a great altar of Zeus, was regulated by a public health law of a modern type. A great library was collected and schools of literature and philosophy were developed.

Rhodes Rhodes was one of the few Greek cities that maintained its independence and prospered under the new regime. From early times there had been three little towns on the favorite island of the sun god, Helios. Shortly after 400 B.C. the three towns united to form one city at the head of the island, where nature provided two magnificent harbors. Alexander favored the city and deposited treasure there. After his death Rhodes declared neutrality in the wars of succession, and when Demetrius ordered it to unite with Antigonus, it refused. A siege was instituted by sea, but the swift ships of the Rhodians ran the blockade and took in supplies furnished by Egypt. Assaults by land were repulsed. When Demetrius constructed a huge nine-storied wheeled machine, the *helepolis*, equipped with battering rams, catapults, and stands for archers and slingers, and moved by thirty-four hundred men, a Rhodian engineer turned the sewage of the city into its path. Demetrius gave up the siege after ten months, and thereafter Rhodian neutrality was respected.

The Nike (Victory) of Samothrace. This is one of the most beautiful of Hellenistic sculptures. Musée du Louvre. (Service de Documentation Photographiques, Réunion des Musées Nationaux)

With the spoils from the *helepolis* Rhodes erected a colossal statue of the sun god at the entrance to the harbor. This famous Colossus of Rhodes, one hundred and five feet high, had stood only a few years when it was destroyed by an earthquake.

Rhodes was the chief port of call for all ships sailing between the East and the West. A 2 per cent port tax on its transit business brought great wealth to the city. Its fleets became guardians of the sea and suppressors of piracy. When Byzantium in 220 B.C. endeavored to tax ships passing through the Bosporus, Rhodes, interfering to protect the freedom of the seas and its own commercial interests, punished the presumptuous city. Many cases were submitted to the neutral city for arbitration, which developed and enforced the Rhodian law of shipwreck dealing with salvage, taken over later in Roman law. Rhodes became famous for its school of philosophy, much visited by Romans, and for its sculptors, who produced colossal statues and the renowned Laocoön.

Reproduction (Cast) of the Borghese Warrior by Agasias Second or First Century B.C. Original found at Antium and now in the Musée du Louvre. (The Metropolitan Museum of Art, Cullum Collection, 1895)

Delos   Another island community that gained advantage under the new regime was Delos. This island, sacred to Apollo and once the center of the Ionian amphictyony, then the meeting place and treasury of the Confederacy of Delos, had been consecrated by the Athenians, who removed all dwellings and made it into a sacred place. After it gained its freedom from Athens in 314 B.C. Delos speedily became an important city. Its central location among the Cyclades, its small but well-sheltered harbor, and the wealth of its temple, always a favorite depository for men of wealth, gave it great advantages. Beautiful houses were built on its hillsides and fine porticoes and halls in its market place. Merchants and artisans from the Greek lands and from the Orient flocked there in such numbers that there was a house famine during the middle of the third century B.C. It became the chief market for slaves. When the Romans abolished its 2 per cent export and import duty after

168 B.C. and made it a free port, Delos' trade and prosperity surpassed that of Rhodes.

Its buildings, excavated by the French School at Athens, afford a fine example of a Hellenistic city, and its inscriptions, particularly the temple accounts, provide much information about economic conditions — prices, rents, wages, and rates of interest—in the Hellenistic age.

Seleucid Asia   Asia, the central and largest of the succession kingdoms of Alexander's empire, occupying most of the area of Persia and Babylonia, in 301 B.C. passed definitely into the hands of Seleucus, cavalry commander under Alexander. He was the cornerstone of the resistance to Antigonus, was one of the victors at Ipsus, captured Demetrius in 285 B.C., and defeated Lysimachus in 281 B.C. Under his successors the large and widely scattered domains tended to break into pieces. Not only Pergamum but Bithynia, Pontus, and Cappadocia became independent kingdoms in Asia Minor. In the East a number of independent states were formed, and the plateau of Iran was held by the Parthians, whose kings claimed to be successors to the Persians. Southern Syria was the subject of contention between Egypt and Asia, with the latter finally victorious. Ptolemaic Egypt controlled the area until 201 B.C. in spite of a series of wars. The most interesting of these was the struggle culminating in the battle of Raphia in 217 B.C. Over a hundred thousand men and numerous war elephants (Indian and African) were engaged. Ptolemy IV won, but in the next war Antiochus III took Palestine and Syria from the boy-king Ptolemy V. Further advance brought Antiochus into unsuccessful conflict with Rome, which marked the collapse of the Seleucid Empire.

The Seleucid Kings   The Seleucid kings claimed power over some thirty million people of many nationalities scattered over a million square miles of territory. The sole unifying force in this great empire was worship of the king. To the Orientals he was the vicar of the gods and successor to the kings of Persia. To the Greeks he was the descendant of Apollo, founder and patron of the Seleucid Empire. The Seleucids took such titles as *Theos* (God), *Soter* (Saviour), and *Epiphanes* (God Manifest). The empire was divided into many small satrapies in which civil, financial, and military powers were carefully separated. Local government of the natives was in the hands of officers of the king or of native rulers. The Greek communities were given constitutions and governed themselves. The administration was financed from a land tax, duties, and gifts, and from the large royal domains. Much of the land remained in the possession of the ancient temples and some in the hands of the Persian nobility. Most of the noble estates of the older regime, however, were handed over as possessions to the Greek city-states.

Seleucid Culture   For the Seleucids, civilization meant Hellenism. Hellenization was therefore a program of unity. Many cities were founded, Seleucus alone establishing some sixty—Seleucia, Antioch on the Orontes, Apamea, and Laodicea being the most famous. Seleucia, on the Tigris, took the place of Babylon as the great city of Mesopotamia. It is said to have had a population of six hundred thousand. Greatest of all was Antioch, capital of the empire, with a population of half a million Greeks, Syrians, and Jews. The Persian road and postal system was maintained. The Royal Road ran from Sardis to Antioch, crossed the Euphrates by a bridge at Doura, where a flourishing town developed, and continued to Seleucia. A fleet was maintained on the Persian Gulf, and trade connections were established with India, where the emperors Chandragupta and Asoka reigned.

In the attempt to spread Hellenic culture, Greek law was advanced, Greek gods were worshiped, philosophy and science were studied, and theaters and stadia erected. At that time Greek curiosity led to a revival of interest in the old cuneiform literature and in Chaldean divination and astronomy. By the side of Apollo flourished the Great Mother, Ishtar, with her religious prostitutes. But the Greeks in the interior were being slowly absorbed. Loss of contact with the motherland, whence sprang inspiration, broke down their Hellenism, and all attempts to Hellenize the natives failed. The effort of Antiochus IV to Hellenize the Jews led to open revolt and to the establishment of the independent Maccabean kingdom (p. 519). The Seleucid Empire was too vast, too unwieldy, and too diversified to be successfully united into a permanent structure by the policies used. The Parthians in the east (pp. 345, 352) and the Romans in the west (p. 451) delivered the death-blows.

Ptolemaic Egypt Our knowledge of the history, administration, and social life of Ptolemaic Egypt is richer than that of any of the other Hellenistic states, because of the abundance of papyri and because of the literary and scientific pre-eminence of Alexandria. Egypt was the richest and most long-lived of all the succession kingdoms. Alexander appointed Cleomenes, a Greek from Naucratis, as financial administrator in 332 B.C. This able man organized the tax system of Egypt along Greek lines and in 330 B.C. gained great wealth for himself by cornering the grain market. He shut down on the export of Egyptian grain, bought up the crop, being careful to pay well for it, and then sold it abroad at famine prices.

In 323 B.C. Ptolemy was made satrap in Egypt. The year following the death of Alexander, he murdered Cleomenes and seized his treasure. By a clever trick Ptolemy I had obtained the body of Alexander and housed it in a magnificent tomb in the city of Alexandria. It promptly became the major tourist attraction of the Hellenistic world. In the wars of succession Ptolemy played a minor part. He had no ambition except to be recognized as a ruler of Egypt where, in 305 B.C., he assumed the title of king but rejected the offer of regency over the rest of

One of a Pair of Stone Plaques Shaped as Lions, Ptolemaic Period,
Third Century B.C. They were obviously mounted on some larger object.
(The Brooklyn Museum)

Alexander's empire. He aided Rhodes against Antigonus, annexed
Cyrene, tried to hold southern Syria, and established himself in the
Aegean by sending grain to the island states in a famine year. For this
deed he received the title of *Soter*, "Saviour." Ptolemy Philadelphus and
his sister-wife Arsinoë (283–246 B.C.) followed their father in power.

Under these rulers and their successor, Ptolemy Euergetes, Egypt
gained its greatest power since the days of Thutmose III. For a brief
period the Ptolemies controlled Syria and the coast of Asia Minor; their
fleet dominated the Aegean and the Hellespont; their money stirred up
the Chremonidean War and enabled the Achaean League to hold Macedon at bay. But Macedonian naval power proved too strong for them in
the Aegean. On the mainland Aratus betrayed the Greeks to Macedon
at Sellasia (p. 347), and Ptolemaic influence in Greece was completely
destroyed. The Ptolemies also lost Palestine and Syria. Ptolemy IV,
Philopator, had used native troops at Raphia. Afterward there was
unrest and revolt among the economically depressed Egyptians. Egypt
began to decline, and the kingdom became a protectorate of Rome with
decadent Ptolemies ruling there until the dynasty passed in a blaze of
glory with the great Cleopatra.

The ruling Ptolemy was accepted by the native Egyptians as pharaoh, divine son of Amon-Re. He bore in hieroglyphs the five names of the ancient kings, and from the time of Philopator went through the ancient ceremonies. Old temples were repaired or enlarged and new ones built, upon whose walls inscriptions were cut and reliefs carved of the Ptolemaic pharaohs in ancient garb and style. The reigning Ptolemy was acknowledged as a god-king, successor to the pharaohs and the divine Alexander.

Under the king were the vizier, the directors of finance, the chief justice, and a host of secretaries organized into an elaborate bureaucracy. The ancient division of the land into nomes and smaller subdivisions of districts and villages was maintained under Egyptian officials. By the side of the natives, however, were Greek military and police magistrates who overshadowed them and soon took their place. Finances were in Greek hands. Separate systems of courts for the Greeks and the Egyptians and mixed courts for cases that involved both were established. The Ptolemies did not follow the policy of urbanization pursued by Alexander and the Seleucids. In fact, Alexandria was the only important Greek city. The Greeks and the Jews who thronged into Egypt were settled in the villages under separate corporate organizations of their own, which they managed under the watchful eye of the central administration. Both peoples intermarried freely with the Egyptians and were soon fused with the native population.

The government was supported by produce, excise, sales, and poll taxes. In addition there were a number of state monopolies, particularly banking, and the manufacture of paper, perfumes, leather goods, and oils, all of which were farmed out under careful supervision. Foreign trade was likewise in the possession of the Ptolemies, and protective tariffs were levied on olive oil, wines, and woolens to protect the royal profits. Greek administrative ability put the governmental machine in order and kept it under such careful supervision that no more complete system of regimentation has ever been seen. The status of every individual, the condition of every piece of property was carefully defined and recorded. Local administration was directed to the full development of the economic wealth of the land, and Egyptian foreign policy was motivated by commercial ends—the promotion of trade with the Aegean, with Syracuse and the West, with Syria, and with distant India.

As of old, the land and all it produced were the property of the king, but granted by him to his subjects and classified according to its terms of grant—the royal domains, the sacred land of the temple, land in grant or gift to officials, nobles, and private citizens, and cleruch land, which was given to soldiers. The Greeks who became farmers seem to have controlled the land as their own; some were able to estab-

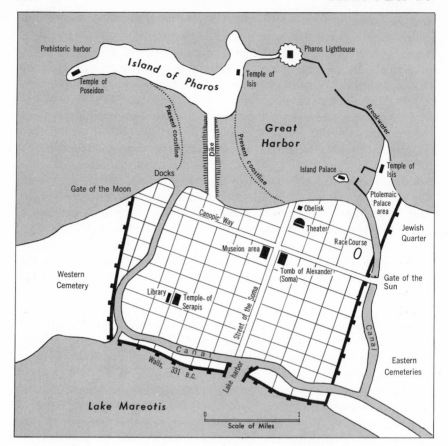

Probable Reconstruction of Alexandria Under the Ptolemies, ca. 200 B.C. Grid plan by Dinocrates. Blocks were labeled by letters of the Greek alphabet.[1]

lish great estates, while the natives were, for the most part, serfs. Greek genius applied itself to farming, to manufacturing, and to exploiting the commercial wealth of ancient Egypt. While still clinging to the old lines of activity, it improved ancient methods, expanded the markets, and created extraordinary wealth.

Alexandria   The capital of Ptolemaic Egypt was the city of Alexandria, with its broad Canopic Way, lined with palaces, and its museum and library, its harbor and famous Pharos lighthouse. A large, self-governing Greek colony occupied one quarter, and a similar group of Jews another. The wealth, literature, and science of the world met in this city of Alexander, under the generous patronage of the Ptolemies,

[1] From *Alexandria: A History and a Guide* by E. M. Forster. Copyright © 1961 by Edward Morgan Forster. Reprinted by permission of Doubleday & Company, Inc.

and it became the cosmopolitan cultural center of the Hellenistic world. The work of its scholars, scientists, and writers will be described later.

The West   The history of the western Greeks followed the careers of three leaders—Agathocles, Pyrrhus, and Hiero. Out of the confusion that followed the ultimate failure of Timoleon's settlement of 338 B.C. (p. 322), an able tyrant, Agathocles (317–289 B.C.), rose to power in Syracuse. He regained control of Dionysius' empire in Italy and Sicily, fought with Carthage, and invaded Africa. In the last enterprise he was unsuccessful, and peace was made again on the basis of the division of Sicily between the powers. When Agathocles died, Syracuse once more collapsed.

In 281 B.C. Pyrrhus, king of Epirus, entered Italy on the invitation of Tarentum (p. 398) but with dreams of a great western empire. After his first battles with Rome he turned to the conquest of Sicily. Here he won some successes, but his methods and plans displeased the Sicilian Greeks and they failed to support him. He returned to Italy, was defeated at Beneventum, and returned to the East to become king of Macedon for a brief period.

Trouble with mercenaries, the Mamertines, in Messana led to the choice of Hiero (269–215 B.C.) as ruler of Syracuse. This wise man handled the affairs of the city well during the long war between Carthage and Rome that followed. He entered into close relations with Egypt, organized his lands on the Ptolemaic model, and imported the papyrus plant that still grows wild in the marshes near modern Siracusa. His successor broke with Rome during the Hannibalic War, and Syracuse was conquered by Rome.

Alexander had carried Macedonian power and Greek ideas from the Aegean to the borders of India. The unity of his empire was dissipated by his successors in the wars they waged with one another, but out of the final settlement emerged the great powers of Egypt, Asia, and Macedon, and the little kingdom of Pergamum. Athens and Sparta, leading states of the classical period, declined and in their place, as centers of political power, stood the Achaean and the Aetolian leagues. Rhodes, Delos, and Corinth succeeded to the commercial position once held by Athens, while the newly founded cities of Antioch and Alexandria became the cultural and commercial centers of the East.

17 · Hellenistic Civilization

IN THE WIDESPREAD HELLENISTIC WORLD TWO CURRENTS of civilization, Greek and Oriental, met and mingled. Though they did not blend and become one, they acted upon each other like chemical reagents. The stronger element, however, was the Greek. For most Greeks the city-state, whether one of the older cities or one of the colonies in the Oriental world, remained the center of loyalty for the individual. At the same time the world was bound together by a sense of unity, the product of the expansion of Hellenism. Greek religion, Greek art, and the ever-present Greek artistic and dramatic festivals drew the Greeks together, while the bond was completed by the spread of a common language—not the literary Attic prose of Plato, but the *Koine*, the spoken language of the common man. Philosophers talked of *homonoia*, a union of minds: "The educated man is a citizen of the world." After contact with other peoples they were ready to say that "Above all nations is humanity." The leagues and the great kingdoms were in a measure expressions of these concepts. "There are many cities, but they are all one Hellas." The wide use of arbitration in the settlement of disputes, the exchanges of citizenship, the granting of honorary citizenship or of the titles of friend and benefactor, the development of legal uniformity and of a recognized body of commercial law, the universal welcome to the Dionysiac artists who traveled around giving dramatic performances—all these and more were at once the symptoms and the products of *Hellenismus*.

The Cities Though the independent city-state was declining, the number and size of cities were increasing. Everywhere the successors of Alexander had founded new cities, some of which attained astounding size. Alexandria, Seleucia, and Antioch approached or even passed the half-million mark.

Rhodes, Delos, Ephesus, and Corinth grew into large and wealthy emporia. In these cities wealth ruled, for Greek democracy had gone with the passing of the greatness of Athens. Wealth, however, respected

neither family, tradition, nor sex. The new alignment of society was rich
and poor, not aristocrat and commoner, oligarch and democrat. Women
of wealth who so desired were able to secure freer participation in public
life; higher education was open to them; many secured election to public
office and some were voted honorary citations.

Greek intelligence showed itself to good advantage in the new cities.
These settlements were carefully laid out with proper attention to
water supply, sanitation, and drainage. They were equipped with fine
buildings in the market places, splendid temples, theaters, and stadia.
Market commissioners regulated weights, measures, and prices. Schools
endowed by the rich or supported by the city offered opportunities
for education. Many cities hired doctors to tend the sick, and state aid or
private benefaction often brought relief to the very poor. Religious
associations, social and athletic clubs, trade and industrial federations
provided companionship and gave individuals dignity.

The God-Kings The power of the god-kings spread over all.
Upon them prosperity depended. In times of disaster they might be
counted on to come to the rescue, and thus earn the title of saviour or
benefactor. They might not be offended, nor their will crossed, even by
the older cities of the Aegean. Ever present was the hope that one day
a god-king might right the wrongs, put an end to the injustices of the
world, and bring universal prosperity.

Commerce In the economic world expanding commerce and
localities specializing in agricultural and industrial products were the
most striking features. Throughout the Mediterranean, trade developed north and west along the routes from Alexandria and Antioch.
Egypt, Asia, and Macedon contended in wars for control of these routes.
Rhodes, jealous of its interests, attempted to preserve the freedom of
traffic and to suppress piracy. Syracuse and Messana prospered because
of their trade contacts with Egypt. Trade in the western Mediterranean
was still in the hands of Carthage, while the Ptolemies and Seleucids both
turned to the East. The Seleucids established a fleet in the Persian Gulf,
sent envoys to India, and maintained a prosperous traffic with that
fabulous country. The Ptolemies reopened the canal from the Nile
to the Red Sea, renewed the caravan route from Coptos to the coast,
established several ports on the Red Sea and controlled an active trade
in its waters with southern Arabia. The commerce between there and
India was firmly and jealously held by the Arab merchants until the last
century B.C., when direct contact was definitely established between
Egypt and India. Much of the trade from southern Arabia passed north
by land in the hands of the Nabataeans through their famous "rose-red"
city, Petra, and from there to Alexandria, Gaza, or Antioch. The
Ptolemies exploited the coast of Africa as far as Cape Guardafui. Silk
from China reached the Mediterranean by way of India until after the

establishment of the Han dynasty when, about 126 B.C., direct contact was established by way of Bactria and the overland route. So much silk came into the Mediterranean that the city fathers of Messana found it necessary in 91 B.C. to pass a law prohibiting the women of that city from wearing transparent silk dresses.

From the Far East came silk, pepper, spices; from Africa, ivory and fine woods. Arabia produced frankincense and myrrh. Gold was supplied by India, Nubia, and Spain; silver by Macedon and Spain. Copper, as of old, came chiefly from Cyprus. Egypt and the Black Sea area were the granaries of the world. Wool from the highlands and purple dye from the shellfish kept Tyre and the Syrian cities prosperous.

Industry   Industry expanded and became specialized with the development of trade. Though in all the cities there were, as always, countless small shops that supplied local needs, establishments of larger size grew more and more frequent in the great cities. The royal monopolies in Egypt and Pergamum were organized for mass production and distribution, and many private men of wealth owned and operated large workshops. At the same time there was much regional specialization: Egypt supplied linen goods, paper, glassware, and vegetable oils; Pergamum produced textiles and parchment; though Athenian pottery had lost its pre-eminence, Athens still controlled the Mediterranean market with its excellent olive oil.

Slavery   The Hellenistic age brought no fundamental changes in the types of slavery and in the employment of slaves. Increased wealth added to the number of slaves who were in domestic service, and the growth of great estates in Sicily and Italy led to the expansion of agricultural slavery in the West. But in Egypt and in Asia the native systems of serfdom were an effective bar to the extension of slavery there. Industrial slavery was introduced into the newer cities, but the large number of free workers and the low rate of wages made it unprofitable and led to a general decline in its use. The sources of slaves remained the same: in spite of the efforts of Alexander and his immediate successors, prisoners of war were still sold; victims were still enslaved by pirates; debtors and exposed children still appeared in the market. As the slave trade became international in scope, with Delos as its chief center, the creation of new markets in Italy and Sicily led, in the Roman period (p. 427), to a westward shift in the traffic.

Hellenistic Law   Both the political and economic structure of the Hellenistic world contributed to the development of uniformity in law: the kings rendered decisions for the peoples under their control; the leagues fostered conformity among their members; and the great extension of commercial transactions made the formation of a recognized if unwritten body of contractual law an absolute necessity. The request of states for commissioners from without to adjudicate suits with even-handed justice created a rather large group of lawyers who made it their business to study legal systems. The informal method these men used in their courts led substantially to an interstate system of equity and to a general understanding of obligations. This body of law was taken over by the Roman jurists as the *jus gentium* (p. 471).

Money Money of gold and silver was plentiful after Alexander had turned loose the flood of Persian treasure, with a resultant rise in prices and decline in interest rates. The world-wide character of trade led to an enlargement of banks and an extension of banking transactions greater in volume, if not more complex in character, than those of the fourth century B.C. (p. 328). Through surviving papyri the records of the state-owned banks of Egypt disclose almost every kind of financial practice—deposits, checks, drafts, loans, and letters of credit. Many private banks in the Greek cities had international connections and carried on a widely diversified business. Curiously enough, as this financial skill developed, public finance in the cities reached a low ebb. The cities spent far beyond their income and borrowed so continually from temples or bankers, pledging their revenues and the property of their citizens, that most of them were on the verge of bankruptcy and were constantly calling on wealthy citizens and friends for aid.

Rich and Poor The inflation during the period brought prosperity to many and enabled some to build fortunes far beyond the dreams of earlier times. Yet untold suffering was the lot of the poor. Far from keeping up with prices, wages actually declined. The competition of slaves and of the many poor for work dragged free labor down to the subsistence level until wages became so low that it was cheaper to hire freemen than to own slaves. Hence industrial slavery declined, particularly in Egypt. Though the wealthy man was generous in his gifts to the state, he was far from liberal in the wages he paid. That the conditions of the poor did not escape notice is demonstrated by the fact that some states, particularly Rhodes and Samos, distributed grain to the indigent; others acted at times to lighten the load of debt, and the philosophers planned ideal states in which poverty would be abolished.

The disparity between the classes and the growing burden of debt and poverty produced a constant threat of social revolution in many of the Greek cities. Such a revolution actually took place in Sparta, initiated by Agis and executed by Cleomenes and Nabis (p. 347). The leaders of the Achaean League probably opposed these men because of their fear that, if successful, the revolutionary movement would spread to their states rather than because of a fear of the rebirth of Spartan power.

CULTURE

Royal patronage, private wealth, and civic pride contributed in this period to the development of a culture which a common language and the growth of travel made universal. As demand arose, scholars, scientists, literary men, and artists traveled about, forming groups, especially in Alexandria, Antioch, Rhodes, and Athens. The departures of this period from the standards of purity, idealism, and devotion to the gods, in contrast to the glorious period of the fifth and fourth centuries B.C., have caused admirers of the classics to regard the works of the Hellenistic age as decadent. Such a question of progress or decline is a matter of taste; each must answer it for himself. Certainly, excellence in technique and a universal appeal to the educated of the day, and at times even to the ignorant classes, were to be found in the works of the Hellenistic leaders of arts, letters, and thought.

Architecture and Art

The Hellenistic City   Architecture and art in the Hellenistic age were essentially secular in character. Allusion has already been made to the careful planning and construction of a Hellenistic city. Sites were carefully chosen for the market place, the theater, stadium, gymnasium, baths, and temples; and, in checker-board plan, the streets were laid out with attention to these sites. On three sides of the market were *stoae*, long colonnades, usually in two aisles with rooms behind and sometimes with two stories. Theaters and stadia were equipped with stone seats. The temples of the age, of which the most famous was the temple of Apollo at Didyma near Miletos, were large and elaborately decorated, the ornamental Corinthian capital being preferred to the older Doric and Ionic. Though still simple in style — an inner court surrounded by rooms in one or two stories — private houses were much more lavish and elegant than were the houses of the classical period. Walls were adorned with pictures in stucco or painted on the plaster, and the pavement of the court contained elaborate and beautiful mosaics.

Architecture and the other arts showed trends that have been described as "Orientalizing." In brief, there were tendencies toward monumentalism (huge buildings and statues), realism (dying, aged, or drunk subjects), and decorative art (flower designs, backgrounds, and ornamental borders). Only the gods continued to be portrayed idealistically.

Sculpture   Sculpture demonstrated a complete mastery of technique and of subjects. Lysippus (*ca.* 330 B.C.), favorite sculptor of Alexander, bridges the period between the great artists of the fourth and of the third centuries B.C. Greatly idealized portraits were carved of the leaders of the age and of the great men of the past, and idealized figures represented the cities. The Fortune of Antioch, for example, is a beautiful statue of "a gracious and charming woman with a pensive face, seated on her mountain with the river-god Orontes at her feet; she was fully draped and wore a turreted crown . . . and held a palm leaf in her hand."[1] A long line of unveiled Aphrodites of great beauty followed the famous Aphrodite of Cnidos. These were especially popular in the second century B.C. Statues of shepherdesses, fishermen, boxers and wrestlers, and children were also popular. The Rhodian school of sculptors sought for colossal effect; the famous Laocoön and the Farnese Bull belong to the period of the decadence of this school. The sculptors of Pergamum displayed marvelous technical skill, a thorough knowledge of anatomy, and an extraordinary ability in achieving realism in the famous statues of the Dying Gaul, and the Gaul and His Wife, remnants in copy of a great group made to glorify the first victory of Attalus I over the Gauls. Most beautiful of all the Hellenistic works of art were the glorious Aphrodite of Melos, the graceful Apollo Belvedere, and the noble Victory of Samothrace.[2] In the latter, Victory has just alighted on the galley's prow, bearing in her upraised right hand what is probably the victor's crown. The wind is sweeping through her draperies and as one looks up at her in the Louvre today she seems to be floating through space on outstretched wings.

Painting The painters of the Hellenistic age were masters in the handling of line and color, securing effect by means of realism and the expression of emotion. Where earlier painters had chiefly painted portraits, the Hellenistic artists gave their scenes backgrounds of natural scenery or of architecture. Scenes of daily life — sometimes brutal, often vulgar — and even pieces of still life were popular. The wealthy acquired collections of paintings and hired artists to decorate the walls of their houses with murals. Of all this art, however, only a few echoes have survived in mosaics and in the later frescoes of the Roman period.

Literature

The intellectual life of the Hellenistic period was noteworthy for the production of books and the formation of libraries. Since the production of papyrus, under the royal direction of the Ptolemies, was plentiful and slave copyists were numerous, books could be produced and sold at fairly low prices to a large reading public. Libraries were established not only in the great centers but in many of the smaller cities as well. The famous library at Alexandria is said to have amassed a total of seven hundred thousand rolls, and that at Pergamum, two hundred thousand. The great masters of the past were copied, read, and studied,

[1] William W. Tarn, *Hellenistic Civilization*. Third Revised Edition. New York: Meridian Books, 1961, p. 319.
[2] The date of the last is doubtful. Possibly it was erected by Antigonus Gonatas to celebrate his victory over Ptolemy II at Cos (*ca.* 258 B.C.). See p. 350.

and the output of the authors of the age itself was most varied and prolific. Drama, poetry, history, philology, science, mathematics, philosophy, and religion—in short, all branches of human knowledge and intellectual activity—were represented in the Hellenistic period.

Drama   The drama was never more universally popular. Every city apparently had its theater, and traveling groups of actors, the Dionysiac artists, went from place to place putting on favorite plays of the great dramatists. The texts that have survived are probably from these actors' collections. Tragedies were written during this period but, like those of the fourth century B.C., they were of such little consequence that they have completely disappeared. Comedy received a fresh impulse from the Athenian Menander (fl. 300 B.C.), fragments of whose plays have been recovered in the Egyptian papyri. In exquisite language, he composed comedies of manners, plays of society dealing with love intrigues, and dramas about exposed children who by chance become slaves in their own families, rescue their kindred from difficulties, and are at last recognized. These plays had great influence on the Romans, Plautus and Terence. In style and in content they are far different from the plays of Aristophanes. Sophisticated mimes and plays were produced, many of them indecent, dealing with incidents of daily life. Of these a little sketch written by Theocritus and dealing with the adventures of two women in Alexandria at the Feast of Adonis has survived.

Poetry   The poets were masters of all kinds of verse. The Alexandrians, Theocritus in particular, employed the older verse of Alcaeus and Sappho and experimented with a wide variety of exotic meters. Particularly popular was the miniature epic, sometimes called the epyllion, which dealt usually with some local myth. Apollonius of Rhodes composed a long, rather dry epic poem on the subject of the Argonauts. The astronomer Aratus of Soli employed epic verse to describe the stars in a poem that influenced Vergil's *Georgics.* These epyllia were written chiefly by scholars and did little more than display the erudition of their scholarly composers, who vied with one another in producing short, witty epigrams or in writing love poems or epitaphs for their friends or for men of the past.

The idylls, another form of expression in vogue at the time, were short but graceful pictures of life. Masters of these poetic forms were Callimachus of Cyrene and Theocritus of Syracuse, both of whom lived and wrote in Alexandria under Ptolemy II. The poems of Callimachus were excellent in form and wording but were lacking in heart and substance; Theocritus, on the other hand, loosed his very soul in a series of pastoral idylls portraying in verse the fishermen, shepherds, and lovelorn girls of his native Sicily. His poems have furnished inspiration and served as models for many later-day poets.

Prose Prose flourished under the dual impulse of rhetoric and science. Books of history and geography, travel accounts and memoirs, pamphlets, letters and stories, philosophic and scientific treatises made their appearance, some appealing to the learned, others to the lay public. The writer of Ecclesiastes, who lived during this period, fittingly remarks, "Of the making of many books there is no end, and much learning is a weariness to the flesh." In most of these works rhetoric dominated. The manner in which a fact was stated was more important than the fact itself, and contact with reality was frequently sacrificed to literary style. However, books that were strictly scientific tended to be difficult, dry, and almost unreadable. It is nevertheless a great tragedy that almost all of these many productions have been destroyed by the vicissitudes of time.

History The most important branch of prose was history. Many of Alexander's followers, notably Ptolemy, wrote memoirs or histories of their own period. Writers produced literary histories covering the period of the conquests and the struggles that followed, or dealing with particular phases thereof. Scientific historians presented careful studies of their own states, such as the *Atthis* of the Athenian Philochorus. Some scholars, after collecting and studying inscriptions, wrote on the antiquities of the cities.

The greatest names in scientific history are Timaeus of Tauromenium (died 264 B.C.) who wrote, after careful study, a monumental history of the western Greeks; Hieronymus of Cardia, assistant of the first three Antigonids (p. 348), who covered the period of the Alexandrian wars; and Polybius of Megalopolis (*ca.* 198–117 B.C.), who recorded the history of Rome and of the Greek leagues during the period of the Punic Wars and the Roman conquest of the East. Such fragments as we have of the first two we owe to Diodorus the Sicilian, who drew chapters from them for his historical library.

Of the forty books of Polybius, only the first five and fragments of others have survived. His philosophy of history is set forth not only by the character of his writing, but by his digressions when he turns aside to criticize previous historians for their shortcomings and to expound his own views. He agrees with Thucydides that history is a useful subject written for the instruction of future generals and statesmen. However, his concept of the universality of history gives his work a broader base than is inherent in the Thucydidean devotion to a period. Though in his earlier pages he alludes to "chance" as a dominant force, his ideas of causation grew to such an extent that not only did he come to realize the importance of geographic and climatic elements, the significance of men and of institutions, but also to declare that nothing happens without a natural cause. He distinguishes, too, between motive, cause, and occasion. He was most specific in his statements of the obligations of the historian, the first object of whose search must be the truth, for "if you take truth from history, what is left is but an idle tale." To arrive at the truth, he said, the first requisite is a careful study and criticism of all sources; the second is knowledge based on travel and on the scrutiny of the sites of the events described; and the third is that practical experience of politics and warfare which alone makes possible the understanding and explanation of history. Polybius himself had been active in the affairs of the Achaean League until captivity in Rome interested him in the history of Rome and inspired him to commence his great work. He criticized his predecessor Timaeus as a bookworm historian, "When history is written by the book-learned, without technical knowledge, and without clearness of detail, the work loses all its value. For if you take from history its element of practical instruction, what is left of it has nothing to attract and nothing to teach."[3]

Polybius' style is dry, matter-of-fact, and uninteresting, and his composition lacks the artistry of Herodotus and Thucydides. Yet the greatness of his subject, his concept of history, and his devotion to his work place him in the front rank of historians of all times.

Science

Hellenistic thinkers made extraordinary advances in philology (a science they created), in botany, biology, and medicine, in geography, astronomy, and mathematics. Their work, studied and expanded by scholars during the Roman imperial period, became the basis of knowledge during the Middle Ages.

Alexandria was the center of scientific achievement. In 294 B.C. Ptolemy I founded the museum as a home for scholars who were subsidized by the government. "Fatted fowls in a coop," an envious rival called them. In this city the great librarians established the canons of literary criticism; they collected and arranged the epic poems and started the never-ending discussion of the Homeric problem; they issued texts with critical commentaries of the great masters; they studied grammar, style, and word usage—they founded, in short, the science of philology.

Natural Science   Beside the philologists stood a great group of natural scientists, not all of whom were Alexandrians. Biologists continued the work of Aristotle. In Athens Theophrastus (*ca.* 320 B.C.) studied botany, and Ptolemy Philadelphus built in Alexandria a great zoological garden filled with little-known animals among which was a polar bear. Physicians contributed to the knowledge of drugs. Heroph-

---

[3] Polybius, *History*, 12. 25. 7. Trans. by Evelyn S. Shuckburgh. London: Macmillan & Co., Ltd., 1889.

ilus of Chalcedon (fl. 300 B.C.) learned that the arteries carry blood, not air, on impulse from the heart; he learned the significance of the pulse in disease and discovered the nervous system. He performed major operations, practiced dissection, and is said to have practiced vivisection on criminals furnished him by Ptolemy I for the purpose. Other physicians made advances in treatment and without the use of drugs cured many by dieting, massage, exercise, and baths. Popular medicine was still dominated, however, by magical cures effected in the temples of the gods.

Geography Alexander's march had rekindled the interest in geography which Hecataeus and Herodotus had started. Nearchus, admiral under Alexander, (fl. 325 B.C.) wrote a treatise on his voyage from India to Babylon. Subsequently many exciting tales and descriptions of India were brought back from the court of Chandragupta by Megasthenes (fl. 290 B.C.). Another contemporary of Alexander, Pythias of Marseilles, sailing north along the coast of Europe to Britain and Jutland, learned there of the existence of the Arctic Ocean. The greatest of the geographers was Eratosthenes of Cyrene (275–200 B.C.), who lived and worked in Alexandria. He was a man of amazing versatility in every branch of knowledge, but his geographic studies were astounding. He drew a map of the known world in which he utilized parallels of latitude and longitude. Deciding that the earth was round, he measured the noontime shadows at Alexandria and Syene and then computed its circumference at 252,000 stades, probably 24,662 miles (the true measure is 24,857)—a remarkable achievement.

Astronomy The astronomers based their work on the discoveries of the long line of Babylonian, Egyptian, and Greek scientists who preceded them. Aristarchus of Samos (*ca.* 310–230 B.C.) learned from earlier scholars that the earth turned on its axis, and declared that the sun was some three hundred times larger than the earth. From these facts he evolved the heliocentric theory of the solar system many centuries before Copernicus. Unfortunately, his contention that the earth and the planets moved in circles did not accord with known facts, and his theory was rejected. Hipparchus of Nicaea (fl. 140 B.C.) offered in its place a complicated series of cycles and epicycles to explain the motion of the heavenly bodies. Learning much from the Babylonians, he explained, if he did not discover, the precession of the equinoxes, calculated the length of the year, and made a catalogue of the stars. His erudition made it possible for him to correct errors in the latitude and longitude of Eratosthenes' map.

Last in the succession of geographers and astronomers before the Roman Empire was Poseidonius of Rhodes (135–51 B.C.). This famous scientist journeyed to Gades to study the tides, attributing their cause to the wind but their variations to the phases of the moon. He calcu-

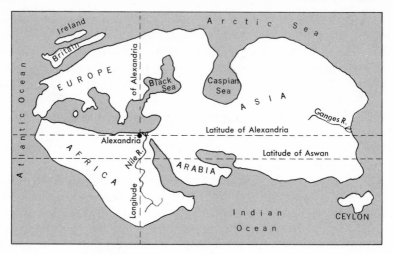

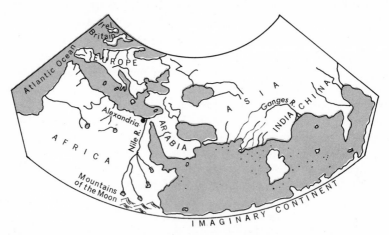

Work of the Alexandrian Geographers. *Upper:* The World According to Eratosthenes, 250 B.C. *Lower:* The World According to Claudius Ptolemy, A.D. 100.

lated the size and distance of the sun and the circumference of the earth. Furthermore, he argued that a man sailing west could reach India. On this statement Columbus later based his hopes of a western voyage to India.

Mathematics and Physics   Mathematics kept pace with and made possible many of these studies. Euclid (fl. 300 B.C.) collected geometric theorems and prepared the textbook of geometry which was used down to the twentieth century and which is the cornerstone of all modern handbooks of geometry. Apollonius of Perge (*ca.* 250 B.C.) wrote a book on conic sections and began the study of trigonometry which Hipparchus further developed.

In mathematics and mechanics Archimedes (*ca.* 287–212 B.C.) towers over all the Greeks. He advanced the study of geometry, calculated the value of π, and began the study of calculus. On his tombstone was engraved the figure of a sphere within a cylinder. His law of floating bodies, based on his discovery of specific gravity and still known as Archimedes' principle, he is said to have discovered by noticing the water he displaced in his bath and to have jumped out and run home naked, shouting "Eureka" ("I have found it"). He invented the double pulley and the water screw, both of which are still in use. He understood the principle of the lever. "Give me where to stand," he declared, "and I will move the earth." He held a Roman force at bay with grapnels and, tradition says, with burning glasses. By the irony of fate, he died at the hands of a Roman soldier.

After his death some progress was made in hydraulics; and clocks, mills, and organs worked by water were invented. One scholar produced a catapult operated by compressed air, and Hero of Alexandria (fl. 100 B.C.) discovered the expansive power of steam.

That these scientific achievements were not put to actual use was due to two circumstances. In the first place, they were made by men who regarded themselves as philosophers and who thought it beneath them to apply their discoveries practically. (Even the inventions of Archimedes were partly incidental to his theoretical studies.) In the second place, labor was so cheap and so plentiful that machinery was unnecessary, unprofitable, and undesirable. In the period of the Roman Empire an inventor presented to Vespasian a road-making machine. The emperor thanked and rewarded him but put the machine aside with the remark, "What would I do with my poor people?"

Philosophy

It was to the problems of these poor people and their betters in a complex world that philosophers and religious teachers, following in the train of Socrates, addressed themselves. Men were but little individuals in an overwhelming cosmos, composed of great kingdoms, huge cities, and decadent communities. When a bad harvest or a cornered market in Egypt might ruin a good man in Greece, the well-being of an individual was no longer dependent upon his own labors but upon the will of a mighty king or upon a capricious providence. The old moral sanctions of the family and the state had been destroyed by the collapse of the state and by the migration of many families. Men everywhere, rich and poor alike, felt the helplessness of the individual. On all sides men were asking the question: "What must I do to be saved?" To this problem philosophy and religion endeavored to give an answer.

The Philosophic Schools Under such conditions philosophy became ethics with enough cosmology to explain or justify the ethical position. On one thing all philosophers were in agreement: the aim of living is the good life, which may be termed happiness or virtue. On the definition of these terms, however, and on the method of attaining the good life there was much disagreement. Out of the attempts to solve this problem arose many new schools of philosophy, while the old schools declined. Aristotle's Lyceum, for example, survived its founder by but a brief period, while the Academy of Plato devoted itself to dialectic and became barren as method asserted its authority over content. Among the new schools the Cyrenaics taught that happiness was sensual pleasure. They were the true founders of the dictum, "Today let us eat, drink, and be merry, for tomorrow we die." The Skeptics in Athens denied the possibility of knowledge and accomplished nothing beyond an attack on superstition; their most illustrious exponent was Carneades, who went to Rome. The three most important schools were the Epicurean, the Cynic, and the Stoic, and these dominated philosophic thought to the close of antiquity and beyond.

Epicureanism   Epicurus set up his school in Athens in 306 B.C. To him the world was a soulless mechanism. Atoms flying through space swerve and meet to create life; they fly apart to cause death. Men share this common fate with all of nature. Since men have always believed in gods, then gods may well be, but they live apart in perfect happiness, and have nothing to do with men. Consequently all human hopes and fears, all prayers, charms, and magic arts are but idle fancy. Man, once convinced of this and thus freed from the weight of superstition, may raise his head from the earth and see it and himself for what they are, simply mechanisms. The chief end of life is indeed happiness. But, Epicurus taught, happiness is not sensual pleasure. On the contrary, it is negative: the avoidance of pain, an escape into a gentle, quiet world of the intellect, typified by the garden in which Epicurus taught and which gave its name, the Garden, to the school. Epicurus' teaching appealed, and has appealed since, to the few of strong intellect. But it furnished no salvation for the masses.

Cynicism   The Cynics ministered to the masses. Antisthenes, pupil of Socrates, founded in Athens in the Cynosarges gymnasium the school of which Diogenes, whose name has become a legend, was the most famous exponent. The Cynics taught that the end of life is virtue; virtue is knowledge; and knowledge concerns oneself alone. All the conventions of society, all the ties of state and family are as nothing to the free individual. The cares and worries about friends, fortunes, reputation, and even daily living must be laid aside. Whatever is, is right; therefore take what comes. When Alexander the Great offered a boon to Diogenes' at the Isthmian games, the philosopher simply asked the king to step to one side because Alexander's shadow blocked him from the warm sunlight. Until late in Roman imperial times, the Cynics traveled, usually in pairs, carrying a message of endurance to the poor and simple. Their disregard of the amenities of life offended the rich and the intellectual, few of whom became Cynics.

Stoicism The Stoics, taking possession of the best elements in Cynicism, developed a vigorous and popular system of philosophy. Zeno, a Phoenician from Cyprus, began to teach the Stoic philosophy in the Painted Porch in Athens in 302 B.C. His followers, Cleanthes, Chrysippus, and Panaetius of Rhodes, clarified and systematized his teaching. Stoic philosophy received from its founder a religious tinge and a missionary fervor. The world of inert matter, it taught, is animated by a divine fire that is God; all living and moving things partake there-fore of the divine. God has established for the world, according to his divine and perfect wisdom, a perfect universal law. Virtue and therefore happiness depend upon obedience to that law. But the flesh is material and blunts the vision. Life, as a result, becomes a struggle to overcome the flesh, an upward climb toward virtue by means of knowledge. The truly wise man, said the Stoics, will know the law and be sincerely happy. To him affairs of the body and the problems of daily life will be of no importance when compared with matters of the mind and soul. He will understand that whatever comes must be endured as a part of the divine plan, and he will know that the inner man which is the mind can only be injured by itself. But the Stoic went further than that. Since all men partake of the same divine element, he argued, it follows that all men are brothers, and all are parts of one divine and universal state. Each man has, therefore, his obligations to his fellow men, his duties to this ideal fatherland. Like an actor, he is given a part to play on the stage which is the earth, and whatever part it is, he must play it like a man. When it comes his turn to leave the stage, he must go willingly and cheerfully. The Stoic insistence on individual moral growth and on the performance of duties in the world make it a practical, livable philosophy of never-ending value. It was a noble creed, but its appeal was essentially intellectual: the Stoic was but trying to save himself by the powers of his own reason. It was only natural therefore that the great mass of the people should turn from Stoicism and its rival schools to religion, where they might find salvation by faith in gods and by the performance of ancient rituals.

Religion

The New Gods The old gods of Greece were divinities of the city-state. Philosophy and criticism weakened their position, and their mythology nearly destroyed them, but their real failure was due to the collapse of the city-state on which they depended. The individual in a great world needed a more personal religion than they could offer him. Some men cast religion aside, sought no gods but gold and silver, and worshiped material success. Others worshiped *Tyche*, Fortune, Lady

Luck, and sought to win her favors with charms and amulets or to learn her will by attending oracles, practicing divination, or reading the stars. While the power of the old oracles of Dodona and Delphi was declining, new oracles were springing up on every hand. Charlatans peddled amulets and books of magic charms and secret names. Astrology came from Babylon to fasten itself on the Western mind with a grip that has not yet been entirely broken.

The worship of the god-king provided a center of devotion and a hope of economic salvation. At the same time there came into the Greek world a flood of Oriental divinities whose appeal and promise of help was more personal and satisfying than that of the old gods of Greece. Greeks going east readily identified the divinities of the lands to which they came with those of Olympus and worshiped them, but the Orientals settling in the Aegean brought their gods with them. While the Orientals rejected the Greek divinities, the Greeks, in their search for religious satisfaction, accepted what the Orient might teach. In every Greek community there appeared many little religious associations in which, as in the modern fraternal order, men found under the protection of a friendly deity brotherhood and dignity in a bewildering and humbling world. Such an association was the Jewish synagogue. The part the Jews played in the Hellenistic world, however, will be considered later (p. 518f).

Mystery Religions   The so-called mystery religions had the most universal appeal of all. These, basing their dogma and ritual on ancient myth, by their initiatory rites awakened in their converts a sense of sin and of purification; they established an insistent order of elaborate ceremonials and a code of ethics; and they promised to the faithful the rewards of a glorious immortality. While Demeter continued to be worshiped at Eleusis, Dionysus ranged the earth with renewed vigor. The dramatic festivals were in his honor, and his artists were everywhere in demand. Moreover, the Orphist Neo-Pythagoreans had dramatized the legend of his earthly life, death, and resurrection, and furnished to his worshipers the magic words by which they might escape the ever-turning and recurring wheel of life and enter into the Elysian Fields of eternity. In Egypt, Ptolemy I created a god, Serapis, out of a combination of Osiris, Apis, and elements of Zeus and Dionysus, associated him with Isis and Anubis, and set him up as the god of the Greeks in Egypt. He was a god of healing, a kindly god who protected his followers and led them to the fields of Yaru.

The Mother Goddess   Among the throng of goddesses, the most beloved were the mother goddesses. In Anatolia men and women prostrated themselves before Cybele, or Ma, and her divine son, Attis, and men mutilated themselves in her orgiastic rites. The worship of Cyprian Aphrodite inspired Theocritus' lovely ode on the mythical death of Adonis. But loveliest, greatest, and most widely worshiped of the goddesses was Isis. Faithful wife and mother herself, she presided over marriage and childbirth, and to the weary and worn she extended a mother's arms. Human beings found in her the culmination of all their desires. "I am all that is, all that has been, and all that shall be," she said in her ritual. Rome, too, was destined to fall under the spell she cast over the Mediterranean world.

Conclusion Independent Greek history draws to an end with the close of the Hellenistic age and the Roman conquest of the East. The Greeks of the classical period had achieved greatness in their city-states and had taught the world the lessons of democratic government and of the nobility and power of man both as a citizen and an individual. Though the later period saw the city-states decline, and though many fell under the sway of god-kings, the leagues proved the advantages of federalism, and men rose above local feelings of city and of race to concepts of cosmopolitanism and the unifying force of a world culture. The standard forms and principles of art, architecture, and literature were developed and lifted to extraordinary heights. Philosophic studies resulted in great products of human thought, in the advancement of science, and in the study of ethics. Continuing failure to solve the problems of unity and at the same time to preserve the civic and religious institutions that were the mainspring of culture was perhaps the chief contributing force to the downfall of the Greek city-states. Yet the story of Hellenic culture does not end with the Hellenistic age. There were Greek architects, artists, scientists, and men of letters of great ability under the Roman Empire. Greek influence on the development of the Christian Church was strong, and a genuine revival of Hellenism took place in the Byzantine period. Mingling with the currents of civilization in the Western world from the time of the Romans to the modern age, the Hellenic stream is still a potent element in our culture today.

18 · The Rise of Rome

WHILE THE GREEKS IN THE AEGEAN, IN SOUTHERN
Italy, and in Sicily were attaining the heights of classical
culture, a community on the banks of the Tiber in Italy
was developing in the fire of tribal warfare and internecine strife those institutions and traits of character that were to make
it the conqueror and lawgiver of the Mediterranean world and the
civilizer of Western Europe. Within the space of five centuries Rome
was to rise from insignificance to such power that it became and remained for centuries the center of civilization.

SOURCES

Literary Sources The sources for the history of Rome are similar
in character to those for the history of the Greeks. For the period of
growth we are dependent upon the Roman Livy, and upon such Greeks
as Polybius, Diodorus the Sicilian, Dionysius of Halicarnassus, Plutarch,
and Dio Cassius. Other books that dealt with Roman antiquity, such as
those of Cato, Varro, and Verrius Flaccus, survive only in fragments.
For the late republic, the historical works of Sallust and Caesar, the
orations, letters, and essays of Cicero, and other literature help to fill
in the details. The *Deeds of Augustus*, the works of Tacitus, Suetonius,
the later *Historia Augusta*, and Ammianus Marcellinus provide the history
of Rome under the empire, a history illuminated by the essays, letters,
plays, and poems of the writers of the great ages of Latin literature.
Commentaries on the law, now known chiefly from the Digest of Justinian's Code (p. 584), along with references scattered throughout the writing of other Romans, provide information about Rome's most enduring
contribution to the world.

Archaeology Archaeology contributes substantial information.
There are remains, though few, from the early period—the cemetery,
remains of early villages on the edge of the Forum and on the Palatine

374

Hill, and the Black Stone in the Forum, fragments of walls erected during the republic, foundations of temples and houses. Elsewhere in Italy, especially in the Etruscan area, the finds are so numerous that museums can hardly contain the materials. Revolutionary methods have made it possible, too, to explore tombs and buried chambers without excavation. Cameras are inserted and pictures taken of the contents. If worth it, the chamber may be excavated. Aerial photography has also provided a vast amount of new knowledge about the location of prehistoric and historic sites. For the later ages the remains of temples, arenas, theaters, arches, houses, statues, mosaics, and pottery are found in great abundance, not only in Rome and Italy but throughout the empire. The Italian government continues to uncover the ruins of the imperial city and to push forward the excavations at Pompeii, Herculaneum, Ostia, and many other Italian cities. For this later period the great quantities of Roman coins also supply much information.

Inscriptions Inscriptions, however, are the chief aid to the Roman historian. Scant for the early republican period, they gradually increase in number and in value until under the empire they bring knowledge of events, organizations, and social and religious activities from every corner of the Roman world. For the Etruscan and Roman, as for the Hellenistic period, the papyri of Egypt give information about the administration and life of Italy and of the Roman Empire.

GEOGRAPHY

The Mountains Just as Egypt, Babylon, and Greece were influenced by their respective environments, so Rome shows the effect of the geography of Italy. The long, narrow, boot-shaped Italian peninsula lies northwest to southeast, with the Alps on the north, and Sicily at the toe. Its dominant feature is the range of the Apennines, which rises to the northwest behind Genoa, curves in crescent shape the length of Italy, and terminates in the mountains of Sicily. Along its western slope were many volcanoes. Those that lay to the north were active until about 1200 B.C., but since that time they have become extinct. To the south, Vesuvius, Aetna, and Stromboli still maintain their fires. As a result, while the basic rocks of the mountains are granite, limestone, and sandstone, on the western side there is a deposit of volcanic rocks.

The Plains The mountains divide Italy into four parts. To the north is the broad fertile valley of the Po, protected against the cold winds of Germany by the Alpine mass. Because of racial differences and geographic obstacles this area was not considered a part of Italy by the Romans of the republic. Instead it was known as Cisalpine Gaul, from the Celts or Gauls who occupied it during the fifth century B.C. On the east the mountains reach their greatest height and approach so closely

Early Italy, ca. 400 B.C.

to the Adriatic that their slopes and sandy coasts are adapted only for the raising of cattle. Southern Italy and Sicily face the east. Their history was bound up from very early times with that of the Aegean and of the Greeks on the other side of the Ionian Sea. The coastal plain to the west of the Apennine curve is the heart of Italy. Here lie the most fertile lands, the richest and loveliest regions. The plain is cut by transverse hills into the three sections of Etruria, Latium, and Campania, watered by three fine rivers, the Arno, the Tiber, and the Volturnus, respectively.

Agriculture Italy was destined by nature to agriculture. In contrast with the many inlets that tempted the Greeks to the sea, in all of its two thousand miles of coast line there were but two real harbors in Italy, the Bay of Tarentum and the Bay of Naples. Raw materials for industry were localized: copper and iron in Tuscany and in the island of Elba, and some clay suitable for pottery in a few places. On the other hand, the mild and equable climate had a sufficiently wide range from north to south and from the sea level to mountain valley to favor the production of a variety of foodstuffs. The soil in the western plains, enriched by volcanic ash, was exceedingly fertile, particularly in Campania. The richness and the extent of the arable land in Italy were particularly noteworthy in contrast to the small plains and the poor soil of Greece.

The land made very definite demands on the farmer, however. Although the soil was rich, it was young and thin, easily eroded, and quickly exhausted. When the torrential waters of the spring rains were allowed to course over the fields, when the working of the land was neglected or the hills were bared of their trees, the farms were soon destroyed. The hillsides above Rome are covered with a network of ditches dug in early times to prevent erosion. Further, the river beds were not large enough to contain the full waters of the rainy season, and unless the water was controlled the lower lands were subject to floods. The basic volcanic rock was porous and absorbed great quantities of water which, as the land approached sea level, came out again to form great marshes, breeders of mosquitoes and sources of fever. Epidemics were a constant menace to the peoples living along the coastal plain.

Thus to secure the great rewards of the land, hard work was necessary. The Italian gods of agriculture were jealous gods, and the farmer's religious calendar was full of ceremonies designed to secure their favor. In fine, the lessons the Italians learned from their land were the need for discipline and the values of conservatism.

"Beyond the Alps lies Italy!" The sunny skies, the mild climate, the fertile soil of Italy have always attracted outsiders. Over the Alps, whose northern slopes are gradual and easy of ascent, across the narrow Adriatic and the sheltered Ionian seas, from Africa by way of Sicily and the calm shallow Tyrrhenian Sea, have come wave after wave of peoples, to remain in and to be absorbed by this pleasant land.

THE PEOPLES OF ITALY

Prehistoric Peoples

Early Inhabitants Throughout the long centuries from the first appearance of man in Europe down to the beginning of recorded times, Italy was inhabited. Flint tools of the lower Paleolithic Period have been found on the hills, but as yet few traces have appeared of the finer tools and art of the later Old Stone Age. Among them, however, are the cave paintings in Apulia and on the island of Levanzo. In the Neolithic Period men of Mediterranean stock entered the land, some from Africa by way of Sicily, where once there existed a land bridge. Other peoples came by way of Spain and Gaul, and from the Danube Valley. Still others crossed the Adriatic Sea. They lived in small round huts clustered in villages, farmed in crude fashion, tended their herds of cattle and sheep, worshiped the Earth Mother, and buried their dead in pit graves.

The Bronze Age brought fresh invasions into the south and the north. Into the south came men from across the Adriatic and Ionian seas. Ancient legends record Minoan contacts with southern Italy and Sicily; archaeological remains of pottery, implements, and beehive tombs indicate that this area had begun its long history of contact with the Aegean (p. 379). After the Minoans came the Greeks; hence the region came to be known as Magna Graecia (pp. 189, 322, 398).

Neolithic Culture   Among the earliest Neolithic peoples to enter Italy were farmers from the Danube Valley and the Swiss lake regions. They built villages in the marshy areas of the Po Valley which were protected by moats, and rowed daily to their nearby farms. However, this culture was localized and of no lasting significance. The central Po Valley was occupied by farmers who built round huts and whose culture spread over a wider area. The rest of Italy, by 1700 B.C., was settled by a people whose culture is called Apennine. They made fine pottery and small figurines that show Balkan influence, and they used very little copper or bronze. The oldest village sites at Rome were Apennine, and the language of this people is believed to have been an Indo-European dialect.

Bronze Age Culture   New settlers entered Italy about 1700 B.C. Among them were the people using fine bronze tools who have been called the Terremaricoli (people of Terremaricoli culture) because of the rich, black earth that covered their ancient village sites. Italian farmers of recent generations have found the *terre mare* (black earth) useful as fertilizer. Early archaeologists confused the Terremaricoli with the earlier lake and marsh dwellers, but extensive excavation has shown that the culture of the Terremaricoli was distinct, later in date, and quite superior. Their huts were made of post, wattle and daub, and they were breeders of cattle, pigs, and horses. They were also skilled workers in bronze. Their art and technology were similar to those of contemporary Hungary, so they probably entered Italy from that direction. The Terremaricoli were nearly overwhelmed by Indo-European expansion early in the first millennium B.C., and they ceased to play a large role in Italy's development.

Indo-Europeans entered Italy in several waves between 1700 and 1000 B.C. but it is not clear what routes they followed or exactly when they arrived. At the time for which written documents are first available, peoples of three major dialect groups were settled in the country. These Indo-European groups were: (1) Sicel and Latin; (2) Umbrian, Sabellic, and Oscan; and (3) Venetic, Picene, and Iapygian. The speakers of these various dialects were so arranged geographically that their boundaries resemble a giant wedge, thrust from east to west, with its point penetrating halfway through Sicily. On either side of the wedge, and beyond its tip in Sicily, the inhabitants continued to speak non-Indo-European tongues such as Ligurian and Sican.

Culturally, the Apennine folk advanced under the influence of trade and other contacts with the eastern Mediterranean. A bronze industry, whose techniques and styles were strongly influenced by Mycenaean models, grew up, and the villages in southern Italy and Sicily grew richer in material possessions. This "developed" Apennine culture is called Ausonian, and there were many local variants of it.

During the latter part of the Bronze Age the practice of burning the dead instead of burying them was widely adopted—by Apennines, Terremaricoli, and other peoples alike. The change cannot be assigned to any one culture, nor can the fashion be accounted for, unless it spread in connection with new religious ideas. A few conservative tribes rejected cremation and continued to use inhumation. Both practices were used in later Rome.

The Iron Age The technique of working iron came to Italy with fresh invaders about 1000 B.C. Two fresh tribes of Indo-Europeans, known respectively as the Villanovans and the Fossa People, with their superior iron weapons took lands from earlier settlers. Alternatively, both iron cultures could have evolved from the advanced Apennine. The evidence is by no means clear. Oddly enough, the earlier examples of the Villanovan and Fossa cultures have been found in western Italy from where they later spread north and east. It is possible that, like the Dorian Greeks, these invaders came by sea.

The Villanovan villages are characterized by the use of funeral urns shaped like double cones, or sometimes like huts; by iron swords, razors, and other tools; and by bronze helmets and ornamental brooches. Their designs and ornaments have Balkan affinities. The earliest Villanovan villages were scattered about Latium and Etruria, and one of them underlies Rome.

Side by side with the Villanovans in Etruria and Latium lived the Fossa People, so called because they buried their dead in trenches (*fossae*). The designs on their pottery and metal work show a multiplicity of influences: Balkan, Sicilian, Greek, and Italic. Perhaps they also were seafarers. The theory has been tentatively offered that the Villanovans are the ancestors of the historical Latins and the Fossa People of the Sabines. Both peoples were to form—along with a group of later invaders from Anatolia and the Aegean area—the historical people known as Etruscans.

The Italic Tribes   The first written records, from approximately the fifth century B.C., show that Italy was occupied at that time by a diversity of tribes produced by the various invasions and the consequent blending of stocks. In the mountains back of Genoa dwelt the Ligurians, descended from or related to the Neolithic peoples. The Po Valley was occupied by Celts, who had come over the mountains from southern Gaul. At the mouth of the Po dwelt an Illyrian tribe, the Veneti. The eastern coast of Italy was likewise occupied by Illyrians who had crossed the Adriatic. Sicily still contained Elymi, Sicans, and Sicels, the last named of Indo-European stock. The heart of the peninsula was in the possession of tribal groups descended from the Indo-Europeans but blended in varying degrees with the older peoples.

Lack of unity made these peoples easy prey for highly skilled invaders. Into the southern area came the Greeks; into the valley of the Arno, probably from Anatolia or the Aegean islands, the Tyrseni, who were to give that land the names it still bears, Etruria or Tuscany, from their Latin name, *Etruscus.*

The Etruscans

Origin   As early as the Augustan period there were questions about the origins of the people the Romans called Etruscans. Dionysius of Halicarnassus disputed the statement of Herodotus that they came from Lydia and insisted that they were indigenous to Italy. Archaeologists and linguists have found no final solution to the problem other than

Etruscan Chariot of Wood Covered with Bronze. The wheels have iron tires, ca. 550–540 B.C. From Monteleone. (The Metropolitan Museum of Art, Rogers Fund, 1903)

to point out that the Etruscans were obviously a mixture of peoples, some of whose antecedents derive from Villanovan, Fossa, and other Italic predecessors, some from the Aegean and Anatolia. The most likely reconstruction of the evolution of the historical Etruscans is this: During the tenth and ninth centuries B.C. bands of displaced people from the eastern Mediterranean, perhaps resembling the Philistines in the diversity of their origins (p. 146), made their way by sea to the west coast of Italy and secured footholds on the Etrurian coast. Their superior techniques and advanced culture made them acceptable, if not welcome, to Villanovan and Fossa neighbors, and they intermarried to a degree. Used to an urban existence, the newcomers established city-states with organized political institutions appropriate to them. They admitted the Italians to citizenship and were in turn accepted in Italic villages, which they helped to change into urban centers. They introduced ships of eastern type, new techniques in metallurgy, and art styles with middle eastern affinities. Their language came to dominate the older Indo-European dialects in Etruria.

Conquests By 700 B.C. the typical Etruscan culture, blended from eastern and Italic elements, was well developed, and the people who practiced this culture had combined their cities into a league of twelve city-states. In the years thereafter the Etruscans expanded south across Latium into Campania, where Capua and Pompeii were among their settlements, but further movement in that direction was checked by the Greeks (p. 189). In the sixth century B.C. they moved north into the Po Valley and settled such towns as Bologna, Parma, Verona, Placentia, and Cremona. In both Campania and the Po Valley this expansion, though it was not organized conquest, resulted in the formation of loose leagues, or confederations. Apparently Etruscan families with their retainers struck out in search of new lands, and with superior knowledge and better weapons they were able to conquer, control, and organize native communities. But they never attained a strong, federal union of states with a centralized government.

Cities The Etruscans followed a careful ritual in the founding of their cities. A furrow was dug by a plow drawn by a cow and heifer, creating a sacred moat and wall around the city. The plow was carefully carried over the places where the gateways were to be placed. Walls with arched gateways were raised within the sacred boundary and constructed with polygonal or rectangular stones carefully fitted together. Within, an area was set apart for the gods; streets were carefully laid out; drains were dug; and houses were constructed. The houses belonged to what is called the atrium style, the feature of which was a large room whose ceiling sloped inward with an opening in the center to draw the rain into a cistern that lay below in the room. Around this room were arranged smaller rooms, sometimes with a second story above them.

An Etruscan Tomb at Cerveteri. (Italian Government Travel Office)

Life Etruscan civilization rested upon sound economic foundations in agriculture, industry, and commerce. The iron mines of Elba and the copper and tin deposits of Etruria were exploited, and a profitable metal industry was developed. Etruscan bronze and iron wares were sold in Spain and Gaul and throughout the Mediterranean world. In exchange Etruscans received amber, tin, and other raw metals, and wines and oils from the Aegean. The workers in industry were supplied by abundant products from farms and forest. The arable land was improved and expanded by drainage systems, terracing, dams, and the reclamation of swamps. Vineyards and olive groves were planted along with grains, flax, and vegetables. Horses, cattle, and sheep were bred and pastured on the upper hill slopes. The surplus products found ready markets in Italy and abroad. Shipbuilding kept pace with the needs of trade. The virgin forests of hardwood and pine supplied the timbers and masts for a large cargo fleet.

Energetic economic activity brought luxury to the nobility and prosperity to a growing middle class. The thousands of Etruscan tombs

An Etruscan Necropolis (Cemetery) near Bologna. (Italian Government Travel Office)

testify that it was not alone an aristocracy that could afford comforts in both life and death. Scenes of daily life, as well as pictures of religious import, decorated the tomb walls, and these along with the objects buried with the dead provide a good view of Etruscan life. Men and women were social equals. Both sexes had fine clothes of linen and wool, beautiful jewelry, bronze mirrors, exquisite tools of metal, luxurious tableware, and many other beautiful objects. They enjoyed banquets and games.

In tombs of the early period, the subjects of the tomb paintings are usually joyous, but in the later period, coincident with Etruscan political and economic decline, they are gloomy and forbidding, filled with monsters and demons of the underworld.

Religion The Etruscans believed in many gods, each of whom controlled a part of the "sacred space" into which the cosmos was artificially divided. This sacred space could be laid out anywhere: in the sky, in the plan of a city, on the liver of an animal, or on a holy spot. The concept of it is expressed by the Latin *templum*. When laying it out, an Etruscan priest would visualize a circle halved by a line running north and south, called in Latin the *cardo*. An intersecting line running east and west, in Latin the *decumanus*, then quartered the circle. Each quarter was subdivided into smaller, equal portions, and each of these

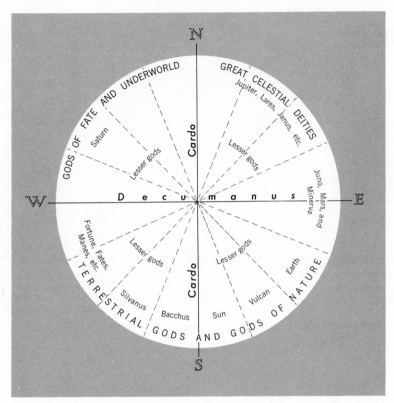

General Outline of the *Templum*, or Sacred Space, Used by the Etruscans and Romans. This chart, imposed by imagination on the sky, permitted the priest who was taking the omens to determine which god sent a given sign, and also helped him to determine its meaning. For example, an eagle appearing from the area governed by Jupiter was supposed to bear a message from that god — in this case the omen would be deemed favorable. A vulture from the section governed by the gods of the underworld would be deemed extremely unfavorable.

was assigned to a specific deity. Through this device the priest consulted the gods for omens. The great gods of the sky controlled the northeast and east, the gods of earth and nature ruled the south. If the *templum* was laid out in the sky, unusual phenomena or the flights of large birds would be watched. Any significant event appearing in Jupiter's (Tin's) sector was believed to be sent by that god, and the omen was probably good. If the *templum* was laid out on the liver of an animal, suspicious bumps, bulges, or indentations in a given sector had meaning. In general, good omens were expected from the northeast, east, and southeast; unfavorable signs came from the west, particularly the northwest, which was controlled by the inexorable gods of fate and the

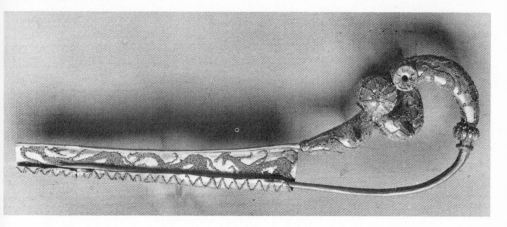

Etruscan Gold Fibula (Safety-pin) Showing Animals in Filigree. (The Metropolitan Museum of Art, purchased by subscription, 1896)

dread deities of the underworld. The idea of the *templum* and its use was transmitted to the Romans and affected their city plans, their religious beliefs, the organization of their priesthoods, and the very fate of the city of Rome itself.

Central to the Etruscan ritual were the great gods Jupiter (Tin), Juno (Uni), and Minerva (Menerva). The rites by which men must

An Etruscan Bowl of Bucchero Ware, Showing Lions in Relief, Seventh to Fifth Centuries B.C. (The Metropolitan Museum of Art, purchased by subscription, 1896)

worship them and the other gods were carefully worked out and set down for general use. This compilation, known to the Romans as the *disciplina* (discipline), contained rules for offering sacrifices, for propitiation, methods of invoking the gods, the means of divination, and the order of festivals. Writings devoted to religion formed a large branch of Etruscan literature, though only fragmentary bits have survived in tomb inscriptions, on a mummy wrapping found in Egypt, and in the works of later Roman writers.

Collapse of Power   When the Etruscans were at the height of their power, western and northern Italy lay at their feet. They combined with the Carthaginians to halt the Greek advance (p. 189), and they drove a colony of Phocaeans out of Corsica. They failed, however, to produce an organization stable enough to achieve unified action by their cities. Within many of the communities they were never more than a ruling class surrounded by retainers and supported by serfs. Defeats by Aristodemus of Cumae at Aricia in 525 B.C. and by Hiero I of Syracuse at Cumae in 474 B.C. cost them Campania. During the fifth century B.C. the Celts drove the Etruscans out of the Po Valley. Native reaction deprived them of many Latin communities. After the Romans had learned the basic lessons of civilization from the Etruscans, they expelled them from Rome and finally overwhelmed and conquered them. The Etruscans continued, however, as a wealthy, distinguished, and respected people, much sought after as soothsayers, until the days of the Caesars. Their place as the unifiers and civilizers of Italy was taken by Rome, the leader of the Latin peoples who lived just across the Tiber.

The Latins

The low hills and plains to the south of the Tiber were occupied by the Latins, a blend of Villanovan and Fossa peoples. The higher hills that surrounded Latium in the east and south were occupied by tribes called Aequians and Volscians. The tribes cannot be identified with certainty with the groups designated by archaeological names, but some scholars doubtfully identify Latins with southern Villanovans and Sabines with Fossa folk.

The Latins placed fortified towns (*oppida*) on the hilltops, and digging hillside drains to protect the soil, they settled down to farm the land intensively. They were united by the worship of Jupiter Latiaris and by a league centering in the temple of Diana of Aricia and commanded in time of war by a dictator. Many of their towns were seized by Etruscan nobles in the seventh and sixth centuries B.C. and so were brought into the current of Italian commercial life. Though their trade was in the hands of the Etruscans or Greeks, at about the end of the sixth century B.C. the Latins threw off the Etruscan yoke and began a more vigorous, independent development.

THE EARLY DAYS OF ROME

Sources   No other period of human history of equal importance is so lacking in contemporary or even in trustworthy sources as are the centuries from the founding of Rome to its rise to importance in Italy. The Romans did not become history conscious until they found it necessary to explain themselves to the Greeks. The first Roman annals were written by Romans in Greek about 200 B.C. after Rome had risen to supremacy in the western Mediterranean. Other annalists, who wrote in Latin, followed during the second century. Of all of these, however, only fragments have survived. The earliest consecutive books that have come down are those written in Latin by Livy and in Greek by Dionysius and Diodorus, all of whom lived in the last century B.C., but who depended for the most part on the works of the annalists. The problem that confronts the modern historian is therefore the nature and the authenticity of the sources these earlier writers used.

Sources of a public nature were available, such as local traditions and records of the kings, lists of magistrates, of triumphs, and of extraordinary events, kept by the priests throughout the history of the republic; documents such as laws and treaties which were recorded on lasting materials; and institutions and customs, political and religious, which survived into later times. Much of the written material was destroyed about 390 B.C., when Rome was burned by the Gauls. Archaeological evidence indicates, however, that a good deal survived the catastrophe and probably much was replaced from memory. Private family traditions of great deeds were preserved in the *laudationes funebres*, speeches delivered at family funeral ceremonies. By 200 B.C. Greek mythmakers had been at work drawing the Romans into the framework of the Heroic age. Poets, such as Ennius, and annalists also embellished their work by transferring to Rome stories from the Greek epic and even tales from Herodotus. Out of such material, these men created the history of Rome. Livy himself acknowledged the weakness of the sources on which he depended.

The Tradition   The tradition, given by Livy in detail, asserts that Aeneas, fleeing from Troy after it fell to the Greeks, found his way via North Africa to the west coast of Italy. He married the daughter of the king of Latium and had a son Iulus (later claimed to be an ancestor of Julius Caesar). After several generations twins called Romulus and Remus were born to a daughter of the family. Their father was supposed to be the god Mars. Their wicked uncle exposed the twins to die, but they were suckled by a wolf and rescued by a shepherd. On reaching manhood they rid Latium of the wicked uncle, then went away with a band of young men to found Rome. A quarrel brought about the death of Remus and made Romulus king of the new town, which bore his name. Livy continues by describing how the young men kidnaped wives from the neighboring Sabines and through the peaceful intervention of the women welcomed Sabines into Rome as citizens.

Romulus, according to tradition, did not die but ascended bodily to heaven and became the god Quirinus. There were six succeeding kings, and Livy ascribes specific developments, events, and the formation of Roman institutions to each. Servius Tullius, next to the last king, was believed to have established a reformed constitution and to have built a wall around the growing city.

Criticism of the Tradition The tradition concerning the early days of Rome contains some probable elements of truth, many possibilities, many myths, and many stories invented to explain later names and customs. The Aeneas story, a good example of Greek mythmaking, pleased the Romans because it brought them within the circle of Greek civilization. Romulus himself is clearly an eponymous creation, the very steps of which can be traced, and the stories of his reign are attempts to explain the origin of later institutions and customs.

The facts provided by archaeological investigation, while more prosaic than Livy's narrative, reveal a normal picture of a city growing within the Etruscan confederation. Of the seven kings listed by the Roman tradition, the last three were historical and were Etruscan. They were Tarquinius Priscus, Servius Tullius, and Tarquinius Superbus, all of whose names were Latinized.

Before the Etruscan conquest the hills of Rome were dotted with several small villages overlooking the winding Tiber, which at that point flowed around a large island. The presence of Tiber island made bridges across the river possible, and it has been established that such bridges were very ancient and served inland peoples going to and from the salt marshes at the Tiber's mouth. The crossing at Rome along the Old Salt Road (*Via Salaria*) was both safe and convenient. Aside from the salt merchants, the villagers had little contact with outsiders. They lived principally by herding sheep and cattle and by growing a few patches of spelt and beans. They did, however, form some sort of league or agreement by which they lived peacefully together in close proximity. The first four kings according to tradition — Romulus, Numa Pompilius, Tullius Hostilius, and Ancus Martius — may be semihistorical figures from the period of the league.

The Regal Period

Rome was conquered by the Etruscans about 575 B.C. and through their efforts was transformed into a city-state. They drained the marsh between the Palatine and Capitoline hills and made a *forum* (market place and civic center) for the new city. The Capitoline, which had never been inhabited, was fortified and turned into the principal reli-

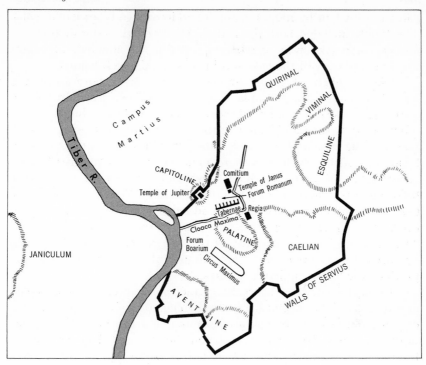

Early Rome, ca. 350 B.C.

gious area by the construction of a temple to Jupiter. The city was laid out in four quarters (*Roma Quadrata*), following the general plan of the *templum*, and many public buildings were erected.

The total area of the state was greatly increased, and the economy of its citizen body prospered because of Rome's membership in the Etruscan confederation. Better tools, better methods of agriculture, and new industries were introduced, and the surpluses produced could be readily sold in the expanded markets available. Rome's population is believed to have grown to about one hundred thousand during the reign of its last king.

Social Organization   Roman social organization was affected by Etruscan domination. The inhabitants of the city-state were arranged at first in three tribes, called the Ramnes, Tities, and Luceres. As industrial and commercial developments brought changes, tribes and clans disintegrated and the family (*familia*) became the basic social unit throughout the Etruscan-held regions. The Etrusco-Roman family retained many of the older clan characteristics. It was ruled by the *pater familias* (father), who controlled the family's common property and the actions of each of its members. Membership in the family could be gained by birth or by adoption, and it had its own gods (ancient totems). The family included both the living and the dead, and only the *pater familias* could take away membership once it was attained. The overweening authority of the *pater* was incorporated into Roman law.

The members of a big, undivided family (*gens*) bore a common name, the *nomen* (for example, Claudius or Julius). Individual males were given a personal name, *praenomen* (Appius or Gaius), but girls were often called by the family name in the feminine case (Claudia or Julia). Later, as big families broke apart, the elder branch was distinguished from the cadet branch by variant personal names (Appius Claudius versus Tiberius Claudius) or by a hereditary nickname, or *cognomen*, following the family name (Tiberius Claudius *Nero*, or Gaius Julius *Caesar*). Additional *cognomena* were added if a son was adopted, or if because of signal service the Senate granted one by honorary decree. The name of the emperor Augustus is an excellent example of both practices. By adoption he became Gaius Julius Caesar Octavianus — to which the Senate added Augustus.

In regal Rome only the wealthier and more powerful families could afford to fulfill the religious and social obligations of the *gens*, so gentile organization came to be characteristic of the aristocracy. The leaders of the *gentes* became very powerful men and were called *patres* (fathers). From among them, the king selected his senate. From the word *patres*, the nobility which had thus developed derived the name *patrician*. The rest of the people were called *plebs* or *plebeians*, which seems to mean the filling or the mass.

Clientage was associated with the *gens*. The clients (*clientes*) were dependents who may once have been vassals, serfs, emancipated slaves, or strangers who attached themselves to a *gens* in order to gain civic rights and residence in Rome. The *pater familias* automatically became the patron (*patronus*) of the clients as the family system developed, and the relationship remained hereditary. The patron looked after the legal interests of the client and secured him means of support. The client, in turn, voted for, attended, and served his patron. The relationship also had religious significance. The great families owed much of their power to large numbers of such retainers. There were few slaves.

The plebians formed the growing middle class of regal Rome. They were property owners, possessing either small farms within the borders of the state or businesses in Rome itself. They were craftsmen and traders. Many of them came to regal Rome from other parts of Italy to seek economic advantage. Their occupations were as varied as the business of the city, but they shared a common condition. They were not bound to the gentile system, and they were favorable to the Etruscan monarchy and to the Etruscan confederation.

Government   Governmental organization comprised king, senate, and assembly. The king had two fundamental powers: *imperium*, the right of issuing commands which had to be obeyed under penalty of death; and *auspicium*, the right of consulting the gods to learn their will. Rome's location at the crossing of the Tiber was vulnerable from a military standpoint. In case of sudden menace, therefore, Rome needed the strength of leadership which the military character of the imperium afforded. Too, by virtue of the imperium, law and justice were in the king's hands. It is significant that for military reasons also the king and not a priest had the second power, auspicium. The king might and did use priestly officials called *augurs* to interpret the signs, but he alone might see them. No priest could hamper the free action of the government. Because Rome needed strong leaders at all times, the kingship was elective rather than hereditary, and a definite machinery was established for the election. It was said that when the king died, the imperium returned to the people, the auspicium to the senate. The senate elected an *interrex* who "took the auspices" and served for five days. During that period he nominated, with the approval of the senate, a king on whom the people voted. If the vote was negative, that man served as interrex, and the process was continued until a king was elected and the assembly conferred the right of command upon him by the *lex curiata de imperio*.

The senate was composed of the *patres* of the great *gentes*, traditionally one hundred in number. Its primary function was to advise the king by a *senatus consultum*, "advice of the senate." It gave its consent to measures and nominations submitted to the people by the *patrum auctoritas*, "authority of the fathers."[1] It took the leading part, as we have seen, in the choice of a king. Patricians and plebeians alike took part in the assembly. The plebeians were represented by the assembly, which was organized by wards (*curiae*) of which there were thirty. Each man voted within his own ward group; the majority vote controlled, whereupon the ward vote was cast in the assembly as a unit. The chief function of the assembly was the election of the king; it dealt also with such family matters as wills and adoptions, and gave its consent to the declaration of war.

The Army The Romans remained divided into three tribes: the Ramnes, Tities, and Luceres, organizations of military rather than political character. The nobility served in the cavalry, two companies from each tribe, while commoners were marshaled by tribes and curiae. The widespread changes of the Etruscan period dictated a change in military organization and tactics. The Etruscans borrowed the heavy-armed infantry formation of the phalanx from their Greek enemies, and it was introduced to the Romans (most likely by the first Etruscan king, though tradition gives the credit to Servius Tullius).

---

[1] These were the powers of the senate during the early republic. To what extent they were exercised under the monarchy is a matter of question.

Instead of the thirty tribes of the tradition, however, there were probably twenty—four in the city and sixteen in the country. The five
classes ascribed to Servius seem to have been a later development. The
people were divided at this time into two military classes: the *classis*,
or "summoning," and the *infra classem*, or "below the summoning."
The members of the *classis*, which consisted of those able to buy arms,
were organized into centuries of sixty men within a total army of
thirty-six hundred. Their armor and weapons were like those of the
Greeks.

Economy As a member of the Etruscan Confederation, Rome
shared in its general prosperity. Romans traded articles of metal, clay,
leather, and wool in exchange for wheat, luxuries, and metal wares not
available locally. The text of a treaty negotiated at the end of the monarchy between Rome and Carthage (which is preserved by Polybius)
indicates the existence of some foreign trade, however negligible in quantity. Contacts with the Greeks of south Italy were frequent enough to
bring Greek ideas, artistic designs, and religious beliefs to the city.[2]

Religion Etruscan religious beliefs were mingled in Rome with
native Latin ideas and some Greek notions coming in with the trade.
The Latins believed originally that everything in nature had a "spirit,"
or "power," called a *numen*. The animistic Latin did not personify these
powers, but they were no less real to him for being invisible. He believed
that a *numen* had "will" and that it could be persuaded to act to his
advantage. He therefore sacrificed to it both to encourage it to be-
neficent action and to increase its power to carry out that action. The
Etruscan *disciplina* was superimposed upon this Latin belief, and the
major *numina* were identified with Etruscan gods. The methods of
sacrifice, ritual, festival, and divination were adopted and used with
rigid perfection by the Romans. When performing any rite in Rome,
the words and acts had to be perfect. A single mistake made it necessary
to stop instantly and repeat the entire procedure from the beginning.

The chief Greek influences on early Roman religion caused the
adoption of the god Apollo as a major deity and brought the Greek
Dionysus to Rome under the name Liber. He was accompanied by Demeter, as Ceres, and by Persephone as Libera. Also important was the
growing popularity of the Oracle at Cumae. Pronouncements by the
Sibyl of Cumae were collected to form the basis for the Sibylline Books,
consulted by Romans on the orders of the senate in times of grave
emergency or disaster.

Gods of the Family The Romans were not highly imaginative,
and their religion, though deeply spiritual, had none of the beauty and

[2]If archaeologists are correct in estimating the population of Rome at one hundred
thousand under Tarquin the Proud, economic life must have been healthy indeed.

color of Greek mythology. The Roman family gods remained *numina* who were not personified. The most important of the household gods was the *genius*, guardian spirit and reproductive power of the *pater familias*, head of the family. The *lar* took care of the farm, and the *Penates* were the spirits of the storeroom. *Janus* was the power resident in the door; and *Vesta*, in the fire. The dead lost personality and merged with the ancestors, whom the family worshiped as the *di manes*, divine shades of the underworld. During certain festivals of the year, these shades returned to earth to visit the living members of the family.

Gods of the State   In similar fashion a group of divinities protected the state. Of these the greatest was Jupiter, who gave it power and prosperity. Vesta protected the hearth-fire, as in the family, and was served by maidens. Mars guarded it with his martial power. The doorway of the state was represented by the shrine of Janus, of which the door stood open when the army was away at war. A number of powers looked after the crops and herds: Saturn was the spirit of sowing; Robigus kept away the mildew; Consus and Ops were deities of the harvest; Faunus and Pales guarded the sheep. The Roman calendar was full of simple festivals designed to win the favor of the powers. The priesthood did not form an organized hierarchy. Individual gods and special festivals had priests assigned to them; the most powerful religious officials of the Romans were the pontiffs, whose peculiar domain was care of the law.

Rome at the End of the Monarchy   The Etruscan rulers of Rome built a thriving city-state out of a cluster of small villages. The territory at the time of Tarquin the Proud included some three hundred and fifty square miles of arable and pasture land, and the well-built, well-guarded city had a large citizen body and a sturdy citizen army. The great sewer (*cloaca maxima*) drained the Forum, around which stood substantial public buildings. At the upper end, with the Capitoline looming above, stood the *rostrum* from which the king could address the assembly. Nearby was the meeting place of the senate. On the heights of the Capitoline was the magnificent temple of Jupiter with its long flight of steps, deep porch, and colonnades decorated with colorful terra cotta. Looking from it over the Forum to the right, the Roman could see handsome mansions climbing the steep Palatine at whose foot stood the royal palace, or *regia*.

The patrician revolution that drove out Tarquin did not and could not destroy the achievements of the Etruscan monarchy. Rome was a strong state with solid institutions, possessing a vital culture strongly held, and able to weather the storms that followed.

19 · The Early Roman Republic

THE REVOLUTION THAT ESTABLISHED THE ROMAN Republic caused confusion. Rome recovered, however, and within a little more than two centuries made itself the center of a confederation that controlled all Italy. Contemporary with the conquest, influencing it and affected by it in turn, went an internal class struggle and a constitutional development.

THE FOUNDATION OF THE REPUBLIC

Sources The validity of the sources for the early republic to the time of the Gallic catastrophe (p. 397) has, like that of the sources for the monarchy, been seriously questioned. The truth of many of the stories has been denied, and to others later dates have been assigned by scholars. Institutional history has been reconstructed from allusions by classical writers and from inferences derived from later practices. Answers to the questions of historicity depend in large measure on ascertaining how great was the destruction of records by the Gauls, which is itself a matter of controversy. Historians like Livy, Diodorus, and Dionysius made use of the *fasti*, or official annals, which were kept by the Roman magistrates and filed every year. Many of the originals were ill preserved by the second century B.C., but about 123 B.C. an attempt was made to collect and preserve them. Existing tablets were published in eighty books. This work was used by the historians and by the composer of the Capitoline *fasti*, which was incised on the Arch of Augustus. The inscription, while fragmentary, is invaluable to supplement the works of Roman historians. Neither the *fasti* nor the historians are particularly reliable for the early history of Rome, but their accuracy increases from the third century B.C. onward.

The Overthrow of the Monarchy The events of the revolution that overthrew the monarchy are known only through legend. The stories told by Livy about Lucretia, Brutus, and Horatius at the Bridge

Bronze Italic Cinerary Urn in the Form of a Hut, Late Eighth Century B.C. (The Metropolitan Museum of Art, Fletcher Fund, 1938)

must be considered literature rather than history. Still, the later hatred borne by Romans, particularly Romans of senatorial rank, for the title king (*rex*) bears witness to the fact that the struggle was painful and deeply disturbing to the state.

Everything about the traditional account is questioned, even the date. By tradition, the beginning of the crisis occurred in 510 or 509 B.C., and it has been suggested that it might be connected with the Etruscan defeat at the hands of the Greeks a few years earlier (p. 386). The date might equally well have been 474 B.C., but there is no proof available to resolve the problem. With reservations, therefore, it seems best to keep to the traditional account.

The overthrow of Tarquin was initiated by the patricians who, supported by their clients, suddenly expelled the king. It was not a social revolution and, though supported by some of the plebeians,[1] the object was obviously to enable the patricians to control the government themselves. Marcus Brutus, with a private army of eight hundred men, led the revolt.

Tarquin got help from Etruscan allies led by Lars Porsenna and from the Latins, and a prolonged struggle took place in which Rome was recaptured at least once by the Etruscans. But the state freed itself again, and a Roman victory at Lake Regillus in 493 B.C. put an end to

---

[1] Without some plebeian help—or at least neutrality—the revolution could hardly have succeeded.

the Etruscan danger. A peace treaty with the Latins followed, and they were thereafter allies of Rome. The treaty, a famous document that survived into historical times, was an offensive and defensive alliance between Rome and the Latin League, and it provided for alternation in command of the army, for rights of trade and of intermarriage, and for prompt settlement of suits of law. The principles it embodied formed the cornerstone of Rome's foreign policy for over two centuries.

Republican Organization   With peace came the establishment of a new government. Two generals of the army, called consuls ("consulters") and elected annually by the people from among the nobility, succeeded the king as magistrates. They possessed his imperium and auspicium, but their power was checked by the principle of collegiality, that is, the division of powers between two men and the right of one to veto the action of the other. To secure unity of command in times of crisis, the consuls, with the consent of the senate, nominated a dictator, who possessed absolute power for six months, the normal period of a campaign. Control over the law passed into the hands of the aristocratic pontiffs. The senate, increased to three hundred patricians named by the consuls, soon assumed a dominant position in the government. A new assembly, composed of wealthier citizens who had fought in the army, took over the function of electing the consuls and voting on measures submitted to it by the consuls, subject to approval by the senate. Whether it continued for a time the older curiate organization or assumed a new form based on the centuries of the army is not certain.

The First Conquests

Thus organized at home under an aristocratic rule, the Romans defended their own and the Latin lands. For a hundred years they were beset by a ring of enemies: the Volscians in the hills to the south, the Aequians and the Sabines to the west and north, and the Etruscan cities, particularly Veii, on the other side of the Tiber. During the first half of the fifth century B.C. Rome's enemies took advantage of internal disorders in the city to raid its territories for plunder. When the local troubles were temporarily settled, Rome gained the upper hand; the hill people were defeated, and colonies of Romans and Latins were placed in their territory to act as permanent garrisons. In 396 B.C. the famous dictator Camillus captured Veii, after which he confiscated and divided among the Romans a large area of Etruscan land. The celebrated story of Cincinnatus bears repeating here. In the crisis that arose when the Aequians had trapped a Roman consul and his army, Cincinnatus was named dictator. He received the message while he was plowing, left his plow, organized an army, defeated the enemy, celebrated a great triumph, resigned his post, and returned to his farm—all in sixteen days.

The Gauls The end of the first century of wars found Rome victorious over its neighboring enemies. Scarcely had this been achieved when a devastating blow was struck. In 390 or 387 B.C. a horde of Gauls, barbarian warriors who had invaded the Po Valley and expelled the Etruscans during the fifth century B.C., crossed the Apennines and besieged Etruscan Clusium. Angered by Roman intervention, they marched against Rome, defeated the Roman army in the battle of the Allia River, and took and sacked the city. The citadel alone held out against them.

There are many celebrated stories of this sack; the most famous follows. The Romans agreed to ransom the city for a thousand pounds of gold. When a dispute arose about the weights, Brennus, the Gallic leader, threw his sword on the scales, exclaiming, *"Vae victis"* ("Woe to the conquered"). According to Roman tradition, however, Camillus drove the Gauls out without paying the ransom. At all events, the barbarians retired to the Po Valley, where they remained a perpetual threat against the peace of Italy. The stories tell of later invasions which were repelled.

The Latins After the retreat of the Gauls, Rome appeared to be stricken. Its old enemies quickly tried to take advantage of the situation, but they soon learned that they had miscalculated, for Rome had lost little but prestige. The citizens promptly rebuilt their houses, and the army constructed a fine stone wall to enclose the city, making it one of the most strongly fortified cities in the West.[2] The annexation of the Etruscan territory had led to the formation of two new tribes and the addition of at least ten thousand men to the army. Order was quickly restored on the borders of Latium, but the Latins themselves had become disaffected. In 358 B.C. the old treaty between them and Rome was patched up and renewed. But when in 340 B.C. the Latins' demands for citizenship and seats in the Roman senate were refused, war broke out afresh. Rome's success was sure and swift. In 338 B.C. the Latin League was dissolved, and in its place Rome substituted treaties with each individual state.

The Samnites The conquest of the hill country to the south had brought Rome into contact with the fertile lands of Campania, and Capua was brought into alliance. From it grain was purchased in years of shortage, and the earliest Roman silver coins were struck in the Capuan mints. Such an expansion of Roman power seemed intolerable to the Samnites, a powerful mountain tribe that itself coveted the Campanian land. There are traditions of a treaty of alliance in 354 B.C. between Romans and Samnites and of a short war for the control of

---

[2] This wall was assigned by tradition to King Servius Tullius, and is still called the Servian Wall.

Capua (343–341 B.C.) in which the Romans were victorious. The great Samnite Wars (327–290 B.C.) were caused by Roman interference in Naples, which had a large Samnite element in its population. The Romans, although disgracefully defeated at the Caudine Pass in 321 B.C., eventually won. After a peace made in 304 B.C. had provided a breathing spell, a great alliance of Samnites, Umbrians, Etruscans, and Gauls attacked Rome in 300 B.C. The Roman general Decius Mus led his forces to a decisive victory at Sentinum in 295 B.C. By 293 B.C. Samnium was conquered and annexed, and Etruria was annexed in 283 B.C. After arresting a raid of Gauls called Boii at Lake Vadimon in 283 B.C., the Roman army crossed the Apennines and took possession of Picenum with the northern boundary at the Rubicon River. Apart from the expansion of Roman territory, the most important results of the war were the building of the Appian Way and the transformation of the Roman army from the phalanx to the manipular legion, a reform that will be described later (p. 408).

The Greeks   Only the southern end of Italy remained outside of Roman power. After the Samnite wars the cities of Magna Graecia had fallen on evil days. They had been materially weakened by the conquests of Dionysius (p. 321) and had suffered much from the raids of the Italic tribes in the interior, until only Tarentum retained any vestige of its former power. The Romans had made a treaty with this city in which they promised to send no ships into the Gulf of Tarentum. Nevertheless, when Thurii appealed to Rome for help against the Lucanians in 282 B.C., the Romans, in violation of the treaty, sent an army and some ships. Tarentum at once declared war, and called upon Pyrrhus, king of Epirus, (p. 357) for aid. This warrior, with a vision of a great western empire for himself, brought over an army trained to the Macedonian phalanx. He defeated the Romans at Heraclea and at Asculum, but lost so many men that a victory whose cost is too great has ever since been called a Pyrrhic victory. After unsuccessfully trying to make terms of peace, Pyrrhus attempted the conquest of Sicily in a war with the Carthaginians and failed again. He returned to Italy, was defeated in the battle of Beneventum in 275 B.C., and left for home. The Greek cities, surrendering in 272 B.C., were added to the Roman confederation, and Rome was master of all Italy south of the Po.

The Roman advance to power had been evolutionary rather than planned. In theory, at least, all of the wars had been defensive. The conquest of one territory established a new frontier, and this caused new difficulties and led to new conquests until the natural boundaries of Italy had been attained. Land hunger on the part of the Roman populace and the desire of the leaders for military glory lay in the background as effective causes for all the wars. It was but a short time before similar causes involved Rome in wars outside the peninsula.

The Organization of Italy

During the years of Rome's conquest of new lands the senate had developed a system of organization which appears in its completeness at the end of the Greek War. In many communities land was confiscated and given to land-hungry Romans until the number of tribes had been increased to thirty-five and Roman citizens had been scattered over all of Italy. All of the cities within annexed territories were drawn within the Roman state and organized. Certain seacoast towns, twenty-two in number, were garrisoned with three hundred Roman veterans and their families and were called Roman colonies. The veterans retained full rights as citizens of Rome. Other towns received charters from the senate and were known as *municipia*, municipalities. Of these some, *municipia optimo jure*, had full Roman rights: the people were Roman citizens, could vote and hold office in Rome, paid taxes, and served in the legions. Since they were subject to the Roman magistrates, their local organization was simple and provided merely for local needs. The greater number of municipalities were *municipia sine suffragio* — municipalities without vote. They had full local autonomy under a government prescribed by the senate and modeled on that of Rome. Their citizens paid taxes and served in the army, could trade and intermarry with Romans, but could not vote or hold office in Rome. In the Roman colonies, it should be noted, the original inhabitants occupied this position also. This type of organization, whereby citizens might carry the burdens but not enjoy the privileges of citizenship, had been instituted as a punishment for Gabii, an ally that had revolted, and it proved a most successful method for the Romanization and absorption of conquered peoples.

The allies were divided into two classes, Latin and Italian. Many of the old Latin cities had been annexed; others were allowed their freedom and given a privileged status of equal alliance with Rome, all of the rights of the *municipia sine suffragio* without the burden of taxation. The Latin colonies were of the same status as the Latin cities. In conquered territories the Romans settled garrisons of Roman and Latin veterans, giving them grants of land for their support. The Romans in such a community gave up their Roman citizenship, and all acquired Latin rights. The colonies were legally Latin allies.

The Italian communities were united to Rome each by a separate treaty. They paid no taxes, retained complete local autonomy, even to the right of issuing coins, worshiped their own gods, but gave all control over foreign affairs to Rome.

All the allies, both Latin and Italian, furnished the Roman army with contingents commanded by their own officers. The federation, with a population of about three million, could muster, after 272 B.C., a fighting force of about seven hundred and fifty thousand men. Italy under Roman control has been likened to a telephone exchange with Rome in charge at the switchboard.

INTERNAL CONFLICTS AND CONSTITUTIONAL DEVELOPMENTS

Causes of the Conflicts   The patrician aristocrats, having been the leaders of the revolution, garnered to themselves its fruits. The basis of their claim to power was their right to consult the gods through the auspicium. Since this was the necessary counterpart of the consular imperium, it followed that patricians alone could hold office, and establish, know, and apply law. It followed that patrician blood could not be contaminated by intermarriage with lower classes, lest the gods be angered. After the admission of the Sabine, Attius Clausus (Appius Claudius), who moved to Rome in 504 B.C. with a great throng of retainers, the patricians became a closed caste. They endeavored and eventually succeeded in making a rule forbidding intermarriage between the classes, which later was made law in the Twelve Tables.

The plebeians found themselves in a difficult position. The wealthier of them felt keenly the stigma of political and social inequality. They desired the share in government to which they felt their political and military abilities entitled them, and they resented the prohibition of intermarriage between the classes. The small farmers suffered from raids of the enemy as well as from the constant war tax and the annual military levy of men which took them away from their fields.

The collapse of industry and trade that followed in the train of the revolution wrought great hardships on the city population. The situation was aggravated by the fact that in years of scarcity the patrician leaders sold at famine prices grain that they had imported from Campania and Sicily. The severe law of debt was strictly applied by the patrician magistrate-judges, so many plebeians were sold into slavery for debt. The rigid requirements of procedure in Roman legal custom, control of the law by the aristocratic pontiffs, and the absence of written law made it exceedingly difficult for the commoners to secure justice in the courts.

Yet in the ensuing struggle for political and legal equality, success rested inevitably with the plebeians. They were needed for the army, and their economic well-being was essential to the welfare of the state. As soon as they had learned to act in unison and had acquired leaders, they were sure to win, though indeed the wealthier plebeians gathered the major fruits of the victory (p. 403). The striking character of the struggle is that plebeian success partook of the nature of a gradual evolution, of a series of timely surrenders and intelligent compromises on the part of the patricians. Though there were riots and secession, there were no bloody civil wars, tyrannies, or exiles, nor any of those wild excesses that mar the history of most of the Greek states. Roman sense of discipline and Roman obedience to tradition kept the ship of state on a fairly even keel.

Triumph of the Plebeians The story of the plebeian triumph is confused by contradictory sources, by historical problems arising from later traditions, and by knotty constitutional and legal problems. The first plebeian achievement was certainly that of organization. The natural rendezvous of the plebeians was the temple of Ceres, the Earth Mother, patron divinity of farmers. Under the presidency of the care-takers of the temple, the aediles, whom they elected, the plebeians met together on the basis of the old curiate assembly and formed them-selves into an unofficial assembly called the *concilium plebis tributum* (tribal council of the plebs). Tradition tells of a strike or secession, which supposedly took place in 493 B.C., when the plebeians withdrew in a body to the Sacred Mount to found a new city. The more likely date, however, is 471 B.C. They were brought back to Rome by the patricians' offer to allow them to elect protectors, called tribunes, who would have the right to veto any oppressive act of a magistrate. The tribunes were to be elected by the *concilium plebis*.

A few decades later the number of tribunes was established at ten, and was never changed thereafter. To be eligible for the office, one had to be of plebeian rank. The council of the plebs continued also to elect aediles to assist the tribunes. It is worthwhile to emphasize that the plebeians were middle-class citizens. Since only landholders were listed in the tribes, the landless clients of the patricians were excluded from the plebeian deliberations.

The plebeian assembly elected the tribunes and under their pres-idency passed measures called *plebiscita* ("decisions of the plebs"), which were binding on its members. The tribunes, in response to personal appeals, could stop any magistrate in his actions, and the sacred character which they claimed for themselves protected them from violence. At once they began agitation for the writing down of the laws, their method of procedure being to veto the annual levy. After several years of confusion and military disaster the patricians yielded. The result of this victory for the tribunes was the Twelve Tables of the Roman law, the great achievement of the board of ten men, decemvirs, which ruled Rome in 451–449 B.C. Difficulties with the second board of decemvirs led to a second plebeian secession and to the Valerio-Horatian laws. By these, the plebeian assembly probably became the *comitia tributa* ("tribal assembly"), and the sacred character of the tribunes was legally recognized. Citizens were given the right of appeal to the tribal assembly from a death sentence imposed by the consul within the city.

From that time forward plebeian advance was rapid, concessions being made by the patricians in all phases of the struggle. The social stigma, felt most keenly by the wealthier plebeians, was removed by the Canuleian Law of 445 B.C. which repealed the prohibition of marriage between the classes. Possibly to satisfy the demand of the plebeians for higher office and more certainly to meet the exigencies of wars, provision was made for the election in certain years of military tribunes with consular power to serve in the place of consuls; among these might be plebeians.

At the same time (443 B.C.) the power of the consuls was lessened and their duties were made less onerous by the establishment of the censorship, consisting of two *censors*, patricians, elected every five years and usually holding office for eighteen months. The censors took the census of the people, assigned each man to his tribe and class, and let and supervised public contracts. Later they acquired the right to draw up the list of senators, and to disenfranchise a citizen on moral grounds, which made them an important political factor in the state.

It was probably also at this time that those listed as *infra classem* in the earlier period were divided into four classes according to their wealth, making five classes in all, so that every man might be called upon to serve the state as his means allowed and might also have a share in the centuriate assembly.

During the following generation the debt problem was met by prohibiting slavery for debt, and on several occasions by lessening or remitting debts. The economic pressure on the poorer plebeians was eased by introducing pay for soldiers, possibly to prevent them from serving as mercenaries in the armies of the Sicilian cities, and by providing land for the landless in the conquered territories.

During the conquests considerable portions of enemy territories were confiscated and made public land. Some of this land was used for the establishment of colonies and some was divided into small farms and given to Roman citizens. This was the case after the conquest of Veii, for example, when four new tribes were created from the Veientine land. Tracts that were not allotted to small farmers were leased to wealthy landowners who in return for small rents were allowed to pasture their cattle and sheep on lands unfit for cultivation.

Agitation, arising annually when it was found that the senate regularly fought any proposal for the election of military tribunes and that the ruling class was still occupying the greater part of the public land, resulted in the Licinian-Sextian Laws of 367 B.C. These laws contained provisions that limited the amount of public land any one man might occupy and the number of cattle he might keep on the public pastures; they decreed that henceforth one consul should be a plebeian; but they also created a new patrician office, the praetorship.

The praetor had the right of military command, subject to the superior power of the consul, but his chief duty was to relieve the consul of all his judicial duties. By the praetorship the ruling class met the growing needs of government, weakened the consular office by further separation of its powers, and reserved for the patricians control over the law.

Nevertheless, the patrician cause was lost. In the years that followed one office after another was opened to the plebeians until in 300 B.C. the Ogulnian Law made them eligible for the priesthoods. Political and economic controversies arising chiefly from the condition of the debtor group led to a great plebeian secession in 287 B.C. and to the passing of the Hortensian Law. This measure settled the debt controversy and also gave the tribal assembly authority to pass laws binding on the entire population. The *comitia tributa* (tribal assembly) thus became an official organ of the state. Exactly how the debt problem was solved by this law is not known, but no more is heard of it for one hundred and fifty years.

Apparently the plebeians had won a complete victory. The burden of debt had been lifted from them; they had been assured a part in the public lands; their votes put men into office and into the senate; furthermore, the offices were now open to all men; and they had the right to pass laws under the presidency of their tribunes, whose power of intercession protected them in all their rights.

As a matter of actual practice, however, the facts were far different. Since no office carried any pay, only the well-to-do could afford an official career. Consequently, in place of the patrician aristocracy there developed an officeholding nobility (men who were "known") composed of about one hundred wealthy families, both patrician and plebeian, who, through their prestige and their power over the timocratic centuriate assembly, were able to control the elections. Tribunes who looked for advancement found it wiser to follow the policies of these leaders than to serve the people. In addition, since the enforcement of the land provisions of the Licinian-Sextian Laws was in the hands of these wealthy landowning officials, the limitations on public land were disregarded and the law became a dead letter. Although ostensibly in the hands of the people, in actuality the government of Rome was controlled by the wealthy officeholders — the large landowners — who composed the senatorial group.

Roman Institutions

A century later the Greek Polybius declared that Rome's rise to power was based on its institutions, which, he said, combined the best features of monarchy, aristocracy, and democracy, each checking the others. A survey of these institutions as they appeared at the end of the Italic Wars (272 B.C.) will explain his conception.

The Magistracies   The magisterial system provided the monarchical element in the Roman constitution. The higher magistrates possessed such power of command that they were literally masters, as the word *magistratus* implies. They wore robes with purple borders; on official occasions they sat on ivory chairs; and they were attended by lictors bearing the *fasces*, bundles of rods, symbolizing magisterial power to compel obedience. When displayed outside of the city, the fasces contained an ax, indicative of the power of life and death.

The most important limitations in the power of the magistrates arose from the principle of collegiality and from the one year term of their offices. To these restrictions should be added the powerful right of veto of the tribunes in the action of any magistrate except the dictator.

Cursus Honorum   Tradition required that an aspirant for high office in Rome pass through a regular succession of positions from the lowest to the highest. In 180 B.C. the *lex Villia annalis* established the succession—quaestor, praetor, consul—called the *cursus honorum*, "succession of offices," with required intervals between offices; holding two offices at the same time and re-election to the same office within ten years were prohibited. In addition to these required offices most young men served as tribunes and aediles if plebeian, and curule aedile if patrician. The place of these in the *cursus* was not fixed. Many young plebeians, especially in the early period, must have begun their official careers by being elected tribune. Some never went beyond this office. In the later republic, however, the usual sequence for plebeians became quaestor, tribune, aedile, praetor, consul and for patricians, quaestor, curule aedile, praetor, consul.

A young Roman ambitious for an official career began by serving for at least ten years as a junior officer in the army. He would then post his name with the proper official, consul or tribune, as a candidate for office.

Quaestors   The quaestors were originally two in number, but were increased to four in 421 B.C. and to eight in 267 B.C. They were at first assistants of the king, and then of the consuls, in criminal cases. To that duty the care of the treasury and the management of funds on campaigns came to be added. They also presented appeals of citizens before the assembly. In the early period they were appointed by the consuls; later they were elected by the tribal assembly.

Tribunes   The power of the tribunes, who were ten in number, had steadily increased. They could come to the aid of any individual citizen when called upon; they could veto any proposal of a magistrate before an assembly or any action of the senate. For a period they sat outside the senate door to listen; later they were allowed to enter the senate, and finally, even to convoke that body and present measures to it. They presided over the tribal assembly, presented measures to it, which, if passed, became *plebiscita,* and called magistrates before it for criminal trial in cases of malfeasance in office. Thus they were the cornerstone of democracy in checking the ruling classes.

Aediles In early days the two plebeian aediles had been assistants of the tribunes. Gradually they developed a set of separate duties of such importance that the parallel patrician aedileship was established. The aediles were charged with the care of public buildings, the supervision of the grain market, and the task of providing the games for the people. In later days the games gave them an opportunity to curry popular favor by lavish expenditures from their own means beyond the money provided by the state.

Praetors The praetorship, established in 367 B.C. to relieve the consuls, was the lowest of the offices that carried with them the imperium. Though the praetor often exercised military command, his activities were normally confined to the city, where as *praetor urbanus* he dealt with civil and criminal cases arising under the law. In 242 B.C., a second praetor, the *praetor peregrinus,* was added to take cognizance of cases involving non-Romans. At the beginning of his term the praetor issued an edict in which he stated the principles of law and the rules of procedure he would apply.

Consuls The consuls were chief executives and commanders of the army. Their power was in theory autocratic, for they were masters (*magistri*) of the state. In actual practice limitations on their power developed. First there was the limitation of collegiality: in case of dispute between the two consuls, the negative vote prevailed; that is, if one said "go," and the other said "stay," they stayed. Though not legally bound to follow the advice of the senate, custom decreed that the consuls consult that body and abide by its decisions. In fact, the control which the senate exercised over the raising and allotment of money made such action necessary. Furthermore, the consul knew that he would be consul for but one year and senator for the rest of his life; consequently he was not likely to jeopardize his future career by actions that would weaken the power of the senate. Within the city there were definite restrictions that regulated the consul's imperium: his actions might be vetoed by a tribune; appeals from his decisions in capital cases might be taken to the tribal assembly; and he might be brought before that assembly for an account at the end of his office. But in the field on a military campaign, his power (*imperium militiae*) was supreme and brooked no interference.

Dictator In times of great emergency the consuls, usually after consultation with the senate, named a dictator, whose power was truly monarchical, for all guarantees of appeal, intercession, or veto were suspended. His term of office was limited to six months, but many dictators prided themselves on completing their task and surrendering their power in less time. The record belongs to Cincinnatus. It is a noteworthy evidence of the strength of Roman tradition that no dictator used his power to make himself king or tyrant in early Rome. The dictator's title was *magister populi* and he could choose an assistant called "master of horse" (*magister equitum*).

Proconsuls The chief disadvantage that accrued to Rome from this magisterial system arose from the fact that command of the army changed hands annually. This problem was solved and additional commanders were provided during the Samnite Wars (327–290 B.C.) by the practice of prorogation. The senate, with consent granted by the tribal assembly, might prolong the imperium of a consul or reappoint an ex-consul for purposes of military command. The official so designated served *pro consule*, in place of the consul, and was later called *proconsul*. His imperium was limited, however, to a specific task and was subject to the superior command of the consuls.

The crowning honor of an official career was election to the censorship, the duties of which office have already been described (p. 402).

Senate The senate became the chief administrative body under the Roman constitution. It was made up of three hundred senators, appointed at first by the consuls and later, after the Ovinian Law (*ca.* 300 B.C.), by the censors. In early times its membership was patrician, but when public offices were opened to the plebeians, seats in the senate were yielded to them also. The senate had no responsibility to the people and so was aristocratic in character. Since it was understood that admission to the senate should preferably be given to ex-magistrates of the grade of quaestor or above, the senate was composed of a body of experienced men. Experience was emphasized by the fact that in its deliberations the presiding official called on the *consulares*, ex-consuls, to express their opinions first.

The senate's powers, never clearly stated, developed gradually through custom, often more potent among the Romans than law. The senate advised the consuls and gave its consent to legislation. Its approval was necessary for the validation of contracts let by the censors. It provided for the levy of armies, the raising of taxes, and the allocation of funds; it appointed proconsuls and it assigned commands. It controlled and directed foreign affairs, received embassies, and regulated the affairs of the Italian federation. In times of emergency it could suspend constitutional guarantees of personal liberty by the *senatus consultum ultimum* ("final decree"), a declaration of martial law. It has been maintained that no finer body of men has ever directed the course of any state with greater success than did the senate during Rome's rise to power.

The *Comitia Curiata* The old curiate assembly used under the monarchy continued to exist though its functions and powers were increasingly curtailed. By 287 B.C. thirty lictors, representing the old *curiae*, carried out the formalities for which it was still responsible. They ratified wills and adoptions and formally conferred the imperium on the magistrates elected by one of the other assemblies. This formal ratification of election was called the *lex curiata de imperio*.

The *Comitia Centuriata* Throughout the period of the Italic Wars, the centuriate assembly was the dominant voice of the people. It was composed of 193 centuries arranged by classes, as they were arranged also in the army.

ORGANIZATION OF THE COMITIA CENTURIATA[3]

	JUNIORS (17–46 years), in centuries	SENIORS (above 46 years), in centuries
Cavalry		18
Class I	40	40
Class II	10	10
Class III	10	10
Class IV	10	10
Class V	15	15
Musicians and workmen } unarmed		4
Landless		1
Total		193

The cavalry, which was always composed of the wealthiest men, voted first and was followed by the classes in their order. Since the cavalry and the first class together had a majority, ninety-eight votes, this assembly was timocratic in character, that is, it was controlled by the well-to-do. It elected the magistrates, voted on laws submitted to it, declared war, ratified treaties of peace, and heard appeals from capital decisions of the consuls. It had no rights of nomination or of initiation of legislation, since no one could invoke it or address it save a magistrate. Candidates for office presented their names to the consuls; if acceptable to them, officeseekers then campaigned in a white toga, *toga candida*, to solicit votes. The presiding consul presented the candidates' names to the centuries for their votes. Legislation was proposed by the magistrates, after discussion and consent by the senate. If popular debate was deemed necessary, a less formal meeting called a *contio* was

[3] G. W. Botsford, *A History of the Ancient World*. New York: The Macmillan Company, 1912, p. 341. Revised by Lily Ross Taylor, "The Centuriate Assembly in the Light of New Evidence," Thomas Spencer Jerome Lecture, March 18, 1965.

summoned, which private citizens might address with the consent of the presiding magistrate. The action of the centuriate assembly could be controlled by religious devices, for if the direction of affairs displeased the magistrate, he could conveniently observe an unfavorable omen and terminate the deliberations. If a man was stricken with a fit of epilepsy, all action was suspended. So frequently was epilepsy feigned that it was called "comitial sickness." The whole process was cumbersome and unwieldy, so after 287 B.C. many functions of the *comitia centuriata* were transferred to the tribal assembly, with its simpler voting procedures.

The *Comitia Tributa* The more democratic *comitia tributa* elected tribunes under the presidency of a tribune, and quaestors under the presidency of a consul. It dealt with judicial cases brought before it by tribunes or aediles. It voted on laws presented to it by tribunes (*plebiscita*) or by consuls (*leges*) with the previous consent of the senate. This senatorial restriction was reduced to a formality in 339 B.C. and was removed by the Hortensian Law of 287 B.C. In 312 B.C. the censor Appius Claudius enrolled the landless in the tribes; however, after 304 B.C. they were confined to the four city tribes. The major constitutional measures of the period up to 287 B.C. were passed by the centuriate assembly; but many laws and plebiscites, particularly those that dealt with debts, emerged from the tribes. The tribal assembly ratified the senate's recommendations for the appointment of promagistrates for particular tasks, and eventually took over the right of the declaration of war. In the later years of the republic it was the principal assembly for all purposes.

The Army The Roman army of the early republic was a phalanx composed of those able to furnish arms, assisted by the rich as cavalry, and the poor as light-armed troops. The introduction of pay for service enabled all to buy armor and thus broke down the military distinction between the classes. The defeat at the Claudine Pass in the Second Samnite War brought an end to the phalanx (p. 398). The Romans adopted their enemy's formation and also their arms: the dart, *pilum*; and the oblong shield, *scutum*. Henceforth, instead of being massed into a single body, the Roman troops were organized into maniples, mobile companies of one hundred and twenty men each. There were thirty such companies to a legion, deployed, checkerboard fashion, in three lines.

The men fought in open order, about eight feet apart. The first line was composed of recruits, the second of experienced men, the third, or reserve, of veterans. Each man wore heavy body armor and carried two darts and a short sword. As the line advanced, the men threw their darts and then closed in with their swords. At this close fighting the Romans were supreme. The open order of the legion proved in the end superior to the Macedonian phalanx of Pyrrhus. Four legions made up the normal annual levy, to which would be added troops from the allies. Training was rigid and exacting, discipline absolute. Perhaps the most famous of the Roman rules of war was that which required the army to build a carefully planned camp complete with moat and mound, wherever it stopped for the night.

The Roads   A most renowned Roman accomplishment was the system of roads which was begun in the early republic and extended with conquest throughout Italy and eventually across the Roman Empire. While salt was being transported over the *Via Salaria* ("Salt Way") from the marshes beside the lower Tiber northeast into the Sabine country and the *Via Latina* climbed over the hills to Capua as early as the fourth century B.C., the famous Appian Way, built in 312 B.C. by the censor Appius Claudius established the method and the precedent for Roman road building of later generations. The Appian Way crossed the Pontine Marshes on solid foundations and then ran near the coast to Capua. Later it was extended to Beneventum, Tarentum, and Brundisium. It was famed not only for its directness but also for its durability. The roads built in later periods clearly show the Roman method of road building. Gravel was laid on hardpan or on a solid foundation; over that lime was poured to form a sort of concrete; on this base were laid huge paving blocks with convex surface to provide drainage. The roads were built for military purposes, but they were used by travelers and merchants as well. By providing means of communication and trade routes, the roads helped greatly to bind Italy, and in later times the Mediterranean world, together.

The Family   The basic Roman institution for the development of character was the family. The Roman *familia* consisted of the father and mother, sons and sons' wives, unmarried daughters, grandsons, and so on, and all clients and slaves. Over the *familia* presided the *pater familias*, father of the family. His *patria potestas* gave him power to inflict punishment for disobedience, even to the penalty of death; the latter was usually imposed only after a trial before a family court.

The father had full charge of the family estate, and it was his pride to hand on to his sons at his death an estate larger than it was when he had received it. The sons were educated by their father in reading, writing, and arithmetic, in the family traditions, which inculcated the stern Roman virtues, in the law, and in the management of affairs. Only

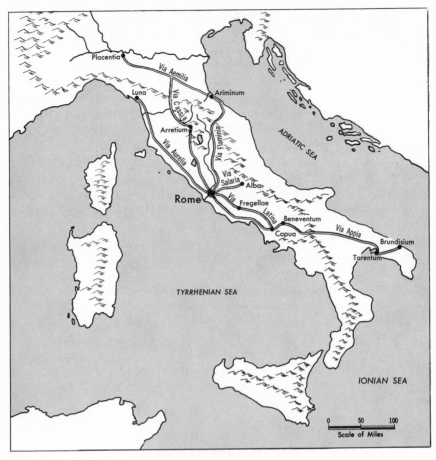

Colonies and Military Roads of Italy, ca. 265 B.C.

at the father's death, or after he had gone through the fiction of selling them into slavery three times, were the sons free of his control and independent. At his death they divided the property[4] and became *patres* in their own right.

Daughters learned household affairs from their mothers. Women and their possessions were always under the control (*in manu*) of their father, brothers, or husband.

Family life was very simple. The house was characterized by the *atrium*, a large central room with a roof that sloped to an opening which let rain water into a cistern in the center, and in the rear of which stood the bed of the father and mother. Around the atrium were built smaller

─────────

[4] In early times indivisible family ownership prevailed.

rooms for various household uses. Food consisted of vegetables, milk, bread, pork, and perhaps a little beef. Women wore a long garment, the *stola*, which reached their feet, and for out-of-doors added the *palla*, a large rectangular woolen garment which they draped around them. Men wore the tunic, which reached just below the knees, and the *toga*, the characteristic Roman woolen cloak.

The Growth of Rome The city of Rome must have been very un-prepossessing. Its best feature was the fine wall built after the Gallic disaster. The houses had been hastily rebuilt after that occurrence; streets were crooked and dirty; the temples of local volcanic stone could not have been very attractive. The fine buildings of the later Forum had not yet been erected. The lower ground, where lived the poor, was frequently flooded and the buildings there destroyed. Marshes and cisterns were constant sources of fever, and epidemics were frequent. The city was served by two aqueducts, the Aqua Appia, built by Appius Claudius in 312 B.C., which brought good water from the hills and distributed it in fountains, and the Anio Vetus, whose water from the Anio River was not potable, but could be used for washing.

Economic Life Economic conditions were slowly improving. The necessities of an important and expanding city led to the development of the industries essential to its life: pottery manufacture, leather working and metallurgy, particularly the manufacture of weapons and armor. Contact with the Italic tribes and with the Greek cities contributed to the development of trade. The period of conquest witnessed the first appearance of Roman coins, the copper *as*, weighing twelve ounces. After a brief period during which silver coins were minted in Capua, Rome established in 269 B.C. a silver coinage with the standard a *denarius*, a silver coin equivalent to the Athenian drachma; a smaller coin, one-fourth its size, was called the *sestertius*; an *as*, made of two ounces of bronze, was one-tenth of a *denarius*.

In spite of these developments trade and industry were of less importance than agriculture; the Romans were pre-eminently farmers. Lands acquired from the conquered tribes were distributed among the poorer Romans for the creation of new tribes; others were given in allotments to the Roman and Latin colonists; and much more came into the possession of the ruling class in leasehold in spite of the restrictions of the Licinian-Sextian Laws. Agrarian rather than commercial interests controlled Roman policies and motivated the program of expansion.

Conquest and the acquisition of land led to a very rapid increase in the citizen body. Accurate figures are lacking for the early period, but the first reliable census, dating from the year 318 B.C., gives two hundred and fifty thousand men of military age, which indicates a total population of approximately a million citizens scattered throughout Italy. Estimates of the city population are little more than guesses.

Mores Majorum   Controlling all Roman activities were the *mores majorum*, the customs of the ancestors. Tradition prevailed in the constitution, in law, religion, education, and daily life. Discipline and conservatism were the keynotes of these customs. Yet Roman conservatism was not blind. It made constitutional progress slow, but it did not block necessary improvements. It did not prevent the Romans from adopting the Samnite military system when it proved better than their own. The lessons tradition taught the people are evident from the large number of Latin words representing qualities: *constantia, diligentia, continentia, fides,* and pre-eminently *virtus, gravitas,* and *pietas. Virtus* is valor, illustrated by the story that on the battlefields of Heraclea all the Roman dead received their wounds in front, and by the ancient legends of Scaevola and Horatius. *Gravitas* is seriousness of outlook, characteristic of the Romans in all their dealings, as contrasted with the lightheartedness and changeability of the Greeks. *Pietas* is loyalty, the culmination of all virtue, the performance of all duties and obligations due to the family and its gods, to the state and the great gods that made Rome great.

Appius Claudius   Appius Claudius (censor in 312 B.C.), surnamed Caecus, the Blind, whose vivid personality made an impression on his own and succeeding generations, stands out among the many famous heroes of the period as the symbol and epitome of the period, as does Pericles for his age in Athens. Three times military tribune, quaestor, aedile, three times praetor, three times interrex, twice consul, dictator, and censor, serving with distinction in the Samnite Wars, he had a long and honorable career. During his censorship he caused something of an uproar by enrolling the landless in the tribes and by putting even freedmen in the senate. He had his own freedman publish the pontifical rules of procedure of the law. His greatest achievement was the building of the Aqua Appia and the Via Appia, immortalizing his name. To him was ascribed the authorship of many an ancient maxim such as "Each man is the blacksmith of his own fortune." He was the first great Roman orator whose orations were preserved in later times. When the senate was about to accept the offers of peace from Pyrrhus after Asculum (279 B.C.) (p. 398), Appius Claudius, by that time over ninety and so blind that he had to be led by a boy, entered the senate house and thundered, "Rome never makes terms of peace with a victorious enemy on Italian soil."

During the first centuries of the republic the fundamental principles of the Roman government had been developed and the once discordant peoples of Italy had been welded together into a most potent confederation. The same evolutionary process that led to these accomplishments next drew Rome into the vortex of Mediterranean affairs and thereby raised a whole new series of problems — imperial, constitutional, and economic.

CONQUEST OF THE MEDITERRANEAN, 264–133 B.C.

The Roman conquest of the Mediterranean is one of the most astounding stories in all history. In 272 B.C. Rome completed her conquest of the Italian peninsula. Eight years later the first war with Carthage began, and within less than a century and a half Rome possessed or controlled nearly every country around the periphery of the Mediterranean. This extraordinary achievement had profound and lasting effects on the Roman constitution, on Roman society and culture, and on the conquered lands as well—effects that still influence the world today.

The First Punic War, 264–241 B.C.

Causes of the War In 264 B.C. the Mamertines, mercenaries in Messana, were attacked by Syracuse and appealed to both Carthage and Rome for aid. Carthage responded, but in Rome the senate hesitated. Affirmative action would violate agreements with Carthage to leave Sicily alone and would certainly arouse resentment and lead to war with the Carthaginians. Refusal meant that Carthage, in coming to the assistance of the Mamertines, would not only gain possession of Messana and control over the Straits, a blow to the Greek cities in Italy, Rome's new allies, but would be a constant menace to the peace of the peninsula. The people, however, did not delay. The victors over the Macedonian phalanx of Pyrrhus did not fear the mercenary armies of Carthage, and in Sicily there was rich booty to be had. The centuriate assembly voted to send aid, and so began the long duel with Carthage.

Carthage Carthage, rich and powerful, ruled over what is now Tunis, and was allied with the Numidians to the west. Controlled by it were the western half of Sicily, Sardinia, Corsica, the smaller islands of the western Mediterranean, and the southern coast of Spain. Its fleet, dominating the western sea, restricted the trade of others and prevented passage through the Straits of Gibraltar without Carthaginian permission. To the smaller states of the region, such as Rome, Carthage had dictated treaties that limited their activities while demonstrating its own pre-eminence. In the wars that had been fought at intervals in Sicily over a period of nearly three centuries Carthage, though never able to conquer the Greeks, had more than held its own against them. Occupation of Messana would have given the Phoenician city an important advantage over the Greeks, and therefore it could not brook the interference of Rome in Sicily. Its aristocratic rulers were confident that their fleet, their generals, and their wealth were sufficient to stop the advance of Rome. Carthage's chief weakness, the mercenary character of the

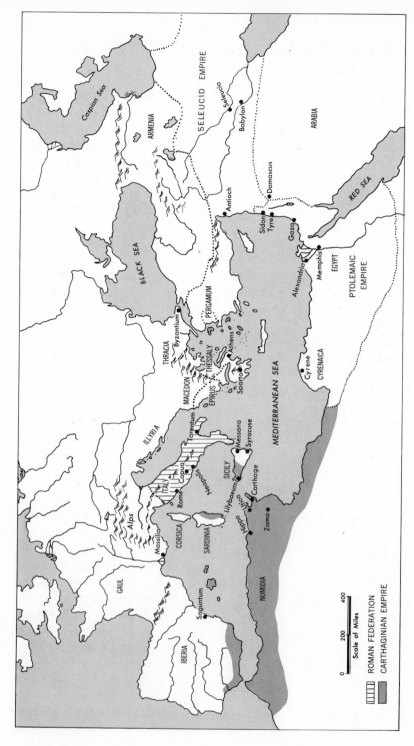

The Mediterranean World in 265 B.C.

SELEUCID EMPIRE
ARMENIA
Caspian Sea
Seleucia
Babylon
ARABIA
Damascus
Antioch
Sidon
Tyre
Gaza
RED SEA
Memphis
Alexandria
EGYPT
PTOLEMAIC EMPIRE
BLACK SEA
PERGAMUM
Byzantium
THRACIA
MACEDON
THESSALY
Athens
EPIRUS
Sparta
Cyrene
CYRENAICA
MEDITERRANEAN SEA
ILLYRIA
Tarentum
Messana
Syracuse
Neapolis
Capua
SICILY
Rome
Lilybaeum
Carthage
ITALY
Hippo
Zama
GAUL
CORSICA
SARDINIA
Massilia
NUMIDIA
Saguntum
IBERIA

Scale of Miles
0   200   400

ROMAN FEDERATION
CARTHAGINIAN EMPIRE

army, need cause no concern, they thought, so long as the troops were paid.

The Roman Position   Rome's interests were not so directly involved as those of Carthage. Its commercial activities were comparatively slight, and it had readily signed the treaties Carthage had requested, even entering into alliance with Carthage against Pyrrhus. The Greek cities of southern Italy, however, were allies of Rome, and it was incumbent upon Rome to protect them against the advance of Carthaginian power. Long-standing relations between Rome and Syracuse would be endangered if Carthage closed the Straits, and with Carthage in Messana peace in Italy would be forever threatened. In resources Rome seemed pitifully weak. Without fleet, money, or tribute from the allies, its wealth was solely in the produce of its land and its strength in the citizen-soldiers of the legions and the levies of the Italian allies.

The War   Rome met with immediate success on land. The Carthaginian and Syracusan forces were driven from Messana and the city was occupied. Hiero II of Syracuse, who had joined with Carthage at first, immediately changed sides and remained Rome's faithful ally until his death in 215 B.C. The Romans then, in 262 B.C., besieged and conquered Agrigentum (the Greek Acragas), which had become the center of Carthaginian power in Sicily.

Their experiences in this siege demonstrated to them the need of a naval force, and they at once proceeded to build a fleet. There is a famous story which relates how Roman carpenters, using a wrecked Carthaginian quinquereme as a model, built the ships, while oarsmen were being drilled on benches on the shore. Each battleship was equipped with unusual grappling devices, called "crows," and provided with a boarding party of one hundred and twenty soldiers — an innovation in naval warfare. With a fleet of one hundred and twenty ships Duilius in 260 B.C. won a great battle off Mylae on the north of Sicily.

The Romans then determined upon the invasion of Africa, and in 256 B.C., after a second naval battle off Ecnomus had cleared the way, they dispatched an expeditionary force under Regulus. The fate of this invasion revealed the weakness of the Roman military system. Though the consul won a victory, he failed to take Carthage or to secure a treaty of peace. Then in the fall, according to Roman custom, the greater portion of his army went back to Rome, while he remained in Africa with a small force awaiting the consul who would take his place and bring fresh troops. During the winter a wandering Spartan, Xanthippus, coming to Carthage, reorganized and drilled the Punic army. In the spring he tempted Regulus to battle before reinforcements came and succeeded in destroying the Roman forces, taking their commander prisoner. The fleet that was sent to the rescue was wrecked off Sicily.

After the failure of the African expedition the war dragged on interminably in Sicily. At sea two Roman fleets were wrecked by storms and one was defeated in the harbor of Drepana. On land the Carthaginian force commanded by Hamilcar Barca waged guerrilla warfare and kept the Romans in continual difficulty. Meanwhile Carthage, its trade at a standstill, was forced to borrow money from Egypt. In Rome the treasury was empty and the currency depreciated. Polybius compared the contestants to two gamecocks who have fought to exhaustion. Rome, however, was the first to recover.

The End of the War   In 242 B.C. a group of wealthy Romans built and equipped a fleet of two hundred vessels. Catulus, the commander, trapped a Carthaginian transport fleet on its way to Sicily and destroyed it off the Aegates Islands. Thereupon Carthage yielded, and in 241 B.C. a treaty of peace was signed by which Carthage surrendered its possessions in Sicily to the Romans and agreed to pay a large indemnity. Immediately after the war Carthage, unable to pay its mercenaries, found itself involved in a fearful struggle with these warriors, a struggle that required all of Hamilcar Barca's genius to suppress. Rome took advantage of the situation to occupy Sardinia and Corsica, and when Carthage attempted to regain these possessions declared war and forced the cession of the islands and the payment of an additional indemnity. The story is told that Hamilcar Barca thereafter caused his son Hannibal, before the altar of Moloch, god of Carthage, to swear eternal and undying enmity toward Rome, and then took him off to Spain to gather men and money for a war of revenge.

The Second Punic War, 218–201 B.C.

Rome Between the Wars   The victory over Carthage did not end the advance of Roman power. Rome fought two wars in Illyria to check piracy in the Adriatic and to protect the trade of her Greek allies. These conflicts brought about friendly relations with the Greek leagues and hostility with Macedon. A fresh invasion of Italy by Gauls in 225 B.C., after terrifying Rome, was barely stopped in a fierce battle at Telamon. The Romans promptly retaliated by conquering the Boii and Insubres in the Po Valley and pushing the Roman frontier to the Alps. A new agrarian policy developed by a popular leader, Flaminius, was adopted, and Latin colonies, with large allotments to the colonists, were established at Placentia and Cremona after which, to strengthen the Roman hold on this region, the Flaminian Way was built. Scarcely had the Romans entered upon the exploitation of these rich lands when war with Carthage began for the second time. The occasion was the Carthaginian advance in Spain, where Hamilcar Barca had gone to secure the rich mineral wealth and the assistance of its able fighters.

Hannibal   The Roman occupation of Sicily, Sardinia, and Corsica deprived Carthage of markets for the sale of its articles of export and import as well as of sources of its mercenary troops. To compensate for

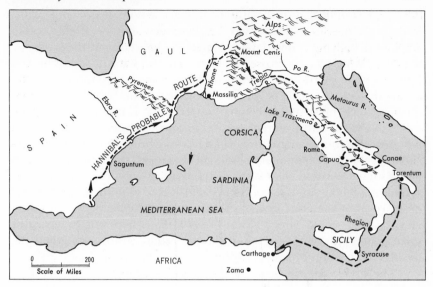

Hannibal's March, 218–203 B.C.

these losses Hamilcar Barca developed Carthaginian control over southern Spain, a land rich in metals and inhabited by warlike tribes whose men proved a valuable addition to the forces of Carthage. Through the resources so obtained the Carthaginian hoped to crush Rome and re-establish the greatness of his city. After his death in 229 B.C. his son-in-law, Hasdrubal, founded Cartagena and sent wealth back home from the silver mines. He readily agreed to a treaty with Rome requested by the Massaliots and limiting Carthaginian power to the Ebro River on the north. In 221 B.C., at the death of Hasdrubal, Hannibal, at the age of twenty-six, succeeded to his brother-in-law's power in Spain. The history of the next twenty years is largely the biography of this remarkable man, in some respects the greatest of all military tacticians. A born leader of men, he understood the psychology of his own troops and of his enemy's as well. He knew how to use the terrain of a battlefield to the fullest advantage, and he was a master in the disposition of his troops on the field of battle. Ever since his time great generals, from his opponent Scipio to von Hindenburg, have studied his campaigns. His abilities were first manifested in 219 B.C. when he besieged and took Saguntum, a Spanish city allied to Rome. Angered by this presumption, Rome forthwith declared war in 218 B.C.

The Invasion of Italy The Roman plans were quickly made. One consul, Sempronius, was to gather an army in Sicily and invade Africa, which could easily be done since Rome controlled the sea; the other, Publius Cornelius Scipio, was to proceed with two legions to Spain and deal with Hannibal directly. But Hannibal's actions upset both plans. With great precision he crossed the Pyrenees and the Rhone, while Scipio was dallying a few days at Marseilles, and entered the passes of the Alps. What pass he crossed by is not known, but it was possibly the Little Saint Bernard. After a difficult time owing to the hostility of the mountaineers, the lack of proper roads, and the September snows, during which most of his elephants were lost, Hannibal entered the valley of the Po with twenty thousand infantry and six thousand of the best cavalry (Numidian) in the world. His route brought him into the territory of the newly conquered Boii and Insubres, still hostile to Rome. He planned to rouse the Gauls, to break the Italian confederation by promises of liberation from Rome, and to accomplish thereafter the destruction of the city itself. To attain his ends he needed resounding victories that would offer to Gauls and Italians hopes of success. But great general that he was, Hannibal underestimated the strength of the ties that bound the Italians to Rome.

The Trebia River   Scipio, after sending his army into Spain under his brother's command and returning to Italy to raise fresh troops, was defeated on the Ticinus River. Sempronius, recalled from Sicily, sent his army north in small detachments, reassembled it two months later at Ariminum, and joined Scipio at Placentia. Hannibal defeated the combined armies on the Trebia River in December, 218 B.C. By a clever ruse he engaged the Roman troops before breakfast and then drew them through an icy mountain stream into an ambush from which few escaped.

Lake Trasimeno   For the following year the Romans elected to the consulate their popular hero Flaminius. He took his stand at Arretium. Hannibal crossed the Apennines at Bologna, led his army for three sleepless days and nights through the marshes of Etruria, and placed himself between Flaminius and Rome. By well-designed atrocities, such as the burning of farmhouses, he brought the Romans down upon him, only to lead them into the hills around Lake Trasimeno, where he trapped them by placing his troops on the mist-covered slopes and by blocking the road before and behind them. The Roman army was annihilated. Italian prisoners were sent home with promises of freedom, but the Italians were not yet ready to exchange Roman leadership for Carthaginian promises.

Fabius, the Delayer   Amid great consternation at Rome, Fabius Maximus was chosen dictator. His policy of delay and refusal to attack, while continually harassing the enemy, has given the name Fabian to policies of slow advance, and Fabius himself earned the nickname *Cunctator* (Delayer). Hannibal fell into a trap laid by Fabius in the Campanian hills and again showed his resourcefulness in his clever escape. He tied lighted faggots to the horns of cattle and drove them up the slopes at night. When the Roman guards rushed to stop this seemingly rash move, Hannibal and his men marched out by the pass. Minucius, master of the horse, elected co-dictator by the impatient Roman people, was soundly defeated but was rescued by Fabius.

Cannae, 216 B.C.   Hannibal spent the winter in Apulia and in the spring met the Romans on the banks of the Aufidus River near Cannae. Rome put its greatest army into the field — traditionally eighty thousand men, but certainly not so large — led by Aemilius Paullus, conservative, and Terentius Varro, popular leader. They expected to sweep Hannibal off the field with their overwhelming numbers. But Hannibal allowed his weakened center to fall back, swung his wings of heavy-armed Africans around the Roman flanks, and sent his cavalry against the Roman rear. Only ten thousand Romans escaped. The plan of Hindenburg's great victory over Russia in 1914 at the Mazurian Lakes was based on Hannibal's tactics at Cannae.

Hannibal made no attempt to attack Rome, which doubtless he could not have taken, but his original purpose seemed nearly achieved. Philip V of Macedon made an alliance with him; Syracuse, with Hiero dead, came over to him; Capua joined him, and he was later able to secure Tarentum save for its citadel. One more such victory and he might win! But that victory he never achieved.

Though he remained in Italy until 203 B.C. and fought many skirmishes, he never again met the Romans in pitched battle. Instead, Rome, standing like a rock, sent troops to watch and harass him, while it dealt singly with his allies. By timely assistance to the Greeks, Rome kept Philip V busy at home. Marcellus, overcoming both the bravery of the Syracusans and the genius of Archimedes, took Syracuse and carried its treasures to Rome. Carthage, either from inability or unwillingness to act, failed to support its great commander or his ally in Sicily. Even so, when the Romans besieged Capua, Hannibal made a sudden raid on Rome. But the army stood firm around Capua, and, though mothers might frighten their children into good behavior with the cry, "Hannibal is at the gates," Rome remained unharmed behind its walls, while Capua fell to the Romans and was destroyed.

The Metaurus River   The last great threat of the Carthaginians came, like the first, from Spain. Hasdrubal, Hannibal's brother, after gaining successes over the Roman forces in Spain, eluded the Roman army and sped to Italy to join Hannibal, in the hope that the union of their forces might strike a deathblow at the war-weary Romans. His messenger to Hannibal was caught, however, and the Roman armies, hastening north, defeated and killed Hasdrubal on the banks of the Metaurus River in 207 B.C. Hannibal withdrew into the hills of Bruttium, where he stayed until 203 B.C.

The Rise of Scipio   The genius of a young man, Publius Cornelius Scipio, son of the Roman commander at the battle at the Trebia River, finally brought victory to Rome. In 211 B.C. Scipio, though too young to be eligible for high command, was given proconsular power by special act of the centuriate assembly and sent to Spain to replace his father and uncle, who had been killed in battle the preceding year. Though he let Hasdrubal slip through his fingers with almost fatal consequences, he seized Cartagena, the Carthaginian stronghold, expelled the Punic forces from Spain, and entered into friendly relations with the Numidians, who had supplied Carthage with its fine cavalry. Returning to Rome a hero to the populace, he was elected consul. Straightway he proposed an invasion of Africa. With Hannibal in Italy, the senate hesitated; but when Scipio threatened an appeal to the people, it yielded, and Scipio crossed over in 204 B.C. The Carthaginians sought for peace, and during the armistice that followed Hannibal returned home in 203 B.C.

Zama For fifteen years Hannibal had lived in an enemy country, had won great victories, and had held Roman forces at bay. His return to Africa brought fresh hopes to the Carthaginians, who at once renewed the war. In 202 B.C. he met Scipio on the battlefield of Zama. The Roman commander used Hannibal's favorite weapon, the Numidian cavalry, against him, and won a victory that brought the war to an end. By the terms of peace dictated by Scipio and agreed upon by Hannibal in 201 B.C., Carthage surrendered its possessions in Spain and its alliance with Numidia, disbanded its army, destroyed its fleet, promised to wage no war without Rome's consent, and agreed to pay an enormous indemnity. Scipio was rewarded by the *cognomen* Africanus, and Rome was mistress of the western Mediterranean.

Consequences of the War From the long struggle with Carthage Rome emerged victorious but indelibly scarred by the conflict. The loss of men had been appalling. The ravages of Hannibal's army and the demands of the long years of constant military service had led to the abandonment of many small farms, especially in southern Italy, and this in turn led to the further development of the great estates of the senatorial class. The services of supply for the armies and the fleet, the tasks of management of the finances of newly acquired territories, and the appearance at Rome of a large supply of mobile capital gained from booty and indemnities led to the appearance in Rome of a new class of capitalists and men of business who were ready at the end of the war for new fields of exploitation, and whose interests eventually clashed with those of the ruling group of senators.

In the meantime senatorial power had consistently advanced. During the period between the wars the popular leader Flaminius had challenged it successfully. He had secured the passage of laws reorganizing the centuriate assembly on a more democratic basis and restricting the activities of individual senators in trade. Democratic interest in the land program was evidenced by the provision of farms larger than customary for colonists in the Po Valley. But the need for consistent direction of military affairs, the wretched failure of Flaminius and his follower Varro in the struggle with Hannibal, and the firm strength the senate displayed — all combined to crush this nascent democratic movement and leave the senate in control of the state. The powers of the senate, however, depended not on legal sanctions but on its prestige and that of its members and on Roman adherence to custom and precedent.

The victory over Carthage made the Romans rulers of the western Mediterranean and almost inevitably involved them in the troubled waters of the Hellenistic East. When the opportunity arose, the senatorial leaders, jealous and fearful of their newly acquired position, but avid for wealth and military glory and abetted by the business leaders, who looked for new outlets for their capital and recently discovered abilities, were ready to seize it and to draw the war-weary but still rapacious populace with them. The declaration of war on Macedon in 200 B.C. launched them upon a series of wars which made Rome mistress of the Hellenistic world.

The Eastern Wars

The reason or excuse for the first entrance of Rome into Hellenistic affairs is hard to find. Until Pyrrhus came to Italy the Romans had few relations with the Aegean. The Illyrian wars, fought during the interval of the Punic wars for the protection of Adriatic commerce, led to favorable relations with the Greek leagues and hostile feelings on the part of Macedon. But neither this nor Philip V's abortive alliance with Hannibal in what is called the First Macedonian War gave the Romans any real interest in the East.

Yet Rome's position as the first power of the western Mediterranean in control of Sicily and the western waters made it almost inevitable that it would be drawn into the maelstrom of Eastern politics. The occasion was a crisis in Eastern affairs, which arose in 203 B.C. When Ptolemy IV died in that year leaving his throne to an infant son controlled by a corrupt and weak regency, Antiochus III of Asia (p. 352), flushed by the success of his eastern campaigns, immediately advanced upon southern Syria, while Philip V in agreement with him set to work to capture the Ptolemaic possessions in the Aegean area. Egypt, thus beset, appealed to Rome for aid. True, there was no reason why Rome should go to the rescue of Egypt, since so far the only relations between these states had been the sale of Egyptian grain to the Romans at exorbitant prices during the Hannibalic war. When, however, to the appeal of the Egyptians was added the request of Attalus of Pergamum, of Rhodes, and especially of the Aetolians, who had been Rome's allies during the First Macedonian War, all alarmed by the advance of Macedon, the Romans ordered Philip to cease harassing the Greeks and Ptolemy V and to arbitrate his differences with Pergamum and Rhodes. Philip's refusal was followed by a declaration of war.

The senate persuaded the assembly to change a negative to a positive vote by presenting the danger, indeed remote, of a Macedonian invasion of Italy. Many modern authorities believe that Attalus aroused Roman fears by pointing to the growing might of Antiochus and exaggerating the danger presented to the whole Mediterranean by the alliance between Macedon and Asia and its threatened conquest of Egypt. It is sometimes argued, but without sufficient evidence, that the real basis of the senate's action was the sentimental desire on the part of some Roman senators to be recognized as civilized people by the cultured Greeks. Rome apparently desired, by establishing protectorates over the Greeks and Egypt, to preserve a balance of power in the East, to check the advances of Macedon and Asia, and yet to avoid the problems and perils of territorial aggrandizement.

The Second Macedonian War The Second Macedonian War (200–197 B.C.), after lagging for a period, was brought to a victorious conclusion when in 197 B.C. Titus Flamininus, a young philhellene serving as proconsul, secured the aid of the Achaean League and forced and won a battle at Cynoscephalae in Thessaly. Philip at once agreed to evacuate Greece, the Aegean, and Illyricum and to ally himself with Rome. When at the Isthmian games in 196 B.C. Flamininus announced the freedom of the Greeks, he was nearly overwhelmed by the enthusiastic people. Flamininus restored order, settled disputes between cities, arranged boundaries, and recalled his troops. The Greeks quickly learned, however, that they were bound by his decisions and that Rome intended quietly but firmly to interfere with their foreign relations to keep peace. In short, the Greeks had merely exchanged masters. The irritation that inevitably resulted helped to bring on later wars.

The Aetolians, greatly aggrieved because they had secured neither the spoils nor the power they felt was their due from the wars with Philip, and resenting the postbellum interference of the Romans, invited Antiochus III to come to their assistance, and Antiochus, who had emerged unscathed from the previous war, foolishly consented. He crossed to Thrace after conquering several Anatolian cities. Although Hannibal, banished from Carthage in 196 B.C. on the order of Rome, was at his court, the king did not avail himself of Hannibal's services and experience. A small Seleucid force was defeated in 191 B.C. at Thermopylae, and in 190 B.C. a Roman army commanded by Lucius Scipio and his brother, the great Africanus, won a decisive victory at Magnesia in Asia Minor. Antiochus III was forced by the treaty to surrender all Asia Minor.

Continued irritation against Rome resulted in 171 B.C. in the formation of an anti-Roman alliance of Macedonians and Greeks, led by Perseus, son of Philip V. After the Romans had suffered a number of defeats due to incapable leaders, Aemilius Paullus won a great victory at Pydna in 168 B.C. Macedon was thereupon divided into four tribute-paying republics; its treasure, the royal domains, and mines became the property of Rome. The Achaean League suffered for its attitude in the war when one thousand of its leading citizens were taken to Rome as hostages; at the same time, for an unfortunate offer to arbitrate, Rhodes was punished by the loss of its Anatolian possessions and by the ruin of its trade when Rome opened Delos (p. 352) as a free port. Though Rome had not annexed a single foot of territory, its will was supreme throughout the East. The order of a single Roman envoy was strong enough to compel Antiochus IV to retire from Egypt. He was forced also to recognize the independence of the Maccabean state in Palestine, which became an ally of Rome in 161 B.C.

The Roman program of control without annexation was, however, a failure in Greece. Revolts led in 146 B.C. to the formation of a province of Macedonia. When in the same year the Achaean League refused to obey orders, Mummius, the Roman commander, sacked the city of Corinth, dissolved the Achaean League, and placed the Greek cities under the supervision of the governor of Macedonia. This first period of Roman expansion in the East reached its climax and end when in 133 B.C. Attalus III died. Having accepted the inevitable, he left Pergamum in his will to the Roman people. From it the rich province of Asia was formed.

The Third Punic War, 149–146 B.C.

Meanwhile, the Roman legions had been engaged in consolidating Roman control over the West. Cisalpine Gaul was recovered after the Hannibalic war, and more roads were built and new colonies founded. In spite of the heroic resistance of the native tribes, particularly under the Spanish hero, Viriathus (147–139 B.C.), Roman power steadily advanced in Spain, until 133 B.C. the capture by Scipio Aemilianus of the city of Numantia, which had defied and defeated the Romans, brought the struggle to an end. In the following years Roman fleets secured control of the Balearic Islands, and in 121 B.C. southern Gaul was annexed to protect the land route to Spain.

For two generations Carthage remained the traditional foe of Rome and the constant object of Roman suspicion. When Hannibal, after Zama, reorganized the state and restored its prosperity, the Romans in alarm ordered his banishment. Their enmity followed him to the court of Antiochus and to Bithynia, where he fled after the battle of Magnesia and where he took poison rather than be led a captive to Rome. Still Carthaginian prosperity aroused the fears of conservative Romans, possibly also the jealousy of Roman landowners, who resented the com-

petition of Carthaginian olive oil, and almost certainly it aroused the
land hunger of the agrarian interests at Rome. Cato, farmer and leader
of the senate, is said to have ended all his speeches with the words,
"Carthage must be destroyed."

At length pretexts were found for war, which began in 149 B.C.
After two years of failure in the field, the Romans again elected a young
Scipio as proconsul. This youth, son of Aemilius Paullus, victor of
Pydna, and adopted by the son of Scipio Africanus, is known to history
as Scipio Aemilianus (p. 430) or as Africanus Minor, the latter adjective
to distinguish him from the first Africanus. Carthage fell before him in
146 B.C., was utterly destroyed, and its very site accursed. Its territory
was organized into the province of Africa; much of its land was confiscated and handed over to Roman settlers, and the great estates of its
aristocrats passed into the hands of Roman landlords.

In the same year Corinth also fell. The forces of Carthage and the
East, dependent upon mercenaries, disunited and weak, had proved no
match for the vigorous action of the Roman legionaries, guided wisely
by the senate and led in their victorious campaigns by a series of brilliant
commanders. Of the Hellenistic powers only Seleucid Asia and Egypt
were left; Egypt was a protected ally, however, and Asia was crushed and
humiliated. The entire Mediterranean world lay at the feet of Rome.

THE EFFECTS OF ROMAN IMPERIALISM

Within the space of one hundred and thirty-one years the entire
structure of the Mediterranean area had been completely transformed
by the meteoric rise of Rome. Political, economic, social, and cultural
changes, accompanying and reacting upon one another, appeared
everywhere and affected life in the conquered lands, in Italy, and most
vitally in Rome itself.

The Provincial System   The Roman provincial system was an
emergency product. At the end of the First Punic War Rome found
itself with Sicily, and soon thereafter with Sardinia and Corsica, on its
hands. Since to include them in the Italian confederation was impossible, the senate decided to treat them as subjects, literally as *praedia
populi Romani* ("estates of the Roman people") and to exact tribute from
them. Two new praetors were elected to take these territories as their
provincia, or sphere of duty. When Spain was organized into two provinces in 197 B.C., two more praetorships were established. As the number of provinces increased, proconsuls and propraetors were regularly
assigned to them by the senate.

Each province was an aggregate of local communities whose status
was carefully defined in the *lex provinciae*. This important document

was drawn up at the time of annexation by the conquering general and a committee of ten senators subject to approval or amendment by the senate. A few ancient cities of great honor such as Athens, Rhodes, and Marseilles were recognized as allies of Rome and were theoretically free from interference and from all burdens. To some others the senate granted, in return for services rendered, immunity from taxation. The great majority were tax-paying communities that governed themselves according to their ancestral customs. But their foreign relations were strictly under Roman control, and they paid to Rome either 10 per cent of their annual produce, as in Sicily, or a fixed annual sum, as in Asia.

The provincial governor's duty was to protect the frontier, to keep order, to see that taxes were paid, and to judge cases involving Roman citizens. His imperium, or right of command, was limited by the borders of the province. He was assisted by three *legati*, lieutenants, appointed by the senate, and by a number of *comites*, young men who went out with him at their own expense to gain experience. Royal monopolies, mines, and domains, and all confiscated properties were worked under lease or contract by Roman businessmen usually acting in partnerships. The system of itself was not burdensome. The taxes were no more than most of the cities had already been paying. Peace and order, uniform systems of law and coinage should have brought great prosperity; yet, in point of fact, the situation was quite different. The Romans regarded the provinces as so much booty. Not only did commanders and soldiers plunder freely at the time of conquest, but the tax collectors rapaciously seized more than was their due. Roman businessmen exploited the provincial resources mercilessly and lent money to cities at exorbitant rates of interest. Many of the governors corruptly levied exactions and extortions to enrich themselves. As a result many of the provincials were impoverished and men of intelligence either were drawn to Rome or became so discouraged by Roman interference that progress in the Hellenistic world slackened materially.

Rome and Italy The conquest of an empire made itself felt in every phase of Roman life. The agricultural revolution vitally affected the lives and property of the senatorial and the popular classes, while the demands of imperial finance gave added impetus to the development of a new class of businessmen. Significant constitutional changes took place as the government of a city-state tried to adapt itself to the needs of imperial control. The wealth of empire created new standards in social life, and contact with the Greeks led to the absorption of Hellenistic culture, the growth of Roman literature, and the appearance at Rome of Hellenistic religions and philosophic systems. Rome of the early period had been a community of farmers ruled by an agricultural aristocracy, with only such trade or industry as local demand required.

The city of the late republic was imperial and populous, active in the affairs of the world, replete with wealth and all wealth's embellishments and refinements, and with poverty and all its problems.

Agriculture   The agricultural revolution was marked by the decline in the number of small farms and the growth of great estates devoted to cattle raising or to the production of the olive and the grape. There were several reasons for these changes. Many of the soldiers who had fought for years in Sicily, Africa, Spain, or the East had no desire to return to the humdrum life of the ancestral farm. Some who did desire to return found it difficult if not impossible to do so because of the condition of their farms. Large areas of southern Italy had been so thoroughly devastated by the forces of Hannibal that they never recovered; others had declined or had suffered soil erosion as a result of neglect; on still others the soil had been exhausted by generations of intensive cultivation. The competition of foreign, particularly Sicilian grain, though not serious except in Rome itself, made grain farming less lucrative than previously. On the other hand, the more profitable raising of cattle or growing of olive orchards and vineyards required larger areas and greater outlays of capital than were possible for the small farmer. Slave labor was preferred on the large estates. There was constant pressure to sell land to the aristocracy who, forbidden by law to engage directly in commercial activities, were compelled to invest their wealth in land. Finally, some small farmers were doubtless forced off their lands illegally by rapacious senators. These developments hurt Romans and Italians alike, though southern Italy suffered most. A great part of its land area was good only for pasturage, and large ranches became characteristic of the region. Census lists of propertied citizens declined steadily from 209 B.C. onward.

The growth of *latifundia* ("great estates"), beginning with the conquest of Italy, continued unchecked, since the restrictions of the Licinian-Sextian Laws were not enforced. Large tracts of abandoned or confiscated land were turned over to great landowners after the Hannibalic war, and the process of growth continued throughout the second century B.C.

Much of our information about the management of estates comes from Cato, who wrote *De Agricultura*. To Cato the most profitable type of farming was cattle raising, and the large cattle or sheep ranch tended by gangs of slaves became common. The careful attention Cato paid to the handling of olive orchards and vineyards is indicative of the great importance of the growth of these phases of agricultural activity in Italy, particularly in the southwestern and central areas. In the raising of grain and vegetables Cato laid emphasis upon specialization to suit the soil or the market and advised fertilization and the rotation of crops.

The management of the estate, according to Cato, should be strictly regulated in all its details; at the head should be a slave bailiff and his wife; free laborers were to be hired for special tasks and at harvest time; the rest of the force, mostly slaves, should be worked until old or worn out, when they should be turned out like cattle to die; household and farm equipment and food should be simple and doled out only as required. Cato made a careful list of everything that should be needed and allowed. Cato's book, drawn in part from Italian tradition and in part from Greek and Phoenician sources, and the translation into Latin of the agricultural manuals of Mago of Carthage are evidences of the interest of wealthy landowners in the development of scientific and income-producing farming on their estates. Wine became one of Italy's most profitable exports. A six gallon jug sold in Gaul was equal to the price of a slave.

Slavery Slavery first became an important factor in Roman life through the period of conquests. The demand for labor on the great estates together with the presence of large numbers of prisoners of war combined to accelerate the development of slavery as an institution. Piracy in the Hellenistic world contributed to the number of slaves. Thracians and Illyrians were in great demand as herdsmen on the cattle ranches, and Greeks and Syrians, experienced in the culture of the olive and the vine, were eagerly sought for by owners of large vineyards. Many highly skilled slaves served as clerks, secretaries, or artisans in the city; others were employed in ever-growing numbers in the households of men of wealth. Slaves were by no means so numerous, however, as entirely to dispossess free labor, some of which was still used on the estates or employed in the city. Manumission, except on the great ranches, was easy and frequent, and the freedmen secured citizenship along with release from servile status. Still, the number of slaves was large and continued to increase.

The menace the great extension of slavery presented to the Roman state was evidenced by a serious outbreak in Sicily in 134–132 B.C. The slaves on the Roman and Greek estates of that island, terribly oppressed by their owners, found leaders in a Syrian named Eunus ("Well-wisher") and in a Cilician named Cleon who headed a revolt that rapidly spread over the whole island. After killing their owners and being joined by peasant farmers who rejoiced in the destruction of great estates, they successfully met detachments of the Roman army. The rebellious slaves endeavored to establish an independent kingdom of their own in Sicily with Eunus as "King Antiochus" and Cleon as his chief general. Vigorous action by the Roman consuls in person was required to suppress the revolt. After fearful engagements and wholesale executions of captives, the slave forces were subdued, order was restored, and the working of the great estates resumed. No effort was made to redress the grievances that had led to the outbreak, and the slave question remained a pressing and unsolved problem for the Roman senate.

The *Optimates* The senatorial group, *Optimates* ("Best men") as they came to be called, thus emerged from the war period as a group of aristocrats who derived their wealth from great estates which they managed for profit. Their chief occupation was with the offices and affairs of government, which they monopolized. The wars gave them opportunities for military glory and booty, and the provincial governorships provided openings for recouping or increasing their wealth at the expense of the provincials. Though the law forbade them to engage in business or to own a ship larger than a small yacht, many individuals who desired increased incomes circumvented the law by investments or loans through agents.

The glory and prestige that accrued to the *Optimates* made them more conscious than before of their position as a class, so they drew the lines more closely about themselves. Through control of the election machinery they made it impossible for any but men of extraordinary ability and tenacity like Cato to break into their class. At the same time, affected more than any other group in Rome by Greek culture, they began, despite the opposition of some conservatives, to ignore the traditions of their ancestors, to depart from ancient ideals and standards of simplicity, to live in luxury, and to seek intellectual attainments. Devotion to their own interests as individuals and as a class took the place of loyalty to the best interests of the state and they failed, as time passed, to manage successfully the affairs of Rome and the empire.

The *Equites* Commerce and industry remained relatively undeveloped in the city of Rome, partly because of the aversion, both traditional and sanctioned by law, of the ruling classes for those forms of occupation, and partly because of the competition of the highly developed Eastern centers. Not until the last century of the republic did Roman merchants dominate Mediterranean affairs. The requirements of war and of imperial management, however, led to the rapid expansion of a class of businessmen as contractors for the construction of roads, bridges, and public buildings, for the transportation of troops and supplies, and as managers of mines and state properties in the provinces. These men had a share in the collection of taxes, though their most celebrated activities in this sphere and in the exploitation of the provinces belongs to the succeeding period of the Roman revolution. The influx of mobile wealth which poured into Rome as booty or as tribute resulted in the appearance of bankers who invested it and who also lent money to needy senators or to provincial cities. For larger undertakings the businessmen formed "societies," partnerships comparable to joint-stock companies, in which senators secretly invested and even poorer men sometimes had shares. Those who engaged in the public or private phases of these business affairs were called *publicani* or *negotiatores*, respectively, although, since men of wealth doubtless acted in both capacities, these groups overlapped. The class as a whole was called *Equites*, knights, or horsemen, because they had sufficient wealth to qualify for the cavalry, though their actual occupations prevented them from taking any part in this military service. Since they did not hold office and had no social standing with the aristocracy, their only measure of success was money. Consequently they were distinctly imperialistic and increasingly inclined to be grasping and corrupt. The rival activities of the *Optimates* and the *Equites* in the provinces led eventually to controversies of vital importance to the Roman state.

The *Populares* While some of the expropriated peasant farmers remained in the country as hired laborers, many of them drifted into the city where, with returning veterans, they formed a landless and poverty-stricken proletariat. They were supported by such employment as they might find, assisted by the charity or the bribes of the wealthy, who expected applause and votes in return. Since landownership was still a prerequisite for military service, the census lists of eligible soldiers steadily declined as the restless and turbulent mob of the city increased to the detriment of civic and political life. This group, the *Populares*, which found its leaders in the liberal group in the senate, presented to the ruling class of the state problems — military, economic, and moral — that were the starting point of a revolutionary movement.

Political Changes The senate reached the acme of its powers in the strain and stress of conflict. The obvious need of wise and consistent direction in war and in the management of conquered lands led to silent acquiescence in a senatorial control that far transcended its legal powers. The senate assumed full control of military affairs, the assignment of commanders and provincial governors, dealings with foreign and allied states, and finance. At home it kept a watchful eye on manners and morals, and developed its right to establish extraordinary judicial commissions and, at times of crisis, to suspend constitutional guarantees of appeal by the *senatus consultum ultimum*, equivalent to a decree of martial law. The senate showed itself to best advantage in the Second Punic War, when the courage and tenacity of the ruling class saved Rome from collapse. In the following century, jealous of its prerogatives, torn by factions, and with its members greedy for money, the senate far too frequently displayed weaknesses in the management of the wars, even though success crowned its efforts in the end. Not only did it fail lamentably and completely in the control and direction of the provinces and even more disastrously in the handling of the complex problems presented by the Italian allies, the city mob, and the political corruption of Rome itself, but by its treatment of these questions it aggravated the existing evils.

At the same time the power of the magistrates declined, and the system of choosing them proved utterly inadequate. Admirably adapted to produce men trained in the traditions of command and rule and competent to deal with ordinary affairs, the system had no means of providing an extraordinary man for a crisis without striking a dangerous, even disastrous blow at the constitutional machinery. Regularly elected consuls like Flaminius, Varro, and Paullus failed completely against Hannibal. The time-honored institution of the dictatorship[5] was abandoned after the command of Fabius because it did not meet the needs of the situation. The use of experienced men in continued command as proconsuls, although helping to solve the immediate difficulties, proved to be the opening wedge that eventually destroyed the old governmental machine.

The first open step toward one-man rule was taken when Scipio, who had been given proconsular power in Spain before he was quaestor, was able to force from the senate permission to go to Africa. Under the pressure of circumstance the great man had become more powerful than the constitution. The senate realized its danger and fought vigorously to retain its strength. Charges of mismanagement of finances were brought against Scipio when he returned with his brother from the Asiatic War, and, though Scipio disdainfully tore up the accounts, he passed into eclipse. The events of the Greek wars further revealed the weaknesses of the machine. Offices that promised to be lucrative from spoils became the prize of political struggles between factions within the senate, with the result that incompetent men were often chosen. Consuls, elected in ordinary course, failed wretchedly against Philip V and against Perseus, while the brilliant proconsuls Flamininus and Aemilius Paullus succeeded. In the Third Punic War, likewise, the regular magistrates were incompetent, and Scipio Aemilianus, though only a candidate for the aedileship, was sent as proconsul against Carthage.

In response to this pressing need for better machinery to choose able men without unconstitutional action, the senate merely attempted to strengthen the constitutional tradition against the rise of individuals stronger than the state. The succession of offices (*cursus honorum*) — quaestorship, praetorship, and consulship with fixed age limits (twenty-eight for the quaestorship) and a two-year interval between successive magistracies — was established by law in 180 B.C. Yet in the election of Scipio Aemilianus in 146 B.C. this law was completely ignored.

Another problem that the senate failed to solve was the control of provincial governors. The promagistrates in the provinces held the

[5] The later dictatorships of Sulla and of Caesar were of different character.

imperium and though the senate made the assignments and might punish the governors on their return, they were virtually independent during their term of office. The consuls, eventually finding their power restricted to Italy, were likewise unable to check the overseas officials. Appointments were made on principles of favoritism or for political motives without regard to ability or to honesty. As a result, the mismanagement, graft, and corruption that followed from the attempts of the governors to pay off the expenses of their political career at Rome and to gain great wealth at the expense of the provincials became an open scandal. An attempt to correct the evil by the *Lex Calpurnia de repetundis* of 149 B.C., which provided a jury of fifty senators presided over by a praetor to try cases of extortion, was almost a complete failure. The expenses of prosecution at Rome were so great as to discourage provincial action, and convictions were hard to secure from a jury of men who had been, or hoped to be, governors in their turn. Furthermore, provincial graft had an unfortunate effect on Rome since the opportunities thus afforded for the attainment of great wealth increased the competition for offices and induced bribery and lavish expenditures on games to curry favor with the populace. Finally, the unrestricted power of promagistrates in command of great armies in the provinces proved, in the next period, to be a force greater than the constitution and eventually brought the republic to its end.

The grievances of the Latin and Italian allies were intensified when the senate cut in half their share of the booty after victory and gave conquered lands only to citizens, and also when individual magistrates demanded entertainment from Italian towns through which they passed. More and more the Italians approached the status of subjects. Efforts to deal with the problem of the proletariat by putting them back on the land were blocked to protect the vested interests of the ruling class. Senatorial power likewise prevented any attempt to secure reform by action of the assemblies. The popular movement led by Flaminius and Varro during the interval of the Punic wars attained a small success in the settling of citizens on lands in the Po Valley. It was their program also which secured the restrictions against senatorial entrance into business. To break down the influence of wealth in the centuriate assembly, they passed a law redividing the centuries among the tribes and providing for the choice by lot of a century to cast the first vote. Their movement collapsed, however, with the death of its leaders in the war, and for almost a century no strong leader of the popular element appeared. Tribunes who looked forward to a political career found it necessary to obey the wishes of the senatorial machine, and vetoes of colleagues were always available to stop any who might prove recalcitrant. Small attendance, bribery, and influence rendered worthless the reform of the centuriate assembly. As the farmers ceased to come to the city to vote, the tribal assembly degenerated even more than the centuriate into a venal city mob easily controlled by skilled politicians. Laws were passed to prevent bribery, and secret balloting was established, but to no avail. In spite of the presence of many honorable men who still clung to the ancient standards, Roman politics were unmistakably corrupt.

ROMAN CULTURE

The wealth derived from conquest began, during the period of the wars, to affect the city, the living standards of its inhabitants, and their intellectual, artistic, and religious interests. In the earlier period the Romans had possessed the foundations of a Roman culture. In literature they had begun the development of legal writings, of maxims, and of oratory. Rude verses of loose construction and ribald content were composed in the so-called Saturnian meter, and for drama they had the native Italian puppet show, the *fabula Atellana.* Unlovely death masks of great men took the place of portrait sculptures. Under Etruscan and, to a lesser extent, Greek influences they had erected temples and statues on Etruscan models. For example, the Scipio family at the time of the Samnite Wars possessed a tomb with an inscribed and decorated sarcophagus of Etruscan style. Roads and aqueducts, practical arts, were the great Roman contributions to architecture. But these modest beginnings were completely surpassed when Rome, conquering the Hellenistic world, fell under the spell of Greek culture.

The Hellenization of Rome

Graecia capta ferum victorem cepit. "Captive Greece took her barbarian conqueror captive." So wrote the poet Horace. The long years in Sicily during the First Punic War and the continued campaigns in the East during the second century acquainted Roman officers and soldiers with the beauties of Hellenistic art and literature, the amusements of the Greek theater, the intricacies of Greek philosophies, and the consolations of Hellenistic religions. Prisoners of war, bought as slaves, became secretaries to wealthy Romans or tutors to their sons. Greek doctors began to practice in the city, and rhetoricians and philosophers found it profitable to set themselves up as teachers. The ambassadors from the Greek cities were frequently learned men, and one of them, Carneades, the Skeptic, gave lectures while waiting for the senate to hear his cause. Among the thousand Achaean hostages (p. 423) were many scholars who became attached to noble families and planted the seeds of culture in Roman soil. The greatest of these was Polybius, the historian, friend and teacher of the younger Scipio.

Art and Architecture Empowered by wealth and enlightened by contact with Hellenistic culture, the Romans began to refurbish their

The Temple of Vesta near the Tiber, with Modern Rome in the Background. Here burned the "eternal flame" of the Romans. (Italian State Tourist Office)

physical and intellectual surroundings. Though temples were still erected of tufa or of concrete covered with stucco and adorned with terra-cotta ornaments and though most houses were still simple *atria*, at the same time basilicas (p. 537) were erected in the Forum, while a few nobles had pictures painted on the walls and added peristyles to their dwellings. A fine new aqueduct was built on arches to bring water to the city. Statues, brought from Greek cities, especially from Syracuse by Marcellus and from Corinth by Mummius, were placed in temples, and Roman gentlemen liked to possess galleries of Greek objects of art. Of creative work in this field by Romans there was little. Tapestries, rugs, silverware, fine gowns and jewelry were new luxuries and signs of Hellenistic influence. Laws were passed to outlaw luxury and forbid extravagance, and Cato as censor in 186 B.C. vainly tried to check these vices by vigorous action. From the old city a new and beautiful Rome was slowly rising.

Literature Roman literature passed rapidly under Greek influence from its crude beginnings to the time of its flowering. After the First Punic War, Livius Andronicus (fl. 220 B.C.), a Greek freedman, translated the *Odyssey* into Saturnian verse and wrote and produced in Latin plays taken from the Greek. At about the same time Naevius,

possibly a Campanian, made translations, wrote plays on Roman subjects, and composed an epic poem on the First Punic War. Plautus (*ca.*
254–184 B.C.) wrote comedies based on Menander's works but with a
broad Roman flavor. Terence (*ca.* 195–159 B.C.), his follower, adhered
more closely to the Greek originals. That the Roman populace had
little understanding or interest in the Greek theater is well illustrated
by the story of how an audience once made a chorus engage in mimic
battle on the stage. Ennius (239–169 B.C.), the greatest of the poets of
the time and friend of Scipio Africanus, composed a great epic, *Annals
of Rome*, and translated into Latin works of philosophy as well as plays.

History appeared when the Romans found it necessary to explain
themselves to the Greeks, and during the Second Punic War a number
of annalists, notably Fabius Pictor, wrote histories of Rome in Greek.
Cato, in addition to his treatise on farming (p. 426), composed the
first Latin history of Rome, *Origines*, for his son. These writings made the
Romans conscious of their own past and served in a later period as
sources for the great historian, Livy. The loss of all except a few fragments of these early historical works has made the task of reconstructing
early Roman history difficult for modern historians.

Philosophy   Philosophy, as well as literature, made its appeal to
the Roman mind. But what the Greek teachers who brought the thought
of the Hellenistic world to Rome chiefly accomplished was the under-
mining of the simple and narrow, though virile, Roman tradition.
Ancestral customs and ideas no longer satisfied the men of the new
age, introduced as they were suddenly to wealth, luxury, and freedom
of thought. One group endeavored to draw from Greek culture the
best there was in it: this was the famous Scipionic circle led by Scipio
Aemilianus and his friend Laelius, who were advised by Polybius.
They studied and discussed history and philosophy, invited Panaetius,
the Stoic, to Rome, and through their influence made Stoicism the
dominant Roman philosophy, aided, of course, by the fact that its
principles best coincided with the Roman traditions of valor and endurance. But many of the younger generation misinterpreted the teachings of the philosophers and with pseudointellectual nonchalance
claimed freedom from the restraint of ancient sanctions on the authority
of intellectualism.

A vigorous faction in the senate, however, fought against the Greek
influences as well as against the forces of corruption and the new luxury.
Cato, its leader, affected to despise all things Greek and wrote in Latin
for his son, though he made use of Greek sources in his *De Agricultura*.
In 173 B.C. two Epicureans were expelled, and in 161 B.C. all Greek
rhetoricians were dispatched from Rome. When Carneades in his lectures (p. 370) proved that justice was relative and not absolute, Cato
urged the senate to finish his business and send him back to Athens.

But the tide was irresistible, and soon all educated Romans were learning Greek. Even Cato did so, for business reasons.

Religion The effect of Greek influence on Roman religion was distinctly bad. Down to the end of the Italic Wars, Roman religion, in spite of accretions, had retained much of its simple spirituality. Thereafter Roman and Greek gods were identified with each other — Jupiter with Zeus and Juno with Hera, for example — and the whole gorgeous imagery of mythology was handed over to the literal-minded Romans. But instead of making the gods more human and appealing, these changes tended to destroy them. The Romans, failing to penetrate through the story to the experience behind it, lost confidence in gods who possessed human weaknesses. Greek philosophy removed the faith of the educated classes in the ancestral gods, and the Punic wars also wrought untold havoc in the old Roman religion when, in the crisis of the second war, it seemed as if the gods themselves had deserted the Romans. The people turned to such barbaric practices as human sacrifice, and finally on the advice of the Sibylline books, invited the Great Mother, Cybele, to Rome. The conservative senate, shocked by the orgies of her religion, forbade any Roman to become her priest; nevertheless many people found solace in her emotional worship. In southern Italy, in Sicily, and in the East, Roman soldiers became aware of other emotional cults. Among the western Greeks the secret bands of Orphist worshipers of Dionysus had always been strong. The Romans called the god Bacchus, his festivals, Bacchanalia. So strong did this hidden and emotional cult become that the senate ordered an investigation in 186 B.C. and suppressed the society, though individuals who felt themselves bound by religious scruples to worship the god were, with special permission, allowed to do so. It proved as impossible, however, to stop the coming of Eastern religions to Rome as it was to halt the advance of Greek education. Rome was becoming a cosmopolitan city.

Games The wealth acquired by conquest and the changes in the character of religion revealed themselves in the amusements of the people. Many festivals and games provided the city populace with relaxation from the toils of life. Originally there had been frequent festivals connected with the religious life of early Rome, but with the growth of the city many of these were abandoned. The most beloved, however, was kept, the feast of Saturnalia on December 17, when all the people, freeman and slave, exchanged gifts and made merry together. Games, *ludi*, took the place of festivals that had lost their meaning. At these functions, which were public and therefore free to the populace, processions were held, followed by chariot races in the Circus, and by exhibitions and hunts of wild animals. The aediles were in charge of the games, and those who hoped for political preferment spent much more money on them than the state granted; in fact in the later republic young men went heavily into debt to please the people. Gladiatorial combats were introduced from Etruria in 264 B.C. The gladiators were usually slaves, trained in special schools and offered for hire. For a long period they were exhibited at funeral games held in honor of great men and at the expense of the family. Until the close of the republic they were exhibited almost exclusively by private persons, but in the imperial period the combats became great public spectacles. In addition to the games of this sort there were many dramatic presentations which, apparently, were never very popular with the mob (p. 434).

Conclusion   Rome gained an empire, but the institutions and character by which, as Polybius said, it rose to power failed to meet the tests imposed by victory. Senatorial failure to produce and to control competent leaders in times of crisis and to develop an intelligent, well-directed system of provincial administration made possible, even essential, the rise of men with power superior to the constitution. The acquisition of great wealth by the senators and the growth of a capitalistic class of businessmen resulted in the decline of the Roman traditions of simplicity and even of honesty. Hellenistic ideas, poorly comprehended, destroyed the spiritual and social bases upon which the traditions rested. The populace was slowly degenerating from a class of independent farmers into a city proletariat, poverty-stricken and, at least in part, venal in politics.

The failure of Rome's leaders in the senate to rise to the occasion, remodel the government, and correct the social and economic evils resulted in a century of revolution which ended with the fall of the senate and the rise of one-man power, Caesarism. As Scipio Aemilianus stood on the hill overlooking burning Carthage, he turned to his friend and recited the words of Hector: "The day shall come when this our sacred Troy shall fall, and Ilium, and Priam's towering citadel." Troy had fallen; Carthage was falling; the symptoms of decay that he had observed convinced him that Rome also would fall in the cycle of time; and as censor he prayed to the gods to preserve rather than to increase the state.

20 · The Roman Revolution

THE ROMAN REVOLUTION WAS AN EPOCH-MAKING
series of events which transformed the Roman Republic into
an empire ruled by the Caesars. It was caused by the failure of
the ruling class to solve the economic and social problems that
had developed with the conquests, or to adapt or expand the constitutional machinery of the city-state to meet the needs of empire.

THE DEMOCRATIC REFORMERS, 133–88 B.C.

The problems Rome faced at the end of the period of expansion
were varied and difficult enough to daunt the most intelligent and sincere leaders of the state. Rome and Italy suffered from the general inflation affecting the entire Mediterranean world during the Hellenistic
period, but certain distinct problems were specific to Rome. The equestrian order of businessmen, growing rapidly in numbers and in wealth,
was already causing difficulties for the senatorial governors in the
provinces. Jealous of the political and social prerogatives of the aristocracy in Rome, this class was eager to share in directing the destinies
of empire to its own profit. The debts youthful aspirants for political
power owed in increasing amounts to the moneylenders contributed
to the friction. Rivalry between the classes runs as a continuous thread
throughout the century of revolution. The decline in the number of
small farmers threatened not only the economic health of Italy, but
also the recruiting strength of the Roman army. The growth of an urban
proletariat for whom gainful occupation was not available presented
great political and social questions pressing for an answer. To these was
added the difficult task of absorbing into peaceful pursuits the veterans
returning from the wars. Unemployment rose steadily. The spasmodic
slave revolts indicated new dangers resulting from the growth of great
estates and offered new problems to the leaders of Rome. The Italian
allies were demanding a fuller share of the benefits of empire, which

437

their arms had helped to win, and their insistent requests for citizenship could not long be resisted without disaster.

Imperial control, repression of piracy, which had flourished after the fall of Rhodes, proper regulation of provincial governors, the suppression of graft and plundering in the provinces, and the need for a good method of selecting able men to meet difficult situations without recourse to unconstitutional procedure were all essential for the political and economic well-being of the empire and of Rome itself.

The revolution began with the attempt of a young reformer to secure agrarian reform against the opposition of the vested interests. It witnessed bitter struggles for control between the classes, a series of economic crises, rioting in the city streets and threatened revolts, the formation of professional armies ready to follow their leaders even against the state, and the rise of great personalities who proved stronger than the constitution. In the end it became a contest not to determine whether the senate or the great man should rule, but to decide which of the leaders should succeed. Since the personalities and programs of individuals were the decisive factors in the events, even though problems of economic and imperial significance were the fundamental circumstances that made their activities possible, the political history of the period is largely biographical.

The Gracchan Reforms

Tiberius Gracchus   Tiberius Sempronius Gracchus, a young man of illustrious but Plebeian family, was elected tribune for 133 B.C. The safe future of a Roman aristocrat lay before him; his father had gained renown as consul and proconsul; his mother was the patrician Cornelia, daughter of the great Scipio; his wife was the daughter of Appius Claudius.[1] He had been brought up in the Scipionic circle, educated by the best Greek teachers of the day, and had served creditably as quaestor in Spain. With youthful confidence he undertook to carry through a vital reform.

The Public Land   The solution Gracchus proposed for the economic problems of Rome was a distribution of state lands to the city proletariat (p. 429). For this he had ample precedent in Greek experience and in Roman tradition. The program of Agis and Cleomenes in Sparta was doubtless well known to him through his Stoic teachers. The Roman tradition of homestead distribution dated back to the conquest of Italy, when considerable portions of confiscated lands were distributed to Roman farmers (p. 402). The Licinian-Sextian Laws of 367 B.C. were an attempt to regulate this distribution and prevent the ruling class from securing too large a share, but since the enforcement

---

[1] Descendant of the famous censor.

of these laws depended upon the plutocratic officials who benefited by their violation, they speedily became dead letters and the greater portion of the state-owned lands in Italy became the virtual possessions of the senatorial class.

Flaminius, as tribune in 232 B.C., revived the older policy and distributed lands in the Po Valley among the citizens, but after his death at Lake Trasimeno his program was abandoned. The alarming decline in the number of small farmers revealed by the census lists of the second century B.C. caused much discussion because of its military significance, and the Scipionic circle agreed among themselves that the proper remedy for this decline was renewed distribution of land. Laelius, in 145 B.C., went so far as to draft a bill to that end, but withdrew it because of opposition.

The Gracchan Land Law   Tiberius Gracchus returned to the program of Laelius. He drew up a bill that provided for the reenactment of the Licinian Law limiting the holding of public land by any individual to five hundred *jugera*,[2] with two hundred and fifty more for each of two sons, for the repossession by the state of such lands as were held in violation thereof, and for the distribution of these lands to needy citizens in small lots, inalienable and subject to a quitrent. Three commissioners were to carry out the examination of land titles and the distribution of land. The bill aroused a storm of opposition. Title deeds had been lost; lands had changed hands; and determination of ownership was exceedingly difficult. Senators who saw their cherished estates threatened claimed that the bill would rob them. Accordingly they persuaded the tribune Octavius to veto the bill. Tiberius, however, was convinced that his proposed reform was vital to the well-being of Rome, and he therefore persuaded the tribal assembly to take the unprecedented step of removing Octavius from office as a betrayer of the popular will. The bill was then passed.

The commission, composed of Tiberius, his brother Gaius, and his father-in-law, Appius Claudius, went directly to work. Tiberius challenged senatorial control over public finance when he proposed to use the money from the recently acquired treasury of Attalus III of Pergamum to equip the restored farms. In order to carry this measure through the assembly and to protect himself and his cherished reforms from senatorial enemies, he determined to make a further break with custom by offering himself for re-election. When the consul refused to take action to stop him, a group of senators attended by armed slaves and clients descended upon the Forum. In the ensuing riot Tiberius and some three hundred of his followers were killed. Others of his supporters were punished by a senatorial investigating commission.

---

[2] A *jugerum* was approximately three-fifths of an acre.

The Years of Reaction   The following years were filled with strife between the senate and the popular party, which now had a program and a martyred leader. The land law remained in force for a brief period; the committee proceeded to work, reclaimed much land and made many allotments, as is shown by a decided increase in the census lists. To senatorial opposition, however, were added the complaints of wealthy Italians whose lands had been taken by the commissioners. Scipio Aemilianus, returning from Numantia, espoused the conservative side and secured the passage of a law depriving the three commissioners of their judicial powers, thus putting an end to their activities. The popular party, on the other hand, secured recognition of the right of re-election to the tribunate.

Gaius Gracchus   In 123 B.C. Gaius Gracchus, younger brother of Tiberius, a polished and forceful orator, entered upon the tribunate. He was re-elected for the following year. In these two years he presented an extensive and carefully thought-out program by means of which, he hoped, the political and economic ills of Rome would be corrected. He proposed: (1) to center the civil administration in the tribunate, somewhat in the manner in which that of Athens had been centralized in the office of general in the days of Pericles; (2) to break the political power of the senatorial machine, at the same time punishing the murderers of his brother; (3) to put in its place an effective combination of business and popular interests strengthened by admission of the Italians to citizenship; and (4) to provide economic opportunities for the poor of the city.

As tribune, Gaius presented a series of measures to the tribal assembly and took upon himself direction of their administration. These measures prohibited extraordinary courts, the putting of Roman citizens to death without trial, and denial of the right of appeal. The senate was ordered to assign provinces to the consuls before their election, thus losing its most effective means of control over those magistrates. Political power was given to the business leaders by a law providing that juries were henceforth to be drawn from businessmen of wealth who were listed as *equites*, or knights. This move not only gave political recognition to this new group, but also provided an effective means of checking senatorial aggrandizement. The knights were further pleased by an act that changed the taxes of Asia from a fixed sum to a percentage basis and which, by allowing the contract for collection to be paid in a lump sum at Rome, gave them a monopoly of this lucrative business. Gaius provided that grain received in payment of taxes be sold to the poor at a very low price. This was in accord with Greek precedent and had the further merits of binding the city proletariat firmly to him and of relieving the poor from the economic dependence upon the rich which was in part the basis of senatorial control. He worked steadfastly, however, to remove the necessity for this dole. A public works and road building program was inaugurated; Tiberius' land law was re-enacted, and many of the poor were placed on farms. A *Lex Militaris* (military law) required the government to arm and clothe soldiers without deduction from their pay. In addition Gaius proposed to locate commercial colonies at Tarentum and near Crotone in Italy and on the site of Carthage in Africa, where citizens who could not benefit from other measures could make a fresh start.

Finally, the Latins were to be given full citizenship and the Italian allies, Latin rights. The last two measures, indispensable for the success of his program, cost Gaius his hold on the city mob, which did not wish to share with the Italians their cherished rights as Romans. While Gaius was in Africa superintending the planting of the colony Junonia at Carthage, the senate, having induced another tribune, Drusus, to bid against him by proposing twelve colonies of the older type, gained control over the populace; the businessmen, alarmed by the prospective competition of commercial colonies deserted Gaius; and in the elections for 121 B.C. he failed to be reelected. When attacks against the Gracchan laws increased, Gaius endeavored to defend them. The senate however decreed martial law; a riot ensued; and Gaius in despair committed suicide in order to avoid capture by his enemies.

Results of the Gracchan Program   Estimates of the value of the Gracchi and their program have varied since their time, chiefly in accord with the political and economic sympathies of the observer. They have been lauded as heroes and martyrs who would have saved Rome; they have been condemned as revolutionaries, destroyers of the Roman constitution, who debauched the people by a dole. Tiberius certainly broke with Roman tradition when he deposed Octavius and ran for re-election. On the other hand, the will of the people was law and technically, therefore, his acts were not unconstitutional. In this connection it might be noted that in the death of each brother the conservatives violated the law by provoking violence.

The Continuing Struggle

No answer can be given to the question of whether the agrarian program was feasible or advisable. It was not given a fair chance. Within ten years after the death of Gaius, division had ceased, the lots had been declared private property, and the land was reverting to the possession of the wealthy. That the knights, following senatorial precedents, abused their power in the courts and in Asia to enrich themselves was not a fault of the law. It is significant that the rest of the Gracchan program was carried out substantially, most of it by Caesar and Augustus, both of whom used the tribunician power as the basis of their civil administration. For the time, however, the reform movement was stopped by the death of Gaius. But the knights had tasted political power and were more than ever a force to be reckoned with. The popular party also had a program and two martyrs to venerate. The senate, though seemingly victorious, was both weakened and alarmed. The revolution advanced as a three-cornered struggle broke out between the senators, the knights, and the followers of the Gracchi.

The War with Jugurtha   The coalition between the senatorial and equestrian classes which had finally caused the downfall of Gauis Gracchus lasted but ten years. It was broken by the failure of the senate to regulate the affairs of Africa.

The throne of Numidia had come by intrigue and assassination into the hands of an able but unscrupulous prince, Jugurtha. The destruction of the town of Cirta, an incident in the rise of Jugurtha, led to the death of many Roman and Italian merchants. Senatorial incompetence and corruption were responsible for the disaster. Second-rate men sent to deal with Jugurtha were defeated or bribed, and when the senate in 109 B.C. finally sent to Africa an able and honorable commander, Metellus, it had already lost the confidence and support of the business element.

This class found a leader in a new man on whom they and the popular party united, Gaius Marius, a lieutenant in Metellus' army. Marius, a native of Arpinum, belonged to a plebeian family. He had demonstrated his ability in warfare and in finance and had risen to the rank of praetor. His marriage with Julia of the family of the Caesars had gained for him a measure of recognition among the aristocrats. Nevertheless he was regarded by the *nobiles* (families, one of whose members had attained the consulship) with disdain as a "new man"; and his request for support for the consulship was abruptly refused by his patron and commander, Metellus, with whom he was serving as lieutenant in Numidia.

Marius therefore broke with Metellus and with the support of the knights and the democrats was elected consul for 107 B.C. Furthermore, by action of the tribal assembly and in defiance of the senate he was appointed to supersede Metellus. He was successful in bringing the African war to a brilliant end. His lieutenant, Sulla, captured Jugurtha through treachery, and in 104 B.C. Marius returned in triumph to Rome.

The Germans   While Marius had been gaining victory and glory in Africa, another crisis in the affairs of empire had arisen with which the senatorial leaders had proved incompetent to cope. Southern Gaul had been made into a Roman province in 121 B.C.; a Roman colony was established at Narbo in 118 B.C., and a military road was constructed from Italy to Spain. Hardly had this been accomplished when the Gallic province was seriously threatened by the appearance of Germanic tribes —the Cimbri, Teutones, and related groups—on the Roman frontier.

After a series of minor defeats the Roman army suffered a great catastrophe at Arausio (Orange) in 105 B.C. The way to Italy lay open, and Rome, with visions of a second sack, was in a panic. Marius, the hero of the hour, was available, and in defiance of all precedent he was elected consul successively for 104, 103, 102, and 101 B.C. Fortunately for him and for Rome the Germans turned aside to plunder Gaul and Spain.

The Army of Marius These years under the consulship of Marius reveal not only a marked step toward one-man rule in the reliance of the state upon a military hero, but also the creation of the machine by which future leaders were to rise to power. Marius established a professional army by enrolling volunteers for a term of sixteen years without regard to property qualification, drawing many from the proletariat of the city. He put his recruits through a rigorous regime of military training, thus securing an efficiency impossible with the annual levies of citizen soldiers of former years. The former distinction among the three lines of the army, based on military experience, was thereby destroyed, enabling Marius to replace the maniple as the unit of tactical maneuver by a larger body, the cohort, which corresponded in size and use to the battalion of a modern army.

The legion contained six thousand men divided into ten cohorts. *Esprit de corps* was achieved by giving each legion a silver eagle as its standard. This became the idol of the soldiers and the center of legionary tradition. The political danger of this professional soldiery arose from the fact that the loyalty of the men was given not to the state but to their commander, to whom they looked for rewards in fighting and for lands and pensions at the end of their term of service. Marius had three years in which to organize, equip, and drill his army. In 102 B.C. he defeated the Teutones at Aquae Sextiae in Gaul, and in 101 B.C. he annihilated the Cimbri at Vercellae in northern Italy. Again he returned to Rome in triumph to be hailed as the saviour of the city and the third founder of Rome.[3]

While Marius had been winning victories, the state had been involved in a second slave revolt in Sicily (105–101 B.C.) and in piratical raids in the Mediterranean. After a number of small outbreaks among slaves in southern Italy had served to remind the senate of the dangers of plantation slavery, the slaves in Sicily again rose against their masters. As before, a slave, Sabius, was chosen king with the name Tryphon, and efforts were made to conquer and organize the land. Again, also, vigorous efforts and ruthless executions were necessary to restore peace and order. The eastern pirates, too, were suppressed, but only for the moment. Neither of these affairs brought glory to the senate or renown to any leader who might rival Marius.

---

[3] Romulus was the first and Camillus the second.

Marius the Reformer Marius now felt called upon to become a democratic leader and to solve the political problems of Rome, as he had dealt with its imperial difficulties. He formed an alliance with Saturninus and Glaucia, the leaders of the popular party, and, as a democratic reformer, he was elected consul for the sixth time for the year 100 B.C. The program upon which he and his allies embarked was based on that of Gaius Gracchus. But as a politician, Marius proved a complete failure. He lost the support of his equestrian followers, and when disorder arose out of the elections for the year 99 B.C. Marius was maneuvered by the senate into enforcing martial law (*senatus consultum ultimum*). In the ensuing difficulties his own supporters, who were popular leaders, were killed, and Marius, disappointed and discredited, went out of office.

Rutilius Rufus For a brief period after Marius' defeat the senatorial and equestrian combination dominated Roman politics. But the equestrian control of the juries made this an unnatural alliance, and a scandalous episode of 93 B.C. was to shake it. A Roman noble, Rutilius Rufus, a Stoic renowned for his probity and honor, had served as lieutenant of Scaevola, proconsul in Asia for the year 98 B.C. There he had sternly repressed the illegal exactions of Roman businessmen. Accordingly they attacked him in Rome and in 93 B.C. he was brought to trial on the charge of extortions. In defiance of all the evidence, an equestrian jury convicted him. He retired into exile, spending the rest of his life in the province he was said to have despoiled. The scandal of his conviction made clear to thoughtful men the dangers of the situation in Rome.

Livius Drusus From the ranks of the senators arose a new reformer to correct conditions. Livius Drusus, probably the son of the opponent of Gaius Gracchus, elected tribune for the year 91 B.C., set forth a program that had the support of a portion of the senate. Three hundred leading knights were to be enrolled in the senate, and from this enlarged body the juries were to be chosen. To please the people, he added a grain dole and colonial settlements to his program. When an opportunity arose, he submitted a proposition for the enfranchisement of the Italians, which he had apparently promised to accomplish. At this the opposition became vehement. Drusus, accused of being involved in an Italian secret society in defiance of the law, lost support on every hand and was finally murdered by an unknown assassin. With Drusus' death perished the last attempt that had any real hope of succeeding in the reformation of the Roman constitution by legal and peaceful means. Future reforms were destined to come from military leaders supported by armed force.

The Social War, 90–88 B.C. The Social War followed immediately on the death of Drusus. A large group of the Italian allies (*socii*), disappointed in their hope of enfranchisement, determined upon a struggle for independence. They revolted and formed a new state, Italia, with two consuls, twelve praetors and a senate of five hundred. Their armies, composed of veterans of Roman wars, were generally successful in a bloody war against Rome. The senate, yielding to superior force and impelled by a critical situation in the East, gave citizenship by the *Lex Julia* of 90 B.C. to all Italians who had not revolted, and by the *Lex Plautia Papiria* of the following year conferred it on all who would register with a Roman praetor within sixty days. A third law, introduced by the consul Pompeius, extended citizenship to all Italians south of the Po River and gave Latin rights to those north of the river. Their end achieved, most of the Italians yielded. To their great chagrin, however, instead of being distributed among the thirty-five tribes where their numbers would make their influence strong, they were enrolled together in eight new tribes with little resultant political power.

THE CIVIL WARS

The Rise of Sulla   The year 88 B.C. saw the senate in full control with Sulla as consul. He had shown his ability as lieutenent of Marius and as commander in the Social War, and his loyalty to the senate was unquestioned. Senatorial leadership, however, did not remain long unchallenged. There was a crisis that same year in the East when Mithradates, king of Pontus, invaded Asia, gained control of the Aegean Sea and of Athens, and then ordered the massacre of all Romans resident in Asia. The senate quickly assigned Sulla to deal with him.

The loss of men, property, and revenues produced a panic on the Roman market; interest rates rose and many senators found themselves in difficulties. To protect them, a praetor revived an obsolete law against usury. He was thereupon murdered, but the proposal completed the breach between the senators and capitalists, which had begun with the trial of Rufus. The knights now thoroughly aroused, turned for a leader to their hero of former days, Marius, who, at his own request, was to be chosen to displace Sulla in the Mithradatic command.

The popular leaders at the same time were disappointed by the citizenship provisions made for the Italians, which broke down their hopes of new voting power for their party. The tribune Sulpicius combined the two interests (popular and equestrian) by proposing to distribute the Italians among the thirty-five older tribes and to supersede Sulla with Marius as general in the war. When word came to Sulla of his deposition after he had already started from Rome, he wheeled his army about and marched upon the city to deal with his opponents. Marius escaped, but Sulpicius and many of the leading knights were killed. After introducing a few measures designed to place the senate again in full control, Sulla left for the East. Military power had been used for the first time by a leader of the conservative forces to settle political problems in Rome.

The First Mithradatic War, 88–85 B.C.   Sulla invaded Greece in the spring of 87 B.C. After a bitter siege he took Athens in 86 and defeated the forces of Mithradates in two battles at Chaeronea and at Orchomenus. After his quaestor Lucullus had cleared the seas, Sulla invaded Asia where another Roman army had won victories in northern Anatolia. Anxious to return to Rome, he failed to follow his victories to their logical conclusion and made peace with Mithradates. The king surrendered his conquests, paid a small indemnity, and retired to his kingdom. The cities of Asia which had aided him suffered the penalty of an enormous indemnity, which brought great profit to Roman capitalists who lent them the money with which to pay it. Greece, devastated and despoiled, suffered long from the effects of the war.

The First Civil War   Meanwhile the democratic forces had regained control of Rome. Cinna, a popular leader, was elected consul for 87 B.C. and met opposition by calling upon Marius for aid. The aged general raised an army, seized the city, put his leading enemies to death, and was elected consul for the seventh time. Hardly had he assumed the office in 86 B.C. when he died. The following years were consumed with useless bickering among Cinna, Carbo, and the younger Marius. The only real achievement of these leaders was the completion of the political unification of Italy by the final enrollment of the Italians in the thirty-five tribes. Plans to deal with Sulla in the East failed, and the senatorial champion returned in 83 B.C. to begin the First Civil War. He won a series of victories in Italy, culminating in a fierce battle at the Colline Gate in Rome. His victory was followed by a terrible proscription. Lists of names were posted to indicate that their bearers might be killed without judicial action and their property confiscated. Not only were equestrian and popular leaders marked out for murder but many names were added to please Sulla's friends. Nearly five thousand persons were murdered; their property was confiscated and sold at public auction; and their descendants were disenfranchised. Those Italians who had sided with Cinna and Marius saw their lands taken from them and given as rewards to Sulla's veterans, who were thus provided for by a return to the land.

Sulla, victorious and all-powerful, turned to problems of state. He secured his own election for an unlimited time as *dictator legibus scribundis et rei publicae constituendae* (dictator for writing the laws and establishing the republic) with full power over the constitution. This office found its precedent in the powers of the decemvirs of 451–449 B.C. rather than in the ancient military dictatorship. Sulla's constitutional reforms were calculated to establish the senate in full control. The consul's power was limited to Italy; the praetors were increased to eight and given charge of a number of permanent courts to deal with extortion, bribery, treason, murder, and similar offenses, with juries composed entirely of senators; the number of quaestors was increased to twenty. Definite age limits were established for each grade in the *cursus honorum* (the succession of offices) and re-election was forbidden within a ten-year period. Most important of all, the tribunate was rendered negligible by forbidding those who had been tribunes to run for any other office and by re-establishing the senatorial veto over legislation. The proconsuls and propraetors received their provinces from the senate with power strictly limited to the province. If they crossed its bounds without consent of the senate, they lost their power of military command and might be declared public enemies. The senate, increased to six hundred by Sulla's enrollment of prominent *equites*, was in full control of imperial administration. Sulla then resigned his office in 79 B.C. and retired to Campania, where he died the following year. The senate was thus given its last chance at control, but its own weaknesses and the forces of history were against it. The succeeding years were filled with struggles, on the outcome of which depended not the power of the senate but the choice of the leader who would succeed Sulla as dictator of Rome.

The Rise of Pompey A new set of leaders arose after Sulla's time. The center of the stage was occupied by men like Pompey, Crassus, Cicero, Cato, Caesar, and Catiline. The most pre-eminent of these men, the "first man" in Rome, from the death of Sulla to the battle of Pharsalus, was Pompey. Yet beneath the surface the struggle of the classes continued. The problems produced by debt and poverty, the agrarian situation, unemployment and the urban proletariat, the retired veterans, the mistreated slaves, and provincial control still remained unsolved.

Pompey had already made his appearance as an able lieutenant of Sulla. Though vain and pompous, he was a military leader of great ability and a gentleman of honor, and had won the youthful admiration of Cicero and Caesar. History has dealt harshly with him because he failed. Pompey as a youth had entered the First Civil War as a supporter of Sulla with an army of his own which he had raised. Though he had not held public office, he was sent as propraetor to Sicily and Africa, where he crushed remnants of the Marian party. For this success he demanded a triumph and the title Magnus, "the Great," both of which were accorded him by Sulla.

Sertorius Shortly after the death of Sulla, Pompey was sent to Spain, this time as proconsul, though he was not yet old enough to be consul according to the law. Sertorius, Marian governor of Spain, had established himself as ruler there. Regarding himself as a true Roman, acting in the best interests of his country and the equestrian order against the power of the senate and the Sullan faction, he gathered around him the followers of Marius, organized a senate, and ruled the Spaniards so tactfully and well that they followed him willingly. He seems to have intended the formation of a state in Spain independent of the senate, from which he might return to Rome to establish a democratic rule over an empire in which Romans and provincials would share in a common rule and a common culture. Sertorius defeated Roman armies sent against him and withstood the forces of Pompey for several years (78–71 B.C.). At length his Spanish allies weakened and many of his Roman supporters, by their mistreatment of the Spaniards, proved a detriment rather than an aid. Finally he was assassinated by one of his lieutenants, and Pompey victoriously regained Spain for Rome.

Spartacus Meanwhile a slave revolt in Italy had given Crassus, the financier, an opportunity to appear as a rival to the pre-eminence of Pompey. The rebellion revealed a new danger in Italy in the presence of slaves trained to fight as gladiators in addition to the permanent menace of the servile groups on the great estates. In 73 B.C. Spartacus, a Thracian gladiator, led a band of his fellows in a search for freedom. When they had fortified themselves on the slopes of Vesuvius, large bands of runaway slaves joined them. Spartacus had planned to lead his followers beyond the Alps with the hope that they might return to their original homes in freedom. His followers preferred, however, the plunder of Italy and refused to follow him. After two consular armies were defeated by Spartacus in 72 B.C. Crassus, given the task of defeating the rebel leaders, succeeded in defeating and killing Spartacus the following year. Though Crassus was the victor, Pompey, returning from Spain, reached Italy in time to kill five thousand slaves and to claim a share in the success.

Crassus Crassus proved his real ability by his handling of the Spartacan trouble. Like Pompey, he had been a lieutenant of Sulla. He had reaped his reward during the proscription, when he had bought up large quantities of confiscated property for very low prices and had thus accumulated a huge fortune. Plutarch recounts other tales that show Crassus' reputation for financial greediness. There was no public force to fight fires in Rome, and when they broke out, Crassus was able to buy the burning and surrounding properties at ridiculously low prices, whereupon a private fire department of slaves owned and trained by him speedily extinguished the conflagrations. One cannot help wondering how many fires were started by his agents.

Pompey and Crassus as Consuls Rivals under Sulla, Pompey and Crassus found themselves face to face in 71 B.C. Both demanded triumphs for their campaigns as well as consulships for 70 B.C. The senate rejected both. Thereupon they united, overawed the opposition with the threat of military force, and secured the election. As consuls they restored the tribunician power, by repealing Sulla's law, and reorganized the juries, which were henceforth to be drawn one-third from the senate, one-third from the knights, and one-third from a lower class of businessmen, known as *tribuni aerarii.*

Cicero and Verres   The year 70 B.C. saw the rise of the third new leader, Cicero. Son of a knight of Arpinum, educated in Rome and in Athens, he had already shown courage and ability in the defense of Roscius during the Sullan regime. He had been honest and successful as quaestor in Sicily in 75 B.C., and the Sicilians gave him his great opportunity when they engaged him to prosecute Verres, propraetor of the island in 73–71 B.C., who had been shamelessly corrupt in his handling of Sicilian affairs. Verres was a member of the inner circle and with the leading Roman orator Hortensius, to speak for him, he had no doubt of the outcome. Cicero, however, gathered evidence with unusual speed, and it was so overwhelming that Verres retired into exile before he was condemned. Cicero afterward published his undelivered *Orations against Gaius Verres*, a complete exposé of the methods and materials of provincial corruption. His success brought him prominence in Rome and he was elected praetor for the year 66 B.C.

Caesar   Caesar, who had made himself notorious as an exquisite in dress and a roué in conduct, made his entrance on the political stage in 69 B.C. at the funeral of his aunt Julia, widow of Marius, with an address in which he proclaimed his championship of the Marian cause, of the disenfranchised, and of the popular party. There are earlier stories of his defiance of Sulla and of his defeat of the pirates in the East, but in 69 B.C. he gave little evidence of his ability, no foreshadowing of the power that was subsequently his.

The Pirates   The inability of the Sullan political machine to deal with emergencies, which had been made apparent by the appointments of Crassus and Pompey, showed itself again in the case of the pirates. For centuries the naval powers in the Aegean had kept piracy under control. With the collapse of Rhodes this protection for sea-borne merchandise had ceased. The Romans failed to comprehend the necessity for permanent policing, and so allowed the fleets that had served in the Punic and Greek wars to decay.

The piratical residents of Cilicia and Crete were quick to take advantage of their opportunity. Temporarily suppressed in 104–102 B.C., they returned as soon as the Roman fleet was withdrawn. They raided Italy, even entering the mouth of the Tiber and stopping the grain fleets that carried supplies to Rome. When the regular officials failed to deal with them, it became apparent that an extraordinary command was necessary. Pompey was clearly indicated for the task, but the senate, ostensibly out of respect for the constitution but jealous of Pompey, refused to act.

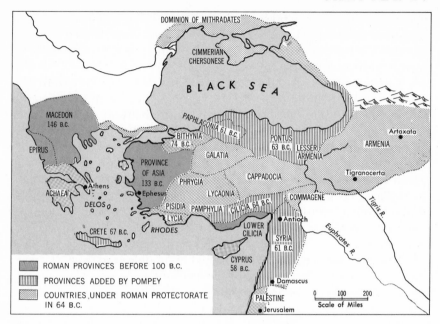

Rome in the East, 146–58 B.C.

Again a combination of *Equites* and *Populares* took the initiative, depriving the senate therewith of its traditional right to imperial administration. The tribune Gabinius in 67 B.C. proposed and carried a law in the tribal assembly to create an extraordinary command, the holder of which would control the entire Mediterranean and a strip of territory fifty miles wide around it in Roman provinces for three years, with authority to appoint his lieutenants and to enlist an army and a naval force.

Pompey was the man, and his appointment, forced upon the senate, resulted in an immediate drop in the price of grain. Within three months he had accomplished the task with brilliant success. The pirates were completely crushed, and many of them were settled as farmers on abandoned lands in the provinces.

The Second Mithradatic War, 74–63 B.C.   A second need for Pompey's services immediately arose in the East. Mithradates had renewed the war with Rome when Nicomedes III of Bithynia had willed his kingdom to Rome in 75 B.C. In this war Rome was well served by the proconsul Lucullus, a member of the senatorial group. He defeated Mithradates, drove him out of his realm, invaded Armenia, and took its capital, Tigranocerta. Lucullus, however, offended the business element by interfering with their exorbitant interest charges and offended his army by preventing excesses of plunder. While his soldiers mutinied in

Armenia and he was forced to retire, his enemies attacked him bitterly in Rome. At this crisis Manilius, tribune in 66 B.C., proposed to add to Pompey's power the command of Bithynia and Cilicia and of the war against Mithridates. The senate opposed it. Cicero, praetor for that year, needing powerful support for the consulship and motivated by an unbounded admiration for Pompey, supported the bill with a panegyric on Pompey, *On the Command of Gnaeus Pompey*. The bill was passed, and the great general again showed his ability: he reduced Pontus to a province in 64 B.C. and made Armenia a client kingdom; turning south he entered Syria, brought the dynasty of the Seleucids to an end, and made Syria a province to which he added Judaea after the capture of Jerusalem (63 B.C.). Setting the affairs of the East in order in regal fashion, he prepared to return to Rome in 62 B.C., a conquering hero, the most powerful citizen of the state—at least in his own estimation. A rude awakening was prepared for him.

Cicero's Consulship Throughout the years of Pompey's wars in the East, the political pot of Rome had been kept boiling by the attempts of leaders to place themselves in impregnable positions before Pompey's return. Caesar, serving as aedile in 65 B.C., and backed financially by Crassus, made an extravagant display in the games and brought to public view the trophies and statues of Marius in an effort to curry favor with the mob and to make his own position clear. He and Crassus found a ready tool in a ruined aristocrat Catiline, whom they backed for the consulship for 63 B.C. against Antonius and Cicero. This backing forced the senate to throw its support to the "new man," and Cicero was elected with Antonius as his colleague.

Thus defeated, Caesar and Crassus turned to other measures. A will, no doubt forged, had given Egypt to Rome. The senate had refused to recognize it and had allowed Ptolemy Auletes, "the Flute Player," to assume the throne. Crassus, as censor in 65 B.C., had suggested the annexation of Egypt but had been blocked. In 63 B.C. a tribune, Rullus, proposed an agrarian bill to give extraordinary power—military, legal, and financial—to a commission of ten to confiscate or purchase lands for distribution among the people, the funds for the project to be secured by a sale of public property throughout the empire. This bill would have made possible the conquest of Egypt as a state possession, and Caesar and Crassus, if appointed commissioners, would have been strongly entrenched as rivals to Pompey. Cicero, however, attacked the bill so vigorously that it was never brought to a vote. Caesar, a realist, then turned his back on grandiose schemes and although, like many of his contemporaries, utterly without religious beliefs or scruples, secured his own election as *Pontifex Maximus*, head of the Roman religion.

Catiline Catiline, failing to attain the consulship and deserted by Caesar and Crassus, determined upon a daring revolutionary program of cancellation of debts and the establishment of a democratic regime. He found supporters among aristocrats who like himself were heavily in debt, among poverty-ridden members of the populace, and among the Sullan veterans who, unsuccessful as farmers on the lands assigned to them, had become aggrieved and turbulent. Defeated again as consular candidate for 62 B.C., he organized a conspiracy and planned a *coup d'état*, the murder of the consuls and the seizure of the government. His movement is an indication of the critical economic conditions in Rome. Cicero, becoming aware of the plot and of its program through the mistress of one of the conspirators, was ready for it. He secured from the senate a decree of martial law and with a brilliant and famous speech (the first oration against Catiline, November 8) so confounded Catiline that he left the city. In a second speech the following day Cicero exposed the plot and described the conspirators to the people.

Catiline and his followers continued their work, but their final plans for action were betrayed by a group of Gallic Allobroges to whom the conspirators in Rome had given letters for Catiline. The conspirators were called before the senate, where Cicero presented the evidence. That evening (December 3) he reported the events of the session to the people in the third Catilinarian oration. When in a later session (December 5) the question of punishment was discussed, Caesar argued for a sentence of imprisonment, but Cicero, backed by Cato, that Stoic philosopher and rigid conservative, who now appeared as a senatorial spokesman, called for the sentence of death, which was enforced.

By this action Cicero, though he gained considerable renown, put himself definitely on the side of the *Optimates*, who distrusted him. Henceforth, he worked for a program of the "harmony of the orders," the union of senators and leading knights—"the best men of Rome"—to run the state. He was inordinately proud of his victory over Catiline and even wrote a poem on his consulship.

The First Triumvirate   Pompey returned to Rome in the winter of 62 B.C. He failed to capitalize on his position and become dictator when, in obedience to the law and relying upon his prestige, he disbanded his army. The senate refused to recognize Pompey's acts in the East without examination in detail, and pushed him aside. At the same time the senate, on the advice of Cato, declined to release the business group led by Crassus from an unfortunate contract for the taxes in Asia, where harvests had been poor. Once more therefore Pompey and Crassus were forced to combine. Caesar, returning from a successful propraetorship in Spain and needing their support for the consulship, engineered the combination. Thus was formed the first triumvirate, a political alliance, which has been described as a "union of genius, position, and capital against the law." No real community of interests beyond jealousy of senatorial power held the three men together. Rather, the achievements of each had created a balance of power among them, and in the jockeying for position they found that through union they could best attain their immediate ends — prestige and recognition of his treaties and land for veterans for Pompey, financial protection and political backing for Crassus, political advancement for Caesar.

THE PERIOD OF THE TRIUMVIRATE

Caesar's Consulship   The triumvirate began at once to pay returns to its members. Caesar, with the powerful backing of Pompey and Crassus and through his own vote-getting ability, secured election as consul for the year 59 B.C. with Bibulus, a conservative, as colleague. Caesar forced legislation through the assembly over the opposition of Bibulus and in utter disregard of the constitutional checks Bibulus invoked. Pompey's acts in the East were ratified, and his veterans were settled on lands in Campania. Crassus and his associates were granted a rebate of one-third on their contract. The throne of Egypt was conferred on "the Flute Player," for a large price. Caesar, in spite of senatorial efforts to block him, was granted a provincial command for five years in Illyricum and the two Gauls, where trouble threatened from the Helvetians and the Germans. Before he left Rome he consolidated his position by arranging a marriage between his daughter Julia and Pompey and by removing Cato and Cicero, his two most dangerous opponents, from Rome.

The Banishment of Cicero   Cato was easily dealt with by giving him the task of reorganizing Cyprus, which he felt he could not honorably refuse and which took him three years to accomplish. Caesar offered Cicero an opportunity to join with the triumvirate through a lieutenancy in Gaul. When he refused this offer, Clodius, a brilliant product of the fast younger set and the able leader of Caesar's political clubs, was given a free hand against him. Clodius had earlier committed sacrilege, and at the time of his trial, in 61 B.C., Cicero's testimony had destroyed his alibi. To secure acquittal, Clodius had been forced to resort to wholesale bribery, and he therefore had his own score to settle with Cicero. In 59 B.C. he secured a transfer for himself to plebeian status, was elected tribune for 58 B.C., and carried a measure to banish all who had put Roman citizens to death without trial, as Cicero had done with the followers of Catiline. Cicero at once went into exile in Macedon, and his property was confiscated.

Caesar in Gaul   Caesar's success in Gaul, recounted in his own *Commentaries*, revealed him a military genius. He defeated the Helvetians and the Germans, conquered northern and western Gaul, invaded Germany, after building a famous bridge, and later crossed into Britain. The first revolts against his conquest were put down with ease. In 52 B.C., however, a revolt led by an able youth, Vercingetorix, caused Caesar much trouble. Finally, however, he besieged the Gallic leader in Alesia near modern Dijon, drove off a relieving host, and secured his submission. By 50 B.C. Gaul had been thoroughly pacified, and Caesar, now very wealthy, was ready to return to Rome, where he had won prestige with the people as a result of his victories, and popularity with the business element, who had reaped riches from the spoils of his conquest. More important, he had with him a loyal army of veterans who had shared in his campaigns.

Rome, 58–56 B.C.   In Rome, however, all had not gone well. The triumvirate was substantially an unnatural alliance of three potential rivals. With Caesar present, it had worked well; with Caesar away, it verged on collapse. Clodius, Caesar's agent, was a vigorous leader of the mob, opposed to all that Pompey and Crassus represented. From the poorer section of the populace, who still hoped for improvement in their economic and political status, he organized armed groups with which he dominated the assemblies, where he passed laws to suit himself, and created such confusion in the streets that Pompey himself did not dare leave his house.

Pompey, to regain power, secured the election of Milo as tribune for 57 B.C. Milo armed groups of his own and contended with Clodius in riots to secure political control over the Roman government. To strengthen himself further, Pompey obtained the recall of Cicero, who received a tremendous ovation on his joyous return. Cicero immediately paid his debt to Pompey by persuading the senate to grant him control of the grain supply of Rome for five years together with proconsular imperium in the Mediterranean. Pompey with his usual efficiency dealt well with this problem. The senate, however, not yet willing to recognize his pre-eminence in the state and rejecting proposals that would have made him in effect the first emperor, drove him once more into the arms of Caesar.

The Conference at Luca   Cicero, in the hope of splitting the triumvirate, began an assault on Caesar's agrarian laws. Caesar, with troublesome problems in Gaul on his hands, did not welcome the open breach threatened by Cicero's attack, and accordingly he invited Pompey and Crassus to meet him in April, 56 B.C., at Luca in Cisalpine Gaul. There they journeyed, attended by some two hundred senators, and there the affairs of empire were settled and the spoils divided. Pompey and Crassus were to be consuls for 55 B.C. and were to be given five-year provincial commands the following year; Crassus was to receive Syria and the command of a war against the Parthians, who were disturbing that province; Pompey was to be governor of the two Spains, but he was to manage his provinces through *legati*, while he remained in Italy and kept watch; Caesar's command in Gaul was to be renewed for another five-year period. Clodius was ordered to behave himself, and Cicero was forced to acquiesce in the plans of the ring. To appease Cicero, his brother was made one of Caesar's lieutenants in Gaul, where he speedily won distinction. In return the orator delivered a brilliant speech in favor of the provincial commands.

The Principate of Pompey

These well-laid plans soon went awry. Crassus left for the East in 54 B.C. with highest hopes of returning with a military glory equal to that of his colleagues. In 53 B.C., however, he was drawn into the desert, defeated, and slain at Carrhae. The influence of Pompey was not sufficient to keep order in Rome, and Caesar was too busy with revolts in Gaul to interfere. Clodius and Milo fought in the assembly and in the streets; elections could not be held; the authorities were powerless. In 52 B.C. Clodius was slain by Milo's group on the Appian Way, and in the riot that followed the senate house was burned. In despair the senate turned to Pompey and caused his election as "sole consul." Since at the same time Pompey still had charge of the grain supply and ruled the Mediterranean and the provinces of Spain through his lieutenants, he had at last attained the long-desired position as the indispensable man, *princeps*, first citizen of the state. In the meantime, Julia, through whom he had been held close to Caesar, had died (54 B.C.). In his new position he could not brook a rival; accordingly he severed relations with Caesar. The one man who might have prevented an open break, Cicero, was absent in 51 B.C. as governor of Cilicia, where he won an enhanced reputation for honesty and efficiency in provincial administration.

The Second Civil War   The issue between Caesar and Pompey came to an open break over Caesar's position at the expiration of his provincial command. Caesar had no intention of returning to Rome as a private citizen and exposing himself to the attacks of his enemies, so he demanded the right to remain in Gaul until the end of 49 B.C., though his command terminated in the first of March of that year, and to run for the consulship for 48 B.C. *in absentia*. At first Pompey agreed but then withdrew his consent. Throughout December, 50 B.C., there was spirited debate in the senate, enlivened by compromise offers from Caesar and by vetoes imposed by Caesarian and Pompeian tribunes. Finally, Caesar offered to lay down his powers if Pompey would do the same. When Pompey refused, Caesar prepared for action. On January 7, 49 B.C., the senate passed a decree of martial law and declared Caesar a public enemy. Antony and Cassius, Caesarian tribunes, vetoed the law and were forced to flee for their lives. This enabled Caesar to act in defense of the sanctity of the tribunician office.

With the famous remark, "the die is cast," Caesar crossed the Rubicon River, boundary of his province on January 10, 49 B.C. "*Hoc voluerunt; tantis rebus gestis Gaius Caesar condemnatus essem nisi ab exercitu auxilium petissem."* "They wished it; after the great things that I had accomplished, I, Gaius Caesar, would have been condemned, had I not sought aid from my army."[4] The senate had sealed its own fate.

The Rivals Caesar had a large following in Italy among the equestrian and popular parties, and a loyal army at his back. Pompey had the senate, finally and reluctantly supporting him, and the administration with its experience and prestige to add to his own record. He had one army in Spain, another in Epirus, which he had been gathering for the Parthian War and to which Caesar had sent two legions. He also controlled the sea. However, he had no troops in Italy, and he did not foresee the speed with which Caesar would advance. Hampered rather than helped by his senatorial advisers, he failed to act with his customary precision.

Italy and Spain Caesar moved with such speed and such success, as the Italian communities went over to him, that Pompey was forced to abandon Italy for the East. There he planned to close in on Caesar from both sides. The latter, however, after failing to cut Pompey off from Brundisium, went at once to Rome. There he called together what was left of the senate, demanded funds, and when they were not granted seized the treasury. He satisfied the business element by announcing that there would be no proscription.

After eight days in the capital, he left for Spain. In a hazardous campaign around Ilerda he defeated Pompey's lieutenants and absorbed their armies; on the way home he received the surrender of Massilia, which had resisted until besieged. Back in Rome as dictator, he devoted eleven days to his own election as consul for 48 B.C., to easing the debt situation by a moratorium and by the application of interest payments to principal, and to the grant of citizenship to the Transpadane Gauls. Then at the end of October he left for the East.

Pharsalus Though Bibulus controlled the Adriatic with his fleet, Caesar managed to slip part of his army across to Epirus. Bibulus died during the winter, and Antony had little difficulty in crossing with the rest of the army in March. After a failure to besiege Pompey in Dyrrhachium, Caesar led his army into Thessaly in search of supplies, and there Pompey's senatorial officers, anxious to return to Rome, forced him into battle with Caesar at Pharsalus. Caesar's veterans, though outnumbered two to one, defeated the Pompeian forces with ease. Pompey fled to Egypt, where he was murdered by agents of the young Ptolemy.

Egypt Caesar, following Pompey to Egypt, found himself quickly involved in the tangled affairs of that kingdom, where two children of "the Flute Player," Ptolemy and Cleopatra, were contending for the

---

[4] Suetonius. *Julius* (in *Lives of the Twelve Caesars*), 30. 4.

rule. Won by the youth and charm of the famous Cleopatra, Caesar placed her on the throne. He suppressed riots in Alexandria and with aid from Syria defeated an Egyptian force in a battle on the Nile. Then while there was rioting in Rome and the Pompeian forces were gathering in Africa, Caesar dallied with Cleopatra in Alexandria until June.

Zela, Thapsus, and Munda Once on his way Caesar acted with dispatch. He defeated Pharnaces of Pontus at Zela with speed and sent his famous message: *"Veni, vidi, vici."* In April, 47 B.C., he was back in Rome. There he again dealt with the debt problem, put down a mutiny of his veterans, and engineered his own election as consul for 46 B.C. In April of that year he defeated the Pompeians and their ally Juba, king of Numidia, at Thapsus in Africa. Cato, unwilling to surrender and unable, as he thought, to live longer with honor, committed suicide at Utica, a manner of death which made him a hero to later ages. Numidia was made a province with Sallust, the historian, proconsul. A final concentration of Pompeians in Spain was defeated at Munda in March, 45 B.C. After Thapsus, Caesar, elected dictator for ten years, held a great fourfold triumph over Gaul, Egypt, Pontus, and Africa. Statues symbolic of the Rhone, the Rhine, the Ocean, and the Nile were carried in the procession. Games were celebrated and presents distributed to the people. The following year a three-day festival glorified the final victory at Munda.

CAESAR, EMPEROR

Caesar's Powers From the crossing of the Rubicon in January, 49 B.C., to his death on the Ides of March, 44 B.C., Caesar was in Rome but sixteen months in all. During this time he carried out a series of reforms calculated to change the aspect of the Roman world. He gathered into his own hands the major power of the Roman constitution. He was elected dictator (of the Sullan type) for brief periods in 49 B.C. and in 47 B.C., for ten years after Thapsus, and for life after Munda; he was consul in 48 B.C. and from 46 to 44 B.C.; he held the tribunician power (by special grant) with its right of presidency over the assemblies and its sacrosanctity; he had proconsular power with full command over all the armies of the state. He had the right to nominate magistrates and appoint all provincial governors. As *praefectus morum* he had not only supervision of public morals but full censorial control over citizen and senatorial lists. The office of *Pontifex Maximus* gave him control over the machinery of religion and the religious law. In addition, by vote of the senate, he bore the title *Imperator*, signifying a victorious general, and was hailed by the senate as *pater patriae*. He wore the laurel wreath of triumph continually and showed his superiority to the senate by receiving it while seated. In addition to these titles and powers which belonged to the Roman tradition, he was granted a series of honors which placed him in the succession of Hellenistic monarchs. *Venus genetrix* was established as a goddess by edict to indicate his divine ancestry and was given a temple. His statue was placed in the temples, his portrait on the coins. The month, *Quintilis*, was renamed July in his honor. His liaison with Cleopatra, who came to Rome in 46 B.C. and remained in his house and gardens across the Tiber until his death, gave color to a rumor that he intended to marry her and establish an eastern monarchy with its capital at Alexandria or on the ancient site of Troy.

The significance of Caesar's titles and powers was revealed in the autocratic character of his policies in the administration. He, Caesar, was above parties and was, indeed, not merely a magistrate of Rome but ruler of the world.

Caesar's Reforms In an all-embracing program of reform Caesar endeavored to cure the ills that beset the Roman body politic. He ended the long struggle between the senators and the knights by using the latter widely in the administration and enrolling great numbers of them in the senate, thus awarding them the palm of victory over the senators. He added provincials to the senate as well, increasing its numbers to nine hundred in an attempt, his opponents said, to degrade it, but actually to break down the republican tradition of the rule of Rome and of the senatorial class and to make the body representative of the empire. He abolished the political clubs through which he himself had risen to power.

Through his supreme command of the military forces and his right to nominate and appoint his assistants, Caesar was able to control the magistrates and the provincial governors and thus end the confusion and corruption of the preceding century. By this act and by conferring citizenship on many Spaniards and Gauls, he began a program intended to destroy the distinction between Italians and provincials and so level off the Mediterranean world in fulfillment of the hopes of Sertorius. For the same purpose Caesar proposed but did not carry out a census of the entire empire. A uniform charter was provided for the Italian communities by the *Lex Julia Municipalis*, probably drawn by Caesar but made law after his death by Antony. Carthage and Corinth were re-established as Roman cities.

In Rome Caesar improved the administration by increasing the number of magistrates and reforming the law courts; he also planned a codification of the Roman law. The influx of wealth from Gaul and the moratoria and reductions of debts during the Second Civil War had brought relief to the overburdened debtors. For the proletariat and the veterans he returned to the program of Gaius Gracchus, and settled many not only on Italian lands but in colonies throughout the empire as well. Laws compelling the use of free labor on the great estates provided employment for many poor in Italy and lessened a little the dangers of slave revolts. At the same time the list of recipients of public grain was investigated and reduced to 150,000. Caesar had many plans in mind for the imperial city, such as the enlargement and beautification of the city, the gathering of a great library, the regulation of the bed of the Tiber, and the development of Ostia as a port for Rome.

His entire program was calculated to establish unified and orderly imperial control under himself as autocrat; provincial misrule and the threat of civil war were to be removed; local government was to be put in order and local prosperity secured in Italy and throughout the empire; the economic ills of Rome were to be healed; and Rome was to be made a city worthy of being the capital of an empire. Even time, as represented by the calendar, was to be made correct in Caesar's world. In the most lasting of his reforms Caesar, with the assistance of a Greek astronomer, and modeled on the Egyptian calendar, brought the official year into accord with the sun and established a year of 365 days with every fourth year a leap year. The Julian calendar, with certain minor changes made by Pope Gregory XIII in 1582, is the one still used in the West.

The Conspiracy For the year 44 b.c. Caesar and Antony were consuls, and Brutus and Cassius praetors. The latter pair were to be governors of Macedon and Syria the following year. Officials were also designated for 43 b.c. and 42 b.c., and Caesar prepared to leave for the Parthian War. The Sibylline Books declared that only a *rex* could conquer Parthia, and in accordance with this prophecy Antony, at the feast of the Lupercalia, offered Caesar the crown. But popular opposition showed itself, and Caesar refused.

On the Ides of March he went, unattended by a bodyguard as was his custom, to address the senate. At the foot of Pompey's statue he was surrounded by a band of conspirators and murdered. The conspiracy responsible for Caesar's murder was composed of Pompeians, disappointed Caesarians like Cassius, and republican doctrinaires who objected to his tyrannical powers and the trend toward monarchy. The leader of the last group was Brutus, traditionally descended from that Brutus who had expelled the Tarquins. The self-styled liberators planned to address the senate and declare the restoration of the republic; but when the senate fled in alarm, and confusion reigned in the streets of Rome, the liberators retired to the Capitol where they barricaded themselves.

The Achievements of Julius Caesar Caesar has left an indelible imprint on the pages of history. School children still read his commentaries; scholars have followed his career and scrutinized his every act; generals have studied his campaigns and sought to learn the secrets of his victories; kings have envied his power and sought to equal it. His very name has come to mean emperor and has been borne proudly by the Roman Caesars and the Russian czars and German kaisers.

He was without doubt a man of extraordinary potentialities, whose abilities and character developed with his opportunities. The young Caesar, first known for his irreverence and his escapades, matured into the scheming but skillful politician who knew how to charm men by the force of his personality so that they would do his will and at the same time how to organize and get out the vote. His powers of organization and leadership were best revealed when, though over forty years of age, he won his first military campaign and became one of the world's great generals. He knew the value of speed and surprise, and was the first general in antiquity to make proper use of trenches and siege engines. His calculated daring in warfare was based on a full knowledge of his capabilities of his men and on an understanding of the psychology and weaknesses of his opponents. Ultimate success made him a great statesman, the mighty Caesar, organizer and ruler of empire, who did indeed "bestride the narrow world like a Colossus." His deeds and his ideas survived him, and later Caesars carried his plans to completion.

THE LAST STAGE OF THE REVOLUTION

Antony The conspirators had failed lamentably to make plans for dealing with Caesar's lieutenants — Lepidus, master of the horse, and Antony, consul. Lepidus at once occupied the Forum with troops, while Antony secured possession of Caesar's papers and money. The stalemate that resulted was temporarily solved by a meeting of the senate at which a general amnesty, engineered by Cicero, was proclaimed. Again a mistake was made when Antony was given permission to make an address at Caesar's funeral. With a skillful speech Antony inflamed the mob so that they burned Caesar's body in the Forum. Rome became unsafe for the conspirators, and Brutus and Cassius soon left for the East, where they hoped to secure men and money for the struggle with Antony which they saw was soon to come.

Octavian Antony's advance to power received a rude check, however, when the young Octavius came to Rome. Caesar's will had revealed, in addition to royal gifts to the Roman people, that he had adopted his grand-nephew Octavius, who had been waiting in Epirus to join him for the Parthian War. On learning of the murder, the eighteen-year-old boy, with his friend Agrippa, left at once for the capital city. When Antony rebuffed him, he raised enough money to pay Caesar's bequests, and in 43 B.C. he secured the formalities that made him Julius Caesar Octavianus. Cicero supported Octavian, rallied the republican forces with letters and speeches, and in his famous *Philippics* opened a savage attack on Antony which drove him to his province of Cisalpine Gaul.

In the war with senatorial troops which followed, Antony was defeated, but both the consuls commanding the troops were killed. Octavian, as he should be called after the adoption ceremonies, thereupon demanded the consulship for himself. When this was refused, he seized Rome with an army of Caesar's veterans which he had raised and forced his election. He left at once to deal with Antony, but instead of fighting he came to terms.

The Second Triumvirate

Antony, joined by Lepidus, met Octavian near Bononia, and the three laid plans for the future. In accordance with these plans they seized Rome and secured legal election as triumvirs with dictatorial powers for five years. Thus the second triumvirate was established as a legal office. The triumvirs divided the western provinces among them and prepared for the war with Brutus and Cassius. Because they desired vengeance and needed money, they declared a proscription. Many tales of horror and heroism have survived from this butchery; among the victims was Cicero, whose death Antony desired. In the summer of 42 b.c. Antony and Octavian defeated Brutus and Cassius in two battles at Philippi. Cassius committed suicide after the first, Brutus after the second. Antony then remained in the East, while Octavian returned to restore order in Rome and to deal with the piratical Sextus Pompey, son of the Great, who had seized Sicily and was interfering with Rome's grain supply. Lepidus, to whom had been given the office of *Pontifex Maximus* and the province of Africa, became and remained a negligible factor.

In spite of their apparent agreement, the future portended a struggle between Octavian and Antony for the rule of Rome. The hopes of the liberators and of Cicero could no longer be realized. One-man rule supported by the army and relying upon control of the provinces was firmly entrenched, and the republican forces were entirely too weak to make possible any restoration of the ancient constitution. The care with which the triumvirs took over the provinces and divided them among themselves indicates their realization of the powers, dangers, and potentialities of the situation.

Octavian in the West   Octavian faced the difficult tasks of providing for the veterans, restoring order and prosperity to Italy, which had been ravaged by the late war, dealing with Sextus Pompey, and handling the remaining republican leaders and the populace in Rome. His path to success in these matters was rendered difficult by the watchful jealousy and constant interference of Antony and his adherents. When Octavian confiscated much land in Italy, to provide farms for the veterans, Lucius and Fulvia, the brother and the wife of Antony took advantage of the unpopularity of the act to lead a revolt, known as the Perusian War, against him. After Lucius had been besieged in Perusia and starved into submission, Octavian with undue severity destroyed that ancient Etruscan town.

Antony returned, but when the veteran armies refused to fight against each other, peace was made at Brundisium. By formal agreement Octavian received the West and Antony the East, and the agreement was sealed by a marriage between Antony, Fulvia having died, and Octavia, sister of Octavian. Another quarrel that broke out over the war with Sextus was patched up by Octavian at Tarentum in 37 B.C., and the triumvirate was renewed for five years.

In the face of these difficulties Octavian met with great success. After several difficult campaigns his lieutenant Agrippa defeated Sextus Pompey in Sicily. In Italy, Octavian laid aside his former ferocity and showed himself a wise statesman. He put an end to confiscations of land, restored order by wiping out brigandage, fostered agriculture, and brought prosperity back to Italy. With careful regard for republican tradition and skillful use of propaganda in his own favor and against Antony he secured the support of the Roman people and became the hero of the day in Rome.

Antony and Cleopatra   The story of Antony in the East is far different. On his first trip to the East after Philippi he showed he had inherited Caesarian ideas when he allowed the cities to give him divine honors as the New Dionysus. Requiring money of Egypt, he summoned Cleopatra to meet him at Tarsus. He succumbed so completely to the charms of the lovely Egyptian that he retired to Alexandria with her, where they both reveled in luxury while his lieutenants struggled with the Parthians. Recalled to Italy by the Perusian War, Antony, apparently putting Cleopatra aside, married Octavia and spent three years in Athens with her, a model Roman husband and governor. When he finally set out for the Parthian War in 36 B.C., however, he sent Octavia back to Rome and renewed his alliance with Cleopatra. The Parthian expedition was a complete failure and only a skillful retreat saved Antony and part of his army. In 36 B.C. Antony openly married Cleopatra and in 34 B.C. he bestowed the Oriental provinces as kingdoms on her children by Caesar and himself.

These affronts to Rome enabled Octavian to arouse the city against his ancient enemy. Many of Antony's Roman followers deserted him when he refused to abandon Cleopatra. Open war broke out and in the spring of 31 B.C. Agrippa succeeded in blocking Antony's fleet in the harbor at Actium and in cutting his army off from supplies. To break the blockade the battle of Actium was fought. A part of the fleet, led by Cleopatra and bearing the treasure, succeeded in getting through and left for Egypt, whereupon Antony, fearing defeat, followed her, abandoning the rest of his fleet and his army to their fate; these, left with no choice, went over to the victor.

When Octavian advanced upon Egypt the following year, Antony, unable to establish a strong defense, committed suicide and died in Cleopatra's arms. The queen, after her pleas for clemency for her children and herself had failed, took poison rather than grace Octavian's triumph in Rome. Plutarch has made the death scenes of the "Inimitable Livers" (as he called them) immortal in literature and history. Octavian was crowned Pharaoh of Egypt.

Antony's ability had been frittered away by dissipation and by a dream of power for which, as Caesar's fate had shown, the world was not ready, while the shrewd statesmanship and propaganda of Octavian had triumphed. Cleopatra remains an enigma. Her charm was great, though her portraits indicate that she was not particularly beautiful. Caesar and Antony neglected imperial duties for her, and her Roman contemporaries, both hating and fearing her, could not say too much evil against her. As administrator of Egypt she showed ability, energy, and wisdom, and she certainly had great dreams of a world empire in which she would be queen. Whether she really loved Caesar and Antony or whether she played a shrewd and mercenary game with them is a matter of opinion. Her whole story is clouded with romance and, as Plutarch said of her death, "the truth no one knows."

The victory of Octavian ended the revolution. The democratic reformers had not succeeded in establishing their program. The senate, despite the bolstering power of Sulla's enactments, had failed to handle the problems of empire and had been cast down from its high estate. Caesar's attempt at dictatorship had resulted in conspiracy and assassination, and the attempt of the triumvirs to divide the world between them had ended in civil war. The triumph of Octavian at Actium brought to an end the Rome ruled by the "senate and the Roman people" and marked the beginning of the Roman Empire under the Caesars.

21 · Roman Life During the Revolution

ENORMOUS INCREASES OF WEALTH AND ATTENDANT luxuries and the continued absorption of Hellenistic culture mark the life of the upper classes of Rome during the revolutionary period. In addition, the reforms of Augustus established a frankly monetary basis for the senatorial and equites classes.

The Senatorial Class   Senators brought home large sums acquired from booty or extortion in the provinces. With these they built fine houses in Rome and villas in the country, which they adorned with the finest products of Eastern craftsmanship. They held elaborate banquets and made great displays of wealth. By making loans or investments through freedmen secretaries or agents who regularly managed their estates, they evaded the law that forbade them to engage in industry and trade. Thus Brutus, through an agent, lent money to Salamis on Cyprus, at the exorbitant interest rate of 48 per cent and protested bitterly when Cicero, as governor of Cilicia, interfered.

In contrast to this picture of wealth was the problem of debt. The way to office was expensive; standards of living were high; and moneylenders considered senatorial youths good risks. Caesar is said to have owed as much as two million dollars before he became consul. Those who failed to rise found themselves overwhelmed, and many were ruined. It was such a situation that gave rise to Catiline's conspiracy. In fact it was the debt problem that caused many of the difficulties which arose between the *Optimates* and the equestrian moneylenders.

Problems of the possession and inheritance of wealth, coupled with newer ideas, led to the decline of the old-fashioned Roman family. Heiresses, unwilling to be under the control of any man, secured freedom from the ancient restrictions of the law. Marriages were arranged for financial or political reasons, and divorce became easy and frequent.

The spread of Stoic and Epicurean philosophies destroyed the belief of educated Romans in the ancestral religion; ancient standards

464

The Ancient Senate House in the Forum Romanum. It is built of warm, rose-colored brick. (Photograph by Mary Francis Gyles, reproduced by Frank D. Grande)

were therefore laid aside. A younger group, led in the later period by Clodius and his sister Clodia, used their wealth and skepticism as excuses to engage in fast living and in every kind of vice. On the other hand, there were some, like the Metelli and Cato, who in spite of all followed the old tradition. The stories of the proscription of 42 B.C. are filled with evidence of family devotion and honorable behavior. Similarly, not all provincial governors were as corrupt as Verres.

The senatorial group failed not because of their vices but because they clung blindly to the traditional constitutional forms and refused to establish an effective system of imperial administration. Their policy of unbending resistance to change played directly into the hands of Pompey and of Caesar. The proscriptions of Sulla and of the triumvirate weakened them by depriving them of many of their bravest and most intelligent leaders and by cowing the remainder.

The Equites The business element as a whole prospered, in spite of proscriptions and disasters, as their leaders came into political power and they obtained a large share in the profits of the wars in the East and in Gaul. The contract system of tax collection for which "societies," joint-stock companies, were formed brought them great wealth, whereupon they began to play a leading part in Mediterranean commerce and to invest their means in industrial establishments. They acquired real estate in Rome, Italy, and the provinces; bought or leased from the state the mines and former royal monopolies of the East; and owned great numbers of slaves, whom they employed or leased for multifarious activities. The capitalists served as money-changers and as bankers to receive deposits, issue letters of credit, and make loans, especially to senators and provincial cities. Their major interest in politics was the protection and extension of their financial transactions.

The Common People   Detailed information about the commoners of the city is lacking. They lived in huge tenements, called *insulae*, where rents were low. Though faced with slave competition, many must have found employment as laborers. Others engaged in the ancient crafts, particularly in the manufacture of arms, for which there was great demand, and some kept small stores, bakeries, and wineshops to supply the needs of the city. The state assisted them with cheap grain and amused them with free shows, and they could always count on gifts from office seekers who desired their votes. Their poverty made them fair spoil for politicians like Catiline, Clodius, and Milo, and they were easily induced to join the political clubs and to riot in the streets.

The Slaves   The slave population of Rome and Italy increased enormously with wealth and conquest. Skilled slaves from the East were in demand for the olive and grape plantations, and rougher barbarians for the cattle ranches. In the city there were slave architects, builders, copyists, readers, chefs, and craftsmen. Some were employed in their owner's establishments; others were rented out; many had shops of their own under the patronage of their masters. Slaves who became wealthy often possessed slaves of their own. Work in the wealthy households was directed by slave stewards and performed by menials of

A Roman Lamp of Green Glazed Pottery, 100 B.C. — A.D. 100. A wick was inserted through the hole in the "nose" and the lamp filled with olive oil. It burned with a clear flame and little odor. (The Metropolitan Museum of Art, Fletcher Fund, 1942)

A Section of Roman Mosaic Pavement of Colored Marble, 100 B.C.–A.D. 100. (The Metropolitan Museum of Art, gift of Mrs. W. Bayard Cutting, 1932)

servile status. Other slaves did the clerical work of the officials and of the business houses. Some were secretaries who, like Cicero's Tiro, a freedman, looked after the correspondence and managed the estates of their masters or served as tutors for the children of the family. Manumission was easy and frequent; indeed, Sulla is said to have freed ten thousand slaves in one block for political and military purposes. As the result of such occurrences the grant of citizenship, which in earlier times had accompanied freedom, was restricted toward the end of the period to the traditional Latin rights, which precluded voting or holding office.

Rome Rome itself was still far from being a worthy capital of a great empire. The houses of the nobility were fine structures, but the *insulae* of the poor were hastily constructed and liable to collapse or catch fire. Though new basilicas and temples were built and covered with marble veneer, many of the older buildings were in a sad state of disrepair, and the streets were narrow, dirty, and crooked. The administration of the city was in utter confusion, without any effective police or fire department, and the government proved itself incapable of handling street disorders without recourse to military aid.

Italy The political situation of Italy was thrown into confusion by the wholesale grant of Roman citizenship which followed the Social War, and the civil wars made conditions worse. Until Octavian restored order, there was much brigandage, as runaway slaves, dispossessed farmers, and dissatisfied veterans plundered unwary or unattended travelers. The economic condition of the peninsula is more difficult to assess. The great estates of wealthy Romans and Italians continued to grow in size and in the number of the slaves employed, though there are evidences that the great landowner was beginning to find it more profitable sometimes to let his land out to tenants than to work it with slaves. The small farming class was badly upset by the series of confiscations and resettlements, but the eagerness of veterans for a piece of Italian land indicates that farming on a small scale was still profitable and prevalent. The industries that existed in Campania in imperial times—the manufacture of pottery and of copper and iron wares—had already made their appearance. Puteoli prospered as the chief port of Rome.

The Provinces   The provinces suffered most during the revolution. Sicily was terribly impoverished by the slave wars and by the plundering of its governors, and Africa was just beginning to recover from the ravages of the Third Punic War. The continuous wars kept Spain in turmoil, while Gaul was ravaged by Caesar's conquests. The East, plundered in turn by its governors, by pirates, by Mithradates, by Sulla, Cassius, Antony, and Octavian, also paid heavy tribute to the Roman businessmen in the form of interest payments on the debts the monetary exactions created. At the same time the demand in Rome for Eastern manufactures brought much of the wealth back. Also the increase of maritime business and of commercial banking, which, in spite of the appearance of Roman merchants and bankers often remained in the hands of skilled Greeks, brought new opportunities and wealth to many individuals. The provinces poured extraordinary sums in tribute into Rome which were spent on public works, the pleasures of the Roman mob, the army, and imperial administration. Since the treasury was in the hands of quaestors, most of them without much experience in administration, much of the tribute was squandered, and the provinces failed to get in return the efficient management and protection that were their due. Real prosperity came to the empire only under the well-organized system of the Caesars.

Roman Law   Roman civil law, Rome's greatest and most enduring contribution to the civilization of the world, was developed during the republican period into an instrument readily adapted by the Caesars for the ordering of an empire. Later it was to dominate the law of the Middle Ages and to be the model for European and Latin-American civil codes.

Roman law had its beginnings in the regal period under the authority of the king and in the hands of the pontiffs who probably acted as his advisers in legal matters. It was at that time primarily *fas*, religious law or custom, which the state controlled to preserve the favor of the gods. Certainly in very early times, however, the king served as arbitrator or judge in private disputes, and so there developed methods of procedure and principles of private law for citizens, the *jus civile*, or civil law, which, like *fas*, was held under the guardianship of the pontiffs. The difficulty of access to these patrician priests and, as a consequence, the difficulty of securing justice in the courts were among the chief grievances of the plebeians (p. 401), whose agitation resulted in the writing of the Twelve Tables. This famous document, with its rules, maxims, definitions, and remedies, was in the language of the Roman jurists, the basis of the *jus civile*. It stated the fundamental rules of procedure, giving the plaintiff the right to summon the defendant into court and compel his attendance by force if necessary, and likewise to force him to obey the decision of the court. If the debtor failed to make his payments after proper judicial procedure, he became the property of his creditors and might be sold or killed. The famous provision, "Let him be cut into pieces; if anyone cut too much or too little it will not be a crime," was characteristic of the rigid logic of the code rather than a statement of actual practice. The creditors fared better if they sold the debtor and divided the proceeds.

The section of the Tables which dealt with family law established the power of the *pater familias* over his wife, children, clients, and slaves. It recognized marriage by religious rites, by a ceremony of purchase, and by cohabitation, and it provided for the inheritance of the property, together with the religious duties that belonged to the family, by the direct heir or close relations, or in default of legal heirs it permitted a man to adopt or designate an heir so that the continuity of family life might not be lost.

In its definitions of property, the law distinguished between that kind of property which required legal forms of transfer in the presence of witnesses, such as land, slaves, and cattle, and less valuable things which might readily be bought and sold without technicalities. For the former it provided the procedure of conveyance and by establishing contractual rules it created forms of bond and mortgage.

In respect to injuries the code rested on the ancient principle of retaliation, modified, as were the earlier Oriental codes, by provisions for restitution or payment. A famous article, still the rule, ran, "If a thief breaking in and stealing at night be killed, let him be killed rightly." The rigidity of the law as applied to contracts, oral or written, is illustrated by the phrase, "As the tongue hath pronounced, so shall the law be."

Those articles of the Tables that dealt with public law, in part derived from Greek codes, forbade illegal assemblies at night; provided the death penalty for murder, arson, libel, false witness, and similar offenses; and prohibited the burning or burying of the dead within the city and the burial of gold with a dead man save that which was in his teeth.

The Twelve Tables were the product of a people, literal-minded and narrow, but with a great sense of justice. The code represented a community in the economic stage of agriculture and herding. The landless man (*proletarius*) had to have a landowner as security in court. Interpretation, procedural reform, and expansion were needed to adapt the Twelve Tables to the needs of economic and intellectual growth, as was done in time.

For a period the power of interpretation of the code and the knowledge of procedure under it remained in the possession of the pontiffs. Litigants and judges alike turned to them for information and opinions (*responsa*) about the law. Roman procedure (*legis actiones*), including the summons, the charge, and the execution of the judgment, were all carefully regulated. There were five such procedures by which a case could be taken to trial. The plaintiff haled or hauled the defendant into court, where his case appeared *in jure*. He recited a formal charge, the wording of which had to be exact, for if he used the wrong formula or word in his statement, his case was lost and he could never bring it again. After this formal proceeding the magistrate turned the case over to a private judge, *judex*, who, *in judicio*, examined the facts and applied the law as he received it from the Tables, or in case of doubt from the pontiffs. The victor in the suit then executed the judgment himself. The ridigity of this procedure and the necessity of securing the wording from the pontiffs prevented many from securing justice, and the limited number of *actiones*, due to the early period of their formulation, blocked the development of the law to meet new needs.

The first break in this system came in 304 B.C. when Flavius, freedman of Appius Claudius (p. 412), published the *legis actiones*. Tiberius Coruncanius, the first plebeian pontiff (*ca.* 250 B.C), by public lectures made known to all the science of interpreting the law, and in 204 B.C. Aelius composed a treatise containing the Twelve Tables, the interpretations, and the *legis actiones*. As a result, knowledge of the law became general property, and there developed a number of lay jurists, *prudentes*, who made knowledge of the law their specialty and pride and who gave *responsa* freely to all.

After the creation of the office of *praetor peregrinus*, the methods of procedure were reformed under praetorian influence in order to deal with cases involving foreigners. Since foreigners could not be expected to know or to use the exact Latin wording of the actions, this praetor adopted the practice of calling litigants before him and, after a discussion of the case, of drawing up in writing a formula which stated its nature and which he turned over to the *judex*. This simplified procedure was so advantageous that it was made available for citizens by the *Lex Aebutia* (*ca.* 150 B.C.), which allowed action *per formulam* as an alternative to *per legis actionem*. Use of the *legis actiones* rapidly declined thereafter, and it was ended by Augustus.

Expansion of the law to meet new conditions was the work of the magistrates, primarily the praetors, and particularly after the passage of the Aebutian Law. The praetor had a good deal of power over the law. If it worked injustice, he might set it aside in effect, though not directly; or if new cases developed, he might evolve through the formulary process new rules of law. The aediles, who possessed judicial authority in minor cases, followed the praetor's example, and the law that developed through this process of legislation by magistrates was called *jus honorarium*. Since the largest part of it was created by the praetors, however, it is often spoken of as *jus praetorium*. The *jus honorarium* received formal statement and sanction in the edicts. Upon entrance into office each magistrate issued an edict in which he stated the principles by which he would be guided in carrying out the duties of his office. In the case of the praetor this consisted of a statement of the *formulae*, upon which he would accept action at law. Normally he simply took over the edict of the preceding year with such additions or changes as his own knowledge, or the experience of his predecessor, made him feel were desirable. Thus through the praetor's edicts the *jus civile* was kept up to date and developed to fit changing needs, while through the habitual continuity of the edicts and the recognized, though not legal, authority of the *responsa prudentium* it held to its traditional character of a law founded on custom and inherited from the fathers.

The *praetor peregrinus* made a further contribution to Roman jurisprudence in the development of the concept of the *jus gentium*, "law of all nations," fundamentally a new idea. In antiquity law was commonly regarded as the peculiar possession of the citizens of a state, and foreigners had no part in it. Thus Greek cities had agents to represent their citizens in the courts of other states (p. 196), and metics in Athens had patrons to aid them in legal cases (p. 277). Rome, respecting this concept, allowed local codes to remain in force in conquered territory. Nevertheless there developed in the Hellenistic period (p. 361) certain recognized principles of commercial relations between citizens of different states, generally understood and enforced throughout the Mediterranean. The foreign praetors discovered these principles in their discussion of cases involving aliens, and called them *jus gentium*. The principles of equity, of innocence until proved guilty, and of the equality of free men before the law were developed in their courts in Rome, and the experience of the Roman governors in the provinces established them. Technically, the *jus gentium* was never more than a body of principles, since its provisions received the force of law only when recognized by the praetor or by the provincial governor and embodied in the edicts these magistrates issued. When so stated, however, they became *jus honorarium*. Thus, they had their part in laying the broad foundations of the Roman law on which the world continues to build.

LITERATURE IN THE CICERONIAN AGE

In the momentous last years of the Roman Republic, Latin literature began to attain the full heights of its greatness. Catullus and Lucretius, poets, Caesar and Sallust, historians, Nepos, biographer, Varro, antiquarian, and Cicero, orator, essayist, and letter writer, were the chief ornaments of a literary period that has been called after its greatest writer, the Ciceronian period.

Catullus (*ca.* 84–54 B.C.)   The influence of the Alexandrian poets on Roman literature is most clearly revealed in the works of Catullus. He was a master of verse, skilled in the lore of the Greeks and able to adapt their varied meters to Latin, particularly the lively eleven-syllable verse. He composed many lyrics, a miniature epic, and an elaborate wedding hymn. But his fame rests on a group of short poems which reveal him as one of the sweetest of love poets. Madly in love with Clodia, he addressed her as Lesbia in impassioned verse.

> Let's live, my Lesbia, and love.
> Let's value not a whit above
> A penny all that dotards grey
> In tones of condemnation say.
> The sun can set, the sun can rise;
> Once let the brief light quit our eyes,
> And we through endless night must keep
> The couch of one unbroken sleep.
> Give me a thousand kisses — more!
> A hundred yet: add to the score
> A second thousand kisses: then
> Another hundred, and again
> A thousand more, a hundred still.
> So many thousands we fulfil,
> We must take care to mix the count —
> Bad luck to know the right amount —
> Lest evil eye impose its spell
> When it can all our kisses tell.[1]

[1]John Wight Duff, *A Literary History of Rome from the Origins to the Close of the Golden Age.* New York: Barnes & Noble, Inc., 1953, pp. 233–234. Reprinted by permission of Barnes & Noble, Inc., and Ernest Benn Limited, publishers.

When she proved unfaithful, he poured out his heart in reproaches
and endeavored to steel himself to renunciation:

> I hate yet love: you ask how this may be,
> Who knows? I feel its truth and agony.[2]

Equal depth in feeling and beauty in words are revealed by his poetic
greeting to his home on Lake Garda and his address to his dead brother
ending with the famous line

> *Atque in perpetuum, frater, ave atque vale.*
> "And so forever, brother, hail and farewell."

Lucretius (*ca*. 99–55 B.C.)   Though equally under Greek influence,
Lucretius was an exact opposite of the passionate Catullus. In most
beautifully written Latin hexameter he endeavored to bring to the
Romans the Epicurean message of quietude. In *De Rerum Natura*,
"On the Nature of Things," he appealed to men with evangelistic fervor
to lay aside their troubles and worries and find rest in Epicureanism.

> Naught sweeter than to hold the tranquil realms
> On high, well fortified by sages' lore,
> Whence to look down on others wide astray—
> Lost wanderers questing for the way of life—
> See strife of genius, rivalry of rank,
> See night and day men strain with wondrous toil
> To rise to utmost power and grasp the world.[3]

Praising the Greek as the man who first liberated men from the
weight of superstition, he explained the atomic and mechanistic universe that Epicurus had portrayed. He described the evolutionary
growth of the world and of man and endeavored to explain the processes of nature. With a deep religious feeling he tried to free the Romans
from the fears that were even then driving them to the emotional religions of the East, and especially from the fear of death. In the third
book he discusses the problem of the soul and marshals his arguments
against immortality.

> "Soon shall thy home greet thee in joy no more,
> Nor faithful wife nor darling children run
> To snatch first kiss, and stir within thy heart
> Sweet thoughts too deep for words. Thou canst no more
> Win wealth by working or defend thine own.
> The pity of it! One fell hour," they say,
> "Hath robbed thee of thine every prize in life."

[2] *Ibid.*, p. 231.
[3] *Ibid.*, p. 205.

But he does not let pathos daunt him; his comment is that of the philosopher:

> Hereat they add not this: "And now thou art
> Beset with yearning for such things no more."[4]

His work was great poetry, and it was extraordinary in its value to science. From it the modern world of scholarship has derived most of its knowledge of the philosophy of Epicurus.

The Historians   Caesar recounted his deeds in Gaul and in the civil wars in terse, clear prose, with words and phrases handled like cohorts on the field of battle. Though his *Commentaries* were campaign documents written to explain and defend his own actions, they were composed with such apparent detachment and impersonality that it is rarely possible to separate propaganda from fact and to prove that Caesar distorted history for his own justification. Nothing has survived of his orations, essays, or poems.

Sallust (86–35 B.C.), quaestor, proconsul of Numidia, and follower of Caesar, devoted the closing years of his life to historical writing. In two brilliant monographs—one on the Jugurthine War, which was a glorification of Marius; the other on the Catilinarian conspiracy, a virulent excoriation of Catiline—both of which have survived; and in the *Histories*, which covered the decade after Sulla's death, now lost except for fragments, he abandoned the annalistic method of composition and wrote readable, if inaccurate, works of history.

Nepos (*ca.* 100–*ca.* 25 B.C.)   A Gaul from the Po Valley, Nepos became a learned member of Cicero's circle and contributed a long series of biographies of which only a few, mostly of famous Greeks, have survived. Though not scientifically composed, they are lively, popular, and clear, and hence are often read by students of Latin.

Varro (116–27 B.C.)   Varro, "the most learned of the Romans," wrote encyclopedic works covering a wide range of subjects. Modern scholars estimate that he produced seventy-four different works consisting of six hundred and twenty single volumes. Of these the most famous were *Antiquities* and his books on farming and on the Latin language. Though he was studied and quoted throughout the imperial period and often referred to by early medieval scholars, only fragments of his works have survived.

Cicero (106–43 B.C.)   Statesman, orator, and philosopher, Cicero looms large in the political history of the period and in the history of the humane studies. He was a master of Latin prose and of rhetorical form. His orations disclose the crosscurrents of Roman politics and society. The characters of Verres, Catiline, and Antony have never recovered from the fierceness of his invective. His tribute to the liberal arts in the

[4]*Ibid.*, pp. 209–210.

defense of Archias is one of the noblest expressions in any language. Though not a profound thinker, he carried the message of the Greek philosophers to his own generation through his essays and at the same time contributed much to modern knowledge of ancient thought. He created a vocabulary for philosophy in Latin which has descended through the medieval schools to our own time. He was an inveterate letter writer and his freedman-secretary Tiro and his friend Atticus preserved and published his correspondence. The letters reveal the man — vain, at times hesitating, even weak, but ever sincere, honest, and patriotic. The noble character of the statesman shines through his defects. His hopes for the preservation of the Roman Republic were shattered by the onslaught of Caesarism, but like Demosthenes in Athens he stands in history's hall of fame ennobled by the courage of his failure. Augustus' comment on him was a fitting epitaph, "A great orator, and one who loved his country well."

22 · The Age of Augustus

HE TRIUMPH OF AUGUSTUS CAESAR (THE NAME BY which Octavian was known after he became ruler of the Roman world) brought to a close a century of revolution and civil war and ushered in an era of peace and prosperity for the Mediterranean world which lasted for two centuries and which was due in large measure to the wisdom and statesmanship of the victorious Augustus. During his reign he reorganized the imperial government, achieved the political and economic rehabilitation of Rome, Italy, and the provinces, regulated the frontiers, and undertook a broad program of moral and religious reform and artistic and literary advance. Because of his achievements his generation has been called the age of Augustus.

THE IMPERIAL SYSTEM

When Augustus returned to Rome after the battle of Actium, he was faced with the difficult tasks of fitting a system of one-man rule into the republican constitution without doing outrage to Roman sensibilities. He also had to secure a body of loyal and efficient supporters for the rule of the provinces, the command of the army, and the administration of the empire. He had no intention of giving up his own power, which rested basically on his control of the military forces, but his pride in the Roman tradition and his comprehension of the needs of the situation made him cling to established forms and avoid the autocratic ideas and actions of Julius Caesar which had resulted in conspiracy and assassination. He desired rather to perpetuate the idea of a Rome that would rule the world and in which he would be the "first citizen." The system he established therefore followed the programs of Gaius Gracchus and of Pompey, rather than those of Sulla or of Caesar. The dictatorship had been abolished, and Augustus made no attempt to revive it. In its place he assumed a position that assured him command of the army and control over the civil administration. He was careful, however, to refuse

476

all offices inconsonant with republican custom. In addition to these formal powers he received a number of titles indicative of his influence, and he surrounded himself with an aura of sacrosanctity which bound the people of the empire to his person.

Powers and Titles   For some years after the legal expiration of the triumvirate in 32 B.C., Augustus continued to rule by virtue of the consular office and by common consent. In January, 27 B.C., however, he announced to the senate the end of his extraordinary powers and the restoration of the republic. Thereupon the senate conferred upon him that series of offices and titles which made him in effect the ruler of Rome. He was annually elected consul (with a colleague). At the same time he was given not only proconsular power over certain of the provinces where an army was required, being allowed to remain in Rome and govern these provinces through lieutenants, but also the tribunician power[1] with its important privileges of intercession, of calling and presiding over the senate and the assemblies, and of making nominations.

When the consular office proved to be too much of a burden because of its ceremonial obligations and his tenure prevented the rise of many senators to the coveted honor, he surrendered the position in 23 B.C. As proconsul, however, he was allowed a seat between the consuls, and by an extension of the tribunician power he was given primacy over them in the deliberative bodies. The emphasis he laid upon this position is indicated by the fact that from that time he and later emperors dated the years of their rule by the annually renewed *tribunicia potestas.* Though he refused to accept a perpetual censorship because of its unrepublican character, he did take the census several times, and in addition he took charge of the grain supply and of the administration of the city of Rome, in which he established police and fire departments. By virtue of his tribunician power he reformed the senate and tried by a series of laws to secure moral reform. When Lepidus died in 12 B.C., Augustus was elected *Pontifex Maximus*, head of the Roman religion.

In addition to these powers he bore a group of titles which expressed his prestige and influence in Roman affairs. As *princeps* of the senate and the people, he was consulted first on all nominations and on all questions of policy or of legislation, and he was thus able to dominate the activities of the state. His military prestige was expressed by the word *imperator*, "victorious general," which he had inherited from Julius Caesar as a personal name. *Augustus*, a name conferred upon him by the senate, signified "consecrated" and carried with it the implication of divinity or of divine protection. It is significant that this name had never before been conferred upon any living person. His lofty

---

[1] Since he was a patrician, he could not be tribune.

Portrait Bust of a Young
Man, Perhaps Augustus,
ca. 30 B.C. (The Metro-
politan Museum of Art,
Rogers Fund, 1919)

position and his great services to the world in the restoration of peace
and order made him the natural recipient of those divine honors which
the Hellenistic East had learned to confer on its rulers. In that region
therefore he allowed himself to be worshiped as a god in temples dedicated to *Roma et Augustus*. This imperial cult throughout the provinces
proved a great unifying center of patriotic devotion to the person of
the ruler. In Italy, however, not Augustus but the *Genius Augusti* associated with the *lares* received worship. Augustus himself laid great
stress on the divinity of Julius Caesar and associated the great deities,
particularly Apollo and Vesta, with his household. By ceremonies and by
reliefs on monuments throughout the empire he fostered the conception that his rule had brought a new age of peace and plenty to a
troubled world. Opposition to such a man, or even criticism of him,
verged on sacrilege and became an injury to the majesty of the Roman
people, whom he represented, and was punishable by death. The
veneration with which he was held received further expression when

in 2 B.C. the senate hailed him as *pater patriae*, "father of his country." After his death he was formally deified and listed among the gods of the Roman state.

In theory, the senate and the Roman people ruled the world under his leadership. Perhaps it was the desire and intention of Augustus that this be so. But in actuality, his military command, his control of the civil administration, his extraordinary wealth (for he was by far the richest man in the world) and the prestige of his personality made him an autocrat — the first of the long line of Roman emperors.

Problem of the Succession   The greatest failure of Augustus, his failure to provide a proper means of choosing his successor, was due to the anomaly of his own position. The ideal of his system called for the selection of the ablest man by the duly constituted authorities of the state. In actual fact the power was certain to descend to the man who inherited the Augustan wealth and who received the support of the army. Roman ideas of inheritance combined with the natural wishes of Augustus to keep the position in the possession of his family. Though he seems to have expressed a certain unwillingness to found a dynasty, his own actions and the attitude of the people indicated a belief that the person he designated as his personal heir would inherit the position of *princeps* as well. When his nephew Marcellus was married to Julia, only child of Augustus, and was advanced to high office in early manhood, the world assumed that these actions were equivalent to designation for succession. After the death of Marcellus in 23 B.C. Agrippa, chief assistant of Augustus in his rise to power and recipient of the latter's signet ring during his illness of 23 B.C., was married to Julia and received proconsular and tribunician powers almost equal to those of Augustus.

It is evident that Augustus planned to bridge the gap between his own reign and that of his successor by conferring these powers with the concurrence of the senate. Fatality, however, dogged the footsteps of Augustus. When Agrippa died in 12 B.C. the princeps turned to his stepsons, Tiberius and Drusus, children of his third wife, Livia, and designated them as guardians for his grandsons, Gaius and Lucius, who had been born to Agrippa and Julia. After Drusus died in 9 B.C., Tiberius was compelled to divorce his wife and marry Julia. He received the proconsular and tribunician powers by grant of the senate. The marriage was not a happy one, and when Augustus began to advance Gaius and Lucius, Tiberius retired to Rhodes. Julia, equally unhappy, engaged in a series of love affairs which resulted in her banishment. When, however, Lucius died in A.D. 2 and Gaius in A.D. 4, only Tiberius was left. Recalled from Rhodes, he received the tribunician and proconsular authorities again, was the actual ruler during the last ten years of Augustus' life, and succeeded to power when the great princeps died

A Section of the Frieze on the Ara Pacis (Altar of the Augustan Peace) Showing Members of Augustus' Family. (Photograph by Mary Francis Gyles, reproduced by Frank D. Grande)

in A.D. 14. By Augustus' wish, Tiberius adopted Germanicus who was a grandson of Octavia and husband of Julia's daughter Agrippina. But the problem of succession remained undetermined and returned to vex later generations.

The Senate   The great deliberative body of the republic was theoretically still the guiding force from which Augustus received his powers and to which he rendered account. In reality the senate became one of the agencies the autocrat used to execute his will. A great deal of trouble during succeeding reigns was caused by Augustus' failure to define clearly the relations between the princeps and the senate. This omission was due, perhaps, to his understanding of the conflict between theory and reality and his unwillingness to offend senatorial feelings. He offered various suggestions to encourage the senate to clear its membership of provincials and undesirables who had secured enrollment during the civil wars, but after these methods failed he assumed a personal control over the senatorial list which made him master of that body. He organized a council composed of certain of the magistrates and fifteen (later twenty) senators to assist him in administrative matters and to prepare measures for senatorial discussion and action. Through this he was able to sense the feelings of the senate, avoid opposition, and at the same time make his own wishes known in a tactful but effective manner. Though he showed great deference to that body and referred important problems to it for legislation, it is doubtful if he would have allowed really independent action. In any case the members, except for a few outspoken malcontent republicans, were so overawed by his power and cowed by their revolutionary experiences that they hesitated to act or to speak freely and instead merely ratified his wishes. As a result the famous *senatus consulta* in actuality came to be legislation by Augustus which was merely consented to by the senate. Though some measures were still carried to the assemblies for legislation, the power and activities of these bodies declined rapidly. Imperial control of nominations made even their elective function formal, and in the reign of Tiberius both legislation and elections were transferred *in toto* to the senate. Control over foreign affairs, the reception of embassies, and the negotiation of treaties passed naturally into the hands of Augustus. However the senate during his reign assumed as a body the functions of a high court of justice, taking cognizance of cases involving its members under charges of corruption or malfeasance in office, or offenses against the majesty of the emperor or the state.

Officials of the Empire In accordance with his stated adherence to republican tradition Augustus continued to use members of the senatorial order in military and political positions as officers of the legions, governors of the provinces, and magistrates in Rome. The old senatorial career continued therefore with some additions. The aspirants to office served in minor military commands and judicial positions (the latter a new feature), held the magistracies in Rome in proper order, and then served as governors of provinces or lieutenants of Augustus. The holding of the quaestorship carried with it membership in the senate. To these duties Augustus added administrative positions by creating senatorial curatorships, permanent boards to look after such functions as the care of roads, public buildings, aqueducts, and the bed and banks of the Tiber.

The republican magistrates, however, gradually declined in power. Imperial appointees overshadowed the quaestors in the provinces, while in Rome care of the treasury was given to two senators of consular rank. Though the praetors retained their judicial functions, their powers became circumscribed and gradually declined until later in the empire they were merely city magistrates. The consuls likewise lost most of their administrative duties as Augustus assumed charge of the direction of the city and entrusted its care to prefects of equestrian rank.

The senators retained withal their lofty social position, and public opinion demanded of them high standards of wealth, morals, and manners. Accordingly Augustus revised the senatorial list and reduced the number of senators to six hundred once more. Proscriptions and small families had brought to an end many of the great houses of early times, and the old patrician class, still needed for certain priesthoods, had almost disappeared. Moreover, many of the senators had lost the financial means of maintaining their position; manners and morals had grown distressingly lax; skepticism had broken down religion; the old glory of service to Rome had been lost; and senators who still clung to the ancient ideals were openly critical of Augustus and the new regime. Reorganization of the senate and reawakening of its old religious and patriotic loyalties were imperative. To meet these needs Augustus established a high property qualification for the office, provided pensions for worthy but impoverished senators, elevated many to the patriciate, and took measures to revive religion and morals and to secure support for himself. By these means he built up a senatorial class which, in spite of the dissensions and troubles of succeeding reigns, served the Roman Empire well and loyally.

For the higher posts in the civil service and for efficient management of imperial finance, Augustus turned to the equestrian class, which thus reaped the fruits of its long struggle with the senatorial order and of its support of Caesar and Augustus. The class of *Equites* was definitely established to include all Roman citizens of means, excluding senators, but with a property qualification much lower than that required of the senatorial order. The knights bore special marks of distinction and passed through a definite series of offices. After service in the army with the auxiliary forces, they entered upon secretarial and financial positions, becoming procurators in the various bureaus of government and governors of such minor provinces as Judaea. (Pontius Pilate was such a procurator.) The summit of their career was the holding of one or more of the great imperial prefectures by which the rule of Egypt, the command of the watch and of the imperial bodyguard, or the care of the grain supply was entrusted to them. In these capacities they gradually assumed the functions of the republican magistrates and became powerful officials in the empire. The knights could be depended upon for loyalty to the system which brought them prosperity and recognition.

For the lower posts in the financial and secretarial service, skilled freedmen were widely used. They entered this service as secretaries of great men or as clerks performing duties the Romans regarded as beneath their dignity. Of their ability and their loyalty to the new regime there was no doubt. Their opportunities in the imperial service and in business were unrestricted, and many acquired important posts and great wealth. The municipalities in which they served conferred high distinction upon some of these freedmen when they were chosen as *Augustales*, priests for the worship of Augustus.

The Army   The army, the real foundation of Augustus' power, was the object of his greatest solicitude. Great numbers of the revolutionary troops were dismissed and given land as pensions. A permanent army of three hundred thousand men was established. Twenty-five legions of six thousand citizens each formed the main body, to which were added an equal number of provincials, who were enrolled as auxiliaries. In addition to their numbers and standards, the legion and the auxiliary cohorts received names expressive of their achievements or of their place of enlistment. Thus Legion III Gallica was organized in Gaul, and XX Valeria Victrix received its name from its general Valerius Messalinus and its victory under his command in the Pannonian revolt of A.D. 6. Similarly Cohort I Gallica was raised among the provincials in Gaul. A select body of nine thousand troops drawn from Italy was stationed in the vicinity of Rome under two prefects as the praetorian cohort or bodyguard of the princeps. Soldiers, enlisted for fixed terms of years, were entitled to bonuses or lands at the end of their service. Auxiliaries received the grant of Roman citizenship. When the cost of the army bonuses and pensions proved too great for the treasury, Augustus established the *aerarium militare*, "military treasury," a special fund supported by a 5 per cent inheritance and a 1 per cent sales tax. A permanent fleet with headquarters at Ravenna and Misenum was organized to keep down piracy.

Italy   The Augustan peace brought political order and economic restoration to Italy and the provinces. The problems of Italy had been solved during the time of the triumvirate when, after the period of confiscations and resettlement, Augustus had entered upon a definite program for the encouragement of Italian agriculture. In this he made use of the erudition of Varro, who composed *De Re Rustica*, a textbook on farming, and of the poetic skill of Vergil, whose *Georgics*, written at imperial behest, form both a textbook on farming in poetic form and a glorious tribute to the beauties and richness of the Italian land.

The Empire   Augustus divided the provinces between himself and the senate. He took all the newer and the frontier provinces where an army was required as imperial provinces to be governed by his lieutenants. Provinces that were thoroughly pacified were retained by the senate and governed as before by promagistrates.

The senatorial provinces were Asia, Bithynia, Cyprus, Crete with Cyrene, Macedonia, and Achaea in the East; Sicily, Africa, Hispania Baetica, and Gallia Narbonensis in the West. Edicts found at Cyrene prove that Augustus possessed the power of interfering in the affairs of the senatorial provinces, "until the senate comes to a decision on the subject or I find a better plan." The control he exercised over the appointment of governors to the imperial provinces and this practice of supervision in the others enabled him to check the malpractice of republican years and to repress any tendency toward revolutionary action. The establishment of a paid secretariat to collect certain taxes and supervise finances removed at the same time the worst burdens of corruption

The Mausoleum (Tomb) of Augustus. The dome that originally covered
this imposing brick building has disappeared — probably as a result
of vandalism rather than structural deficiencies. (Photograph by Mary
Francis Gyles, reproduced by Frank D. Grande)

under which the provincials had suffered at the hands of the *Equites*.
He clung to the republican idea of Roman rule in the hands of men of
senatorial rank, and departed from the precedents and ideas of Caesar,
who had extended citizenship to provincials and allowed provincial
representation in the senate.

Augustus spent the years 27–24 B.C. in the West and 22–19 B.C.
in the East setting provincial affairs in order. While the older province
of Gaul, modern Provence, was left as Gallia Narbonensis under senatorial control, Caesar's conquests were organized into three imperial
provinces with a common center at Lyons. Out of Spain, whose conquest
was finally ended after two centuries of warfare by the subjugation of
the mountain tribes in 16 B.C., three provinces were created. Two were
imperial; the third, in the south, was senatorial. The romanization of
Gaul and Spain proceeded apace as both regions became prosperous.
In later generations many men of letters and even some of the emperors
were of Spanish or Gallic descent. Africa, a senatorial province with one
legion under its proconsul to guard the frontier, speedily became
wealthy once more. Though Carthage was a Roman colony — the
remains of cities, temples, and aqueducts prove that it was well Romanized — the older Phoenician elements in the population remained strong,
and the Phoenician language continued to be spoken down to Christian

times. Herod the Great (p. 520) was permitted to remain as king of Judaea, but shortly after his death the kingdom became a province (A.D. 6) under a procurator of equestrian rank subject to the supervision of the governor of Syria. Egypt was unique among the provinces. Since Augustus feared to entrust its wealth and its control over Rome's grain supply to an ordinary governor, and since its own system of government did not fit into the Roman scheme, Augustus kept it as a personal possession and ruled it as pharaoh. For actual administration he appointed a prefect of equestrian rank; he even went so far as to forbid senators to visit Egypt without permission. As pharaoh, his statues were set up and his name was written in hieroglyphs in the temples.

The Frontier　　The Augustan frontier policy was one of completion and pacification. The southern frontier of Egypt was made secure by a war with the Ethiopians, and although an expedition in southern Arabia failed, the Romans gained control of the Red Sea trade. In Asia Minor, Galatia was annexed; Armenia became a client kingdom under a native ruler nominated by Rome; and peace was made with the Parthians, who surrendered the standards and captives of the earlier wars. The northern frontier was extended to the Danube by a series of expeditions in the Balkans and in the Alps. Britain was definitely abandoned, but Augustus planned to shorten the Rhine-Danube frontier by extending the boundaries to the Elbe. A series of brilliant campaigns led by Drusus and Tiberius, the stepsons of Augustus, brought the region partially under Roman control. But by a sudden revolt in A.D. 9 under a Roman-trained chieftain named Arminius, the Germans succeeded in defeating and destroying a Roman army of three legions under Varus in the Teutoburg Forest. The loss of men was serious, and Augustus gave up the idea of reconquest.

Finances　　The state treasury received its income from the tribute of the senatorial provinces, collected as of old, although Augustus corrected the worst evils of the tax-farming system by proper supervision. The expenses of the government were too great for this income, however, and Augustus was constrained on several occasions to come to the rescue with substantial contributions from his own wealth. The management of the personal property of Augustus and of the finances of the imperial provinces was in the hands of procurators—secretaries who were knights or freedmen. No fixed rule was laid down for the collection of taxes: many were still sold to tax farmers, others were handled directly by imperial agents. To facilitate imperial collections, Augustus decreed a census of the entire empire. An echo of this order is to be found in the story of the birth of Christ.[2]

---

[2] The date of this census, probably 9–8 B.C., and the date of the death of Herod, in 4 B.C., indicate that the medieval chroniclers made a mistake in their dating of the birth of Christ, which is variously placed by modern scholars as between 8 and 4 B.C.

Economic Rehabilitation The restoration of peace and order was accompanied by general economic rehabilitation. With security of property assured, farmers throughout the Mediterranean world were able to work their lands and reap the fruits of their toil. With piracy suppressed, with the road system repaired, extended, and policed, and with the world at peace, merchants and goods could pass freely by sea and land from one corner of the empire to the other. Private enterprise was free to act and develop without fear of governmental interference, and, indeed, with the assurance of imperial support. The relations with Parthia and the campaign in Arabia were both based primarily on a desire to secure the benefits of trade. Large-scale factories appeared, particularly in the pottery, metal, glass, and paper industries, though many small shops continued to prosper in filling local needs and in manufacturing goods for profit. Mass production was achieved by increasing the number of workers in any given industry.

Italian pottery (the famous Arretine ware) and metal goods were exported along with wine and oil into other sections of the empire. The papyrus, glassware, and linens of Egypt, the silk, wine, and fruits of Syria, the textiles of Phoenicia and Anatolia, the grain, meats, fruits, and vegetables of Sicily, Africa, and Gaul, and the metals of Spain traveled far from their places of origin.

Roman capitalists invested in provincial concerns, and Roman merchants vied with Greeks and Syrians for a share in the trade. New partnerships were established, centers for the exchange of market information were developed, and banking kept pace with the needs of commerce. Many in the world had, indeed, reason to be grateful to the princeps for the restoration of peace and for the latitude he allowed to individual action in the economic field.

Yet slavery was widely used in industry and agriculture, save in regions like Egypt where free labor was cheap. The low scale of wages did little to relieve the condition of the poverty-burdened lower classes of the empire. In Rome though a free man could usually secure some occupation, Augustus found it necessary to aid the populace by giving free grain and occasional sums of money, and to provide games and shows to keep the people contented.

Moral and Religious Reform To restore the older standards and at the same time to secure support for himself, Augustus tried many devices. Clubs composed of the youth of the aristocracies in the cities of Italy and of the upper classes in Rome provided the new generation with military and athletic exercises along with patriotic training. Laws in 19 and 18 B.C. and again in A.D. 9 laid heavy penalties on adultery and on celibacy, encouraged marriage and the bearing of children, and forbade marriage between the senatorial and freedmen classes. Men and women with three children were given special preference in all positions

A Room from a Villa near Boscoreale, ca. 40–30 B.C. The furnishings and pavement are from the first and second centuries A.D. (The Metropolitan Museum of Art)

of honor or power. The older senators opposed these laws as contrary to the republican tradition. The legislation, however, proved generally ineffective. Not even the imperial family respected the laws, for Augustus had to banish his own daughter and granddaughter for violations of the law concerning adultery.

At the same time Augustus tried to bring about a religious revival by rebuilding old temples and reviving obsolete priesthoods. At his behest Ovid wrote *Fasti*, a poetic account of the Roman festivals; Livy's *Roman History* and Vergil's *Aeneid* were literary attempts to acquaint the Romans with their great past and to arouse their dormant patriotism; and many of Horace's *Odes* praising simple ways and civic loyalties were written in the same service. In 17 B.C. the secular games were held, a jubilee festival to celebrate the revival of Roman power under Augustus. For this occasion Horace composed a hymn to be sung by a chorus.

But to what extent the whole Augustan program met with success it is difficult to say. While Augustus and his successors were well served in the administration of the empire, in Rome jealousy and discontent remained to vex and harass both princeps and senators.

CULTURE

Architecture   Meanwhile the city of Rome was being rebuilt to make it a worthy capital of an empire. Augustus boasted, "I found Rome a city of brick, I left it marble." Eighty-two temples were repaired; the Capitoline Temple of Jupiter and the Senate House were rebuilt. Near the spot where Caesar's body had been burned, a temple to the "Deified Julius" was erected. The Forum of Julius Caesar was completed and the new Forum of Augustus constructed. In the latter, as the Hall of Fame for imperial Rome, was the temple of Mars Ultor, guardian of the Augustan Peace. On the Palatine near the home of Augustus were erected temples to Apollo, with libraries attached, to the Great Mother, and to Vesta. Older theaters and basilicas were repaired, and the new theater of Marcellus was added. In the Campus Martius, Agrippa built the Pantheon, dedicated to the Stoic "All-divine." Most beautiful of the monuments and symbolic of the new order was the Altar of the Augustan Peace, ornamented with pictures symbolizing peace, prosperity, and plenty, and with a processional relief containing portraits of the imperial family and the leading men of Rome.

Latin literature reached its climax, its golden age, under Augustus. Its great historian, Livy, and its poets, Vergil, Horace, and Ovid, masters of language and form, produced works filled with the richness and peace of the Augustan era.

Livy (59 B.C.–A.D. 17)   A native of Padua, Livy composed a magnificent history of Rome, *From the Founding of the City*. He wrote this prose epic of the greatness of Rome with the avowed purpose of calling the Romans back from the vices of the day to ancient virtues by a recital of the glorious deeds through which Roman power was obtained and increased. Though a literary artist interested primarily in the telling of a great story, and without Polybius' stern conception of history as a textbook for generals and statesmen, Livy nevertheless showed ability as a historian. He was intelligent in the handling and criticism of his sources. He recognized the lack of accurate information for the earlier period and the weaknesses of the family traditions on which the annalists from whom he drew had depended and which he himself was forced to use. When he found varying opinions, he chose that which seemed best founded. With a clear and vivid historical imagination, he wove so well the strands of information collected by his predecessors or his erudite contemporaries that no ancient historian was ever able to rival his magnificent achievement. In fact, those who wrote later of republican Rome leaned heavily upon him. His style was vigorous, at times poetic and dramatic; Tacitus proclaimed him renowned for eloquence and truthfulness, "and it must be remembered that his very art attains a truth of its own. He possessed gifts of real historical worth—the gift of reverence for the majesty of Rome; the gift of enthusiasm for olden times, olden heroes, olden virtues; the gift of imagination through sympathy which feels, even if imperfectly, the spirit of the past."[3] The modern student may still feel the thrill that comes from reading Livy's account of Rome's rise to power and of the men whose virtues made Rome great. His work remains our chief source, at times our only source, for the early history of Rome. The disappearance of all but thirty-five books of his history, save for a late epitome, is an irreparable loss.

Vergil (70 B.C.–19 B.C.)   Vergil was an epic poet of the first rank. Born in Mantua of a farmer father, he went to Rome for an education. There, by his group of pastoral poems called *Eclogues*, written after the style of Theocritus, he attracted the attention of Maecenas, friend of Augustus and patron of letters. The fourth of these poems, containing a prediction of the return of the golden age to the world, has been called the Messianic eclogue, and because of the unlikely supposition that it referred to the birth of Christ it gave Vergil an important place in Christian history. More probably, it anticipated an heir to Augustus.

> On thee, child, everywhere shall earth, untilled,
> Show'r, her first baby-offerings, vagrant stems
> Of ivy, foxglove, and gay briar, and bean;
> Unbid the goats shall come big-uddered home,
> Nor monstrous lions scare the herded kine.
> Thy cradle shall be full of pretty flowers:
> Die must the serpent, treacherous poison-plants
> Must die; and Syria's roses spring like weeds. . . .
>
> The pilot's self shall range the seas no more;
> Nor, each land teeming with the wealth of all,
> The floating pines exchange their merchandise.
> Vines shall not need the pruning-hook, nor earth
> The harrow: ploughmen shall unyoke their steers.
> Nor then need wool be taught to counterfeit
> This hue and that. At will the meadow ram
> Shall change to saffron, or the gorgeous tints
> Of Tyre, his fair fleece; and the grazing lamb
> At will put crimson on. . . .[4]

[3] John Wight Duff, *A Literary History of Rome from the Origins to the Close of the Golden Age*. New York: Barnes & Noble, Inc., 1953, p. 473.

[4] George Howe and Gustave Adolfus Harrer, *Roman Literature in Translation*. New York; Harper & Row Publishers, 1924, pp. 342–343.

Maecenas, securing for Vergil means of support, encouraged him to compose *Georgics*, a poetic treatise on farming. Inspired by the Augustan age and prompted by Augustus himself, the poet wrote the *Aeneid*. While this great poem dealt with the story of the trials of Aeneas as he journeyed from Troy to Italy, it was really the epic of Rome's past. It consecrated that *pietas*, "devotion to duty," which had made Rome great, and it declared the mission of Rome to conquer and organize the world. In it poetic skill was blended with the poet's deep feeling for humanity to produce many memorable pictures and unforgettable lines. "In no other poetry are the chords of human sympathy so delicately touched, its tones so subtly interfused. In none is there so deep a sense of the beauty and sorrow of life, of keen remembrance and shadowy hope, and, enfolding all, of infinite pity."[5]

> Let others better mould the running mass
> Of metals, and inform the breathing brass,
> And soften into flesh a marble face;
> Plead better at the bar; describe the skies,
> And when the stars ascend, and when they rise.
> But Rome! 'tis thine alone, with awful sway,
> To rule mankind, and make the world obey.
> Disposing peace and war thy own majestic way;
> To tame the proud, the fetter'd slave to free;
> These are imperial arts, and worthy thee.[6]

Horace (65–8 B.C.)   Horace, the friend of Vergil, was of humble birth (his father was a freedman) and, like Vergil, he owed his means of living to the patronage of Maecenas. He became a skilled writer of lyrics and an urbane interpreter of his own age and of the art of living. In matchless verse he portrayed the pleasures of the simple life, trifled with mild affairs of the heart, glorified the civic virtues, and sang the praises of Augustus. He has been studied, translated, and paraphrased by other poets down to our own times, and many of his poems ring as true today as they did when they were written. In a famous ode, "Snatch the day" (*Carpe diem*), the eleventh of the first book, he expressed his attitude toward life.

> Do not ask—it is not for us to know—what end
> Will be given to me or to you, Leuconoe,
> Nor meddle with Babylonian numbers,
> Whether you live more years or this be the last assigned by Jupiter
> In which the Tyrrhenean Sea eats away its rocks.
> Be wise, strain the wine and prune away hope of a long life.

---

[5] John W. Mackail. *Vergil and His Meaning*. New York: Cooper Square Publishers. 1963, p. 110.

[6] George Howe and Gustave Adolfus Harrer, *Roman Literature in Translation*. New York: Harper & Row Publishers, 1924, p. 318.

> Our span is short, and even as we talk
> Envious time will flee.
> Snatch this day. Expect little from the future.[7]

In another poem he offered the poet's prayer to Apollo:

> Health to enjoy the blessings sent
>   From heaven; a mind unclouded, strong;
> A cheerful heart; a wise content;
>   An honored age; and song.[8]

The Elegiac Poets Among a number of youths of wealth who amused themselves and delighted their friends by producing polite love songs written in the elegiac meter were Tibullus, Propertius, and Ovid. Of these the most brilliant and versatile was Ovid (43 B.C.–A.D. 18). Belonging to the younger set who rejected the strict standards of Augustus, he composed a series of verses on love affairs and on the art and remedy of love itself. He wrote *Fasti*, an account of Roman festivals, to please Augustus, and in his celebrated poem, *Metamorphoses*, he presents the greatest myths of the ancient Greeks. Involved in the scandal of the younger Julia, he was banished to an island in the Black Sea, where he portrayed and lamented his sad fate in *Tristia*.

Monumentum Ancyranum Augustus himself composed a résumé of his own achievements and of his services to Rome, which was inscribed on bronze tablets in front of his tomb in Rome. A copy of it in Latin and Greek was found in Ankara, ancient Ancyra, and fragments have since been discovered in other cities. Called *Monumentum Ancyranum*, it is one of our most precious sources for the history of the period.

Epilogue Estimates of the character and the services of Augustus have varied ever since his own time. Admirers of the great Julius have regarded Augustus as a crafty politician, a timeserver who gave Rome not a republic but a monarchy disguised under republican forms, like a sugar-coated pill. Others have seen him as a great statesman, sincere in his protestations of loyalty to the republic, the restorer of order to a troubled world, the "architect of the Roman Empire." It is almost impossible to arrive at any sound judgment of him as a person. In his early years he was indeed crafty and not too honest, as evidenced in his dealings with Cicero. The sanction he gave to the proscription and the destruction of Perusia proved him cruel and ruthless. Accession to power transformed him into a wise, farseeing statesman. He bowed to the sentiment of the times, proclaimed the restoration of the republic, and for the most part observed republican traditions. Yet he guarded his own position carefully. He retained command of the army, allowed

---

[7] Horace, *Carmina* 1.11.
[8] Grant Showerman, *Horace and His Influence*. New York: Cooper Square Publishers, 1963, p. 33.

A Table Support of Decorated Marble from the Augustan Period. (The Metropolitan Museum of Art, Rogers Fund, 1913)

himself to be worshiped as a Hellenistic god-king, and planned the hereditary succession to his power. At the same time with carefully considered policies he brought tranquillity and wealth to the Mediterranean world. The system he established endured through the vicissitudes of two centuries, and when it was finally overthrown, Rome began her decline. Augustus, therefore, must always occupy a place in the front rank of the statesmen of the world.

23 · The Great Age of the Roman Empire

URING THE YEARS THAT ELAPSED BETWEEN THE accession of Tiberius in A.D. 14 and the death of Marcus Aurelius in A.D. 180 the Roman Empire flourished and expanded under the guidance of the successors of Augustus. The age is readily divided into three periods: from A.D. 14 the Julian-Claudian house held the office of princeps; after a year of civil war the Flavian family, Vespasian and his two sons, ruled from A.D. 69–96; the third division is the age of the Antonines, A.D. 96–180.

The successive emperors were concerned with the varied problems of empire—the direction of provincial affairs, the control of the army, the defense of the frontiers, the building of roads, bridges, aqueducts, and triumphal arches throughout the empire—with the management and adornment of the imperial capital, with the difficult relations between the ruler and the senate, with the social life of the court, and with the problem of succession.

Sources Two types of sources, literary and archaeological, contribute information of varying sorts about the period. Surviving Roman literature furnishes accounts of the lives and the wars of the emperors, and pictures of the imperial court, with its intrigues, scandals, and murders; and of the busy and exciting life of the capital city. The archaeological sources include the inscriptions, papyri, coins, and remains of buildings, monuments, and public works which provide revelations of economic conditions and of governmental activities, both imperial and local. They disclose also the occupations, thoughts, and religions of the inhabitants of the empire.

THE JULIAN-CLAUDIAN EMPERORS, A.D. 14–68

Tiberius, A.D. **14–37** Fifty-six years of age when he succeeded to power, Tiberius was, by virtue of his character and experience, an excellent administrator. Under his guidance order was maintained in

493

Rome, and the governors of the provinces were held sternly in check. The northern frontier was definitely established at the Rhine. Though Germanicus, his nephew, adopted son, and recognized heir, avenged the defeat of Varus with three victorious campaigns in Germany, Tiberius refused to allow him to complete the conquest to the Elbe River because of the difficulty and the expense. On the eastern frontier friendly relations were maintained with Armenia and Parthia, and two small client kingdoms were changed into provinces to protect communications with these states.

Looking back, the most important event in Western history that took place under Tiberius was the trial and execution in Jerusalem of Jesus of Nazareth. But its significance was so little understood at the time that it passed unnoticed by imperial chroniclers until the rise of Christianity and the passage of years brought it to their attention.

Tiberius was unfortunate in his personal relations with the senatorial class. The bitterness and suspicion engendered by the disappointments of his earlier years had not softened a character naturally reserved and austere. His difficulties were intensified when, after the death of Germanicus in the East in A.D. 19, Agrippina, widow of Germanicus, accused him of removing his nephew from Germany because of jealousy, and of complicity in a supposed plot to poison him. Disgusted with the quarrels and recriminations that followed, Tiberius retired to Capri in A.D. 26, leaving his praetorian prefect Sejanus in charge of the city. Sejanus, an able man but deluded with dreams of grandeur, set out to secure the succession for himself. He poisoned Tiberius' son Drusus and obtained the exile of Agrippina and the death of two of her sons on charges of treason. Tiberius, learning of Sejanus' plans, removed him from office and had him and his followers executed. In the last years of his reign Tiberius struck at rebellious senators. The law of treason, *lex majestatis*, with its penalty of death, was extended to include any expression critical of the emperor, and paid informers watched for violations. The historian Tacitus, likening the events under Tiberius to his own experience in the last years of Domitian's reign, paints Tiberius' last years as a reign of terror. The facts he presents do not fully justify the charge. With the death of Tiberius in A.D. 37 the senate conferred his powers upon Gaius, sole surviving son of Germanicus and Agrippina.

Gaius Caligula, A.D. 37–41   Gaius, born in camp, was known to the army affectionately as Caligula, "Little Boot." His reign started auspiciously with promises of peace in Rome and renewal of imperial expansion into Britain. But it soon became clear that he was insane. Regarding himself as a god, he built a bridge from his house on the Palatine to Jupiter's temple on the Capitoline and ordered his statue to be set up in the Temple of Jerusalem. He murdered innocent people,

View of a Ruined Aqueduct near Rome. The details of the true arches constructed in stone are very clear. Bridges were built in the same way. (Photograph by Mary Francis Gyles, reproduced by Frank D. Grande)

gave wild entertainments, and spent all the imperial monies, so laboriously collected by Tiberius, in less than two years. In A.D. 41 he was murdered by an officer of the praetorian guard, his mad career ended.

Claudius, A.D. **41–54** A soldier of the guard looting in the palace discovered Claudius, brother of Germanicus and uncle of Gaius, hiding behind a curtain. Recognizing him as a member of the imperial family, the guard hailed him as emperor. The whole cohort took up the cry and forced the senate to consent to the accession of Claudius. Crippled in youth and reputed to be a half-wit because of his stammer and his ungainly appearance, Claudius had lived quietly and safely in the troubled times of Tiberius and Gaius and had pursued undisturbed his studies in the histories of Etruria and Carthage. But Claudius proved to be no fool. During his reign the empire was well and shrewdly managed. His most important administrative achievement was the creation of a permanent bureaucracy for the civil administration. Pallas, his freedman-secretary in charge of finance, concentrated the funds of the imperial provinces and estates in a single treasury, the *fiscus*; other freedmen took charge of correspondence, of petitions, and of information. Together they exercised a powerful influence on the mind and activities of the princeps.

Claudius constructed two new aqueducts at Rome, the Aqua Claudia and the Anio Novus, to bring more water to the city, and tried, by the construction of breakwaters and docks at the mouth of the Tiber, to make Ostia a suitable port for Rome. Returning to the policy of Julius Caesar, he conferred Roman citizenship and Latin rights on many Gauls and made some Aeduan nobles members of the senate. During his reign, southern Britian was conquered and Thrace was added to the list of Roman provinces.

Claudius married Messalina, by whom he had a son, Britannicus, and a daughter, Octavia. Messalina's reputation was shockingly bad, and when in A.D. 48 the freedman Narcissus claimed to have discovered her in a plot to overthrow the princeps, Claudius ordered her execution. The following year he married his niece Agrippina, daughter of Germanicus and the elder Agrippina. This ambitious woman, gaining complete dominance over the aging Claudius, caused him to adopt her son, Lucius Domitius. He took the Claudian name Nero and became the emperor's elder son. When Claudius died in A.D. 54, all Rome believed that Agrippina had murdered him.

Nero, A.D. 54–68 Nero, who had married Octavia, succeeded to power without opposition. He promised a return to the Augustan principles of senatorial rule and a wise administration. Under the guidance of his tutors and advisers, the philosopher Seneca and the praetorian prefect Burrus, the promise was kept for eight years. An intelligent reform of the coinage was effected; measures were taken to assist Italian agriculture; able governors were selected to manage provincial affairs; and in Britain the dangerous revolt of Boudicca was put down.

Nero's private life was filled with scandalous behavior. Nightly revels in the streets and taverns of Rome led him into all kinds of excesses, and Agrippina, who tried to restrain him and to keep the power she had enjoyed under Claudius, was sent away from the court and was murdered in A.D. 59. After first divorcing, then banishing, and finally executing Octavia, Nero married Poppaea Sabina, the most celebrated beauty of the day. When Burrus died in A.D. 62 and Seneca lost all control of his pupil, Nero turned to fresh dissipations with the assistance of the new prefect, Tigellinus. Preferring music and drama of the Greek type to gladiatorial shows, in curious opposition to Roman tastes, and regarding himself as a great artist, he began to appear in public in his own compositions.

A great fire in Rome in A.D. 64, which began in the shops at the east end of the Circus and burned ten of the fourteen wards of the city, involved Nero in serious trouble. Though he hastened to take proper relief measures, it was said that during the fire he sat in his palace on the Palatine, played his lyre and recited verses from his own tragedy on the fall of Troy. The city was rebuilt with wider streets and better materials, but when he reserved a large area between the Palatine and the Esquiline for a park and an imperial palace, the Golden House, beautifully designed and decorated, he was accused of starting the fire. Though it was an idle accusation, he looked for a scapegoat and found it in an obscure sect called Christians. These unfortunates, convicted of arson, were put to death in most horrible fashions to satisfy public clamor. Tradition records that St. Peter and St. Paul met their deaths at this time.

The years that followed were difficult. To obtain money to pay for rebuilding the city and to provide for his own extravagances, Nero revived the law of treason, struck down wealthy senators, or trumped up charges against them in order to confiscate their estates. A plot against him in A.D. 65 was discovered and ruthlessly suppressed; among the victims were Seneca and his nephew, the poet Lucan. In A.D. 66 Nero left for Greece to appear as a contestant in the national games where, in a burst of enthusiasm, he declared the freedom of the Greek cities. While in Greece, he sent Vespasian to suppress a serious revolt in Judaea. When Nero returned to Italy he heard graver news of an uprising in Gaul, not against Rome but against himself. Hated by the senate and deserted by the praetorians, he fled from Rome, was declared a public enemy, and was killed by a faithful servant at his own command. His name has ever since been a symbol of excesses of all kinds and an object of execration to Christian writers. Yet by his interest in, and patronage of, the arts he did much to stimulate a second creative age, called the silver age. With the death of Nero the house of Caesar became extinct. As his successor, the senate recognized Galba, the able, experienced, but aged governor of Spain, who was already on the march to Rome.

The revolt against Nero, with his interests in Greece and in Hellenistic culture, signaled an interimperial shift of power from the Greek East to the Latinized West. The succeeding reigns were to see Spaniards and Gauls increasingly powerful and important at Rome. But the year A.D. 68, following Nero's death, brought one crisis after another, and the deaths in turn of Galba, Otho, and Vitellius.

The events that followed the death of Nero revealed at once the consequences of Augustus' failure to provide for an orderly succession, the weakness of the senate, and the fundamental military basis of the principate. Galba was the candidate of the praetorian guards, who had already revealed their power in the selection of Claudius. When Galba proved unfit for the imperial task after a rule of seven months, the guards overthrew him and placed Otho in power. After a reign of eighty-eight days Otho fell on his sword when the Rhine legions took Rome and established their commander Vitellius as princeps. Vitellius was even less capable than his two immediate predecessors, and while he indulged in banquets of extraordinary cost, Italy was being plundered by his army. He was easily overthrown in A.D. 69 by the armies of the East, who hailed Vespasian as emperor. Not the votes of the senate but the civil war between the military forces of the empire settled the question of who was to rule Rome.

The Colosseum. This huge arena was built by Vespasian on the site formerly occupied by a colossal statue of Nero; hence its name. Its partly ruined condition is due to vandalism in the post-imperial era rather than to faulty construction. (Italian State Tourist Office)

THE FLAVIAN DYNASTY, A.D. 69–96

Vespasian, A.D. **69–79**   The Eastern armies, jealous of the army of the Rhine, chose as their candidate Vespasian, commander in the war against the Jews. After the army of the Danube had killed Vitellius and had sacked Rome, the senate yielded, and in one act, the famous *lex de imperio Vespasiani,* conferred upon Vespasian all the powers that had been held by his predecessors.[1] An able ruler, he proceeded at once to restore order to the empire, and by strict economy and new taxes, carefully collected, to rebuild the shattered finances of the state. The senate received a needed infusion of new blood by the admission of provincials from Gaul and Spain. The ravages of the sack of the city were erased; the Capitoline Temple was rebuilt; a Forum and Temple of Peace were erected; and on the walls of the new Temple of the Sacred City was placed a marble map of Rome. Nero's Golden House was partly demolished and in its park Vespasian began to build the famous amphitheater, the Colosseum. To establish a high intellectual level for his court, he patronized men of letters and founded professor-

[1] Drawn up by the senate and ratified by the assembly.

ships of Greek and Latin rhetoric. The chief event of Vespasian's reign in the provinces was the Jewish War, which he had begun and which his son Titus brought to a victorious conclusion by the destruction of Jerusalem in A.D. 70 (p. 521).

Titus, A.D. **79–81** Titus, who had been associated in power with Vespasian, became princeps at his father's death. He was a man of great charm, ability, and universal popularity, and was well trained in administration. After confirming his father's acts and gifts, he erected baths and completed the Colosseum, which he dedicated with a hundred days of games. His reign is best known for a catastrophe, the eruption of Vesuvius which buried Pompeii and Herculaneum. Titus died of a fever in A.D. 81 and was succeeded by his brother, Domitian.

Domitian, A.D. **81–96** Excluded from a share in the administration by his father, Domitian spent his youth in a study of history, particularly of the memoirs of Tiberius. The sound conception which he thus secured of the resources and the dangers of the empire was reflected in his policies as emperor. In Rome he followed a policy of adherence to tradition. As perpetual censor, he endeavored to revive old practices in morals and religion. Scandalous actions and writings were suppressed, and a vestal who had broken her vows was buried alive according to the ancient law. Attempts to restore the old religion brought the Christians to his attention, and there were several executions. He continued the imperial attempts to improve the condition of Italian agriculture by encouraging the growing of grain and by restricting vineyards.

The northern frontier occupied much of his attention. Agricola, a competent general whose renown is due to Tacitus' biography of him, finished the conquest of Britain but was recalled when he planned a costly expedition to Ireland. To improve the frontier defenses on the Rhine, where the restlessness of German tribes were a presage of coming events, Domitian built the *limes,* a line of forts across the base of the triangle formed by the Rhine and the Danube. Trouble with the Dacians north of the Danube was settled by a compromise. Decebalus, the Dacian king, recognized the sovereignty of Rome and was promised a subsidy to assist him in his struggles with the wilder tribes to the east.

Domitian's rule marked a long step forward to the monarchical principle, with a demand for a clear recognition of the supremacy of the emperor over the senate. A thoroughgoing autocrat, he assumed control over the appointment of senators through the perpetual censorship and insisted that he be addressed as *"dominus et deus,"* "lord and god." The dynastic principle by which he had attained the purple and which he emphasized by building a temple to the deified Vespasian offended the senators and was regarded with hostility by the Stoic philosophers, who wanted the rule of the "wisest man." Criticism was intolerable to Domitian, and the friction which inevitably resulted between him and the senators from his policy of suppression produced a reign of terror toward the end of his reign that Tacitus compared to the last years of Tiberius. After the discovery of a plot against Domitian, philosophers were banished and senators were put to death, while literary men who had been encouraged to write in the early years of the reign no longer dared to express themselves. Finally a plot, in which his wife had a share, was successful, and Domitian was assassinated in A.D. 96. By order of the senate his name was erased from his monuments and his memory forever cursed. The historians Tacitus and Dio Cassius record the terror of these years of oppression. The senate chose Nerva, a senator over sixty years of age, to succeed him. The army accepted the nomination.

During the Flavian period the monarchical principle of the Roman Empire made a great advance. The military foundation of the ruling family, the principle of dynastic inheritance, and the policies of Vespasian and more particularly of Domitian made clearly evident the real mastery of the emperor in the Roman state.

THE AGE OF THE ANTONINES, A.D. 96–180

The accession of Nerva ushered in a period known as the age of the Antonines, or the age of the Good Emperors. The superior power of the princeps, immensely strengthened by the Flavian dynasty, was definitely recognized by the senate, and dreams of republican liberty were forgotten. The rulers left individual senators alone and received in return wholehearted cooperation in the administration of the empire and in the various commissions and offices which were created. Tacitus declared that Nerva combined the principate and liberty, two elements once considered opposites. The care taken by the emperors to secure the best man available to succeed them pleased the philosophers. Under the five emperors from Nerva to Marcus Aurelius the empire was well governed and prosperous.

Nerva, A.D. 96–98 Nerva appointed senatorial commissions to reorganize the finances and to further the cause of Italian agriculture. The latter aim was combined with a measure to increase population, by which money was distributed to municipalities to be loaned to farmers at low rates of interest. The income therefrom was applied to helping the children of the poor. Some of this income was used to support local schools. Nerva adopted as his successor the ablest of his generals, M. Ulpius Trajanus, governor of Upper Germany.

Trajan, A.D. 98–117 Trajan was born to a Roman family long resident in Spain and hence was the first non-Italian emperor. He was by character and training a soldier – sharp, precise, and practical. The

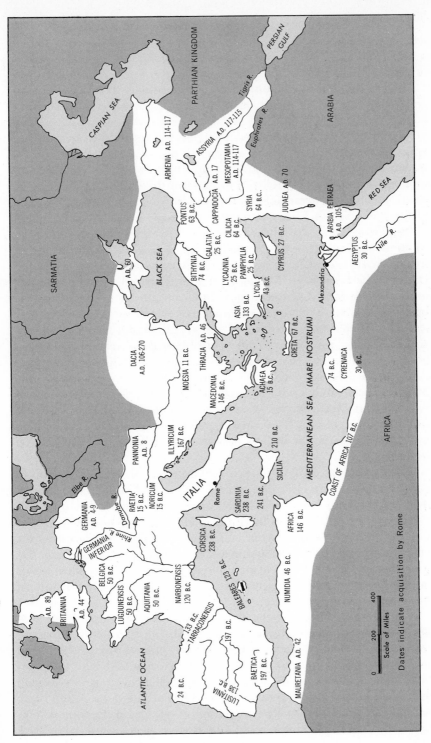

PARTHIAN KINGDOM

PERSIAN GULF

CASPIAN SEA

SARMATIA

ARABIA

ARMENIA A.D. 114-117

ASSYRIA A.D. 117-115

Tigris R.

Euphrates R.

RED SEA

MESOPOTAMIA A.D. 114-117

CAPPADOCIA A.D. 17

PONTUS 63 B.C.

BLACK SEA

SYRIA 64 B.C.

JUDAEA A.D. 70

ARABIA PETRAEA A.D. 105

A.D. 60

GALATIA 25 B.C.

CILICIA 64 B.C.

BITHYNIA 74 B.C.

LYCAONIA 25 B.C.

CYPRUS 27 B.C.

Nile R.

AEGYPTUS 30 B.C.

PAMPHYLIA 25 B.C.

Alexandria

LYCIA 43 B.C.

DACIA A.D. 106-270

ASIA 133 B.C.

THRACIA A.D. 46

MOESIA 11 B.C.

CRETA 67 B.C.

MACEDONIA 146 B.C.

ACHAEA 15 B.C.

CYRENAICA

74 B.C.

30 B.C.

PANNONIA A.D. 8

ILLYRICUM 167 B.C.

MEDITERRANEAN SEA (MARE NOSTRUM)

Elbe R.

RAETIA 15 B.C.

Danube R.

NORICUM 15 B.C.

SICILIA 210 B.C.

COAST OF AFRICA 107 B.C.

GERMANIA A.D. 49

ITALIA

Rome

Rhine R.

GERMANIA INFERIOR

SARDINIA 238 B.C.

AFRICA

BELGICA 50 B.C.

CORSICA 238 B.C.

241 B.C.

AFRICA 146 B.C.

A.D. 89

A.D. 44

LUGDUNENSIS 50 B.C.

AQUITANIA 50 B.C.

NARBONENSIS 120 B.C.

BALEARES 123 B.C.

NUMIDIA 46 B.C.

BRITANNIA

ATLANTIC OCEAN

133 B.C.

TARRACONENSIS

197 B.C.

24 B.C.

BAETICA 197 B.C.

MAURETANIA A.D. 42

LUSITANIA 138 B.C.

0   200   400

Scale of Miles

Dates indicate acquisition by Rome

The Roman Empire Under Trajan, A.D. 117

letters he wrote to his diligent governor Pliny display these characteristics and at the same time indicate his interest in the smallest details
of provincial and municipal government.

His reign was distinguished by extraordinary building activities
and by frontier wars that carried the Roman Empire to its furthest
bounds.

In Rome Trajan constructed a magnificent forum with colonnades,
apses, basilica, libraries, and a temple. In one of the courts still stands
the great column (dedicated after his death) on which his Dacian Wars
were recorded in spiral relief. Throughout the empire he built many
roads, including a great military highway from Gaul along the Danube
to the Black Sea. A bridge that bears his name is still in use in Spain.

He completed the northern frontier by the conquest of Dacia,
where Domitian's program of subsidization had become a source of
irritation. In two wars during which Trajan built a bridge across the
Danube, the Dacians were conquered and destroyed, and the land was
so thoroughly settled with Romanized provincials that it bears today the
name Romania. Trajan endeavored to extend the empire on the
eastern frontier as well. One of his generals added to the empire
Arabia Petraea, important for its control over the caravan routes from
Southern Arabia to the Mediterranean, and famous today for the
ruins of the rose-red city of Petra. When trouble arose with Parthia,
Trajan himself conquered and annexed Armenia, created a province of
Assyria, and captured the great cities of Babylonia. Before the war
could be brought to a victorious conclusion, however, he was recalled
by a revolt in Syria. On his way back to deal with this problem he died
in Cilicia in 117.

Hadrian, A.D. **117–138** Hadrian, a cousin of Trajan, and probably adopted by him as he lay dying, was recognized by the army and
the senate as his successor. Four generals who quarreled with this
decision were put to death by order of the senate. The new emperor
was far different in character and ideals from his predecessor, for
Hadrian was a scholar and administrator rather than a conqueror. He
spent fourteen out of his twenty-one years of rule in the provinces or
on the frontier, and his reign is of great importance in the history of
Roman imperial organization.

His general policy on the frontiers was one of consolidation and
defense. The Roman wall was built across the northern end of Britain;
the defenses (limes) of the Rhine-Danube line were extended, and
forts were built to protect Dacia, which was organized into two provinces. The tribes beyond the border received native rulers educated
at Rome and named by Hadrian. A number of kingdoms in the Black
Sea region submitted to Roman power when Arrian, famous scholar
and officer of the emperor, led the Roman fleet around the Black

The Pantheon from the Front. The dome can just be seen, but if the picture had been taken from ground level, it would not be visible, as was, apparently, the intention of the architect. The inscription of Marcus Agrippa, Augustus' son-in-law, who paid for construction of the Pantheon, shows clearly. Hadrian repaired and rebuilt the temple ca. A.D. 125. It is the oldest domed building of Roman construction and is presently used as a Christian church. (Photograph by Frank D. Grande)

Sea. In the East, Armenia was re-established as a client kingdom, Assyria was abandoned, but Arabia was kept, and peace was maintained with Parthia. Hadrian suppressed a Jewish revolt, built a temple on Mount Zion, and forbade the Jews entrance to the temple area.

The army was extensively reorganized. Hadrian placed cohorts in permanent camps along the frontier and allowed recruiting in the region around them. At the same time he completed the organization of the detachments of engineers and of the hospital service. He introduced a solid formation, a modification of the older phalanx system, to secure the steadiness necessary for meeting the wild charges of the barbarians. Hard drills and three long marches each month kept the soldiers in condition.

The central administration was put on a sound basis. Since the days of Claudius, the secretariat had been filled with freedmen or with knights at the choice of the individual princes. Hadrian established a permanent equestrian bureaucracy opening to the knights a definite civil career (p. 509). The civil service thus established developed traditions of its own apart from the military, and served the empire well during the confusion of the third century. Hadrian's legal reforms, the codification of the praetor's edicts and the formation of a council of jurists, belong to the history of Roman law.

Hadrian, like Trajan, was a great builder. In Athens, where he spent much time discussing philosophy, he completed the Peisistratean temple of Olympian Zeus. In Rome he built a great temple to Venus and Rome, and also his own tomb, which, after many transformations during the Middle Ages, was renamed the Castello Sant' Angelo and is now used as a military museum. At Tibur (Tivoli), in the Sabine Hills, he erected a splendid villa in which he endeavored to duplicate parts of the great buildings he had seen in the provinces. After his first heir died, Hadrian adopted Titus Aurelius Antoninus, who succeeded him in 138.

Antoninus, A.D. **138–161** Antoninus, surnamed Pius because of his character and his devotion to the memory of Hadrian, was of Gallic descent. Under his rule the empire reached its acme of peace and prosperity. A few difficulties on the frontiers, the necessity of building a second more advanced wall in Britain, and the killing of a handful of Christians as a result of local uprisings were but minor episodes. The law was humanized. Aid, heretofore given only to boys, was extended to poor girls. Antoninus had adopted two sons, Marcus Aurelius and Lucius Verus, and when he died in 161 the former succeeded him.

Marcus Aurelius, A.D. **161–180** Marcus Aurelius, the last of the Good Emperors, remains one of the great names of ancient times. From his boyhood he had been a student of philosophy and he looked at the problems of empire from the viewpoint of a Stoic. On the whole he grappled with them successfully. It was his misfortune that two great catastrophes descended upon the empire under his rule. After a successful war with the Parthians, the returning army in 166 brought with it a terrible plague which lasted twenty years, destroyed many thousands of people throughout the empire, and had incalculable effects on the courage and livelihood of the remainder. In the midst of the epidemic a group of Germanic tribes, led by the Marcomanni, pushed across the Danube in 167 and even invaded Italy itself. Marcus Aurelius met the challenge heroically and spent most of the remainder of his life on the frontier. He defeated the invaders, settled some on abandoned lands within the empire, re-established the frontier, and was on the verge of the conquest of Bohemia when he died in 180.

Throughout his life even in camp it was his custom to record his thoughts of life and its meaning. These *Meditations*, a most precious human document, have been preserved and have offered as much comfort to men in succeeding ages as they did to the emperor who wrote them. With his death the great age of the Roman Empire came to an end. Succeeding generations witnessed its transformation from a principate into an undisguised military autocracy and the later, gradual decline of ancient civilization. During the great age, however, Roman political institutions, Roman law, economic and social life, and culture had developed under the rule of the successive emperors and had been carried north and west to establish the foundations on which Western civilization still rests.

24 · The Early Empire

THREE CULTURAL STREAMS OF THE ANCIENT WORLD — Oriental, Greek, and Roman — met and mingled in the Roman Empire. Rome, having created an empire by conquest, gave it an admirable set of institutions and laws. From the Greeks came not only science and art, but a philosophic theory of the unity of the world which affected even the masses and gave organic vitality to the Roman creation. The Orient, contributing religious beliefs and attitudes rooted in its distant past, was destined to play a major role in the transition from the ancient to the medieval world.

ROMA AETERNA

The city of Rome, the capital of a great empire, was filled with splendid palaces and public buildings. Its populace was feasted and entertained with the tribute of the provinces. Rome was the center of arts and letters, the goal of every ambitious man's dreams. It's power centered in the Mediterranean Sea, extended from the Arabian Desert on the east to the Atlantic Ocean on the west, from the Sahara Desert on the south to the Rhine, the Danube and the Carpathian Mountains on the north, and even reached across the channel to include England. Within its frontiers were Syrians, Jews, Phoenicians, Egyptians, Greeks, Iberians, Celts, Germans, and numerous other tribes of peoples.

To the people of the empire Rome was more than a city. Its name stood for the civilized world, membership in which was gained by the magic phrase used so proudly by St. Paul, "I am a Roman citizen." The many and varied peoples of the empire were united into one organic structure by a common citizenship and a common allegiance. The Stoic concept of a universal state, ruled according to the divine law of nature by the wisest citizen, seemed to have found fulfillment in the Roman Empire. So strong was the idea of unity, thus made fact, that it persisted after the collapse of Roman power. The Greeks of the early

Byzantine period called themselves Romans, and the peoples of Western Europe in the Middle Ages clung to a belief in a world church and in a world state long after actual unity had disappeared.

The center and focus of the Roman world was the princeps, the source of all law, the fountain of all wisdom and power, united with divinity as living ruler, and god, indeed, after death. The imperial cult was the symbol of imperial unity. When the provincial offered sacrifice to or for the emperor, or cast a handful of incense on the altar before his statue, he was but asserting himself a partaker in Roman universality and proclaiming his loyalty to the world in which he lived.

Augustus had apparently endeavored to establish himself as the first citizen in a Rome that ruled the world, but Julius Caesar's idea of an emperor superior to Rome and the provinces prevailed. Men of provincial origin succeeded to the throne during the Antonine period and, though holding Rome as their capital, considered themselves as supreme rulers over the empire. Though the senate was, as has been said, "an imaginative symbol of the glory of Roman power" and though it became in a measure representative of the empire as provincials were drawn into it, it had lost its effectiveness and had been made an advisory and assisting rather than a ruling body.

The Emperor The emperors bore the names *imperator* and *Caesar* and the title *princeps,* emblematic of their power. They became imperator by acclamation of the army upon their accession and received the formal grant of power which made them Caesar and princeps by acts of the senate. As holders of the imperium they were commanders-in-chief of the army and navy, and supreme judges in all matters of law. The tribunician power gave them direction of civil affairs of state and, by the ancient right of intercession, made them the center of all appeals. The office of *Pontifex Maximus* gave them control over taking omens and over religious practices and laws. The title *pater patriae* conferred on them the added prestige of Roman tradition. They controlled all nominations for offices in Rome, appointed the prefects, curators, procurators, legati in the imperial provinces and in the army, and lesser officials of the state. Their commands, speeches, letters, and decisions had the full force of law. Pliny described Trajan as "he who may at his will dispose of all that others possess."

The wide extent of imperial power as it developed from the Augustan establishment during the Julian-Claudian period is displayed by the famous *lex de imperio Vespasiani,* a part of which has been recovered from an inscription.

> Let it be permitted him to make treaties with whom he will wish, as was permitted to the divine Augustus, to Tiberius Julius Caesar Augustus, and to Tiberius Claudius Caesar Augustus Germanicus. Let it be permitted him to hold the Senate, bring matters before it, to dismiss it, and to make

decrees of the Senate through the presentation and division as was permitted to the divine Augustus, Tiberius Julius Caesar Augustus and to Tiberius Claudius Caesar Augustus Germanicus. When the Senate shall meet in accordance with his wish, authority, order, or command, or in his presence, let him have and preserve the right of all things therein as if the Senate had been proclaimed and called by law.

To whomsoever of those seeking a magistry, power, command or care of anything whom he shall commend to the Senate and the Roman people and to whom he shall have given or promised his suffrage, let extraordinary consideration be given in the comitia.

Let it be permitted to him to move and extend the boundaries of the *pomoerium* when he shall decide that it is for the benefit of the state as was permitted to Tiberius Claudius Caesar Augustus Germanicus.

Let him have the right and power to do whatever he may deem best to serve the interest of the state and the majesty of all things divine and human, public and private, as had the divine Augustus, Tiberius Julius Augustus, and Tiberius Claudius Caesar Augustus Germanicus.

By whatever laws or plebiscites it was written that the divine Augustus, Tiberius Julius Caesar Augustus, and Tiberius Claudius Caesar Augustus Germanicus should not be bound, let the imperator Caesar Vespasianus be freed from these laws and plebiscites. Whatever it was permitted by any law or rogation to the divine Augustus, Tiberius Julius Caesar Augustus, and Tiberius Claudius Caesar Augustus Germanicus to do, all those things let it be permitted to imperator Caesar Vespasianus Augustus to do.

Those things which have been performed, done, decreed or ordered by the imperator Caesar Vespasianus Augustus or by any one at his command or order, these things are henceforth right and ratified as if they had been done by order of the people or the plebs.[1]

The legislative and administrative powers of the emperor become apparent from this decree. It is evident that the princeps is not thought to be above the law but to be exempted or given power to act in special cases which have the authority of precedent.

The overwhelming power of the princeps cast a shadow over the aspirations and activities of men throughout the empire. No freedom of political action was possible for the individual. Provincials of independent mind were sternly checked by the ever-watchful agents of the emperor, and men of ability who would bow the knee were drawn into the imperial circle. Renown in government or in war could only be attained in the service of the emperor and at his order, and leaders like Germanicus and Agricola who sought to transgress the limits laid down for them were speedily recalled. The only avenue of success for the ambitious general, as the events of the years A.D. 68–69 showed, was the attainment of the imperial purple, and many who tried to achieve it were ruthlessly suppressed. In the sphere of economic pur-

---

[1] Herman Dessau, *Inscriptiones Latinae Selectae I*. Trans. by Wallace E. Caldwell and rev. by William C. McDermott. Berlin: Weidmannos, 1892–1935, p. 244.

suits, the attainment of great wealth made Romans and provincials alike objects of suspicion and envy. In fact, in times of hardship the mere possession of wealth often led to the death of its owner and to the confiscation of his property. Freedom of thought was as dangerous. Emperor-worship made loyalty to the emperors and obedience to their will a matter of religious duty, and even criticism became a crime against their majesty. Many of the emperors, using this as a weapon against their enemies, wielded despotic power, throttled free expression of opinion, and at times instituted reigns of terror.

The Magistrates The chief assistants of the emperor were drawn from the senatorial and equestrian orders, according to the nature of their duties. Military and political positions were still held by senators who, in accordance with the tradition, passed through the republican offices from quaestor to consul. With the exception of the praetorship, which involved judicial duties, these were but honorary posts, stepping-stones to the imperial service. Under Trajan six pairs of consuls holding office two months each were elected every year. Members of the senatorial class served as officers in the army, as judges in the lower courts, as proconsuls in the senatorial provinces, and as curators in the bureaus of administration.

In addition to the Augustan curatorship of the roads, public works, aqueducts, and care of the bed and banks of the Tiber the Antonines had established senatorial commissions to regulate finance and to supervise the management of the relief program for the poor of Italy. The prefect of the city, whose care of the urban government of Rome involved important judicial duties, was regularly a senator. In spite of occasional difficulties in Rome, the senators proved to be faithful and competent servants in the work of the empire. The senatorial class was recognized as superior and its members received the distinguishing title *clarissimus,* "most noble sir."

The civil administration of the empire was in the hands of the secretariat organized under Claudius by his freedmen, and transformed into a civil service of equestrian rank by Hadrian. The five great secretariats were *a rationibus,* finance; *ab epistulis,* correspondence, with separate secretaries for Greek and Latin; *a libellis,* petitions; *a cognitionibus,* investigations; and *a studiis,* intelligence and records. The minor posts in the central offices were held by knights, freedmen, and slaves. Under the secretaries were the procurators, who had charge of tax collections or the management of imperial lands or other properties, subprocurators, and the *advocati fisci,* prosecutors for the treasury. These procuratorships were grouped in four salary classes by Hadrian, and a fairly definite equestrian career was established. The business of government in the empire was well centralized and efficiently managed by this system. In recognition of their position and services, members of the equestrian class were hailed with the title *splendidus eques Romanus*, "glorious Roman knight."

The great prizes of the equestrian career were the prefectures, the most powerful official positions in the Roman Empire. The praetorian prefect, commander of the bodyguard, became the emperor's personal representative and acquired by custom great judicial authority. The prefect of the watch kept order in Rome and the prefect of the grain supply kept Rome's granaries full. The prefect of Egypt was the Roman pharaoh's viceroy. Another prefect commanded the Roman fleet.

Though the freedmen were demoted from the chief offices by Hadrian, they still held posts within the secretariat. Their great glory, however, was in the order of *Augustales*. Leading freedmen chosen for this order served in Italy and in the provincial towns as priests for the celebration of the festivals of the imperial cult.

System of Imperial Finance   At the accession of Tiberius there were two treasuries, the republican treasury, *aerarium Saturni*, and the military fund, *aerarium militare*. The accounts for the imperial provinces belonged to the former. Pallas, secretary of Claudius, however, established the *fiscus* as a central treasury for the public finance of the princeps and refused to render an accounting to the senate. The republican treasury continued to exist as the depository of funds from the senatorial provinces but steadily declined in importance. The *fiscus* absorbed the military fund.

Revenues were derived from port duties and tolls, income and rents from state lands, mines, and quarries. A 5 per cent inheritance tax was collected from Roman citizens; there were also a tax on auction sales (the per cent varied), a 4 per cent tax on the sale of slaves and a 5 per cent tax on their manumission. These taxes, at first levied in Italy, were later extended to the provinces. The provincials paid the land tax, usually a tithe, the poll tax on all noncitizens, and a tax on the income of artisans and small tradesmen. For the purpose of levying these taxes a census was taken every five years (after Hadrian, every fifteen years) in which all persons and properties were recorded. The collection was in the hands of procurators who at some times and in some places collected directly. Elsewhere the taxes were farmed locally. In many cases the municipalities were made responsible, and the collection was carried out by local officials, who often had to advance the revenue themselves before collection. The taxes were not burdensome in themselves, and the imperial system corrected the abuses of republican times and prevented or checked extortion. Most of the money was spent in the provinces on roads, on public works, on supplies for the army, and on the defense of the frontier. The price of the Roman imperial service in the flourishing days of the empire was not exorbitant.

Another branch of the treasury of great importance was the "patrimony of Caesar." Augustus had become the richest man in the world. By legacies and confiscations the property of the princeps had grown to extraordinary size by the time of Nero's death. Vespasian assumed it as "crown property" and established a special procurator to control it. Family property of the Flavians was kept separate. Eventually the *fiscus* absorbed the patrimony, and the personal wealth of the emperor was set up in a department known as the *res privata*.

The Law The greatest and most enduring achievement of the empire was the law, both administrative and civil. After the reign of Tiberius, the assemblies ceased to meet, except for the formal vote of the princeps's imperium and for the approval of such measures as the emperor wished (usually for reasons of tradition) to submit to them.[2] Until the time of Hadrian, the senate continued to meet and pass *senatus consulta*. But since to an ever-increasing degree all the senate did was to discuss, sometimes formulate, and ratify the wishes of the emperor as expressed in his *oratio*, the emperor's words came to have the force of law by themselves. After the time of Hadrian the power of the senate as a legislative body decreased steadily and the *orationes principis* (statements of the emperor) became fully recognized as law. To these were added the *constitutiones principum*, consisting of *edicta* (proclamations), *decreta* (decisions in particular cases), *rescripta* (answers to questions from officials or private citizens), and *mandata* (orders to imperial officials). The rescripts dealt often with particular cases and did not acquire the force of general law or become important until after Hadrian's reign.

Civil law came under the control of the emperor. The *jus honorarium* (p. 471), developed by the republican magistrates through their edicts, was fully recognized by imperial officials, and throughout the early empire the praetors continued to issue edicts, doubtless controlled and supplemented by the edicts and decisions of the emperor. The Cyrenaic edicts of Augustus (p. 483), which dealt with the rights of noncitizens in the province, are a case in point.

One of the sources of contention between the senate and the earlier emperors had been the interference of the princeps in the courts. Claudius, particularly, had liked to preside over the hearing of cases and render decisions. By Hadrian's time it had been definitely established that the princeps, usually represented by the praetorian prefect, was the highest court of appeal. Since the power of legislation inherent in the praetor's edict was inconsonant with the principle of autocracy, Hadrian removed the power and with the assistance of Salvius Julianus codified the edictal law and issued the Perpetual Edict. Thereafter changes were made through the imperial constitutions. For the same reason it became essential for the emperors to control the work of the *juris prudentes*, the jurists who through their advice influenced the

---

[2] Thus Nerva submitted an agrarian law to the tribal assembly.

interpretation of the law. Augustus permitted only qualified men, whom he licensed, to give opinions with the force of law, and Hadrian formed a council of these jurists to advise judges and to assist the imperial court in the decision of its cases.

The writings of the jurists were carefully preserved and selections from them appear as definitive law in the Digest of Justinian's Code. Of these and the many legal commentaries composed during the empire, only *Institutiones* ("Principles of the Civil Law") of Gaius, written in the reign of Antoninus Pius, and fragments of the writings of Paul and Ulpian, who lived in a later period, have survived apart from the Digest.

An important development in the character of the law took place in the imperial period, since the concept of Rome as a world state led inevitably to discussions of the Stoic idea of a world law emanating from the divine principle and based on universal reason. This, called by the Romans *jus naturale*, natural law, was never recognized as formal, but its philosophic ideas inevitably reacted on the interpretations of the *jus gentium* and on the principles of the civil law itself. The power of the father of the family was weakened; the harsh rules regarding slaves were softened; women gained control over their property; and the principle that an accused was innocent until proved guilty was firmly established. An interesting growth was the appearance of distinctions between the privileges and obligations of the *honestior* (noble) and the *humilior* (commoner). Caracalla's edict in a later generation extending citizenship to all provincials made Roman law the rule of the civilized world.

Between the years 529 and 535 Justinian (p. 584) issued the famous *Corpus Juris Civilis* containing an elementary treatise on the principles of the law, a digest (actually a series of selections) of the written opinions of the great jurists, and a code made up from the *constitutions* of the earlier emperors. In the course of his reign a fourth book, called *Novellae*, was added, containing new rulings that were found necessary. This great collection of documents provided the cornerstone for the structure of medieval, and much of modern, law.

The Army   While the law went with Roman citizenship and Roman governors into every corner of the empire, the most evident symbol of empire was the army. It was a far different organization from the citizen body of republican or even of Augustan times. Since recruits from Italy barely filled the ranks of the imperial guards of the city, provincials were drawn in under a system of voluntary enlistment. Those so enlisted were usually citizens of the towns; they were at least partially Latinized and either were Roman citizens or received citizenship upon enlistment. A rigorous course of training made them competent professional soldiers. The Latin language used in the legions and their distinctly Roman tradition speedily completed the process of Romanization. While they were not allowed to marry until their discharge, illicit unions were permitted. The soldiers served enlistments of twenty years, keeping order in the provinces, executing many public works, and defending the frontier. At the end of that time they were entitled to retirement with a grant of land or a pension. Other provincials were enlisted in the auxiliary forces organized in cohorts. They served for twenty-five years and received citizenship and a bonus on retirement. Each legion had its number, its name, and its eagles. During the early empire it was customary to transfer legions and cohorts from the area in which they had been recruited to other frontiers. Hadrian changed that to a principle of territorial defense, recruiting and employing troops in the same district.

The frontier was defended by a long series of walls of stone or earth, the *limes*, on the north, and elsewhere by forts and watch towers strategically placed with connecting roads and permanent legionary camps at convenient points. The most famous section of the northern line was the Roman wall in Britain, built by Hadrian and improved by later emperors. Moats protected the advances to the wall on either side; towers were placed four to the mile with guardhouses at the mile posts and seventeen garrison stations at regular intervals behind the seventy miles of wall. Around the great camps clustered the *canabae*, or huts of camp followers, traders, and women who accompanied the army. Many of the camps developed into permanent communities, some of which, surviving to the present, have preserved their names, such as Chester in England. Cologne, Coblenz, Mainz, and Vienna were famous centers along the Rhine-Danube frontier.

The camps served as Romanizing influences over the surrounding territory and with the purchase of supplies, particularly grain and meat, did much to disseminate prosperity among the provincials. In times of peace the army was employed in constructing roads, bridges, aqueducts, and many other public works which likewise made their contributions to the civilization and prosperity of the empire.

The navy was a permanent establishment in imperial times under the command of prefects, with stations at Ravenna and Misenum and with fleets of small boats on the Rhine and the Danube. The personnel, drawn chiefly from the eastern provinces, consisted of free men who received citizenship after a service of twenty-six years. It was effective in its control of piracy.

The Provinces Of the forty-five provinces in the time of Hadrian, eleven were recognized as senatorial and were governed by promagistrates, who held office for a year. Asia and Africa normally received ex-consuls, the other provinces ex-praetors, but all senatorial governors had the title of *proconsul*. They received assignments from the senate according to lots, and each was assisted by three legati and a quaestor. The right of imperial interference, indicated by the often-cited Cyrenaic decrees, and the presence of imperial procurators of equestrian rank, who took care of imperial property and supervised the collection of taxes, made senatorial control illusory.

The remaining provinces were imperial, and their governors, senators of praetorian or consular rank called *legati Caesaris propraetore* (propraetorian lieutenants of Caesar), were chosen with great care by the emperor and held office at his will. The normal term of office was five years, but there was no fixed rule. The governor was assisted by the commanders of the legions and by the equestrian procurators who, directly responsible to the emperor, served, as in the senatorial provinces, as a check on the governor. Smaller provinces were governed by procurators, who in such provinces performed military and judicial as well as financial duties.

Though provincial conditions were far better than under the late republic, there were still occasional venal governors and grasping

View of the Interior Court of a Private Home in Pompeii. Part of the original roof tiles can be seen above the colonnade in the center, an unusual feature, as the hot ash and shower of stones from the eruption of Vesuvius that buried the city in A.D. 79 destroyed most roofs. (Photograph by Mary Francis Gyles, reproduced by Frank D. Grande)

A View Looking South Across the Civil Forum in Pompeii with Mount Vesuvius in the Background. (Italian State Tourist Office)

procurators who proved as rapacious as the equestrian tax collectors of earlier periods. At times discontent led to provincial uprisings. In many regions local feelings persisted or racial antagonisms led to clashes between discordant elements in the populace.

In most of, if not all, the provinces, there existed local councils, representative of the communities. These organizations, whose purpose was religious, met once a year to hold festivals in connection with the imperial cult. Nevertheless they acquired some political importance. Matters pertaining to the whole province were discussed; representations may have been made to the governor; and embassies were certainly sent to Rome to praise or to accuse the imperial agents.

The Municipalities The preferred unit of local government in Italy and in the provinces was the municipality. The East was already a land of cities, and all that was necessary for Rome to do was to recognize the existing order. The Greek cities continued therefore to be ruled by their magistrates, councils, and assemblies, as in earlier times. The franchise, however, was restricted to men of property. The West had been for the most part a region of tribal or rural communities. Such cities as existed were drawn into the Roman system and, though

The Via (Street) dell' Abbondanza in Pompeii. A smooth sidewalk permitted pedestrians easy passage on each side of the roughly paved
street, and stepping stones set at intervals provided convenient cross-
ings. (Italian State Tourist Office)

the Romans utilized the pre-existing cantonal forms of government
under aristocratic rule, as in Gaul, efforts were made to develop urban
organizations in country districts. Market places and court houses
were erected at crossroads, and the people in the surrounding territory were listed and encouraged to settle around them. The *canabae*
around the great camps received a city form of government, and
colonies of Roman veterans were settled in the provinces.

The excitements of city life, with its elections, shows, games in the
arena, schools, and libraries, proved so attractive that the West rapidly
became transformed into an aggregation of cities. To cities that were
sufficiently Latinized was granted a charter which prescribed the form
of government and gave Latin or Roman rights. These grants freed the
citizens from the poll tax. The land tax, however, was removed only
by the grant of the *jus Italicum,* rarely given except to Roman colonies.

The charters regulated local citizenship, which was based on birth.
Citizenship so acquired was never transferred except by gift of the city
or of the princeps. St. Paul was to the end of his life a "citizen of Tarsus,
which is no mean city," but at the same time he had Roman citizenship.
This assured him of the protection of Roman law, of full rights to

participate in civic affairs if he went to Rome, and other advantages accruing to the Roman citizen. Voting depended upon the possession of property in the community of one's residence. In the East the Greek custom of voting by head was followed, while voters in the West were organized into groups on the Roman model. Chief magistrates were the *duoviri*, patterned after the consuls, assisted by aediles and quaestors, all drawn from the upper class. The charters also established age limits and financial qualifications. The expenses of officeholding were great, for the magistrate was expected to make a gift on taking office, to hold games, and to undertake other expenditures of similar nature. The rewards of a magistrate were membership in the local *curia*, or senate, and full Roman citizenship. Every fifth year the magistrates took a census of the people and drew up the list of the *curia*, usually to the number of one hundred. Ex-magistrates were entitled to membership, and other citizens of wealth and good repute might be enrolled to fill out the number. The council assumed general direction of the affairs of the city and was usually held responsible for the collection of imperial taxes. Members were very proud of their titles and position. The towns frequently hired doctors and schoolteachers to serve their people, and they sometimes possessed hospitals and libraries.

Throughout the first century of the empire, political life flourished in the cities. Echoes of a vigorous political campaign have survived in

An Aerial View of the Amphitheater at Pompeii. The principal entrances to the arena are visible, as are the stairs that gave spectators access to the upper tiers of stone seats. (Italian State Tourist Office)

the notices on the house walls of Pompeii. Offices were eagerly sought
for, and gifts were generously made by officeholders and citizens of
wealth. The status of municipal finance, however, was never satisfac-
tory. The income of the town depended chiefly upon its property, local
tolls and fines, and the contributions of the officeholders. Accounts
were poorly kept; public property was often mismanaged; debts once
incurred proved difficult to meet; and the increasing burdens caused
men of wealth to avoid officeholding. Accordingly, later charters contained provisions for the drafting of candidates. As a result of ineffi-
cient management and financial confusion, correctors or curators,
Roman citizens, were appointed in many cities during the second century to direct or advise the municipal officials. Such interference aggravated the decline of political vitality in the cities of the empire.

THE JEWS IN THE EMPIRE

The Jewish nation was brought under Roman control by Pompey
the Great, but long retained a semiautonomy and a measure of self-
government greater than were accorded most other subject peoples.
The conditions under which the Jews were brought into the Roman
Empire and the organization of their state grew from events and
developments in the history of the Jews after the return from exile in
Babylon (p. 166).

When the Persians allowed the re-establishment of Jerusalem by
those exiles who cared to return, Judaea became a small, theocratic
state governed by its priests. The Temple was reconstructed, the
walls were rebuilt by Nehemiah, and, most important, the Law, center
of Judaism, brought from Babylon by Ezra, was codified and sworn
to by all of the people in a great covenant with Yahweh. Probably in
the same period the history of the kingdom was rewritten by the
Chronicler and the sacred literature was gathered into a collection.
Since it was all-important that the people know the law, synagogues,
"houses of the law," were established in the cities and villages, the law
and the prophets were read, and liturgies of prayer and praise were
developed for the Sabbath gatherings. Scribes, sometimes priests but
often laymen, learned the law and began to interpret it in the schools
they established in the synagogues and to apply it to specific cases, a
service similar to that rendered by the Roman jurisprudents. The most
famous of these masters, or rabbis, as they came to be called, were
Hillel and Shammai, who lived during the reign of Herod the Great.
From the teachings of the scribes there grew a body of traditional
unwritten law developing out of, but distinguished from, the Torah,
or Law of the Pentateuch. Though later disputes arose over the validity
of their teaching, they served to keep alive and growing the religion
which the Jews had inherited from Moses and from the Prophets.

Though Jewish teaching was restricted to an emphasis upon its own people and an insistence on strict adherence to the law, it was deeply penetrated and enlivened by the prophetic assurance that God was a universal deity whose name would become great among the Gentiles and who would raise His chosen people to dominion with Him. Filled with longing for the great days of David and Solomon, the Jews dreamed of a Messiah of Yahweh who would re-establish their independence, make Jerusalem the spiritual capital of the world, and therewith bring about a golden age. Writers who saw visions of the coming of this Kingdom of God, hence called apocalyptic, "revealing," took the place of the prophets of old among the people.

The events of the second century B.C. promised fulfillment of their hopes. After the conquest by Alexander in 331 B.C. and the long rule of the Ptolemies, as the spoils of war in 199 B.C. the Jews passed into the possession of Antiochus III of Asia. Under this monarch and his successor the question of Hellenization became acute. Many of the wealthy and cultured Jews had come under the seductive influence of the Greek manner of life. They learned Greek in order to read its literature, they admired its art and its architecture, and the athletically inclined youth among them delighted in the Greek games. When Antiochus III allowed the establishment of a palaestra in Jerusalem, many young Jews scandalized their elders by attending it and by even assuming the broad-brimmed hats, characteristic of Greek youth but contrary to the Jewish custom.

The work of the scribes, however, had been well done. There was a vigorous reaction against Hellenization, and when Antiochus IV made war on Egypt, Jewish sympathies were openly with the Ptolemies. Antiochus, understanding well the source of hostility, determined to wipe out the Jewish religion and secure the unification of his realm by the spread of Greek culture. But when he set up a statue of Zeus in the Temple at Jerusalem and ordered celebration of Greek festivals, the Jews revolted under the leadership of a priest, Mattathias, and his four sons. The oldest son, Judas, surnamed Maccabaeus, "the Hammer," was the hero of the war and gave the name of Maccabee to the family. After twenty-five years of struggle, during which Rome aided them, an independent kingdom was established in 143 B.C. But the Messianic hope was not fulfilled; the Maccabean kings, allied with Rome, ruled over their little state amid constant dynastic confusion while dreamers wrote new revelations of the "Day of Yahweh" when the Messiah, a godlike figure coeval with God, would establish not a political restoration but a spiritual kingdom on earth.

The religious crisis, however, resulted in the appearance of two famous sects, the Pharisees and the Sadducees. The latter were chiefly members of the upper class associated with the priests in the Temple, and were believers in ritual and in a strict adherence to the Mosaic

Law. They denied the validity of the scribal tradition and of the growing belief in immortality. Their influence ceased when Jerusalem fell and the Temple was destroyed by the Romans. The Pharisees, on the other hand, were followed by the great mass of the people and supported the scribes. With the greatest scholars in Judaism among their number, they were progressive and liberal in their interpretations of the Law to meet the changing needs of the time. In contradistinction to the Sadducees, they believed in a future life. The work they accomplished survived to become the foundation of later Judaism.

When Pompey appeared in the East, there were two factions in the kingdom, headed by the brothers Hyrcanus and Aristobulus. The latter had the backing of the Sadducees, while the former enjoyed the support of the Pharisees and the advice of the Idumaean Antipater. Pompey, intervening in the quarrel, took Jerusalem in 63 B.C. and made Hyrcanus high priest. But in following years Antipater was the actual ruler of the land, and Caesar made him procurator of Judaea. His son Herod, who succeeded him in 43 B.C., killed the last of the Maccabees and received the title "King of the Jews" from the Roman senate on the advice of the triumvirs. He supported Antony and Cleopatra until their overthrow, and then by a frank statement of his past and a promise of future loyalty he won confirmation of his power from Augustus.

Herod's achievements as king gave him the surname "the Great." Though he offended the Jews by his nonobservance of the Jewish law and by the celebration of Greek rites and games, he pleased them by refortifying Jerusalem and rebuilding the Temple on a magnificent scale. Many tales are told of his marital difficulties and of the splendor and corruption of his court. After Herod's death in 4 B.C. his kingdom was divided into four parts and, as a result of disorders that followed, Judaea was made a procuratorial province in A.D. 6. Claudius restored it to his friend Agrippa, grandson of Herod, but shortly after Agrippa's death it became again a province.

Meanwhile there had taken place the great *Diaspora*, the scattering of the Jews throughout the civilized world. There were many in Babylonia, descendants of exiles who had not returned to the homeland, and during the Hellenistic period great numbers moved into the cities of Syria, Asia Minor, and Greece. Egypt, a haven of refuge for many at the time of the Babylonian exile, received great additions during the Ptolemaic period. Under the aegis of Rome Jews also moved west into Africa, Spain, and Gaul, and a large colony gathered in Rome on the Janiculum side of the Tiber. In many cities they lived in special quarters and in some, certainly in Alexandria, were governed by their own officials.

Wherever they went they carried with them their religion, their sacred writings, and the synagogue. Though it became necessary to translate the law and the scriptures into Greek for the use of Jews in Egypt,[3] they resisted Hellenization or Romanization. The Jews presented a difficult problem to the Roman government not only because of their religious peculiarities but because of the quarrels that arose between them and the other peoples of the provinces. Caesar and Augustus confirmed the status which the Hellenistic rulers had conferred upon them and tolerated their presence in Rome. Their ancestral pride and exclusiveness, their devotion to their own God, their refusal to conform to the religious and social customs of their neighbors made the populace regard the Jews with suspicion and derision, at the same time being jealous of the special privileges they enjoyed. Amid constant disorders and occasional persecutions the Jews managed to cling tenaciously to their religion and customs and to their faith in the coming of the Kingdom. They even proselyted among the Gentiles, and those they gathered into their fold were called God-fearers.

The Jews were freed from obeisance to the imperial cult and from attendance at the public festivals on the ground of religious scruple and were permitted to substitute prayers for the well-being of the emperor. They were even allowed to collect a small temple tax and send it to Jerusalem. But the authorities frowned on proselyting, and when a flagrant case, combined with sharp practice, appeared in Rome in A.D. 29, Tiberius expelled the entire Jewish population of the city—but they soon returned. Caligula caused an uproar by ordering the Jews to worship his statue. Only his timely death saved them. Claudius, influenced by Herod Agrippa, confirmed their privileges of self-government in Alexandria in edicts mentioned by the Jewish historian Josephus, as well as in a letter of the emperor recently found among the papyri. He even extended these rights to other Greek cities.

In Judaea, however, where Roman rule bore hard upon them, the Jews were discontented, and radical sects kept the people in constant ferment as one leader after another claimed to be the Messiah. Finally in A.D. 66 war broke out against the Roman governor Florus, as the result of a quarrel over the desecration of a synagogue in Caesarea by a Greek. The Judaeans expelled the Roman garrison and put the land in a state of defense. Vespasian, sent against them by Nero, started methodically to reduce their strongholds. At Jotapata he captured a young priest, Joseph, who became his client, and was henceforth called Flavius Josephus. Josephus later wrote a history of the war and a book on Jewish antiquities. Titus assumed command when his father became emperor, and completed the conquest. After a fearful siege Jerusalem fell in A.D. 70. According to Josephus the city and the Temple were accidentally burned, and thousands of Jews were sold into slavery. The ornaments

[3] This was traditionally done in the reign of Ptolemy II by seventy-two scholars, hence called *Septuagint* (Seventy). Philo of Alexandria in the first century A.D. tried to explain Judaism by allegory in the light of Platonism.

of the Holy of Holies were carried to Rome, where they are depicted in relief on the Arch of Titus.

Troubles between Jews and Greeks and general hatred of the Romans involved the Jews in revolt against Trajan (A.D. 115–117). When Hadrian settled Romans in Jerusalem, called it Aelia Capitolina and built a temple to Jupiter on the site of the Temple, a great uprising took place led by a priest, Eleazar, and a popular hero, Simon, called Bar Kochba. Hadrian pitilessly suppressed the revolt and forbade the Jews entrance into the Temple area. From that time Judaism, though preserving memories of past glories and never giving up the hope of a restoration to Israel, centered its devotions in the law and its interpretations. The legal teachings of the scribes, codified into the Mishna, and the expositions and tales of later authorities were gathered together into the collections known as the Talmud, the source not only of the law but also of the strength of medieval and modern Judaism. Christianity, likewise freed from attachment to its place of origin by the destruction of Jerusalem, was the more easily adapted into a religion for the Gentiles.

ECONOMIC LIFE

"Regions, once desert solitudes, are thickly dotted with flourishing cities. . . . The world has laid the sword aside and keeps universal festival, with all pomp and gladness. All other feuds and rivalries are gone, and cities now vie with one another only in their splendor and their pleasures. Every space is crowded with porticoes, gymnasia, temple fronts, with studios and schools. Sandy wastes, trackless mountains, and broad rivers present no barriers to the traveler, who finds his home and country everywhere. The earth has become a vast pleasure garden."[4] Such was the description of the Roman world by Aristides, a rhetorician of the age of the Antonines. The *Pax Romana* made the civilized world one. A common code of laws and a uniform system of weights, measures, and coins made trade between distant areas easy. Greek remained the language of the East, but the spread of Latin in the West established for the empire a two-language system far easier for the merchant of the period than the polyglot character of the same area today. Military roads facilitated commercial travel by land, and policing of the seas protected the transport of goods by water.

Travel Throughout the empire Rome followed its republican policy of good roads, built with a substantial and elastic substructure, and paved with stone or materials available locally. The roads radiated from

---

[4]Sir Samuel Dill, *Roman Society from Nero to Marcus Aurelius.* New York: Meridian Books, Inc., 1958., pp. 199–200. Paraphrased from Aristides, 14.

Rome to the seaports and borders of Italy, and from central points in the provinces to the frontiers. Every mile was marked by a milestone, usually carrying upon it the name of the emperor under whom it was erected, the number of miles from the provincial center, and sometimes the number from the Golden Milestone, center of the world, in Rome. More than thirteen thousand miles of roads are said to have been constructed in Gaul alone. The road from the Atlantic to the Black Sea was over a thousand miles long. In the East the older roads of the Persians and the Greeks were kept in use and new ones were added. Important roads were maintained at imperial expense; others were kept up by local communities.

The roads followed natural routes, as straight as possible without regard for grades. The average speed of travel for horse-borne traffic was probably about five miles an hour, though we hear of a journey of eight hundred miles in eight days and of one extraordinary trip of three hundred and thirty-two miles in thirty-six hours. Travelers were provided with maps and roadbooks. Inns, which seem to have had a reputation for uncleanliness and dishonesty, sprang up at convenient points. Some innkeepers were thieves, and there were occasional highwaymen. Refreshment and post stations, set at twenty mile intervals, were controlled by the imperial government. Unwary travelers were sometime kidnaped and sold as slaves, though the penalties for such crimes were severe. The roads were policed, and there was probably less brigandage than in the same area in the eighteenth century.

The Post   The imperial post, provided with relays of horses and riders, carried public dispatches from Rome to every corner of the empire. At first the expense was borne by the provincials, but Hadrian placed the burden on the imperial *fiscus*. Businessmen maintained corps of secretaries who carried their documents. Private letters had to depend on chance travelers who might be willing to carry them.

Travel by sea had not changed much since Hellenistic times; indeed the sea captains of the imperial period were still mostly Greeks and Orientals. Piracy, which had caused so much trouble in the last century of the republic, was repressed by the vigilance of the fleet, and navigation had only natural perils to face. Ships sailed the Mediterranean with reasonable safety in the summer. Spring and fall were dangerous, however, and in the winter navigation ceased save in cases of dire necessity. Speed depended entirely upon the winds. The ordinary voyage from Puteoli to Alexandria took eighteen or nineteen days; the return trip, against the wind, an average of fifty, and often many more. The usual size of merchantmen may be estimated from the ship on which St. Paul sailed for Rome, which carried a load of grain, 276 passengers, and its crew. Wrecked vessels explored by deep-sea divers, especially the French, have provided details of shipbuilding and of cargoes. Puteoli was the port of Rome until the first century when Claudius and Nero built Ostia. Corinth again became an important port of call and transshipment between East and West. Ephesus was the greatest port in Anatolia, Antioch in Syria, and Alexandria in Egypt.

Commerce   By land and by sea men traveled on errands of trade from one corner of the empire to another with a universal law to protect them, no tariff barriers to hinder them, and only regional collection of small tolls to bother them. Italians appeared in the East, and Greeks and Syrians carried their goods to Gaul and even to distant Britain. The striking feature of imperial development in commerce was its universality, which bore in its train decentralization, extreme individualism, and freedom of enterprise. Alexandria, Antioch, Ephesus, Carthage, centers of earlier times, and Lyons, as the distributing center for wealthy Gaul, became rivals of Rome itself in wealth and size; Corinth flourished again; and many other lesser provincial cities prospered.

Most business activities were carried on by single individuals. Partnerships might be formed for single enterprises, but there is no evidence of large-scale corporations engaged in trade. The merchants' associations were social and religious clubs, employed by the government for such regulations as it deemed necessary. Apart from the exchange of information and the erection of common buildings like that at Ostia, they served no economic purposes. Most of the great fortunes were founded on commerce and moneylending. Within the empire, trade handled chiefly foodstuffs and products of industry— metal wares, lumber and its products, textiles, and pottery. For Rome proper the most important trade was that which brought the grain of Egypt and Africa to the city. The emperors kept careful watch over it, offered bounties to the grain merchants, and in time of shortage gave special rewards to those who would sail in winter. The great grain warehouses still standing in the ruins of Ostia are sufficient evidence that it was primarily for the purpose of this trade that the port of Rome was developed.

Banking expanded its services to meet the needs of commerce. The royal banks of Ptolemaic Egypt were turned over to private enterprise and participated in the active life of that province. There and throughout the empire men of wealth engaged in money changing (for Greek coins were standardized on the Attic drachma and permitted to circulate). The need for money-changers lessened after Nero's currency reforms because these reforms equalized the values of the Latin and Greek coins, but business opportunities abounded through the receipt of deposits, in the making of loans, and in the transfer of credit from one section of the empire to another.

Commerce was not limited to the confines of the empire. Ships sailed the Atlantic coasts of Africa and Europe; traders penetrated

Germany as far as the Baltic Sea; others sought the markets of Turkestan to buy Chinese goods. The canal from the Nile to the Red Sea was kept open; a Red Sea fleet protected merchants in those waters; and ships sailed to and from India with the monsoons, which Hippalus had discovered in the first century A.D. The great bulk of Eastern goods came by this route. Fragrant Mediterranean wines, pottery, glass and other Western wares filled the outbound ships. Goods from India which were landed in southern Arabia were carried by the Nabataeans through Petra to Mediterranean ports. Chinese records show that a Roman embassy reached the court of the Chinese emperor in the reign of Marcus Aurelius. The silks and spices that came from the East were paid for with goods and with coins, hoards of which have been found in India. Roman merchants had a fine reputation for honesty among the Eastern peoples with whom they did business.

Industry Industry, like commerce, profited from the prosperity of the provinces and became decentralized. Save for the mines, which in large measure became the property of the imperial patrimony, the monopolies in industry and trade, once assiduously maintained by the Ptolemies and Attalids, were surrendered by the Roman emperors. The advanced industrialization of the Hellenistic East gave that region a continuing pre-eminence in the practical arts, particularly in the production of textiles, glassware, and metal goods. For a period the West was primarily a source of raw materials, especially of metals, which came from the Spanish and British mines. Gradually, however, the West advanced in importance as a manufacturing region. In the Augustan age the great pottery works in Campania, north of Naples, produced a red ware and captured the imperial markets from the Greek potters, but during the first century similar vases from southern Gaul displaced the Italian. Furnaces and warehouses excavated in the Auvergne indicate that from twenty-five to thirty thousand people were employed in this industry. At the same time the cost of transportation made profitable the development of local industries. Gallic clothing and Spanish metal and leather goods appeared, and many skilled Greeks and Syrians moved to the West to establish shops for the production of such objects as glassware and silks. In spite of the appearance of some large centers of production manned by slaves, industry remained characteristically a small shop business employing both free and slave labor in proportions that varied with local conditions of supply. In competition with the city shops industrial establishments also appeared on some of the great estates to serve the needs of the people there.

As in the case of commerce, the associations of artisans, with a few exceptions like the silversmiths of Asia Minor, were not trade unions but were social and religious in character and paid no attention to hours, wages, or conditions of labor. Slavery, a plentiful supply of cheap labor, and the absence of industrial organizations combined to strip the laboring class of industrial weapons and to hold it to very low levels of subsistence.

The chief purchasers of goods were the urban population and the peasants on the great estates. Though the wealthy demanded fine goods, most of the sales were made to the very poor. In satisfaction of their needs for low-priced products, technique and ornamentation declined and standardization was introduced in the interest of cheapness.

The decentralization of commerce and industry contributed to the urbanization of the West and to the decline of Italy, which, always more a purchaser than a seller of goods, lost to local centers its market in the empire. The process of urbanization was accompanied by the formation of a class of wealthy merchants, shop owners, and landholders, who had invested their wealth in farms for income. They presided over a large group of pauperized laborers—free, slave, or freed—who, like the populace at Rome, looked to the upper stratum for gifts and shows to help them to live and to keep them amused and contented. At the same time a great body of tenant peasants were appearing on the farms.

Agriculture   In spite of the growth of trade, industry, and towns throughout the empire, agriculture remained the basic source of wealth and the chief occupation and interest of the greater part of the population. Its products were essential to life. Men of wealth invested their means in it; soldiers returned to it after their period of service; and poor men sought in it a relief from the uncertainties of labor in the cities.

Throughout the period agriculture was generally in a prosperous condition. While the greater portion of the grain supply of the city of Rome came from Africa and Egypt, the cost of transportation made it possible for Italian farmers to compete with their produce in the markets of Rome and of the smaller Italian cities, and the same element of price protected provincial farmers from world competition. The growth of urban communities provided local markets, and the agriculturalists behind the frontier prospered from sales to the army commissariat. This was particularly true of northern Gaul, of Britain, and of the Danubian region. Around Rome, and presumably near the other cities of the empire, were many small farmers who did a flourishing business in vegetables and flowers. In Greece, however, where population was decreasing amid a general decline, there were many abandoned farms.

No estimate is possible of the number or proportion of small independent landowners. The various measures taken by the emperors to protect them and the alimentation program of the Antonines (p. 500) are proofs of their presence in Italy. The practice of giving lands to veterans must have augmented their number in the provinces. The pressure of the wealthy, who wished to secure or expand great estates, and the attractiveness of city life, on the other hand, operated against them. The Hellenistic and republican tendency to the formation of great estates continued with increasing force under the empire, as senators and businessmen invested their surplus wealth in land. The greatest landowner was the emperor. Large tracts came into the possession of Augustus by legacy and confiscation, and the amount increased under succeeding emperors. In Africa, for example, Nero, finding six men owning more than one-half of the province, condemned them and confiscated their possessions.

The great estates, however, changed in the character of their operation. During the late republic and the early empire most of the estates in Italy were worked by slaves herded in gangs and often imprisoned in fearful underground dungeons called *ergastula*. The wasteful character of this type of farming, the imperial ban on *ergastula*, and the increasing cost of slaves, as conquests diminished, caused the system to decline. Owners found it more profitable to settle their slaves on a piece of land, sometimes giving them freedom, to be paid for with produce. The literary sources for our knowledge of agricultural conditions cease to deal with the handling of slaves and treat instead of the problems of tenant farming.

In Egypt and the Eastern world tenant farming had a history that went back to the early millennia. The systems of management which had developed in early times, modified somewhat by the Ptolemies and Seleucids, continued into the Roman period. The tenants on the royal estates or the temple possessions of the earlier periods simply transferred their allegiance to the Roman masters. Eastern methods of control, somewhat changed to meet new conditions, were adapted by the emperors for their Western estates into a system of tenancy under procuratorial control. The land in each province was divided into tracts, the tracts into regions, and each region into estates. The lessee of an estate was called a *conductor*, his tenants, *coloni*. Each *colonus* rented a lot, usually 200 *jugera*, on a five-year lease and paid a quota of his produce and a small sum per head for cattle on the common pasture. In addition he was compelled to work a fixed number of days for the *conductor* at plowing, seeding, and harvesting, and occasionally also on buildings and fortifications. The *coloni* lived in the *vicus*, village, around the villa of the *conductor*. There stood the bakery, mill, barns, pleasure grounds, and shrines. Leases were normally renewed after the five-year period, both tenant and *conductor* being protected by law in their respective rights, which could be transmitted by inheritance. Wastelands could be occupied and worked for a period of five or ten years without payment. This system developed by the emperors spread to the private estates, where freemen and slaves alike became *coloni*. In the third century the peasant population sank everywhere from the rank of small farmers into tenantry, but it was not until the following century that the tenants were reduced to serfdom.

The first notable result of imperial agriculture for profit was the wide extension of those familiar sources of income, the olive tree and the vine, until Gaul and Spain produced their native brands and competed successfully in the world market with the Italian oil and wines. In regions adapted for grazing, especially those close to the army camps, cattle and sheep were raised for their meat and their hides.

The decentralization of industry, which had resulted in urbanization, particularly in the West, along with the formation of great military centers created great local demand for the growing of cereals, and for this tenant farming was best adapted. Attention to scientific farming, the rotation of crops, and the fertilization of the soil declined, however, as the tasks of labor passed into the hands of ignorant, poor, and unambitious peasants.

All economic activities bore their share of the tax burden. Commerce contributed to the tolls, for which the empire was divided into districts; industry paid special license fees levied on trades and occupations; landowners paid the land tax according to its produce. All transactions were subject to the sales tax; and the estates of citizens were subject to the 5 per cent inheritance tax. Provincials who were not citizens or landowners paid the poll tax, which fell heaviest upon the urban proletariat and upon the impoverished tenant farmers. Moreover, the provincials were obliged to supply goods and services upon requisition, for which they were paid but which nonetheless proved burdensome. The imperial service, agriculture, industry, and commerce brought prosperity and its attendant comforts to the upper and middle classes of the empire; but below them were a multitude of the proletariat in the cities and the tenant farmers in the country, miserably paid, wretchedly housed, overtaxed, continually exploited, often dependent, at least in part, on charity, unhappy and hopeless in the midst of plenty.

SOCIAL LIFE

The Imperial City Rome was the focal center of all men's eyes, the goal of every ambitious provincial, the hub of all activities. Its population, composed of elements from every corner of the empire, had spread far beyond the republican wall.[5]

[5] Estimates of the population based on known numbers of houses and tenements, though made by competent scholars, vary all the way from two hundred and sixty thousand to a million.

On the Palatine stood the splendid imperial palaces. At the foot of the hill was the republican Forum and beyond it, the fora of the emperors. The Circus Maximus lay between the Palatine and the Aventine, the Colosseum, on the other side, at the foot of the Esquiline. Temples, theaters, and baths dotted the city. The fine houses of the men of wealth were erected on the hills, while the huge *insulae* where the poor lived stood on the lower ground. Aqueducts supplied the city with water, which overflowed in the many fountains that still add charm to modern Rome. Water was carried into private houses by lead pipes, bearing the emperor's stamp to show payment.[6] The paved streets, wider after the fire of Nero's reign, were filled all day with throngs, and at night the noise of the carters conveying the city's supplies kept the restless or the visitor awake. The poems of Juvenal and Martial resound with the bustle and excitement of imperial Rome.

The Aristocracy   On the income from their landed estates the aristocrats lived in magnificent style. The *atria* of their houses were constructed with marble pilasters and columns. The walls of the rooms were adorned with paintings; the floors were covered with beautiful mosaics; the gardens in the peristyle contained many plants and flowers; Greek statuary or copies of the great masters gave an atmosphere of refinement; and draperies and tapestries added color. The decorative furniture was elegant and costly. For convenience they had water, piped in from the aqueducts to faucets and fountains, and heat, supplied by flues built into the walls.

After an early morning breakfast of a roll and a cup of sour wine, the rich man received his morning callers and then went about his business. Lunch at eleven was followed by a siesta, and the afternoon was devoted to exercise and the bath. In the luxurious *thermae* (baths) the Roman met his friends, discussed the topics of the day, and enjoyed the pleasures of libraries, hot rooms, hot and cold water baths, and massage. The chief social event of the day was the dinner, which frequently lasted three or four hours and was made noteworthy by a wide variety of food brought from all corners of the empire. Fish and oysters were considered such delicacies that many men kept private fish ponds; grouse, thrush, peacocks, and cranes pleased the taste of the epicure; melons and fruits, pastry and nuts were served as desserts. Good chefs were highly valued and cookbooks became popular. Mosaics which represent bones, shells, and vegetables scattered on the floor are indications of a rather low standard of table manners. The entertainment that followed the food depended upon the taste of the diners. Frequently the time was passed in gambling with dice. For the frivolous there were music, girls, and shows, while the reading of poems,

---

[6] Pipes occasionally found without the stamp are indications of illegal connections.

A Part of Hadrian's Villa at Tivoli, Built as a Summer Residence. The group of buildings originally covered many acres of ground.

essays, or orations, and the discussion of ancient authors or of the standards of rhetoric and the meaning of words occupied the erudite.

Women in high society enjoyed greater freedom than in earlier periods. The strict laws that placed women under male control had been relaxed and customs had changed. The new woman participated freely in the social and intellectual life of the time. In spite of imperial discouragement, divorce was easy, and in a society where marriages were arranged there was much moral laxity.

The moralists inveighed against the luxury and corruption of Roman society. Stories of orgies, of expensive feasts, and luxurious appointments were ever popular. There is ample evidence, however, that these were the exception rather than the rule, that many of the customs against which Juvenal thundered, and which Petronius ridiculed, were simply advances in the standard of living. Many of the aristocrats had no part in the luxuries of Nero's court. The group that surrounded Vespasian and the circle of the younger Pliny were simple in their tastes, reserved, and intellectual. Inscriptions show that family affection and loyalty were abiding qualities of Romans of the better class. Conservative traditions, still living and enforced by maternal wisdom, prevented Agricola from pursuing the study of philosophy further than "was fitting for a Roman and a senator." The very fact that the Roman aristocracy served the emperor so well in the armies and provinces of the empire and in the administration of Rome is ample evidence of the stability of the class and of the continuing strength of the old Roman tradition of devotion to the state.

The Business Class   The men of business, *Equites*, and the freedmen found great opportunities for amassing wealth in commerce and industry and in the offices in the civil administration. Their social activities, imitations of senatorial society, were often marked by the vulgarity and ostentation with which they displayed their wealth. These qualities are brilliantly portrayed in the novel *Satyricon* by Petronius, who was a friend of Nero, in a scene that describes the life of a successful freedman. Venality was the chief fault of this group, arising from the fact that money alone could gain them social distinction. Yet in the work they did and in the offices they occupied they too proved themselves able and loyal servants of the empire.

The City Populace   Juvenal portrays the Roman populace as a mob in which all the peoples of the Roman Empire were mingled and which sought only "bread and shows." Rome was an imperial city to which came men from all corners of the empire, but the city populace was far from being an idle and pampered mob. Two hundred thousand people received from the state a grant of grain, which assisted them to live but did not provide entire sustenance. Some received gifts of money or of food from men of wealth. But for the most part they occupied themselves in the industries, the small shops, the tasks of transport, and all the various activities of a busy metropolis. They lived in huge tenements sometimes five stories in height and always subject to fire or collapse, though Nero's building code had lessened the dangers. For amusement the state provided regular festivals, with chariot races, wild-beast shows, gladiatorial combats, and even naval contests in the Colosseum and the Circus. Plays were produced in the theaters, and puppet shows were presented on the street corners.

The *Collegia*   The common man in Rome and in the provincial municipalities found companionship, a sense of security, and a small opportunity for distinction in the *collegia*, or clubs. Some of these were artisan and trade organizations that dated back to the early days of Rome; others were newly organized societies of similar sort; still others were social or sporting clubs or religious associations. All probably had religious features, and all had to have legal charters with the permission of the senate. Secret meetings and all unlicensed associations were strictly forbidden. Trajan frowned on all new organizations as likely to be centers of sedition or disturbance, but other emperors fostered them, and Marcus Aurelius gave them the right to receive bequests. Groups of Christians often hid under the guise of such clubs.

The *collegia* differed from medieval guilds or modern trade unions in the objects of their organization. They made no attempts to regulate methods or conditions of work or to raise wages. But they provided for those in the lower walks of life companionship and a measure of recognition from their fellow men, and gave dignity and meaning to their lives. Their organization was the Roman state in miniature. Some had clubhouses; others met in the houses of their wealthy patrons to whom all paid great deference. Most of them provided burial places for their members. The dead were cremated and the cinerary urns placed in niches in the great underground passages, known as the catacombs, along the Appian Way. Members often left small sums so that the brothers could celebrate their memory with feasts on the anniversary of death.

Slaves and Freedmen   Slavery continued as a legally recognized and widely prevalent institution under the empire but under changing conditions. Wars within the Mediterranean area, once the great source of Roman slaves, had almost ceased. However, rebellious provincials were still sold, and Titus threw thousands of Jews on the market after the fall of Jerusalem. Piracy and brigandage, though checked by the government, continued to feed the supply, though any person who could prove he had been so enslaved was instantly freed. Exposed children were still raised by dealers, and some poor people sold their children and themselves into slavery. But in general these ancient sources were drying up, and most of the slaves were born into slavery to slave mothers whose status they acquired. As a result, the prices of slaves rose appreciably. A man in Claudius' reign paid 30,000 sesterces for a cook.

Slaves were used widely in all sorts of activities. In the household they were, as always, menials, tutors, and secretaries, many of the latter acquiring a knowledge of shorthand. Imperial and municipal clerks and the laborers on public buildings were slaves belonging to the state. Many worked in the industrial or retail shops of the cities, at times managing them for the profit of their owners and even owning slaves of their own. Barbarians from the frontier were apt to be recalcitrant and suited only for the rougher work of the cattle ranches or the mines. Agricultural slavery, however, was declining.

The treatment of slaves varied, of course, with the character of the master; but in general slaves born in the household were kindly treated, and sometimes held in real affection. In any case the law protected them from cruelty. Slaves who were guilty of crimes or who revolted, however, were punished severely, often being sent to the mines. Many belonged to clubs restricted to freedmen and slaves, and enjoyed a social life of their own. They had a right to their *peculium*, a sum of money derived from tips or gifts or sometimes from a share of their wages, and could either spend it for their own pleasure or save it to purchase their freedom. Manumission was easy and frequent. Sometimes it was bought, but often it came by gift of the owner, the result of gratitude or of a desire to have a large following of clients, or for economic reasons, or to save the expense of maintenance, or because of sentiments of universal brotherhood induced by a study of Stoic philosophy. The grant of freedom by will was especially popular.

Freedmen no longer received full citizenship, except by grant of the emperor. They were given a Latin status, and were, as always, attached to their former owner who acted as patron. This relationship involved legal protection on the part of the owner, and loyalty on the part of the freedman, including attendance upon the patron, the protection of his interests, and often services rendered to him in accordance with the provisions of the grant of freedom. Ungrateful freedmen who did not perform these duties might be sold into slavery again. Though their freedom was thus restricted and they could not attain high office in the empire after Hadrian's reforms, the world of business and the lower branches of the imperial service were open to them, and many of them achieved great wealth and power or were renowned as scholars and philosophers.

Provincial Life Superficially the provincial communities presented small-scale replicas of life in the capital. Fora, temples, and administrative buildings were erected; aqueducts supplied water, and sewers provided drainage. The wealthy lived in fine houses, elegantly decorated and furnished, and enjoyed the pleasures of sumptuous bath houses and rooms, heated by furnaces. The poor lived in hovels or were concentrated in tenements. Schools, libraries, medical service and hospitals, and frequent or regular donations of grain were provided for the people through the civic funds or by the gifts of public-spirited men of wealth.

On the great estates the landowners built handsome villas elaborate in plan, ornamented with mosaics and wall paintings, and luxurious in their appointments. Temples, pleasure parks, and exercise grounds provided centers of social life for the tenants whose villages surrounded the great houses.

Yet amid this seemingly prosperous and happy life there was much discontent and misery, and under the surface appearance of uniformity was a wide diversity. The ever-watchful imperial agents hindered freedom of thought or expression and independence of action. Fear of confiscation, the load of taxation, and the expenses of public careers limited the acquisition of wealth by the middle class, while to the poor the burden of living was terrible.

Political diversity was in large part the product of the Roman system of provincial administration. In the first place the Romans willingly recognized and perpetuated local forms of government: the nomes and villages of Egypt; the peculiarities of rule of the Jewish groups; the popular assemblies and boards of archons or generals among the Greeks; the rule of chieftains or princes (as clients of the empire) over tribes and states along the frontier; and the cantonal form of rural government in Gaul, Spain, and Africa. The differences among the charters to the colonies and municipalities produced many variations. The concessions to traditional practices tended to foster rural pride and patriotism and to produce a healthy balance between centralization and local control. Local pride, however, was thus accentuated, and jealousy among neighboring communities became the cause of frequent wranglings and at times of disturbances. The beginning of imperial interference in the reign of Trajan was a first step toward the end of local independence and the triumph of centralization.

Historical differences—arising from local characteristics of race, language, and religion and varying with the extent and character of the impact of Roman culture—persisted between regions of the empire, between provinces, and even between sections of the provinces. The most striking and fateful of these was the division between the Eastern and Western halves of the empire. Though the West was Romanized, the East remained Hellenistic. There Greek was the language of daily life and of literature; architecture and art preserved their Hellenic character; classical plays were produced in the theater; the great games and the historic festivals of classical time were still celebrated, while the gladiatorial contests and the circuses of the Roman arena received scant applause. Indeed the first century witnessed a distinct revival of Greek culture, and Athens continued long to be the center of philosophic studies.

Though the Greek motherland, while remaining the mecca of students and tourists, declined in population and wealth, the cities of Anatolia thrived as wealth accrued from the products of the rich lands, from industry, and from the trade that still flowed overland from Asia. Antioch in Syria, cosmopolitan in its population, was one of the large cities of the empire, and the remains of many cities in the interior of Syria bespeak the prosperity of that region. The Roman government fostered the Hellenization of the mixture of peoples who lived in Asia Minor and of the native Semites of Syria. Yet particularistic elements were strong; native languages persisted; and contemporary religious tendencies brought the Eastern religions into prominence, thereby strengthening the Oriental aspects of civilization. The Jews were a constant source of trouble, and the revolt which recalled Trajan from his victorious campaign in Mesopotamia was caused by a wave of religious fanaticism.

In Egypt the institutions and social conditions that had developed under the Ptolemies continued almost unchanged under Roman domination. The administration and the management of commerce and industry were almost entirely in Greek hands. Indeed, though Romans were at the head of the government, though Roman tourists visited the temples and pyramids, and though Roman businessmen had investments in Egypt, senators, following the order of Augustus, were carefully excluded. All pieces of property were carefully registered and the status of every individual inhabitant was recorded. The natives, bound to the soil, overworked and heavily taxed, still clung to their ancient practices and beliefs; the Egyptian language, writing, methods of work, and religion persisted. Roman emperors repaired the temples on whose walls their pictures and hieroglyphic titles appeared after the manner of pharaonic times. The cults of the gods, though deprived of much of the land which they had once possessed, even of that which the Ptolemies had left to them, continued, and Isis-worship spread throughout the Roman world.

The same story of local variations amid general uniformity is to be told of the West. Though Sicily remained predominantly Greek, elsewhere the Latin language and Roman culture spread. Roman senators bought land, and Roman colonists settled in Africa, Spain, Gaul, and Britain. Agriculture, industry, and trade were developed. Cities were built or enlarged; aqueducts, roads, and bridges were constructed. Seneca, Lucan, Quintilian, and Martial were the leaders of a Spanish school of Latin literature in Rome, and in later centuries literary works of note were produced in Gaul. Spain provided Trajan and Hadrian as rulers of the empire, and Antoninus and Marcus Aurelius were of Gallic descent.

Yet in these regions local traditions were also strong. The native tribes of Sicily, Sardinia, Africa, and Spain continued in the use of their native dialects; Phoenician was still spoken in Africa and local gods, though generally identified with Roman deities, preserved much of their pristine strength.

Of all the Western lands Gaul was most thoroughly Romanized. Its Celtic elements were almost completely submerged; the Druids were suppressed, and Celtic religion assumed a Roman aspect. The Roman policy of urbanization was especially effective, and the presence of army cantonments on the northern frontier with their incessant demands for the products of the fields and the workshops of Gaul brought prosperity to the people.

Along the Rhine and the Danube and in Dacia, camps and colonies provided centers from which Roman influence spread among the provincials to the rear and to the Germanic peoples beyond. Newly conquered and often troublesome, these regions created many problems for the imperial administrators, and the restless barbarian tribes proved a constant menace, which became a positive danger in the reign of Marcus Aurelius. Of local conditions along the frontier, little is known. Yet it is certain that when at last the flood could no longer be stemmed, the Germanic invaders had secured a veneer of Roman culture and an appreciation of the institutions and customs of the Romans.

Such, in brief survey, was the empire which the might of Roman arms had secured and which Rome, through its military force, its emperor worship, its bureaucracy, its roads, and its work of civilization, not only taxed and exploited but also endeavored to hold together, administer, and protect.

CULTURE

Throughout the territory of the empire still stand the symbols of its prosperity and greatness. The ruins of Ostia, Herculaneum, and Pompeii, in Italy; of Carthage and Timgad (Temesa) in Africa; the temples and arenas and aqueducts at Nîmes, Arles, and Orange in southern Gaul; the remains of towns and villas and the great wall in Britain; traces of the *limes* across the northern frontier; the buildings of Roman times in Athens, Eleusis, and Corinth, in Asia Minor and at Baalbek in Syria; hieroglyphs of the Roman emperors in the temples of Egypt; and everywhere the remains of roads and bridges and thousands of inscriptions—all convey to the modern student the message of the imperial majesty of Rome.

Art and Architecture

The achievements of Rome in architecture are amply represented in the many structures that have survived and in the traditions that influenced the architects of the Middle Ages. The Romans learned the basic elements—the column, the arch, the vault, and the dome—from their Oriental, Greek, and Etruscan predecessors, and with a shrewd sense of the practical and the effective they developed and combined them in the great works of the empire.

The column, derived from the Greek, was used profusely, not only for structural needs but also for ornamental purposes in the façades of great buildings and in the piers of triumphal arches. The Romans liked the ornate Corinthian style and endeavored to make it even more luxuriant. They delighted in colored marbles and often omitted the fluting. By combining elements of the Greek orders, they produced the so-called Composite or Roman order.

The arch, which came to them from the Etruscans, was used for the construction of bridges and thence for the erection of aqueducts like the Aqua Claudia at Rome and the celebrated Pont du Gard near Nîmes in southern Gaul. The great memorial arches of imperial triumphs were a Roman creation. As a structural element the arch was used in the lower courses of massive structures and in the exteriors of the Colosseum and other amphitheaters.

The barrel vault for the covering of passageways and even of rooms was essentially a Roman contribution. The intersection of two barrel vaults at right angles produced the groined or cross vault which was employed to great effect in the ceilings of the great halls of the baths and the basilicas. The use of the dome as a roofing device, though known to the Orientals, was first developed on a magnificent scale by the Romans. The greatest domed structure in the world was a round building, the Pantheon. But the architects learned to erect on arches triangular segments called *pendentives*, and so to place the circular dome over a square space. The semicircular apse, covered with a half dome on the side or at the end of temples and public buildings, became a favorite device of the designers. These achievements in the use of the dome and the vault made possible the development of the Byzantine and Romanesque styles of the Middle Ages.

For basic materials the Romans used bricks and concrete. The surfaces, however, were covered with a veneer of tiles or, in the finer buildings, with slabs of granite or marble. Thus were achieved buildings with great vaults or lofty domes massive in size and magnificent in appearance. Interiors were plastered or sometimes veneered.

The temple, the theater, the stadium, and the stoa were the structural productions of the Greek architects. To these the Romans added the triumphal arch, the basilica, the bath, the amphitheater, and the great *insula*, or apartment house.

The triumphal arch, with its massive piers often adorned with columns, its arched openings, and its superstructures that bore inscriptions, medallions, and bands of relief, was characteristically Roman.

The basilica was a large, colonnaded building with a two storied, or one and a half storied, central nave often covered with barrel or groined vaulting and side aisles of lesser height. Arches, resting on piers beside the nave, raised the central roof above the sides to admit light, creating a clerestory like that used in Egyptian temples. With the addition of an apse at one end, the basilica became the ancestor of later Christian cathedrals.

The distinctive feature of the bath and, it should be added, of the imperial palaces was complexity of plan. A variety of rooms for different purposes were disposed to produce an effective, useful, and harmonious whole. The *thermae* contained dressing rooms, hot rooms to induce perspiration, a hot bath, and a cold plunge. In addition there were frequently exercise rooms, lounging places, and even lecture halls and libraries. Heat was carried from the furnace by flues set into the floors and walls. The basic construction was like that of the basilica.

The amphitheaters, oval in form, contained tiers of seats resting upon rows of arches. Ramps, stairways, and vaulted passages gave access to the spectators. Underneath the central arena were extensive substructures containing the dens of the wild animals, dressing rooms, and rooms for the storage of scenic materials. The Colosseum, most celebrated of the amphitheaters, was 57 meters high and 527 in circumference. Four great stories resting on piers, arches, and vaults supported the seats. Spacious stairways and eighty arcades made rapid ingress and exit possible, and each of the seats bore a number or the name of its occupant. Awnings, drawn by ropes and supported by huge beams, protected the spectators from rain and sun. The building held about 45,000 spectators.

> While stands the Colosseum, Rome shall stand;
> When falls the Colosseum, Rome shall fall;
> And when Rome falls, the world.[7]

The *insulae*, chief feature of city architecture, were huge apartment houses of many stories. The first floor contained shops or business offices. In front of these, arches supported the façade of the upper stories and provided a sheltering arcade. The higher levels contained apartments of varied size and elegance. In early days the inner supports were of wood or cheap stone, so there were many fires and collapses. After the great fire, however, the law required brick or better materials in the lower courses, and though many were still poorly constructed, the general improvement was marked. Similar to the *insulae* in construction were the huge *mercatori* of Rome and Ostia, where business concerns had offices. These arcaded buildings are still characteristic of Italian cities.

Sculpture   Though in sculpture, as in architecture, the Romans learned lessons of technique from the Greeks, they infused it with their own spirit. In reliefs they portrayed historical scenes and processions and added elaborate floral ornaments for decorative purposes. Of this character are the carvings on the Altar of the Augustan Peace representing members of the imperial family and their attendants, and the sacrifice with symbolic figures, wreaths, and flowers. The procession on the Arch of Titus and the reliefs of Trajan on balustrades in the Forum are famous examples of reliefs of historical significance. The memorial column covered with bands of relief in spiral, like those of Trajan and of Marcus Aurelius, was a Roman creation. Portrait sculp-

---

[7] A maxim attributed to the Venerable Bede. Compare: Edward Gibbon, *Decline and Fall of the Roman Empire, III.* Ed. by J. B. Bury. London: Methuen & Co., Ltd., 1930, p. 317.

Portrait Bust of the Emperor Antoninus Pius. The Antonine emperors followed the fashion, which had begun with Hadrian, of wearing carefully trimmed beards and mustaches. (Metropolitan Museum of Art, Fletcher Fund, 1933)

ture was distinctively Roman in its realistic faithfulness to life in contrast to Greek idealization. It had its origin in Etruscan sculpture and in wax death masks of great men, which were carefully kept by leading families as evidence of their nobility. From these influences sculpture acquired a sense of naturalness and an adherence to the details of appearance, even to the furrowed lines of the face. As a result, the portraits have made familiar to the modern world the appearance of the emperors and the women of their families.

Literature in the Silver Age

Post-Augustan Latin literature belongs to the so-called Silver Age, the chief characteristic of which was the development of rhetoric. As patronage, on the one hand, and fear of the tyrannical power of the princeps and his informers, on the other, discouraged free expression of opinion, the writers in general paid greater attention to the words and the forms they employed than to the substance of what they wrote. Nevertheless, they produced great works of literary value and erudition. Significant of the spread of Roman culture is the fact that many of the ablest writers came from the provinces, notably from Spain.

Of the voluminous writings of histories, memoirs, treatises, essays, poems, and plays not much has survived. The loss of the memoirs of Tiberius and of Agrippina, mother of Nero, is particularly to be deplored. Seneca, stoic philosopher and tutor of Nero, composed literary tragedies and philosophic essays of lasting value. Petronius, *arbiter elegantiarum* of Nero's court (pp. 496, 531), in *Satyricon* created the Latin novel. Seneca's nephew Lucan wrote a historical epic of the civil war between Caesar and Pompey, *Pharsalia*, famous for its portrayal of the great leaders and for its striking and poignant lines.

"Heaven loved the winning side, Cato, the lost."

"For those who are to live the gods conceal
The bliss of death; so they endure their life."[8]

Vespasian's friend and helper, the elder Pliny, was the author of a history of the German Wars, no longer extant, and of an encyclopedia of miscellaneous information called *Natural History*. Many tales are told of the energy and erudition of this distinguished man. He read continuously even while being carried about the city in his litter, dictating to a writer of shorthand as he read. Lest he lose a moment of time he had someone read to him during his bath. Scientific curiosity, incidentally, was the cause of his death at the eruption of Vesuvius.

The tyranny of Domitian brought about a temporary silence, but in the period of the Antonines a new group of literary men appeared: Pliny the Younger, the historian Tacitus, the biographer Suetonius, and the poets Martial and Juvenal. Pliny, nephew of the naturalist, servant and loyal supporter of Trajan, regarded himself as a second Cicero and composed orations, most of them now lost, and letters, which have been preserved. Pliny's correspondence is of great value for its pictures of Roman life, for the description of the eruption of Vesuvius, and for the very important book of letters between himself and Trajan which deals with provincial and municipal problems and policies.

Tacitus (*ca.* A.D. 55–120)   Tacitus is one of the great figures in Roman history. In matchless style and with an extraordinary gift for epigrammatic terseness, he wrote *Annals*, a history of Rome from the death of Augustus to the death of Nero, *Histories*, on the events from

[8]John Wight Duff, *A Literary History of Rome in the Silver Age*. New York: Barnes & Noble, Inc., 1960, pp. 261, 262. Reprinted by permission of Barnes & Noble, Inc., and Ernest Benn Limited, publishers.

Galba to Domitian, a treatise on Germany, a biography of his father-in-law Agricola, and an essay on oratory. A large part of *Annals*, the first books of *Histories*, and the shorter works have survived. His pages reflect bitter indignation at the tyranny of the emperors and the luxury and vices of the aristocracy. His characterizations of Tiberius, Claudius, Nero, and Domitian, though extremely prejudiced, are indelibly fixed on the pages of literature.

History, in the opinion of Tacitus, had a moral purpose. "This, I regard as history's highest function, to rescue merit from oblivion and to hold out the reprobation of posterity as a terror to evil words and deeds."[9] To this end he devoted some of his most brilliant epigrams with which he characterized the deeds of the Romans. "They make a solitude and call it peace," was a description of conquest. "This among the ignorant is called civilization, when it is really the badge of slavery," portrayed the Romanization of Britain. "The persecution of genius fosters its influence," was his comment on the tyranny of Tiberius.

Suetonius (*ca.* A.D. 75–150) Suetonius was a biographer rather than a historian. Of the many works he composed, only *Lives of the Twelve Caesars* from Julius to Domitian has survived, except for scattered fragments. As Latin secretary to Hadrian he had access to the imperial archives and might have written biographies of outstanding merit. He preferred, however, to write character studies filled with gossip and episodic materials paying little attention to chronology or to the great affairs of state. Nevertheless, his manner of writing became the pattern for later Roman and medieval biographers, and his work remains a valuable, if irritating, source for the history of the first century of the empire.

Apuleius *The Golden Ass* of Apuleius is a novel of magical adventure written in the Antonine period by a native of Africa. It deals with the experiences of a youth traveling in Greece who, through misadventure, is turned into an ass and passes through a series of mishaps until he is finally rescued through the intervention of Isis. The romantic character of the narrative, the tales of magic, and the religious devotion to Isis distinguish it from other classical works. From this viewpoint Apuleius might be called the first medievalist.

Martial (*ca.* A.D. 40–102) Born in Bilbilis in northeastern Spain, Martial went to Rome as a young man, made his mark there as a man of letters, and returned in his old age to his native town. The Greeks had developed the epigram; Martial established it as a Latin form and gave to it the content of pungent Roman satire. In a series of brilliant verses, sometimes noble, sometimes biting, he describes the life of

---

[9] Tacitus, *Annals*, 3. 65.

Rome in his day in both its finer and shadier aspects. One of his loveliest epigrams follows:

> Your birthday, April first, is here,
> A day I love, yes, Quintus dear,
> Love much as my own natal day —
> The first of March — and well I may.
> Red letter days are both for me,
> Both days I welcome gratefully.
> One gave me life, dear Quintus, — true;
> But one gave more, it gave me you.[10]

Juvenal (ca. A.D. 55–130)   Juvenal, a younger friend of Martial,
employed the satire for the same purpose that Tacitus used history,
and Martial the epigram. The noise and confusion of the city streets,
the crime, the self-seeking, the graft, the favoritism and corruption of
the imperial city were the themes of his poems.

> For since their votes have been no longer bought,
> All public care has vanished from their thought,
> And those who once, with unresisted sway,
> Gave armies, empire, everything, away,
> For two poor claims have long renounced the whole,
> And only ask — the Circus and the Dole.[11]

In the famous tenth satire on "The Vanity of Human Wishes"
he mocked the desire of men for power, eloquence, beauty, wealth, and
fame. The standard he proclaimed — *mens sana in corpore sano* — has
become the ideal of modern education.

In addition to these works of literature a number of specialized
treatises by other writers have survived: Columella on agriculture,
Frontinus on aqueducts, Vitruvius on architecture, Celsus on medicine,
Gaius on law, and Quintilian on oratory. Quintilian, professor of Latin
rhetoric under Vespasian, gave to the world the ancient literary canon
and at the same time composed a textbook of educational principles
that are still valid. He laid emphasis on the choice of the best teachers,
on the beginning of education in infancy, on proper training of the
memory, and on the value of cultural subjects. The purpose of the
training of an orator, he held, was not only to produce a competent
public speaker, but to make him the best man in culture, in ethics, and
in devotion to the state.

---

[10] Paul Nixon, *Martial and the Modern Epigram.* New York: Longmans, Green & Co.,
Inc., 1927, p. 46.

[11] George Howe and Gustave Adolfus Harrer, *Roman Literature in Translation.* New
York: Harper & Row, Publishers, 1924, p. 582.

Greek Literature

Greek literature continued under the impulse of the Hellenistic age and in the forms and patterns of that period it is represented by many famous men. *Library of History*, an annalistic collection of excerpts and comments, was composed by Diodorus, the Sicilian, during the revolutionary period. In the Augustan age Dionysius of Halicarnassus wrote on rhetoric and composed a book on the antiquities of Rome which is a chief source for the early period of Roman history. His contemporary Strabo provided a mine of information in a descriptive geography of the Mediterranean world. For the tourists who thronged to Greece to enjoy the ancient glories, Pausanias under Hadrian composed a guidebook which remains the chief aid to archaeologists. Ptolemy's *Geography* and Galen's treatise on medicine, both composed in the period of the Antonines, were the texts of the Middle Ages. Hadrian's reign is noteworthy, in addition, for Appian, a civil servant, who composed histories of Rome's foreign and civil wars, and for Arrian, likewise an official of the emperor, who wrote a life of Alexander the Great and an account of a voyage around the Black Sea.

Plutarch In the list of names of Greek men of letters in the Roman period two are pre-eminent—Plutarch and Lucian—and of these the most familiar to the modern world is Plutarch. Born about A.D. 50 in Chaeronea, he was prouder of holding in his native city a local office that Epaminondas had once held than of any position or title Rome could confer upon him. In quiet, refined leisure he discussed historical and moral problems and composed a number of essays on them. To discover the secret of greatness he studied the lives and wrote biographies of illustrious Greeks and Romans, arranging them in pairs and making comparisons for purposes of elucidation. His *Lives* are not only historical sources of immeasurable value; they form one of the greatest pieces of the world's literature. Believing in the old gods, the old ways, and the ancient city, he remained a classical Greek in a changing world.

Lucian Lucian, a Syrian born about A.D. 125 in Samosata, was more a product of his generation. Rhetoric, he said, "made a Greek of him," and he used the dialogue form as a means of expression. His dialogues are one-act plays in which gods and men discuss every sort of problem, natural and supernatural, and in which the religious and philosophic thought of the age is reviewed and dissected with keen and brilliant sarcasm. Lucian's ultimate conclusions are that human life and ambition are alike worthless and that virtue must be its own reward.

Morals and Religion

It is at once apparent that morality is the absorbing interest of most of the Latin and Greek men of letters in the early empire. The arbitrary and uncertain power of despotism, the restraint on intellectual discussions about questions of public policy, and the lack of any real political activity or opportunity for social service as outlets for the energies of the leisure class made men introspective. Luxury and wickedness in high society and abject poverty and the degradation of slavery at the base aroused in thoughtful minds considerations of the problems of humanity. In the midst of prosperity the wealthy became afflicted with an abnormal consciousness of sin, a *taedium vitae*, "weariness with life"; while the poor and enslaved, with little hope of economic betterment, sought every means of mental and emotional escape from the hard facts of life. In answer to the cries from all strata of society, moralists, philosophers, and missionaries of a multitude of religions went from one end of the empire to the other and found audiences ever ready to listen to their messages. There is hardly an age in all history that has seen more discussion of the nature and problem of human life than the most flourishing epoch of the Roman Empire.

To meet the needs of men, the moralists and teachers cast aside the scientific elements of the Greek philosophic systems and turned philosophy into ethics. Great moral preachers like Dio Chrysostom went about teaching temperance and justice, the reality of virtue, and the freedom of the individual who, released from the tyranny of illicit desires, gives himself over to simple pleasures in a confident reliance upon the fatherhood of God. Epicureans endeavored to bring contentment and freedom from superstition by means of the messages of Epicurus and Lucretius, which taught release from vain desires and superstitious fears through the acceptance of a materialistic universe. But hated and feared by the populace as atheists and almost as subject to persecution as the Christians, they made little headway except among the intellectuals. On the other hand, pairs of Cynic philosophers, though often obscene and corrupt, carried to the poor the lesson of the wise man who searches for the life according to nature, after he has renounced vain desire and has liberated himself from evil. Neo-Pythagoreans, talking of virtue and knowledge of hidden words and signs and the recurrence of life, promised to their converts rest in the underworld and eventual release. In a later period Philostratus wrote the life of the great leader of this sect, Apollonius of Tyana, who according to his credulous biographer visited the Brahmans in India, conversed with Egyptian sages, slept in temples, wrought miracles, and preached sermons of virtue with revivalist force.

The dominant philosophy of the empire, however, was a Roman version of Stoicism, which, laying aside interest in the nature of the world and all thought that had no bearing on conduct, turned its attention fully to the position and duties of man and the power and character of that "Pantheon," all-divine world god, the all-in-all. The great spokesmen of Roman Stoicism were Seneca, Epictetus, and Marcus Aurelius. To the jaded aristocrats of Nero's court, Seneca preached the Stoic doctrines of self-control, of moral self-discipline, of obedience to a "rational law of conduct," and of social obligations. "No one outside the pale of Christianity has ever insisted so powerfully on the obligation to live for others, on the duty of love and forgiveness as Seneca has done."[12]

In the next generation lived Epictetus, a poor, lame Phrygian freedman, whose golden sayings drew crowds to Epirus to listen to him. Recorded by Arrian, they are still a source of comfort and delight to many. He taught personal cleanliness, decent behavior, freedom from worry, and reliance upon the will of a wise creator. The thoughts of Seneca and of Epictetus recur in *Meditations* of the philosopher-emperor, Marcus Aurelius, wherein he describes himself as a citizen of the world ruled by a divine Providence. He was confident that though life was but a play whose lines were written and whose limit was set, the inner will was free. He felt that no man could do him injury save himself alone, and that to live fully as befitted a man he must serve his fellow men as far as his abilities and resources permitted.

Religion Though many of the philosophers had drawn religious dependence upon the gods or upon a Divine Being into their systems, their message was still the intellectual demand that men save themselves by the power of thought. Someone has pointed out that Stoicism, despite all its force and values, had no message for children. As in the Hellenistic age, men, weary of philosophic thought, turned to religion, where emotion ruled and where salvation might be found by faith. The great gods of old were no longer vital forces, for they had been slain by the skepticism of the philosophers, by the failure of the civic institutions they had once served, and by their very elevation to supremacy over a world empire. Emperor worship was more real and gave a deeper sense of hope and satisfaction than did the festivals of Jupiter himself. The provincial prayed to the god-emperor for economic betterment, and participation in that worship carried with it a sense of patriotism, of community in a civilized world.

Amid the decay of classical religion, both Greek and Roman, superstition was everywhere rife, from the highest to the lowest ranks of

[12] Sir Samuel Dill, *Roman Society from Nero to Marcus Aurelius*. New York: Meridian Books, Inc., 1958, p. 326.

society. Men and women sought charms to secure good luck or to avoid evil; they thronged the wonder-working shrines of Asclepius in search of health; they crowded the oracles and poured money into the hands of fortunetellers. A widespread belief in miracles made them the victims of many clever fakers, and even the emperors consulted astrologists, believed in horoscopes, and feared unhappy omens. Only when philosophy would compromise itself by alliance with magic did it become acceptable to the people. By so doing, however, it lost all dignity and value as philosophy.

Though many turned for contentment to the little gods of early times, the lares and penates of the Romans and the deities of springs or trees or countryside of the Hellenic or Italian world, most of the people of the world sought salvation in the mystery religions. These, with their initiatory ceremonies, their ecstatic rituals, their calls to service, and their promises of immortality, spread throughout the empire. Traders, soldiers, travelers, and missionaries carried their doctrines from the eastern frontier to the wall in Britain. Pre-eminent among them were two religions: the worship of Isis (p. 373), whose maternal loveliness captured the hearts of men and women, and the soldier religion of Mithras. Mithraism was an adaptation of the Zoroastrian worship of Ahura-Mazda. Mithras was the chief agent of that great god of light, general of his forces. His initiates, passing through a series of seven degrees, were soldiers in the battle of life fighting for Light and Truth under their heroic leader. The chapels of their lodges represented caves and contained reliefs and pictures of scenes drawn from the myths of their god. They are found in Rome (one can still be seen in the baths of Caracalla) and in the ruins of the camps of the Roman legions. One such chapel excavated at Doura on the Euphrates still contains these portrayals. In the third century Mithraism became the chief rival of Christianity.

Christianity In scattered places in the empire, particularly in the East, there began to appear groups of people called Christians. They attributed the foundation of their religion to Jesus of Nazareth, who was crucified during the reign of Tiberius. His message and the belief in the divinity of the Risen Christ was spread and firmly planted in the Roman world by St. Paul and the Apostles.

In the struggle with the pagan cults Christianity had certain advantages. In place of the nature myths on which most of them were based, it had as its background the fine creation story of Genesis and the grand theological concepts of the Hebrew prophets. Its code of morals, with its greater emphasis on behavior than on ritual, was of a higher order than any possessed by its rivals. It claimed fulfillment of the Jewish Messianic hope and gave definite promises of immortality in a glorious Paradise. Above all, in place of a mythical founder, it looked back to a Personality who had fixed himself on the minds and hearts of the Apostles and who remained vivid and living. Freed from the burden of Jewish law by the efforts of Paul and by the destruction of Jerusalem, it made a universal appeal. The poor and oppressed flocked to it, and even members of the imperial family of the Flavians became converts. For a period the Roman government paid no attention to it. The Christians in Rome in Nero's reign were punished as incendiaries, not as Christians. Domitian's religiosity led him to punish a Christian member of his own family on the charge of "leading a Jewish life."

However the Christians were in constant trouble in the provinces. They took no part in festivities; they failed to worship the gods; and they refused to sacrifice to the emperor. Such persons were regarded as certainly guilty of the *odium generis humani*, "hatred of the human race," which Tacitus imputed to them. They broke the law against unlicensed assembly unless they disguised themselves falsely as a *collegium* established for some other purpose. In addition, in the regions where they were strong, the sale of sacrificial animals and votive offerings of silver declined and business suffered. Accordingly, there were sporadic outbreaks and some executions. Charges against them were brought before Pliny, who wrote to Trajan for a ruling. Trajan's reply was direct and clear. If accusations were properly made (no anonymous charges were to be heard), the governor should investigate and punish in accordance with the offense. A rescript of Hadrian confirmed this ruling. All Christians perforce violated the law by belonging to associations for an unlicensed religion, by holding secret meetings, and by offending the majesty of the emperor, and for these offenses they were punished when brought to trial. There was, however, little interest in them in the imperial administration, and no concerted effort was made to destroy them.

Of the organization of the Christian church before the third century little is known. The Christians were organized into groups under bishops (i.e., overseers) and presbyters (i.e., elders). Finances and the care of the poor and sick were in the hands of deacons. The Christians at Rome buried their dead, as did other societies, in the underground catacombs, and they probably held meetings in the chambers where lay the bones of their martyrs. Early Christian art produced pictures of Biblical scenes, of the Good Shepherd, and of a fish, symbol of Christ. The initial letters of the Greek words for Jesus Christ, of God, the Son, Saviour, formed the word *Ichthus*, a fish. The period of trial and triumph for Christianity was the third century.

25 · Civil Wars and Recovery

THE SUCCESSORS OF MARCUS AURELIUS WITNESSED the end of the dream of universal peace and prosperity of the Antonine age and the triumph of those forces of disruption which had always been present though latent in the imperial structure. As the martial basis of the principate came into greater prominence, the empire passed into the hands of military rulers; the armies, localized on the frontiers, rose to claim the imperial office for their commanders and to secure for themselves the rewards of booty; civil wars wracked the empire; and for the greater part of the third century the throne was the prize of victorious generals. With the armies thus engaged, the barbarians broke through the frontier and laid waste the border provinces. Political disorder, civil war, the advance of economic decentralization, an increase in the number of self-sufficient estates, and the overwhelming burdens of taxation and of exactions by generals and their armies were accompanied by the decline of towns and general economic decay. Intellectual life became sterile, and religious controversies and persecutions brought confusion and dismay. It was a dark period in the history of the Mediterranean world.

Unfortunately, good literary sources for this period are almost entirely lacking. For the first third of the century the works of two contemporaries, Dio Cassius and Herodian, have survived. The last part of Dio's history of Rome exists, however, only in the form of a late epitome. Herodian's work, marred by inaccuracies and distortions due in large part to a striving after literary effect, is at best scarcely reliable. A series of biographies, known as *Historia Augusta* and probably composed in the next century as a continuation of Suetonius' work, presents many problems to the historian. While it contains many facts that can be verified from coins or inscriptions, which are probably authentic, its overemphasis on personal anecdote and tales of wonder and the presence of many forged documents, letters, and speeches make it difficult to use. Some information may be gleaned from the writings of the great jurists. Papyri provide facts about Egypt and occasionally information or verification about incidents of imperial interest. Coins verify or add facts about the emperors, and inscriptions carry scattered bits of information about the provinces, the army, and the workings of imperial officials. Some knowledge may be gleaned from the writings of early Christians, but the scarcity of written material has made exceedingly difficult any clear and certain explanation of the problems of this century. Archaeology supplements the record but scantily.

THE EMPERORS

The worthless Commodus succeeded to his father's power in 180. He made terms of peace with the Germanic tribes with whom Marcus Aurelius had been fighting and returned to Rome to enjoy his favorites and to appear in public as a gladiator. Murdered in 192, he was succeeded by Pertinax. He in turn was killed by the praetorians, who then sold the throne to the highest bidder, Didius Julianus. Once more the armies asserted their authority, and the army of the Danube, led by Septimius Severus, was victorious over the forces of the East and of Gaul. Local feeling which animated these military activities was indicative of the increasing decentralization of the empire and portended the dissension that came later. With the triumph of Septimius Severus, the military side of the principate emerged triumphant, and the title *imperator*, with which armies hailed victorious generals, became dominant over that of *princeps*.

Septimius Severus, 193–211 It was Septimius, an African of equestrian family, who, having risen to power on the basis of his military ability, openly made the government of the empire a military institution. With utter disregard for the traditional position of the senate and the privileged status of the Italians, he put members of the equestrian order with the title "prefect of the legion" into high command in the army and reconstructed the imperial bodyguard, hitherto drawn from Italy, into a military reserve picked from the elite of the entire army. To gain the support of the soldiers, he increased their pay and allowed them to contract legal marriages, creating a new treasury department for the purpose. The latter reform enhanced a tendency toward an hereditary military caste and made the armies more than ever local in character.

Of greater significance than the military reforms was the work of Papinian, the praetorian prefect. The great jurist made this office the center of the judicial structure of the empire. His decisions, along with those of his pupils and successors, Paul and Ulpian, were a major contribution to the final development of Roman law.

A Leaping Tigress, Perhaps Serving as the Handle of an Ornamental
Metal Vase, Second to Fourth Centuries A.D. Found in Asia Minor.
(The Brooklyn Museum)

The cultural interests of Rome were left in the capable hands of
the emperor's wife, Julia Domna, daughter of the priest of the sun at
Syrian Emesa. At her court and under her patronage lived Philostratus, biographer of Apollonius of Tyana; Diogenes Laertius, who
wrote *Lives of the Philosophers*; Athenaeus, an anthologist of poetry; and
Dio Cassius, whose history of Rome from the beginning to his own
time has survived in fragments and epitomes.

Caracalla, 211–217   The process that reduced Rome and Italy to
the level of the provinces was begun by Julius Caesar. Extended by
the acts of many emperors, particularly Claudius and Hadrian, and
accelerated by the military reforms of Septimius, it was completed by
the son of Septimius, M. Aurelius Antoninus, better known as Caracalla. In 212 he issued a proclamation conferring Roman citizenship
on all freemen in the empire. This act had the merit and probably the
purpose of unifying the administration and equalizing taxation. To
secure funds with which to meet the increased needs of the military

establishment, he issued coins seriously debased in value. The economic crisis that resulted in part from this inflation continued without surcease throughout the century. Apart from these measures Caracalla is known chiefly for the magnificent baths he built at Rome, the ruins of which are still standing.

Caracalla was murdered in 217 by the order of Macrinus, praetorian prefect, who succeeded him. After Macrinus had ruled a year he was overthrown, and the Syrian army put on the throne the priest, Elagabalus, grandnephew of Julia Domna. Under this degenerate the imperial office sounded the depths of degradation. When he was murdered in 222, his cousin, Alexander Severus, became emperor.

Alexander Severus, 222–235   In the reign of Alexander Severus the senate made its last appearance as a ruling force in the empire when a council of senators was appointed to assist the emperor's mother, Julia Mamaea, and the prefect Ulpian during the youth of Alexander. At this time the imperial government regularly sought the advice of the senate. After a brief period, however, the senate lost its favored position, and as a body it remained henceforth little more than a municipal council in Rome. Septimius had taken from the senatorial order its pre-eminence in the administration, and during the following period the time-honored division of the empire into senatorial and imperial provinces was completely ignored. The title of senator during the later centuries was conferred on certain men because of their wealth or for services rendered the emperor. For the most part the senators lived not in Rome but on their estates scattered throughout the empire.

In an attempt to remedy the economic conditions in Rome resulting from the financial disorder, Alexander commanded the wine merchants, greengrocers, and shoemakers of the city to form associations through which their activities might be regulated. Taxes were reduced and primary education provided everywhere, even in villages, throughout the empire.

Alexander's reign was marked by the appearance of enemies on the frontiers, who in succeeding generations threatened the life of Rome. In the East appeared the second Persian Empire. After long centuries of Parthian rule the Persians reasserted themselves and under the leadership of a family called Sassanids established their second empire in 227. The kings, claiming to be descendants of Darius, planned the restoration of ancient imperial glory. Zoroastrianism was made the official religion and the writing of the *Avesta* (p. 170) was completed. Again in the name of Ahura-Mazda the Persian emperors beautified their capital, Ctesiphon, with palaces and temples and went to battle in an effort to regain the territory and greatness of the fifth century B.C. In a continuing series of wars with Rome and later with the Eastern emperors, though the Persians failed in their aim of conquest, they acquitted themselves creditably until they were finally overthrown by the followers of Mohammed. In spite of unruly and undisciplined armies, Alexander won a victory over the Persians sufficient to protect the Roman frontier. At the same time the German Alemanni threatened to cross the Rhine. The emperor held them back by negotiation and purchase, but a mutiny of the army, which was indignant at his seeming lack of energy against the enemy, led to his execution in 235.

The Anarchy From 235 until 285 civil war and near anarchy prevailed in the empire. One emperor after another was elevated by the armies, which had become local in outlook and greedy for rewards. The soldiers had learned of their power over the imperial throne and of the booty and high position to which they might attain. Accordingly claimants to the purple were established in the provinces by armies that hailed their commanders as *imperatores.* Emperors in Rome followed one another with great rapidity, the nadir being reached at the succession of Gallienus (260–268), when there were as many as nineteen candidates for the throne. They are sometimes called the Barracks Emperors.

This disintegration of the political and military structure of the empire resulted in calamities on the frontier. During these years the Franks and the Alemanni crossed the Rhine and devastated Gaul and Spain; the Saxons began to raid Britain; the Goths from Russia occupied Dacia and in 251 defeated and killed the emperor Decius (249–251). On the eastern frontier the Persians under Sapor seized Armenia and invaded Syria, defeating and taking prisoner the emperor Valerian (253–260). The West, forced to defend itself against the Germans, set up an independent state in Gaul. In the East, Odaenathus, ruler of Palmyra, defeated the Persians and established himself as an independent monarch. In the midst of these troubles there were wide-scale persecutions of Christians, pestilence again decimated the populace, succeeding rulers debased the coinage and overtaxed the towns, and commerce almost ceased. The Roman world was threatened with collapse.

The great vitality that two centuries of peace and power had given to the empire made possible a rebirth of imperial strength under the able men who succeeded Gallienus, though their reigns were short and their ends violent. Claudius Gothicus (268–270) defeated the Goths. Aurelian (270–275) overcame Tetricus, ruler of the Gallic empire, and repulsed the Germanic tribes on the Rhine frontier. Abandoning Dacia to the Goths, he succeeded in protecting the line of the Danube, and finally, conquering Zenobia, widow of Odaenathus, he re-established the unity of the Roman world and the defense of the frontier. Still, cognizant of the perils of barbarian invasion which threatened even the imperial city, he built a wall around Rome. Though

Roman Sarcophagus of Marble, Second or Third Century A.D. (The Metropolitan Museum of Art, Rogers Fund, 1947)

he tried to strengthen his own position by proclaiming himself to the superstitious soldiery as the earthly incarnation of the sun god, whose worship he established as the official religion of Rome, he was murdered in 275. Four emperors followed Aurelian in quick succession until in 285 Diocletian was elevated to the throne by the eastern army and entered upon a program of reform which gave new life to the Roman Empire.

THE REFORMS OF DIOCLETIAN

The period of the anarchy had revealed many weaknesses in the imperial system and had aggravated the economic problems, which were already acute. In a well-ordered state the position of the ruler could not be allowed to depend on the whim of an army which could elevate its commander to power by acclamation and the force of arms, and with equal readiness overthrow him by mutiny and assassination. If the empire was to continue as a unit, the attempts of the provincial armies to establish local kingdoms like those of Tetricus and Odaenathus had to be rendered impossible. At the same time the increasing pressure of the German barbarians and the Persians on the northern and eastern frontiers called for decisive action if the life of the empire was to be maintained. Within the empire both political and economic reorganization was required to restore order; to revive industry and the flow of commerce, which had suffered severely in the confusion of the anarchy; and to provide for the regular collection of taxes so that the administration and the army might function effectively.

Diocletian (285–305), a Dalmatian soldier who had risen by sheer ability from the lowest ranks to the imperial purple, determined to carry out a reorganization of the imperial structure which would correct these political and economic evils, prevent civil wars, and secure adequate protection for the frontiers.[1]

His first reforms were the logical conclusions to the militarization of the empire by the Severi and its orientalization by Aurelian. Though recognizing the army as the basis of his power and providing a coherent structure for the military rule of the empire, he endeavored to break down the control which the soldiers had exercised over the imperial office by expanding Aurelian's policy and setting up an Oriental court with himself as a divine ruler surrounded by a host of palace officials. In the interests of more efficient direction of military affairs, and with the realization that one man could not hope to defend the entire frontier, he associated with himself Maximian, to whom he gave the title Augustus. Without any formal division of the empire and steadfastly maintaining his own pre-eminence, he entrusted the West to his colleague, while he himself resided in and looked after the East. To secure further assistance and to prevent wars of succession he appointed two assistant emperors, called Caesars, Constantius Chlorus in the West and Galerius in the East, with a further provision that after a period of years the Augusti should retire, the Caesars become Augusti, and new Caesars be selected.

Along the frontier Diocletian established small bodies of border troops, called *limitanei*, in permanent stations with lands for their support and a system of local drafting which, completing the process of the preceding century, made the troops definitely local in composition and virtually hereditary. The necessary strength of the armies was maintained by forcing the enlistment of able-bodied men not engaged in essential occupations, as well as by voluntary service. Sons of German settlers were drafted as well as any other eligible citizens. To assist the frontier guards in resisting sudden onslaughts of barbarian tribes, each of the rulers was provided with a large mobile force of *comitatenses* placed at strategic points within the empire to be available for emergencies. In place of the praetorian cohort, the emperor and his assistants maintained imperial guards of young men drawn chiefly from the upper class and trained to be future officers. The frontier forces were thus no longer of sufficient size to continue the third-century practice of elevating their commanders to the purple or of establishing local kingdoms. The commanders of the larger armies were placed in such a secure line of succession that, it was hoped, their

---

[1] The reorganization was begun by Diocletian and finished by Constantine and his successors. We will survey it in the completed form.

rivalries and ambitions could be satisfied without recourse to war. In addition, the division of the command was planned to provide efficient direction of the long line of the frontier.

The administration of the empire was rebuilt on a civil basis entirely distinct from the military. The provincial system was completely revamped. The division between senatorial and imperial provinces had disappeared during the preceding century, and Diocletian proceeded to wipe out the older provinces themselves. The empire was redivided into more than a hundred small provinces controlled by civil administrators. These were grouped into thirteen dioceses, ruled by *vicarii*, and these in turn into four prefectures, each under a praetorian prefect. The duties of these magistrates were judicial and administrative, including general supervision of finance and, in the case of the provincial governors, control over municipal affairs, but without any military authority. Thus Diocletian hoped to secure efficient administration and to remove the menace of the revolt of provincial commanders. The bureaus of the central administration were reorganized to accord with this new system, and many agents and spies were assigned to the divisions or traveled about keeping check on local administrators and on each other. At the head of the civil services was a group of palace officials: the master of offices, who had general supervision over the bureaus, superintended military factories and arsenals, and commanded the imperial bodyguard; the quaestor or chancellor, chief judge and legal adviser of the emperor; the count of the sacred bounty, director of imperial finance; the count of the private estates, who managed the imperial domains; and the great chamberlain, who had charge of the imperial palace. From the highest group of officials and nobles was drawn the consistory, a body of twenty men who formed the supreme council of advisers to the emperor.

The city of Rome was governed by the city prefect with the assistance of the senate, which continued to meet as the local governing body of Rome. The senatorial order, however, was spread over the entire empire as great landowners and higher officials received the title *clarissimi*, which entitled them to membership in the order. The powers of local government within the provinces were both municipal and rural. The cities still maintained their local *curiae*, senates, and magistrates, but actual government was in the hands of imperially appointed curators, who had supervision of public finance. In the country districts the senators had secured immunity from municipal control and were allowed to act as magistrates and tax collectors on their own estates.

A large and steady income was needed to support the tremendous number of officials. Diocletian cleared away the chaotic system of indirect taxation, used since the time of Augustus, abolished emergency levies and requisitions established in the third century, and imposed a new system. Taxes in money were levied upon tradesmen, municipal aristocrats, and senators. But their value varied so greatly because of the debasement of the coinage and the wide fluctuation of prices that Diocletian collected payments in kind from the landowning class. Land, capital, labor, and livestock were assessed by units arranged according to value. The amount to be raised, announced annually in a proclamation called the *indictio*, was apportioned over the empire according to the units in each region. In addition, communities were compelled to render services in the support of the imperial post and of the army, and merchants were forced to transport without payment the taxes in kind.

These taxes worked to the advantage of the bureaucracy and the army, which were thus assured of a steady income of fixed value within a fixed budget. Although they conferred considerable power on the great senatorial landowners, they constituted a heavy burden on this class, whose produce was essential to imperial well-being. At the same time, of course, they wrought even greater hardships upon the smaller landowners and upon the municipal councilors, the *curiales*. Many of the small farmers surrendered their farms to near-by senators to evade the exactions. The *curiales*, however, compelled to pay taxes on their own property, to render governmental services, and to be responsible for the collection of taxes in their own communities, were allowed no relief. Diocletian did not iron out all the difficulties in the new system. The new tax laws were not equally applied everywhere, and both individuals and groups often sought to evade their responsibilities. Constantine, Diocletian's successor, was forced to take stringent action to force local officials and citizens to fulfill their obligations. When they endeavored to escape by resigning or by moving to another city, Constantine, in 332, interfered and by the law of *origo* (origin) compelled them to stay in their native city and to hold office as long as they possessed sufficient property. On the same principle of *origo*, which involved the performance of service to the community, merchants and artisans were forced to remain members of their associations (*collegia*), pay the taxes, and render the required labors.

To the tax burden was added the further expense caused by graft and corruption. This continued everywhere in spite of spies and spies on spies. When a later emperor (Valentinian I) appointed a *defensor plebis* to protect the people from illegal exactions, he merely added one more official to be paid or to be bribed.

In an era of confusion when coinage was debased and the state was again resorting to collections and payments in kind, prices varied greatly between regions and fluctuated widely within them. In 301, to secure stabilization and to prevent undue excess, Diocletian issued the celebrated Edict of Prices, which fixed the maximum cost of goods and labor under penalty of death but which proved impossible to enforce for more than a short period.

Possibly to restore imperial unity and to magnify his own claim to divinity, Diocletian, on the persuasion of Galerius, opened warfare on the Christians. During the preceding century the Roman government had taken sporadic steps against the Christian menace to imperial worship. Decius and Valerian, in particular, had ordered all persons to offer sacrifices to the emperor or to suffer death. Many Christians lapsed and secured certifications (*libelli*) of sacrifice, while others suffered martyrdom. But the enforcement of the decrees varied between provinces and periods according to the interests of local administrators and the demands of the populace. In 302 Diocletian ordered the confiscation of all church property and the enforcement of imperial worship. In the East, Galerius was particularly vigorous in enforcing the edict, while in Gaul, Constantius, whose wife was a Christian, paid no attention to it. When the persecution came to an end with the Edict of Toleration of Galerius in 311 and Constantine's Edict of Milan in 313, which placed Christianity on a level with the other religions, the church could exist in security for the first time.

Diocletian succeeded in restoring order throughout the empire, in re-establishing the northern frontier in Britain, on the Rhine and the Danube, and in defeating the Persians. In 305 he retired, forcing Maximian to resign at the same time. His system of succession thereupon proved a failure. Rivalries arose over the appointment of the new Caesars, and wars broke out afresh.

Constantine

From these wars Constantine (306–337), son of Constantius, emerged triumphant. The century and a half that followed this event may well be considered as a period of transition during which the Roman Empire of Augustus and its religions suffered their death throes while the new powers, Byzantine-Christian in the East and German-Christian in the West, were increasing in strength and influence.

Constantine won Rome from Maxentius, son of Maximian, by the battle at the Milvian Bridge where, according to Christian writers of the time, he saw in the skies a cross bearing the words *in hoc signo vinces* (by this sign, conquer) and accordingly provided his soldiers with Christian standards. For seventeen years he ruled in the East, while first Galerius (305–311) and then Licinius (312–323) ruled in the West. At Milan (313) Constantine seems to have agreed with Licinius on the issuance of a new edict of toleration of Christianity for the entire empire. In 323 he defeated Licinius and became ruler of the reunited empire. Except for the system of double emperors he took over entirely

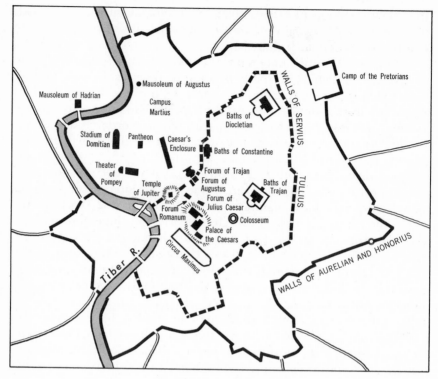

The City of Rome Under the Emperors, A.D. 325

the reforms of Diocletian and enforced them. Oriental monarchy became the order of the day, with an emperor surrounded by a great court and bearing all the trappings of divinity and with almost complete regimentation of economic life controlled thoughout the empire by an elaborate bureaucracy. Two of Constantine's deeds stand out as significant of the times and portentous for the future. In 325 he called the leaders of the Christian church together at Nicaea to standardize church procedures and to resolve certain doctrinal differences that had arisen among them (p. 575). By so doing he completed the recognition of the Christian church as an imperial institution, brought it within the realm of imperial politics, and made it an important instrument of government.

In 330 he founded Constantinople on the site of the ancient Greek city of Byzantium and made it his capital. Situated on an easily defended promontory and equipped with a magnificent harbor, it provided an excellent base for the defense of the Danube and the Euphrates. From it the cities of the Greek East, still highly industrial, populous, and wealthy, could easily be controlled. With its erection

Rome and Italy sank into the background and throughout the ages that followed, Constantinople as capital of the Eastern or Byzantine Empire, remained the center of civilized life, the source of imperial activity.

ECONOMIC AND POLITICAL LIFE

The failure of the Roman imperial system, beginning under the Severi and continuing with cumulative effect to the reign of Diocletian, was the product of a number of forces so inextricably interwoven that they can scarcely be separated or followed. Agriculture on the small farm or on the great estate, industry and trade in the town and commerce along the great roads or on the highways of the seas, the political and economic status of landowners and peasants, financiers, shopkeepers and merchants, the political life of the municipalities and the provinces, the efficiency of the central administration, the size and composition of the population, the composition and the attitude of the army, the defense of the frontier, the fortunes, fates, and wars of emperors and of aspirants to the imperial purple, and the mental outlook of the inhabitants of the empire—all were interrelated and affected one another. A survey of each of these phases of life as they appeared during the third century will provide a key to the historical phenomenon called the decline of ancient civilization.

Agriculture The process of the formation of great estates, which had been prevalent in the Orient from the time of the Sumerians and the early Egyptians, reached its climax in the Western world during the third and fourth centuries A.D. Land had always been the major form of investment in ancient times, and its stability as a source of income made it particularly attractive to men of wealth during the confusion and fluctuations of the last centuries of the empire. In addition the control which its possession enabled them to exercise over the essential supplies of food for the army placed them in a position of power, particularly after the introduction of taxes and payments in kind. During the centuries of decline the great landlords throughout the empire became Roman senators and a potent group in the state.

The Villa System The same forces that contributed to the power of the great landowner wrought the destruction in the West of the free farmer, who fell under the burdens of increased taxation, the plundering of officials, the collapse of municipal markets, and the constant pressure of greedy senators. Many a farmer gave up the struggle and surrendered his farm to the nearest landlord, receiving it back as a leasehold. Others, compelled by the law of *origo* to remain on their farms, became virtual serfs of the state. The landless men, however, found opportunity for themselves by receiving grants of land and becoming tenants. On the imperial estates, likewise, in response to governmental demands for grain, the peasants were compelled to remain on their leaseholds and transmit them to their sons. The practice of settling Germans, called *inquilini*, on imperial lands with the hereditary obligation of military service added another class of tenants. The peasant farmer class all over the empire was becoming a serf class. To be sure, free farmers never entirely disappeared. But the result of the growth of hereditary tenancy was a general decline in agricultural technique. Scientific farming was a thing of the past.

The first aim of management, no longer the capitalistic desire for income of a city-dwelling absentee landlord, was self-sufficiency. In its interest the senators built factories, mills, and ovens and fostered the development of industry to serve the needs of their tenants. Likewise, in order to advance their own power, they secured rights of local government and immunity from municipal control. Many became so powerful through the size of their estates and the number of their tenants that they were able to resist with armed force the imperial tax collectors. The decline of urban industry and markets and the prevalent desire for self-support led generally to a decline in the culture of the olive and the vine, except for local needs, and to an increased production of cereals, vegetables, and cattle, any surplus of which was in great demand for the army. This was particularly true in Italy, where agricultural prosperity suffered an almost complete collapse.

Commerce and Industry   Commerce, industry, and town life suffered together, especially in Britain and Gaul. Though the presence of Constantinople and the renewed vitality of Greek life, which displayed itself in the later Byzantine Empire, preserved the Eastern urban centers for several centuries, industrial and commercial activities in the West suffered a marked decline. The civil wars of the third century made travel unsafe and dislocated the course of commerce, while the localization of industry tended to prevent its renewal. Governmental compulsion, in an effort to revive trade and to keep in operation the necessary service of supplies for the city of Rome and for the army, laid heavy burdens on the merchants' associations, which resulted in their ruin. Industrial establishments, losing their distant markets with the collapse of trade, and their rural sales with the growth of industry on the great estates, decreased in size and in technique. Heavy taxation also contributed to their woes. Again the government interfered through the *collegia* in an endeavor to keep them at work. The system of trade associations was extended for purposes of governmental control, and the members were compelled to carry on their crafts and to teach them to their sons.

The Towns   Commerce, industry, and agriculture had been the life of the towns, and the decline of the first two and the transformation

A Six-sided Glass Pitcher of the Late Roman Period. Manufactured in Syria or Egypt (Coptic). (The Brooklyn Museum)

of the last brought fearful hardships to their population. Political stagnation had already become their lot. In the first years of the empire men had eagerly sought office, and the people had taken an active part in elections. Gradually but surely this vitality had diminished. Later town charters contained provision for the drafting of officials. The populace had lost interest in voting and then, as elections were transferred to the councils, the right to vote. The paternalism of the Antonines, which expressed itself in interference in the rectification of finance and the appointment of *curators*, broke down local independence and pride. The troubles of the third century aggravated the situation, and the reforms of Diocletian almost destroyed the political activities of the local units of the empire. Public spirit vanished; the common people were indifferent save as they clamored for the gifts and shows of more prosperous times; and the curial class, oppressed by the central administration and no longer proud of their position or of their communities, sought to avoid rather than to gain office.

In the third and fourth centuries men abandoned the towns to escape the heavy taxation and incessant government supervision.

Industries moved to *villae* (great self-sufficient estates) scattered about the countryside. Archaeologists believe that the total volume of production in the province of Britain remained about the same as it had been in the second century, but instead of being centered in towns, factories were built in the country. The same phenomenon is characteristic of parts of Gaul, Italy, and other western provinces. The towns, abandoned by large numbers of their citizens fell into disrepair. Theaters crumbled, aqueducts ceased to function, and business establishments lay idle and vacant. It was, of course, this trend which forced Constantine to issue the law of *origo*, but it came too late. The villa system could not be eradicated in the West, for markets had disappeared; industry had become too decentralized and capital too scarce to permit a reversal of the economic trend. In addition, the law of *origo* was, in this sense, self-defeating. By its provisions no man was free, even if he possessed the necessary ambition and capital, to move to a place of his choice and establish a new business.

At a time when the income of individuals was decreasing, the demands of the government upon the local aristocrats were becoming greater. The loss of old endowments for public service, due to economic decline and monetary confusion, increased the cost of local government. The burden of taxation, the third-century exactions of generals, and the depredations of booty-hungry soldiers made the condition of the upper class almost unbearable. On the aristocrats fell the heavy burden of local expense; they were subject to heavy taxes in money on their own account; the ten richest among them in a town had to advance the amount of the imperial taxes, and when the burden became too great for ten to bear, it was laid on the shoulders of the entire group.

From this intolerable situation the *curiales* had but two avenues of escape. The first was to rise in the imperial service or to gain additional wealth and become a senator, a road open only to a few; the second was to become bankrupt and lose membership in the group. The government endeavored to block the first avenue of escape; it refused to allow them to resign, and by enforcing the law of *origo*, which obliged them to remain in their native cities and render the required services, it prevented their removal to another municipality. As the *curiales*, faced with this outlook, became tyrannical in their handling of the lower classes and corrupt in their dealings with the imperial officials, bribery and misdealing became the order of the day. The inevitable end of the system was the ruin of the middle class of the empire.

The Coinage   Debasement of the coinage accentuated this economic crisis. In the first century Nero had reduced the quantity of gold in the aureus and of silver in the denarius, adding copper alloy. His reform, which was intended to make the Latin and Greek coins more equal in value, was beneficial in its effects but set a bad precedent for future emperors. Trajan and Marcus Aurelius increased the quantity of copper without materially affecting the value of the money, but Caracalla caused a financial panic when he issued silver coins that were half copper. The supply of precious metals in the Mediterranean, while by no means exhausted, was no longer mined efficiently. Citizens, trying to keep some measure of security, had resorted to hoarding. When the needs of government and the army led Caracalla to debase the coinage, hoarding increased and matters became worse. The emperors of the period of the anarchy, requiring funds for their wars and unable to secure the regular collection of taxes, followed Caracalla's example. The value of the coins declined still further until in the time of Gallienus they were little more than copper dipped in acid to resemble silver. The double denarius was 2 per cent silver, and the smaller coins were almost worthless. Under such conditions prices fluctuated, chiefly upward; it became impossible to conduct business affairs successfully, and taxes became so hard to collect that the government under Diocletian was forced to requisition services and to accept payments in kind. Creditors and investors suffered tremendous losses; municipal and charitable foundations dependent upon investments for their income were completely destroyed. Aurelian, Diocletian, and Constantine endeavored with some success to restore coinage to a sound basis of value. Monetary economy was partially restored but the former prosperity was never regained.

The Caste System The efforts of the government were directed to the collection of taxes and the preservation of needed services. Taxes were put on everything. Every man, woman, slave, every head of cattle, every unit of land was taxed; fees and forced labors were levied upon merchants and artisans; the *curiales* were forced to pay "crown-gold" to the emperor, and the senators to make "free-will" gifts. The cost of the enormous bureaucracy erected by Diocletian and the system for the collection and handling of taxes in kind increased the amount to be raised. As a result, the burden of taxation destroyed the purchasing power of the people in the West, and by making impossible an adequate revival of trade and industry played an important part in economic decline.

The general enforcement of the law of *origo* created a caste system in the empire. Trade, the crafts, the soldiery, and even the municipal aristocracy became fixed and hereditary. Free enterprise and intelligent workmanship, like the proper cultivation of land, became impossible and unprofitable under such a system of regimentation. The Western empire degenerated into a society of wealthy senatorial landowners and a great mass of peasant serfs with only a small struggling caste-ridden middle class and a dwindling proletariat still demanding "bread and

shows" left in its cities. The city-state, pride of the Hellenes, characteristic unit of classical polity, and source of inspiration for so many
great achievements, was gone in the West. Wretched towns and huge
rural units, worked by an ignorant peasantry and governed by an
arbitrary bureaucracy, had taken its place.

In generalizing it is very easy to exaggerate the picture of decline.
Some areas undoubtedly suffered greater economic hardships than
others. Conditions were worse in the older regions such as Greece,
Italy, and Sicily, where intensive cultivation for centuries had exhausted the soil. Gaul and Britain, on the other hand, were fairly
prosperous. In Africa, the bishop Cyprian in the middle of the third
century devoted a large part of his sermons to inveighing against the
luxury and self-seeking of wealthy Christians. Egypt, likewise, was still
a rich land, eternally renewed by the inundations of the Nile, and the
industrial cities of the East showed a remarkable power of recuperation.
Many of the Western senators were men of culture and ability who
made contributions of lasting merit to civilization. In fact the bureaucracy had a vitality of its own.

The Bureaucracy   The civil administration, well established by
Hadrian, carried on much of its work even during the disorder of the
third century. Diocletian's reorganization infused it with new life. In
the East it continued to function for centuries; in the West, until it was
taken over and perpetuated by the Germanic kings. In spite of its
oppressive character it provided order and a fair amount of justice for
the people. Able men were attracted to it by its freedom from military
burdens in a period of confusion, and they found in it power and a
career worthy of their talents.

The Army   The army had fallen from its once high estate. In the
early republic it had been the body of citizens in arms. Marius had made
it a professional force without, however, destroying its citizen character.
During the early empire the traditions of the Roman legions were
transmitted to urban provincials under the command of Roman
senators. Intelligent, highly trained, and well disciplined, the legionaries withstood with unbroken ranks the wild charges of the barbarians
and overawed them by their efficiency, speed, and engineering achievements.

Changes in personnel during the third century destroyed much of
this effectiveness and were in a large measure responsible for the military disorders of the period. Marcus Aurelius, to fill the gaps left by
the plague, settled Germans on lands within the empire on the condition that they should furnish men to serve in the Roman army. Succeeding emperors followed his example. Septimius Severus drew his
soldiers from the provinces or, by allowing them to marry and to acquire lands along the frontier, made peasants of them. The resultant
army, composed of Germans, provincials, and peasants, was without

the intelligence and the culture of the municipal classes, which it hated, envied, and was ever ready to plunder. It possessed local attachments and a feeling of personal loyalty to its commander which, replacing patriotic allegiance to the empire, made the army corps ready for rebellions. The soldiery seized the opportunity to establish provincial kingdoms like that of Tetricus or to make their general emperor of Rome.

Discipline suffered along with intelligence in leadership and soldiery. The new personnel did not yield readily to the iron rule that had made the Roman army great, and when the soldiers discovered that they had the power to make their generals into emperors and profit thereby, they were less ready than ever to subject themselves to regulation. Those commanders who endeavored to restore the *disciplina Augusti* were speedily overthrown and killed. This process of decline continued as the border forces of Diocletian and the armies of his successors were increasingly filled with Germans. At the same time constant fighting against the Romans taught lessons in warfare to the Germans, and when the two opposing forces became equal in the qualities of discipline and intelligence, the superior numbers of the invaders prevailed, and the Western empire was overwhelmed. The Eastern, being better served and less open to invasion, survived.

CULTURE

Cultural productions of lasting merit were almost entirely lacking during the troubled times of the third century. The emperors were provincials, many of them peasants, with no knowledge of, or interest in, literature and art. The confused political conditions and the economic situation were not conducive to intellectual or artistic work. The literary productions that appeared were works of erudition and book learning, rather than of creative thought. The group of writers which surrounded Julia Domna, wife of Septimius Severus, including Dio Cassius, Philostratus, Diogenes Laertius, and Athenaeus, was distinctly second-rate. Anthologies of poetry, collections of maxims and quotations, and *scholia*, which were commentaries on the writings of classical authors, were characteristic of the age. There was some provincial literature. In the Gallic empire of Tetricus oratory of a bombastic style was developed, and in the court of Zenobia, queen of Palmyra, the sophist Longinus wrote a famous essay, "On the Sublime." Christian literature, vigorous in character, appeared in the polemical diatribes of Tertullian and in the letters of Cyprian, bishop of Carthage.

Amid the general decay, however, juristic writing advanced. The opinions and treatises of the great jurists—Papinian, Ulpian, and Paulus—marked a great advance in the law and became the foundation of the later code of Justinian (p. 584). One of the contributions the jurists made to law, however, was the principle of autocratic control, the product of the period in which they lived, but used by lawyers as a justification for the despotic power of the European kings of later ages.

Architecture and art suffered from the same conditions that affected literature. The Severi, though lacking in taste, were active builders. Septimius did much work of restoration in Rome, added to the imperial palaces on the Palatine Hill, and erected an arch in the Forum. The baths of Caracalla, overwhelming in their size and magnificence, and the temple of Jupiter at Baalbek in Syria remain today among the great monuments of Roman architectural skill. The succeeding reigns, however, were almost barren of worthwhile achievements. Diocletian built a huge palace at Salona in Dalmatia and a set of baths still standing on the Viminal Hill in Rome, now used as a vast museum. Maxentius added a basilica in the Forum, and Constantine, an arch near the Colosseum. These structures are ponderous and without great artistic value. The best reliefs on the arch of Constantine were taken from works of an earlier period. In comparison with them the contemporary sculpture was clumsy and crude. Cultural, like political and economic, vitality seemed to have passed.

Philosophy and Religion

The psychological aspects of the decline appear most clearly in the trends of philosophy and religion. The Antonine period had revealed a weariness with life, a conviction that the world was growing old and tired, and a willingness to turn to philosophy or religion for escape. The insecurity of life during the next century augmented this feeling. The pestilence that ravaged the empire at intervals throughout the third century; the depopulation of Greece, Sicily, and some sections of Italy, due to economic decay, disease, and decline in the population; the triumph of the uncultured provincial armies and their rude generals — all contributed to the depressing conviction that the world was a place of darkness, that mankind was evil and life a burden.

Neoplatonism The stern philosophies of the classical age were not an adequate defense against these convictions. To meet them Plotinus of Alexandria and his student Porphyry evolved, during the third century, the philosophic system known as Neoplatonism. Adopting the mystical aspects of Plato's teaching, these philosophers taught the baseness of matter and the reality of the spiritual world of "ideas." By the successive stages of reason, intuition, and ecstasy, and with the assistance of gods and spirits (*daemones*), individuals might escape from the world and commune with the sublime and perfect supernatural realm. Greek philosophy, which had begun in Ionia with a denial of the gods, had at last surrendered completely to them.

The Pagan Religions Religion witnessed a great revival. The worship of the old gods, great and small, from Jupiter to the lares and penates of the Romans and the local divinities of the provinces, was actively renewed. The Oriental mystery cults gained ever more adherents. Isis and the Great Mother had their devotees. Mithraism (p. 546), coalescing with the worship of the Syrian sun god, became the official worship of the military emperors. A Babylonian priest, Mani, who lived in the third century, developed from Babylonian and Persian doctrines a religious dualism of good and evil, symbolized by light and darkness. His cult, called Manichaeism, attracted many, and even St. Augustine turned to it in his youth. It is characteristic of the cosmopolitanism of the period in its search for gods that Alexander Severus, according to report, suggested the erection of statues to Abraham and Christ along with the gods of Rome. Religiosity was accompanied by a belief in all kinds of superstitions; prodigies and signs were multiplied; and all possible devices were used to appease angry gods. Yet with this multiplication of divinities there came a syncretism, a growing feeling that all the gods and daemons were but manifestations or perhaps assistants of the one divine ruler of the universe.

The conviction that the world was evil, which both religion and philosophy held and taught, drove many to lives of asceticism and celibacy. Some went into the desert to live as hermits or into retirement as members of pre-Christian monastic sects.

The Christian Church Meanwhile Christianity firmly held its ground and advanced amid the fires of persecution with a dogged intolerance of its pagan rivals that gave it much of its strength. Throughout the third century the Christian religion spread into all sections of the empire and attracted a growing number of adherents in all classes of the population, but especially among the poorer people. A small Christian chapel of the third century has been excavated at Doura on the Euphrates. It contained a recess that almost certainly served as a baptismal font. On its walls were pictures (based on the Old Testament) of Adam and Eve, the tree and the serpent in the Garden of Eden, and David and Goliath. The New Testament was represented by the Good Shepherd over the font, by the scene of the healing of the paralytic, the miracle of the lake where Jesus and Peter walked upon the water, the Samaritan woman at the well, and by a picture of the three Marys at the sepulcher on Easter morn.

These and similar portrayals of Biblical scenes show that the Church was creating its own art. It also produced intellectual leaders of great acumen like Irenaeus of Lyons, Tertullian and Cyprian of Carthage, Clement and Origen of Alexandria. Amid discussions arising from many concepts considered heretical, it evolved its body of doctrine, its ceremonies and ritual. Its organization also developed as the clergy became distinguished as a separate group from the laity and as the supremacy of the bishops, now heads of great churches and administrators of defined geographical areas, was recognized.

Perhaps the most striking and important feature of Christian history was the growth of the power of the Church at Rome. In addition to the prestige natural to an establishment in the capital of the empire, the Roman Church possessed the advantage of a tradition that it was founded by St. Peter and St. Paul. During a period when the Eastern churches were torn by heresies which seem to have been indigenous to their region, the Roman Church held steadfastly to what it considered the basic doctrine. By the time of Constantine, the bishop of Rome was on the way to being recognized as the leader of the Western Church. Throughout the empire the Church set itself steadfastly against any compromise with the pagan religions or with the demands of the imperial government. Many of its members suffered martyrdom rather than yield. No estimate can be made of the total number of Christians at the time of Constantine, but they were a large, well-organized minority of the imperial population. The Church was powerful, well organized, and militant, ready to assume a position of leadership in the new era. Constantine, by the Edict of Milan, gave it legal status and then brought it into the realm of the imperial administration.

THE ROMAN WELFARE STATE

The reforms of Diocletian and Constantine made the Roman Empire into something resembling a modern welfare state. No particular theory had guided them in this arrangement, but rather the exigencies of economic and political necessity. They sought to stabilize the economy and halt trends that threatened to tear the empire to pieces and destroy it, rather than to create a "planned economy." The government interfered in the life of every citizen to restore unity and to end military anarchy and economic disintegration, and to maintain the stability so precariously achieved.

By and large the reforms were successful, but they were successful at great cost. Economically, the East — never so badly hurt — recovered prosperity, but the Western provinces did not regain what they had lost. Politically, the new arrangements, while revised by Constantine, who had upset them, provided for a stable bureaucratic hierarchy that could and did administer the tremendous governmental machine. And the government had become a kind of "machine." Its working parts, the officials — down to the least of them — were necessary to keep it running. Taxes, collected in food and produce, had to be transported to government warehouses. Government officials were responsible for getting the goods housed, sold, and converted into money. The mines had to be supervised and the foundries making arms and weapons had to be overseen. The mints were closely regulated. And since the government necessarily had to control most metallic resources, a close surveillance was kept over metals going to private industry. Inevitably, the Roman government was involved in every major economic activity of the empire's citizens. The necessary army of bureaucrats kept the citizen bound to his job. Each individual was a cog in the vast machine made up of so many millions of interdependent parts.

No one had much time for cultural or intellectual activity under such a system, even if one had the heart and inspiration for it. Artists were working craftsmen commanded to do a job about which they did not get excited. Students, bent on getting a hasty education, were satisfied with brief summaries, *epitomes*, instead of the complete works of masters. In the West, where many towns had died, these forces were strongest, and the last centuries of imperial control in the Latin West did nothing to reverse the pattern. An informal, but very real division of the empire had taken place.

26 · The End of the Empire
in the West

BETWEEN THE DEATH OF CONSTANTINE IN 337 AND THE accession of Justinian in 527, the Roman Empire was plagued by a host of troubles, by attacks of foreign enemies and domestic and civil strife. The eastern half emerged from the turmoil intact though shaken and was able to recover, but the western half disintegrated into a group of German states. This difference in fate, under similar blows, has called forth the efforts of many minds to explain it. It is generally conceded that internal weakness in the West must account for the empire's dissolution, but what internal weakness is to be blamed? Answers have ranged from Gibbon's accusation of the Christians[1] through "class struggle," depopulation, decentralization of industry, racial exhaustion or mongrelization, and a loss of spirit, to the divisive forces of an "internal-external proletariat." But the truth must lie in an interlocking multiplicity of factors from which no single one can be isolated and held responsible. The social, economic, and political ills that were already visible in the age of Constantine were aggravated in succeeding years and played a large part in the decline of the West, as did mischance and poor judgment by responsible officials. But the sources do not permit a detailed reconstruction. If they did, there would be no more mystery attached to the decline of the Roman Empire than there is about the disintegration of any other empire, before or since its day.

The Sources The historical sources for the two centuries between Constantine and Justinian are sparse, and they leave gaps which cannot be filled. They consist of biographies, eulogies, an excellent history written by Ammianus Marcellinus under the emperor Julian, some inscriptions, poems, two great law codes, and the works of a number of

[1] The present writer, contrary to Gibbon, would eliminate Christianity from the list. The Christian church in the West, unlike the church in the East, served as a unifying factor in the fourth and fifth centuries. It supported and held together the people and their government.

Christian writers—from Eutropius under Constantine to Procopius under Justinian. The Christians, however, with a few exceptions were more interested in theology, morals, or religious controversy than in history. Archaeology does little to supplement the picture, except to describe war panoplies buried with German chiefs and to reveal the architectural details of buildings constructed in a few well-known periods.

Division of the Empire   Constantine had destroyed the tetrarchy established by Diocletian and had ruled alone, but he left the empire divided among his three sons, who were brought up Christians, and two nephews. Quarrels broke out among the five immediately, and after a series of deaths through battle and murder Constantius was left to rule his father's empire. He was deposed and killed in 361 by his rebellious nephew Julian. Julian, who was called "the Apostate" because he

Colossal Marble Head of the Emperor Constantine. (The Metropolitan Museum of Art, Bequest of Mary Clark Thompson, 1926)

attempted a revival of the Roman religion in the face of growing Christianity, immediately chose a colleague to rule in the West. Neither emperor reigned long, but their successors, chosen by the army, maintained Julian's east-west division. Duplicate but separate administrations were created for each part, and from this time onward no one emperor tried to rule the whole empire, save for short intervals created by bitter necessity.

THE EMPIRE IN THE EAST

Until A.D. 422 the chief enemies of the Romans in the east were the Persians (Parthians), now reorganized under strong kings. But the Danube frontier on the north often had to be defended against the powerful Goths and other Germanic peoples. In 375 crisis rose on the Danube, brought about by the swift, unexpected attack of the Huns, who, coming from the east, defeated and destroyed the Ostrogoths. The remnants of this tribe and their panic-struck kinsmen the Visigoths fled to the Danube and sought admittance to the empire. The Huns continued their drive into central Europe with terrified Germans of various tribes fleeing before them.

The Huns   The people known as Huns in the West are identified with the *Hiung-nu* of the Chinese annals. They were Turks living in Mongolia along the Chinese borders as early as the sixth century B.C. Their restless inroads into China were checked by a great wall built about 214 B.C., and they were thereafter held back by the strong resistance of the Han and Tsin emperors. In the fourth century A.D. the Huns streamed westward across the steppes. One of their hordes turned south to ravage the Iranian plateau; the other hurled itself upon Europe.

Like other peoples of Mongolia, the Huns were nomads whose possessions were completely portable. Both men and women learned to ride horseback before learning to walk, and they wandered about from pasture to pasture in "families" (camps of four or five tents), several of which formed a clan. A number of clans made up a tribe, and several tribes a "people." Occasionally an ambitious chief would organize a group of peoples into a "horde," upon which he became a "khan." If he led his horde to profitable plunder at the expense of settled farmers, he became increasingly powerful, and his horde grew in numbers.

The organizer of the horde that struck the Ostrogoths in 375 was probably Rugila, who was khan at that time. He was succeeded by Attila[2] after the horde had penetrated into central Europe. The Huns

---

[2] Attila is the Latin form of his name. It was properly something like "Etzel."

liked to make surprise attacks in mass, and they were usually successful. On the rare occasions when they failed, they found it easy to out-distance pursuers.

The Goths The first victims of the Huns among the Germans were the Ostrogoths ("Bright" Goths), who lived along the Dnieper River in southern Russia. Their chiefs were killed and the tribe was split in two. One part submitted to the Huns and served them so long as their dominion lasted, but the other part fled west to the Visigoths ("Wise" Goths) beyond the Dniester. The Visigoths did not wait for the Huns, but fled also. Part of them took refuge in the Carpathian Mountains, but a large body (which incorporated the refugee Ostrogoths) appeared on the Danube to seek safety within the Roman Empire.

An agreement was reached with the Romans, and the Visigoths crossed over, but the terms of the treaty were broken by both sides from the beginning. A year later the dissatisfied Goths plundered Macedonia. The emperor Valens met them in battle at Hadrianople, and was defeated and killed. His successor, Theodosius I, using alternate force and persuasion, managed to settle them on assigned lands in Illyria and to enlist their men into the Roman army. But he mistakenly permitted them to live in their own separate villages under their own chiefs, and to retain their tribal autonomy. It was a dangerous precedent that was followed when other Germans entered the empire, and it left the Visigoths free to act again as a nation. They did so in 401, setting out on a trek that took them into Italy and back again, and on to Gaul and Spain (map p. 574).

Master of the Militia Under Theodosius I, who was forced to rule briefly over the entire Roman Empire, the office of master of the militia was established in both East and West. The holder of the office, who was also called Patrician, served as commander-in-chief of the armies. Theodosius left a master of militia to be regent for each of his two sons, Arcadius in the East and Honorius in the West, and the office thereby became so powerful that no later emperor could be rid of it. Indeed, neither emperor nor master of militia could eliminate the other save by treachery and murder. In the West the master of militia was always a German, probably because the army was more and more re-cruited from German tribes, but in the East after 400 he was of any origin except German.

Death of Attila Eastern emperors bribed Attila with huge sums to keep out of the empire, but occasionally the Huns raided to force the price up and to remind the Romans of their superior power. The emperor tried to save face by making Attila a master of militia, though everyone knew it was pretense. The only comfort for Constantinople while Attila lived at Vienna was the successful negotiation of a peace treaty with Persia in 422. The Persians, also under attack by Huns, were

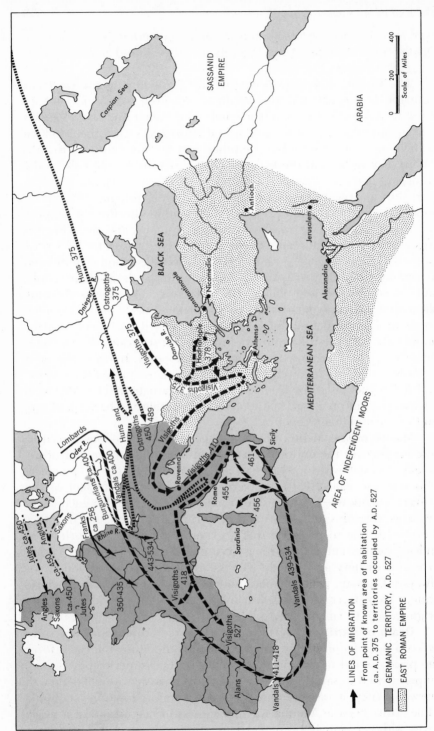

German Migrations into the Roman Empire, A.D. 375–527

LINES OF MIGRATION

From point of known area of habitation
ca. A.D. 375 to territories occupied by A.D. 527

GERMANIC TERRITORY, A.D. 527

EAST ROMAN EMPIRE

Scale of Miles
0   200   400

as eager for peace as the Romans, and the settlement lasted for a hundred years.

Freed from danger on the eastern frontier, the brave emperor Marcian left off payments to Attila and prepared for war, but the Huns surprisingly turned west, hurling themselves on Gaul and Italy. They were driven back from the one, and bribed away from the other in 451, and the next year Attila died in Vienna. There was no other leader capable of assuming the khanate and the horde broke up. The Ostrogoths who had submitted to the Huns resumed their tribal autonomy and followed their kinsmen into the empire. The Huns disappeared, though Hungary bears their name.

The dissolution of the empire of the Huns brought new troubles for the Romans. Wandering Germans, Iranians, Slavs, Bulgars, and Avars battered ceaselessly at the Danube defenses. Diplomacy, bribery, and warfare in turn kept them at bay, while the emperors in Constantinople struggled with problems at home.

Christian Disputes   In the Eastern empire theology was a topic of passionate interest to emperors and populace alike, and disputes on theological problems occasionally reached proportions disturbing to the government. The first major schism in the Christian community began under Constantine when the Alexandrian deacon Arius questioned the relationship of Christ to God. The orthodox view of the nature of the Trinity — God the Father, God the Son, and God the Holy Spirit — was upheld by the bishop, Athanasius, and this view prevailed at the Ecumenical Council of Nicaea called by Constantine in 325. The council issued a statement which, though later shortened and simplified, has been the accepted doctrine of most Western Christians (Catholic and Protestant) ever since. Recited in many churches, it is still called the Nicene Creed. But the council's action did not end the dispute. Controversy continued for generations, aided and abetted by various emperors. By the end of the fifth century the schism was at last resolved for Romans in favor of the Athanasian (Nicene) Creed, but it was prolonged beyond that time because the Visigoths and Ostrogoths were converts to Arian Christianity[3] — a situation that kept them long unassimilated after they moved into the empire.

On the heels of the Arian-Athanasian dispute came, in the Eastern empire, the divisive doctrines of Nestorius and of the Monophysites. A majority of the Christians in Syria and Egypt were converted to the latter teaching, and their ties to Constantinople were thereby loosened. In general, these disputes swayed mobs and factions and brought frequent riots, confusion, and even the deposition of emperors.

[3] Bishop Ulfilas converted the Goths before they were attacked by the Huns. The Gospels were translated into Gothic for their use and written in the Gothic (runic) script — a script later adopted by peoples in Scandinavia.

Panel from a Fourth-Century Christian Sarcophagus of Marble. The scene in relief shows the separation of the sheep from the goats at the Last Judgment. (The Metropolitan Museum of Art, Rogers Fund, 1924)

The Theodosian Code   Theodosius II (408–450), grandson of the first emperor of that name, received credit beyond his due for the achievements of his reign. He was weak and indolent and interested mostly in theology. It has been said that he never read the code bearing his name. Still, he permitted his officials to found a university in Constantinople, to build better fortifications for the city, and to carry out an extensive codification of Roman law. The Theodosian Code was the most comprehensive collection so far achieved, and it was to serve as a valuable basis for the more extensive work under Justinian.

Between 451 and 527 a series of usurpers occupied the throne in Constantinople. Their personal qualities were not outstanding, but they dealt with the internal and external problems of the empire with reasonable success. The emperor Zeno (p. 580) theoretically became the sole ruler of a reunited empire after 476, and his successors continued to claim that office and title even though they exercised no real power over the German kingdoms that had formed in the West. When Justinian succeeded his uncle in 527, the Eastern empire was intact and he spent the greater part of his long reign in an attempt to reassert direct imperial authority over the lost western provinces. He had only partial success, and that proved to be ephemeral, for soon after Justinian's death, the recovered territory was lost again. But in spite of military failure, Justinian's achievements were such that he succeeded in passing to European peoples of both East and West much that was good in the great Roman heritage.

THE EMPIRE IN THE WEST

The external enemies of the Western empire were often the same as those in the East, except that Persia posed no threat. In place of that danger were the Picts and Scots in Britain. Otherwise, Germans, Huns, Slavs, and Iranians (Sarmatians) directed their attacks without apparent discrimination against the eastern or western frontiers. The wall in Britain, the English coast, the Rhine frontier, and the Upper Danube defenses were seldom left in peace. But while the Eastern empire shook off its enemies and emerged intact, the Western empire gradually dissolved under the continuing impacts of barbarians.

The Germans in the West The most formidable and successful of the German tribes that were to parcel out the provinces of the Western empire were the Franks, the Saxons, the Burgundians, the Vandals, and the Goths. Of these, only the Goths could be called semicivilized in Roman terms. They, both Visigoths and Ostrogoths, were Arian Christians, and through trade and close contacts with Constantinople they had attained to some knowledge and appreciation of Roman culture. The rest were non-Christian and non-Romanized. They were primitive farmers who had been long resident in the forests of northern Europe, and were without the thinnest veneer of civilization.

The first of these peoples to gain a successful foothold in Roman territory was a Frankish tribe. During the civil wars between Constantius and his enemies (350–353) the Franks, along with another strong tribe of Germans (the Alemanni), seized the Rhine Valley. Constantius and Julian drove the Alemanni out but permitted the Salian Franks to settle along the lower Rhine as *foederati* (allies) of the Romans. Their men were enrolled in Roman armies and occasionally rose to high office.

The entry of the Huns into central Europe brought new and increased pressures upon the imperial defenses, and the German tribes were held at bay with great difficulty by Roman armies that were increasingly recruited from among Germans. Stilicho, a staunch master of the militia (p. 573) under the Western emperor Honorius, beat the attackers back again and again until he was treacherously murdered in 408. Honorius had immediate cause to regret his complicity in the crime. The Visigoths, who had abandoned their eastern lands under their king Alaric, poured into Italy, and at the same time the Franks, Vandals, and Burgundians crossed the Rhine and penetrated Gaul. The Vandals moved across Gaul and the Pyrenees into Spain. Meanwhile two usurpers, commanding respectively the armies of Britain and of the Rhine, proclaimed themselves emperors, and civil wars began.

Honorius survived the disasters through a mixture of luck and diplomacy. He married the daughter of his most formidable opponent for the crown, and with his help defeated the claimant from Britain who had invaded Gaul. The combined forces of Honorius and his father-in-law also stopped the tidal wave of Franks and Burgundians, but they were forced to permit the settlement of tribes of both peoples

Interior of the Dome in the Tomb of Galla Placidia, Mother of Valentinian III and sister of Honorius, at Ravenna. The ceiling shows the
lovely mosaic work characteristic of the fifth and sixth centuries A.D.
(Italian State Tourist Office)

in Gaul. The Ripuarian Franks occupied the upper Rhine Valley, and
Burgundians occupied the northeastern section of Gaul, which still
bears their name. Both were proclaimed *foederati* and owed nominal
allegiance to the emperor in Italy.

Meanwhile, the Visigoths had wandered the entire length of the
Italian peninsula. They were unable to touch Honorius, who was
barricaded behind the impregnable walls of Ravenna, but they sacked
Rome in 410. The psychological effects of this terrifying event were
greater than the damage to the city, for the Visigoths held it only a few
days and left without doing much harm. They carried away valuables
and portable objects, but did not resort to burning, needless destruction, or annihilation of the citizen body.

Somewhere in southern Italy Alaric died, and the Visigoths thought
better of continuing to Africa. They retraced their steps to the north and
entered southern Gaul with the intention of settling there. Honorius'

agents persuaded them to invade Spain and rid it of the Vandals. They complied willingly and ousted the Vandals except in an area of the south, afterward called Vandalusia (modern Andalusia), then returned to Gaul to settle in Aquitaine. They also became *foederati* of the Western emperor (map, p. 574).

In the following years Britain, whose protecting army had been withdrawn in 410 or 411, fell piecemeal to various enemies. The Picts and Scots attacked the north, while the Saxons, Angles, and Jutes penetrated England along the entire east coast. By 450 the peaceful, Romanized Britons had been annihilated. Those who survived fled into the mountains of Wales. Unlike the Germans in Gaul, the conquerors of Britain were not even nominally committed to an alliance with the Romans.

Africa fell to the Vandals even more quickly. Driven from the greater part of their Spanish conquests, these Germans took to the sea and in the space of ten years (429–439) conquered Mauretania, the province of Africa, and the island of Sicily.

Aetius, the master of the militia, fought lionlike to save what he could, but was kept so busy in Gaul and Italy that he could do nothing for Britain or Africa. He fought restless Franks and Burgundians and contained the Visigoths within their assigned boundaries. So desperate was his situation that he hired Huns as mercenaries to serve with the Roman-German armies. It was with such a mixed force that he drove Attila from Gaul in 450, but he could not stop Attila's sudden turn into Italy. Attila had to be bribed to leave without despoiling the peninsula. Yet Aetius, by whatever means, preserved the heart of the West: Gaul and Italy. For this he received the usual reward from the emperor. He was murdered in 454. His loyal followers took quick vengeance, assassinating the emperor a few months later.

The double murder ended any hope of recovery. The Vandals raided Italy from their Sicilian base and sacked Rome in 455. The senseless destruction they wrought was so great that "vandalism" has remained a synonym for such damage in the ages since. The Germans who were settled in Gaul expanded their territories to take the entire province, while the Visigoths spilled greedily over into Spain (map p. 574).

A sordid drama played by emperors and masters of militia, jockeying for power and murdering one another, filled the years until 476. Odovacar, the German master of the militia, who had made and unmade emperors, decided in that year to depose the puppet he had himself elevated to power. He told the last so-called Emperor of the West, a boy called Romulus Augustulus, that he must abdicate. At the same time Odovacar proclaimed himself master of the militia whose sole allegiance was to the emperor (Zeno) in Constantinople. After a hesitation of several years Zeno accepted this solution and confirmed Odovacar in office. Theoretically the Roman Empire was one and whole, and again ruled by one emperor.

Odovacar did not long enjoy his power. He fought hard to preserve Italy, but was treacherously murdered by Theodoric the Ostrogoth. The Ostrogoths thereupon took Italy and Theodoric ruled it until his death in 526. His daughter succeeded him.

Theodoric interfered as little as possible with the political and administrative institutions of Italy, and indeed he attempted a renascence of Roman culture by patronizing artists and writers and by using Romans in high office. The Ostrogoths themselves remained aloof from the civil population, and their men served as a defending army, fighting off all enemies. They took Sicily from the Vandals and defended the islands off the Italian coast. Theodoric concerned himself to obtain necessary grain for Rome. His people and his descendants fought Justinian for eighteen years and were largely responsible for that emperor's failure to achieve his goal.

German Kingdoms By 527, the Western empire existed in name only. It had broken up into a group of Germanic states independent of the emperors and of one another. Except in Britain and Africa, the kings of these states recognized the emperor at Constantinople as their overlord and considered themselves *foederati* of the Romans. Everyone concerned recognized that this arrangement was a farce, but it gave legal coloring to the German regimes and saved face for the emperor; and it in no way hindered the Germans from ruling as they pleased in their respective kingdoms. There was considerable diversity. The Visigoths, like the Ostrogoths in Italy, preserved and used Roman institutions and law in Spain and the areas of southern Gaul which they occupied. Also like the Ostrogoths, they held aloof from the Romanized population because of religious differences.

The Vandals, Burgundians, and Franks were less attracted by Roman culture and institutions, and they destroyed much of the Roman system. Yet the Franks, led by their remarkable king Clovis, in accepting orthodox Christianity were more quickly intermixed with the Gallic peoples over whom they ruled.

The Western Church Christianity in the Western empire was not torn by the theological disputes that fragmented the Church in the East. Athanasius' doctrines were firmly held and supported everywhere. The Church became stronger with every generation, and in 392 when the emperor Theodosius I forbade the continuance of any pagan rite, Christianity became the state religion. Church members were subjected to criticism only from an outside source, not from within. Their efforts, missions, and writings were directed toward the nonbeliever and not, as in the East, toward one another. This internal harmony directed to a common aim produced some remarkable leaders in the Western church.

Ambrose of Milan While the bishops of Rome (popes[4]) were uniformly strong leaders and staunch defenders of Christianity, the most outstanding Western church fathers during these two centuries were not in Rome. Ambrose, bishop of Milan (died 397), was the best known Christian leader of his day. He pioneered in the development of ritual, and composed music, hymns, and prayers. His work stimulated a continued interest in the rites and services of the Church. His most courageous action was taken when he defied and humbled the emperor Theodosius, forcing him to do penance for an imperial action that horrified the Christian community.[5] Ambrose became a saint in the Roman Catholic Church.

Jerome Jerome (died 420), one of the greatest scholars of the age, lived in the generation after Ambrose. Proficient in both Greek and Hebrew, he translated the Old and New Testaments into Latin, making them available to the ordinary people of the West. His edition of the Bible, called the Vulgate, is now the official Latin Bible of the Roman Catholic Church. He, too, became a saint in the Church.

Augustine of Hippo The greatest theologian was Augustine, bishop of Hippo, in North Africa (died 430). From an early interest in Neoplatonic philosophy, he was converted to Christianity. His analyses, explanations, definitions, concepts, and tremendous vision have left their imprints on Western Christianity into our own day. His *City of God* and *Confessions* are the only works of this period that are still read widely by a contemporary audience.

Other writers, poets, and theologians were produced by the Christian communities of both the East and West, but neither produced good historians. The Christian writer, in the attempt to justify himself against pagan charges, wrote *apologiae* (defenses) rather than history. Alternatively, the so-called history written by Christians was indelibly colored by the belief that the world was coming to an end. Even St. Augustine of Hippo shared that view and thought that the Roman Empire marked the last age of the world.

General Culture

The reforms of Diocletian and Constantine had turned the class structure of the empire into a caste system in which sons inherited their father's status and occupation. Men even had to marry within their class. The system virtually ensured the enrollment of non-Romans

---

[4] The first Roman bishop to insist on the title Pope was Leo the Great in about 450.
[5] Theodosius massacred the inhabitants of Salonica in revenge for the death of one of his officers.

into the army to replace the losses of the fifth century which reduced the professional military caste. Recruitment within the empire, above a certain level, endangered the structure of society and affected the financial system upon which the government rested. The hereditary "workers" of every type lost all knowledge of the art of war. Nor had they arms or weapons. Consequently, whether living in Gaul, Britain, Africa, Spain, or Italy, the average Romanized citizen fell easy prey to the warlike German.

The caste-ridden structure of the empire, while it engendered little creative activity, worked well enough to supply the material needs of its citizen body, its officials, and its professional armies. Every individual had his part to play in the working of the huge machine.

Especially characteristic of much of the Western empire were the *villae* (p. 562). They continued to increase in number and in economic significance. The landowners formed small private armies from among their retainers and tenants. With these troops they beat off wandering bands of Germans, and sometimes also the imperial tax agents. They intimidated and browbeat the free men in their neighborhoods, and gradually assumed legal jurisdiction over them as over their own tenants. Emperors tried in vain to lessen the landlords' power.

Art   Art and architecture declined in direct ratio to the decline of cities and towns. Fewer buildings were erected. This quantitative decline was accompanied by a change as Christianity became the dominant religion. It has been said that Christians did not kill ancient art, but rather buried it. Certainly they transformed it. Christians avoided the nude figure and all pagan symbolism, though they readily used Roman buildings and columns at hand. Also, they continued Roman techniques and forms but used them to build churches or to portray Christian subjects in mosaic and painting. The lesser arts, handicrafts, and music were similarly transformed. Decorative elements increased and the humanistic values were submerged.

Literature and Philosophy   Literature, aside from theological works, was largely uninspired. The works of earlier authors were collected, copied and epitomized (abbreviated). Insipid novels were written, and encyclopedic collections of information and misinformation, often copied from earlier writers, were popular. In spite of Julian's last great effort to revive it, the ancient pagan spirit was dead. Christian works, a few poems, and the great law codes stand as isolated monuments of the age.

The Army   The Roman army, from the time of the Severi, had tended to become increasingly a professional force. The reforms of Diocletian and the pressing needs of the fourth and fifth centuries had transformed it into a mercenary army. In the West most of the hired soldiers were Germans. In the East the armies were recruited from

Copy of a Mosaic Panel from the Church of San Vitale in Ravenna (A.D. 536–547), Showing the Empress Theodora. (The Metropolitan Museum of Art, Fletcher Fund, 1925)

among Macedonians, Isaurians, and other mountain and barbarian peoples. Military tactics, armor, and weapons had also undergone a change. Early in the fourth century the use of heavy-armed cavalry spread from Persia to the Romans. The invention of the saddle with stirrups made it possible for a heavily armored man to fight from horseback using heavy weapons. By the end of the fifth century the heavy-armed cavalry was adopted even by Germans. The ancestors of the medieval knights had appeared.

THE REIGN OF JUSTINIAN

Justinian (527–565) had been associated with his uncle Justin in imperial affairs, and was an experienced administrator when he ascended the throne in Constantinople. He has been called the last Roman-minded emperor, and he was the last who used Latin as the official language. Aided by his remarkable empress, Theodora, Justinian championed orthodox Christianity and regarded himself as the rightful heir of the Caesars. It was his ambition to restore and reunite the entire Roman world under his direct control, and he made supreme efforts to realize that aim.

Reconquests Justinian, served by two excellent generals, Belisarius and Narses, reconquered a part of the west. Africa was wrested from the Vandals; the islands and the Spanish coast were dominated by the Roman fleets; and after eighteen years of war with the Ostrogoths Italy came under his control. But the costs were too great. No more could be attempted.[6] Gaul and the interior of Spain, to say nothing of Britain, remained under their Germanic masters. Moreover, Italy was so reduced by the long and intense struggle that it could not be defended against new enemies after the death of Justinian. Rome had lost all political significance and its population was sharply reduced. Its citizens lived by catering to tourists and pilgrims or on the charity of popes. Only the papacy stood between Rome and outside enemies, and that not always successfully. Northern Italy fell during the next generation to the Lombards. Soon after (632–711), North Africa and Spain were overrun by the Moslems.

Buildings In Constantinople, in Ravenna, and other cities, Justinian sponsored an enormous building program. The basilica of San Vitale at Ravenna was crowned with a high dome raised on pendentive arches, a feature characteristic of this era, and decorated inside with beautiful mosaics. Even more magnificent was the huge Cathedral of the Holy Wisdom (Hagia Sophia) in Constantinople, still one of the most famous buildings of the world. Its huge dome soared high above the city, nestled amid surrounding half-domes. The mosaics inside are as beautiful as the finest artists and the finest materials could make them.

Justinian's Code The most enduring monument to Justinian's reign was the complete codification of the Roman law, together with its precedents and interpretation. A commission chaired by the jurist Tribonian labored for years on the work. First to be published was the *Codex*, containing more than four thousand laws. It was followed by a later section embodying the legislation of Justinian, called the *Novella*.

[6] New wars with Persia in the East absorbed part of his resources.

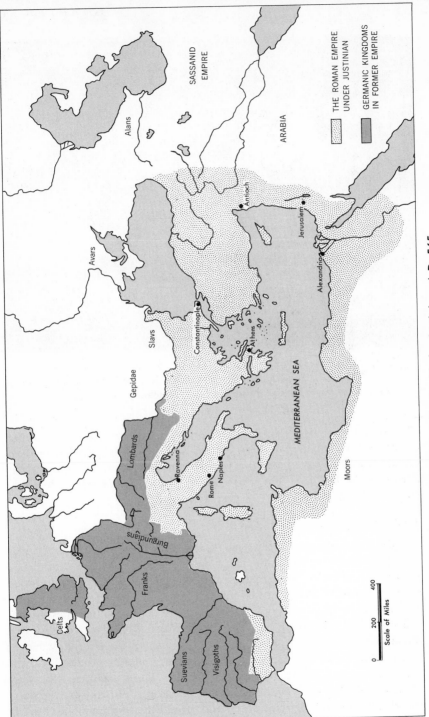

SASSANID
EMPIRE

Alans

ARABIA

THE ROMAN EMPIRE
UNDER JUSTINIAN

GERMANIC KINGDOMS
IN FORMER EMPIRE

Avars

Antioch

Slavs

Jerusalem

Gepidae

Constantinople

Alexandria

Athens

Lombards

MEDITERRANEAN SEA

Ravenna

Rome

Naples

Burgundians

Moors

Celts

Franks

Suevians

Visigoths

0   200   400

Scale of Miles

The Roman Empire Under Justinian, A.D. 565

Copy of a Mosaic Panel from the Church of San Vitale in Ravenna
(A.D. 536–547), Showing the Emperor Justinian and Members of His
Court. (The Metropolitan Museum of Art, Fletcher Fund, 1925)

The interpretations established by Roman jurisprudence were codified
in fifty books called the *Digest*, or *Pandects*. This in turn led to a revision of the *Codex* and to the publication of a textbook of principles
known as the *Institutes*. The whole of this tremendous work made up the
Corpus Juris Civilis, or Body of Civil Law.

The Legacy of the Ancient World

In a curious way the *Corpus Juris Civilis* incorporated much that
was good and useful from all of the ancient world, for Rome had
absorbed and ruled the greater part of it. Its laws were compounded
of all the older laws into a vast international scheme. Here lay customs
established by the traders of the East and Greece, and here lay also the
rules by which men dealt with men in the West. This great code, passed
through later states and through the canon law of the church, serves as
the basis for many European and American codes. Justinian's was the
last attempt to reunite the Roman world. The empire in the West
was irrevocably lost. Yet the idea of unity would not die. It remained
the dream of kings, emperors, and popes throughout the Middle
Ages. Moreover, in spite of the Germanization of the West, much of

Roman culture and many ancient institutions survived. Germanic rulers appointed Romanized subjects to important civil posts and learned administration from them. The Church preserved ancient books and educational methods, passing them lovingly from one generation to the next.

Constantinople preserved the Greek heritage, together with elements from the Roman and the Eastern traditions. These traditions were compounded anew to flourish in the continuing Roman Empire in the East, called Byzantine because Greek became the language of government after the age of Justinian, and because the old Roman tradition made up only one component of a different and distinctive culture. Works of the ancient Greeks were as cherished by scholars of Constantinople as the Latin authors were by the Western churchmen, and these scholars were to return the Greek works to the Western world, directly or through the Moslems, before Constantinople fell to the Turks in 1453.

The ancient world had indeed come to an end in the West. The characteristic urban, trading cultures that had developed before 3000 B.C. in the middle east and had spread and expanded to flourish around the shores of the Mediterranean, and even in far away Britain, had been undermined, eclipsed, and ruined. The Roman imperial government, so long the guardian and preserver of the urban culture, had failed. The ancient middle east like the Roman West was overrun with peoples following a more primitive tribal pattern. The Christian thinkers proved both right and wrong: the Roman Empire had ended, and with it the culture typical of many peoples and many centuries, even though the world survived.

TABLE I. THE ORIENT

	EGYPT*		MESOPOTAMIA	
7000				
	Neolithic period		Neolithic villages in hills	
			Settlement of valley	
	Fayum and other valley villages			
5000				
	Predynastic period		Uruk period	
			Sumerian and Semite settlers	
			Jamdat Nasr period; cuneiform invented	
	ca. 3400 Two Kingdoms			
	ca. 3200 Union of Egypt		*ca.* 3200 Growth of cities and strong	
	First Dynasty		city-states	
3000				
	Second Dynasty		Domination of Kish	
	ca. 2700 *Third Dynasty*		*ca.* 2700 Domination of Erech	
			Gilgamesh	
	ca. 2620–2500:		*ca.* 2600 First dynasty of Ur; royal tombs	
	Fourth Dynasty		*ca.* 2500 Lugalannemundu unites Sumer	
	Great Pyramids			
	ca. 2480 *Fifth Dynasty*		*ca.* 2400 Urukagina of Lagash	
	ca. 2340 *Sixth Dynasty*		*ca.* 2350 Sargon of Akkad	
			ca. 2300 Naram-Sin; Guti conquest	
			ca. 2250 Gudea of Lagash	
	ca. 2200			
			ca. 2050 Sumerian revival; Erech leads revolt	
			Third dynasty of Ur, Ur-Nammu	
	ca. 2134 *Eleventh Dynasty*			
2000	*ca.* 1991 *Twelfth Dynasty*			
			ca. 1950 Dynasty of Isin	Babylon founded; first Assyrian expansion
			Dynasty of Larsa	
			Rim-Sin of Larsa	
	ca. 1780			
	ca. 1750 *Thirteenth Dynasty*		*ca.* 1750 Hammurabi; law code	Fall of Indus Valley cities
	Fifteenth and Sixteenth Dynasties			
	Hyksos conquest (*ca.* 1730)		Decline of Sumer	
			ca. 1600 Hittite raid on Babylon	

(Egypt: *Old Kingdom* — Third through Sixth Dynasty; *Feudal Age* — ca. 2200 to ca. 2134 Eleventh Dynasty; *Middle Kingdom* — ca. 1991 Twelfth Dynasty to ca. 1780)

SYRIA	ASIA MINOR (ANATOLIA)	AEGEAN
	Neolithic period Small villages in hills and along coasts	
Neolithic period Jericho I		Neolithic period
		Villages on islands and Greek mainland
Villages in Fertile Crescent and in Lebanon and Anti-Lebanon	Villages grow steadily in size and comforts	Culture similar to that of Asia Minor
Cities of Biblos, Sidon, Ras Shamra, etc.	Troy I Coastal towns fortified	Fortification of villages
Strong state of Mari (records *ca.* 2500–1750)		
	ca. 2300 Troy II destroyed along with other towns	*ca.* 2300 Destruction of many towns
Amorite rulers in Mari	Indo-European migrations Troy VI; Hittites take plateau *ca.* 1900–1800: Assyrian traders live in Anatolia Hittite capital at Hattusas	Early Minoan { First palace period in Crete Indo-European migrations *ca.* 1900 Achaeans in Greece
ca. 1750 Conquest of Mari by Hammurabi *ca.* 1730 Hyksos conquest of south Cities of Phoenicia and Canaan fortified by Hyksos *ca.* 1575 Destruction of Mari by Aryans and Hurrians, who form state of Mitanni	*ca.* 1740 Hittite Old Kingdom { Millewandas (Miletos) founded	Middle Minoan { Growth of palaces in Crete Dominance of Knossos in Crete *ca.* 1580 Minoan thalassocracy

[589]

| EGYPT* | MESOPOTAMIA |

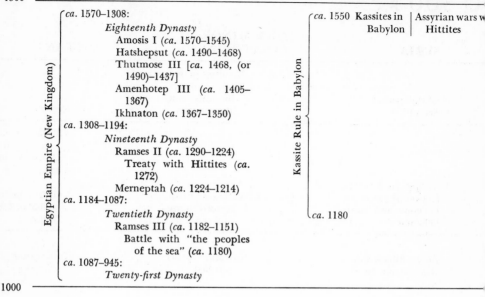

1500

EGYPT*

Egyptian Empire (New Kingdom)

ca. 1570–1308:
   Eighteenth Dynasty
   Amosis I (ca. 1570–1545)
   Hatshepsut (ca. 1490–1468)
   Thutmose III [ca. 1468, (or 1490)–1437]
   Amenhotep III (ca. 1405–1367)
   Ikhnaton (ca. 1367–1350)
ca. 1308–1194:
   Nineteenth Dynasty
   Ramses II (ca. 1290–1224)
   Treaty with Hittites (ca. 1272)
   Merneptah (ca. 1224–1214)
ca. 1184–1087:
   Twentieth Dynasty
   Ramses III (ca. 1182–1151)
   Battle with "the peoples of the sea" (ca. 1180)
ca. 1087–945:
   Twenty-first Dynasty

MESOPOTAMIA

Kassite Rule in Babylon

ca. 1550 Kassites in Babylon | Assyrian wars w Hittites

ca. 1180

1000

ca. 945–715:
   Twenty-second to Twenty-fourth Dynasties

ca. 715–668:
   Twenty-fifth Dynasty
   Ethiopian pharaohs
   Assyrian conquest (ca. 670)
   Necho I of Sais
ca. 663–525:
   Twenty-sixth Dynasty
   Psamtik I (ca. 663–609)

   Necho II (ca. 609–593)

   Psamtik II (ca. 593–588)

   Apries (ca. 588–569)

   Amosis II (ca. 569–525)

   525 Persian conquest

Assyrian Supremacy 885–612

Assurnasirpal II (ca. 885–85

Tiglath-pileser III (ca. 746–7?

Shalmaneser V (ca. 727–722)
Sargon II (ca. 722–705)
Sennacherib (ca. 705–681)
Esarhaddon (ca. 681–669)
Assurbanipal (ca. 669–626)
ca. 612 Fall of Nineveh
ca. 676–539:
   Chaldean dynasty in Baby▮
ca. 604–561:
   Nebuchadressar
ca. 633–550:
   Median kings

ca. 550–530:
   Cyrus
   539 Fall of Babylon
   529–522:
   Cambyses
   522–486:
   Darius I

500

* Dates for Egypt follow Sir Alan H. Gardiner, *Egypt of the Pharaohs.* Oxford: Clarendon Press, 1961.

SYRIA	ASIA MINOR (ANATOLIA)	AEGEAN	
ca. 1468–1437: Conquest by Thutmose III; forms part of Egyptian empire	Hittites develop iron industry	ca. 1480 Achaeans at Knossos	
ca. 1340 Mitanni taken by Hittites	ca. 1460 Hittite expansion in Southern Anatolia	ca. 1400 Knossos destroyed	Late Minoan
Hittites take North Syria	ca. 1375–1335: Suppiluliumas' conquest of Mitani		
ca. 1290 Battle of Kadesh	ca. 1290 Muwatallis defeats Ramses II		
	ca. 1272 Treaty with Egypt		
ca. 1250 Philistines attack coast	ca. 1250 Fall of Troy VII	ca. 1250 Fall of Pylos	
ca. 1250–1182: Exodus of Israelites and entry into Palestine	ca. 1200 Phrygian conquest of plateau	Dorian invasions Dorians found Sparta	
ca. 1150 Tyre founded	ca. 1200–1100: Ionians settle coast		
Judges in Israel Saul, king of Israel		ca. 1100 Dorians in Crete and Rhodes	
1000–961: David	ca. 1000–967: Hiram of Tyre	Phrygian kingdom	
ca. 961–922: Solomon			
ca. 922 Division of the kingdom			
ca. 869–850: Ahab		ca. 900–500: Rise of Greek states (see Table 2)	
ca. 842–815: Jehu	ca. 800–546: Lydian kingdom		
ca. 750 Amos and Hosea		ca. 800–600: Adoption of Phoenician alphabet by Greeks	
ca. 732 Fall of Damascus			
ca. 722 Fall of Samaria			
ca. 715–687: Hezekiah Isaiah			
ca. 639–608: Josiah Jeremiah			
ca. 598 Capture of Jerusalem	585 Battle with Medes		
ca. 587 Destruction of Jerusalem Babylonian Exile	560–546: Croesus		
539 Return to Jerusalem	546 Persian Conquest		
ca. 450 Ezra and Nehemiah			

TABLE 2. THE GRECO-ROMAN WORLD TO 133 B.C.

THE EAST	THE GREEKS	THE WEST
3000		
	Aegean civilization (see Table 1)	Neolithic peoples
	1250–1200:	ca. 1800–ca. 1000:
	Dorian invasion	Apennine culture
	1200 Dorians at Sparta	ca. 1700–ca. 1200:
	1100 Dorians in Crete and Rhodes	Minoans and Mycenaean trade in Sicily and South ern Italy
	1100–800:	Formation of Italic tribes
	Ionians in Asia Minor	
1000–500:	*Homer* (fl. *ca.* 800)	1000 Iron age of Villanova an Fossa folk
Phrygian kingdom	800–600:	1000–800:
885–612:	Colonial expansion	Entrance of Etruscans
Assyrian empire	776 First Olympiad	ca. 825 Carthage founded
	725 First Messenian War	800–600:
800–546:	*Hesiod* (fl. *ca.* 700)	Greeks in southern Italy and Sicily
Lydian kingdom	682 Athenian archon list begins	753–509:
		Regal period of Rome
	Archilochus (fl. *ca.* 670)	ca. 664 Zaleucus of Locri
	650 Second Messenian War	
	Trytaeus and Alcman	
	627 Periander, tyrant of Corinth	
	621 Draco's code	
	Alcaeus and Sappho (fl. 610–595)	600–509:
		Etruscan domination of Rome
	594 Solon's reforms	
	Thales (fl. *ca.* 585) *Glaucus of Chios* (fl. *ca.* 566) *Anaximander*	
560–546:	560–527:	
Croesus	Peisistratus, tyrant of Athens	
550–529:	*Anaximenes* (fl. 540)	
Cyrus		
546 Cyrus conquers Lydia	*Pythagoras* (fl. 535) *Xenophanes* *Anacreon* *Theodorus of Samos* *Thespis* *Theognis of Megara*	
		525 Battle of Aricia
529–523:	527–512:	510 Sybaris destroyed by Crotone
Cambyses	Hippias, tyrant of Athens	509 Roman republic established
521–485:	514 Murder of Hipparchus by Harmodius and Aristogeiton	508 Treaty between Carthage and Rome
Darius I	508 Cleisthenes' reforms	ca. 504 Attius Clausus moved to Rome

[592]

THE EAST	THE GREEKS	THE WEST
	500 Hecataeus	
	500–494:	497 Battle of Lake Regillus
	Ionian revolt	493 Treaty of Spurius Cassius
	494 Destruction of Miletos	First secession of the plebs
	493–492:	
	Themistocles, archon	
	492 First Persian expedition	492 Gelon, tyrant of Gela
	490 Battle of Marathon	490–400:
	487 Archons chosen by lot	Wars between Rome and the
485–464:		hill tribes
Xerxes		485 Gelon conquers Syracuse
	483 Ostracism of Aristides	
	480 Battles of Thermopylae	480 Battle of Himera
	and Salamis	
	479 Battles of Plataea and	478 Hieron, tyrant of Syracuse
	Mycale	
	477 Confederacy of Delos	474 Battle of Cumae
	468 Revolt of Naxos	471 Tribunate established
	Battle of Eurymedon	
464–424:	464 Revolt of helots	
Artaxerxes I	462 Ostracism of Cimon	

Generation of Marathon, 490–461

- *Pindar (520–441)*
- *Aeschylus (525–456)*
- *Simonides*
- *Calamis*
- *Myron*
- *Polygnotus*
- *Panaenus*
- *Micon*
- *Parmenides*
- *Zeno*
- *Heraclitus*
- *Temple of Zeus at Olympia*
- *Temple of Aphaia on Aegina*

THE EAST	THE GREEKS	THE WEST
462–454:	459 Settlement of Naupactus	
Egyptian	457 Battle of Tanagra	
revolt	456 Completion of Long Walls	
	454 Defeat in Egypt	
	451 Law of citizenship in	451–449:
	Athens	Decemviri
	449 Cimon's victory in Cyprus	449 Twelve Tables Valerio-
	448 Peace with Persia	Horatian Laws
	447 Battle of Coronea	
	445 Thirty Years' Peace	445 Canuleian Law
	440 Revolt of Samos	443 Censorship established
	438 Parthenon completed	
	437 Propylaea begun	
	435 Alliance of Athens with	
	Corcyra	
	432 Megarian Decrees	

Age of Pericles, 461–431

- *Sophocles (496–406)*
- *Herodotus (484–425)*
- *Meton*
- *Anaxagoras (500–428)*
- *Empedocles (495–435)*
- *Leucippus*
- *Phidias*

THE EAST	THE GREEKS	THE WEST

424–404:
  Darius II
	430 Plague at Athens
	429 Death of Pericles
	428–427:
	  Revolt of Lesbos
	425 Capture of Pylos
	421 Peace of Nicias
	416 Capture of Melos
	415–413:
	  Syracusan expedition
	411 Four Hundred in Athens
	410 Battle of Cyzicus
	407 Erechtheum constructed
	406 Battle of Arginusae
	405 Battle of Aegospotami
	404 Fall of Athens
	  Rule of Thirty Tyrants
	403 Restoration of the Democracy
	  Ionic alphabet
	  Code of Laws
	
	  Thucydides (460–395)
	  Euripides (480–406)
	  Aristophanes (450–385)
	  Socrates (469–399)
	  Democritus
	  Protagoras (490–415)
	  Gorgias (480–395)
	  Hippocrates
	  Polyclitus
	  Zeuxis
		415–413:
		  Syracuse attacked by Athenians

404–359:
  Artaxerxes II
401 Expedition of Cyrus
  Battle of Cunaxa
	401 Anabasis of the 10,000	

	400–394:
	  War in Asia Minor
	395–387:
	  Corinthian War
	393 Long Walls rebuilt
	387 King's Peace
	382 Sparta seizes Thebes
	379 Olynthian League destroyed
	378–377:
	  Second Athenian Confederacy formed
	378–371:
	  War with Sparta
	371 Peace Conference
	  Battle of Leuctra
	371–362:
	  Hegemony of Thebes
	362 Battle of Mantinea
		405–367:
		  Dionysius of Syracuse
		390 (387):
		  Battle of Allia River
		  Gauls sack Rome
		
		367 Licinian-Sextian Laws

359–338:
  Artaxerxes III
	359–336:
	  Philip II of Macedon
		358 Treaty with Latin League

(Peloponnesian War, 431–404)

THE EAST	THE GREEKS	THE WEST
	357–346: War between Athens and Philip	354 Treaty with Samnites
	356–346: Second Sacred War	
	346 Peace of Philocrates	
	340 Philip attacks Byzantium	343–341: First Samnite War
	339 Third Sacred War	339 Publilian Laws
	338 Battle of Chaeronea	338 Latin League dissolved
	Xenophon (430–350) *Lysias* (440–380) *Isaeus* *Isocrates* (436–338) *Demosthenes* (384–322) *Plato* (428–347) *Aristotle* (384–322) *Scopas* *Praxiteles* *Lysippus* *Parrhasius* *Apelles*	344–338: Timoleon at Syracuse
338–330: Darius III	338–337: Hellenic League formed at Corinth	
Alexander's conquest	*Alexander, 336–323* { 335 Destruction of Thebes 334 Battle of Granicus 333 Battle of Issus 332 Siege of Tyre 332 Conquest of Egypt Cleomenes, administrator 331 Battle of Arbela 330–327: Invasion of the East 327 Defeat of Porus 323 Death of Alexander }	327–290: Samnite Wars
	323–322: Lamian War	
	323 Ptolemy, satrap of Egypt	
	323–276: Wars of Succession	321 Battle of Caudine Pass
	317–307: Demetrius of Phalerum in Athens	312 Censorship of Appius Claudius
	305 Siege of Rhodes	304 Landless enrolled in city tribes at Rome
	301 Battle of Ipsus	300 Ogulnian Law
323, 305–283: Ptolemy I	Aetolian League organized	317–289: Agathocles of Syracuse
305–281: Seleucus I		295 Battle of Sentinum
281 Battle of Co- rupedium	281 Lysimachus, ruler of Thrace, killed at Coru-pedium	293 Annexation of Samnium
283–247: Ptolemy II		287 Hortensian Law
		283 Annexation of Etruria Battle of Lake Vadimon
	280 Revival of Achaean League	282–275: War with Pyrrhus
	279 Gauls raid Macedon	

THE EAST	THE GREEKS	THE WEST
Founding of Pergamum	277–239: Antigonus Gonatas of Macedon	279 Battle of Asculum
		275 Battle of Beneventum
		269 First Roman coinage
281–261: Antiochus I		269–215: Hiero II of Syracuse
263–241: Eumenes of Pergamum		264 First gladiatorial games
		264–241: First Punic War
261–247: Antiochus II	266–262: Cremonidean War	262 Siege of Agrigentum
	258 Macedonian victory at Cos	
		260 Battle of Mylae
		256 Battle of Ecnomus Expedition of Regulus
247–221: Ptolemy III	251 Rise of Aratus of Sicyon	249 Battle of Drepana
	244 Agis IV of Sparta	242 Battle of Aegates Islands *Praetor peregrinus* establish
241–197: Attalus I of Pergamum	239–229: Demetrius II of Macedon	241 Treaty with Carthage
		232 Flaminius, tribune
	229–221: Antigonus Doson of Macedon	
		230–228: Illyrian Wars
	226 Reform of Cleomenes in Sparta	229 Death of Hamilcar Barca
		225 Battle of Telamon
222–187: Antiochus III	222 Battle of Sellasia	
221–203: Ptolemy IV	221–179: Philip V of Macedon	219 Siege of Saguntum
		218–201: Second Punic War
217 Battle of Raphia		218 Battle of Trebia River
		217 Battle of Lake Trasimeno Fabius, dictator
		216 Battle of Cannae
	215–202: First Macedonian War with Rome	215–205: First Macedonian War
		214–212: Revolt of Syracuse
	207 Nabis, tyrant of Sparta	207 Battle of Metaurus River
		202 Battle of Zama
	200–197: Second Macedonian War with Rome	200–197: Second Macedonian War
197–159: Eumenes II of Pergamum		197 Battle of Cynoscephalae
191–189: War of Antiochus III with Rome	191–189: Aetolian League joins Antiochus III against Rome	191–189: War with Antiochus III
		186 Bacchanalia episode
		186 Cato, censor

THE EAST	THE GREEKS	THE WEST

175–163:
    Antiochus IV
	179–168:
	    Perseus of Macedon
	171–168:
	    Achaean League joins Per-
	    seus against Rome
	168 Delos, a free port
		173 Epicureans expelled
		
		171–168:
		    Third Macedonian War
		
		168 Battle of Pydna

166–132:
    Maccabean
      wars
159–138:
    Attalus II of
      Pergamum
		150 *Lex Aebutia*
		149 *Lex Calpurnia de repetundis*
		149–146:

	146 Annexation of Macedon
	    Destruction of Corinth
	      by Rome
		Third Punic War
		147–139:
		    War with Viriathus in Spain

138–133:
    Attalus III
	Nearchus
	Megasthenes
	Theophrastus
	Herophilus of Chalcedon
		146 Destruction of Carthage
		143–133:
		    Numantine War in Spain
		134–132:

133 Pergamum
    united to
    Rome
	Menander
	Euclid
	Diogenes
	Epicurus (in Athens, 306)
	Zeno (in Athens, 302)
	Aristarchus (310–230)
	Eratosthenes (275–200)
	Archimedes (287–212)
	Aratus of Soli
	Timaeus (d. 264)
	Callimachus
	Theocritus
	Apollonius of Perge
	Apollonius of Rhodes
	Polybius (198–117)
	Poseidonius of Rhodes
	    (135–51)
	Carneades
	Hero
		Slave revolt in Sicily
		133 Annexation of Pergamum
		
		    Plautus (254–184)
		    Livius Andronicus (fl. 200)
		    Naevius (fl. 200)
		    Ennius (239–169)
		    Terence (195–159)

TABLE 3. ROME, 133 B.C.-A.D. 337

133–121:
  Reforms of T. and C. Gracchus
121 Province of Gaul organized
111–105:
  War with Jugurtha
105 Disaster at Arausio (Cimbri and Teutons)
104–101:
  Consulship of Marius; army reform
102 Battle of Aquae Sextiae
101 Battle of Vercellae
105–101:
  Slave revolt in Sicily
104–102:
  War with pirates
100 Sixth consulship of Marius
99 Saturninus and Glaucia
93 Trial of Rutilius Rufus
91 Drusus the reformer
90–88:
  Social War
89 *Lex Plautia Papiria*
88–85:
  First Mithradatic War
88 Sulla, consul; Sulpicius, tribune
87 Consulship of Cinna
86 Seventh consulship of Marius
86 Siege of Athens
83–82:
  First Civil War
82–79:
  Dictatorship of Sulla
78–71:
  War with Sertorius
75 Cicero, quaestor
74–67:
  War with pirates
74–63:
  Second Mithradatic War
73–71:
  Revolt of Spartacus
70 Consulship of Pompey and Crassus
  Trial of Verres
69 Caesar at the funeral of Julia
67 Gabinian Law
66 Manilian Law
  Cicero, praetor
65 Crassus, censor
63 Pompey in Judaea
63 Cicero consul; conspiracy of Catiline
62 Return of Pompey
60 Formation of the First Triumvirate
59 Caesar, consul
58–51:
  Conquest of Gaul by Caesar
58 Clodius, tribune; Cicero banished
57 Milo, tribune
56 Conference at Luca
55 Consulship of Pompey and Crassus

53 Battle of Carrhae
52 Death of Clodius; Pompey, sole consul
51 Cicero, governor of Cilicia
49–44:
  Second Civil War
48 Battle of Pharsalus
46 Battle of Thapsus
45 Battle of Munda
44 Assassination of Caesar
44–43:
  War of Mutina
43 Formation of Second Triumvirate
  Death of Cicero
42 Battle of Philippi
40 Perusian War
  Treaty of Brundisium
40–36:
  War with Sextus Pompey
37 Treaty of Tarentum
36 Parthian War
31 Actium

  Cicero (106–43)
  Varro (116–27)
  Nepus (100–25)
  Lucretius (99–55)
  Catullus (84–54)
  Augustus (27 B.C.–A.D. 14)

27 Restoration of Republic; establishment of
  Principate
27–24:
  Augustus in Spain and Gaul
23 Revision of government (Augustus receives
  proconsular imperium)
22–19:
  Augustus in the East
17 Secular games
15–9:
  War in Germany
12 Augustus, Pontifex Maximus
9 Death of Drusus
8 (or 4):
  Birth of Christ
6 B.C.–A.D. 4:
  Tiberius at Rhodes
A.D. 4 Death of Gaius (Augustus' last heir); recall
  of Tiberius
6 Creation of *aerarium militare*
  Judaea, a province

  Livy 59 B.C.–A.D. 17
  Vergil 70 B.C.–19 B.C.
  Horace 65 B.C.–8 B.C.
  Ovid 43 B.C.–A.D. 18

14–37:
  Tiberius
19 Death of Germanicus
26 Tiberius retires to Capri

Conspiracy of Sejanus
7–41:
Gaius Caligula
1–54:
Claudius
3 Conquest of Britain
3 Death of Messalina
4–68:
Nero
9 Death of Agrippina
4 Burning of Rome; Christians blamed
5 Conspiracy of Piso
6–70:
Jewish War
8 Galba, Otho, Vitellius
9–79:
Vespasian
0 Destruction of Jerusalem
8–85:
Agricola in Britain
9–81:
Titus
9 Eruption of Vesuvius; destruction of Pompeii
   and Herculaneum
0 Dedication of Colosseum
1–96:
Domitian
5 Recall of Agricola
6–89:
Dacian War

Petronius
Seneca (4–65)
Lucan (39–65)
Pliny the Elder (23–79)
Quintilian (35–95)

96–98:
Nerva
98–117:
Trajan
05–106:
Second Dacian War
11 Pliny, governor of Bithynia
13–116:
Wars in the East
15–117:
Revolt in the East
17–138:
Hadrian
22 Wall in Britain
25 Perpetual Edict
32–135:
Revolt of Bar Kochba
38–161:
Antoninus Pius
61–180:
Marcus Aurelius
62–166:
Parthian War
65–166:
Plague throughout the Empire

167–180:
Germanic wars

Tacitus (55–120)
Suetonius (75–150)
Martial (40–102)
Juvenal (55–130)
Plutarch (50–125)
Lucian (125–192)
Epictetus (50–120)
Arrian
Dio Chrysostom (40–115)
Appian

180–192:
Commodus
193–211:
Septimius Severus
211–217:
Caracalla
212 Edict of Citizenship
218–222:
Elagabalus
222–235:
Alexander Severus
227 Sassanid Empire established in Persia
233 Invasion of Alemanni
240–251:
Decius
250 Plague; persecution of Christians
251 Invasion of Goths
253–260:
Valerian
257 Persecution of Christians
260 Valerian captured by Sapor of Persia
260–268:
Gallienus
268–270:
Claudius Gothicus
270–275:
Aurelian
271 Wall of Rome built
272 Zenobia captured
285–305:
Diocletian
301 Edict of Prices
303 Persecution of Christians
306–337:
Constantine
311 Edict of Toleration of Galerius
313 Edict of Milan
325 Council of Nicaea

Diogenes
Eusebius
Philostratus
Athenaeus
Dio Cassius (155–240)
Papinian (d. 212)
Ulpian (d. 228)
Paulus
Plotinus (204–270)
Porphyry (233–304)

[599]

TABLE 4. THE ROMAN EMPIRE, 337-565*

THE WESTERN EMPIRE	THE UNITED EMPIRE	THE EASTERN EMPIRE
337 Death of Constantine Civil wars between Constantine II (d. 340), Constans (d. 350), and Constantius Franks settled along Lower Rhine 350 Constantius 361 Julian		337 Constantius
	Constantius (sole emperor 350–361) Julian (sole emperor 361–363) War with Persia	361 Julian
363 Jovian	Jovian (sole emperor 363–364)	363 Jovian
364 Valentinian I Wars with Franks and Burgundians 375 Gratian Wars with Franks Revolt in Britain 383 Valentinian II 392 Theodosius I	Gratian (sole emperor 378) Theodosius I (sole emperor 392–395)	364 Valens Valens killed in Battle Hadrianople (378) 378 Gratian 379 Theodosius I Suppression of all pagan rit and institutions (383)
395 Honorius Stilicho, master of militia *St. Ambrose* (d. 397) *St. Jerome* (d. 420) Vandals in Spain Angles and Saxons in Britain Visigoths sack Rome (410) and move on to southern Gaul (418) 423 Valentinian III Aëtius, master of militia *Orosius* (fl.) *St. Augustine* (d. 430) Visigoths drive Vandals from Spain (429) Attila invades Gaul (451) Vandals sack Rome (455) Pope Leo I (440–461)		395 Arcadius 408 Theodosius II Code of Laws University of Constantinopl
455 Maximus 456 Avitus 457 Majorian Ricimer, master 461 Severus of militia and real 465 No emperor ruler of Italy, 455– 467 Anthemius 472 472 Olybrius 473 Glycerinus 474 Nepos 475 Romulus Augustulus (deposed 476) 476 Odovacar, king of Italy 477 Zeno acknowledged emperor by Odovacar, who continues as actual ruler of Italy	Zeno (sole emperor 477–?)	450 Marcian Death of Attila (452) and dis appearance of Huns 457 Leo I 473 Leo II 474 Zeno 491 Anastasius

THE WESTERN EMPIRE	THE UNITED EMPIRE	THE EASTERN EMPIRE
3 Invasion of Italy by Ostrogoths Theodoric, king of Italy		*St. John Chrysostom* (fl.)
Boethius (fl.) *Cassiodorus* (fl.) *Symmachus* (fl.)		
Clovis the Frank conquers most of Gaul (496–508)		518 Justin I
6 Athalaric, king of Italy		527 Justinian
4 Amalasuntha, queen of Italy		
0 Justinian		*Corpus Juris Civilis*
Justinian's armies recover Africa and the coast of Spain (554–565)	Justinian (sole emperor 554–565)	Hagia Sophia
Church of San Vitale at Ravenna		*Procopius* (fl.)
		Conquests in the West War with Persia
Gaul, Britain, and Spain remain independent German kingdoms		
5 Death of Justinian		565 Death of Justinian

* Dates give the beginning of the independent reign of the respective emperors. There was frequent overlapping. For example, Valentinian made his son Gratian "Augustus" in 367, but Gratian's independent reign began in 375, at his father's death, as given above.

BIBLIOGRAPHY

An attempt has been made to select books and articles that will best meet the needs of the elementary student. Books in foreign languages are included when no adequate work on a subject exists in English; the only exceptions are a few classics that should be known at least by name to every student of ancient history. Many older books that have lost their value have been omitted. The more general works are listed separately and are not repeated in the special chapter bibliographies. Paperback books are starred.

Chapter 1. PRELITERARY HISTORY

Bandi, H. G., and Maringer, J., *Art in the Ice Ages*, London, 1953. Good survey and excellent photographs.

Barker, H., "Radio Carbon Dating: Its Scope and Limitations," *Antiquity* 32 (1958), pp. 253 ff. One of the most lucid accounts of this dating method.

*Benedict, Ruth, *Patterns of Culture*, New York, 1946.

Boas, Franz, *The Mind of Primitive Man*, New York, 1938. An irreplaceable study of men still organized in primitive social groups.

*Braidwood, Robert, J., *Prehistoric Men*, Chicago, 1963. An excellent survey of the evidence illustrating human evolution and development.

Breuil, H., *Four Hundred Centuries of Cave Art*, London, 1952. Detailed exposition and analysis by a scholar familiar with his subject. Well illustrated.

Clark, J. D., *The Prehistory of Southern Africa*, London, 1959.

Clark, W. E. Le Gros, *History of the Primates*, London, 1958. A study of the relationships among the great apes and their likenesses and differences as compared to human beings.

*Cole, Sonia, *The Prehistory of East Africa*, Harmondsworth, England, 1954. Not so detailed as other works on the subject but a good summary and readily available.

Coon, C. S., *The Races of Europe*, New York, 1939. An old book but still valid for study of early men on the European continent.

Daly, R. A., *The Changing World of the Ice Age*, New Haven, Conn., 1934. This book makes real to the reader the variations in climate, fauna, and flora during the ice age.

Daniel, G., *The Megalithic Builders of Western Europe*, London, 1958. A fascinating study of the cultures that built huge stone monuments from Sicily to Scandinavia. The ruins in Brittany and at Stonehenge are related to others less well known.

Gardiner, Sir Alan, *The Theory of Speech and Language*, New York, 1951. An interesting study (though not necessarily final) of the problem of sounds and their realization as languages.

Garrod, Dorothea A. E., *Environment, Tools and Man*, New York, 1946. A general but interesting book on the lives and cultures of early man.

———, "Relations Between Southwest Asia and Europe in the Later Palaeolithic Age," *Journal of World History* I (Paris, 1953), p. 13.

———, and Bate, D. M., *The Stone Age of Mount Carmel* I, New York, 1937. A record of one of the most important archaeological discoveries bearing upon the relationship between Neanderthal and modern men.

*Hawkes, Christopher, and Hawkes, Jacquetta, *Prehistoric Britain*, Harmondsworth, England, 1952.

Hawkes, Jacquetta, and Woolley, Sir Leonard, *Prehistory and the Beginnings of Civilization*, New York, 1963. Available also in a paperback edition in two volumes. A monumental undertaking of international scholarship. It is conservative in approach and, as one can discover from the notes, controversial in some of its interpretation.

Hawkins, Gerald S., *Stonehenge Decoded*, Garden City, N.Y., 1965. The author develops his idea that Stonehenge was a giant "computer." Few archaeologists and historians of science will agree with all his conclusions.

James, E. O., *Prehistoric Religion*, London, 1957. A good survey of the little that is known about the subject. The deductions are sane and logical.

Laming, A., *The Lascaux Cave Paintings*, London, 1949.

Leakey, L. S. B., *Adam's Ancestors*, London, 1953. An interesting account of the author's discoveries. Detailed but not overburdened with minutiae.

*Lowie, R. H., *Primitive Society*, New York, 1961. A good study and readily available.

McCown, T. D., and Keith, Sir Arthur, *The Stone Age of Mount Carmel* II, New York, 1939. A study of the physical remains and other evidence described in the first volume (see Garrod, Dorothea A. E.).

Mellaert, James, "Roots in the Soil" in Stuart Piggott (ed.), *Dawn of Civilization*, London, 1961. A short interesting study of early farmers and farming.

Movius, H. A. L., "Palaeolithic Archaeology in Southern and Eastern Asia," *Journal of World History* II (Paris, 1954). p. 257.

Oakley, K. P., *Man the Toolmaker*, London, 1958. There are studies of primitive tools that are more detailed but this is excellent for the beginning student. Clear exposition of a complicated subject.

Oakladnikov, A., "Le Néolithique en Siberie," *Journal of World History* VI (Paris, 1961), p. 476. One of the few publications on Siberia available in a language other than Russian.

"Radio-Carbon Supplement," *American Journal of Science* (1961). This extremely useful volume covers all aspects of the methodology, problems, and achievements of radio-carbon dating up to the date of publication.

Warmington, H., *Ancient Man in North America*, Denver, Colo., 1957. Describes most of the ancient cultures of North America, but not in great detail.

Zeuner, F. E., *The Pleistocene Period, Its Climate, Chronology and Faunal Succession*, London, 1959. A detailed, scientific study.

THE ANCIENT MIDDLE EAST: GENERAL WORKS

*Albright, William Foxwell, *From the Stone Age to Christianity*, New York, 1957. A general though fairly detailed account of developments in the middle east by an outstanding American archaeologist. The author possesses wide knowledge but his interest centers on Palestine.

Braidwood, Robert J., *The Near East and the Foundations of Civilization*, Eugene, Ore., 1952. An account of discoveries made by the author and by others in the hill country of northern Mesopotamia. Concerned chiefly with the most ancient herding and farming communities.

The Cambridge Ancient History (12 vols.), London, 1923–1939. Invaluable for its bibliography and notes as well as detailed history. A new edition of volumes I and II is in preparation; sections of these volumes are being published in fascicles and are available in paper covers from Cambridge University Press, New York.

Clark, Grahame, *Archaeology and Society*, London, 1939.

———, "Horses and Battle-axes," *Antiquity* 15 (1941), pp. 50–70. An interesting article on the art of war as practiced by ancient peoples.

Chardin, Pierre Teilhard de, *The Phenomenon of Man*, New York, 1959. Sparkling with ideas and theories concerning the continuing evolution of man — and especially of the human mind.

*Childe, V. Gordon, *New Light on the Most Ancient East*, London, 1934. Not all of the author's ideas and theories are now accepted, but this book is still immensely useful as an inquiry into the origins of civilization.

*———, *What Happened in History*, Baltimore, 1964. Valuable for the mass of archaeological evidence presented.

Driver, G. R., *Semitic Writing from Pictograph to Alphabet*, London, 1954. Well illustrated and easy to follow.

*Frankfort, Henri, *et al.*, *Before Philosophy*, Baltimore, 1964. This group of essays was originally published as *The Intellectual Adventure of Ancient Man* (Chicago, 1946). It was designed to provoke thought and succeeds in doing so.

———, *Kingship and the Gods*, Chicago, 1948. A brilliant study of ancient ideas of kingship, their origin and relation to religion.

*Frazer, Sir James G., *The New Golden Bough*, edited and annotated by Theodore H. Gaster, Garden City, N.Y., 1961. A welcome revision in the light of evidence available since the original work was published.

*Forbes, R. J., and Dijkterhuis, E. J., *A History of Science and Technology* I, Baltimore, 1963.

———, *Studies in Ancient Technology*, Leiden, 1955. Excellent book for the beginner who wishes to become familiar with the materials and methods used by ancient peoples.

Gadd, C. J., *Ideas of Divine Rule in the Ancient East*, London, 1948.

*Gaster, Theodore, *The Oldest Stories Ever Told*, Boston, 1958. The title is misleading as no Sumerian or very early Egyptian stories are included. However, the Hittite and Syrian stories are delightful.

*———, *Thespis — Ritual, Myth, and Drama in the Ancient Near East*, Garden City, N.Y., 1961.

Heichelheim, F. M., *An Ancient Economic History from the Palaeolithic Age to* the *Migrations of the Germanic, Slavic, and Arabic Nations*, trans. by J. Stevens, Leiden, 1958.

*Hooke, S. H., *Middle Eastern Mythology*, Baltimore, 1963.

Kantor, Helene J., *The Aegean and the Orient in the Second Millennium B.C.*, Bloomington, Ind., 1947. A careful and useful correlation of the relationships among different peoples in this period.

*Kramer, Samuel Noah, *Mythologies of the Ancient World*, Garden City, N.Y., 1961.

Mendelsohn, Isaac, *Slavery in the Ancient Near East*, New York, 1949.

*Moscati, S., *Ancient Semitic Civilization*, New York, 1960. A very general survey.

*Mongait, A. L., *Archaeology in the U.S.S.R.*, Baltimore, 1961. Difficult to use as the organization is based on geography rather than chronology or topic. Thus one jumps from Siberia in the Middle Ages to Armenia in the Neolithic period. One of the few works on Russian explorations available in English.

Neugebauer, O., *The Exact Sciences in Antiquity*, Providence, R.I., 1957. A detailed study of the evidence and easy to read.

*Lloyd, Seton, *The Art of the Ancient Near East*, New York, 1963. One of the most beautiful books of its kind. The magnificent photographs are located historically by the accompanying text.

Sigerist, Henry E., *History of Medicine* I, New York, 1951. One of the better histories of medicine, though it may not do complete justice in every area.

Ullman, Berthold Louis, *Ancient Writing and Its Influence*, London, 1932. A useful and charming small book illustrating the development of writing.

Chapter 2. MESOPOTAMIA: THE LAND OF THE
TWO RIVERS

Agrawal, D. P., "Harappa Culture: New Evidence for a Shorter Chronology" in *Science* 143 (February, 1964) pp. 950–951.

*Chiera, Edward, *They Wrote on Clay*, Chicago, 1957.

Finegan, Jack, *Light from the Ancient Past*, Princeton, N.J., 1946.

Gadd, C. J., *Teachers and Students in the Oldest Schools*, London, 1956. An intriguing reconstruction based on original sources.

Hammurabi, *Code of Hammurabi*, trans. by C. H. W. Johns, Edinburgh, 1903. A standard translation of the code which is readily available.

*Heidel, Alexander, *The Babylonian Genesis*, Chicago, 1963. Significant account of early Mesopotamian civilization.

Jacobsen, Thorkild, *The Sumerian Kinglist*, Chicago, 1939. One of the most valuable original sources for Sumerian history.

Kramer, Samuel Noah, "Dilmun: Quest for Paradise," *Antiquity* 37 (1963), p. 111. An important article illuminating Sumerian trade.

*———, *History Begins at Sumer*, New York, 1959. A series of essays on Sumerian institutions and customs.

———, *The Sumerians*, Chicago, 1963. The only full-length history of the Sumerians.

*———, *Sumerian Mythology*, New York, 1961.

Luckenbill, D. C., *Ancient Records of Assyria and Babylonia* (2 vols.), Chicago, 1926–1927. A valuable collection of original sources.

Mallowan, M. E. L., "The Excavations at Nimrud (Kalhu) 1953," *Iraq* (1954) part 1, p. 59.

Marshall, Sir John H., *et al.*, *Mohenjo-daro and the Indus Civilization* (3 vols.), London, 1931. Excavation reports.

New Oxford History of Music, vol. I, *Ancient and Oriental Music*, New York, 1957.

Oppenheim, A. Leo., *Ancient Mesopotamia: Portrait of a Dead Civilization*, Chicago, 1964. Good recent general history of the area.

———, "The Seafaring Merchants of Ur," *Journal of the American Oriental Society* 74, 1 (Jan.–March 1954), pp. 6–17. An important article illuminating trading methods and relationships.

*Piggott, Stuart, *Prehistoric India*, Harmondsworth, England, 1950. General summary of the excavations and history of the Harappa culture.

Sachs, Curt, *The Rise of Music in the Ancient World, East and West*, New York, 1944. An important study of early music, musical instruments, and musicians.

Wheeler, R. E. M., *Five Thousand Years of Pakistan; an Archaeological Outline*, London, 1950. A valuable historical summary.

Woolley, Sir Leonard, *Excavations at Ur; A Record of Twelve Years' Work*. These excavation reports contain the essential facts from which a history of Ur is to be constructed.

Chapter 3. EGYPT: THE TWO LANDS

Aldred, Cyril, *The Development of Ancient Egyptian Art*, London, 1962.

Breasted, James Henry, *Ancient Records of Egypt* I–V, Chicago, 1906. Still the best place for students to find original sources translated into English. Texts discovered after 1905 are of course not included.

———, *The Development of Religion and Thought in Ancient Egypt*, New York, 1959. The interpretation is interesting though not every Egyptologist or historian will agree with it.

Drioton, Etienne, and Vandier, J., *L'Égypte*, Clio Series, Paris, 1952. Includes an excellent bibliography with works in all languages up to 1949.

*Edwards, I. E. S., *The Pyramids of Egypt*, Baltimore, 1964. A good survey.

*Emery, W. B., *Archaic Egypt*, Baltimore, 1963. Immensely valuable summary of excavations of early dynastic sites.

Erman, Adolf, *The Literature of the Ancient Egyptians*, trans. by Aylward M. Blackman, London, 1927.

*Frankfort, Henri, *Ancient Egyptian Religion*, New York, 1961. Probably the best and most readable book on the subject in English.

*Gardiner, Sir Alan H., *Egypt of the Pharaohs*, New York, 1961. The most recent history of Egypt by one of the greatest Egyptologists. Largely factual with little interpretation.

———, *Egyptian Grammar*, New York, 1957. The Egyptian-English text for the student of hieroglyphics. Also valuable for historical *excursi*.

Lucas, A., *Egyptian Materials and Industries*, London, 1934. Old but still valuable study of technology.

Parker, Richard A., *The Calendars of Ancient Egypt*, Chicago, 1950. Sheds new light on the difficult problem of Egypt's different calendrical systems.

*Smith, W. Stevenson, *A History of Egyptian Sculpture and Painting in the Old Kingdom*, New York, 1946. Valuable survey and well illustrated.

Reisner, G. G., *The Development of the Egyptian Tomb down to the Accession of Cheops*, Cambridge, Mass., 1936. Excellent illustrated study. The author disagrees in some of his ideas with I. E. S. Edwards.

Vandier, J., *La Religion Égyptienne*, Paris, 1944. One of the best studies on Egyptian religion.

*Wilson, John A., *The Culture of Ancient Egypt*, Chicago, 1963. Particularly important for ideas and interpretation, some of which are controversial.

Winlock, H. E., *The Rise and Fall of the Middle Kingdom in Thebes*, New York, 1947. A detailed study by one of the principal archaeologists specializing in this period.

Chapter 4. THE FERTILE CRESCENT AND THE PEOPLES OF THE SEA

Syria and Palestine

*Albright, W. F., *The Archaeology of Palestine*, Baltimore, 1963. A very important summary.

Contenau, G., *La Civilisation des Hittites et des Hurrites du Mitanni*, Paris, 1948. A history based on French archaeological studies.

Driver, G. R., *Canaanite Myths and Legends*, Edinburgh, 1956. Valuable study of little known material of early Syrian peoples.

Gray, John, *The Canaanites*, New York, 1964. Readable account based on recent work in Syria and Palestine.

Greenberg, Moshe, *The Hab/piru—The American Oriental Series* XXIX, New Haven, Conn., 1955. Detailed and exhaustive study of the evidence with logical conclusions.

*Kenyon, Kathleen, *Archaeology in the Holy Land*, New York, 1960. A handsome, informative, and well illustrated account.

———, *Digging up Jericho*, London, 1957. A summary of archaeological investigations.

Kupper, J. R., *Archives Royales de Mari* (6 vols.), Paris, 1954. The records of Mari with a French translation.

Mallowan, M. E. L., and Rose, J. C., *Prehistoric Assyria*, New York, 1935. A useful summary of excavation results.

Olmstead, A. J., *History of Assyria*, New York, 1923. Old but still important for ideas and interpretation.

Özgüç, Tahsin, "An Assyrian Trading Outpost," *Scientific American* 208, no. 2 (Feb. 1963), p. 97. Readable account of early Assyrian trade, trade routes, and business practices.

Anatolia

Akurgal, Ekren, *Art of the Hittites*, New York, 1962. Excellent illustrations and good explanation.

Bittel, Karl, *Die Ruinen von Bogasköy*, Berlin, 1937. A good summary of archaeological discoveries.

Blegen, C. W., *Troy and the Trojans*, London, 1963. Interesting account based on Blegen's own excavations at Troy.

——, *Troy: excavations* (4 vols.), Princeton, N.J., 1950, 58. Official excavation reports.

Dussaud, R., *Prélydiens, Hittites et Achéens*, Paris, 1953. Important study of the relationships among peoples in Anatolia in the second millennium B.C.

*Gurney, O. R., *The Hittites*, Baltimore, 1962. A general historical account.

*Lloyd, Seton, *Early Anatolia*, Baltimore, 1956. A companion book to Gurney, *The Hittites*. Together the books provide an excellent survey of ancient Anatolian development.

Mellaert, James, "A Neolithic City in Turkey," *Scientific American*, 210 (April 1964), p. 94. Important article on the early farming societies of Anatolia.

——, "The end of the Early Bronze Age in Anatolia and the Aegean," *American Journal of Archaeology* 62 (1958), p. 1.

Vieyra, M., *Hittite Art, 2300–750 B.C.*, London, 1955.

Crete

Evans, Sir Arthur J., *The Palace of Minos at Knossos* (5 vols.), London, 1921–1936. Beautiful account of the excavations.

Gordon, Cyrus H., "The Decipherment of Minoan," *Natural History* 72, 9 (Nov. 1963), p. 22. An attempt to decipher Linear A that is not widely accepted.

*Hutchinson, R. W., *Prehistoric Crete*, Baltimore, 1963. A summary of excavations.

Pendlebury, J. D. S., *A Handbook to the Palace of Minos*, London, 1954. Short, extremely useful guide with good plans of the palace.

——, *The Palace of Knossos*, London, 1935. A summary of the discoveries at Knossos. Easily used and provides clues to the use of Evans' fine volumes (see above).

Greece

*Chadwick, J., *The Decipherment of Linear B*, Baltimore, 1961. An account of the work of Ventris and Chadwick on Linear B. Texts are illustrated and translated.

Dow, Sterling, "The Greeks in the Bronze Age," *Rapports II*, XIe Congrès International des Sciences Historiques, Stockholm, UNESCO, 1960. An important study of the interrelationship between Minoan Crete and the Mycenaeans of Greece.

Kohler, Ellen L., and Ralph, Elizabeth K., "C 14 Dates for Sites in the Mediterranean Area," *American Journal of Archaeology* 65 (1961), p. 357.

Ventris, M., and Chadwick, J., *Documents in Mycenaean Greek; Three Hundred Selected Tablets from Knossos, Pylos and Mycenae*, New York, 1956.

Wace, A. J. B., *Mycenae; An Archaeological History and Guide*, Princeton, N.J., 1949. An important revision of earlier ideas and interpretations of the archaeological evidence from Mycenae.

Webster, T. B. L., "Mycenaean Records, A Review," *Antiquity* 31 (1957) p. 4.

Chapter 5. THE EGYPTIAN EMPIRE (See also Chapter 3)

Černy, J., *Ancient Egyptian Religion*, London, 1952. The most recent study in English on the subject.

Fairman, H. W., "Town-Planning in Pharaonic Egypt," *Town Planning Review* 20 (1949), p. 33. Based chiefly on Tell el 'Amarna excavations.

Faulkner, R. O., "The Installation of the Vizier," *Journal of Egyptian Archaeology* 41 (1955), p. 18. An examination of the texts, especially those concerned with Rekhmire.

Fox, P., *Tutankhamun's Treasure*, New York, 1956. A general and readable account with fair illustrations.

Gardiner, Sir Alan H., *The Kadesh Inscriptions of Ramesses II*, New York, 1960. Text, translations, and commentary.

Kees, Hermann, *Der Götterglaube im alten Aegypten*, Leipzig, 1941. A study in depth of Egyptian myth and religious belief.

Mace, A. C., *Egyptian Literature*, New York, 1928. Selections from Egyptian literature.

Mercer, S. A. B., *The Tell-el-Amarna Tablets* (2 vols.), Toronto, 1939. The most recent translations of the texts.

Pendlebury, J. D. S. *et al.*, "City of Akhenaton," in *Memoirs* of the Egypt Exploration Society (2 vols.), Series 44, New York, 1951. Excavation report.

———, *Tell-el-Amarna*, London, 1935. A readable account based on the excavation of Akhetaton.

Pirenne, Jacques, and Van der Walle, Baudouin, *Histoire des Institutions et du Droit Privé de L'Ancienne Egypte* (3 vols.), Brussels, 1932–1935. Texts with French translation.

Sauneron, *Les Prêtres de l'Egypte Ancienne*, Bourges, France, 1957. A definitive study of Egyptian priesthoods.

Steindorff, Georg, and Seele, Keith C., *When Egypt Ruled the East*, Chicago, 1947. Beautifully illustrated and highly interpretive.

Wilson, John A., "The Texts of the Battle of Qadesh," *American Journal of Semitic Languages*, 43 (1927), p. 266.

Chapter 6. THE CONFLICT OF EMPIRES
(See also Chapter 4)

*Albright, W. F., *The Biblical Period from Abraham to Ezra*, New York, 1963. A thoroughly documented study.

Brewer, Julius August, *The Literature of the Old Testament*, (3d ed.), completely revised by Emil G. Kraeling, New York, 1962.

Bright, John, *A History of Israel*, Philadelphia, 1959. Regarded as one of the best recent histories of Israel.

Cameron, George Glenn, *History of Early Iran*, Chicago, 1936. Detailed account of the pre-Persian and early Persian periods.

Driver, Godfrey Rolles, and Miles, John C. (eds.), *The Assyrian Laws*, New York, 1935. Texts, translation, and commentaries.

———, and Miles, John C., *The Babylonian Laws*, New York, 1952. Texts, translation, and commentary.

Frye, R. N., *The Heritage of Persia*, Cleveland, 1963.

*Gray, J., *Archaeology and the Old Testament*, New York, 1965. Incorporates recent excavation reports.

Gyles, Mary Francis, *Pharaonic Policies and Administration, 663 to 323 B.C.*, Chapel Hill, N.C., 1959. The only work in English covering the subject.

Harden, O., *The Phoenecians*, New York, 1962. One of the few works on the subject available in English.

Herzfeld, Ernst Emil, *Archaeological History of Iran*, London, 1935. Interpretation based largely on archaeology.

Heschel, A. J., *The Prophets*, New York, 1962.

Macalister, Robert Alexander Herbert, *The Philistines; Their History and Civilization*, London, 1913. The only general work on the subject available in English.

Meek, Theophile James, *Hebrew Origins*, New York and London, 1936. A scholarly and highly useful study.

Meulenaere, Herman de, *Herodotos over de 26ste Dynasties (II.147–III.15)*, Louvain, 1951. A critical study in Dutch of the second book of Herodotus in the light of middle eastern sources.

*Olmstead, Albert Ten Eyck, *History of the Persian Empire* (Achaemenid Period), Chicago, 1959. The most recent and extensive history of Persia. Originally published in 1948.

*Orlinsky, Harry, *Ancient Israel*, Ithaca, N.Y., 1964. An interpretive general history.

Pritchard, J. B. (ed.), *Ancient Near Eastern Texts Relating to the Old Testament*, Princeton, N.J., 1955.

Ross, Sir Edward Denison, *The Persians*, New York, 1931. A readable history but not exhaustive in scope.

Smith, John Merlin Powis, *The Origin and History of Hebrew Law*, Chicago, 1960.

Waterman, Leroy (ed. and trans.), *Royal Correspondence of the Assyrian Empire* (4 vols.), Ann Arbor, Mich., 1930–36. Commentary, texts, and translation.

Wiseman, D. J., *Chronicles of Chaldaean Kings (626–556)*, London, 1956. Commentary, texts, and translation.

Wright, G. Ernest, and Freedman, David Noel (eds.), *The Biblical Archaeological Reader*, Garden City, N.Y., 1961. A useful group of essays covering all periods and many subjects related to the history of Palestine.

*Wright, G. Ernest, *Biblical Archaeology*, Philadelphia, 1960.

Chapter 7. THE RISE OF THE HELLENES

Sources   Homer: *Iliad* and *Odyssey*
                   Homeric Hymns

Blegen, Carl W., *The Mycenaean Age*, Cincinnati, 1962. Important discussion of the problems of dating the Trojan War, the Dorian invasions, the fall of Pylos, and the Fall of Mycenae.

Chadwick, Hector Munro, *The Heroic Age*, New York, 1912.

*Finley, M. I., *The World of Odysseus*, New York, 1965.

Fontenrose, J., *Python: A Study of the Delphic Oracle and Its Origin*, Berkeley, Calif., 1959.

*Forsdyke, John, *Greece Before Homer*, New York, 1964.

Glotz, Gustave, *The Greek City*, New York, 1930. An old book but still valuable for its study of the *polis*.

Huxley, G. L., *Early Sparta*, Cambridge, Mass., 1962. One of the most significant works on the subject. Sparta's evolution becomes normal and comprehensible.

Lang, Andrew, *The World of Homer*, London and New York, 1910.

Leaf, Walter, *Homer and History*, London, 1915.

*Murray, Gilbert, *The Rise of the Greek Epic*, New York, 1960.

Nilsson, Martin D., *Homer and Mycenae*, London, 1933. Valuable for discussion of the historical place of the Homeric poems and their value to history.

*———, *The Mycenaean Origin of Greek Mythology*, New York, 1963.

*Otto, Walter F., *The Homeric Gods*, Boston, 1964.

*Page, Denys, *History and the Homeric Iliad*, Berkeley, Calif., 1963.

Persson, A., *Religion of Greece in Prehistoric Times*, Berkeley, Calif., 1942. Conclusions in this work must be modified in the light of information given by Linear B texts but it is still a useful work for the beginner.

Scott, John Adams, *Homer and His Influence*, New York, 1963.

*———, *The Unity of Homer*, Berkeley, Calif., 1921.

Starr, Chester G., *The Origins of Greek Civilization 1100–650 B.C.*, New York, 1961.

Weinberg, Saul, "The Relative Chronology of the Aegean" in R. W. Ehrich (ed.), *Relative Chronologies in Old World Archaeology*, Chicago, 1954.

GREEK HISTORY AND CULTURE

General Works

Botsford, George Willis, and Robinson, Charles Alexander, *Hellenic History*, New York, 1957. One of the best general histories.

*Brown, Truesdell S. (ed.), *Ancient Greece*, New York, 1965.

Bury, John Bagnell, *A History of Greece to the Death of Alexander the Great* (3d ed.), rev. by Russell Meigs, London and New York, 1959. A good revision of a standard work.

*———, *The Ancient Greek Historians*, New York, 1958.

Cary, M., *A History of the Greek World 323–146 B.C.*, London, 1959. Very detailed and useful history.

Cohen, Robert, *La Grèce et l'Héllenisation du Monde Antique*, Clio Series, Paris, 1939. Excellent bibliography, with works in all languages, and notes.

*Finley, M. I., *The Ancient Greeks*, New York, 1964. General history. Well written and interesting for the beginning student.

Hale, William Harlan, *Ancient Greece*, New York, 1965. A beautiful book with striking photographs. Highly interpretive.

*Kitto, H. D. F., *The Greeks*, Baltimore, 1962.

Laistner, M. L. W., *A History of the Greek World from 479 to 323 B.C.*, New York, 1957. Especial emphasis on cultural life and achievement.

*Toynbee, Arnold J., *Greek Historical Thought from Homer to the Age of Heraclitus*, New York, 1964.

Source Collections

Bakewell, Charles Montague, *Source Book in Ancient Philosophy*, New York, 1939.

Botsford, George Willis, and Sihler, Ernest Gottlieb, *Hellenic Civilization*, New York, 1929. An old but very useful collection of translations from various Greek writers.

Cary, Max, *The Documentary Sources of Greek History*, New York, 1927.

*Finley, M. I. (ed.), *The Portable Greek Historians: The Essence of Herodotus, Thucydides, Xenophon, Polybius*, New York, 1959. Well selected readings. Serves as a useful introduction to these historians.

Godolphin, F. R. B. (ed.), *The Greek Historians* (2 vols.), New York, 1942.

Gomperz, Theodor, *Greek Thinkers* (4 vols.). Vols. 1–3 trans. by Laurie Magnus, (vol. 4 by G. G. Berry). London, 1901–1912.

Harsh, Philip Whaley, *A Handbook of Classical Drama*, Stanford, Calif., 1944.

Howe, George, Harrer, Gustave A., and Epps, Preston Herschel, *Greek Literature in Translation*, New York, 1948.

*Kagan, Donald (ed.), *Sources in Greek Political Thought from Homer to Polybius*, New York, 1965. The readings are well chosen and of great interest to the beginning student.

Tod, Marcus N. (ed.), *A Selection of Greek Historical Inscriptions* (2 vols.), New York, 1948. One of the best group of inscriptions available in English translation.

Political, Economic, Social, and Judicial Institutions

Adcock, Sir Frank Ezra, *The Greek and Macedonian Art of War*, Berkeley, Calif., 1957.

Agard, Walter Raymond, *What Democracy Meant to the Greeks*, Chapel Hill, N.C., 1942.

Andreadēs, Andreas Michaēl, *A History of Greek Public Finance*, revised edition, trans. by Carroll Neide Brown, Cambridge, Mass., 1933. Vol. I only.

Balogh, Elmer, *Political Refugees in Ancient Greece from the Period of the Tyrants to Alexander the Great*, with the collaboration of F. M. Heichelheim, Johannesburg, 1943.

Barker, Ernest, *Greek Political Theory*, London, 1960.

Bonner, Robert Johnson, and Smith, Gertrude, *The Administration of Justice from Homer to Aristotle* (2 vols.), Chicago, 1930–1938.

Calhoun, George Miller, *The Ancient Greeks and the Evolution of Standards in Business*, Boston and New York, 1926.

———, *The Growth of Criminal Law in Ancient Greece*, Berkeley, Calif., 1927.

*Fustel de Coulanges, Numa Denis, *The Ancient City*, Garden City, N.Y., 1956. An exhaustive study of the ancient city state from the literary sources. This book, originally published in 1894, has become a classic.

Gittler, Joseph Bertram, *Social Thought Among the Early Greeks*, Athens, Ga., 1941.

Glotz, Gustave, *Ancient Greece at Work*, New York, 1926. Useful in its account of the technological achievement of the Greeks.

———, *The Greek City and Its Institutions*, trans. by N. Mallinson, New York, 1930.

Michell, Humfrey, *The Economics of Ancient Greece*, New York, 1957. A general work that is useful as an introduction to the subject. Some confusion is possible in trying to distinguish the changes from one period to another.

Seltman, Charles Theodore, *Greek Coins: A History of Metallic Currency and Coinage Down to the Fall of the Hellenistic Kingdoms*, London, 1960.

Tod, Marcus Niebuhr, *International Arbitration Among the Greeks*, New York, 1913. One of the few studies available on this topic.

Vinogradov, Sir Pavel G., *Outlines of Historical Jurisprudence* (2 vols.), London, 1923. An important study of legal institutions and their evolution.

Zimmern, Alfred, *The Greek Commonwealth*, New York, 1961. A classic study of the organization of the city-state. Sources are drawn largely from Athens.

Religion and Mythology

Cornford, Francis Macdonald, *Greek Religious Thought from Homer to the Age of Alexander*, London, 1923.

Farnell, L. R., *Greek Hero Cults and Ideas of Immortality*, New York, 1921.

*Festugiere, A. J., *Personal Religion Among the Greeks*, Berkeley, Calif., 1960.

Gardiner, Edward N., *Athletics of the Ancient World*, New York, 1930. The Greek games were held to celebrate religious festivals, but, as this study makes clear, athletics were taken very seriously.

*Graves, Robert, *The Greek Myth* (2 vols.), Baltimore, 1961.

Guthrie, W. K. C., *Orpheus and Greek Religion*, London, 1952.

*———, *The Greeks and Their Gods*, Boston, 1962.

Hadas, Moses, and Smith, M., *Heroes and Gods*, New York, 1965.

*Hamilton, Edith, *Mythology*, New York, 1963.

*Harrison, Jane, *Themis: A Study of the Social Origins of Greek Religion*, New York, 1962.

*Murray, Gilbert, *Five Stages of Greek Religion*, Garden City, N.Y., 1951.

Mylonas, George E., *Eleusis and Eleusinian Mysteries*, Princeton, N.J., 1961.

Nilsson, Nils Martin Persson, *A History of Greek Religion*, trans. by F. J. Fielden, New York, 1949.

———, *Cults, Myths, Oracles, and Politics in Ancient Greece*, Copenhagen, 1951.

*———, *Greek Folk Religion*, New York, 1961.

*Oliver, J. H., *Demokratia, the Gods and the Free World*, Baltimore, 1960.

Science and Philosophy

Bailey, Cyril, *The Greek Atomists and Epicurus*, New York, 1964.

Casson, Lionel, *The Ancient Mariners*, New York, 1959. Interesting study of ships, shippers, and methods of navigation.

*Dodds, E. R., *The Greeks and the Irrational*, Berkeley, Calif., 1963.

*Farrington, Benjamin, *Greek Science* (2 vols.), Harmondsworth, England, 1949. Valuable for details of little known Greek scientists and thinkers.

*Guthrie, W. K. C., *The Greek Philosophers from Thales to Aristotle*, New York, 1960. Excellent summary of what is known of the lives and works of the Greek philosophers.

Singer, Charles Joseph, *Greek Biology and Greek Medicine*, New York, 1922.

*Snell, Bruno, *Discovery of the Mind; the Greek Origins of European Thought*,

New York, 1960. Useful for the student interested in the history of philosophy.

Warmington, Eric H., *Greek Geography*, London, 1934. An account of the explorations and geographical knowledge of the Greeks.

Zeller, Eduard, *Outlines of the History of Greek Philosophy* (13th ed.), rev. by Wilhelm Nestle and trans. by L. R. Palmer, New York, 1960. A good revision of one of the best short histories of Greek philosophy.

Literature and the Arts

Allen, James T., *Stage Antiquities of the Greeks and Romans*, New York, 1963.

*Ashmole, Bernard, *The Classical Ideal in Greek Sculpture*, lectures in memory of Louise Taft Semple, Cincinnati, 1964. Important essays on the aims and purposes of the Greek sculptor.

Beiber, M., *History of the Greek and Roman Theater*, Princeton, N.J., 1961. One of the best books covering the means and methods of dramatic production in the ancient theater.

*Boardman, John, *Greek Art*, New York, 1964. A beautifully illustrated book.

Bowra, Sir Cecil Maurice, *Ancient Greek Literature*, New York, 1960. A general historical survey.

*Devanbez, Pierre, *Greek Painting*, New York, 1962. Beautiful illustrations but very brief narrative.

Hadas, Moses (ed.), *Greek Poets*, New York, n.d.

———, *History of Greek Literature*, New York, 1950.

*Kitto, H. D. F., *Form and Meaning in Drama*, New York, 1960.

*———, *Greek Tragedy*, Garden City, N.Y., 1954.

Lawrence, Arnold Walker, *Classical Sculpture*, London, 1944.

*———, *Greek Architecture*, Baltimore, 1957. Historical approach to the development of Greek architecture.

Murray, Gilbert, *The Literature of Ancient Greece*, Chicago, 1956.

Norwood, G., *Greek Tragedy*, London, 1948.

Richter, Gisela M. A., *A Handbook of Greek Art*, London, 1960. An extremely valuable account and well illustrated.

———, *The Sculpture and Sculptors of the Greeks*, New Haven, Conn., 1957. One of the best recent studies on the subject.

Books of Interpretation

*Agard, W. R., *The Greek Mind*, Princeton, N.J., 1957.

*Bowra, C. M., *The Greek Experience*, New York, 1963.

Cary, Max, and Haarhoff, T. J., *Life and Thought in the Greek and Roman World*, London, 1957.

*Dickinson, G. L., *The Greek View of Life*, New York, 1965.

Ehrenberg, Victor, *Aspects of the Ancient World*, New York, 1946.

Gomme, Arnold Wycombe, *Essays in Greek History and Literature*, New York, 1937.

———, *More Essays in Greek History and Literature*, edited by David A. Campbell, New York, 1962.

Hamilton, Edith, *The Greek Way*, New York, 1964.

Jaeger, Werner Wilhelm, *Paideia: The Ideals of Greek Culture* (3 vols.), trans. by Gilbert Highet, New York, 1960–1962.

Murray, Gilbert, *Greek Studies*, New York, 1946.

*Robinson, C. E., *Hellas*, Boston, 1962.

*Smith, Morton, *The Ancient Greeks*, Ithaca, N.Y., 1960.

Tod, Marcus Niebuhr, *Sidelights on Greek History*, New York, 1932.

Whibley, Leonard, *A Companion to Greek Studies*, New York, 1931.

Chapters 8 to 11.   GREECE BEFORE THE FIFTH CENTURY

Sources   Aeschylus: *Persians* and *Oresteia* (trilogy)
Herodotus: *History of the Persian Wars*
Hesiod: *Theogony* and *Works and Days*
Lyra Graeca (3 vols.), edited by J. M. Edmonds, Loeb Classical Library,
Cambridge, Mass., 1922–1928.
Plutarch: Lives of Aristides, Lycurgus, Solon, Themistocles, and
Theseus
Xenophon: *Constitution of the Lacadaemonians*

Bowra, Sir Cecil Maurice, *Greek Lyric Poetry from Alcman to Simonides*, New York, 1961.

Burn, Andrew Robert, *The World of Hesiod: A Study of the Greek Middle Ages, c. 900–700 B.C.*, Ann Arbor, Mich., 1962. A study of Hesiod in relation to archaeological evidence.

Burnet, John, *Early Greek Philosophy*, London, 1958.

Cary, Max, and Warmington, E. H., *The Ancient Explorers*, Baltimore, 1963. Intensely interesting account of geographical exploration among ancient peoples.

Casson, Stanley, *The Technique of Early Greek Sculpture*, New York, 1933.

Dunbabin, T. J., *The Western Greeks*, New York, 1948. Significant study of the colonies in the western Mediterranean.

Ehrenberg, Victor, *The Greek State*, New York, 1960. An analysis of the evolution and nature of the *polis*.

Freeman, Kathleen, *Greek City-States*, New York, 1963.

————, *The Work and Life of Solon*, with a translation of his poems, Cardiff, 1926.

Grundy, George Beardoe, *The Great Persian War and Its Preliminaries*, London, 1901. The only detailed study of the subject. Out of print and difficult to obtain.

McDonald, William Andrew, *Political Meeting Places of the Greeks*, Baltimore, 1943.

Michell, Humfrey, *Sparta*, New York, 1964. Most useful for Sparta in the fifth and fourth centuries B.C.

Randall-MacIver, David, *Greek Cities in Italy and Sicily*, New York, 1931. An important study in an area for which there are few available works.

Richter, Gisela M. A., *Attic Red-figured Vases. A Survey*, New Haven, Conn., 1946.

Seltman, Charles T., *Athens, Its History and Coinage Before the Persian Invasion*, New York, 1924.

Ure, Percy Neville, *The Greek Renaissance*, London, 1921.

——, *The Origin of Tyranny*, New York, 1962. Study in depth of the forces and events behind the rise of tyranny.

Whibley, Leonard, *Greek Oligarchies, Their Character and Organization*, New York, 1896.

Chapters 12 to 14.   ATHENS, 479–404 B.C.

Sources   Aeschylus: Plays
Aristophanes: Plays
Aristotle: *Constitution of the Athenians*
Euripides: Plays
Plato: *Apology, Crito*, and other essays
Plutarch: Lives of Alcibiades, Cimon, Lysander, Nicias, and Pericles
Sophocles: Plays
Thucydides: *History of the Peloponnesian War*
The Old Oligarch: *Constitution of Athens*
Xenophon: *Memorabilia*

Athenian Studies Presented to William Scott Ferguson, Cambridge, Mass., 1940. A collection of valuable essays on various subjects in Athenian history and culture.

Bonner, Robert Johnson, *Aspects of Athenian Democracy*, Berkeley, Calif., 1933.

——, *Lawyers and Litigants in Ancient Athens*, Chicago, 1927. An unusual study based on original sources.

Calhoun, George Miller, *The Business Life of Ancient Athens*, Chicago, 1926. Valuable study from the original sources.

*Cornford, Francis M., *The Origin of Attic Comedy*, New York, 1961. An exhaustive study from the sources.

Croiset, Maurice, *Aristophanes and the Political Parties at Athens*, London, 1909.

Ehrenberg, Victor, *The People of Aristophanes*, New York, 1962. An intensely interesting book on the life and society of fifth-century Athens.

Finley, John Huston, *Thucydides*, Ann Arbor, Mich., 1963.

Gomme, Arnold Wycombe, *The Population of Athens in the Fifth and Fourth Centuries B.C.*, New York, 1933.

Grundy, George Beardoe, *Thucydides and the History of His Age* (2 vols.), New York, 1948.

Headlam-Morley, Sir James Wycliffe, *Election by Lot at Athens*, New York, 1933. Detailed study of election procedure.

Henderson, Bernard W., *The Great War Between Athens and Sparta, a Companion to the Military History of Thucydides*, London, 1927.

Jones, A. H. M., *Athenian Democracy*, New York, 1958.

*Lattimore, Richard, *The Poetry of Greek Tragedy*, Baltimore, 1958.

Norwood, Gilbert, *Greek Tragedy*, New York, 1960.

Pickerd-Cambridge, Arthur Wallace, *The Theater of Dionysus in Athens*, Toronto, 1947.

Taylor, Alfred Edward, *Socrates*, Garden City, N.Y., 1959.

Chapter 15. THE FOURTH CENTURY

Sources   Aristotle: *Nicomachean Ethics, Politics, Rhetoric,* and other works
      Orations of Aeschines, Andocides, Demosthenes, Isaeus, Isocrates,
        Lycurgus, and Lysias
      Plato: *Republic, Laws,* and essays
      Plutarch: Lives of Agesilaus, Demosthenes, Lysander and Pelopidas
      Xenophon: *Anabasis, Cyropaedia, Hellanica* and *Ways and Means*

*Barker, Sir Ernest, *The Political Thought of Plato and Aristotle*, New York, 1959. A convenient summary taken from the collected works of the two philosophers.

Bevan, Edwyn R., *Later Greek Religion*, London, 1927.

Cornford, Francis Macdonald, *Before and After Socrates*, New York, 1960.

Glover, Terrot Reaveley, *From Pericles to Philip*, London, 1919. Valuable as a clear narrative account of a puzzling period.

*Jaeger, Werner W., *Aristotle; Fundamentals of His Development*, trans. by Richard Robinson, London, 1962.

Jebb, Sir Richard C., *The Attic Orators from Antiphon to Isaeos*, New York, 1962.

Laidlaw, William Allison, *A History of Delos*, New York, 1933. Valuable study of the economic and commercial life of a thriving port.

Parke, Herbert William, *Greek Mercenary Soldiers from the Earliest Times to the Battle of Issus*, New York, 1933.

Pickard-Cambridge, Sir Arthur W., *Demosthenes and the Last Days of Greek Freedom*, New York, 1914.

Ross, Sir William D., *Aristotle*, New York, 1964. Useful introduction to the work of Aristotle.

Taylor, Alfred Edward, *Plato, the Man and His Work*, London, 1960.

Chapters 16 and 17.   THE HELLENISTIC PERIOD

Sources   Arrian: *Anabasis of Alexander*
      Euclid: *Geometry*
      Menander: Plays
      Plutarch: Lives of Agis, Alexander, Aratus, Cleomenes, Demetrius,
        Eumenes, and Philopaemon
      Select Papyri (4 vols.) edited by A. S. Hunt and C. C. Edgar, Loeb Classical Library, Cambridge, Mass., 1932–1934
      Theocritus: Poems
      Theophrastus: Complete works

Archimedes, *Works*, edited by Sir Thomas Little Heath, New York, 1953.

Bevan, Edwyn Robert, *The House of Seleucus* (2 vols.), London, 1902.

Bieber, Margaret, *Alexander the Great in Greek and Roman Art*, Chicago, 1964.

Bouché-Leclercq, Auguste, *Histoire des Séleucides (323–64 avant J.C.)*, Brussels, 1963. Detailed account with good bibliography.

Bury, John Bagnell, Barber, E. A., Bevan, Edwyn R., and Tarn, W. W., *The Hellenistic Age*, New York, 1925.

Cary, Max, *A History of the Greek World from 323 to 146 B.C.*, with new selected bibliography by V. Ehrenberg, New York, 1963. Very detailed history with well selected bibliography.

Dickins, Guy, *Hellenistic Sculpture*, New York, 1920.

Ehrenberg, Victor, *Alexander and the Greeks*, trans. by Ruth Fraenkel von Velsen, New York, 1938. Specialized study of considerable use.

Ferguson, William Scott, *Greek Imperialism*, New York, 1913.

——, *Hellenistic Athens*, London, 1911.

Forster, E. M., *Alexandria*, Garden City, N.Y., 1961. A guidebook with an excellent brief historical introduction.

Fyfe, David Theodore, *Hellenistic Architecture*, New York, 1936.

Grant, Frederick C., *Hellenistic Religions*, New York, 1953.

Griffith, Guy Thompson, *The Mercenaries of the Hellenistic World*, New York, 1935. Valuable specialized study.

Hadas, Moses, *Hellenistic Culture: Fusion and Diffusion*, New York, 1959.

Haverfield, Francis John, *Ancient Town Planning*, New York, 1913. Intensely interesting discussion of Hellenistic cities and their facilities for comfort and sanitation.

Heath, Sir Thomas Little, *Aristarchus of Samos, the Ancient Copernicus*, New York, 1959.

——, *A Manual of Greek Mathematics*, New York, 1963.

Hick, Robert Drew, *Stoic and Epicurean*, New York, 1962. Study of the two most important Hellenistic philosophies.

Jones, Arnold Hugh Martin, *The Greek City from Alexander to Justinian*, New York, 1940.

Jouquet, Pierre, *L'Imperialisme Macédonien et l'Héllenisation de l'Orient*, Paris, 1961.

Koerte, Alfred, *Hellenistic Poetry*, trans. by Jacob Hammer and Moses Hadas, New York, 1929.

McEwan, Calvin Wells, *The Oriental Origin of Hellenistic Kingship*, Chicago, 1934. Useful though not exhaustive study of the problem.

Préaux, Claire, *L'Économie Royale des Lagides*, Brussels, 1939. Detailed examination of Ptolemaic finance and economy. Excellent bibliography.

Robinson, Charles Alexander, *Alexander the Great, Conqueror and Creator of a New World*, New York, 1963. General narrative account.

Rostovtzeff, Mikhail I., *The Social and Economic History of the Hellenistic World*, (2 vols.) New York, 1959. Very detailed and exhaustive study from the original sources.

Tarn, Sir William W., *Alexander the Great*, Boston, 1956. Originally published in two volumes, this biography is based on an exhaustive, critical examination of the sources.

*——, *Hellenistic Civilisation* (3d ed.) rev. by the author and G. T. Griffith, Cleveland, 1961.

——, *Hellenistic Military and Naval Developments*, New York, 1930.

*Taylor, Henry Osborn, *Greek Biology and Medicine*, New York, 1963. Particularly useful in discussion of the Hellenistic period.

Tcherikover, Victor, *Hellenistic Civilization and the Jews*, Philadelphia, 1961. A detailed examination of the relationships between the two peoples.

Winter, John Garrett, *Life and Letters in the Papyri*, Ann Arbor, Mich., 1933. Important documentation for social history of Ptolemaic Egypt.

Chapter 18. THE RISE OF ROME

Sources   Livy: *History of Rome*, Book I
          Plutarch: Lives of Romulus, Numa Pompilius, Camillus, and Coriolanus

Bailey, Cyril, *Phases in the Religion of Ancient Rome*, Berkeley, Calif., 1932.

Bloch, Raymond, *The Etruscans*, London, 1958. Excellent study based on extensive source materials.

———, "The Etruscans," *Scientific American*, 206, no. 2 (1962), p. 83. Important article based on archaeological evidence.

———, *The Origins of Rome*, London, 1960. A study incorporating the results of excavations and field exploration.

Conway, Robert Seymour, *Etruscan Influence on Roman Religion*, Manchester, England, 1932.

Fowler, W. W., *The Religious Experience of the Roman People from the Earliest Times to the Age of Augustus*, New York, 1911.

Gilmore, H. W., "Cultural Diffusion via Salt," *American Anthropologist*, 57 (1955). A significant theory on the origin of early Rome.

Gjerstad, E., *Early Rome* (2 vols.) Lund, Sweden, 1953 and 1956. The summary of lengthy excavations.

Homo, Leon P., *Primitive Italy and the Beginnings of Roman Imperialism*, New York, 1927. Still one of the most valuable studies of early Roman development and expansion.

Mayani, Zacharie, *The Etruscans Begin to Speak*, New York, 1964. A general work. Summarizes archaeological evidence.

Pais, Ettore, *Ancient Italy*, trans. by C. Densmore Curtis, Chicago, 1908. An old work but still valuable as introductory material.

*Pallottino, Massimo, *The Etruscans*, Baltimore, 1956. Excellent account and readily available.

Powell, J. G. E., *The Celts*, London, 1958. A very readable summary of the prehistory and early history of Celtic peoples.

Randall-MacIver, David, *Italy Before the Romans*, New York, 1928.

———, *Villanovans and Early Etruscans*, New York, 1924. A valuable study of the interrelationship between these cultures.

*Richardson, Emeline, *The Etruscans: Their Art and Civilization*, Chicago, 1964. One of the best recent works. Well illustrated.

Scullard, Howard H., *A History of the Roman World from 753–146 B.C.*, London, 1961. More detailed than a general history.

ROMAN HISTORY AND CULTURE

General Works

Arnold, William T., *Studies in Roman Imperialism*, Manchester, England, 1906. A valuable specialized study.

*Barrow, R. H., *The Romans*, Baltimore, 1965. General and somewhat abbreviated.

Boak, Arthur E. R., and Sinnigen, William G., *A History of Rome to A.D. 565*, New York, 1965. One of the best one-volume texts.

Cary, Max, *A History of Rome Down to the Reign of Constantine*, New York, 1957.

Fowler, W. W., *The City State of the Greeks and Romans*, New York, 1960. A valuable specialized study.

———, *Rome* (2d ed.) rev. by M. P. Charlesworth, London and New York, 1960.

Gyles, Mary Francis, and Davis, Eugene Wood (eds.) *Laudatores Temporis Acti*, Chapel Hill, N.C., 1964. A collection of essays on special topics.

Heichelheim, Fritz Moritz, and Yeo, Cedric A., (eds.) *A History of the Roman People*, Englewood Cliffs, N.J., 1962. Interpretive. Valuable for extensive bibliography.

*Laistner, Max Ludwig Wolfram, *The Greater Roman Historians*, Berkeley, Calif., 1963.

Mommsen, Theodor, *The History of Rome: An Account of the Events and Persons from the Conquest of Carthage to the End of the Republic*, revised edition by Dero A. Saunders and John H. Collins, Cleveland, 1963.

Pauly-Wissowa-Kroll, *Real-Encyclopädie der classischen Altertumswissenschaft*, Stuttgart, 1894 (continuing). The only classical encyclopedia; now nearing completion.

Piganiol, A., *Histoire de Rome*, Clio. Series, Paris, 1954. Intensely valuable for bibliography and notes.

*Rostovtzeff, Mikhail I., *Rome*, New York, 1964.

Sandys, Sir John Edwin, *A Companion to Latin Studies*, New York, 1963.

Source Collections

Bakewell, Charles Montagne, *Source Book in Ancient Philosophy*, New York, 1939.

Harrington, Karl Pomeroy, *Selections from Latin Prose and Poetry; An Introduction to Latin Literature*, Cambridge, Mass., 1956.

Howe, George, Harrer, Gustave A., and Suskin, Albert I., *Roman Literature in Translation*, New York, 1959. A useful selection of documents illustrating major periods of Greek history.

McDermott, W. C., and Caldwell, Wallace E., *Readings in the History of the Ancient World*, New York, 1951. A selection of documents for the whole of ancient history but especially useful for the Greco-Roman periods.

*Sinnigen, William G. (ed.), *Rome*, New York, 1965. Contains interesting selections from works that are hard to obtain except from specialized libraries.

Political, Social, Economic, and Judicial Institutions

Abbott, Frank Frost, *A History and Description of Roman Political Institutions*, New York, 1963. A valuable specialized study.

——, *Roman Politics*, New York, 1963.

——, *Society and Politics in Ancient Rome: Essays and Sketches*, New York, 1963. Interesting and valuable for the beginning student.

Adcock, Sir Frank Ezra, *Roman Political Ideas and Practice*, Ann Arbor, Mich., 1959. An important specialized study.

Buckland, W. W., *A Manual of Roman Private Law*, London, 1939. A comprehensive source through which the student may become acquainted with an important area of Roman law.

——, *A Textbook of Roman Law from Augustus to Justinian*, London, 1932. A good general history of imperial law.

Frank, Tenney, *An Economic History of Rome*, New York, 1962.

——, *Roman Imperialism*, New York, 1914.

——, T. R. S. Broughton, *et al.* (eds.), *An Economic Survey of Ancient Rome* (6 vols.), Paterson, N.J., 1959. Indispensable for study of the imperial economy. Based on texts not elsewhere available to the beginner.

Heitland, William Emerton, *Agricola: A Study of Agriculture and Rustic Life in the Greco-Roman World from the Point of View of Labor*, New York, 1921. One of the few extensive studies of ancient agriculture.

*Homo, Leon P., *Roman Political Institutions; from City to State*, New York, 1962. One of the classic studies of the subject. Extremely useful.

Jolowicz, Herbert Felix, *Historical Introduction to the Study of Roman Law*, New York, 1961. A useful introduction.

*Louis, Paul, *Ancient Rome at Work: An Economic History of Rome from the Origins to the Empire*, trans. by E. B. F. Waring, New York, 1965. A general, well written work designed as a companion piece to Gustave Glotz, *Ancient Greece at Work* (see bibliography for Greece).

Mattingly, H., *Roman Coins*, London, 1960. A comprehensive study of the numismatic history of the Romans.

Milne, Joseph Grafton, *The Development of Roman Coinage*, New York, 1937.

Ormerod, Henry A., *Piracy in the Ancient World*, London, 1924.

Parker, A. M. D., *The Roman Legions*, New York, 1958. The most comprehensive work on the development of the Roman army, together with a study of armor, weapons, organization, strategy, and tactics.

Rawlinson, H. G., *Intercourse Between India and the Western World*, New York, 1926. An invaluable book covering the Roman period and earlier periods.

Rostovtzeff, Mikhail I., *The Social and Economic History of the Roman Empire* (2 vols.), 2d edition rev. by P. M. Frazer, New York, 1957. The most important book on the subject, though some of the interpretations are not accepted by all students of Roman history.

Schulz, F., *History of Roman Legal Science*, New York, 1953.

Sohm, Rudolf, *The Institutes; A Textbook of the History and System of Roman Private Law*, trans. by J. C. Ledlie, New York, 1937.

Wolff, H. J., *Roman Law: An Historical Introduction*, Norman, Oklahoma, 1951.

Religion and Mythology

Altheim, Franz, *A History of Roman Religion*, trans. by H. Mattingly, London, 1938. One of the best and most comprehensive histories of Roman religious belief.

Baron, Salo, *A Social and Religious History of the Jews*, New York, 1937, vol. 1.

*Barrett, C. K. (ed.), *The New Testament Background: Selected Documents*, New York, 1961.

*Buitman, Rudolph, *Primitive Christianity in Its Contemporary Setting*, New York, 1965. A stimulating and readable book for the beginner.

*Cochrane, C. N., *Christianity and Classical Culture*, New York, 1964.

*Cumont, Franz, *Astrology and Religion Among the Greeks and Romans*, Baltimore, 1960. A valuable introductory discussion. Well documented.

*———, *Oriental Religions in Roman Paganism*, New York, 1956. An examination of the mystery religions prevalent in the empire.

*———, *The Mysteries of Mithra*, New York, 1956. The only detailed study of the cult transplanted from Persia to Rome and spread by the Roman army.

*Daniel-Rops, Henri, *Daily Life in the Time of Jesus*, New York, 1964. This study is useful to the beginning student.

*Enslin, Morton S., *Christian Beginnings* (2 vols.), New York, 1956. A detailed and well documented study of early Christianity within the Roman framework.

Fowler, William W., *Roman Ideas of Deity in the Last Century Before the Christian Era*, London, 1914.

Fox, W. S., *Greek and Roman Mythology*, New York, 1964. A general reference work useful to the beginning student.

*Glover, T. R., *The Conflict of Religions in the Early Roman Empire*, Boston, 1960.

Grenier, Albert, *The Roman Spirit in Religion, Thought and Art*, trans. by M. R. Dobie, London, 1926.

*Hatch, Edwin, *Influence of Greek Ideas on Christianity*, New York, 1957.

Hyde, W. W., *Paganism and Christianity in the Roman Empire*, Philadelphia, 1946.

Laing, G. J., *Survivals of Roman Religion*, New York, 1931. A book that will seem controversial to Christians, but is interesting for its ideas and theme.

*Lietzmann, Hans, *A History of the Early Church* (2 vols.), New York, 1953. A good account and readily available. Good bibliography.

*Nock, A. D., *Early Gentile Christianity and Its Hellenistic Background*, New York, 1964.

*Seznec, Jean, *The Survival of the Pagan Gods*, New York, 1961.

Literature and the Arts

Abbott, Frank Frost, *The Common People of Ancient Rome: Studies of Roman Life and Literature*, New York, 1911. A study derived from the literature.

Beare, W., *The Roman Stage*, London, 1955. Excellent description of the methods of dramatic production and the stage properties available to the Romans.

Cary, M., and Haarhoff, T. J., *Life and Thought in the Greek and Roman World*, London, 1961. A comparative and thought-provoking study of the Greek and Roman cultures.

*Duff, John Wight, *Literary History of Rome: From the Origins to the Close of the Golden Age*, New York, 1964.

*————, *A Literary History of Rome in the Silver Age: From Tiberius to Hadrian*, New York, 1964. Duff's two literary histories are without counterparts and extremely valuable to the student.

————, *Roman Satire: Its Outlook on Social Life*, Hamden, Conn., 1964.

Duckworth, G. E., *The Nature of Roman Comedy*, Princeton, N.J., 1952.

*Grant, Michael, *Roman Literature*, Baltimore, 1958.

*Hadas, Moses, *History of Latin Literature*, New York, 1964. A general, but recent and very excellent history of Roman literature.

*Mackail, John William, *Latin Literature*, rev. by Harry C. Schnur, New York, 1962.

Maiuri, A., *Roman Painting*, Geneva, 1953. A beautifully illustrated and extremely valuable study.

Platner, Samuel B., and Thomas, A., *A Topographical Dictionary of Ancient Rome*, London, 1929. An old book but still valuable to the beginner seeking to orient himself in the ancient city.

Rand, Edward K., *The Building of Eternal Rome*, Cambridge, Mass., 1943.

Richter, Gisela M. A., *Roman Portraits*, New York, 1948. An excellent discussion of Roman portrait sculpture. Good illustrations.

Stahl, William H., *Roman Science*, Madison, Wis., 1962. A general and readable account of theoretical science throughout the Roman period. Little attention is given to technology or applied science.

*Stenico, Arturo, *Roman and Etruscan Painting*, New York, 1963. Handsomely illustrated.

Strong, Eugénie (Sellers), *Art in Ancient Rome* (2 vols.), New York, 1928. These volumes embody the first favorable approach ever made to Roman art. Roman art is treated in the light of its own history and aesthetic value rather than compared (falsely) with Greek art. Extremely important study. Relatively poor illustrations.

*Wheeler, Sir R. E. Mortimer, *Roman Art and Architecture*, New York, 1964. Beautifully illustrated. Very valuable discussion.

Books of Interpretation

Bailey, Cyril, *The Mind of Rome*, New York, 1926. An interesting attempt to describe the Roman view on all subjects.

*Carcopino, Jerome, *Daily Life in Ancient Rome*, New Haven, Conn., 1963. A good introduction to social history.

Grant, Michael, *The World of Rome*, New York, 1961. An extremely interesting interpretation of the Romans, their customs and institutions, and their views of other peoples.

Greene, William Chase, *The Achievement of Rome*, Cambridge, Mass., 1938.

Hamilton, Edith, *The Roman Way*, New York, 1964. Beautifully written and highly interpretive.

Johnston, Harold Whetstone, *The Private Life of the Romans*, rev. by Mary Johnston, Chicago, 1932.

Kerenyi, C., *The Religion of the Greeks and Romans*, New York, 1962. A general work but valuable to the student since it offers the means of comparison between two religious systems.

Showerman, Grant, *Rome and the Romans: A Survey and Interpretation*, New York, 1956.

Chapters 19 to 21. THE ROMAN REPUBLIC

Sources   Appian: *Roman History*
          Caesar: *Civil War* and *Gallic Wars*
          Cato: *On Agriculture*
          Catullus: Poems
          Cicero: Letters, orations, and essays
          Ennius: Poems
          Livy: *History of Rome*
          Plautus: Plays
          Plutarch: Lives of Caesar, Cicero, Crassus, Marcellus, Marcus Cato,
            Tiberius and Gaius Gracchus, Lucullus, Marius, Pompey, Poplicola, Sulla, and others
          Polybius: Histories
          Sallust: *Conspiracy of Catiline* and *Jugurthine War*
          Terence: Plays
          Varro: *On Agriculture*

Adcock, Sir Frank Ezra, *The Roman Art of War Under the Republic*, New York, 1960. A very important discussion of the changes in Roman military organization and of the strategy, tactics, and practices of the republican armies.

Arnold, William T., *The Roman System of Provincial Administration*, New York, 1914. A basic study of the organization of the developing empire. Almost indispensable.

Bailey, Cyril, *Phases in the Religion of Ancient Rome*, London, 1932.

Boren, Henry C., "The Urban Side of the Gracchan Economic Crisis," *American Historical Review* 63 (1958), p. 89. An important article on a hitherto neglected aspect of this period.

Botsford, George Willis, *The Roman Assemblies, from Their Origin to the End of the Republic*, New York, 1919.

Broughton, Thomas R. S., *The Magistrates of the Roman Republic*, New York, 1951–1952. One of the best studies of the Roman administrators and administration.

Carcopino, Jerome, *César*, Paris, 1943. An exhaustive biography of Julius Caesar. Excellent bibliography and notes.

——, *Cicero and the Secrets of His Correspondence* (2 vols.), London, 1951.

*Cowell, F. R., *Cicero and the Roman Republic*, Baltimore, 1962.

Fowler, W. W., *Social Life at Rome in the Age of Cicero*, New York, 1963. A well written and exhaustively documented study.

Frank, Tenney, *Life and Literature in the Roman Republic*, Berkeley, Calif., 1961.

Heitland, William Emerton, *The Roman Republic* (3 vols.), New York, 1923. The most detailed history of the republic in English.

Hill, H., *The Roman Middle Class in the Republican Period*, New York, 1952. A thorough study of the evolution of the middle class and its interest and influence.

Holmes, Thomas Rice, *Caesar's Conquest of Gaul*, New York, 1911.

Marsh, Frank Burr, *A History of the Roman World from 146 B.C. to 30 B.C.* (3d ed.), rev. with additional notes by H. H. Scullard, New York, 1963. An excellent, detailed study amply documented.

Scullard, Howard Hayes, *A History of the Roman World from 753 to 146 B.C.*, London, 1961. A detailed and heavily documented history of the early period.

Sihler, Ernest Gottlieb, *Cicero of Arpinum*, New York, 1933. One of the better and more interestingly written biographies of Cicero.

Sikes, Edward E., *Lucretius, Poet and Philosopher*, New York, 1936. A study of the poet and his work and of the Epicurean philosophy he expounds.

*Syme, Sir Ronald, *The Roman Revolution*, London, 1960. A comprehensive and deeply researched study of an essential period.

Thiel, Johannes Hendrik, *A History of Roman Sea Power Before the Second Punic War*, Amsterdam, 1954. Naval practices and strategy in the First Punic War form the focus of this study.

———, *Studies on the History of Roman Sea-Power in Republican Times*, Amsterdam, 1946. A more general study of Roman navies.

*Warmington, B. H., *Carthage*, Baltimore, 1964. The most complete study of the history of Carthage in the light of recent evidence.

Winspear, Alban Dewes, *Lucretius and Scientific Thought*, Montreal, 1963. An excellent recent study that assesses Lucretius' account of Epicurean philosophy and its place in the history of thought.

Chapter 22. THE AGE OF AUGUSTUS

Sources   Appian: *Roman History*
Augustus: *Res Gestae*
Dio Cassius: *History*
Horace: *Carmina, Epodes, Odes*, and *Satires*
Ovid: *Art of Love, Fasti*, and *Metamorphoses*
Plutarch: Life of Anthony
Suetonius: Lives of Julius and Augustus
Vergil: *Aeneid, Eclogues*, and *Georgics*

Buchan, John, *Augustus Caesar*, Boston, 1937. A good biography.

Marsh, Frank Burr, *The Founding of the Roman Empire*, London, 1927. Good general study of the forces and events that brought Augustus to power.

Hadas, Moses, *Sextus Pompey*, New York, 1930. A valuable study of the brave son of Pompey the Great who held Sicily against Augustus and Agrippa for years.

Hammond, Mason, *The Augustan Principate in Theory and Practice*, Cambridge, Mass., 1933. An exhaustive study of the Augustan "settlement."

Holmes, Thomas Rice, *The Architect of the Roman Empire* (2 vols.), New York, 1928–1931. The best biography of Augustus against the background of his period.

——, *The Roman Republic and the Founder of the Roman Empire* (3 vols.), New York, 1926. An exhaustive study of the events and forces that led to Augustus' success.

Mackail, John William, *Virgil and His Meaning to the World of Today*, New York, 1963.

Winspear, Alban Dewes, and Geweke, Lenore Kramp, *Augustus and the Reconstruction of Roman Government and Society*, Madison, Wis., 1935. A careful study of the reign of Augustus. Amply documented.

Chapters 23 and 24. THE ROMAN EMPIRE

Sources   Dio Cassius: *History*
           Josephus: *Jewish Antiquities* and *Jewish Wars*
           Juvenal: *Satires*
           Lucan: *Pharsalia*
           Lucian: *Dialogues*
           Marcus Aurelius: *Meditations*
           The New Testament
           Petronius: *Satyricon*
           Pliny the Elder: *Natural History*
           Pliny the Younger: *Letters*
           Scriptores Historiae Augustae
           Seneca: Essays, letters and plays
           Suetonius: *Lives of the Twelve Caesars*
           Tacitus: *Agricola, Annals, Germania* and *Histories*
           Velleius Paterculis: *Life of Tiberius*

Abbott, Frank Frost, and Johnson, Allan Chester, *Municipal Administration in the Roman Empire*, Princeton, N.J., 1926.

Balsdon, J. P. V. D., *The Emperor Gaius*, New York, 1934. The life of the insane Caligula.

Bersanetti, G. M., *Vespasiano*, Rome, 1941. One of the few available studies of the life and reign of Vespasian.

Boethius, Axel, *The Golden House of Nero, Some Aspects of Roman Architecture*, Ann Arbor, Mich., 1960. The reign of Nero is reckoned as the peak of Roman architectural expression. The great palace he built for himself was the ultimate expression of the best architects of the age.

Bouchier, E. S., *Spain Under the Roman Empire*, New York, 1914.

Brogan, O. K., *Roman Gaul*, London, 1953.

Broughton, Thomas R. S., *The Romanization of Africa Proconsularis*, Baltimore, 1929.

Crook, J., *Consilium Principis: Imperial Councils and Counsellors from Augustus to Diocletian*, London, 1955. A heavily documented and thorough study of imperial councils.

*Dill, Samuel, *Roman Society from Nero to Marcus Aurelius*, New York, 1962. Interpretive and inclined to share the views of Tacitus somewhat uncritically for this democratic age, but an extremely valuable study of society and social institutions.

Hadas, Moses (ed.), *Essential Works of Stoicism*, New York, 1961. The dominant philosophy of the empire was Stoicism. This collection furnishes a valuable introduction to its thought and teachings.

Hammond, Mason, *The Antonine Monarchy*, Papers and Monographs of the American School at Rome, 19 (1959). A careful study of the period from A.D. 96–180. Thoroughly documented.

Henderson, Bernard W., *Five Roman Emperors*, London, 1927. Relatively brief biographies.

———, *The Life and Principate of the Emperor Hadrian*, London, 1923. A thorough, carefully documented study.

———, *The Life and Principate of the Emperor Nero*, London, 1903. The only exhaustive account of Nero and his reign.

Homo, Leon P., *Vespasien, l'Empéreur de Bon Sens,* Paris, 1949. The title indicates the major approach to the reign of Vespasian. An excellent, well documented biography.

Jones, A. H. M., *The Cities of the Eastern Roman Provinces*, New York, 1937.

Lambrechts, P., *La Composition du Sénat Romain (117–192 A.D.)*, Antwerp, 1936.

Leon, H. J., *The Jews of Ancient Rome*, New York, 1960.

Lepper, F. A., *Trajan's Parthian War*, New York, 1948.

Magie, D., *Roman Rule in Asia Minor*, Princeton, N.J., 1950.

Marsh, F. B., *The Reign of Tiberius*, New York, 1931. The most careful study of Tiberius' reign to date. Marsh goes beyond Tacitus' interpretations to his facts. Combining these with facts from other sources, he shows Tiberius to have been an able administrator.

*Mattingley, Harold, *Roman Imperial Civilization*, Garden City, N.Y., 1959. An excellent, interpretive discussion.

Momigliano, A., *Claudius, the Emperor and His Achievement*, New York, 1934. Excellent, thoroughly documented study.

Nash, Ernest, *Roman Towns*, New York, 1949.

*Nilsson, Martin P., *Imperial Rome*, New York, 1962.

Reynolds, P. K. B., *Vigiles of Imperial Rome*, London, 1926. One of the very few studies of the police force of imperial Rome.

*Richmond, I. A., *Roman Britain*, Baltimore, 1963.

Scullard, Howard Hayes, *From the Gracchi to Nero*, New York, 1963. A history that emphasizes the trend toward one-man rule to redress the ills of the Roman economy and society, and shows how this trend culminated in the Julio-Claudian Principate.

Sherwin-White, Adrian Nicholas, *The Roman Citizenship*, New York, 1939. An indispensable study of the changing attitude toward Roman citizenship, and of the privileges and responsibilities it carried.

Sinnigen, William G., "The Roman Secret Service," *The Classical Journal*, 67 (1961), p. 65. An important article showing how the imperial secret service operated through the grain buyers for the army.

Starr, Chester G., *The Roman Imperial Navy*, New York, 1960. A thorough study of the permanent naval forces of the empire, their organization, stations, and duties.

Sutherland, C. H. V., *The Romans in Spain*, London, 1939.

Wheeler, Sir R. E. Mortimer, *Rome Beyond the Imperial Frontiers*, New York, 1955. The only study of its kind. Archeological evidence from Germany, Africa, and India is examined to gain a view of the extent of foreign trade.

Chapter 25. CIVIL WARS AND RECOVERY

Sources   *The Ante-Nicene Fathers:* Collected works of Christian writers before
               A.D. 325
           Ammianus Marcellinus: *History*
           Aurelius Victor: Works
           Diocletian: *Edict of Prices*
           Eutropius: Works
           Epitome de Caesaribus
           Orosius: *Seven Books of History Against the Pagans*

Boak, Arthur E. R., *Manpower Shortage and the Fall of the Roman Empire in the West*, Ann Arbor, Mich., 1955. A theory not entirely accepted but nonetheless important. Boak documents thoroughly.

*Burckhardt, Jacob, *The Age of Constantine the Great*, New York, 1949. An interesting general account.

Charanis, P., *Church and State in the Later Roman Empire*, New York, 1939. An important study of the early and evolving relationship between Christian organization and the Roman government.

*Gibbon, Edward, *The Decline and Fall of the Roman Empire*, London, 1954. An abbreviated, paperback edition of a classic. Gibbon's interpretations must be modified by later evidence, but he is still worth reading for his ideas as well as his style.

Jones, A. H. M., *Constantine and the Conversion of Europe*, London, 1948. A discussion of the significance of Constantine's reign to Christian history.

————, *The Later Roman Empire 284–602* (3 vols.), New York, 1964. The most detailed history of this period. Well documented.

Katz, S., *The Decline of Rome and Rise of Medieval Europe*, Ithaca, N.Y., 1955.

Kidd, B. J., *The Roman Primacy to A.D. 461*, London, 1936.

Lambrechts, P., *La Composition du Sénat Romain (193–284 A.D.)*, Antwerp, 1937.

Parker, H. M. D., *A History of the Roman World from A.D. 138 to 337*, London, 1958. A comprehensive and detailed study of Roman history from the late Antonine period to the period of the "Barracks emperors." The forces, events, and problems of the period are thoroughly treated.

Platnauer, M., *The Life and Reign of the Emperor Septimius Severus*, New York, 1918. The only important biography of this emperor in English.

Seston, W., *Dioclétien et la Tétrarchie*, French School at Rome, 162. Paris, 1946.

Taylor, L. R., *The Divinity of the Roman Emperor*, American Philological Society Monographs, 1 (1931). A thorough study of the gradual translation of the emperor into a living god.

Chapter 26. THE END OF THE EMPIRE IN THE WEST

Sources Ammianus Marcellinus: *History*
Augustine: *City of God* and *Confessions*
Codex Theodosiani
Corpus Juris Civilis Justiniani
Eusebius: *Ecclesiastical History* and *Life of Constantine*
Orosius: *Seven Books of History Against the Pagans*
The Post-Nicene Fathers: Collected works of Christian Writers after A.D. 325
Procopius: *History* and *Secret History*

*Baynes, Norman H., and Moss, H. S. B., *Byzantium*, New York, 1961. A recent and extremely thorough history.

———, *The Byzantine Empire*, New York, 1943.

Bury, J. B., *A History of the Later Roman Empire, 395–565* (2 vols.), London, 1923. Recent studies make a partial revision of this book desirable, but it remains one of the best and most detailed histories of the period.

Diehl, Charles, *Manuel d'Art Byzantin* (2 vols.), Paris, 1925. Beautifully illustrated history of Byzantine Art.

*Dill, Samuel, *Roman Society to the Last Century of the Empire*, New York, 1962. As with Roman Society from Nero to Marcus Aurelius, the author's work on the earlier period (see bibliography for Chaps. 23–24), one may disagree with certain parts of the interpretation, but this is nonetheless a thorough and readable study.

Downey, Glanville, *Antioch in the Age of Theodosius the Great*, New York, 1962.

———, *Constantinople in the Age of Justinian*, Norman, Okla., 1960. An excellent study of the city of Constantinople and of the reign of Justinian.

Gardner, A., *Julian, Philosopher and Emperor*, London, 1901. The emperor Julian, the last pagan emperor, was an interesting and attractive figure. This biography does him justice.

Gordon, C. D., *The Age of Attila: Fifth Century Byzantium and the Barbarians*, New York, 1960. A study of the intricate political relations between the Huns and the eastern emperors.

Hodgkin, T., *Italy and Her Invaders* (8 vols.), New York, 1916. An exhaustive and comprehensive study that extends well beyond the late Roman period.

Jenkins, Romilly, *Byzantium and Byzantinium*, Lectures in memory of Louise Taft Semple, Cincinnati, 1963.

*Lot, Ferdinand, *The End of the Ancient World and the Beginning of the Middle Ages*, New York, 1961. The most important study of this period of transition for the beginner. Well documented.

Momigliano, A. (ed.), *The Conflict Between Paganism and Christianity in the Fourth Century*, London, 1963.

Ostrogorsky, G., *History of the Byzantine State*, New York, 1956.

Rubin, Berthold, *Das Zeitalter Justinians*, Berlin, 1960. One of the most important and thoroughly documented studies of the age of Justinian.

Runciman, Steven, *Byzantine Civilization*, London, 1933.

Swift, E. H., *Hagia Sophia*, New York, 1940. A detailed study of the architecture and art of the Cathedral of the Holy Wisdom at Constantinople.

Chambers, Mortimer (ed.), *The Fall of Rome, Can It Be Explained?* New York, 1963. The problem of Rome's decline and fall is set forth and answered by several scholars in several ways. The book is designed to provoke thought and does so.

*Ure, Percy Neville, *Justinian and His Age*, Harmondsworth, England, 1951. A good, readable, and dependable account.

Vasiliev, A., *History of the Byzantine Empire* (2 vols.), trans. by S. Ragozin, Madison, Wis., 1952. For many years this was the standard work on Byzantine history, and it remains valuable for the beginner.

Walbank, L. W., *The Decline of the Roman Empire in the West*, New York, 1953. A specific and more detailed study of the problems covered in this chapter.

INDEX

Hellenica, 329

Hellenistic age, 340–357; Alexander and, *see* Alexander; in Athens, 346, 357, 362; in Delos, 351–352, 357, 358, 360; Macedonian, 345, 346, 348–349, 357; in Pergamum, 349; in Ptolemaic Egypt, 355–357; in Rhodes, 349–350, 357–359, 361, 362; Seleucid, 352–353; sources, 340–341; in Sparta, 346–347, 357, 361

Hellenistic civilization, 171–200, 358–373; cities, 358–359, 362; economic character of, 196; evolution of, 185–200; foundation of, 180–181; influence of, on Rome, 425, 432–436; Jews and, 353, 372, 520–521; social life, 358–359; social organization, 361

Hellespont, 101, 188, 189, 215, 216, 219, 243, 246, 263, 354

Helots, 205–206, 255, 256, 264, 320, 325

Helvetians, 453

Hephaestus, 227, 291

Hera, 120, 202, 227, 234, 435

Heraclea, 398, 412

Heraclea in Pontus, 190

Heracles, 119–120, 322

Heraclitus, 308, 309

Herculaneum, 375, 536

Hermae, 262, 276

Hermes, 262, 335

Hero, 369

Herod Agrippa, 520, 521

Herod the Great, 485, 518, 520

Herodian, 548

Herodotus, 32, 63, 79, 160, 161, 165, 172, 199, 202, 239, 244, 305–306, 367, 380, 387

Herophilus, 366–367

Hesiod, 183–184, 194, 210, 229, 236, 239

Hetaerae, 283

Hezekiah, 151, 154

Hieratic writing, 71, 145

Hiero I, 249, 321, 386

Hiero II, 357, 415, 419

Hieroglyphics: Cretan, 91; Egyptian, 65, 68, 71, 145, 536; Hittite, 99, 146

Hieronymus, 365

Hillel, 518

Himera, 248, 249

Hindenburg, von, Paul, 417, 419

Hipparchus, 218, 220, 367, 368

Hippeis, 214, 217, 266

Hippias, 218–220, 238, 241, 242

Hippo, 144

Hippocleides, 199

Hippocrates, 308

Hippodamus, 291

Hiram, 149

Hissarlik, 100

Historia Augusta, 374

Historians: Athenian, 305–307, 329; Greek, 172; Hellenistic, 340–341, 365–366; Roman, 434, 474, 540–541

Hittite Empire, 102–108; collapse of, 175–176; social organization, 103–105

Hittites, 37, 50, 58, 61, 90, 97–99, 127

Homer, 101, 113, 119, 120, 145, 171, 176–180, 185, 207, 228, 229, 235–236, 281, 302, 338, 341

Homo erectus, 5, 6, 9

Homo sapiens, 12, 14–17

Homonoia, 358

Honorius, 573, 577–579

Horace, 432, 487, 490–491

Hor-aha, 68

Horatius, 394–395, 412

Hortensian Law, 403, 408

Hortensius, 449

Horus, 68–70, 72–74, 78, 79, 142

Hosea, 151

Houses: Athenian, 283–284; Egyptian, 23, 62, 67; Etruscan, 381; Greek, 232; Harappan, 53; Hellenistic, 362; Hittite, 108; Mesopotamian, 23, 24, 35; Mycenaean, 120; Neolithic, 23; Paleolithic, 14; Roman, 374–375, 433, 464, 467, 529, 537, 538; Sumerian, 41

Huns, 572–573, 575, 577, 579

Hunters: Mesolithic, 20–21; Neanderthal, 12; Paleolithic, 12, 14

Hurrians, 61, 90, 94, 97–99

Hyakinthos, 227

Hyksos, 88–89, 94, 123–125, 140

Hymettus, 212

Hyperbolus, 261

Hypereides, 331

Hyrcanus, 520

Ialysus, 112

Ice ages, 9, 12, 14, 33

Ictinus, 293

Ida, Mount, 110, 118

Ides of March, 457, 459

Ikhnaton, 102, 130–135

Ilerda, 456

Iliad, 100, 101, 120, 176, 229

Ilissus River, 290

Illyrian wars, 416, 421

Illyrians, 323, 380, 427

Illyricum, 422, 453

Imhotep, 79

Immortality, belief in: Babylonian, 58–59; Egyptian, 79; Greek, 228; Hellenistic, 372; Minoan, 118; Roman, 393

Imperatores, 552

Imperialism: Assyrian, 157–158; Athenian, 255–256, 259; Augustan, 476–488; Roman, 424–432

'88
92

FURS

TIMBER

SLAVES

IRON
LEAD
CATTLE

RED CORAL

TIMBER

Leyden

TIN

SILVER

FISH

AMBER

SLAVES

Vistula R.

GRAIN

Paris
(Lutetia)

Rhine R.

IRON

AMBER

TIMBER

GRAIN

CATTLE

Vienna (Vindobona)

WINE

Rhône R.

GRAIN

OIL

Danube R.

GRAIN

IRON

SILVER

Ebro R.

Massilia

IRON

OIL

SLAVES

IRON

Constantinople

FISH

WOOL

WINE

Rome

WINE

TIMBER

SH

Saguntum

WOOD

WOOL

GOLD

Sardis

SILVER

WINE

Cartagena

HONEY

GOLD

LEAD

Carthage

GRAIN

WINE

Athens

CO

Syracuse

OIL

O

T

SLAVES, IVORY, GOLD

GRAIN

OIL

WINE

Cyrene

Alexandria

SILPHIUM

WINE

Memphis

OSTRICH FEATHERS, IVORY

Oasis of Siwa

CITRON
RICE

FLA

GRAIN

Nile R.

SHEEP